The Youth Labor Force 1945–1995

While the employment of youths in their respective countries varies, this book gathers together voluminous quantities of data in a definitive study that shows the medium-term trends and projections of that participation over the postwar half-century in twelve OECD countries: the United States, Japan, Germany, France, Italy, and the United Kingdom, and the smaller Canada, Australia, the Netherlands, Sweden, Switzerland, and New Zealand. Cross-national comparisons show the proportions of employed youths and out-of-work youths, in various age brackets, in their labor markets, and examines even more minutely such specifics as the participation of students, women, minority workers, and children of guest workers in Western Europe.

Conservation of Human Resources Series: 13

OTHER VOLUMES IN THE
Conservation of Human Resources Series

The Youth Labor Force 1945–1995

A CROSS-NATIONAL ANALYSIS

by

Beatrice G. Reubens
John A.C. Harrisson
Kalman Rupp

Foreword by Eli Ginzberg

LANDMARK STUDIES
Allanheld, Osmun   Publishers

ALLANHELD, OSMUN & CO. PUBLISHERS, INC.

Published in the United States of America in 1981
by Allanheld, Osmun & Co. Publishers, Inc.
(A Division of Littlefield, Adams and Company)
81 Adams Drive, Totowa, New Jersey 07512
Copyright © 1981 by Conservation of Human Resources

Library of Congress Cataloging in Publication Data

Reubens, Beatrice G.
  The youth labor force, 1945–1995.

  (Conservation of human resources series ; 13)
(LandMark studies)
  Bibliography: p.
  Includes index.
  1. Youth—Employment. I. Harrisson, John A. C.
II. Rupp, Kalman. III. Title. IV. Series.
HD6270.R48   331.3'4125   80-67390
ISBN 0-86598-027-6   AACR2

This report was prepared for the Employment and Training
Administration, U.S. Department of Labor, under research and
development grant No. 21-36-76-18. Since grantees conducting
research and development projects under Government sponsorship
are encouraged to express their own judgment freely, this report
does not necessarily represent the official opinion or policy of the
Department of Labor. The grantee is solely responsible for the
contents of this report.

81 82 83 84 / 10 9 8 7 6 5 4 3 2 1

Printed in the United States of America

Contents

Tables

Tables marked with an * have not been printed; they are available from the authors on request. Text and charts include the essential information in the tables which have not been printed.

Charts

Preface

The study of young people and their transition from school to work that began with *Bridges to Work: International Comparisons of Transition Services** is carried forward in the present cross-national analysis of the youth labor force during the postwar period and as projected to 1995. This primarily statistical analysis of the development of numbers and proportions of young people in the population, educational system, and labor force reveals considerable diversity among the twelve industrialized nations, and offers objective bases for some of the variations in national experience and institutional behavior observed in *Bridges to Work*. It also lays the ground for a better understanding of cross-national differences in youth unemployment. To further improve such an understanding, we are continuing our comparative analysis of youth in the labor market with studies of employment trends and occupational concentration of youth compared to other age groups.

The present study owes much to the assistance of the official statistical agencies in the twelve countries and their generosity in making available to us as-yet-unpublished materials as well as unpublished data of various kinds. Through personal meetings, telephone calls, and correspondence, they graciously answered our questions and provided additional information. Other individuals in a large number of countries similarly were helpful in expanding our understanding of the basic phenomena we sought to analyze. An important contribution was made also by the statistical experts of the United Nations, Organization for Economic Cooperation and Development, the International Labor Organization, and the European Communities.

We are indebted to several people who read early drafts of chapters and gave us the benefit of their thoughtful comments. Chapter 2 was read by Cynthia Lloyd and Burkhard von Rabenau, the Appendix to Chapter 4 was expertly reviewed by Constance Sorrentino and Joyanna Moy, and Chapter 6 was read critically by Stephen Hills and Carol Jusenius. Edwin P. Reubens offered helpful advice and read sections of the book. Whatever faults remain are entirely our own doing.

As principal author, Beatrice G. Reubens took major responsibility for the organization, content, and writing of the book. John A.C. Harrisson contributed substantially to the basic research, collection, and interpretation of data as well as the writing, editing, and supervision of the production of a large number of charts and tables. Kalman Rupp's chief function was statistical analysis of the data, including all the regression analyses. At an early stage of the book, Betty G. Fishman supervised the collection and tabulation of data. Research and statistical assistance was furnished by Quentin Hom, George Winslow, Marcia Katzmar, and Peter Rancans. Shoshana Vasheetz and Cheryl Murray Francis were largely responsible for the extensive and demanding typing effort.

We wish to acknowledge our gratitude to the Department of Labor and German Marshall Fund for the initial financing of this book and to the Ford Foundation for supplementary assistance. Rockefeller Foundation support for the continuing

*Allanheld, Osmun, LandMark Studies, 1977.

related studies enabled us to undertake some of the necessary basic research.

We wish to call the reader's attention to the omission from the book of some 45 tables that are listed in the front matter and are cited as references in the text. The content of these tables is available from our printed charts in most cases. The omitted tables are available from the authors on request.

Foreword

Several years ago Nobel Laureate Wassily Leontief, in his presidential address to the American Economic Association, chided his colleagues for investing so much of their time and effort in developing models and so little in collecting the data required to test them. Many heard him but few were moved by his advice, for model-building was accepted, admired, and recommended, while empirical research had lost whatever glamor it once had. Moreover, the collection, sifting, and evaluation of large bodies of data were laborious undertakings that did not attract impatient analysts seeking quick-fix solutions.

Beatrice Reubens, senior research associate at the Conservation of Human Resources, Columbia University, the senior author of the present work, belongs to an earlier tradition led by Wesley Mitchell and J. M. Clark, who long dominated Columbia's economics department. As demonstrated in her two earlier large-scale comparative investigations — *The Hard-To-Employ* and *Bridges to Work* — she has the skill and patience to master large bodies of institutional materials to extract the lessons of history for the purpose of improving public policy.

Dr. Reubens and her colleagues' present undertaking is more empirical and statistical and on a larger scale. They have cast their net wide to capture the experience of no fewer than twelve members of the OECD, including all of the largest economies — United States, Japan, Germany, France, Italy and the United Kingdom, — and some of the medium-sized and smaller nations, including Canada, Australia, the Netherlands, Sweden, Switzerland, and New Zealand.

The central focus of the inquiry was to assess medium-term trends and projections of the youth labor force in these twelve countries, with particular reference to the influence of changes in demographic factors, educational enrollments, and government programs on when young people start to work, how much they work, and when they make the transition into full-time adult work status.

It is easier to state the focus of the inquiry than to convey the complex conceptual and data hurdles that Dr. Reubens and her collaborators surmounted to bring order into the diverse bodies of national and international data so that different series could be meaningfully defined and valid conclusions extracted. It is difficult even for me, who watched the process from close quarters over the past several years, to appreciate fully the amount of effort, energy, and determination required to bring the undertaking from conception to conclusion. There are few, if any, other comparative economic investigations that have dealt with a major issue to a point that it need not be addressed again — at least not for a long period of time.

There is no possible way for a Foreword, unless it were to be extended to an inconceivable length, to summarize the insights and highlights of such a comprehensive comparative analysis. Accordingly, I will limit myself to sharing with the reader a selected number of points that attracted my attention.

As one would suspect from the inclusion of twelve nations in the study, the size and share of the youth labor force differed over time from one country to the next, and often the differences were substantial. But the authors were not overwhelmed by these differences and, without forcing the facts, were able to organize their information into typologies that facilitated the presentation of illuminating and significant comparisons. Supply-side factors seem relevant to explanations of cross-national differences in youth unemployment and perhaps should play more of a role in national analysis.

Another finding speaks more to the parallels than to the differences among the several countries. For instance, in every country more and more young people remained in school for more years: the initial wide gaps between the educational achievements of young men and young women were substantially reduced, and the proportions of young people who complete secondary school and who go on to postsecondary education have increased substantially. While the timing and extent of these important changes varied from one country to the next these transformations occurred in all, without exception.

Much the same pattern was found in the case of the increasing labor force participation of young adult women. Here, too, initial gross differences between men and women narrowed substantially, and while the timing and extent of female participation continues to differ across countries, the pattern clearly is one of greater participation in all countries.

The authors introduced several subjects of considerable importance where they were able to open them up for exploration but had to stop short of treating them definitively. In particular, Dr. Reubens and her associates note that a refined assessment of the labor force participation of young people must consider not only the numbers who work but should also include a measure of how many hours they work during the course of a year. While the authors suggest how this important refinement can be added, the extant data do not enable them to provide comparable and usable estimates for all workers. A similar situation pertains to the labor force participation of students in which the United States leads. Another interesting avenue of inquiry which they open up but which they are unable to treat definitively relates to the parallels and differences between minority youth in the United States and such youth in other countries, including the children of guest workers in Western Europe, who share many if not all of the handicaps that affect young American blacks.

With respect to substantive findings, I was greatly impressed with the following:

Japan has the highest proportion of young people currently enrolled in school.

Despite major efforts of governments to lower the financial barriers to higher education, the children of middle- and upper-income families still account for disproportionate shares of college and university students.

Germany and the United States face the sharpest declines in the numbers of teenagers who will reach working age between 1980 and 1990.

There is no evidence of any decline in the work ethic among young people, as revealed in an important chapter on youth who are neither in school nor the labor force.

If the employment of youth is a matter of substantial economic and social importance to the well-being of individuals, groups, and nations, which few would question, this exemplary comparative investigation into the changing contours of the youth labor supply by Dr. Reubens and her colleagues must be seen as a major contribution to understanding. And with increased understanding should come improved policy. A great many members of the scholarly and policy communities in many countries will be greatly in debt to Dr. Reubens and her collaborators for a major inquiry carried out with breadth and depth. I thank them on behalf of all of us.

Eli Ginzberg

Abbreviations

ABS	Australian Bureau of Statistics
ACE	American Council on Education
AFDC	Aid to Families with Dependent Children (United States)
AMS	Arbetsmarknadsstyrelsen (National Labor Market Board) (Sweden)
BA	Bundesanstalt für Arbeit (Employment Institute) (Germany)
BAS	Bundesministerium für Arbeit-und Sozialordnung (Federal Ministry of Labor and Social Order) (Germany)
BLS	Bureau of Labor Statistics (United States)
BMBW	Bundesministerium für Bildung und Wissenschaft (Federal Ministry of Education and Science) (Germany)
CBO	Congressional Budget Office (see USCBO) (United States)
CBS	Centraal Bureau voor de Statistiek (Central Bureau of Statistics) (Netherlands)
CE	Council of Europe (Strasbourg, France)
CEC	Council of the European Communities (Brussels)
CEDEFOP	Centre européen pour le développement de la formation professionelle (European Center for the Development of Occupational Training) (West Berlin)
CEE	Centre d'études de l'emploi (Center for Employment Studies) (France)
CEREQ	Centre d'études et de recherches sur les qualifications (Center for Studies and Research on Occupational Qualifications) (France)
CERI	Center for Educational Research and Innovation (OECD, Paris)
CETA	Comprehensive Employment and Training Act (United States)
CHRR	Center for Human Resource Research (The Ohio State University, United States)
CLMS	Continuous Longitudinal Manpower Survey (United States Department of Labor)
CPS	Current Population Survey (United States Bureau of the Census)
CWBH	Continuous Wage and Benefit History (United States Department of Labor)
DES	Department of Education and Science (Great Britain)
DHEW	Department of Health, Education, and Welfare (United States) (until March 1980)
DIHT	Deutscher Industrie-und Handelstag (German Industry and Commerce Association)
EC	European Communities
EER	Educational Enrollment Rates
FTE	Full-time Equivalents

GB	Great Britain
GDP	Gross Domestic Product
GHS	General Household Survey (Great Britain)
GNP	Gross National Product
GPA	Grade Point Average
GPO	Government Printing Office (United States)
HMSO	Her Majesty's Stationery Office (Great Britain)
IAB	Institut für Arbeitsmarkt-und Berufsforschung der Bundes-anstalt für Arbeit (Institute for Labor Market and Occupational Research of the Employment Institute) (Germany)
ID	Panel Study of Income Dynamics (University of Michigan, United States)
ILO	International Labor Office (Geneva)
ILR	International Labour Review
IMS	Institute of Manpower Studies (Brighton, England)
IN	Imprimerie nationale (National Publications Office) (France)
INED	Institut national d'études demographiques (National Institute for Demographic Studies) (France)
INPS	Inter Nationes Press Service (Germany)
INSEE	Institut national de la statistique et des études économiques (National Institute for Statistical and Economic Studies) (France)
IPF	Information i prognosfrågor (Forecasting Information) (Sweden)
ISTAT	Instituto Centrale di Statistica (Central Institute of Statistics) (Italy)
IUT	Instituts universitaires de technologie (Technological universities) (France)
LFPR	Labor Force Participation Rate
MDRC	Manpower Demonstration Research Corporation (United States)
MRC	Medical Research Council (London School of Economics, England)
NBER	National Bureau of Economic Research (United States)
NCDS	National Child Development Study (Great Britain)
NCEP	National Commission for Employment Policy (formerly National Commission for Manpower Policy) (United States)
NCES	National Center for Education Statistics (Department of Education, United States)
NCMP	National Commission for Manpower Policy (see NCEP) (United States)
NIE	National Institute of Education (Department of Education, United States)
NILF	Not in the Labor Force
NISLF	Not in School or the Labor Force
NLS	National Longitudinal Survey (United States)
OECD	Organization for Economic Cooperation and Development (Paris)

OLF	Out of the Labor Force
PIB	Presse-und Informationsamt der Bundesregierung (Federal Press and Information Service) (Germany)
R&D	Research and Development
ROSLA	Raising of the School-Leaving Age (Great Britain)
SB	Statistisches Bundesamt (Federal Statistical Agency) (Germany)
SCAP	Supreme Commander Allied Powers
SCB	Statistiska Centralbyrån (Central Statistical Bureau) (Sweden)
SED	Scottish Education Department (United Kingdom)
SES	Socioeconomic Status
SMSA	Standard Metropolitan Statistical Area (United States)
SÖ	Skolöverstyrelsen (National Education Board) (Sweden)
SOU	Statens Offentliga Utredningar (Governmental Published Investigations) (Sweden)
UCCA	Universities' Central Council on Admissions (Great Britain)
UCLA	University of California, Los Angeles
UK	United Kingdom
UN	United Nations (New York and Geneva)
UNESCO	United Nations Educational, Scientific, and Cultural Organization (Paris)
US	United States
USCBO	United States Congressional Budget Office (see CBO)
USDOL/ASPER	United States Department of Labor, Office of the Assistant Secretary for Policy, Evaluation and Research
USSR	Union of Soviet Socialist Republics
WIN	Work Incentive Program (United States)
YEDPA	Youth Employment and Demonstration Projects Act of 1977 (United States)

1 Issues and Context

During much of the postwar period and especially in the booming 1960s, youth unemployment was not a problem in most of the industrialized market economy countries. Many nations could in fact look with satisfaction at youth unemployment rates, which were no higher or were even lower than the negligible rates of adults. High youth unemployment in the United States was an exceptional case, along with a few other countries, and some observers came to believe that deliberate policies and benign institutions in the favored countries were mainly responsible for their low youth unemployment. As one American analyst put it: "The better performance of foreign youth labor markets suggests that the problem in the U.S. is remediable" (Freeman 1976b, p. 43).

At the same time other American analysts developed alternative interpretations of persistently high youth unemployment in the United States, which rested on the demographic bulge in the youth labor force and the marked increase in the labor force participation of adult women (Hall 1970, 1971; Perry 1970, 1972). Implicitly or explicitly, these observed American developments were incorrectly assumed to be unique to the US, or at least more striking than in other countries. It also was assumed that young people always had and would have higher unemployment rates than adults, based on U.S. postwar experience and contrary to the evidence from other countries. Therefore, it was argued that an increased youth share of the labor force inevitably would be associated with higher youth unemployment rates and an upward pressure on the aggregate unemployment rate (Smith, S.P. 1976; Cain 1978, pp. 25–35, 1979; Antos, Mellow, and Triplett 1979; Flaim 1979; Wachter 1980, p. 44). Other analysts pointed to the necessary effects of demography on a worsened youth labor market position, including effects on labor force participation rates, types of employment, and relative earnings (Easterlin 1968, 1973; Wachter 1976, 1977; Adams and Mangum 1978, pp. 19–23; Freeman 1979a, 1979b, 1980b; Welch 1979).

Such American views did not strike a responsive chord in other countries in the 1960s. A few of these countries had had a more intense or prolonged baby boom than the United States, but they had not experienced an increase in youth or overall unemployment. In the years of reconstruction and extraordinary economic growth, some even encountered shortages of young workers when the native labor stock had to be reinforced by foreign workers and permanent immigrants, many of whom were in the youth age groups. Canada, however, had labor shortages and high youth unemployment simultaneously. Moreover, the Canadian adult unemployment rates, reflecting regional disparities, remained so high that ratios of youth to adult unemployment rates were comparatively low, unlike the United States.

The worldwide recession, which began in 1974, brought persistent and historically high youth unemployment to most of Western Europe and Oceania (Australia and New Zealand), and it even diminished the favorable position of youth in the Japanese labor market. As the decade ended without visible improvement in a number of countries and as gloomy forecasts were issued for the medium-term, several points became clear. First, the earlier characterization of most of the industrialized market economy countries as low youth unemployment countries had lost its validity, since almost all now suffered from the high youth unemployment.

1

Second, the earlier view that countries with low aggregate and youth unemployment had achieved this condition mainly through effective policies and institutions became suspect since these countries were unsuccessful in sustaining full employment during the 1970s. Third, by the mid-1970s many countries claimed that the demographic factor was an important explanation of youth unemployment. While the absolute number of young people and their share of the labor force was higher in the mid-1970s than it had been in the 1960s in some of these countries, in others the demographic burden was no greater (or less) than it had been in the earlier days of strong economic growth when demography rarely was mentioned. Finally, the 1970s recession, forcing a reappraisal of the factors that accounted for the earlier negligible youth unemployment in many countries, stimulated new basic studies of the forces underlying youth unemployment. In particular, analyses of trends in the postwar youth labor force appeared to be an essential and somewhat neglected background to youth unemployment. Accordingly, this book is concerned with a cross-national investigation of the youth labor supply from the end of World War II to the present, with projections to 1995.

Beyond the immediate policy relevance are more fundamental reasons to study the youth labor force. Underlying trends may be altering the structure of the entire youth labor market, affecting labor force participation rates and employment patterns as well as unemployment. Moreover, new entrants to the labor force, indeed the entire youth force, constitute the chief source of renewal of the working population. Serving as replacements, more often indirectly than directly, for those who leave the labor force, the new entrants at a minimum add to the total labor force stock. Because of their greater flexibility and mobility, new entrants also facilitate the adaptation of the total labor force to the new geographical, occupational, and skill requirements that result from economic development and change. Of course, the extent of the contribution of the new entrants in each country depends on how well their qualities and preparation match the specific needs of the economy, on the substitutability and complementarity of the new entrants, on the level of demand for labor, on the ease of the transition from school to work, on the degree and effects of segmentation in the labor market, and on the attitudes of employers toward inexperienced workers.

Each year a new cohort of young people enters the labor market, either full or part time. In most advanced countries the movement characteristically is from full-time education to full-time work, although young people in some countries are able to combine educational and labor force activity. The transfer occurs in a concentrated form at a particular time or times of year and has a high visibility. In addition, the annual influx of young people tends to be irregular in absolute and relative size over short and longer periods; this irregularity and the sudden surges and declines in numbers have been conspicuous in the postwar period and give importance to a study of trends in the absolute size of the youth labor force, youth shares of the total labor force, and youth labor force participation rates.

Economists might question the need to consider trends in the absolute size of the youth population and the youth labor force on the ground that the relevant dimension is the youth share of the population and labor force. The underlying assumptions are that young people in the labor force are fully substitutable for other age groups, and that changes in the youth share of the labor force will result in adjustments of their wage rates relative to those of other age groups. If youth wage rates do not adjust as expected, changes in youth unemployment rates relative to adult would be anticipated. In either case, it would be sufficient to measure the trends in youth shares rather than the absolute numbers. If, however, youth are not perfectly substitutable for adults in the labor force, and if, in fact, there exists a distinct youth labor market or segmentation of the labor market which affects a considerable proportion of young people, then a study of the youth share is not sufficient.

It then becomes important to consider the changes in absolute size also, since increased or decreased competition among youth for the youth jobs arises from alterations in the number of young people in the labor force over time. Because our own studies of youth employment, to be published at a later date, as well as other studies indicate that a number of jobs are largely filled by young people, especially teenagers, and that considerable occupational dissimilarity exists, we conclude that substitutability applies only to a part of the youth labor force. To understand the position of the remainder, it is necessary to give considerable weight to absolute changes in the size of the youth population and labor force. This we have therefore done in our study of the youth labor force.

In addition to the impact of the youth labor force on the economy, the study of the youth labor force is significant because of the varied problems faced by young people as they complete compulsory education and choose among the available alternatives: education or training, military service, recorded or unrecorded labor force activity, nonmarket work, inactivity, or combinations of two or more of these. For the youngest cohorts, education is most prominent, and the majority live at home with their parents. By the time they approach their twenty-fifth birthdays, most males and many females are full-time labor market participants, and a large proportion maintain their own homes. Movement among the alternatives accompanies settlement into working life over the course of the first five or ten years after leaving full-time education. Striking changes in the behavior of young women in recent decades give added point to studies of the youth labor force and dictate separate analysis of the two sexes on all issues.

This book deals comparatively with actual and projected medium-term trends in the youth labor force in the half-century from the end of World War II to 1995. Because this study focuses on young people rather than on the total labor supply, it explores only peripherally the central concerns of analyses of the whole labor force and its participation rates which, examining temporal and spatial variations, attempt to determine the nature and behavior of the labor supply and the process by which labor supply and demand are brought into equilibrium (Bowers 1975; Toikka, Scanlon, and Holt 1977). On the other hand, concentration on the youth labor force avoids the assumption, common in treatments of all age groups and found in some analyses of youth (Wachter 1972), that labor force participation begins after all formal education has been completed. Other theoretical and empirical work at the microlevel has stressed the importance of the simultaneity of decisions by young people about continuing their education and labor force participation. The two may be exclusive alternatives or may be combined in various ways, but in any case young people face a different set of choices than their elders. While the concept has been present in labor force analysis for some time, there have been recent advances in developing simultaneous-equation models (Bowen and Finegan 1969, p.380; Blinder and Weiss 1976; Mallar 1976; Stephenson 1977, 1978a; Johnson, T. 1978; Antos and Mellow 1979; Gustman and Steinmeier 1979). The role of trends in education is a key one in our analysis.

Our emphasis on medium-term overall national trends in advanced industrialized market economy countries and on comparisons across nations gives a minor role to the approach taken in studies at the microlevel, in which individual or household decisions in single countries, often based on cross-sectional data, are used to indicate the variables influencing behavior. Findings from such studies, however, are cited where relevant.

Comparative Approach

A cross-national framework has been deliberately adopted to study medium-term trends in the youth labor force. It may be asked whether the current diversity and even greater dissimilarities in history, traditions, institutions, and economic and social structures among the advanced industrialized market economy countries are not obstacles to using the comparative approach. Without underestimating the importance of these questions, it can be said that these are not insuperable difficulties and that the advantages of opening issues to comparative analysis outweigh the disadvantages. It is necessary and advantageous that comparative researchers be well informed about the differences among countries and be able to draw on such knowledge when divergent trends appear. Common trends appear as well, despite the many differences among countries. Here the challenge is to identify the common, overriding explanations of similarity without neglecting the variations in national influences that may account for divergence around the trends. Comparative analysis may thus serve to correct a tendency to assign universal meanings to national phenomena. Similarly, if like trends or developments are found in a large number of countries, the comparative method can sort out those causes that are widely observed and accepted from those that appear to be local or idiosyncratic. A more balanced causal explanation may then emerge for individual countries.

More fundamental advantages of the comparative method may be cited. The diversity of countries allows the testing of general theories and propositions developed for individual countries in a cross-national framework. Empirical tests of causal explanations on the basis of the experience of individual countries are weakened by a lack of variability in some of the parameters. Theories claiming or implying general validity should be valid in the light of the diversity of economic and social patterns, historical trends, and institutional arrangements. Some variables cannot be adequately studied for individual countries. Vigorous tests under diverse circumstances are especially important for judging the merits of ex post explanations. Microeconomic models that focus on household or individual decisions implicitly attach time and place universality to specific historical and national conditions. Cross-national analysis may, therefore, help to offset some built-in biases in microanalysis.

Labor Force Measurement and Concepts

A comparative study of the youth labor force must decide which labor force definitions, concepts, and data will be used, given the national variations. It also must assess whether changes over time in the measurement of the labor force within countries and differences among countries at various points in time adversely affect the continuity of national trends or the comparability of data among countries.

Measuring the Youth Labor Force

Ideally, a comparative study would not deal mainly with the number and proportion of young people willing to supply labor to the market. It would be concerned equally with the number of hours per week and weeks per year supplied or offered to the market by young people, supplemented by qualitative estimates of the skill, knowledge, intensity, diligence, reliability, accuracy, and continuity with which members of the youth force work or seek to work.

Special circumstances affecting youth, in contrast to other age groups, make this approach particularly desirable. Young people, more in some countries than others, are seen as a secondary labor force that is committed to labor market activity, intermittently and often on a part-time basis. Young people are believed to have considerable discretion in making decisions about whether to work, how much to work, how hard to work, where to work, and at what jobs to work. This freedom of choice of youth, relative to the lack of choice about labor market decisions facing adult males, is attributed by some to a lack of pressure to earn a living. Family support or other sources of income make it possible for such young people to work part time or part year. A further contribution to intermittent patterns of youth is made by those who combine or alternate labor force participation, education, and/or nonmarket work (Parnes 1970; Wachter 1972, 1980).

In light of these youth patterns, it is significant that most data and discussions of the labor force deal with the number of individuals, rather than the number of hours offered on the labor market or the amount and quality of effort expended. The latter categories have been widely recognized as more relevant in an economic accounting (Hunter 1970; Parnes 1970; Ashenfelter and Heckman 1972; Wickens 1974). In part, a lack of acceptable data leads to the widespread use of numbers of individuals as the sole measure; but in part the situation arises from the broader interest of sociologists, educators, psychologists, and government policymakers in individuals rather than hours supplied to the labor force.

In practice, the most available and complete comparative data deal with the number and proportion of young people in the labor force at various points in time, unqualified by hours supplied or quality of effort. This data base therefore becomes the mainstay of our comparative analysis, although attention is given to the other measures where comparative data permit. The numbers of young people in the labor force should be modified by the hours and weeks they work or seek to work, both in order to tally the productive resources available to the economy and also to understand the activities of the young people themselves. Even when such modifications cannot be made because of data deficiencies, we attempt to separate the youth labor force by school enrollment status in those countries where the enrolled labor force is significant. If allowance is not made for the composition of the youth labor force and trends in the degree of less than full-time work by young people, misleading comparisons over time and among nations result.

Accepting that the number of young people in the labor force constitutes the basic unit of measurement in this study, we find a compatibility among countries in the basic definitions (Appendix 4:1). Differences among countries in the treatment of youth in the military forces can be reconciled in the data for most countries or be given ad hoc adjustment. Labor force participation by students is, for the most part, treated similarly by countries, especially in labor force surveys (Appendix 4:1). The real differences among nations because of variations in the proportion of students in the population, their propensity to be in the labor force during the school term and/or during vacation periods, and their patterns of work hours and weeks is, of course, a prime subject for analysis in this study, found in Chapter 5.

Nevertheless, there may be trends within countries and differences among countries in the labor force count of certain peripheral categories that affect comparability. Only the labor force as a whole is at issue. If individuals have been counted as employed rather than unemployed or vice versa in some countries but not in others, or at one time but not another, the total in the labor force is unaffected and neither national trends nor cross-national comparisons are impaired. If, however, certain individuals are counted as not in the labor force when they are in fact working (or vice versa) or if they are not counted at all, distortion of the true size of the youth labor force occurs, and it may not be constant over time or among countries. In particular, the incidence and statistical treatment of discouraged workers varies among nations.

An important cause of undercounting youth employment in some countries is the exclusion of "black labor," those whom employers hire unofficially without paying the required social security taxes, or those who work directly for customers without recording the hours or income. Officially they may be unemployed or out of the labor force. If illegal immigrants are in the youth labor force, they might not be recorded, unless they possess false papers. Individuals who work while claiming to be unemployed or out of the labor force (because they are receiving unemployment, illness, or disability benefits or other payments), those engaging in profitable illicit activities, and those who engage in unreported work at home or in barter arrangements add to the total, to the extent that they are otherwise not counted at all or are counted as out of the labor force. By its nature, this category is difficult to estimate (Andersen 1977; Hoagland 1977; Frey 1978; Donaldson 1979, p. 42; GB 1969-80). It is likely that this category constitutes a somewhat larger segment in America and Italy than in most other countries, but it probably is not large enough in any country, except perhaps Italy, to invalidate the acceptance of the officially recorded youth labor force for comparative analysis. It also is unlikely that national youth labor force trends, except possibly for Italy, are seriously distorted by the exclusion of this category. Nevertheless, the existence of the category should be recognized.

On the other hand, unpaid family labor by young people may be recorded so fully in some countries that there is a relative overstatement of employment. Another observation may apply particularly to the four Nordic countries, where employment figures may be swollen by including those who have relatively long leaves of absence from jobs. This probably affects young people less than others. A recommendation for Nordic labor market statistics in the 1980s suggests that such persons should be listed under their actual activity (Farm 1979). On the whole, these additions to employment and the labor force are less important than the exclusions, although the balance between the two varies between countries.

Another source of concern about the continuity of trends in youth labor force size and the validity of comparative analysis arises from the considerable expansion in most countries of government social programs. These income transfer programs are alleged to have an unintended impact on work incentives. Since such programs differ across countries in number, type, coverage, provisions, and in the response of young people to them, a finding that the size of the labor force was significantly affected in individual nations would require some adjustments for comparative purposes.

Most of the analysis and controversial findings regarding such government social programs deal with the impact of income transfers or support programs on the distribution of individuals between employment and unemployment, or more precisely the number of hours of work chosen by individuals, on the dubious assumption that workers are free to reduce or increase their hours at will. The fact is, however, that our major concern is the distinction between in and out of the labor force as it affects trends in the statistics. To the extent that income support programs chiefly affect the division within the youth labor force between the employed and the unemployed, or influence the number of hours worked rather than the decision to be in or out of the labor force, the statistics with which we deal are unaffected. This is not to deny that a policy issue of another kind exists in many countries today. The income guarantee effect of public support programs and the high implicit tax on earnings appear to increase the proportion of the unemployed whose job search is prolonged, if not desultory or insincere, casting doubt on unemployment statistics, income support programs, and broader government policy (Cain 1978, pp. 35–41; OECD 1978h). A later chapter weighs government programs as a factor influencing trends in the proportion of youth out of the labor force.

Labor Force Concepts

Thus far the discussion has dealt with possible distortions of national trends in youth labor force statistics that might affect cross-national comparisons. It has been tacitly assumed that the conventional division of the youth population's nonleisure time activities is valid. That division consists of the following:

In the civilian labor force ("employed" plus "unemployed")
In the armed forces ("employed" *or* "employed plus not in labor force")
In school ("not in the labor force" plus "in the labor force")
Not in school or the labor force ("do not want to work" plus "want to work")

This division is not to everyone's satisfaction. Those who have given particular attention to changes in the structure of the household and family and trends in female labor force participation have raised questions about the traditional categories and definitions (Watts and Skidmore 1978, pp. 40–41). Proposals to the Labor Market Committee of the Nordic Council, a supranational agency of the four Scandinavian countries, recommended the introduction of two new categories to replace the old ones. The economically active would consist of the employed, those in household work, and enrolled students. The economically inactive would consist of the unemployed and all others (Farm 1979). In the proposed treatment of students as economically active, the Scandinavian approach is reminiscent of the treatment in Bowen and Finegan (1969, p. 380) which has not appeared often in later analysis (Wachter 1980, pp. 49–53). In its suggestion that the unemployed and those not in the labor force be combined, the Scandinavian proposal echoes an important new development in American analysis on youth labor markets.

A viewpoint has emerged among a group of influential U.S. analysts that "the unemployment/not in the labor force distinction is virtually meaningless for young people" (Clark and Summers 1979b, p. 9). We give this development considerable attention because, if it should be widely accepted, it would cause the conventional division of the population into "in the labor force" and "not in the labor force" to be replaced by "employed" and "not employed." The conceptual issues must be faced as well as the practical difficulties in gathering suitable statistics for a cross-national comparison in countries which have presented their official data only in the traditional manner.

Four separate strands of analysis can be identified as leading to this new formulation. They are varied in focus and findings. Concern about deteriorating black-white ratios for youth unemployment led some analysts to question whether unemployment rates properly reflected the disadvantage of black youth. These rates were computed on a youth labor force base which itself displayed an independent trend of black youth labor force participation rates that were not keeping pace with white youth LFPR, therefore tending to understate the employment problems of black youth in the form of lower LFPR. As a remedy for this defect in the unemployment rate as an indicator, employment/population ratios were introduced. The residual was called "joblessness" or "nonemployment," a combination of the unemployed and all who were out of the labor force, including those in school (Freeman and Medoff 1978; Freeman 1979a, 1980b).

The second line of approach, which fosters but does not explicitly discern a shadowy line between youth who are unemployed and those who are out of the labor force, stresses the slow maturation process by which young people, especially those from disadvantaged backgrounds, develop labor market attachment on a full-time basis (Osterman 1978, 1979, 1980). This interpretation found official acceptance in planning programs under the Youth Employment and Demonstration Projects Act (YEDPA) of 1977.

A related but more negative view of youth, derived from analysis of both cross-sectional and longitudinal data, considers that many out-of-school youth who claim to be unemployed hardly search for jobs and therefore cannot be distinguished from those not in the labor force (NILF) in regard to their weak attachment to the labor market. Since gross flow analyses of the raw data from the Current Population Surveys indicate frequent movement between unemployment and NILF status among youth, the addition of the unemployed and NILF in a category of "nonemployed" appears to be justified (Ellwood 1979; Feldstein and Ellwood 1979; Meyer and Wise 1979). Some of the resulting studies also offer conventional unemployment data, but others present only the new measure of nonemployment or joblessness. A compatible finding has been that the same categories of individuals who predominate in the NILF category also make up a majority of the unemployed (Hall 1978).

The fourth line of analysis has been influential, forming the basis in part for the first and third views, although its main interpretation has not been accepted. Extending the gross flow analysis of other practitioners who had shown frequent movement, especially by youth, among employment, unemployment, and NILF statuses, Clark and Summers (1978b, 1979b) concentrate on youth; their related studies deal with other age groups as well (1978a, 1979a). Disagreeing with the weak attachment argument, Clark and Summers declare that "the sharp cyclical sensitivity of youth employment belies the suggestion that the unemployed do not really want to work or that they are incapable of working productively. The cyclical evidence suggests that a shortage of attractive jobs is the root cause of the youth non-employment problem" (1979b, p. 2).

Clark and Summers endorse the concept of nonemployment on the ground that it more accurately describes the situation of young people. Urging that "there is reason to doubt the salience of the unemployment not-in-the labor force distinction for young people," they explain:

> Unemployment durations appear to be short in large part because of high rates of labor force withdrawal. The brevity of many spells outside the labor force suggests that many of those who withdraw are in fact sensitive to labor market conditions. Indeed, it appears that our official statistics frequently record two brief spells of unemployment, broken by a period outside the labor force, when a single spell of joblessness would be more appropriate (1979b, p. 19).

The possibility that measurement error accounts for some or much of the observed rapid movement is one of the acknowledged defects of the gross flow data (Pearl

1963; Hilaski 1968; McCarthy 1978; Denton 1973; Smith and Vanski 1978; Bowers 1980, pp. 24–25).

One of the contributions of Clark and Summers in their gross flows analysis is the division of youth into two groups, the enrolled and nonenrolled (1979b, Table 1.1). They computed the probabilities of moving among the various labor force statuses and presented the numbers involved in the average gross flows over a three-month period in 1976. We have constructed Chart 1.1 to represent these flows for youth, with each sex separately represented; stock data for March 1976 have been added. Charts 1.2, 1.3 and 1.4 show similar gross flows for adults in the United States, Sweden, and Canada in various years of the 1970s.

These charts suggest several points. First, youth in the US on average are more likely to move between labor force statuses than the 16 through 59 working-age population. If Canadian and Swedish youth data were available, they would also show this. Second, enrolled youth have higher average movement rates than nonenrolled. This also would be expected in Canada and Sweden. Third, among adults of both sexes, Swedes in one quarter in 1970 had far more month-to-month gross movement than the US in one quarter in 1976 or Canada in the year of 1974. As regards net change, however, Canada and Sweden show a balancing out of the numbers involved in gross flows, while all three age-enrollment groups and both sexes in the US show distinct net movement, mostly in the direction of increased employment.

On the basis of their work with gross flows and other data, Clark and Summers concluded that "the behavior of most of the unemployed and many persons outside the labor force is functionally indistinguishable. . . . The evidence suggests that attention should be focused on the youth non-employment problem, rather than merely on unemployment" (1979b, p. 2). Although Clark and Summers were aware that some youth unemployed did not leave that category until they returned to

Chart 1.1   Stocks and Gross Flows in the U.S. Teenage (16–19) Labor Force, by Sex and School Enrollment Status, March–May 1976

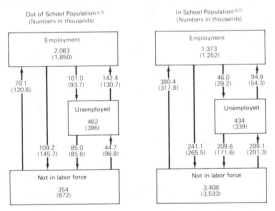

aStocks as of March 1976; bData for females in parentheses.

Source: Stocks: U.S. Department of Labor, Bureau of Labor Statistics, unpublished data. Flows: Calculated from Clark, K.B., and Summers, L.H., The Dynamics of Youth Unemployment, Table 1.1. Paper prepared for the National Bureau for Economic Research Conference on Youth Unemployment, Airlie, Virginia, May 1979.

Chart 1.2   Stocks and Gross Flows in the U.S. Labor Force, by Sex, 16–59 Years Old, March–May 1976

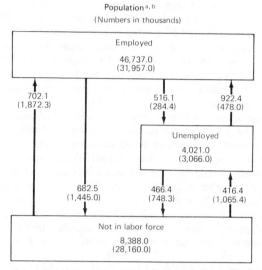

Population[a, b]

(Numbers in thousands)

Employed

46,737.0
(31,957.0)

702.1
(1,872.3)

516.1
(284.4)

922.4
(478.0)

Unemployed

4,021.0
(3,066.0)

682.5
(1,445.0)

466.4
(748.3)

416.4
(1,065.4)

Not in labor force

8,388.0
(28,160.0)

[a]Stocks as of March 1976; [b]Data for females in parentheses.

Source: Stocks: U.S. Department of Labor, Bureau of Labor Statistics, Employment and Earnings April 1976, Table A-3 (Washington: GPO). Flows: same as Chart 1.1.

Chart 1.3   Stocks and Gross Flows in the Swedish Labor Force, by Sex, 16–74 Years Old, 1970 (one quarter)

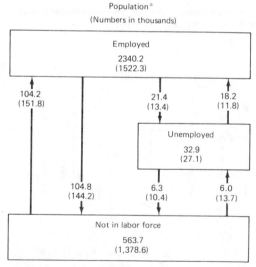

Population[a]

(Numbers in thousands)

Employed

2340.2
(1522.3)

104.2
(151.8)

21.4
(13.4)

18.2
(11.8)

Unemployed

32.9
(27.1)

104.8
(144.2)

6.3
(10.4)

6.0
(13.7)

Not in labor force

563.7
(1,378.6)

[a]Data for females in parentheses.

Source: Sweden. Ministry of Labor, Arbetsmarknads politik i forändring [Labor Market Policy in Transition], Figure 4, p. 119 (Stockholm, 1978).

Chart 1.4   Stocks and Gross Flows in the Canadian Labor Force, by Sex, 16 Years and Older, 1974

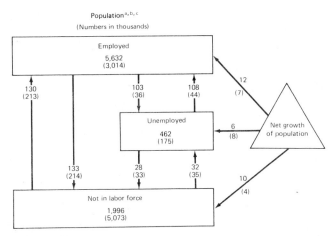

Population[a,b,c]
(Numbers in thousands)

[a]Stocks as of January 1974; [b]Gross Flows are annual averages of monthly data for 1974; [c]Data for females in parentheses.

Source: Canada. Department of Manpower and Immigration, Strategic Planning and Research Division, Research Projects Group, Labour Market Flows in Canada, Table 1.3, Appendix D (Ottawa, 1976).

employment and that many who were NILF did not move to employment or unemployment, the practical effect of their own research has been that other analysts who used cross-sectional or longitudinal data have added the entire category of unemployed and the entire category of NILF, creating the "nonemployed." Often this research has not provided any separate data on the two components.

Without denying that there is a continuum between a segment of the youth unemployed and some of the youth who are NILF, it is possible to question the validity and utility of the nonemployment category, especially if it is unaccompanied by separate information on conventionally defined unemployment (Bowers 1980, pp. 28–29; Wachter 1980, p. 55). Our own scepticism has been stimulated by the results of two studies, one American and one Swedish, which bear on this issue. These studies, which followed individuals over a considerably longer time period than Clark and Summers did, provide a somewhat different perspective on the nonemployment category as an alternative to the unemployed and NILF as separate entities.

Stephen Hills of the Center for Human Resource Research at the Ohio State University utilized that organization's longitudinal survey data for young males to investigate how weeks of unemployment and weeks NILF were distributed among individuals. Hills's unpublished study examined the records of young men who had left high school and college in 1967, 1968, and 1969. He constructed a pooled weighted sample of those who were not employed during the first year after leaving school (t + 1); they constituted 54 percent of all leavers. Hills then computed for each person the ratio of the number of weeks of unemployment in t + 1 to their total number of weeks unemployed plus weeks out of the labor force. Persons who had only weeks of unemployment would register a ratio of 100 while those who had only weeks out of the labor force would have a ratio of 0. Those falling between 0 and 100 would have a mixture of weeks of unemployment and NILF. Hills's calculations indicated that only a small minority of the weeks in each of the three groups of young males were accounted for by individuals whose year-long pattern consisted of a mixture of weeks of unemployment and weeks out of the labor force. As the number of years out of school increased, the proportion with a mixed record decreased.

High school leavers showed only 27 percent of their total weeks in the mixed pattern. Among the 724 sampled high school leavers, 73 percent of the weeks were either entirely weeks of unemployment (30 percent) or entirely weeks of NILF (43 percent). For the 329 sampled college leavers, the total proportion of mixed weeks also was 27 percent; 19 percent were weeks only of unemployment and 54 percent were weeks only of NILF. The control group of 465, which had been out of high school for four years, showed just 11 percent of mixed weeks; 36 percent were weeks only of unemployment and 53 percent were weeks only NILF.

While there were indeed individuals whose year consisted of some weeks of unemployment and some out of the labor force, the majority of individuals (and of weeks) were reported either as in unemployed status or as in NILF status. This division between individuals suggests differences in the composition and reasons for being in the two categories. The experience of this group would have been misrepresented if the nonemployed category had been used instead of the separate categories. Additional longitudinal study is needed of similar youth who had some employment in the follow-up period; an extension to two or more years would be desirable also, as would a separate examination of females from the same data source. The fact that these longitudinal data are collected from the individuals involved, rather than from a household respondent as in the case of the CPS survey, is of some importance.

The Swedish study, going further than Clark and Summers in making longitudinal use of processed and reedited cross-sectional labor force survey data, followed up a rotation group from the survey sample over a two-year period. On the basis of eight entries, each individual was assigned to one of five labor force statuses: two represent stability, two signify modified stability, and one encompasses the changes of status that gross flow data stress. Between 1970 and 1977, six periods of two years each were studied and six sets of separate individuals, divided by age and sex, were followed. For our purposes, this innovative study has only one drawback: enrolled youth are not separated from nonenrolled. In the basic part of the study, those in the labor force are not divided into employed and unemployed, but later portions of the study make that division (Sweden 1979a).

The major finding is significant because the Swedish labor force survey is directed to individuals and is answered by them rather than by family members, and because the Swedish survey may otherwise have lower measurement error than the American (Sweden 1979a, pp. 55-59). It was demonstrated that the youth groups as well as all others had higher proportions in a completely unchanged labor force status over a two-year period (either in the labor force or out of it the entire time) than in the changers' category which consisted of those who had a mix of in and out of the labor force. The other two labor force statuses that expressed a modified stability were called entrants and leavers. Entrants were those who were out of the labor force at the beginning of the two-year period, but who entered and remained in the labor force for the rest of the period. Leavers were those who started out in the labor force, left it, and did not return over the two-year period. These two groups accounted for a minority of the total in all cases (Table 1.1).

Both male and female teenagers show a higher proportion of "changers" than any other age group, as might be expected (Table 1.1). Nevertheless, teenage changers

Table 1.1 Distribution of Population by Labor Force Status Over a Two-Year Period, by Age and Sex, Sweden, 1970-1972 to 1975-1977

Labor force status	16-19 Years Male (percent)			16-19 Years Female (percent)			20-24 Years Male (percent)			20-24 Years Female (percent)		
	1970-72	1975-77	Average six periods	1970-72	1975-77	Average six periods	1970-72	1975-77	Average six periods	1970-72	1975-77	Average six periods
Total	100.0	100.0	100.0	100.0	100.0	100.0	100.0	100.0	100.0	100.0	100.0	100.0
In labor force	32.4	40.2	33.8	28.2	33.8	29.3	61.8	73.9	66.2	44.1	52.9	49.3
Entrants	12.6	13.5	15.6	16.4	18.7	17.5	10.0	8.4	9.4	10.1	10.6	10.6
Changers	37.4	34.4	37.3	36.8	34.3	36.9	19.6	12.9	18.3	24.0	19.5	21.7
Leavers	6.0	4.4	5.0	8.0	5.4	6.9	3.9	2.3	2.7	9.4	7.1	7.6
Out of labor force	11.4	7.5	8.4	10.6	7.8	9.6	4.7	2.6	3.4	12.4	9.9	10.9

Labor force status	35-44 Years Male (percent)			35-44 Years Female (percent)			16-64 Years Male (percent)			16-64 Years Female (percent)		
	1970-72	1975-77	Average six periods	1970-72	1975-77	Average six periods	1970-72	1975-77	Average six periods	1970-72	1975-77	Average six periods
Total	100.0	100.0	100.0	100.0	100.0	100.0	100.0	100.0	100.0	100.0	100.0	100.0
In labor force	92.8	95.5	93.5	54.0	67.3	60.7	79.8	83.6	81.3	44.0	55.7	49.9
Entrants	0.9	0.7	0.9	7.1	5.8	6.3	3.6	2.8	3.4	6.9	6.7	6.9
Changers	3.2	1.4	2.7	18.0	11.8	15.1	9.1	6.8	8.3	21.1	14.2	17.7
Leavers	1.2	0.8	1.0	3.0	2.3	2.7	3.0	2.2	2.6	5.8	4.3	5.2
Out of labor force	1.8	1.6	1.9	17.8	12.8	15.3	4.4	4.6	4.5	22.2	19.1	20.9

Source: Sweden. SCB (Statistiska Centralbyrån), *Strömmarna till och från arbetskraften 1970-1977* [The Flows to and from the Labor Force 1970-1977], Tables 1a–1f. IPF 1979:3 (Stockholm, 1979).

were under 40 percent of all youth at all times, and the proportion tended to decline over time. If it is recognized that enrolled students who worked during the summer contributed to the changers' category, the significance of this group for youth as a whole would diminish. A majority of youth were in the stable or modified stable categories. Attachment of teenagers also is signified by the increase over time in the proportion who were in the labor force or were entrants, while those who were out of the labor force or were leavers decreased their share (Sweden 1979a, Table 33). Although these data do not separate the employed and unemployed, all movements from or to either of those statuses to or from NILF status are captured. These general findings do not portray a youth population dominated by movements in and out of the labor force. While we lack firm evidence that these detailed Swedish results are typical of all other countries, independent information suggests that even greater stability characterizes youth in most of our countries and that a similar analysis for the United States would not find markedly different patterns.

Further findings about employment and unemployment, distinguished by the separate labor force status categories established at the outset, support the initial findings. The Swedish survey, computing the proportions who were employed during all the time they were in the labor force, presented separate data for each of the six two-year periods (Sweden 1979a, Table 5.1). In view of the possibility that some movements from employment to out-of-the labor force may have masked unemployment, the results for the two-year periods of least and greatest stability may slightly exaggerate the extent of continuous employment. A minority of teen-agers, and relatively fewer than in any other age group, enjoyed continuity of employment throughout a two-year period (Table 1.2). The majority had spells of unemployment mixed with employment while remaining in the labor force.

A related analysis for 1975–1977 shows that the proportion with unemployment at some time varied considerably according to the assigned labor force status (Sweden 1979a, Table 5.2). In the youth groups, unemployment fell relatively lightly on the stable and leavers' groups (Table 1.3), but the latter may have had concealed unemployment. On the other hand, many may have returned to school after vaca-tion work.

The Swedish study provides an interesting model that could be replicated in other countries using rotation samples from their labor force surveys. More detail could be collected on the categories of youth identified as engaging in frequent movement among the various labor force statuses in order to determine how much extended unemployment is masked by withdrawal from the labor force in other countries. The whole subject of weak attachment also lends itself to examination in this framework. One of the main contributions of the Swedish study is its establishment of the

Table 1.2 Persons with Steady Employment in a Two-Year Period, Sweden, 1971–1977

Period	16–19		20–24		35–44		16–64	
	Male	Female	Male	Female	Male	Female	Male	Female
	(percent)							
Low Stability	24.6	20.2	56.7	40.9	87.7	52.4	74.8	42.0
High Stability	37.3	28.3	71.2	50.1	94.0	66.1	81.3	54.3

Source: Sweden 1979a, Table 5.1.

Table 1.3   Persons Unemployed at Any Time, by Labor Force Status, Sweden
1975–1977

Age and sex group	Stable	Entrants	Changers	Leavers
		(percent)		
16–19 Male	7.3	15.5	10.3	5.6
Female	16.3	24.5	18.4	17.5
20–24 Male	3.6	21.5	16.5	(13.6)[a]
Female	6.6	17.7	29.7	11.3
25–34 Male	2.6	23.7	19.4	28.6
Female	3.1	18.5	18.4	11.0
16–64 Male	2.6	19.6	14.9	9.2
Female	3.4	18.3	17.5	9.3

[a] Sample too small to be reliable.

Source: Sweden 1979a, Table 5.2.

relative importance for youth of the five different patterns over a reasonable time period. As important as the frequent changers are, they are not the dominant group among all youth, although youth who made at least one change would constitute a majority of all in the labor force at any given time.

The Swedish study presented the following useful diagrammatic scheme, applicable to any population (Sweden 1979a, p.52):

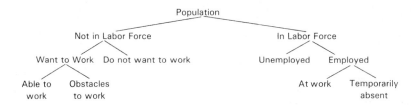

Despite the acceptance by the Swedish analysts of a considerable flow among the categories enumerated above, as a result of their study they did not suggest any changes along the lines of combining the unemployed and not in the labor force. Based on our review of existing evidence, we find it premature to replace the term "labor force" by "employment," and "not in the labor force" by "not employed" or "jobless." We are convinced that the conventional classifications are still valid for our study, especially since our cross-national study concerns the labor force rather than its unemployed component. It is salutary, nevertheless, to bear in mind how inadequately moment-in-time data on youth as a whole reflect the changes in status of individuals over time.

A strong impression conveyed by all of the material we have reviewed on this demarcation issue is that little is known about those who are not in the labor force. It is a major part of our study of medium-term trends in the youth labor force to bring together available information on the subject of the NILF group in a comparative framework. We hypothesize that the youth population that is not in the labor force (and not in school) is a heterogeneous group and that only a part, possibly a minority, are not in the labor force for labor market reasons. If, in fact, it turns out that most or a substantial part of the NILF category is not relevant to the unemployed or nonemployed concept, there will be a strong case against a nonemployed or jobless classification that adds all NILF to the unemployed. A better understanding of the NILF category also will contribute to our basic purpose of studying the youth labor force in a number of countries in the postwar period.

Data Base

This study analyzes data for a large number of countries. Choosing from the member countries of the Organization for Economic Cooperation and Development (OECD), we selected twelve industrialized market economy countries, reasonably diverse in size, geographical location, and demographic, educational, and labor force trends. Europe provided seven countries: France, Italy, the Netherlands, Sweden, Switzerland, the United Kingdom, and the Federal Republic of Germany.* Canada, the United States, Australia, New Zealand, and Japan comprise the remaining five countries. While only some of the industrialized European members of OECD were chosen, all five of the non-European industrialized members are included.

Some background evidence on the diversity of our twelve countries is presented in Table 1.4. Total population in 1978 ranged from a little over 3 million in New Zealand to almost 219 million in the United States. Physical area is in striking disproportion to population, in many cases. Crowding characterizes Japan and the Netherlands, while Australia and Canada have the thinnest settlement, even after allowance for uninhabitable areas. Gross domestic product, expressed in U.S. dollars per capita, was almost three times higher in Switzerland, the leader, than in its neighbor, Italy, which was at the bottom of the distribution. All but three of the countries had a 1977 GDP of over $6000 per capita. These OECD calculations are subject to qualification because of fluctuations in exchange rates and national claims that their relative rankings do them an injustice by not capturing all the social overhead provisions and the qualitative aspects of life.

National rankings for total civilian employment are similar to those for population, although Japan and Sweden have higher than the average ratio of employment to population, and Italy and the Netherlands are on the low side. Employment distribution by sector in 1954 and 1978 indicates that the declines experienced by all countries in the share of total employment attributable to agriculture, forestry, and fishing have reduced the differences among the countries. By 1978, only three countries — Italy, Japan, and New Zealand — had over 10 percent of civilian employment in these primary industries, and none had over 16 percent. Increases in the employment share attributed to services in every country resulted in only three countries, Italy, Germany and Switzerland, with less than half of all employment in the service sector by 1978. Canada, with almost two-thirds of the employed in this category, was highest, followed closely by the United States, with Australia, the Netherlands, and Sweden also showing relatively high proportions.

This study defines young people as those under 25 years of age. National data are not uniform in regard to the lower cutoff age. Most countries choose the age at which compulsory schooling ends or the age at which young people may legally enter full-time work. While these are usually identical, some countries have a higher age limit for leaving school than for obtaining a work permit, often of a limited type. Italy has been unusual in that youngsters are permitted to leave school at 14 but can-

---

*Hereafter referred to as Germany.

Table 1.4 Basic Indicators for Twelve Countries, 1978

| | | | | | Percent of civilian employment in | | | | |
| | | | | | Agriculture, forestry, fishing | | Services[b] | | |
	Population (in thousands)	Area (in 1000 sq. km.)	Gross domestic product per capita[a] (US $)	Total civilian employment (in thousands)	1954	1978	1954	1965	1978
Australia	14,249	7,686.8	7,660	5,975	n.a.	6.4	n.a.	n.a.	62.0
Canada	23,499	9,976.1	8,740	9,972	19.0	5.7	47.8	56.2	65.6
France	53,278	549.1	8,850	20,921	27.9	9.1	35.1	41.1	53.8
Federal Republic of Germany	61,327	248.6	10,420	24,679	18.8	6.5	35.2	39.4	48.4
Italy	56,697	301.2	4,590	19,932	43.1	15.5	26.4	33.3	46.2
Japan	114,920	372.3	8,480	54,080	40.6	11.7	34.6	42.3	53.3
Netherlands	13,937	41.2	9,380	4,569	n.a.	6.2	n.a.	46.2	61.3
New Zealand	3,129	269.1	5,880	1,215[c]	n.a.	11.6[c]	n.a.	n.a.	53.8[c]
Sweden	8,278	450.0	10,550	4,115	14.4[d]	6.1	n.a.	45.9	60.9
Switzerland	6,337	41.3	13,340	2,839	16.5[e]	8.4	36.7[e]	39.2[f]	48.9
United Kingdom	55,902	244.0	5,530	24,610	9.7	2.7	46.4	49.0[f]	57.6
United States	218,548	9,363.1	9,660	94,373	10.7	3.7	54.1	60.9[f]	65.1

[a] At 1978 prices and exchange rates (new standardized national accounts).
[b] All activities other than agriculture, forestry, fishing, mining and quarrying, construction, public utilities, and manufacturing.
[c] 1977.
[d] 1961.
[e] 1950.
[f] OECD Secretariat estimates.

Source: OECD Observer, February 1967 (annual series of tables on member countries), March 1980; OECD, Manpower Statistics 1954–1964 (Paris: OECD, 1965).

not secure work permits legally until they are 15. In federal countries, variations among political subdivisions in school-leaving and work-permit ages cause us to use the most common age in such countries. International agencies also set a single cutoff age in their data, in keeping with current practice in most member countries. Their choice of 15 as the lower age limit is reasonable, but it is necessary to allow for countries where 14 to 16 is the more usual age, both in historical trends within countries and in cross-national comparisons.

This span of nine to eleven years embraces young people who are pursuing a wide variety and ever-changing balance of activities. The aging of cohorts and changes in activities over the years are a crucial part of the youth story, although youth data usually do not permit close examination of differences across single years of age. Most countries and the international agencies divide the youth group into teenagers and young adults. These two age groups are the most frequent units of analysis in the chapters which follow, although it is desirable to separate the flow of new entrants into the labor market from the total youth labor force in a given age group. Only a few countries have a usable data series on new entrants to the labor market, however.

The study requires basic statistics relating to demographic, educational, and labor force developments in the twelve countries. On the whole, the national statistical variations are a less important constraint on comparisons than are institutional and organizational differences. Comparability of data is not a problem for most of the demographic variables, particularly live births and infant mortality. In the case of educational enrollments and labor force data, definitions and measurement methods do vary across nations. While recognizing that the comparability of national concepts, definitions, and data is a significant issue, we find that the nature of the project reduces the number of specific problems we confront. The reliability of a data base depends on the particular questions to be answered; data problems are diminished when cross-national comparisons refer to the direction and steepness of trends rather than absolute levels. Moreover, the amount of cross-national variation over time in the relative magnitudes of several of our most important variables is fairly large, making it likely that measurement bias is small. In order to reduce comparability problems in national data, we made some adjustments directly, and in other cases used national series while taking account of differences in coverage and method.

Furthermore, the increased statistical activity of the international organizations, especially the Organization for Economic Cooperation and Development (OECD), the International Labor Office (ILO), and the United Nations (UN), has aided our comparative study. We have utilized data developed by the international agencies because they have made efforts to establish a uniform basis for country tabulations. Each of these agencies has set up detailed forms requesting data from member countries, accompanied by clear instructions and standardized definitions and concepts for all respondents. In spite of these efforts by international agencies, the day of complete and reliable uniformity in national statistics is not yet at hand. The data sent in by countries frequently are not precisely those that were requested and may be inconsistent with country responses made in earlier years.

Some of the reasons for this unsatisfactory performance are: the lack of national data in the requested form, which entails time and money to comply properly and results in a mixture of existing data and estimates; the assignment of the response to national officials who are not authorities on the subject; the frequent turnover of the national personnel in charge of making the responses; the large number and duplication of requests, sometimes identical and sometimes with minor variations, emanating from a group of international organizations that do not pool information, cooperate on requests, or plan jointly. Within the international organizations, the processing of the country responses falls to a remarkably small staff who, however competent, often lack the time and resources to check on or improve the data they have received. Where countries do not respond at all, some international agencies leave blanks or make estimates. Despite these drawbacks, this attempt at comparative analysis could hardly be undertaken without data from the international agencies. In other cases, the existence of international data permitted a less laborious and time-consuming effort than the use of national data would have required.

Raw data from national and international sources are supplemented by relevant published and unpublished empirical studies based on cross-sectional and longitudinal data for national or subnational samples. Most of these secondary sources deal with one country, but a few provide comparative materials. Our citation of studies made in a single country often is directed toward encouraging similar lines of inquiry in other countries in order to widen the comparative data base, resolve unsettled issues, and reexamine answers derived in a national context. Because so much of the theoretical and empirical investigation of labor supply has been undertaken by Americans, we strive to avoid an American bias in framing the issues and finding the answers. It is significant, in this connection, that a recent review of British research on economic activity rates devoted considerable space to American studies on the ground that much of the British work was "secondary literature, deriving its inspiration and methodology from the American work. Another portion of British work, slighted in this review, has drawn on a different theoretical tradition" (Bowers 1975, p. 72).

It would be desirable to undertake comparisons of subnational demographic and labor force trends in geographic regions, extending our brief attempt at subnational analysis of educational enrollment rates and the more detailed discussion of minority and immigrant youth in Chapter 7. A central question still to be answered is whether countries have as much variation in youth labor supply within their boundaries as exists between countries. Although limitations of time and space prevent an investigation at this time, we feel that the subject is important.

Explanatory Factors

This comparative study of medium-term trends in the youth labor force encompassing a half-century—the historical period from the end of World War II to 1975–1980 and projections to 1995—selects as its explanatory variables such basic factors as demographic trends in all age groups, educational enrollment trends, trends in the LFPR of nonyouth groups, the propensity over time for young people to be neither in school nor the labor force, and the impact of government programs. In choosing these supply-size variables, we are hypothesizing that medium-term trends in the youth labor force are more strongly influenced by supply-side than demand-side factors. The latter are important in short-term oscillations around the longer-run trends, although even here supply-side factors, especially demographic changes, have an impact.

Nevertheless, we recognize the importance of factors on the demand side and the interrelations between supply and demand factors. Indeed, it can be argued that the main factors on the supply side reflect interactions and feedback with factors on the demand side. Demographic developments affecting the youth labor force in a given period may be tied to the labor market situation of an earlier period that affected fertility (Easterlin, Wachter, and Wachter 1978). Trends in educational enrollments are directly related to the absolute and relative demand for young workers as affected by changes in aggregate demand, the structure and location of employment, the substitutability of youth for other workers, technology and organization, capital to labor ratios, earnings trends, employer requirements, and hiring procedures.

Changes in the absolute and relative size of successive cohorts reaching labor market age, or completing compulsory education, are postulated to be a major factor in trends in the youth labor force. The relation of population size to the size of the youth labor force is obvious, but changes in the absolute size of cohorts also may exert direct and indirect influence on the choices made by young people among the alternatives available to them in the utilization of their nonleisure time: additional education, labor force participation (including military service), education plus labor force participation, and remaining out of both school and the labor force. Thus, participation rates in education and the labor force as well as the absolute numbers of youth seeking entry to schools or jobs may be altered by long- or short-run variations in the numbers of young people.

The outcomes depend both on the population change and the response to it. A first consideration is the direction, character, and intensity of the population change — whether it is a prolonged upward or downward movement, or brief periods of sharp ups and downs in numbers, or some combinations of the two. The responsiveness of the educational system to a rapid rise or fall in numbers has a decided bearing on whether this alternative can be used by a higher proportion of young people than indicated by the prior trend in enrollment rates. The effects of population change on aggregate demand and output, together with general economic conditions, will determine how the youth labor market responds to population changes and what employment opportunities are available (Russell 1980, p. 28).

It is curious that few studies of labor force participation have introduced the size of the age cohort as a variable, even in time series, although this factor may operate in the same way as the business cycle. A cyclical decrease in employment opportunities has been associated with a temporary decline in youth LFPR and a rise in educational enrollment rates in a number of countries (Duncan 1965; Mincer 1966; Bowen and Finegan 1969; Hunter 1970; Crean 1973; Gendreau 1974; Mack 1975; Cibois 1976; Edwards 1976; Faguer et al. 1977a, 1977b; Mare 1978a; Sandell 1978; Stewart and Avery 1978; Pissarides 1979).

A Swedish statement puts the case well:

> For the young people the educational system functions in some way as a trade-cycle regulator. Education is not only used as a tool of labour-market policy, but many young people when they complete their education are faced with the choice of entering the labour market or of continuing their education. When economic activity is damped down, employers tend not to appoint further staff and the young people have fewer chances of obtaining a job. The best choice for the young people then will be to continue their education, a choice which means too that they will get financial support . . . It must be noted that the decrease in the LF rates for the young people . . . need not mean that any one has left the labour force on account of the labour-market situation. The observed decrease can have been engendered by decreases in the flow of persons joining the labour force for the first time. When demand rises, this flow increases (Sweden 1971a, p. 79).

Changes in cohort size operate in much the same way. Other things being equal, a decline in the number of youth will tend to depress educational enrollment rates and elevate youth LFPR, and vice versa. Three offsets to these expected effects should be noted: constraints on the expansion of educational places, decisions by young people to combine education and labor force participation instead of choosing between them, and the availability of government youth programs for the unemployed or potentially unemployed.

Not surprisingly, public attention is more attracted to the situations that occur with a rise in births than with a decline. Cohorts markedly larger than their predecessors are likely to display crowding and competition for all the goods and services required from infancy through old age. While members of small or thin youth cohorts (compared to predecessors) may find that their education suffers because of economy drives or their options are restricted when the economy's growth rate slackens, the crowded cohorts are likely to experience sharp competition and limited opportunities for education and work, even when the economy maintains its vigor or expands.

It is clear that, under all conditions, the smaller the cohort the more favorable its labor market position is likely to be (Grauman 1960; Easterlin 1968; Wachter 1977). Other things being equal, a large cohort following a smaller one will have trouble fitting into employment quantitatively and qualitatively. A large cohort following soon after another large cohort also will have difficulties, because some of the preceding cohort are still competing for the entry jobs. People of identical ability and background may have quite different lifestyles, career choices, occupational progress, and outcomes, according to the size of their own age cohort and the size of those that precede and follow them, and as these relate to the state of the economy.

The economy's growth and ability to absorb additional young people may offset the effects of a large cohort, as a British writer recently observed about his own generation:

We [those born in the baby boom of 1942-48] have been uniquely lucky, enjoying the first fruits of the NHS [National Health Service] and then of the 1944 Education Act, finding military service abolished just as we were liable for it, and emerging into higher education and the labour market in a period of headlong expansion. The pre-1942 and post-1948 age-cohorts were far smaller than ours and proved only mild competition. So most of my generation is safely ensconced in secure jobs in which they have risen fast . . . The reverse is true of . . . those born in the baby boom of 1955-64 . . . emerging into the shocking labour market of the 1970s (and 1980s?) (Johnson, R.W. 1978).

Similarly, a Danish report on the coming of age of those born in the years of high births, 1943-1947, commented: "This absorption took place quite painlessly, since industry entered a period of high activity in 1957 and the further education system had been considerably expanded" (EC 1976, p. 125).

Many countries were not so fortunate. Educational institutions were hard pressed to accommodate a sudden increase in numbers, and the labor market's capacity was inadequate. A Japanese authority has described vividly the situation of those born in the short but intense baby boom of 1946-1950:

This generation experienced heavy psychological pressures from sheer density . . . their lives were extremely competitive, both in school and in employment. This age group was destined to feel as if they were permanently packed in a commuter subway at rush hour . . . Classrooms were overcrowded, libraries were packed, and campus cafeterias had not nearly enough seats . . . The sense of over-crowdedness combined with democratic idealism to lead this generation easily to overall frustration and resentment . . . The children who were born after 1951, and especially those born after 1958, are less frustrated in many respects . . . they find more "elbow room," both in the physical and in the psychological sense (Kato 1978, p. 55).

The Japanese finding that cohort size has psychological dimensions is supported by an American observation:

Persons born in the low birth rate years of the 1930s found themselves a part of the "silent generation," of the 1950s — "The Organization Man," "The Man in the Gray Flannel Suit," willing to work within the system — while members of the large cohort born after World War II found themselves surrounded by protest and counterculture (Leveson 1979).

Easterlin goes further, attributing major economic, social, and political changes in part to the coming of age of large cohorts:

On the economic side, the unexpected combination of rising unemployment and accelerating inflation . . . On the social scene, there has been an acceleration in divorce, a rise in suicide rates among the young, and an upturn in crime rates. In the political arena, there has been a growth in alienation from the established system . . . Long-established cultural attitudes, too, appear to have changed . . . I think it is possible that these seemingly disparate developments — and, in fact, many others — are, in part (and I stress, in part), due to a common cause, to a new type of relationship between population and the economy centering on changes in the age structure of the working-age population. And, if I am correct about the importance of shifts in age structure, then the near-term future will be different, perhaps strikingly so, from that foreseen by those who are extrapolating recent changes into the future (Easterlin 1978, p. 398).

Thus, changes in cohort size may affect not only the number and type of oppor-tunities open to young people but also their relative attractiveness. Different sized cohorts may develop specific attitudes that pattern their ultimate choices among the available options. Therefore, this study raises the question whether the changing size of a cohort, especially the coming of age of a large cohort, which alters the age struc-ture of the working age population, changes the distribution of the youth cohort among its main alternatives and, specifically, its labor force participation. And for how long in the life of a cohort do the early effects of cohort size persist? Because of the complexity of the factors affecting individual countries and the fact that the de-mand and the supply side interact and also may change independently, the answers are not expected to be clear-cut and uniform.

Educational enrollment rates and educational attainment beyond the compulsory level constitute the second major supply-side variable used to explain the size of the youth labor force and youth participation rates. Educational enrollment rates of age-sex groups can be viewed as the complement of their labor force participation rates, since young people, especially teenagers, enter additional full-time education or training as a major alternative to direct entrance to the labor market. In probing comparative trends in educational enrollments and rates, this study seeks to identify the factors influencing those rates and to relate them to labor force participation rates, taking account of possible effects of cohort size on the propensity to combine education and labor force participation. Changes over time in the levels of educational attainment of young people and comparisons among countries will be examined as an indicator of the quality of the youth labor force.

The LFPR trends of the population 25 years and older as an influence on youth LFPR is captured in the youth share of the labor force. Trends in the propensity to be inactive, that is, neither in school nor the labor force (NISLF), deal with a residual category of youth, capturing trends in youth attitudes, the effects of changes in family composition, educational attainment levels, and family income distribution, and impacts of the government programs and activities that bear on young people's becoming NISLF.

The remainder of this book divides as follows. In Chapter 2 the demographic patterns that underlie the postwar development of the youth labor force are set forth for individual countries and across nations. Particular attention is given to the baby boom—its size, timing, and duration in various countries. Chapter 3 turns to trends in educational enrollments and enrollment rates for the youth groups, divided by sex, socioeconomic status, family income, and geographic area. The youth labor force, again separately for each sex, is analyzed in Chapter 4. Absolute labor force numbers, youth participation rates, and the age groups' changing shares of the total labor force are among the aspects examined. The differences in labor force behavior between the two age groups and the two sexes and the changes over time are analyzed both on a national and cross-national level. In Chapter 5 some special youth labor force subjects are presented, particularly the incidence of and trends in labor force participation by full-time students.

Chapter 6 deals with those young people who are neither in school nor in the labor force. The relative size of this group among countries and the trends over time within and among countries are discussed separately for each sex and the reasons for intercountry differences are explored. Chapter 7 presents the only subject examined at subnational level—the position of minority or immigrant youth. The situation of black youth in the United States from the demographic, educational enrollment, and labor force participation viewpoints is developed at length, and a similar effort is made for other countries, although data are sparser. Chapter 8 contains projections to 1995 of the absolute and relative size of the youth population and the youth labor force, as well as forecasts of labor force participation rates and their impact on the position of youth. The final chapter provides a summary of findings and some policy implications.

2 *Demographic Influences*

Demographic factors are basic to the changing size of a country's youth labor force. Chief among these influences is the annual number of live births. While the postwar baby boom has attracted the most attention, all variations in births, from year to year or over a period of years, are significant. Deaths in the youth age cohorts and net migration of young people modify the data on births, but the changing number of live births is the predominant factor within and across countries. In fact, fertility trends usually outweigh nondemographic factors in explanations of trends in the absolute and relative size of a nation's youth labor supply and in differences among countries.

Given the significance of fertility trends, it is disconcerting that demographers find fertility the least understood, the most variable, and the least predictable aspect of demography. A plethora of theories — sociological, economic, and psychological — has been propounded about the determinants and consequences of fertility. Some are concerned with the interactions between fertility and social and economic forces, but others concentrate on the broader societal factors that shape fertility trends or, alternatively, on the effects of fertility trends on social and economic developments (e.g., UN 1973, Vols. I and II; NBER 1960). Whatever approach is taken to the analysis of fertility and whichever academic discipline is involved, interpretations that view each country's experience as unrelated to that of others are unsatisfactory, as a British writer cautions:

> It is certainly dangerous to take too parochial a view of fertility trends. The pattern has been similar in a host of countries with differing economic and social climates and, unless a mass of idiosyncratic national factors have conspired to produce similar effects, there has been a kind of herd reaction, of which the British experience is a part (Weightman 1978, p. 365).

For present purposes it is unnecessary to explore in detail the causes of changing fertility trends within or among countries, although passing attention will be paid to the explanations where relevant. It is our main concern to examine the demographic trends as they affect the size of the youth labor supply and its share of the total labor force. This chapter presents the points of similarity and difference among the twelve selected countries in regard to trends in births, deaths, and migration, and provides information on the size of the youth cohorts in the postwar period. Comparative trends in marital and fertility rates of the youth group, especially females aged 20 to 24, which are directly related to changing labor force participation rates and variations in the size of the youth labor force are reserved to a later chapter. As a matter of convenience in presentation, this chapter includes some demographic data on American blacks, although this subgroup is discussed in a separate chapter.

Live Births

Trends in annual live births are more relevant to a study of the postwar youth labor force than trends in crude birth rates, although the two series move in a similar manner and birth rates are discussed briefly below. Because the labor market is structured so that young people generally take entry-level jobs and do not usually

Chart 2.1   Live Births in Eleven Countries, 1930–1979

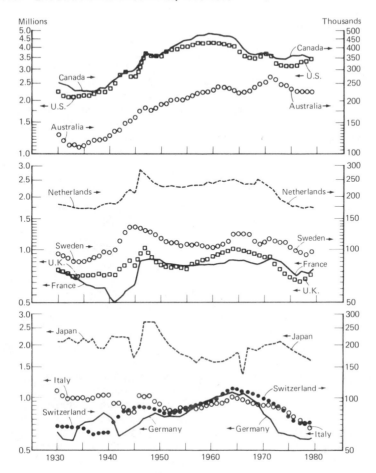

Note: Semilogarithmic scale. Arrows indicate which scale applies to each country.

Source: United Nations, Statistical Office, unpublished data.

replace those who retire from or leave the labor market, the analysis is concerned with the absolute number of young people potentially available to the labor force. In order to reflect the potential youth labor force 1945–1995 by single years of age, annual live birth statistics have been assembled from 1930 to 1979 for the twelve countries (Chart 2.1;*Table A2.1).* New labor market entrants at the beginning of the postwar period, 1945–1950, had been born in 1930 or later. Virtually all who might enter the labor force up to 1995 had been born by 1979.

The overall birth patterns of the twelve countries from 1930 to 1979 suggest greater similarity in the initial period than during the rest of the time span (Table 2.1). Eight

*Tables marked with an asterisk are not included in this volume, but may be obtained from the authors.

of the twelve countries experienced their smallest and second smallest number of births in the depression years from 1932 to 1937. Among the four others, France reached its low points in the devastating war years 1940 and 1941, while the United Kingdom and Italy reached the nadir in 1977 and 1979 respectively. Japan's trough occurred in 1961; the still-lower Japanese figure for 1966 is excluded because it has been attributed to the superstitious avoidance of births in that year, the year of Fire-Horse in the Chinese sixty-year calendar, which foretells that female children born in such a year will grow up to be violent (Aoki and Tomizawa 1968). This episode indicates how much control over births Japanese couples had as early as 1966; Japanese population experts concluded that delays in marriage and family planning, rather than induced abortions (which actually declined in 1966) accounted for most of the 25 percent drop in births in the single year (Yamaguchi 1967). Furthermore, the sharp rise in Japanese births during 1967, the largest annual percentage change for any of the twelve countries over the period of almost half a century, confirmed that the 1966 reduction had been deliberate.

The years marking the highest number of births in the twelve countries are spread much more widely. Italy's peak occurred in 1930, and Sweden's appeared during World War II. Japan, the Netherlands, and the United Kingdom had their highest number in the immediate postwar period. Canada, the United States, West Germany, New Zealand, and Switzerland peaked in the period 1957 to 1964. Finally, Australia and France had their highest number of births in 1971 (see Table 2.1). From 1930 through 1979, Australia had the largest number of years (32) in which births were higher than in the previous year. New Zealand, Canada, and the US followed with 29, 28, and 27 years respectively. Italy was lowest with 18 years out of a possible 50 (*Table A2.2).

Sustained periods (at least four consecutive years) in which the number of births was larger each year than the previous year are another indicator of international rank. Using this standard, Australia again takes first place, with a total of 31 years from 1930 to 1979. New Zealand, Canada, and Switzerland follow. Italy (10 years) is fourth from last, followed by the United Kingdom, France, and the Netherlands (Tables 2.1 and *A2.2). When the examination is limited to the postwar years, the three leaders retain their places, with Germany and the United States moving up to join Switzerland in next place. Italy, the Netherlands, and Sweden are all in next-to-last place above France, which experienced no such sustained growth in births in the postwar period.

The number of consecutive years with an increased number of births as well as the rate of annual increase is important. Australia's 1971 peak year of births was 2.5 times larger than its lowest year. By this standard (the ratio of the highest number of annual births to the lowest in the period 1930 to 1979), Australia led, followed by New Zealand, Canada, and the United States, each of which had a ratio of 2 or more. The spread among the countries was not enormous; all had at least a ratio of 1.5. Comparing the number of births at the end and at the beginning of the 1930–1979 period, the ratios are arrayed in much the same way as the aforementioned ratios of highest to lowest year, but now five of the twelve countries show fewer births in 1979 than in 1930, a reflection of the baby bust that followed the baby boom. New Zealand, with a ratio of 1.81, leads Australia, which has the second-highest ratio of 1.74 (Table 2.1).

Another perspective on the intensity of the baby boom experience is offered by the final two columns of Table 2.1. While the earlier columns reflect sustained increases in the number of births, they do not indicate the shock effect of dramatic increases

Table 2.1 Live Births Indicators in Twelve Countries, 1930–1979

	Two years of highest births	Two years of lowest births	Years with four or more consecutive increases in births	Total number of years with four or more consecutive increases in births	Total number of postwar years (1946–79) with four or more consecutive increases in births	Ratio of births in highest year to lowest year	Ratio of 1979 births to 1930 births	Two largest annual percentage increases in births	Two largest annual percentage decreases in births
Australia	1971 1972	1934 1932	1935–47 1949–61 1967–71	31	18	2.52	1.74	9.9 9.2	7.7 6.5
Canada	1959 1960	1937 1936	1938–47 1949–59	25	15	2.10	1.43	14.3 8.5	7.6 7.4
France	1971 1964	1941 1940	1974–77 1942–49	8	0	1.78	1.01	34.9 10.6	12.0 8.0
Federal Republic of Germany	1964 1963	1933 1932	1954–64	11	11	1.93	0.91	23.4 6.6	19.4 10.3
Italy	1930 1940	1979 1978	1937–40 1959–64	10	6	1.63	0.61	27.1 5.8	10.4 7.6
Japan	1949 1948	1961a 1957	1946–49 1962–65 1969–73 1954–59	13	9	1.70	0.80	42.2 40.6	25.4 21.6
Netherlands	1946 1947	1937 1935	1954–59	6	6	1.67	0.96	35.7 10.2	8.9 7.3
New Zealand	1961 1962	1935 1933	1936–41 1944–47 1950–61 1966–69	26	16	2.41	1.81b	14.4 12.4	8.3 5.8
Sweden	1945 1944	1933 1934	1934–39 1941–45 1961–66	17	6	1.59	1.02	14.3 10.0	6.8 5.7
Switzerland	1964 1965	1937 1938	1938–46 1954–64	20	11	1.81	1.05	12.2 9.7	7.2 5.4
United Kingdom	1947 1964	1977 1976	1956–64	9	9	1.57	0.95	19.1 10.0	12.1 8.1
United States	1961c 1957	1932 1933	1940–43 1951–57 1976–79	15	11	2.06	1.58	20.2 12.5	8.4 6.6

a Japan had a still lower year in 1966, which is excluded for reasons discussed in the text.
b 1931–1979.
c According to U.S. national data.

Source: Tables *A2.1, *A2.2.

or decreases in single years. Japan is clearly the leader by this standard, and several of the other countries which ranked low by the earlier measures also show one or more high entries. Among the four countries which lead by the sustained rise criterion, only the United States has a single year with a change of 20 percent or more.

Drawing on the information on births for the entire period 1930–1979, the following classification of the twelve countries results:

Generally increasing number of births from 1930 until about 1960, with a much higher number in 1979 than in 1930: Australia, Canada, New Zealand, the United States.

Generally increasing number of births from 1930s until the mid-1960s, with the same or lower number in 1979 as in 1930: Germany, Switzerland.

Early peak in births (before 1950) then fluctuations up and down, secondary peak in 1960–1971, 1979 about same or lower than 1930: France, the Netherlands, Sweden, and the United Kingdom.

General downward movement, especially from 1950, but with fluctuations: Italy, Japan.

A division of the whole period 1930 to 1979 into five-year intervals corresponds fairly closely to the timing of major events that are associated with changes in fertility: the early and later depression years, World War II, the postwar baby boom, the "baby bust," and finally an upturn in several countries. These five-year periods are described by index numbers of live births in each of the twelve countries, using 1950–1954 as the base period, and by a distribution of the rates of change in live births in selected years (Chart 2.2; *Table 2.2). Both measures show a considerable similarity of direction among the countries from period to period, with some marked individual differences.

In the initial depression year 1930–1931, most countries had a decrease in births (*Table 2.2). As the depression began to lift, in 1935–1936 a bi-modal pattern appeared. The first war years indicated the shift to growth patterns that were more fully demonstrated in 1945–1946. In 1950–1951 the majority of countries showed an annual decrease, a pause in the baby boom. Its strength is shown by the strong leaning toward increases in 1955–1956 and 1960–1961. The beginning of the baby bust, signaled in 1965–1966, showed a temporary reversal in some countries in 1970–1971, but reappeared in 1975–1976. By 1978–1979, an upturn in births had once again become apparent in more than half of the countries. Variations among countries within the several distinct periods result both from differential impacts of widespread events, such as war or depression, and in particular from secular conditions, such as a sharp decline in birth rates (Italy, Japan) or strong economic growth and geographic settlement (Australia).

On the whole, the decline in births during the 1930s depression, experienced to some extent by all countries, was not sustained. By 1940, the level of live births in seven of the twelve countries reached or exceeded the 1930 level; Australia, France, Italy, Switzerland, and the United Kingdom were the exceptions. Despite declines in births in many countries in the war years, by the end of the war, most countries were well above both the 1930 and 1940 live birth levels. In 15 years, Sweden's fertility rates had risen from the lowest ever recorded to the highest in its history (Holmberg 1978). Another neutral country, Switzerland, also had high births in wartime. The exceptions were the defeated Axis powers — Germany, Italy, and Japan — whose war-

Chart 2.2   Indexes of Live Births in Twelve Countries, 1930–1934 to 1975–1979

(1950–1954 = 100)

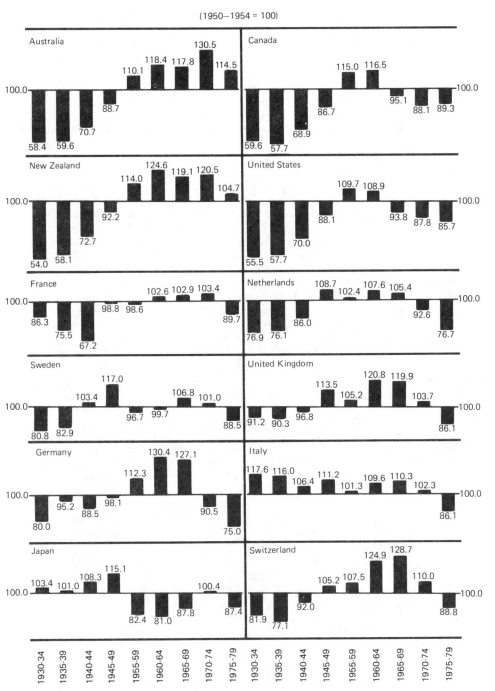

Source: United Nations, Statistical Office, unpublished data.

time births were low, and France, which in 1945 exceeded the 1940 level but did not reach the 1930 number (Chart 2.1; *Table A2.1). Thus, the depression and war did not result in a prolonged decline in the number of live births in most of these countries. There was a deficit between actual births and potential births, however, according to prior trends (the additional births that might have occurred in the absence of depression and war). More specifically, postponed marriages, the absence of men in the military forces, deferred births, and similar factors in the depression and war periods could have limited births (Kirk 1946).

The birth record for the immediate postwar period varies considerably, although this was the most common time for a baby boom. Between 1945 and 1947, most of the countries experienced sharper annual changes in live births for a few years than at any other time in the entire period (*Table A2.2). France, Italy, Japan, and the Netherlands were most conspicuous in this regard. France treated its sudden jump from about 600,000 births a year to well over 800,000 as a far more drastic and difficult change than did other countries with similar or steeper rises. It has been said that France regarded its population as fixed, based on the demographic experience of over a century, and that a change was as disturbing and unexpected as a change in the national boundaries would have been. As the first postwar cohorts came to labor market entrance age, the shock of the added numbers was felt once again (Baudot, Desmotte, and Vimont 1968; Dyer 1977). The Netherlands, long accustomed to high birth rates, viewed its new higher level with equanimity, especially because rapid economic growth ensued before the boom cohorts matured. Italy's substantial 27 percent rise in 1945–1946 was a one-year occurrence, followed by declining numbers, but still at relatively high levels.

The postwar upsurge in births is usually attributed to the recovery from depression and war (UN 1975, p. 10). Alternatively, the baby boom also has been viewed either as a temporary, but explainable, deviation from the expected secular decline, or as a rectification which restored the normal trend after the deviation of the preceding 15 years (NBER 1960; Campbell 1974; Taeuber 1976; Weightman 1978). Other theories for one country or groups of countries have looked to more specific factors, such as the economic conditions affecting the child-bearing cohorts (Durand 1960; Grauman 1960; Kirk 1960; Kuznets 1960; Easterlin 1968, 1973, 1978; Cain 1971; Venieris et al. 1973; Willis 1973; Easterlin and Condran 1976; Wachter 1976; Gibson 1977; Lindert 1977; Simon 1977; Olneck and Wolfe 1978).

The trends in births after the initial postwar years also showed considerable variation among the twelve countries. Rises in live births with new, higher peak years characterized Australia, Canada, France, Germany, New Zealand, Switzerland, and the United States (*Table A2.1; Chart 2.1). Germany, along with Austria, experienced a baby boom in late 1950s and early 1960s because of high births in the late 1930s. The United Kingdom had a second-round baby boom, with a build-up of births from 1956 to 1964, although peaking below the 1947 level. Sweden likewise had such a round from 1961 to 1966, but the levels were lower than in the 1943–1948 period. Italy and Japan had rises and falls, but unlike most of the other countries, births generally were lower than in 1930. Among the factors cited as explanations in the countries where births and birth rates continued to rise were increased numbers of women in the fertile ages; lower marriage ages; increased proportions married; larger families; differences in timing of births; changed age distributions of the population; increase of multiple marriages; declines in the percentage of childless persons; earlier first births; the impact of economic prosperity; interactions between long production swings and long population cycles, the economic calculus of households that children were desirable consumer goods; and the "echo effect," in which a prior large cohort comes to maturity and, without any change in age-specific birth rates, an increased number of babies results simply from the larger number of potential mothers (Kuznets 1960; NBER 1960; Easterlin 1968; UN 1973, 1975, pp. 45–87; Campbell 1974; Ryder 1974; Ward and Butz 1978).

All twelve countries experienced the demise of the period of elevated births and entered the baby bust period of declining numbers, but the timing, persistence, and severity of the drop varied considerably. For present purposes, the period of decline begins in the year after which almost every successive year shows a smaller number of births than the preceding year. Canada, Germany, Italy, New Zealand, Switzerland, the United Kingdom and the United States show a decline starting in some cases in the late 1950s but most commonly around 1965. Australia, France, the Netherlands, and Sweden did not have significant decreases until 1968–1972, and Japan's turning point came in 1974. Explanations of the decline in births and birth rates generally stress long-run factors found in many countries — women's improved educational and labor market position, changes in women's attitudes toward marriage and fertility, liberalized abortion laws, and increased use of reliable contraceptives (Taeuber 1976, p. 130; Keyfitz 1978; Tsui and Bogue 1978; Bogue and Tsui 1979). Some analysts consider specific economic conditions — the recession and the inflationary rise in the costs of raising and educating children — as factors in the downturn (Gibson 1977; Canada 1978a). Reference is also made to ecological considerations (Lindert 1977) and "the subconscious realization that the world is overcrowded" (Benjamin 1978).

Some American analysts have theorized that the deteriorated labor market position of young men, caused by the crowding of those born during the baby boom years, resulted in reduced fertility among young women as they increased their labor force participation rates in order to bolster husbands' incomes. As smaller cohorts of males mature, female fertility in the youth groups is expected to rise again. (Wachter 1976, 1977; Easterlin 1978; Easterlin, Wachter, and Wachter 1979). The behavior of young women of the U.S. baby boom generation, however, was duplicated in other countries with baby booms where, for a number of reasons, the labor market position of young men, measured by their earnings relative to those of adults, improved rather than deteriorated.

Small upturns in live births that appeared in Canada between 1975 and 1977, in the United States from 1976, and in several other countries in 1978 or 1979, have led to speculation about the onset of a new baby boom. To the extent that these slight increases in births are not due to a rise in fertility rates and are temporary, reflecting the echo of the earlier baby boom in larger cohorts of young women, the catching up in postponed births and the new births attributable to remarried divorced persons, a new baby boom was not under way as of 1980 (Eversley 1980). In any case, this book and its chapter on projections is concerned only with persons already born by 1979.

Levels of births characteristic of the different periods were reflected in the entering youth labor force 15 to 20 years later. A reduced number of births in part of the depressed 1930s translated into reduced numbers of potential entrants into the labor market in the first years after World War II up to the mid-1950s. Postwar shortages of youth labor were reported in many countries from the latter part of the 1950s up to 1960–1962, reflecting the low births during some war years. While Japan's severe shortage of young workers in the first part of the 1960s was caused by greatly reduced numbers of births during the war years, it also was due to the remarkable postwar economic growth and a rapidly advancing age of entry to the labor market resulting from increased years of education.

In most countries, the first postwar baby boom cohort was due to enter the labor market from 1960 to 1965; in the United States and a few other countries, the period would extend to 1967. The upsurge in births immediately after the war had seemed sufficiently threatening to prod several international agencies to issue warnings of impending labor market difficulties in Western Europe and make suggestions about preparatory measures (OECD 1955; UN 1956; ILR 1957a, 1957b). That these difficulties did not materialize in most countries, unlike the experience of Germany and Austria in the early 1950s, serves as a useful reminder that the number of young people, whether increasing or decreasing, is not significant in itself. It is the match between the number of young people and the current needs of the labor market that makes for easy or difficult absorption. Labor shortages in the face of rising numbers and surpluses with declining numbers are possible or actual outcomes, although the linkage of increasing numbers with rising youth unemployment and of declining numbers with decreasing youth unemployment is more obvious and common.

Births from 1954 to 1960 affected new labor market entrants from 1970 to 1975. Most countries had level or rising numbers of births, but Japan and Sweden had a declining number throughout, a fact to be borne in mind in evaluating relative unemployment rates. The countries where births continued to rise during most of the period had to cope with larger youth cohorts and in some cases larger shares of youth in the population during the 1970s than they had known before. After the worldwide recession of 1974 and prospects for employment growth seemed gloomy for the medium term, analysts in many countries began to voice the view, developed earlier by Americans, that a rise in the number or proportion of young people was a labor market liability.

In summary, the record of live births from 1930 to 1979 for the twelve countries reveals a high potential for fluctuation in the size of each nation's youth labor force from 1945 to 1990–1995. The baby boom and its successor, the baby bust, command most attention in discussions of trends. Precise and widely accepted definitions of the baby boom are not available, and each country seems to have identified its own experience as an authentic baby boom. In common parlance, the baby boom implied a steep increase from a previous level. This might disqualify Australia and New Zealand, which had gradual increases over a large part of the period, although by most measures they are the clear leaders in the growth of live births and potential youth labor force.

Another common view of the baby boom is that after a period of sustained high births, a recognizable cut-off should occur with a decline of births to some new, lower level. The countries with a more mixed picture of declines and rises in births, such as Japan, seem to rate lower in the baby boom sweepstakes on this account than those whose year-to-year numbers were more regular, as in the United States or France. But it is arguable that uncertainty arising from changing annual numbers of births is inherently more troublesome for a society and economy than a slowly and regularly rising or falling number. It also appears that implicit assumptions about the state and direction of the economy color judgments about what constitutes a baby boom. In fact, most discussions of the youth labor force tend to ignore the demographic factor, except when economic circumstances — be it prosperity or recession — create a situation of surplus or shortage of young people (US 1976c, p. 53). Yet it is clear that in spite of some common tendencies, the patterns, intensity, and timing of variations in live births, and hence of the baby boom and baby bust, did differ among these twelve countries and are significant factors in the size of the postwar youth labor force and in the ease or difficulty with which it was absorbed into the labor market.

Birth Rates

Birth rates relate live births to the size of the population in which the births occur, and are therefore indicative of subsequent youth shares of the working-age population, which are discussed below. Crude birth rates going back to 1920 are presented in Table 2.3. In nine of the twelve countries these rates were higher in 1920–1924 than they would be during the next six decades (Gille 1960). Only France, New Zealand, and the United States subsequently exceeded their 1920–1924 rates: New Zealand in four intervals, the United States in three, and France in one. Although Canada's postwar rates were somewhat below its 1920–1924 level of 28.1 per thousand, it had the highest birth rates of the twelve countries during much of the period 1945–1964, after which New Zealand took the lead. Sweden had the lowest or second-lowest birth rates in most of the time periods.

There is no ground for the belief current in the United States that its postwar birth rates were higher than those of other developed countries (Princeton 1968, p. 5). Nor is a statement about other countries by the U.S. Select Committee on Population of the House of Representatives fully accurate: "Rather than dropping after a few catch-up years, *as happened in most other developed countries* (ed. ital.), U.S. fertility remained high until the early 1960s" (US 1978e, p. 17). Table 2.3 shows that seven of the twelve countries had sustained high birth rates from 1945 through the early 1960s. The United States was not even close to leadership in most of the period 1945–1964; it registered fifth in birth rates in 1945–1949, tied for second in 1950–1954, third in 1955–1959 and 1960–1964, and ranked still lower subsequently, until the end of the 1970s. Data for 1979 show the US with second-highest birth rates.

A strong decline in crude birth rates is apparent from the 1960s in most countries and even earlier in France, Italy, Japan (whose rates rose slightly from 1965 through 1971), the Netherlands, and Sweden. The range in 1979 was from 9.5 to 16.9 per thousand, compared to a range in 1920–1924 of 19.9 to 35.1. Germany's birth rate of 23.1 per thousand in 1920–1924 was more than halved by 1975; in 1979 Germany had the lowest rate among the twelve countries. Italy and Japan, the countries with the highest birth rates in 1920–1924, also more than halved their rates by 1975, as their peoples gained control over their fertility (NBER 1960, p. 35). France, coming from the lowest position in 1920–1924, showed less reduction than many other countries, as have Australia and New Zealand, which started from fairly high rates and now are among those with the highest birth rates. Only the United States showed a higher crude birth rate in 1979 than in 1975.

The data on birth rates confirm the main conclusions drawn earlier about live births. They also show clearly a trend toward secular decline that is less apparent in the live births data. Groupings of countries by secular trends in crude birth rates would place Italy and Japan in one group, Australia and New Zealand in another, with Canada and the US as a subgroup. The remaining six European countries form a group of their own.

Mortality

Differences among countries in the numbers of deaths in the youth cohorts before and after they enter the youth labor market also are indicators of the basic size and variation of the potential youth labor force in the coming years. By far the most important mortality statistic is the death rate under one year of age. It runs far higher

Table 2.3   Crude Birth Rates in Twelve Countries, 1920–1979

	1920–1924	1925–1929	1930–1934	1935–1939	1940–1944	1945–1949	1950–1954	1955–1959	1960–1964	1965	1968	1971	1975	1979
						(per thousand population)								
Australia	24.4	21.6	17.6	17.2	19.5	23.1	23.0	22.6	21.9	19.7	20.1	21.4	16.9	15.5
Canada	28.1	24.5	22.2	20.4	23.2	27.0	27.7	27.8	25.2	21.3	17.6	16.8	15.7	15.3[a]
France	19.9	18.5	17.3	15.1	14.7	20.3	19.5	18.4	18.0	17.8	16.7	17.2	14.1	14.1
Germany[b]	23.1	19.1	16.3	19.4	17.4[c]	16.9[c]	16.1	16.9	18.3	17.7	16.1	12.7	9.7	9.5
Italy	30.1	27.2	24.5	23.2	20.7	21.1	18.3	18.0	18.9	19.1	17.6	16.8	14.8	11.8
Japan	35.1	34.1	31.9	29.3	30.1	30.2	23.7	18.2	17.2	18.8	18.7	19.3	17.2	14.2
Netherlands	26.7	23.4	21.7	20.3	21.8	25.9	22.1	21.3	20.9	19.9	18.6	17.2	13.0	12.5
New Zealand	23.0	20.2	17.5	17.4	21.4	25.1	24.5	24.9	24.4	22.9	22.6	22.6	18.4	16.9
Sweden	20.3	16.3	14.4	14.5	17.7	19.0	15.5	14.5	14.5	15.9	14.3	14.1	12.6	11.6
Switzerland	20.0	17.8	16.7	15.4	17.9	19.4	17.3	17.5	18.5	18.8	17.1	15.2	12.6	11.6
United Kingdom[d]	21.3	17.1	15.3	14.9	15.5	18.0	15.5	15.9	17.9	18.2	16.9	16.0	12.4	12.3[a]
United States	22.8	20.1	17.6	17.2	19.9	23.4	24.5	24.6	22.4	19.4	17.6	17.2	14.8	15.8

[a] 1978.
[b] 1920–44 refers to prewar territory of Germany.
[c] Four-year average.
[d] England and Wales except 1975, 1979.

Source: United Nations, The Determinants and Consequences of Population Trends, Table IV.2 (New York: United Nations, 1973); United Nations, Post-war Demographic Trends in Europe and the Outlook until the Year 2000, Economic Survey of Europe in 1974, Part II, Table V.1. (New York: United Nations, 1975); United Nations, Statistical Office, unpublished data.

Table 2.4   Deaths Under One Year of Age in Twelve Countries, 1930–1979

	1930	1950	1960	1970	1975	1979
		(per thousand live births)				
Australia	47.2	24.5	20.2	17.9	14.3	12.2[a]
Canada	79.8[b]	41.5	27.3	18.8	14.3	12.0[a]
France	83.2	52.0	27.8	18.2	13.8	9.8
Germany	84.0	55.6	33.8	23.6	19.8	14.7[a]
Italy	105.6	63.8	43.9	29.6	20.7	15.3
Japan	124.5	60.1	30.7	13.1	10.1	8.0
Netherlands	50.9	26.7	17.9	12.7	10.6	8.5
New Zealand	49.7[c]	27.5	22.6	16.7	16.0	13.8
Sweden	54.7	20.5	16.7	11.0	8.6	7.3
Switzerland	50.8	31.2	21.1	15.1	10.7	8.6
United Kingdom	63.1	31.5	22.5	18.4	16.0	13.3[a]
United States	64.6	29.2	26.0	20.1	16.1	13.0
U.S. blacks and other races	99.9[d]	44.5	43.2	30.9	24.2	21.7[e]

[a] 1978.
[b] 1930–1934 average.
[c] 1938.
[d] Incomplete coverage.
[e] 1977.

Source: United Nations. Statistical Office, unpublished data. For U.S. blacks and other races: 1930: U.S. National Center for Health Statistics, 1950–75: U.S. Department of Health, Education, and Welfare, *Health 1976–1977*, Table 22 (Washington: National Center for Health Statistics, 1977).

than the rates for subsequent ages up to 25, shows a wider spread among countries, and over the years has declined more within and among countries than the other youth death rates.

The high prewar birth rates and level of live births in Italy and Japan were tempered by markedly elevated infant mortality rates, as the 1930 rates indicate (Table 2.4). A remarkable reduction in the Japanese infant mortality rate since 1960 brought Japan to a rate of 8.0 per thousand in 1979, the second-lowest rate. France and Canada also made striking improvements in their rates. Although Italy has remained in last place since 1950, the gap between its rate and the lowest has narrowed from 43.3 per thousand in 1950 to 8.0 in 1979. The Netherlands, Sweden, and Switzerland consistently maintained rates that were among the lowest of all the countries throughout the period. Since the Dutch birth rate has been high among Western European nations, its relatively low infant and youth mortality rates further add to the numbers coming of age on the Dutch labor market.

Overall, the significance of infant and youth deaths as a modification of live births has diminished over the years in all countries, and the absolute differences among the twelve countries have declined. The decreasing infant and youth death rates have tended to leave the various birth cohorts at higher levels than would have prevailed under earlier conditions, with some countries showing larger gains than others. In a recent evaluation of mortality developments in European countries, the UN stated that death rates are now so low that further large declines are unlikely (UN 1975, p. 22). In general, it has been found that mortality rates respond to medical and public health advances rather than to short-run economic changes (UN 1975, pp. 32–44).

Infant mortality rates, especially in Germany and Italy, still have room to decline, but increasingly, births will determine the number who will survive to maturity and will provide the measure for comparative purposes.

External Migration

The flow of immigrants and emigrants is another factor affecting the actual and potential number of participants in the youth labor force; net immigration of those under 25 means a gain in numbers and net emigration a loss. Since immigrants generally have higher labor force participation rates and somewhat different labor market expectations than natives, especially among males, quantitative and qualitative calculations based on net migration balances require some modification when converting potential youth labor force to actual (Durand 1960, p. 420).

In order to establish the net balance of youth migration for individual countries, it is necessary to obtain annual information on the actual numbers of immigrants and emigrants under 25 years of age by single years of age in the twelve countries. Ideally, such data for the relevant age cohorts would begin in 1930 and continue until the present, as do the data presented for live births. Lacking such data, a more circuitous method is adopted. The direction, size, and trend of each country's external migration in total will be established, and then the relevant age-sex composition will be deduced. The basic source of information is official migration data, supplemented by census counts of the foreign-born by age and sex at fixed times. Migration statistics are far from satisfactory, and are deceptive as to the completeness, accuracy, and comparability of the rates they present (UN 1973, p. 225; UN 1975, pp. 132–35). Emigration and reemigration statistics are particularly lacking or weak in some countries. There is of course no record of illegal entrants and visa overstayers, a source of large undercounting in the United States where the 20 to 24 age group is heavily affected.

International migration has been intensively analyzed in terms of the push and pull of economic, social, and political factors in the sending and receiving countries (UN 1975, pp. 237–45). In the 1930s the outflow from the sending countries in Europe was greatly reduced as the main receiving countries in North America and Oceania (Australia and New Zealand) imposed restrictions during the depression. Thereafter, the war years intervened (Kirk 1946; UN 1973, pp. 225–28, 230–31; UN 1975, p. 132). Migration within Europe also was at a low, as *Table A2.4 shows for Sweden. After World War II there was a resumption of overseas emigration from Europe, but even more significant was the great increase of immigration into northern European countries from southern Europe and other continents. Italy lost population both to overseas countries and to other European nations. Oceania and Canada resumed their intake, mostly of Europeans (UN 1973, pp. 229–33; UN 1975, pp. 132–42).

Estimates of the contribution of net immigration to total population growth show substantial impact. In Switzerland, three-fourths of the total increase in the 1960s and early 1970s was attributed to immigration (UN 1975, p. 147). Legal immigration into the United States currently accounts for about 20 percent of population growth, and some estimates of net illegal immigration would raise the proportion to half or more (US 1978e, p. 23). Between 1947 and 1961, net immigration and the births to immigrants in Australia accounted for half of total population growth (UN 1973, p. 249). Some 30 percent of Sweden's population growth from 1950 to 1970 has been attributed directly to migration. In Luxembourg, net immigration contributed more to population growth than did natural increase in the 1960s and early 1970s (UN 1975,

p. 134). Net immigration was of particular importance in increasing the working-age population in some countries which had a low growth of the indigenous population (UN 1973, p. 249).

Despite the shortcomings of the data, the main directions of migration flow are fairly clear for 1950 onward.* The twelve countries can be characterized as follows:

Japan: Negligible emigration and immigration.

United Kingdom: Considerable emigration and immigration with small, shifting balance.

Australia, Canada, New Zealand: Heavy net immigration.

Germany and Switzerland: Heavy net immigration, followed by net emigration recently.

United States, Sweden, France: Moderate net immigration.

The Netherlands: Net emigration (exclusive of repatriation), followed by net immigration.

Italy: Net emigration (exclusive of return flows).

A fuller picture, starting with 1930 data, might modify the classification of some of the twelve countries. For example, Sweden's record over a longer period indicates that net emigration before 1930 was replaced by net immigration thereafter, except for a few years in the early 1970s. Over the years both immigration and emigration rates increased, reflecting the changing needs for foreign workers and the strong return flows when jobs became scarce (*Table A2.4; Sweden 1977a, pp. 22–24).

Prospects for the future depend on the outcome of the policy shift, in most of Europe in the mid-1970s, to restrict or halt the inflow of foreign workers from countries outside the European Communities. The 1975 migration balance in European countries reflects both these restrictive measures and the recession. This situation might be considered temporary except that most northern European countries assert that they wish to maintain these restrictive policies, even with the return of vigorous economic growth (OECD 1978a). France, Sweden, and Germany forecast no net immigration, and Italy, Switzerland, and the United Kingdom expect net emigration from 1980 to 1990. Only Australia, Canada, and the United States project a continuation of net immigration for 1980–1990. While Australia and the US foresee lower levels than prevailed in the 1950–1970 period, Canada forecasts continuing high rates at the 1975 level.

Although continued massive movements of people across national borders must occur before the age-sex composition of the population of the receiving or sending country will be altered, substantial impacts can be made by transfers of young people under special circumstances. The inflow of children and young people can restore gaps in the population structure left by low fertility or current and earlier out-migration. For France and other European countries, the replacement of young men lost in war through immigration ranks as a particular contribution (UN 1973, pp. 248–49; UN 1975, p. 143). National policies on the immigration of whole families or the reuniting of family members have a crucial effect on the age-sex composition of immigration, modifying the strong tendency of immigrants to be mainly male and in the 20 to 44 age group.

---

*Tables 2.5 and *A2.3 should not be compared to each other. It is possible that revisions in each may still be made by the source agency, bringing them into greater harmony. The results in Table A2.3 can be compared with UN 1973, Table VII.1; UN 1975, Tables VI.1, VI.2, VI.3, Figure 17; OECD 1972a, Table 8.

Table 2.5   Net Immigration Rates in Twelve Countries, 1950-1975, and Projections to 1990

Year	Australia	Canada	France	Germany	Italy	Japan	Netherlands	New Zealand	Sweden	Switzerland	United Kingdom	United States
						(per thousand population)						
(Actual)												
1950	18.7	1.1	0.5	7.9	-1.7	0.4	2.0	4.2	2.1	3.6	-0.3	2.0
1960	8.8	2.4	3.1	6.0	-1.9	-0.3	-1.1	0.8	1.5	15.5	1.3	1.8
1970	9.8	3.3	3.5	9.4	-0.9	-0.1	2.6	3.9	6.1	-1.0	-1.5	2.1
1975	1.0	5.4	0.5	-3.2	1.5	0.0	5.3	7.1	2.1	-10.3	-1.6	2.1
(Projection)												
1980	3.4	5.7	0.0	0.0	-0.7	n.a.	n.a.	n.a.	0.0	-4.8	-0.6	1.8
1985	3.3	5.3	0.0	0.0	-0.7	n.a.	n.a.	n.a.	0.0	-1.6	-0.7	1.7
1990	3.1	5.0	0.0	0.0	-0.7	n.a.	n.a.	n.a.	0.0	0.0	-0.7	1.6

Source: OECD, Manpower and Social Affairs Committee, *Demographic Trends: Their Labour Market and Social Implications*, Table I-6 (Paris: OECD, 1979).

Most of the receiving countries have encouraged or accepted family immigration or the subsequent entrance of the families of male immigrants (UN 1973, pp. 240–43). The result in Australia was that between 1947 and 1961, immigration increased the child population more than the adult; the total working-age population grew by 28 percent and the total population by 39 percent, leaving the ratio between the two slightly higher than it would have been in the absence of immigration (UN 1973, p. 249). Sweden and the United Kingdom have a high proportion of females and married persons in both immigration and emigration (*Table A2.5; GB 1973).

Available international data on the age distribution of immigration and emigration show two age groups of interest: under 15 years and 15 to 34 years (Table 2.6). Going back to the 1920s in some cases and to the 1950s in others, these data reveal a fairly consistent proportion of children (under 15) in total immigration and emigration over time within countries. On the whole, countries have tended to receive a higher share of children as immigrants than they sent out as emigrants; in some countries, emigration is largely a return home of earlier immigrants. In the UK, the sex and age totals and composition of immigration and emigration were similar, according to 1971 data (GB 1973). Comparing countries, Germany has had a low proportion of children in total immigration (under 12 percent) in recent years; Australia, the Netherlands, and the United States had a high share (around 25 percent). In Australia, Germany, Sweden, and the United States, the proportion of children among all immigrants has been rising.

Table 2.6 provides data on ages 15 to 34, going beyond the 15 to 24-year group with which this study is concerned. In each of the countries, probably one-half or fewer of the migrants in the age group 15 to 34 consist of those aged 15 to 24. Nevertheless, infants, children and young people (to age 25) account for a substantial portion of total immigration and emigration. In Sweden from 1951 to 1973, immigrants under 29 years of age constituted two-thirds to three-fourths of the total, and only slightly lower proportions prevailed for the emigrants (*Table A2.5). The comparative youthfulness of the migrants in both directions reflects in part the small proportion of middle-aged and older migrants, due to the recruitment of young workers and immigration policies that initially draw in families, or later permit the reuniting of families.

Detailed evidence of the impact of net immigration on the youth population is available for Sweden. The 16 to 19-year population would have declined from 1965 to 1970 had there been no net immigration. In each year of the period, domestic teenage population decreased and the number of teenage immigrants increased. In the 20 to 24 age group, the domestic population increased in the first three years and declined in the next two, but over the five-year period, the increase attributable to the domestic population was less by several thousands than the contribution of immigration (Sweden 1973, Table 1.2). Unpublished Swedish data on members of the labor force in 1970 indicate that emigration, including repatriation of former immigrants, was substantial among the 15 to 19 and 20 to 24 age groups, partially canceling out the 3 to 4 percent contribution to the labor force from 1970 to 1975 of immigrants in these age groups. In Canada the continued high level of immigration of young people in the years of the baby boom led official researchers to question "whether the market can absorb all of these people" if participation rates remained the same (Canada 1973, p. 5).

In other countries with relatively high birth rates — Australia, New Zealand, and the Netherlands — net immigration added substantially to the youth population and labor force. In the United States, if account is taken of illegal immigration and Puer-

Table 2.6 Share of Youth in Immigration and Emigration, Both Sexes, Nine Countries, 1920–1974

	Years	Immigrants Percent of total[a]		Emigrants Percent of total[a]	
		Younger than 15	15–34	Younger than 15	15–34
Australia	1925–29	18.1	n.a.	n.a.	n.a.
	1931–38	16.8	n.a.	n.a.	n.a.
	1950–54	25.2	48.7	14.5	49.5
	1955–59	25.7	50.9	18.5	48.7
	1960–64	25.7	50.1	21.5	50.1
	1965–69	27.8	49.2	22.9	51.1
	1970–73	26.3	51.4	23.3	52.5
Canada[b]	1950–54	22.0	54.1		
	1955–59	22.6	56.5		
	1960–64	22.6	54.5		
	1965–69	23.5	56.1		
	1970–74	22.4	57.0		
Germany	1960–64	8.0	64.0	7.2	68.0
	1965–68	10.4	60.3	9.8	60.7
	1970–71, 73	11.5	61.4	15.0	56.9
Italy	1965–69	8.3[c]	56.1[c]	12.4	56.8
	1970–72	14.8[c]	44.2[c]	14.1	48.8
Netherlands	1960–64	24.3	50.4	25.1	54.0
	1965–69	20.5	55.4	21.8	56.8
	1970–73	25.3	54.5	22.1	55.5
New Zealand	1922–24	23.1	n.a.	n.a.	n.a.
	1925–29	21.2	n.a.	n.a.	n.a.
	1934–39	17.5	n.a.	n.a.	n.a.
	1950–54	17.8	53.3	16.3	53.1
	1955–59	19.9	51.5	19.2	53.4
	1960–64	21.8	50.7	19.4	56.0
	1965–69	22.6	52.0	21.3	60.2
	1970–73	23.7	54.8	17.9	65.6
Sweden	1950–54	15.5	64.3	19.2	54.6
	1955–59	17.1	63.8	18.8	59.4
	1960–64	19.6	62.2	21.9	56.8
	1965–69	20.7	63.2	22.4	57.6
	1970–73	22.0	60.9	22.6	57.1
United Kingdom[d]	1965–69	20.6	n.a.	26.4	n.a.
	1970–73	18.1	60.4	26.7	56.5
United States[b]	1920–24	18.6[e]	n.a.		
	1925–29	16.3[e]	n.a.		
	1931–38	17.6[e]	n.a.		
	1950–54	21.2	48.7		
	1955–59	22.2	52.4	10.6[f]	49.0[f]
	1960–64	22.4	53.3		
	1965–69	24.9	47.2		
	1970–73	25.9	49.8		

[a] Age groups partially estimated.
[b] No emigration statistics.
[c] Returning emigrants only.
[d] Great Britain.
[e] Less than 16 years old.
[f] 1955–57 estimate.

Source: United Nations, *The Determinants and Consequences of Population Trends* (New York: United Nations, 1973) p. 249; United Nations, Statistical Office, unpublished data.

to Rican migrants, the youth population also has been augmented. Net migration also increased the male youth cohorts in Switzerland and Germany, and both sexes in France. Neither the United Kingdom nor Japan would show much change due to migration, in the former case because of the countervailing effect of out-migration and in the latter because of little movement in either direction. Until the early 1970s, Italian net emigration of children and young people, especially from rural areas, reduced the number of young people competing for insufficient employment opportunities.

The finding that net immigration added to the size of the youth population in nine countries does not establish the precise numerical contribution of the migrants nor does it tell how the immigrant share in the youth population compares with its share of the 15 to 64-year population. Censuses of population that tabulate, by age, resident foreign-born population as distinguished from nonnationals, are one source of information. According to the French Census of 1975, 9.4 percent of the total population were foreign-born, but only 7.8 percent of those under 15, 6.2 percent of those 15–19 years old, and 7.5 percent of those 20 to 24 years old. By contrast, in Sweden in 1976 the foreign-born proportions in the youth groups were higher than in the population as a whole (Sweden 1977a, p. 144). These two countries have low proportions of foreign-born population at all ages compared to Australia, Canada, New Zealand, and Switzerland. More information is needed on the age composition of the foreign-born population by exact date of arrival.

Having explored the main demographic components of the youth population and the differences among the twelve countries, a summary analytic measure is introduced. Regression analysis confirms the hypothesis that changes in births are far more important than changes in infant mortality or net migration in accounting for the later size of the teenage (15 to 19) population. Average annual changes in the log of the size of the starting cohort (the sum of live births that occurred 15 to 19 years prior to the year under consideration) statistically explain 93.4 percent of the variation among the twelve countries in the log of average annual changes in the actual size of the teenage population from 1950 to 1975. Introduction of the immigration and infant death variables does not add significantly and consistently to the strength of the relationship. As Chart 2.3 shows, the predictive power of lagged births for future teenage population is very good for most countries. The residual variation of changes in the size of the teenage population is significant only for Germany, which might have been excluded from the regression; German births from 1930 to 1945 are based on adjusted data for West and East Germany combined, but the youth population from 1945 forward is from direct West German data.

The practical significance of the regression exercise is that one can with confidence use the data on lagged births, which give single years of age, as a supplement to information on the size of the youth population by age groups (15 to 19 and 20 to 24).

Youth Population

Trends in the size of the youth population, divided into the age groups 15 to 19 and 20 to 24, provide the basis for assessing the changing numbers and proportions of young people who are enrolled in educational institutions or are participating in the labor force. These two age divisions, however, are not entirely satisfactory in capturing the exit of young people from various levels of education or in measuring new entrants to the labor market. Smoothed data, produced by the grouping of several years of age, conceal fluctuations in the annual numbers of young people reaching the specific age at which a majority leave the educational system or enter the labor

Chart 2.3   Average Annual Rate of Change and Predicated Rate of Change in Teenage Population in Twelve Countries, 1950–1975

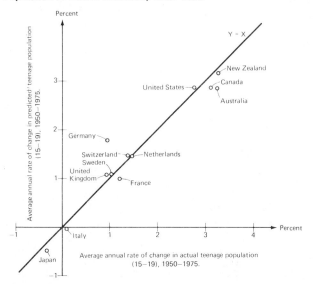

a Predicted teenage population is compiled from births 15–19 years earlier.

Source: United Nations, Statistical Office, unpublished data; OECD, Manpower and Social Affairs Committee, Demographic Trends: Their Labour Market and Social Implications, unpublished revisions (Paris, March 1979).

market of a particular country. For example, in Great Britain the peak year for the number of 15-year-olds was 1962, but the data on 15–19-year-olds in *Table A2.6 show a gradual rise to a later peak, as might be expected. Moreover, in some countries, 15-year-olds are not legally permitted to leave school or to work.

On the other hand, even if a single year of age is most relevant, school-leavers and new entrants to the labor market are never drawn exclusively from a single year of age, but actually span two or three years. In addition, it is difficult to choose a single year of age for analysis because of the changes that have occurred in many countries in the most common year of leaving school during the postwar period. At the outset, 14 would have been the most relevant age in a number of countries, but it became 15 in the 1960s. In most of the twelve countries today, the age would be 16 or older. Finally, the differences among countries at any given time in the typical age of leaving school or entering the labor market suggest the inadvisability, for comparative purposes, of emphasizing a single year of age for the basic population data. This balance of factors makes the 15–19-year interval acceptable for teenagers. For the 20–24-year-old group, two considerations are relevant. National educational sequences at the tertiary level customarily terminate at a wide variety of ages, including ages that go beyond our cut-off point of 25 years. In addition, only a small proportion are new entrants and they are spread over the entire age group, making it a suitable age interval.

Population data for the twelve countries have been drawn from U.N. sources. Published and unpublished population statistics collected by the UN have advantages and disadvantages. The major benefits are the uniform definitions established by the UN and the relative ease of obtaining a large amount of data for twelve countries. The drawbacks are that not all countries supply a consistent series to the UN, and some national revisions may not be communicated to it by the individual countries. Moreover, the UN does not publish all revised estimates. There are other data problems, regardless of source. Some countries adjust estimates backwards when a population census diverges from the earlier estimates for that year, but others do not. For all these reasons, the population data presented may not be entirely consistent with previous data on live births, even allowing for deaths and migration. Also, as is verified for the U.S. data used in Chapter 7, U.N. figures may differ from official national figures, especially those incorporating the latest revisions. Since the major purpose of this section is to show the broad trends and the share of the youth groups in the working-age population, these weaknesses of the U.N. data are not crucial.

The absolute trends for the youth groups contrast with those for the 15–64 group, not unexpectedly (Tables *A2.6, *A2.7). In most of the twelve countries, the 15–64-year population grew fairly smoothly with no decreases year to year; in fact, some of the recorded decreases may be artifacts of the statistics. Annual rates of change were modest, and in most years few countries showed changes of more than 3 percent, especially if exceptional periods are excluded when major postwar population adjustments and relocations occurred.

The youth groups had wider annual fluctuations, including some periods of decline and a large number of years with annual percentage changes, positive and negative, in excess of 5 percent. In fact, at least one change for teenagers of over 10 percent in a single year occurred in France, New Zealand, Sweden, and Switzerland. The elevated rates of increase were concentrated around the period 1959–1962, when the first baby boom cohorts of the late war years in the neutral countries and of the first postwar years in the Allied nations matured; the phenomenon was usually repeated five years later for the 20–24 group.

Two main features distinguish Australia, Canada, New Zealand, and the United States from the other countries in regard to the development of their youth populations. As might be deduced from the record of live births, the countries of Oceania and North America had long periods of uninterrupted increase in the size of the teenage population. Counting only periods of at least four consecutive years of rise (including single years in which slight declines were recorded and years for which missing data are assumed from lagged live births), these four countries had a continuous rise in teenage population in more than two-thirds of the postwar period. Japan and the Netherlands each had three separate periods of increase adding to over twenty years; in both countries the first period of increase occurred before the end of World War II. Germany and the United Kingdom each had two periods of increase, as did Italy, with incomplete data. Switzerland, with some data lacking, France, and Sweden had one period of rise and showed increases in the teenage population in fewer than half of the years. Put another way, the postwar period in nine of the twelve countries was characterized more by rising than by stable or declining teenage cohorts and, in general by larger rates of increase than decrease.

The second main difference between the groups of countries is in the gap between the size of the teenage population at the beginning and the end of the postwar period. The four New World countries, New Zealand, Canada, Australia, and the United States, in that order, had more than doubled to nearly doubled their teenage population in this interval. Among the remaining countries, the Netherlands and Switzerland were the leaders with postwar increases of between 50 and 55 percent.

Germany, France, the United Kingdom, and Sweden showed rises ranging from 45 percent to 20 percent, while Japan and Italy (1947–1977) had gains of only 2 and 3 percent respectively. Several of these countries had higher peaks in intervening years than at the end of the period, however; Japan was outstanding in this regard. By illuminating a slightly different period, 1950–1975, and using the measure of average annual compound growth of the population of two youth groups, Chart 2.4 shows substantial increases for both teenagers and young adults. Somewhat higher growth rates were displayed by teenagers than young adults, in most cases. Patterns of population growth among the countries were similar for both age groups; the four New World countries led the other nations, while Italy and Japan recorded small negative rates for one of the age groups. Using 1975 as a base year, Charts 8.1 and 8.2 in Chapter 8 dramatically portray changes in the postwar period and projected change to 1990.

When the annual average compound percentage changes in youth population are

Chart 2.4   Average Annual Compound Percentage Change in the Youth Population by Age, Both Sexes, in Twelve Countries, 1950–1975

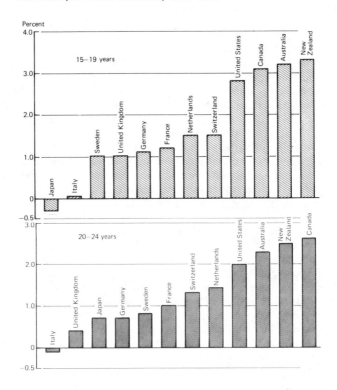

Note: Italian growth rates for 20-24-year-olds cover the period 1951–1975. French growth rates for both age groups are based on OECD estimates for 1975.

Source: United Nations, Demographic Yearbook, 1949–1977 (New York: United Nations, annual); United Nations, Statistical Office, unpublished data; U.S. Department of Commerce, Bureau of the Census, Estimates of the Population of the United States by Age, Sex, and Race: 1970-1979, Series P-25, No. 870, Table 2 (Washington: GPO, 1980).

Table 2.7   Population Change by Age Group, Both Sexes, in Twelve Countries, 1945-1975

	1945-1955			1955-1965			1965-1975		
	15-64	15-19	20-24	15-64	15-19	20-24	15-64	15-19	20-24
	(average annual compound percentage change)								
Australia	1.4	*	-0.7	2.0	5.1	3.3	2.1	1.8	3.4
Canada	1.8	0.5	0.2	2.1	4.5	2.1	2.5	2.7	4.4
France	1.0	-1.0	0.2	1.0	4.2	-0.4	0.8[f]	-0.5[f]	5.5[f]
Germany	2.0[a]	3.1[a]	1.8[a]	0.6	-2.3	1.0	0.6	2.4	0.4
Italy	1.0[b]	0.1[b]	-0.1[d]	0.6[e]	0.3[e]	-0.8[e]	0.2	-0.5	0.4
Japan	2.7	1.0	4.4	2.1	2.3	0.8	1.3	-3.1	*
Netherlands	1.0	0.2	-0.2	1.4	3.8	1.4	1.3	-0.1	2.2
New Zealand	0.9	0.8	1.3	2.7	4.9	3.0	2.1	2.3	3.5
Sweden	0.4	*	-1.8	0.8	3.3	3.6	0.2	-1.4	-0.8
Switzerland	0.5	-0.2	0.1	1.7	4.0	4.2	0.7	*	-1.0
United Kingdom	0.1	-0.7[c]	-1.6[c]	0.5	2.8	1.2	0.7	-0.4	0.6
United States	0.8	-0.4	-1.2	1.3	4.3	2.4	1.6	2.1	3.4

[a] 1946-1955.
[b] 1947-1957.
[c] 1947-1955.
[d] 1951-1957.
[e] 1957-1965.
[f] 1965-1972.

Note: Asterisk indicates less than plus or minus 0.05 percent.

Source: *Table A2.6.

considered at ten-year intervals, clear differences among countries emerge (Table 2.7). In the first postwar decade, the growth rate of all three age groups, 15-19, 20-24, and 15-64, was largest in Germany and Japan. The period 1955-1965 was one of marked growth for the two youth groups in many countries, especially for 15-19-year-olds. In the last decade, 1965-1975, seven countries had larger growth rates than in the previous decade for the 20-24 group; Canada, France, New Zealand, Australia, and the United States had particularly high rates of increase in the 20-24-year group. Growth in the 15-19-year group over the decade was positive in Canada, Germany, New Zealand, the US, and Australia. Japan and Sweden had the highest rates of decline, with slightly negative change in Italy, France, the United Kingdom, and the Netherlands. Switzerland's change was insignificant.

The conspicuous differences among countries in the growth pattern of the youth population are less evident in data on youth shares of the working age population in each country (Table A2.8; Chart 2.5). Youth shares show changes in each youth population in relation to changes in the national working-age population, simulating potential labor supply relationships and eliminating the problems arising from the juxtaposition of absolute numbers for very large and very small countries. Several conclusions emerge from a cross-national examination of the shares of the two youth groups. In any given year, the youth shares in the twelve countries tended to cluster in a fairly narrow range, and large differences were exceptional. Over time the dispersion among countries narrowed and then widened for all but the two countries at the extremes. In individual countries, year-to-year changes were small; and the range between the lowest and highest shares of each age group over the thirty-year

Chart 2.5   Teenage Population (Aged 15–19) as Percent of Population Aged 15–64, Both Sexes, in Twelve Countries, 1945–1977

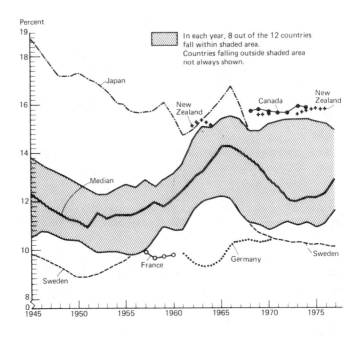

Source: Table A2.8.

period was not wide in most countries, with the exception of Japan. Finally, the countries displayed several different patterns, especially pronounced in the 15–19 group.

Chart 2.5 shows the trends in the shares of the 15–19-year group in the 15–64 population for the twelve countries over a period of thirty years. Changes in the median share, established separately for each year and excluding the extreme cases, indicate the dominant pattern. The degree of variation among the nonextreme countries is shown by the range of shares around the median (shaded area in Chart 2.5). The median line indicates that the teenage share of the working-age population in most countries dropped until 1951, then began an upward movement that was especially marked from 1958 to 1965. Thereafter, the median declined sharply until 1973, when a modest rise appeared. The range for all countries, except the excluded extremes, became narrowest in the late 1950s, when the teenage share in each country was between 11 and 13 percent. From 1966 the range widened perceptibly, and after 1968 the median line was closer to the lower end of the range than it had previously been.

Countries which diverged most from the general pattern (ranked first and last in individual years) are identified in Chart 2.5. Most striking of these is Japan, which had the highest teenage share in each year from 1945 to 1967, with a brief interruption in 1962–1963. But at the same time, Japan's share showed a rapid decline, and by 1978 Japan had the lowest share among the twelve countries. Canada and New Zealand have had the highest shares since the late 1960s. Sweden was at the lower edge of the share spectrum in most years, but was replaced by France and Germany from the late 1950s to 1970.

In individual countries, the range and variability in the size of the teenage shares could be an important indicator of potential labor market difficulty for the teenage group or the labor force as a whole. Four countries — Italy, the Netherlands, Switzerland, and the United Kingdom — had a gap of no more than 3.2 percentage points between the highest and lowest shares of the 15–19 group over the thirty-year period. Seven other countries fell between 3.7 and 4.8 percentage points, with the United States at the high end of this group. Japan's 8.6 percentage point difference between its 1945 and its 1978 shares topped the list. For the 20–24 group, smaller differences between the high and low readings appeared. Seven countries had gaps of 3.5 percentage points or less. The largest spread of 5.4 percentage points appeared in Japan, followed by France with 4.3, Switzerland and the US with 4.0, and Sweden with 3.8 percentage points (Table A2.8).

Despite some dramatic shifts in the teenage share of working-age population in individual countries, there was some stability over time in the ranking of countries, by the size of the teenage share. Spearman's rank-order correlation was +0.75 between the 1945 and 1955 ranks, a relatively high value. For the 1955 and 1965 ranks, the correlation was +0.44, while for the 1965–1975 period it was +0.51. Between the values of 1945 and 1975 — a thirty-year period — a very modest positive correlation (+0.40) was obtained. Together with the overall trends of Chart 2.5, these correlations suggest the presence of common demographic factors in the majority of countries as well as the persistence of differences.

The directions of change in the shares of the 15–19 age group in the working-age population can be categorized into three distinct patterns for the twelve countries:

Shares rising: Australia, Canada, New Zealand, United States.
Shares falling: Italy, Japan.
Shares similar at start and at end, but fall and rise, or rise and fall, in between: France, Germany, the Netherlands, Sweden, Switzerland, United Kingdom.

Classification of the shares of the 20–24 group into the three patterns described for the 15–19 group is not feasible. Shares of the 20–24-year group were not indisputably rising in any country, although the shares in New Zealand and the United States came closest to this description. While Italy's share was falling, in Japan the decline was less clearcut for the 20–24 group than for the 15–19 group. For the remaining countries, the period ended with the same or slightly higher shares than prevailed at the outset, in most cases.

It should be borne in mind that youth shares of the working-age population give a foretaste but are not precisely the same as youth shares of the actual labor force. Therefore, the present finding of relative stability over time in the youth shares of population in most of the twelve countries, and a clustering of shares of different countries around a narrow band, will not necessarily reappear in the shares of youth in the labor force.

Summary

This chapter has established the importance of trends in live births over other demographic factors, such as mortality and net migration rates, in shaping the size of single-years-of-age cohorts as they approach the age of entrance to the labor force. Evaluating the postwar trends in live births, as modified by mortality in the youth ranks and net migration, the twelve countries were ranked by a number of criteria as to the strength of the baby boom in various intervals and the overall change in levels of live births. Australia, New Zealand, Canada, and the United States were in first places in most of the calculations, while Italy and Japan showed more decline than the remaining countries.

Division of the population data into the two age groups required for the subsequent educational enrollment and labor force analysis, 15–19 and 20–24, produces much the same ranking of countries. It also indicates a certain clustering of countries in a narrow band in regard to the youth share of the working-age population (15–64) and relative stability of these shares over time. Differences among countries in the basic demographic levels, trends in the postwar period, and forecasts to 1995 are the foundation for cross-national differences in youth labor force size and participation rates to be discussed subsequently.

Table A2.8 Share of Youth in Working-Age Population (15–64), Both Sexes, in Twelve Countries, 1945–1979

(percent of 15–64 year population)

	Australia		Canada		France		Germany		Italy		Japan	
	15–19	20–24	15–19	20–24	15–19	20–24	15–19	20–24	15–19	20–24	15–19	20–24
1945	12.2	12.6	13.8	13.9	12.4	12.2	n.a.	n.a.	n.a.	n.a.	18.7	13.1
1946	11.9	12.4	13.5	13.7	11.9	11.7	11.7	10.6	n.a.	n.a.	18.2	14.5
1947	11.6	12.2	13.2	13.6	11.8	11.9	11.4	10.8	13.8	n.a.	17.7	15.1
1948	11.1	12.1	13.0	13.4	11.6	11.9	11.0	11.1	n.a.	n.a.	17.2	15.2
1949	10.7	12.1	12.7	13.0	11.5	11.8	10.7	11.2	n.a.	n.a.	n.a.	n.a.
1950	10.4	12.0	12.5	12.9	11.2	11.8	10.8	11.2	13.3	n.a.	17.3	15.6
1951	10.1	11.7	12.2	12.6	10.8	11.7	11.1	11.1	13.0	13.1	17.1	15.5
1952	10.1	11.5	12.1	12.4	10.5	11.7	11.5	10.9	n.a.	n.a.	16.9	15.5
1953	10.2	11.0	12.0	12.2	10.3	11.6	12.1	10.5	n.a.	n.a.	16.6	15.6
1954	10.4	10.6	12.0	12.0	10.4	11.0	12.5	10.4	n.a.	n.a.	16.1	15.5
1955	10.7	10.3	12.0	11.9	10.2	11.3	12.8	10.5	n.a.	n.a.	15.9	15.2
1956	10.9	10.2	12.1	11.9	9.9	11.0	13.0	10.8	12.6	12.1	15.7	15.2
1957	11.1	10.2	12.3	11.7	9.7	10.8	12.9	10.9	12.2	12.1	15.7	15.0
1958	11.3	10.3	12.6	11.6	9.6	10.6	12.4	11.6	11.8	12.2	15.8	14.7
1959	11.7	10.5	12.8	11.4	9.7	10.4	11.8	12.2	11.3	12.3	16.1	14.2
1960	12.2	10.6	13.1	11.2	9.8	10.2	10.8	12.8	11.5	12.2	15.5	13.9
1961	12.6	10.8	13.4	11.1	10.5	9.8	9.8	12.7	11.8	12.0	14.7	14.0
1962	13.4	10.9	13.9	11.2	11.8	9.8	9.4	12.7	11.9	11.7	14.9	14.0
1963	13.9	11.0	14.4	11.4	12.6	9.4	9.3	12.3	12.3	11.6	15.4	14.0
1964	14.2	11.3	14.9	12.2	13.3	9.5	9.3	11.8	12.2	10.9	15.8	14.3
1965	14.5	11.7	15.2	11.9	14.0	9.6	9.6	10.9	11.9	10.7	16.2	13.6
1966	14.6	11.9	15.5	12.3	13.9	9.8	10.2	10.0	11.5	11.1	16.8	12.7
1967	14.3	12.7	15.6	12.7	13.8	10.8	10.3	9.6	11.3	11.3	16.0	13.0
1968	14.2	13.2	15.7	13.2	13.5	11.4	10.4	9.5	n.a.	11.6	14.9	13.7
1969	14.2	13.5	15.6	13.6	13.3	12.1	10.3	9.7	11.2	n.a.	13.7	14.3
1970	14.1	13.7	15.7	14.0	13.1	12.9	10.5	9.6	11.1	11.8	12.7	14.9
1971	13.8	13.7	15.7	14.1	12.9	13.7	10.6	10.3	11.2	11.8	11.9	15.5
1972	14.0	13.5	15.7	14.2	12.8	13.5	10.9	10.6	11.3	11.4	11.4	14.8
1973	14.0	13.4	15.9	13.9	n.a.	n.a.	11.1	10.8	11.4	11.4	11.0	13.9
1974	14.1	13.3	15.7	14.1	n.a.	n.a.	11.4	10.8	11.7	11.0	10.8	12.8
1975	14.1	13.2	15.6	14.3	n.a.	n.a.	11.7	10.7	11.8	11.0	10.4	12.0
1976	14.2	13.1	15.4	14.0	n.a.	n.a.	11.7	10.7	n.a.	10.8	10.4	11.3
1977	14.1	13.0	15.4	14.3	12.7	12.7	12.0	10.8	n.a.	10.9	10.2	10.6
1978	n.a.	n.a.	15.2	14.4	12.6	12.5	12.3	10.9	n.a.	n.a.	10.1	10.2
1979	n.a.	n.a.	n.a.	n.a.	12.6	12.5	n.a.	n.a.	n.a.	n.a.	n.a.	n.a.

Table A2.8 (continued)

(percent of 15–64 year population)

	Netherlands		New Zealand		Sweden		Switzerland		United Kingdom		United States	
	15-19	20-24	15-19	20-24	15-19	20-24	15-19	20-24	15-19	20-24	15-19	20-24
1945	13.4	13.4	12.7	11.1	9.8	11.4	10.5	11.0	n.a.	n.a.	12.3	12.9
1946	13.3	13.1	12.2	11.9	9.7	11.1	10.8	11.4	n.a.	n.a.	12.1	12.8
1947	13.3	13.1	12.0	12.0	9.5	10.7	10.7	11.3	10.2	10.8	11.7	12.6
1948	13.2	12.8	11.7	12.2	9.3	10.5	10.5	11.1	10.0	10.7	11.4	12.4
1949	13.0	12.7	11.5	12.0	9.1	10.2	10.4	10.9	9.9	10.6	11.0	12.2
1950	12.7	12.6	12.0	12.8	8.9	9.8	10.4	10.8	9.6	10.4	10.8	11.7
1951	12.5	12.5	11.7	12.7	8.9	9.8	10.1	10.7	9.5	10.1	10.7	11.6
1952	12.3	12.4	11.8	12.3	8.9	9.6	9.9	10.8	9.4	9.8	10.6	11.3
1953	12.3	12.3	11.9	12.1	9.0	9.4	9.9	10.8	9.5	9.7	10.7	11.0
1954	12.3	12.1	12.1	11.8	9.2	9.2	9.9	10.8	9.6	9.6	10.9	10.7
1955	12.3	11.9	12.5	11.5	9.4	9.1	9.8	10.7	9.7	9.5	10.9	10.5
1956	12.4	11.7	12.8	11.2	9.7	9.0	9.9	10.5	9.6	9.6	11.1	10.4
1957	12.5	11.6	13.4	11.2	10.0	9.0	10.2	10.4	9.7	9.6	11.3	10.3
1958	12.6	11.5	13.6	11.3	10.5	9.1	10.5	10.6	9.9	9.7	11.8	10.3
1959	12.9	11.5	13.9	11.4	11.0	9.2	10.9	10.3	10.2	9.8	12.1	10.5
1960	13.0	11.4	14.0	11.7	12.0	9.4	11.9	11.3	10.5	9.7	12.4	10.1
1961	13.6	11.5	14.1	12.0	12.3	9.5	11.9	11.4	10.8	9.8	12.7	10.5
1962	14.5	11.5	15.1	12.5	12.6	9.8	12.4	12.4	11.6	10.0	13.5	10.7
1963	15.1	11.6	15.4	12.5	12.7	10.3	12.3	12.4	12.0	10.3	13.8	11.2
1964	15.3	11.8	15.0	11.9	12.5	10.9	12.3	13.1	12.1	10.6	14.2	11.5
1965	15.5	11.9	15.4	11.9	12.0	11.9	12.2	13.6	12.2	11.4	14.6	11.7
1966	15.2	12.5	15.5	12.1	11.8	12.2	12.0	14.0	12.1	11.8	15.1	11.9
1967	14.5	13.4	15.4	12.5	11.4	12.6	11.9	14.1	11.5	12.1	14.8	12.6
1968	14.1	14.0	15.3	12.9	11.0	12.8	11.7	14.3	11.1	12.3	14.9	12.9
1969	13.8	14.3	15.6	13.5	10.7	12.7	11.0	12.5	11.0	12.2	14.9	13.2
1970	13.6	14.5	15.6	13.7	10.5	12.5	11.1	12.2	10.9	11.6	15.2	13.1
1971	13.5	14.3	15.3	13.8	10.4	12.2	n.a.	n.a.	11.0	11.2	15.3	13.8
1972	13.5	13.7	n.a.	n.a.	10.3	11.7	11.3	11.7	11.2	11.1	15.4	13.6
1973	13.4	13.3	15.6	13.5	10.2	11.3	11.4	11.5	11.3	11.0	15.4	13.6
1974	13.4	13.1	15.7	13.6	10.2	11.0	11.1	11.3	11.5	11.0	15.4	13.7
1975	13.2	13.0	15.8	13.6	10.1	10.7	11.6	11.3	11.8	11.1	15.3	13.9
1976	13.4	12.9	15.8	13.5	10.1	10.6	11.8	11.4	12.0	11.0	15.2	14.0
1977	13.4	12.8	16.0	13.3	10.2	10.6	11.9	n.a.	12.3	11.1	14.9	14.1
1978	13.4	12.8	16.1	13.3	n.a.	n.a.	n.a.	n.a.	n.a.	n.a.	14.7	14.1
1979	n.a.	n.a.	n.a.	n.a.	n.a.	n.a.	n.a.	n.a.	n.a.	n.a.	14.4	14.1

Source: *Table A2.6.

3 *Educational Enrollment Patterns*

Educational enrollment patterns and trends have been the single most important factor in medium-term trends in youth labor force participation and the best single predictor of cross-national LFPR differences (OECD 1979c). For a substantial proportion of young people, especially teenagers, education or labor force participation are viable alternatives. Notwithstanding the exceptions—teenagers below the legal age for leaving school, young people combining education and labor force participation, those who desire no further education currently, and those who will be neither in school nor the labor force—many youths make a deliberate choice between additional education and labor force participation. As a result, some analysts have described educational enrollment rates (EER) and labor force participation rates (LFPR) as mirror images or reciprocal functions, and statistical series tend to confirm this relationship (GB 1973–79f; Bertrand 1975; Canada 1976d; Wachter 1976).

To test this relation, we regressed full-time EER on LFPR for eleven countries (see Chapter 4). The results support the expectation that over time an increase in EER tends to reduce the relevant LFPR, while a decline in EER will correspondingly augment LFPR. Since some students work while attending school, however, to the extent that they are counted in both categories, there is not an exact reciprocal relation between educational enrollment and labor force participation. In addition, young females, especially in the 20–24 age group, have nonmarket activity as an alternative to both education and labor force participation, and changes in this alternative can affect EER and LFPR simultaneously in the same direction.

Prolonged education influences the youth labor force primarily by delaying or restricting labor force participation and by reducing the number of persons and the hours offered on the youth labor market. Prolonged education also advances the typical age of entry to the labor market, alters the age composition of both enrolled and nonenrolled youth, changes the average age of the youth labor force, increases real or presumed qualifications, heightens aspirations, confers additional credentials on young people, and changes the distribution of nominal education attainment levels across the whole working-age population. It also tends to leave a more conspicuous residual group with low academic qualifications and poor labor market prospects.

The causes of educational expansion are subject to varying interpretations. Viewing education partly or wholly as a consumption activity that rises as income rises and is stimulated by public subsidies that reduce its direct costs, Cain (1977, p. 6) finds an accompanying long-run decline in the labor supply of youth, explained by the "backward bending" supply curve. But as many others emphasize, enrollments in education are not purely a supply-side phenomenon, since EER also reflect important medium-and long-term changes in the educational levels demanded by the labor market and in its rewards. For youth in postcompulsory education, the interaction between educational enrollment and labor force participation rests on a complex and changeable set of perceptions regarding the current and future requirements, type, level, and location of job opportunities, and the relative status and rewards of occupations associated with various levels and types of education. Education is akin to capital investment, in that comparisons can be made of the costs and lifetime streams of earnings that flow from completion of different educational levels.

Major economic and social trends as well as institutional factors and policies also strongly influence the educational decisions of individuals or households. Equally important, such issues affect public and private financial decisions to alter the number and capacity of educational institutions. Clearly, decisions about education are also motivated by elements other than labor market needs and the private and social returns to investment in human capital. Analysis and opinion surveys in many countries confirm the importance of such considerations in private choices and in decisions on the supply of educational institutions and courses.

The numerical aspects of educational enrollment and attainment must be supplemented by qualitative considerations. If educational expansion occurs with a simultaneous dilution of educational standards, qualitative imbalances may arise beyond any possible quantitative mismatch. Similarly, the distribution of subjects studied, the degree to which subject content conforms to emerging employment opportunities, and the correspondence between the educational attainment of the new labor market entrants and actual job requirements are factors that may affect the validity of the qualifications, aspirations, and credentials of young people as they enter the labor force.

Historical Trends

It is difficult to establish analytically a one-way causal relation between medium-term trends in educational enrollments and labor force participation. Historically, however, the dynamic force appears to have been the expansion of education that has encroached on the labor force activity of youth. Educational enrollment rates (EER) have been rising in many of the industrialized countries for a century or more. These long-run trends have persisted to the present despite short periods of little or no change and even slight retrogression. As each new peak was reached in a country, some observers would declare that postcompulsory EER could not increase further, but subsequent enrollment rates did advance.

Educational expansion in the 19th century frequently took the form of an increased number of scheduled days in the school year and stricter supervision of attendance (Long 1958, p. 419; Canada 1978b, Table 9). At the same time, enrollment rates were stimulated by compulsory schooling laws and legislative restrictions on child labor. Once extended attendance patterns were established, progressive advances occurred in the statutory school-leaving age and/or the minimum legal working age. Such legislation was in force in all twelve countries by the 1930s, many nations having initiated these measures in the latter part of the 19th century. Under federal-type governments in which states or other subnational units have jurisdiction over education and child labor, a long interval could separate the first and last enactments by the subnational units. In the U.S., for example, compulsory education laws spread slowly. Only 6 percent of the states had such laws by 1870; this had increased to 49 percent by 1890 and 100 percent by 1920 (Meyer et al. 1979).

Compulsory schooling laws were effective in some countries and quickly brought enrollment rates close to 100 percent for the affected ages, as in Japan. In other countries such as Italy, noncompliance rates were high; years after the passage of compulsory school legislation only a fraction of the age group attended regularly. In still other countries, such as the United States and France, legislation came after the fact and merely confirmed existing enrollment patterns (Prost 1968; Landes and Solmon 1972). At the same time an increased rate of voluntary enrollments in postcompulsory education was another source of rising EER and was often more important than the raising of the compulsory age in overall effect on EER, especially when transfer rates to the next level of education also rose.

Although the general pattern of enrollment growth had been similar for all twelve countries up to the beginning of World War II, the level of enrollment rates varied widely among the countries. At both the upper secondary and higher education levels, EER were markedly higher in the United States than in any other country. Not only previous history, but also the specific wartime and immediate postwar experience of each country affected its subsequent position. The experience of four countries — Japan, the Netherlands, Sweden, and the US — exemplifies the variety of conditions found in the twelve countries.

In Japan during the war years a heavy mobilization of young men effectively truncated their education, while in the final phase of the war, all schooling was disrupted in the heavily bombed areas. Similar conditions existed in Germany and Italy. While the number of births in Japan during the 1940–1944 period was higher than in the late 1930s, sharp declines were experienced in the two European countries (*Table A 2.1; Chart 2.2).* The Netherlands, as a country which was occupied early in the war, faced severe dislocation of its traditional institutions. Wartime births were higher than during the depressed 1930s but below the level which would otherwise have prevailed. France suffered likewise, but experienced a continued decrease in the numbers of births. The United Kingdom, whose birth trends replicated those of the Netherlands, was directly involved in the Allied war effort and had a substantial mobilization. The UK also endured a period when large-scale civilian evacuations contributed to the less effective and consistent functioning of the educational system.

Sweden as a neutral country experienced a boom in both births and education due to the protected circumstances; Switzerland showed similar but less marked effects. In the United States, Australia, Canada, and New Zealand, the large-scale absence of young men on overseas duty adversely affected their education, family formation, and the number of births, but not so severely as in those Allied or Axis nations which were physically part of the war theater.

As a defeated and devastated nation, Japan not only undertook an enormous postwar economic reconstruction, but also revised its educational system in accordance with the guidelines laid down by SCAP (Supreme Commander Allied Powers). The minimum school-leaving age was raised from 12 to 15 in 1947; an increase to 14 had been planned in 1941 but had been delayed because of the war. It is a measure of the high value the Japanese nation places on education and the discipline of Japanese society that as early as 1947, 96.6 percent of the 13–15-year group was enrolled in school (Japan 1971b, p. 101). In some respects, the immediate postwar experience of Germany and Italy resembled that of Japan, but both of these countries were slower to start their educational expansion. Reconstruction was a high priority in the Netherlands as in France and Britain, and rising enrollments were more likely to result from demographic factors than increased EER in the early postwar years. Sweden and Switzerland were able to continue without a break on the expansionary course already set. In the United States and Canada, which began with higher EER

*Tables marked with an asterisk are not included in this volume, but may be obtained from the authors.

levels than Australia and New Zealand, peacetime brought more immediate and rapid expansion than that experienced in the two countries of Oceania.

Educational developments in the postwar period proceeded along generally similar lines in most of the countries. In one sense, nothing more than a continuation of long-run trends occurred; in another sense, the postwar educational explosion sets the quarter-century since 1945 apart from earlier periods, constituting a distinctive interlude in educational history with marked consequences for the quantitative and qualitative development of the youth labor force.

A cross-national study of educational enrollment and EER is complicated by the substantial differences among countries in the structure, sequences, and nomenclature of the various educational systems. A standardized and simplified model of postcompulsory education can be used without excessive distortion of national systems. Such a model makes it possible to deal with the two youth age groups and with three levels of education. Because compulsory education in most countries has come to include all lower-secondary education, the two most relevant postcompulsory sequences are the upper-secondary level (higher education) and the tertiary level (postsecondary education). The postsecondary stage can be divided into the university and nonuniversity sectors; in the United States, for example, this division would be between four-year and two-year colleges. As another simplifying device, those attending all types and levels of educational institutions are called students, instead of observing the distinction made in many countries between pupils and students. In addition, the term "school" is used to designate educational institutions at all levels, including the most advanced higher education. Data and discussion are limited to officially recognized components of the formal education system in each country. As far as possible, information refers to full-time enrollments.

Certain educational trends should be borne in mind, to the extent that they impinge on labor force participation. First, as already has been observed, enrollment and labor force status are not necessarily mutually exclusive categories. As the education process has expanded and become more general, the traditional sequence of completing education before entering the labor force has been modified in a number of countries. The option of simultaneously attending an educational institution and working, either in term-time or during vacations, is of considerable significance in a few countries, and its dimensions will be discussed in the later labor force chapters. Second, it has become increasingly common to delay entry from one educational sequence to another or to the labor force; an increasing trend of alternation between education and labor force participation over a period of years has become apparent.

Because the majority of the enrolled do not make a fresh decision each year to remain in postcompulsory education, but rather commit themselves to several years at a time, the flows of young people into the labor market are best measured through statistics on the completion of various levels of education. On the other hand, the analysis of stocks in the youth labor force is best made with standardized age groups. Both measures are used in the discussion that follows.

Overview

All twelve countries experienced an educational explosion following World War II. While several countries experienced some slowdown or slight reversal in the growth of educational enrollment rates towards the end of the 1960s or in the early 1970s, various indicators of educational expansion reached unprecedented levels by the end of the 1970s.

In many of the countries demographic pressures alone, without any change in enrollment rates, would have produced a notable swelling of enrollments. But what is remarkable in the postwar experience is the upsurge in both enrollments and enrollment rates. In a period when educational institutions had to accommodate the greater numbers of the baby boom, they also expanded in order to permit larger proportions of the age group to attend.

The main developments in education as they relate to the youth labor force over the entire postwar period were:

In many countries the numbers enrolled in upper-secondary or higher education increased much more between the end of the war and the end of the 1970s than they had throughout the previous century. For example, Canadian enrollments in higher education rose by about 90,000 from 1867, the beginning of nationhood, to 1951, but increased by over 520,000 in the much shorter period 1951 to 1977 (Canada 1978b, pp. 16–17).

Most countries entered an era of mass upper-secondary education in which terminal education is provided as well as preparation for entrance to higher education. Enrollment, completion, and transfer rates in each country were considerably higher at the end of the postwar period than at the beginning.

While higher education remains a minor activity for the relevant age group, it also has burgeoned in the postwar period.

As a consequence, the average age at leaving full-time education, the average number of years of completed education, and the average age of entry into the full-time labor force have all risen over the postwar period by two years or more. The generational educational attainment gap has widened.

Increased enrollments and enrollment rates and the strong pressure of the private demand for education led to changes in educational forms and procedures and the creation of new types of educational institutions. In turn, these newer forms, generally offering shorter, vocationally oriented courses, stimulated increased educational participation by groups such as females, low-income, or working class youth, and minority racial or ethnic groups. In most cases, these groups have not achieved parity in enrollment rates, but the gaps have narrowed.

Within countries, disparities in EER between regions or other types of subnational units have been reduced somewhat, but substantial differences remained in some cases.

Among countries, EER for the sexes were closer together at the end of the period than at the beginning.

Trends in Numbers Enrolled

The increase in enrollments over the postwar period was pronounced for both teenagers and young adults in all countries. Enrollment growth occurred as the result of rises in numbers in the youth population and in EER. Educational enrollments would have grown in most countries over the period due to demographic change alone, but the fact that enrollments generally increased at a faster rate than the youth population, in some countries dramatically so, indicates that rising EER were an important factor. An OECD study of 18 countries, including eight of our twelve countries, estimated that approximately one-quarter of the increase in enrollments in postsecondary education between 1960 and 1970 could be attributed to demographic change, while three-quarters was due to changes in EER (OECD 1974a, p. 27). Another study of eleven countries, including seven of our twelve countries, also showed that the increase in higher education enrollments exceeded the rise in the corresponding population. The growth rates of population and higher education enrollments between 1960 and 1970 displayed a weak correlation of + .37, and no positive relationship was found for the 1970–1975 period (US 1978d, p. 82).

Enrollments for both youth age groups increased most rapidly during the 1960s. Teenage enrollments, for the most part, increased at the fastest rates during the late 1950s and early 1960s, while young adult enrollments increased most rapidly during the 1960s. For both age groups, the 1970s were a period of much slower growth, and in a few cases, even of a slight decline in enrollments (OECD 1977b, 1978e; Japan 1979a; US 1979b; Netherlands unpub.). Country data for most of the twelve countries for the whole period by level of education indicate that enrollments in upper-secondary education (usually corresponding to a starting age of 14–16 and a terminal age of 17–19) increased more rapidly in the 1950s than in the 1960s. Similar data for some countries in the early 1970s show a higher growth of enrollments than for the 1960s, though lower than that recorded during the 1950s. Higher education enrollments (usually concentrated in the 18–24 age group) grew faster during the 1960s than the 1950s in most countries, with the slowest growth of enrollments and even some slight year-to-year declines occurring during the 1970s, especially after 1975 (OECD 1974a, 1978e). Were it not for the growth of enrollment rates, several countries would have experienced a more pronounced slowdown or decline in enrollments, especially in higher education (UN 1978; OECD 1979a).

More detailed cross-national comparisons of enrollments for the two youth groups (15–19- and 20–24-year olds) can be drawn from unpublished data for 1960, 1970, and 1975, which the OECD collected from national sources. Covering only enrollments in full-time education, data for both sexes combined are available for all twelve countries, and for each sex separately for all but Switzerland. Since some countries have collected enrollment data only by educational level, the accuracy of data, especially for 1960, is uneven among the countries. Further revisions of the data by OECD may be expected.

Teenage enrollments in all twelve countries were considerably higher in 1975 than they had been in 1960 (Table 3.1). A country-by-country comparison of population and enrollment growth demonstrates how much greater the latter was and how different the country rankings were for the two variables (Charts 3.1, 2.4; Tables 3.1, *A3.1). Five European countries—the United Kingdom, France, Switzerland, the Netherlands, and Italy—led in teenage enrollment growth over the period; each had an increase of 140 percent or more. In the second group were Canada, New Zealand, Australia, and the United States, in that order, exhibiting rises ranging from 80 to 130 percent. The lowest growth in enrollments was recorded by Germany, Sweden, and Japan, with increases of 42 to 50 percent over the 1960–1975 period (Table 3.1). Annual average compound growth rates in teenage enrollments were much higher during the 1960–1970 period than the 1970–1975 span in a majority of countries (*Table A3.1). Growth was stronger for 15–19-year females between 1970 and 1975 than in 1960–1970 in Italy, the Netherlands and Australia. Sweden was the only country which recorded a decline in teenage enrollments between 1970 and 1975, in both sexes.

Analysis of teenage enrollments by sex yields two main conclusions (*Table A3.1; Chart 3.1). First, national patterns of educational expansion dominated over sex differences: changes in teenage enrollments for the two sexes moved in tandem. A division of the countries into three groups according to the amount of growth in teenage enrollments between 1960 and 1975 produces identical groups for each sex, although small variations appear in country ranks within the three groups. The rank correla-

Table 3.1   Enrollments in Full-Time Education, Teenagers and Young Adults, Both Sexes, in Twelve Countries, 1960–1975

| | Teenagers (15–19) | | | | Young adults (20–24) | | | |
| | 1960 | 1970 | 1975 | 1975 as percentage of 1960 | 1960 | 1970 | 1975 | 1975 as percentage of 1960 |
	(000s)				(000s)			
Australia	274.2	457.3	541.5	197.5	8.0	32.5	62.2	777.5
Canada	663.2	1320.1	1529.0	230.5	85.6	252.3	306.4	357.9
France	888.3	1890.9	2251.7	253.5	218.5	390.6	500.8	229.2
Germany	1427.8	1913.6	2144.8	150.2	311.4	385.9	530.5	170.4
Italy	727.4	1252.6	1746.5	240.1	200.8	355.3	655.5	326.4
Japan	4227.1	5846.0	6011.9	142.2	513.0	1273.5	1312.9	255.9
Netherlands	277.6	487.1	668.4	240.8	46.0	103.8	138.4	300.9
New Zealand	57.4	107.5	121.6	211.8	4.3	14.5	16.2	376.7
Sweden	205.1	311.2	306.2	149.3	70.5	106.9	81.5	115.6
Switzerland	130.3	314.2	323.3	248.1	14.9	60.1	66.6	447.0
United Kingdom	581.9	1308.2	1829.3	314.4	160.0	257.5	301.6	188.5
United States	8322.8	14273.6	15140.5	181.9	1270.7	3370.7	4159.4	327.3

Source: OECD, Working Party of the Education Committee on Educational Statistics and Indicators, revised data, unpublished. (Paris: OECD, March 1979). Totals have been obtained by adding OECD data for each sex.

Chart 3.1   Average Annual Compound Percentage Change in Full-Time Enrollments, Teenagers (15-19), by Sex, in Eleven Countries, 1960-1975

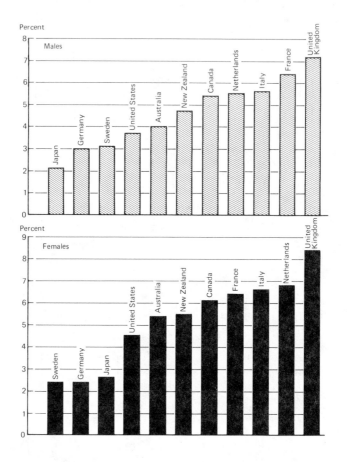

Source: OECD, Working Party of the Education Committee on Educational Statistics and Indicators, revised data, unpublished (Paris: OECD, March 1979).

tion of countries for teenage male and female average annual compound growth rates of enrollments for 1960–1975 is extremely high ($r_S = +.93$); it can be explained in large part by well-established sex similarities in demographic trends. Second, in most countries female teenage enrollments grew faster than male over 1960–1975 and in the subperiods. This was partly due to the fact that in most countries substantially smaller numbers of females than males were enrolled at the beginning of the period; France and Sweden were the only countries in which there were more enrolled teenage females than males in 1960. In Canada, Italy, the Netherlands, New Zealand, the United Kingdom, and the United States, teenage female enrollments grew at a faster rate in both 1960–1970 and 1970–1975, but in Australia, France, and Japan, females led males in only one of the two subperiods. Only in Germany and Sweden did male enrollments grow faster than female for the whole period 1960–1975 and in each subperiod.

Enrollment growth of young adults (aged 20–24) was impressive and exceeded that for teenagers in every country except France, Sweden, and the UK over the 1960–1975 period (Table 3.1). A country-by-country comparison of population and enrollment growth among young adults shows that, as was found for teenagers, enrollments grew more rapidly than population. Unlike the teenagers, however, young adults displayed a fairly close relation between country ranks for the two variables, particularly because the four New World countries, leaders in population growth, also were among the top countries in enrollment expansion. The largest increase for the young adults occurred in Australia, with an almost eightfold growth in enrollments. Switzerland, New Zealand, Canada, the US, Italy, and the Netherlands had a rise of three times or more. In the case of Italy, low starting levels and fast growth in EER offset demographic decline. In Japan and France, enrollments more than doubled between 1960 and 1975, while in the UK and Germany, the growth was a little less than double. Least enrollment growth over the whole period was shown by Sweden, which was the only country to show an absolute decline in enrollments of young adults from 1970 to 1975. This decrease was attributable to demographic factors, a temporary turning away from higher education by this age group because of labor market conditions, and government policy to favor enrollment of those more than 25 years of age.

Analysis of enrollments of young adults by sex (excluding Switzerland for data reasons) reveals, in comparison with teenagers, a wider gap between the sexes in enrollment levels, a greater divergence between the sexes in a ranking of countries and between the sexes in the annual average compound growth rates of enrollments (*Table A3.1; Charts 3.2, 3.3). The range of annual average compound growth rates for young adults over the period 1960–1975 was wide, from 13.2 percent in Australia down to -0.3 percent in Sweden for males, and from 20.9 percent in Italy down to 2.2 percent in Sweden for females. A rank correlation of countries for young adult male and female average annual compound growth rates over 1960–1975 results in $r_s = +.40$, much less association than was found for teenagers. Female average annual compound growth rates exceeded those of males in each time period in each country,

Chart 3.2 Average Annual Compound Percentage Change in Full-Time Enrollments, Young Adult Males (20–24), in Eleven Countries, 1960–1975

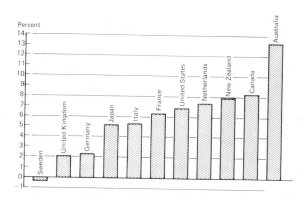

Source: OECD, Working Party of the Education Committee on Educational Statistics and Indicators, revised data, unpublished (Paris: OECD, March 1979).

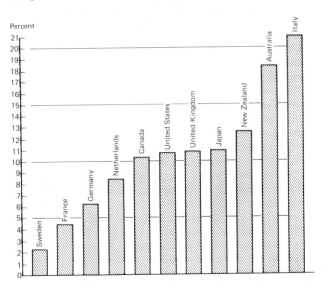

Source: OECD, Working Party of the Education Committee on Educational Statistics and Indicators, revised data, unpublished (Paris: OECD, March 1979).

with the exception of France. While the 1960–1970 subperiod was highly expansionary for young adults of each sex in most countries, between 1970 and 1975 the rate of enrollment growth slowed perceptibly for males in every country except Germany and Italy; a similar downturn was experienced by females with the exception of Australia, France, and Germany. Sweden had fewer young adults, both male and female, enrolled in 1975 than in 1970, while Japan and New Zealand had a smaller number of males only. Changes in both demography and EER were responsible for the slowdown.

Trends in Enrollment Rates

Enrollment rates (those enrolled in educational institutions as a proportion of a specific age group) are in many ways a more important indicator of educational change and a better measure for comparative purposes than the absolute number of enrollments. The latter contains a demographic factor that has been independently analyzed in Chapter 2 and that also affects the size of the youth labor force. Therefore, a clearer view of the distinct educational trends that impinge on youth labor force participation can be obtained from a study of educational enrollment rates.

From the end of World War II to 1980, the proportion of youth enrolled in postcompulsory education showed a rise in all twelve countries; in some cases the increase was dramatic and uninterrupted. Enrollment rates in some countries might have been still higher in the postwar period if all who were academically qualified, financially able, and desired to attend had been accepted. The issue of the availability of sufficient educational places has been a source of controversy in some countries, with those who favor liberal policies and the principle of free access to postcompulsory education opposed by those who advocate high standards, controlled expansion, restrained expenditure, and limitations set by the ability of the labor market to absorb graduates without downgrading them economically or socially.

A lack of availability of sufficient places to accommodate all qualified applicants affected upper-secondary education in some countries. For example, Japanese annual statistics recording the flow from lower-secondary to upper-secondary schools regularly showed that the total number of applicants exceeded the number accepted (Japan 1976a, p. 19). Even at this level, competition to enter certain schools has been extremely sharp. In the United States, on the other hand, it has been taken for granted that a full high school education will be available to all, even though most states' compulsory schooling laws have not extended to the later high school years. Some countries have been unable to provide upper-secondary schooling for all who qualify in the sparsely settled areas. Moreover, the specialized courses that characterize some upper-secondary systems have not all been available in every school, leading some qualified youth to forego postcompulsory education.

In many countries, some qualified and eager candidates failed to enter higher education because of shortages in the number of educational places, whether in total, in given locations, or in types of studies. Among the factors that have commonly contributed to a surplus of qualified and willing applicants over the intake in higher education are: a wholly or largely public system; central control of the number of available places; uniform admissions procedures and standards; early specialization in secondary school; public financing of a high share of all costs, including student living costs; a lack of diversity in the types and duration of postsecondary education; prestige rankings for institutions and courses that inhibit alternate choices; and numerical limits on the number of entrants in many fields.

In Japan the competition for entrance to universities has been so keen that "the mass media calculate the 'competition ratio' of each university, and weekly magazines publish special issues devoted to the entrance examination" (Kato 1978, p. 5). Each year the number of qualified Japanese applicants has exceeded the number accepted, after allowing for multiple applications (Burn 1971, pp. 239–40; *N. Y. Times* f). In Britain also, until recently some qualified applicants were rejected each year (Layard, King, and Moser 1969; Reid 1974; Pissarides 1980).

Some countries have had limited access to certain subjects in higher education. Called *numerus clausus*, this system has been used in many European countries, among them Germany, France, the Netherlands, and Sweden (OECD 1974a). Where difficulties in obtaining admission to a desired course persisted, certain educational patterns emerged. For example, in Germany applicants who were rejected in a chosen field would apply for admission in another subject and attempt to transfer to the original course of study at a later point. Among the effects were a prolonged average length of studies, increased dropout rates, and delays by some youth in entering higher education. In Japan, the disappointed applicants, called *Rōnin*, commonly wait one or more years, often attending cram schools, until they gain admission to a chosen course or institution. Over recent years, about one-third of those admitted to Japanese universities each year have been *Rōnin*; in some fields, they constitute half or more of the entrants (Japan 1976a, pp. 38–39).

The shortfall in the enrollment rate resulting from an insufficient supply of places is impossible to quantify, because it is not known to what extent qualified applicants who were excluded from one type of institution or course were accepted at another in the same year, just as it is not possible to discover to what extent those denied in one year applied successfully in a subsequent year. In any year in which qualified and willing applicants were not admitted, however, enrollment rates would be lower and perhaps labor force participation rates would be higher than under a system with easier access conditions. In recent years enrollment rates have not been reduced because of a shortage of places to the same extent as in the past. Indeed, in some countries, all eligible, willing, and financially able students have succeeded in finding a place, as they have throughout the postwar period in a few countries such as the United States.

Therefore, comparisons of actual enrollment rates over time and among countries should take account of the possibility that EER might have been even higher in some countries at certain times if the number of educational places had matched the eligible demand. The supply of educational opportunities as well as the demand for these places is important, in many countries, in determining educational enrollment rates. Because so much of the analysis has been conducted by Americans and drew on the American situation that appeared to have no real constraints on the supply of places, the question of supply has been somewhat neglected, while empirical and theoretical analysis has been directed to the individual demand for education.

Actual EER are, however, the only hard data that can be examined. Since standardized data are not commonly available for many countries over the full postwar period, a variety of illustrative indicators relevant to upper-secondary and higher education in nine individual countries has been assembled, chiefly from national sources (Table 3.2). While each indicator is a valid measure of change in the specific nation, comparisons of levels and rates of change among countries would be misleading and inappropriate. For example, some of the national data cover full-time enrollments only, while others include part-time enrollments. Not only did the latter differ in importance among countries; but trends in part-time education varied considerably among nations in the postwar period, with a rising proportion of part-timers in higher education in the United States, Canada, and Great Britain, and a declining share in the Netherlands (Netherlands 1967–79; Canada 1978a, Table VII-3; GB 1978d, Tables 2,3; U.S. 1978g, Table 5).

In addition to the earliest and latest available data, Table 3.2 contains data for one intervening year; the peak year has been chosen except in cases where the most recent year is the peak. Each indicator in the nine countries shows considerable growth over the whole period. At the upper-secondary level, or for equivalent age groups, most countries' highest rates were recorded in the latest year cited; for older age groups, or those in higher education, in a majority of the countries the peak appears in the late 1960s or early 1970s, with a subsequent decline to the most recent year. In most countries, teenage EER grew fastest in the 1950s and 1960s (OECD 1970a; Poignant 1973; Passow et al. 1976).

Explanations of Common Trends in Educational Enrollment Rates

Showing a greater rise than occurred in a comparable prewar period, the substantial postwar increase in EER of both teenagers and young adults leads to a search for common causes of the expansion of postcompulsory education in so many countries, beyond those basic factors that underlie the long-run growth of EER over a century or more. Essentially, the basic factors have been identified as the tendency of each generation to acquire more education than its predecessor as family incomes and parents' educational levels rose and family size fell; the rise in Gross National Product, which permitted the whole society to defer entrance to the labor market and to

Table 3.2 Postwar Growth in Enrollment Rate Indicators, Upper-Secondary and Higher Education, in Nine Countries

	Upper-secondary level			Higher education level		
	Indicator	Year	Percent	Indicator	Year	Percent
Canada	Enrolled in upper secondary as percent of 14–17-year-olds	1951	46.4	Enrolled in higher education as percent of 18–24-year-olds	1951	6.0
		1973	98.8[a]		1975	19.9[a]
		1974	98.1		1977	19.6
France	Baccalauréat diplomas as percent of 18-year-olds	1947	3.9	Enrolled in higher education as percent of 20–24-year-olds	1960	8.0
		1975	24.9[a]		1976	24.0
		1976	24.7			
Germany	Upper-secondary diplomas as percent of 18-year-olds	1960	7.3	First-year students as percent of 19–20-year-olds	1960	7.9
		1970	11.3		1974	19.8[a]
		1978	22.6		1979	18.0
Great Britain	Qualified for application to higher education as percent of 18-year-olds	1954[b]	4.3	First-year students (under 21 years old) as percent of 18-year-olds	1961	6.9
		1970	13.2		1973	14.2[a]
		1977	14.9		1979	12.4
Italy	Percent of 14–18-year-olds enrolled	1950	9.2	Enrolled in higher education as percent of 20–24-year-olds	1960	6.9
		1969	37.9		1970	17.3
		1976	53.4		1976	26.4
Japan	Percent lower-secondary graduates (15-year-olds) entering upper secondary	1948	42.5	Percent lower secondary graduates entering higher education three years later	1954	10.1
		1965	70.7		1976	39.2[a]
		1979	94.0		1979	37.9
Netherlands	Percent of 15–17-year-olds enrolled	1947	27.8	Percent of 18–24-year-olds enrolled	1958	5.6
		1964	45.5		1968	11.8
		1977[c]	84.4		1977[c]	20.4
Sweden	Percent of 17-year-old males enrolled	1960	32.6	Percent of 20-year-old males enrolled	1960	12.3
		1966	49.4		1969	21.0[a]
		1978	70.8		1978	15.8
United States	High school graduates as percent of 17–18-year-olds (average)	1950	56.7	Percent of 18–24-year-olds enrolled	1947	13.2
		1970	75.6[a]		1969	28.5[a]
		1978	73.7		1979	28.0

[a] Peak year.
[b] England and Wales.
[c] Estimate.

Source: National data; A.H. Passow, H.J. Noah, M.A. Eckstein, and J.R. Mallea, *The National Case Study: An Empirical Comparative Study of Twenty-One Educational Systems.* International Studies in Evaluation, VII (New York: John Wiley, 1976); OECD, Education Committee, *Educational Trends: Analytical Report* (Paris: OECD, 1978).

enjoy more education as a consumption good; increases in productivity; urbanization; extension of school systems and compulsory education; and the changing character of jobs and growth of the service sector that required a more highly educated labor force, in turn leading to higher economic rewards to the completion of education and encouragement to individuals to invest in human capital (Hirsch 1961; Campbell and Siegel 1967; Tolley and Olson 1971; Poignant 1973; Carnoy and Marenbach 1975; Mare 1977a, 1977b, 1978a, 1978b; Hill 1978; Blau 1980).

Postwar Upsurge

Some analysts see an "absence of clearly established relations between the enrollment trends and outside factors . . . there is always—as with every social subsystem—both a multiplicity of links . . . and a multiplicity of interrelationships between these links. There is also an 'inner logic' of the system" (Hecquet, Verniers, and Cerych 1976, p. 167). In other words, forces within the educational system can explain the postwar expansion.

Those who believe that outside factors are significant have pointed to aspects of the postwar period which reinforced and broadened the basic forces cited earlier. Rapid social change and something as elusive as a postwar spirit of rebirth, improvement, egalitarianism, and equity appeared (*New Society* g). These joined with a growing belief in the importance to economic development and progress of an educated labor force, shaping favorable public attitudes and policy toward educational expansion, including enlarged government expenditures on education (OECD 1978e).

In turn, some categories of individuals who earlier would not have considered additional education as necessary for their lives or careers began to seek and accept educational opportunities. One study of the expansion of postwar higher education in France, Germany, the United States, Finland, and Poland found that young people had decided that higher education was a right, analogous to other rights promised by the welfare state. The analyst declared that the increased educational participation of women and students from the lower classes was the major cause of the expansion in numbers, rather than such factors as the baby boom, rising family income, lower costs of attendance, altered occupational structures, the growth of upper-secondary education, or changes in government policy (*New Society* g).

American analysts have suggested hypotheses about the postwar expansion of EER that might be tested more generally. The unusually rapid initial postwar growth of higher education was due to "a coincidental expansion in requirements for college-educated labor during a period when the educable population was declining" (Weinschrott 1977, pp. 2–3). In turn, the demand for college-educated manpower rose because of a rapid shift in the composition of the final output of the U.S. economy, previously held back by limitations on technological advance during the war and depression; enrollments rose in response (Dresch 1975).

In most countries none of these factors would have produced an educational explosion unless the government, the chief or only educational provider, consciously had altered its educational policies. Among the specific ways in which governments, reacting to the postwar atmosphere, encouraged educational expansion were: extension of the legal age for leaving school; introduction or expansion of comprehensive educational forms; changes in entry requirements and easier transfer procedures from one educational level to another; creation of new types of credentials; introduction of new types of shorter, more vocationally oriented postsecondary education to supplement traditional university courses; special efforts to attract the groups whose participation in upper-secondary and higher education had been low; and provision of facilities in regions and areas of the nation that had been underserved. On the financial side, governments substantially increased their expenditure on postcompulsory education, especially higher education, in absolute and relative terms (OECD 1976b, 1978e; Bishop 1977). They also provided an increased amount of student support in the form of stipends, direct grants, payments to institutions, abolition of tuition or low fees, repayable loans, scholarships, special student employment programs, and tax concessions to students or their parents (OECD 1978d).

While the benefits have chiefly been directed to those in higher education, in several countries upper-secondary students also have been subsidized, especially those from low-income families (Maddison 1975, p. 17). For example, a proposal introduced in Great Britain in 1978 to provide mandatory grants in secondary schools to postcompulsory students from families of low socioeconomic status officially estimated that enrollment rates would rise by 10 percent within four years; however, the plan was subsequently dropped for financial reasons (Harrisson 1978).

In spite of extensive government action, the individual demand for education tended to outrun public educational provision. Attainment of additional education promised wider earnings differentials, greater social prestige in occupational rankings, improved career prospects, and lower unemployment rates. The baby boom was a particular feature in that it created a demand for teachers at every level of education which, in some countries, persisted for long periods of time. Also in selected countries, the increased opportunities to combine education and work had a buoyant effect on enrollment rates.

Some (including government educational planners) who witnessed the postwar burgeoning of enrollment rates foresaw an indefinite expansion, at least until all countries reached the EER levels of the leading nations or, as the popular phrase had it, until an era of mass higher education dawned, replacing elite selection. Reporting that "throughout the 1960s increasing proportions of young people in each age group remained in education after reaching the minimum legal leaving age," a study of OECD member countries observed that "the fact that the pattern was repeated in each country, but beginning at various times, tended to strengthen the impression of a continuous secular trend. Many governments, on the basis of extrapolation of these trends . . . planned the capacity of their upper-secondary and higher educational institutions on the assumption of continuous increase in numbers" (OECD 1976a, p. 1).

Downturn

By the early 1970s it was clear that the assumption was wrong for many countries. In some countries a slowdown in the growth or a small drop of EER occurred. Even though the downward trend had not yet touched all twelve countries by 1980 and chiefly appeared among young adults and at the higher education level, a new period for EER seemed to have arrived. How long it will last and whether it is a short-run or longer-run phenomenon is disputed. Among a number of countries, however, there is a fair degree of similarity in the main identified elements of the downturn, although its timing, extent and form has varied cross-nationally. While the influence of specifically national factors should not be ruled out, it appears that the most important causes have been shared in common.

By all odds, the most pervasive reason for the downturn in EER, especially of young adults, has been the perception on the part of potential students and their families that the relative income, the occupational and social prestige of jobs, and the comparative job security and freedom from unemployment associated with undertaking additional education, chiefly at the higher education level, had become less favorable than for previous cohorts. Decisions were therefore made to delay or forego additional education or to change the subject studied to a more directly vocational one.

The American analysis along these lines has resulted in some dispute about the alleged facts, that is, whether relative incomes of U. S. college graduates have declined (Dresch 1975; Freeman 1975, 1976a, 1977, 1980a, 1980c, pp. 19–22 and 40–44; Freeman and Holloman 1975; Grasso 1977; Weinschrott 1977; Rumberger 1980; Schwartz and Thornton 1980; Witmer 1980). Evidence from other countries tends to support the view, particularly associated with Richard Freeman, that there has been a decline in relative earnings, in acceptable job opportunities, and in job security for higher education graduates, and that these developments are related to the downturn in EER (Williams 1974; Birtig 1976; Canada 1976d; Gordon and Williams 1976, 1977; Bergendal 1977, pp. 38–41; Reubens 1977b; Ritzen 1977; Umetani 1977; Kato 1978, pp. 21–24 and 36–38; Council of Europe *Newsletter* 1/80, pp. 19–20; Pissarides 1980, pp. 31–33; Stegman 1980; Werner 1980; *New Society* h).

The specific causes of the recent job problems of university graduates have received varying emphases in different countries. Some stress the supply of educated persons — either the rise in the number of young people entering higher education or the increased EER, or both. Some stress structural changes in the economy or the recession, or both. On the demand side of available jobs, certain countries are sensitive to particular institutional factors, such as limitations on expansion of employment in the public sector. The vast majority of higher education graduates have been accustomed to enter the public sector, especially as teachers. In Italy there has been a recent voluntary decline in medical enrollments, a truly unusual phenomenon since everywhere the practice of medicine is regarded as one of the most rewarding and prestigious occupations. Italian admissions policy to the medical faculties, however, had been virtually unlimited, in contrast to severely controlled access in all other countries. As a result, the Italian output of doctors, unfortunately poorly trained, grew so large that their incomes dropped. Responding to the relative earnings message, recent cohorts have switched to other, vocationally oriented faculties, such as law and economics (Council of Europe *Newsletter* 1/80, pp. 19–20). The overall decline in Italian EER in higher education also indicates an end to the earlier situation where education was described as a parking lot for those who would otherwise be unemployed (Birtig 1976; de Francesco 1978).

While the change in the economy's balance between supply and demand of suitable jobs is mentioned most frequently in the national sources as an explanatory factor in the downturn of EER in higher education, several other influences are often cited. One is the reduced public financial support to postcompulsory education in absolute and/or relative terms. The recession that began in 1974, the unfavorable medium-term economic prospects in some countries, and fears of the inflationary impact from government expenditures have affected outlays on education (OECD 1978f; Council of Europe *Newsletter* 4/79). Public confidence in education has weakened, and doubt about its alleged beneficial effects on the economy is rife. Moreover, in some countries a redistribution of public education expenditures has occurred — from postcompulsory education to preschool and compulsory as well as adult education (OECD 1978f,g). Another factor was the end of the baby boom, which diminished the market for certain kinds of highly educated manpower, especially teachers. As in the earlier period when the demand for such personnel was increased by the demographic factor, countries were affected to varying degrees by the repercussions of years of low births.

Emphasis has been placed on the downturn in higher education enrollment rates, because these appeared in many countries. Some similar effects have been observed in upper-secondary education, notably in Great Britain, where a disinclination to pursue higher education would be reflected in a reduction of EER at upper-secondary level (GB 1969–80e; Pissarides 1979). Other upper-secondary systems or parts of systems, which are largely engaged in preparation for entrance to higher education, also have experienced a slowdown of growth or decline in EER of the appropriate age group. Even in countries like the United States and Canada, where upper-secondary education has been terminal for many students, the EER and transfer rates, already at a high level, have been adversely affected by the competition from college-educated youth for jobs that formerly were filled by high school graduates.

Whatever conclusions are drawn about the extent, causes, and significance of the downturn in EER, it still remains true that EER at the end of the 1970s was much higher than it had been at the beginning of the postwar period, in almost every case. Moreover, none of the countries has clearly reached the point of enrollment saturation in these age groups. If the forces that produced the downturn are temporary and reversible, as many believe, in the longer run the downturn may appear as a brief interruption in a secular ascent.

Cross-National Differences in Educational Enrollment Rates

Although the shared experiences of countries in the growth and subsequent slowdown of EER are significant, as the previous section suggests, equal importance attaches to differences among the countries in the starting levels of EER and in the timing and rate of change in EER. The later discussion of variations among countries in the size of the youth labor force and in labor force participation rates directly relates to the divergent educational patterns.

US and the Netherlands Compared

Detailed EER data by age for the US and the Netherlands for a long period permit a closer examination of divergent national educational patterns in the postwar period. Annual EER for six U.S. age-sex groups illuminate the postwar course of enrollment rates in a country with high starting levels, while the Dutch data show lower starting levels. U.S. enrollment rates, as presented in Chart 3.4, have been calculated on the basis of the total youth population, including all military personnel. This is done both to make the U.S. data comparable to those of other countries and to avoid the misleading results obtained when there is year-to-year variation in the proportion of the youth population in the armed forces. Inclusion of the armed forces in the U.S. population base reduces EER slightly, compared to rates based on the civilian population. Netherlands EER in Chart 3.5 are also based on total population but are mostly triennial, producing a smoother curve than the American data. Although the six Dutch age-sex groups differ somewhat from the six American, a comparison of Charts 3.4 and 3.5 reveals some of the major differences between the two countries in starting levels and trends in EER.

Chart 3.4   Educational Enrollment Rates, by Age and Sex, United States, October 1947-1979

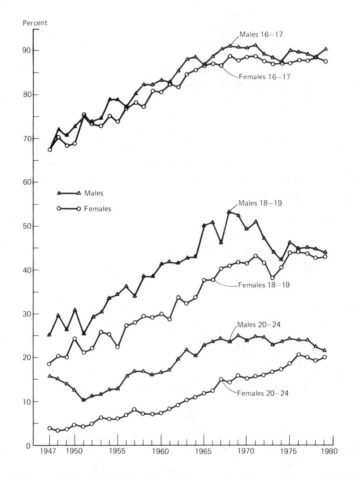

Source: U.S. Department of Labor, Employment and Training Report of the President 1979, Table B-6 (Washington: GPO, 1979); unpublished BLS data; Department of Defense unpublished data on military enlistments (volunteer and conscripted) as of October of each year. Data for 16 and 17-year-olds 1947-1952 provided by Dr. J. P. Mattila. Population base includes military and excludes the institutionalized.

Among the chief contrasts between the two countries are the following:

There is a steep and consistent rise in Dutch EER for each age group, with no tapering off evident by 1977. American EER show a jagged, interrupted, generally upward movement, with downturns and leveling off.

Over time the U.S. sex differentials in EER have narrowed, particularly in the older age groups; but Dutch sex disparities have widened, except for the youngest group, where changes in the compulsory education law play a part in the equalizing effect.

Chart 3.5 Educational Enrollment Rates, by Age and Sex, Netherlands, 1947–1977

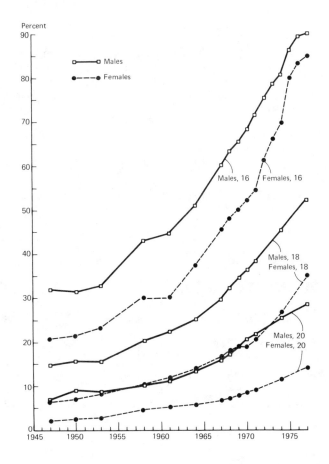

Source: The Netherlands, unpublished data. Population base includes military and institutionalized. 1977 data are derived estimates.

Although Dutch starting levels of EER were lower than American in every case, by the end of the period EER levels were roughly comparable in the two countries for males and the youngest females, after allowing for differences in the ages specified and national educational systems.

While data do not permit the same detailed examination for all twelve countries, comparisons of EER among them can be made for the two main age groups, 15–19 and 20–24, using consistent full-time enrollment rates developed by OECD for the benchmark years 1960, 1970, and 1975. It should be borne in mind that the EER for an age group at various points in time reflect the important but unmeasured influence of changes in the relative population weights of the component single years of age, as well as differing rates of change in EER of several single years in the age group.

Teenage Trends 1960-1975

In 1960 the teenage group in the twelve countries had a wide distribution of full-time EER (*Table 3.3; Chart 3.6). Ranging from a low of 16.6 percent in the United Kingdom to a high of 64.1 percent in the United States, a gap of over 47 percentage points, 1960 EER fell between 30 and 37 percent in seven of the countries. By 1975 the lowest EER, in New Zealand, reached 41.3 percent, only 35 percentage points under Japan's high of 75.6 percent. Not only was the range among countries in EER significantly diminished by 1975, but the rankings of countries according to EER showed some fluidity between 1960 and 1975. For example, Japan moved from third to first place, while the UK moved from twelfth to ninth place.

Chart 3.6   Educational Enrollment Rates, Teenagers (15-19) and Young Adults (20-24), Both Sexes, in Twelve Countries, 1960-1975

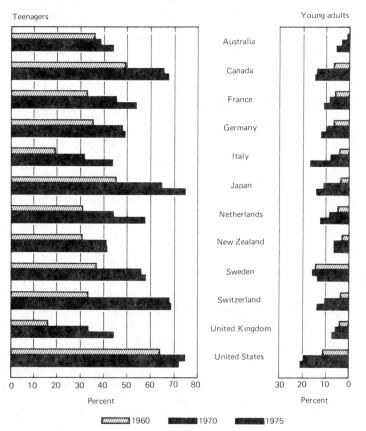

Source: OECD, Working Party of the Education Committee on Educational Statistics and Indicators, revised data, unpublished (Paris: OECD, March 1979).

Between 1960 and 1975 most countries recorded marked growth in teenage full-time EER. Increases over the period ranged up from 7.8 percentage points in Australia to 35.1 percentage points in Switzerland. Teenage EER more than doubled over the fifteen years in Switzerland, Italy, and the United Kingdom; the latter two began the period with the lowest rates. Over the whole period, the countries with the highest teenage EER were Canada, Japan, and the United States, although their relative positions changed over time. Switzerland joined the leading group in 1970. Among the countries with the lowest teenage EER rankings over the period were Italy, New Zealand, and the UK, together with Australia in the 1970s (Chart 3.6). While all twelve countries recorded growth in teenage EER between 1960 and 1970, substantial in many cases, the subperiod 1970–1975 was characterized by much slower growth in some countries. A negative change in teenage EER was recorded in the US, no change appeared in New Zealand, and insignificant rises occurred in Canada, Germany, Sweden, and Switzerland. By comparison, substantial annual average growth continued through the 1970s in Italy, Japan, the Netherlands, and the UK. Japan's remarkable postwar record is confirmed by the official report that 53.9 percent of all high school graduates of March 1979 sought to enter higher education (*Japan Labor Bulletin* b). Although some will fail to attend, Japan's transfer rate and EER will be well above those of any other country.

Young Adult Trends 1960–1975

The postwar upsurge of EER for young adults aged 20–24 began from relatively low levels, with a high of 15.5 percent in Sweden and a low of 1.2 percent in Australia, representing a gap of 14.3 percentage points (*Table 3.3; Chart 3.6). EER in 1975 were still far below those for teenagers, a portion of whom still were affected by compulsory education in many countries. Enrolled young adults mostly are engaged in higher education, which impinges on a more limited proportion of the population than secondary education. Postwar growth in young adult EER, measured by percentage point increase, was not as large as for teenagers, ranging from 11.9 percent in Italy to a negative 1.1 percent in Sweden. In terms of total growth over the period 1960–1975, however, EER more than quadrupled in Australia and rose by over three times in Italy, Japan, and Switzerland.

Among those countries with the highest EER for young adults over the period were the US, Sweden, and Canada (Chart 3.6). Sweden fell from first place in 1960 to fourth in 1975 and was the only country to register lower EER in 1975 than in 1970. Italy and Japan's high growth rates over the period elevated them into the leading group of countries by 1975. Among the countries with lowest young adult EER over the period were Australia and New Zealand, joined by France and the United Kingdom in 1975. Unlike teenagers in the various countries whose EER converged over the 15 years, young adults' EER widened further. By 1975 the spread was 16.2 percentage points between the U.S. high of 21.6 percent and the Australian low of 5.4 percent.

In Canada, New Zealand, Japan, Switzerland, and the United States, growth in young adult EER from 1970 to 1975 was at a slower pace than between 1960 and 1970, while Sweden's EER actually declined. The increased share of older students (25 and older) was a definite factor in Sweden, the US, and possibly some of the other countries. The share of 30–34-year olds in U.S. total college enrollments rose from 5.8 to 9.3 percent for males, and from 5.1 to 10.7 percent for females, between 1970 and 1979. Although smaller, the 30–34-year share of full-time college enrollments also increased, both in two-year and four-year colleges (US 1980a, Table 12). In Sweden 29-year-old students had an EER of 1.5 percent in 1960 and 12.4 percent in 1978 (Sweden 1979b, p. 51). In the six other countries, especially in Italy and the Netherlands, vigorous growth with no signs of downturn characterized the 1970–1975 period.

Compositional Change

National trends in EER for an age group incorporate and reflect a variety of compositional changes. These are mainly changes in the absolute and relative enrollment rates of the two sexes, of different socioeconomic groups, of racial and ethnic subgroups, and of subnational units and separate regions within a country. Such compositional change in the postwar period has been significantly influenced both by altered patterns of demand for education and by developments in the quantitative and qualitative aspects of educational provision. As the composition of educational enrollments and rates has changed, so have the number and types of educational institutions, as well as length and types of courses and other features that bear on the nature and quality of educational opportunity and achievement. These in turn influence labor force participation rates and occupational choices. Postwar enrollment trends for the various compositional subgroups, except for racial and ethnic subgroups which are considered in Chapter 7, are discussed in the following sections.

Sex Differences in Enrollment Patterns

Inequality in education between the sexes has aroused considerable attention and concern in the postwar period. Historical rationalizations for sex inequalities are increasingly questioned and criticized (OECD 1975b; Byrne 1979; Dessaur and Van Vleuten 1979). The pressures for equality center on such considerations as basic individual justice, rapidly changing social circumstances, and economic pressures. Disparities in enrollment trends between the sexes are not only quantitative. As a result of differences in the types of subject studied by the two sexes, even similar enrollment rates would have adverse qualitative educational, labor force, and occupational effects on females.

Explanations of sex differences in EER include the influence of family, the schools, and society in terms of conditioning and expectations, differences in preferences, the structure and length of courses chosen by females, perceived and real discrimination against females in higher education admissions policy, female marriage and child-bearing patterns, unwillingness of the family to finance lengthy further education, and less attractive and rewarding economic opportunities for women than men at various levels of educational achievement. Some believe that innate sex differences in academic preferences and ability explain the divergent enrollment patterns, but scientifically valid evidence is lacking.

During the postwar period, females have made considerable progress toward equality on the quantitative side, but less qualitatively. Change can be measured both through shares of enrollments and through EER. National data extending back into the 1940s and 1950s indicate that the female share of total enrollments, not necessarily full-time, has been increasing over the whole postwar era, both for teenagers and young adults, but especially for the latter. The closer the starting level of the female share was to 50 percent, the smaller the postwar rise was likely to be. Sex disparities in enrollment shares have been at their lowest during compulsory schooling. Indeed, there has been a female majority in some countries, and extensions of compulsory schooling raised the female share in other countries.

As cohorts moved through upper-secondary and higher education, the female share dropped with the advance in educational level. Over time female shares rose. In the United States, for example, the share of 18–19-year-old females rose from 42 percent in 1947 to 49 percent in 1977, while for 20–24-year olds it increased from 20 percent in 1947 to 45 percent in 1977 (US 1979b). By 1979, female college students outnumbered male for the first time, counting all ages, and were equal in number in the under-35 category (US 1980a, p. 10). In Japan, females in senior high schools (generally aged 15 to 18 years) accounted for 37 percent of total enrollments in 1950, rising to 50 percent by 1975. At the higher-education level, the female share of enrollments at Japanese colleges and universities rose from 8 to 22 percent between 1950 and 1975, while for junior colleges, the corresponding increase was from 39 to 87 percent (Japan 1979a). In the Netherlands, 37 percent of 15 to 19-year-olds enrolled in 1947 were female; by 1977 the proportion had risen to 45 percent. For 20–24-year olds the female share rose from 18 to 30 percent over the period, according to unpublished Dutch data. The slowdown of enrollment growth in some countries toward the end of the period was often disproportionately among males, and thus contributed to the continuing improvement in the female share of total enrollments (US 1980a, Table 12).

Female shares of full-time enrollments for eleven countries on a uniform basis also show substantial growth over the 1960–1975 period. Males continued in the majority, however, except that the female share of total enrollments for French teenagers exceeded 50 percent in 1960, 1970, and 1975, while Swedish female teenagers were in this position in 1960. By 1975 the teenage female share exceeded 42 percent in each of the countries and was over 30 percent for young adults, except for the Netherlands at 26.7 percent (Table 3.4). Some countries experienced declines in the female share within the period 1960–1975, but the 1975 share fell below that recorded in 1960 only in Germany and Sweden for teenagers and in France for young adults. The smallest teenage female shares in 1975 were found in the Netherlands, Italy, and Germany, and for young adults, in the Netherlands and Japan (Table 3.4). These are not unex-

Table 3.4   Female Share of Total Enrollments in Eleven Countries, 1960–1975

	15–19 Years			20–24 Years		
	1960	1970	1975	1960	1970	1975
	(percent)			(percent)		
Australia	43.5	41.3	48.2	23.8	23.7	37.3
Canada	45.5	47.7	48.2	30.0	35.6	36.5
France	51.5	54.3	51.7	42.4	34.5	35.9
Germany	45.6	43.7	43.5	26.9	36.2	39.0
Italy	39.9	40.3	43.3	7.1	31.2	37.7
Japan	46.7	48.9	48.8	17.2	25.6	31.0
Netherlands	38.2	39.8	42.8	23.9	24.4	26.7
New Zealand	43.9	46.4	46.5	23.3	25.5	36.4
Sweden	50.1	47.3	47.5	41.8	46.6	49.9
United Kingdom	43.6	47.7	48.8	15.6	33.3	38.7
United States	46.5	48.6	49.2	30.8	32.4	43.2

Source: OECD, Working Party of the Education Committee on Educational Statistics and Indicators, revised data, unpublished (Paris: OECD, March 1979).

pected findings in light of the more general lag of sex equality in these countries.

EER data offer another way of looking at the educational gap between the sexes. As could be expected, sex inequalities in EER have been consistently wider for young adults than for teenagers. For both age groups, female full-time enrollment rates have for the most part remained lower than male rates among the eleven countries, using uniform data for 1960, 1970, and 1975 (Table A3.2). French teenagers are the exception. By 1975 teenage female EER in the UK also surpassed male EER. Parity between the sexes in teenage EER was more or less achieved by 1975 in Australia, Canada, Japan, and the US. Large differences still persisted in Germany, Italy, and the Netherlands. Over time teenage female EER rose more rapidly than male in almost all countries. A certain balance was maintained between the sexes in each country, however, since a rank correlation of countries for teenage EER, separately for each sex, showed high r_s of $+.80$ in 1960 and $+.81$ in 1975.

Over the postwar period, sex differences in teenage EER were more likely to diminish in countries where compulsory education had been lengthened, coeducation and comprehensive education existed or had been introduced, and a varied assortment of options in tertiary education became available. The rise in teenage female participation in postcompulsory education also is related to national differences in the rate of change in female lifestyles. At the same time, evidence is accumulating in the United States that certain subgroups of female teenagers are educationally disadvantaged because of early motherhood (Mott and Shaw 1978; Waite and Moore 1978; Moore et al. 1979). Males are also affected by early marriage and fatherhood, but less than women, on British evidence (Douglas and Cherry 1977).

Higher enrollment rates of teenage males also may arise from the greater tendency in some countries of males to be below modal grade for their age. For example, in the US in October 1976, 27.8 percent of 14 to 17-year-old males but only 17.8 percent of females of the same age were not enrolled in the modal year of senior high school. Similarly, 7.2 percent of 14-17-year-old males were above modal grade, compared with 11.2 of females (US 1978b, Table 12). This type of sex difference has been observed in other countries as well; males tend to remain in school for longer periods than females, without an increase in male educational attainment. This factor accounts for only a small part of the total sex disparity in EER, however.

American national data confirm that the sex difference in young-adult EER has consistently narrowed since the late 1940s (Chart 3.4). Growth in young adult female full-time EER was substantial in 1960–1975 in the eleven countries and was faster than male rates in most countries, especially between 1970 and 1975. By 1975, however, young adult female enrollment rates exceeded male only in Sweden, while females remained particularly disadvantaged relative to males in Japan and the Netherlands (Table A3.2). In terms of percentage point difference, young adult females improved their relative position over the period 1960–1975 in Germany, Italy, Sweden, the United Kingdom, and the United States. A rank correlation of EER for the eleven countries in 1960 and 1975 showed that country ranks for young adult males and females (r_s = $+.67$ in 1960 and $+.75$ in 1975) were less highly correlated than among teenagers.

Inequalities between males and females are also evident in a number of other relevant educational indicators, such as completion rates and transfer rates. In many countries females experience a shorter average duration of education than males, mainly because of trends after upper-secondary education ends. It is more common to find equality or approaches to it at lower educational levels. Thus, the proportion of Japanese male lower-secondary school graduates proceeding to the upper-secondary level exceeded the female proportion over the period 1948 to 1968, but from 1969 to 1979, the female percentage exceeded the male (Japan 1979a, p. 88). While it is true that in a number of countries, female upper-secondary school completion rates have exceeded male rates, this superiority has not generally been reflected in transfer rates to higher levels of education. Evidence for the mid-1960s through the mid-1970s shows that qualified female school-leavers (that is, those qualified for entrance to higher education) were a higher proportion of the equivalent female age group than males were of the relevant male population in a number of countries, among them Canada and the US. Nevertheless, transfer rates to higher education, as a proportion of qualified leavers, were lower for females in all of these countries (Poignant 1973; Hecquet et al. 1976; Canada 1978b). That is to say, females took less advantage of their educational qualifications than males.

An economic analysis has attempted to explain the fact that American females have a higher rate of high school completion but a lower rate of completing college or dropping out of high school or college. These educational differences are attributed to strongly entrenched sex differences in the labor market, especially in regard to earnings and occupational status. Educational differences between the sexes are thus presented as the result rather than the cause of sex differences in job opportunities, and women are seen as responding rationally to their best economic options (Madden 1978). Studies for other countries along these lines would be illuminating. In a number of countries a larger proportion of enrolled female than male students fail to complete higher education (Council of Europe 1979, p. 41).

The female share of earned degrees in higher education has increased over time in some countries. The higher the level of degree, however, the lower the female share usually has been. In the United States, the proportion of bachelor's degrees earned by females has risen from 38 percent to 46 percent, and the female share of master's degrees has risen from 32 percent to 47 percent from 1960 to 1976. The female share of U.S. doctorates (excluding first professional degrees) rose from 10.5 percent in 1965 to 28.6 percent by 1979 (*NY Times* 1; US 1975–80e, p. 196). In Japan the proportion of females earning degrees at all levels of higher education rose from 25 percent in 1960 to 40 percent in 1975. But the female share of master's degrees and doctorates awarded in 1965–1975 was a static 8 and 6 percent respectively (Japan 1976a, pp. 292–95).

Sex inequalities also are evident in the types of postsecondary education chosen and the subjects studied. For example, the female share of higher education enrollments in France has been lowest in those postsecondary educational institutions with the highest prestige; only one percent of all students in the *grandes écoles* were female in the early 1970s. Similarly, women represented 7 percent of the total in French engineering colleges, 26 percent of those in preparatory schools for the *grandes écoles*, 29 percent in university institutes of technology (IUTs), and 33 percent in other forms of higher education (OECD 1976d). In most countries, sex disparities have been more marked in university rather than nonuniversity forms of higher education and in the longer rather than shorter tertiary courses. Indeed, the relative improvement in female higher education enrollment rates has been largely attributed to a rapid expansion of the nonuniversity sector. Thus, the female share of total enrollments has been higher in the nonuniversity sector or shorter courses over the 1960s and 1970s in many countries, among them Australia, Canada, Germany, Italy, Japan, the Netherlands, Sweden, and the United Kingdom. In the US, the female share has been about the same in two-year and four-year colleges (OECD

1970d, 1973a; Hecquet, Verniers, and Cerych 1976; US 1978d, Council of Europe 1979; Germany BMBW 1979).

Sex differences in subjects studied and areas of specialization at all levels of postcompulsory education affect both the length of studies and later labor market outcomes. These differences appear earlier in countries where specialization is introduced at a younger age; for example, it occurs later in the American educational system than in the European. Females tend to be overrepresented in the general arts subjects, such as languages, literature, and fine arts — all subjects with weak occupational links. Such specialization has been interpreted as the result of sex-role stereotyping in relation to career possibilities. For females, the choice of socially acceptable and educationally satisfactory subjects has tended to command priority over career considerations. For males, on the other hand, educational plans are formulated earlier and are more frequently directed toward professional careers and the maximization of social and economic rewards (OECD 1976a).

The strength of the sex division in subject choice is illustrated by the experience in the comprehensive upper-secondary school in Sweden, which has been a leader in official policy to remove sex stereotypes in subject choice. While total enrollments in 1979 were evenly divided between males and females, enrollments in 16 of the 22 subject "lines" were sex intensive (one sex accounted for 60 percent or more of enrollments). Among the seven female-intensive lines were nursing, liberal arts, social science, and clerical studies; the nine male-intensive lines included engineering and technological subjects, agriculture and forestry, and building and construction. Since 1972 when this type of school was established nationally, sex disparity has diminished. In 1972, when females accounted for only 45 percent of upper-secondary enrollments, 19 of the 22 subject lines were sex intensive; seven lines were female intensive and twelve were male intensive. Three lines which had been male intensive in 1972 — agriculture, natural science, and food manufacture — had become sex-neutral subjects by 1979 (Sweden 1978f, p. 187; 1979h).

At the higher education level, sharp sex distinctions in subject specialization have not altered much over time, although a reduction of the disparity has occurred in some countries and fields. Males dominate in medicine, dentistry, engineering, sciences, law, business, economics, and other career-oriented, prestigious subjects with large economic rewards in future occupations (OECD 1976d; Polachek 1978, p. 499; Council of Europe 1979, p. 39; *New Society* e). Teacher training has been the only or one of the few occupationally oriented courses where females usually predominate. Whether this sex distribution in the occupationally oriented fields is the cause or result of labor force patterns is a debated issue.

Socioeconomic Differences in Enrollment Patterns

Disparate EER and other educational indicators among the various socioeconomic groups in each country are an established fact, whether defined by parents' education, father's occupational position, social class designations, or levels of family income. It is less clear how these differences are distributed across countries and how they have changed over time. Moreover, observed differences in students' choice of studies and later selection of occupations according to socioeconomic position add important qualitative elements that have significant repercussions on the quantitative and qualitative composition of the youth labor force. Such disparities have commonly diminished over time, but the process has been a gradual one, and marked differences in all relevant indicators by socioeconomic status (SES) still persist. The importance of such inequality lies in the proposition that "there is a multiple correlation between parental wealth, parental income, access to the best jobs, and 'success' in later life" (Vaizey 1962, p. 45).

Socioeconomic disparities may reflect a number of contributory factors, such as familial cultural practices and values, disposable income, linguistic expression, expectations, and information available on education and the labor market (Husén 1975; Parsons 1975; Levin 1976; OECD 1976a). Parental education, clearly an important influence on the parents' subsequent occupation and SES, has been shown to be strongly correlated with the child's education in a number of countries. Peer group attitudes also play a strong role. French working-class families, for example, have tended to view universities as "bourgeois" institutions; while such attitudes have been changing, a social barrier or antipathy toward university enrollment persists. Similarly, manual workers' families in Germany consider the *Gymnasium*, the select university preparatory school, to be "alien, difficult, geared to men, frustrating and strenuous" (*NY Times* d). Social class origin is related to the amount of education desired and obtained (Husén 1975; Levin 1976; Faguer 1977, 1980; *New Society* i).

Barriers arising from the structures and operations of the educational system also restrict entrants from low SES groups. The main forms are selection processes, screening out through grade-repetition and dropping out, streaming or tracking, curriculum structures that block promotion or access, and systematic differences in educational resources among schools catering to students of various social classes (Husén 1975; Levin 1976).

Out-of-pocket educational costs and foregone earnings, offset by the availability of government financial assistance to students, are further factors affecting socioeconomic differences in EER. The lower the family SES, the more important such considerations are, particularly in higher education. A recent British study found that 42 percent of the boys and 49 percent of the girls who intended to leave school at 16 said they might stay on if a grant were available (*New Society* i). In a recent survey carried out in nine member countries of the European Community, one parent in five said that at least one of their children had had to reduce the amount of education or might have to do so; the most common reason was family financial constraint (EC 1980a).

A 1979 official Japanese report observed that the rise in higher education enrollments was "primarily due to the increase of those going to private colleges or universities . . . the families . . . generally tend to belong to the higher income brackets as opposed to families with children going to public or national colleges or universities who tend to be lower income" (*Japan Labor Bulletin* a). A contrary view of the Japanese situation claims that a majority of the students at the low-tuition national universities come from middle-class families that are able to give their children all the advantages needed to compete successfully for admission to the select national universities, leaving poorer families to pay the high tuition in the private colleges and universities (Kato 1978, pp. 45–46). In any case, the net costs of attending various types of educational institutions influence not only the total number enrolled from various SES levels but also their distribution among institutions.

The extent of disparity among countries in enrollments by SES has been documented in several ways. Ratios have been estimated of the likelihood of entering higher education around 1960, comparing children from the professional and managerial classes with working class children. In France the ratio was 83:1, in the Netherlands 56:1, in Germany 41:1, in Sweden 26:1, in the United Kingdom and the United States 8:1 (OECD 1970b, 1975b, p. 168). Other sources confirm these disparities (Burn 1971, pp. 79, 112, 153). They often are complicated by sex differences and regional or place-of-residence influences. Another measure is the index of dissimilarity by SES between higher education enrollments and the male labor force, which shows the proportion of students or the labor force which would have to shift into another SES category in order to create equality in the distributions. At the start of the 1960s, the proportions were commonly very high, between 50 and 60 percent (OECD 1975b, p. 170).

Both the ratios of SES groups' chances for higher education and the indices of dissimilarity showed striking declines by the early 1970s. Germany, France, and the Netherlands had ratios of 15:1, 18:1, and 27:1 respectively, while the UK and US were down to 2:1 (OECD 1978e). The indices of dissimilarity had fallen by 10 to 15 percent over the decade (OECD 1975b, p. 170). Despite the declines, the large differences in country ratios and dissimilarity indices indicate considerable remaining divergence among nations in the access to education for various SES groups within each country.

While socioeconomic inequalities in enrollment rate trends have declined over the postwar period, a commonly held view is that enrollment expansion has disproportionately benefited youth with middle or higher SES background (OECD 1973a, 1974; Levin 1976; NY Times 1978d). Although cross-national comparisons of enrollments by SES are hampered by definitional problems, national data commonly show that by the early 1970s the upper socioeconomic stratum, commonly comprising less than 10 percent of the labor force, still accounted for between one-quarter to one-half of those enrolled in higher education. These shares were lower than they had been earlier.

Over the same period, the lowest SES or working-class category, constituting approximately 50 to 60 percent of the labor force in most countries, accounted for less than 10 percent of those enrolled in higher education in many European countries in the 1950s, and no more than 15 to 20 percent of students by the early 1970s. In some instances growth has been even more gradual. For example, in Britain the share of university students from the two lowest social class categories rose only from 5 to 7 percent between 1955 and 1976 (New Society d). Swedish evidence, however, indicates that in the downturn in enrollments in the late 1960s, students from working-class backgrounds showed less decline than students from academic family backgrounds (Sweden 1976c).

Appraisals of progress toward the goal of near-equality in educational participation by those from lower socioeconomic groups, low-income families, and disadvantaged groups rest heavily on the expectations and standards set by the appraisers (Husén 1975). Those who believed that the expansion of enrollments and enrollment rates would almost automatically reduce the inequality of access to education have been disappointed (OECD 1976b). Against this type of evidence some call attention to "a substantial mitigation in the privileged status of the upper group in the 1960s because they were much nearer to saturation of their aspirations and educational expansion has been so rapid. The nearer countries approach to universal attendance at a particular level of education, the closer is the convergence in degree of access by social class" (Maddison 1975, p. 15).

It is this last point that explains the greater equality of access in such countries as the United States, where enrollment rates as a whole are high (Busch 1975). Unpublished American enrollment rates for October 1977, by family income level for never married 16–24-year olds living at home (or at school), show a positive relation between income levels and EER. While EER for youth from families with under

$5000 annual income ranged from 25.9 to 68.8 percent for the four age-sex groups, the spread was from 54.1 to 86.1 percent for youth in the top income class, $25,000 and over (Table A3.3). These enrollment rates for the poorest Americans compare favorably with overall enrollment rates for the age group in many other countries.

Disparities by SES do not reveal themselves solely in overall enrollment rates. They are also evident in the different forms of upper-secondary-level education, as Table 3.5 shows for three countries. Although disparities have diminished over time, the more selective types of secondary education clearly have had disproportionately large numbers of students with a higher SES status, compared to the distribution in

Table 3.5   Distribution of Secondary School Students by Socioeconomic Status and Type of School in Three Countries, 1970-1973

Germany
Secondary school students aged 10-15, 1972

Status/Occupation of father	All Youth aged 10-15	Hauptschule	Realschule (aged 10-15)	Gymnasium
	(percent)			
Unskilled manual	24	30	18	5
Skilled manual	26	30	25	13
White collar employee	20	15	23	38
Government official	10	5	9	17
Other	20	20	25	27
Total	100	100	100	100

Italy[a]
Candidates for upper-secondary school final examination, aged 18, 1973

Status/Occupation of father	Total	Technical schools	Primary school teacher training	Vocational and art schools	Scientific lyceum	Classical lyceum
	(percent)					
All occupations	100	46	16	6	17	14
Manual workers	100	61	18	7	9	5
Management	100	20	10	3	32	35

Sweden[a,b]
Pupils' Destinations after ninth year of education, aged 16, 1970

Socioeconomic class	Total	Vocational school	Realskola	Gymnasium	Other
	(percent)				
Upper/Upper-middle	100	6	10	82	2
Middle	100	21	21	46	13
Lower	100	34	21	21	20

[a] Totals may not add to 100 because of rounding.
[b] By 1972 Sweden had adopted a comprehensive upper-secondary school throughout the country, replacing the system in force when the 1970 data were collected.

Source: Germany: Der Bundesminister für Bildung und Wissenschaft (BMBW). *Arbeiterkinder im Bildungssystem* [Workers' Children in the Educational System]. Bonn: Druckhaus Bayreuth, 1976; Italy: OECD. Education Committee. *Educational Trends: Analytical Report.* Paris: OECD, 1978; Sweden: OECD. *Towards Mass Higher Education — Issues and Dilemmas.* Paris: OECD, 1974.

the population at large. Conversely, the technically and vocationally oriented schools are much less likely to be attended by children from high SES backgrounds. In Britain, independent or direct-grant secondary schools, those under private or semi-private control with highest prestige and the most successful higher education transition rate, have been referred to as elitist institutions for the privileged. About 25 percent of professional families' children attend these schools, 20 percent of managerial-class children, but only 1 percent of manual-class children (*New Society* c).

At the higher education level, a number of countries have developed short-cycle higher education. Enrollment rates for lower SES groups in the newer forms of tertiary education have commonly been higher than in the traditional institutions. In Sweden, the reorganization of tertiary education in 1977 to include nontraditional forms of higher education narrowed the overall socioeconomic disparities in that sector (Sweden 1980a). It is claimed, however, that short-cycle education may maintain inequality, inasmuch as the predominantly low SES students may be segregated into an inferior form of higher education (OECD 1973a; US 1978d).

American students from families with high income and occupational background have been much more likely to attend four-year colleges than have those in the moderate-to-low SES categories (OECD 1973a, p. 402). U.S. longitudinal data show that while SES is not a major factor in vocational or technical education, it plays an important role in academic higher education. In 1973, one year after high school graduation, over 70 percent of students from high SES backgrounds were engaged in academic courses, compared with only a little over 20 percent of those with low SES. By 1976, the proportions were still disparate, at more than 25 percent and about 11 percent respectively (US 1976–79).

In other countries, differences in higher education enrollments rates by socioeconomic background are apparent in various forms of education. While 17 to 21-year-old French youth from manual class families accounted for 40 percent of the age group in 1971, they comprised 13 percent of university students, 23 percent of students at university institutes of technology (IUTs) and only 3 percent at business schools. In comparison, French youth of the same age from professional and senior-management backgrounds made up 33 percent of university students, 52 percent of business school students, but only 14 percent of IUT students (OECD 1978e). In Germany 28 percent of polytechnic but only 13 percent of university students came from working class families in 1977, while those from civil service families displayed contrary patterns, comprising 25 percent of all university students and 13 percent at polytechnics (Germany INPS b). In many countries the overall disproportionate enrollment in higher education of students from middle and higher SES is further exaggerated in certain disciplines, such as medicine, law, and business, where subsequent occupational status and earnings are highest (Netherlands 1977a; Sweden 1980a). Working-class students have a limited range of subject and occupational choices, usually opting for those with relatively less prestige and earnings.

The slow progress toward equality will not be aided by a slowdown in growth of EER or the vocational orientation of many current students.

Geographic Differences in Enrollment Patterns

Regions or other subnational units of a country commonly depart from the national average of EER and other educational indicators for any given age-sex group. In fact, the spread between the highest and lowest units within a country may be as marked as the overall difference among countries. Subnational educational differentials are important because, to the extent that they exist and persist, national goals of equality of educational opportunity are not met, and the size and quality of the youth labor force and its mobility are affected.

As significant as it is to look below the national level, this study is able to make only a preliminary approach to a comparative examination of subnational trends in educational patterns. It is difficult to establish which countries have the widest geographical range in educational participation, because the results are influenced by the way geographic boundary lines are drawn; multicountry data for a long and comparable period are scarce; and low average levels in one country permit smaller subnational differences than high EER in another country. In the same way, changes over time are more easily related to the experience of individual countries than to a comparison among countries.

Certain common aspects of subnational differentials in EER are identifiable. Geographic disparities are generally less apparent at and around the compulsory school ages than at more advanced educational levels. Rural youth usually have lower EER than urban or nonrural, although one American study of the 19th century found, counter to popular belief, that enrollments "were generally higher in rural than in urban places, and high enrollments generally preceded industrialization" (Meyer et al. 1979, p. 592). Density of population, on the whole, fosters higher EER.

In several countries geographical differences in EER can also be attributed in part to other variables, such as the socioeconomic status of the population, psychological factors, and racial, religious, or linguistic differences. The same is true for a number of areas of European countries in which recent immigrants are concentrated. Such explanations of geographical disparities are themselves very difficult to quantify since a combination of determinants of regional inequality usually are present (OECD 1970b).

Some explanatory factors appear to have divergent significance in various countries. Thus, proximity to educational institutions usually tends to foster higher EER, but not invariably. In Germany and France, for example, the more higher education places available in a region, the higher has been the EER in that region (OECD 1976a). In Sweden, postcompulsory enrollment rates have been highest among those whose families live within a 50-kilometer radius of the educational institution. Swedish youth living in distant rural areas have half the enrollment rate at universities of those who live close to an institution (Bergendal 1977). An official Japanese report complained that universities and junior colleges are concentrated in Tokyo and Osaka, restricting attendance somewhat (*Japan Labor Bulletin* a). In both Australia and Canada, students mostly have enrolled in higher education institutions in their home state or province. In Australia this has been due mostly to the examination system, geographical quotas, and traditional patterns, while in Canada increasing numbers have sought to minimize educational and travel costs (Burn 1971). Proximity also has been found to affect students' specific choice of subject and type of education (Poignant 1973; OECD 1976a; Bergendal 1977).

Physical proximity may be less important in countries such as Great Britain and the United States, where youth are more disposed to attend college away from home. One American study has observed, for example, that "spatial accessibility to one or more colleges has little effect, for most youth, on whether they will attend college" (Anderson, Bowman, and Tinto 1972, p. 267). At the same time, another analysis of the rise in American EER during the 1950s and 1960s attributed a large part of the growth to the establishment of higher education institutions in areas previously without such facilities (Bishop 1977).

Local availability of education is matched on the demand side by the local availability of employment, as an alternative to education. Here too the evidence varies. At the postcompulsory secondary and higher education level in Italy, the higher proportions enrolled in the south, commonly referred to as the Mezzogiorno, partly reflect the lack of employment opportunities. In comparison, the lower EER in the prosperous, industrialized north than in central Italy can be attributed to the greater availability of jobs for school-leavers (Birtig 1976; de Francesco 1978). Traditional leaving patterns in Britain follow different lines. The northwestern and northern regions have long experienced relatively slow economic growth and high unemployment, which should encourage prolonged schooling. Enrollment rates have been relatively low in these regions, however. The situation has been attributed to negative parental attitudes toward the economic value of additional education, and low rates of movement to more prosperous areas where such schooling might bring larger economic rewards. In comparison, the relatively high enrollment rates in Scotland and Wales, also areas of low economic opportunity and high unemployment, have been explained by strong traditions for learning and by a tendency for young people to emigrate from the region.

Some evidence on geographical disparity and changes over time is available. From the 1950s through the 1970s subnational differences in EER, as measured by an unweighted standard deviation, have widened rather than narrowed. Specifically, increased disparities over various time periods and for different levels of education have been documented in Australia, Canada, France, Italy, Japan, the United Kingdom, and United States. In Germany, regional disparities in the graduation rate from *Gymnasia* narrowed between 1957 and 1964 but widened up to 1974 (OECD 1970b; 1978e). American regional variation in educational attainment has persisted, with the West clearly in the lead and the South in last place (US 1980a, p. 10).

Detailed information for the United States, by urban, rural nonfarm, and rural farm areas, suggests a closing of the EER gap (US 1979a). In 1950, U.S. enrollment rates for males 18–24 were markedly higher in urban areas than in rural areas, especially in farm areas. By 1977 the gap had narrowed considerably, although there was still a ratio of more than 2:1 between those in large SMSAs (standard metropolitan statistical areas) and those in farm areas. The 1950 EER by place of residence were less disparate for females than males, but by 1977, farm-area females 18–19 had a higher EER than those from large SMSAs, and 20–21-year olds nearly had parity. Only 20–24-year-old females had a more unequal geographic distribution in 1977 than in 1950. 16- and 17- year-olds showed virtually no geographic disparity, reflecting the influence on the age group of compulsory schooling.

Table 3.6 presents some suggestive data on geographic differences in educational indicators, mainly EER, for six countries at various times and for a mixed assortment of educational levels and age groups. Using changes in the percentage point difference between the lowest and highest regions over time as the measure of disparity, Table 3.6 shows both increased and decreased disparities. In some countries the top and bottom regions remained the same over time, while in other countries changes in position occurred, although rarely did a country from the bottom group rise to the top group or vice versa. This stability in group position indicates how deeply ingrained are the EER differences within countries. This subject requires additional study, as do many subnational aspects of the youth labor force which this book does not attempt.

Table 3.6 Change in Regional Educational Indicators in Six Countries, 1947-1978

Level/Age	Year	Region with highest EER	EER (percent)	Region with lowest EER	EER (percent)	Difference between highest and lowest regions: Change over period (percentage points)
Increased Disparities						
Canada Postsecondary	1972	Quebec	21.0	Newfoundland	12.7	+4.9
	1977	Quebec	24.5	Newfoundland	11.3	
Sweden Higher education entrants	1947	Stockholm	7.8	N. Sweden	1.4	+3.9
	1960	Stockholm	17.5	N. Sweden	7.2	
Upper secondary	1961	Stockholm	65.1	Gotlands	23.9	+5.1
	1965	Stockholm	78.0	Gotlands	31.7	
United States Higher education	1950	New England	22.7	E. South Central	10.2	+7.4
	1970	Mountain	42.9	S. Atlantic	23.0	
Decreased Disparities						
Germany Upper secondary diplomas (males)	1957	W. Berlin	11.5	Saar	4.3	-2.6
	1964	Hesse	12.6	N. Rhineland/Westphalia	8.0	
(females)	1957	W. Berlin	7.4	Saar	1.8	-2.8
	1964	Bremen	7.3	Bavaria	4.5	
Japan Transfer rates to upper secondary (males)	1965	Tokyo	87.3	Aomori	57.0	-15.8
	1975	Hiroshima	96.9	Iwate	82.4	
(females)	1965	Tokyo	86.3	Aomori	51.5	-23.9
	1975	Hiroshima	97.8	Iwate	86.9	
Great Britain EER 15-19 years (males)	1951	Wales	20.3	North	9.9	-3.3
	1971	South East	40.9	W. Midlands	33.8	
(females)	1951	London & S.E.	18.5	Midlands	10.1	-0.9
	1971	South East	40.0	E. Midlands	32.5	
United States EER 14-17 years	1967	West	96.2	South	90.8	-3.0
	1978	North Central	94.6	South	92.2	

Source: Canada: Statistics Canada, *Education in Canada 1978* (Ottawa: Statistics Canada, 1979); Germany and Sweden: OECD, *Conférence sur les Politiques d'Expansion de l'Enseignement. Rapport de Base no. 4 – Disparités Entre les Groupes en Matière de Participation à l'Enseignement* (Paris: OECD, 1970); Japan: Ministry of Education, Science and Culture, *Educational Standards in Japan, 1975* (Tokyo: Ministry of Education, Science and Culture, 1976); Great Britain: 1951: OECD. op. cit.; 1971: OPCS. *Census 1971, Great Britain, Economic Activity, Part II* (London: HMSO, 1975); United States: 1950 and 1970—OECD. op. cit.; 1967 and 1978—U.S. Department of Commerce, Bureau of the Census, Current Population Reports, Population Characteristics. Series P-20. School Enrollment (October 1968 and 1967); no. 190. *School Enrollment—Social and Economic Characteristics of Students: October 1978.* no. 346 (Washington: GPO, 1969 and 1979).

Summary

The main observations regarding compositional changes in EER over the postwar period are as follows:

In most countries, equality of educational resources between the sexes, between different socioeconomic groups, racial, and ethnic groups, and across geographical regions has been a prime objective of educational policy.

As educational systems have expanded over the postwar period, increased access has occurred. A diminution of compositional disparities is observable, although these remain marked in some cases.

The female share of total enrollments has increased in most countries both for teenagers and young adults, and correspondingly, at all postcompulsory levels of education.

Female EER have risen faster than male over the postwar period so that disparities have narrowed, but male EER still are higher than female in most countries. Sex disparities in EER are greater for young adults than teenagers, and for higher education than upper secondary.

Sex inequalities have been more marked in certain forms of postcompulsory education, and in certain subjects. Enrollment in the most prestigious institutions and specializations continues to be dominated by males.

Socioeconomic disparities in enrollment rates have diminished over the postwar period. They remain greatest at institutions which carry the highest prestige, however. In many countries, the rise in EER of lower socioeconomic group youth has been attributable largely to the establishment and expansion of newer, nontraditional institutions. Similarly, socioeconomic disparities at the higher education level are greatest in those subjects that are most oriented toward prestigious and highly paid professional careers.

Geographic differences in EER have narrowed in some countries but widened in others over the postwar period.

Explanations of Cross-National Differences in Educational Enrollment Rates

Previous sections have shown that the medium-term trends in EER vary among the twelve countries. In this section, regression analysis is applied to the EER data collected by OECD for 1960, 1970, and 1975 in order to test several hypotheses about the growth of EER in the selected countries.

First, the hypothesis was tested that those countries with lower EER starting levels in 1960 were most likely to have the greater growth by 1975. The rationale for this hypothesis about the pattern of growth is twofold. According to the principle of regression toward the mean, countries with extremely high or low EER starting levels might be expected to move toward the mainstream over time (Campbell and Stanley 1963; Tufte 1974). Second, countries with lower EER had greater scope for expansion, being further from the maximum threshold of 100 percent.

This hypothesis was supported in the four linear bivariate regressions, since the slope was negative as expected (Table 3.7). The regressions predicted, for teenage males, that for each 1-percent differential between countries' starting levels, an inverse differential of 0.28 percent would be likely to result in the magnitude of EER growth; smaller inverse effects were shown for the other age-sex groups. Although the regressions were consistent with the hypothesis, starting levels explained a

Table 3.7   Relationship Between Changes in Educational Enrollment Rates, Starting EER Levels, and Youth Population Growth in Eleven Countries, 1960-1975

Subgroup	Dependent variable	Independent variable	Slope	Correlation coefficient (r)	Variation accounted for by independent variable (r^2)
					(percent)
Males 15-19	Δ EER (1975-1960)	1960 EER	-0.28 (1.10)[a]	-0.45	20.3
Females 15-19	Δ EER (1975-1960)	1960 EER	-0.19 (1.08)[a]	-0.32	10.2
Males 20-24	Δ EER (1975-1960)	1960 EER	-0.21 (1.02)[a]	-0.23	5.1
Females 20-24	Δ EER (1975-1960)	1960 EER	-0.22 (0.94)[a]	-0.20	4.2
Males 15-19	EER growth rate	POP growth rate	-0.28** (0.19)[a]	-0.68	46.8
Females 15-19	EER growth rate	POP growth rate	-0.16* (0.19)[a]	-0.49	23.7

[a]Standard error of the estimate of the slope.
*Significant at the 0.25 level.
**Significant at the 0.10 level.

Source: Calculated from OECD, Manpower and Social Affairs Committee, Demographic Trends: Their Labour Market and Social Implications, Annex 2, unpublished revisions (Paris: OECD, March 1979).

relatively small amount of the variation among the eleven countries. The explanatory power was greatest for male teenagers (20 percent) but very small for the 20-24 age group (4 to 5 percent); however, the small number of observations limits the statistical significance of the results.

Based on the regression equations, predicted EER growth rates for individual countries were calculated. The difference between the actual and predicted value for each country (the residuals) controls for the effects of starting levels (Table 3.8). Independent effects of starting levels were indicated by the fact that smaller variations among countries appeared in the residual rates of EER growth than in the actual rates. The remaining large variation among countries in the residuals — for teenage males, ranging from − 12.2 percent to + 13.4 percent — suggests the strength of explanatory forces other than starting levels.

The large positive residuals for Japanese and Dutch teenagers, Italian young adults, and the American young adult females in particular reflected the operation of additional growth forces tending toward higher EER than would be predicted from starting levels. In Japan, for example, the high value placed on postcompulsory education and the intense enthusiasm engendered for educational attainment are likely to be contributory factors. In Italy, the combination of the lack of employment opportunities and the relatively wide access to higher education provide further explanations. For American young adult females as well, availability of education has played an important role together with the established social acceptability of education and social changes, which have been somewhat more advanced for

Table 3.8   Country Deviations from 1960–1975 Changes in Enrollment Rates Predicted by Cross-National Regressions on EER Levels 1960 and Compound Growth Rate of Population 1960–1975, by Sex in Eleven Countries

Independent Variable	1960 EER levels				1960–1975 population growth	
	Males[a]	Females[a]	Males[b]	Females[b]	Males[c]	Females[c]
	15–19 years old		20–24 years old		15–19 years old	
	actual − predicted = residual (percentage points)					
Australia	−12.2	−8.6	+0.3	+0.1	−0.49	−0.30
Canada	+1.4	+2.3	+2.7	+0.8	+0.29	+0.30
France	+0.2	+2.3	+0.6	−3.3	+0.43	+0.35
Germany	−1.8	−9.3	−0.7	+0.5	+0.40	−0.76
Italy	+4.1	−0.3	+5.6	+8.6	+0.24	+0.04
Japan	+13.4	+14.9	+3.8	+1.9	+0.01	+0.41
Netherlands	+9.7	+4.8	+3.1	−1.4	+0.63	+0.45
New Zealand	−9.4	−9.7	−2.2	−1.0	−0.12	−0.30
Sweden	+4.3	−1.0	−7.2	−1.9	−0.36	−0.50
United Kingdom	−4.4	+6.7	−5.0	0.0	+0.35	+0.58
United States	−5.3	−2.2	+3.6	+6.3	−0.58	−0.26

[a] Actual minus predicted values equal residuals.
[b] Based on the following regression equation: Δenr. rate = $a + b \times$ enr. rate$_{1960}$
[c] Based on the following regression equation:

$$\operatorname{Ln}\left(\frac{\text{enr. rate}_{1975}}{\text{enr. rate}_{1966}}\right) = a + b \times \operatorname{Ln}(\text{enr. rate}_{1960})$$

Italy is excluded from the regression equation because of extreme values, but a predicted value is calculated based on the results for the other ten countries.
[d] Based on the following regression equation:
    Δ enrollment rate/year = $a + b \times \Delta$ population/year.

Source: Calculated from OECD, Manpower and Social Affairs Committee, Demographic Trends: Their Labour Market and Social Implications, Annex 2, unpublished revisions (Paris: OECD, 1979); *Table 3.3.

females in the United States than in most other nations. Conversely, the large negative residuals shown by Australia and New Zealand, for example, indicating that actual growth in EER was lower than growth rates predicted from starting levels, could be accounted for by factors such as relatively restrained demand for education by young people, as well as the influence of rapidly expanding economies, which were generating numerous employment opportunities.

The second hypothesis concerns an inverse relationship between the growth rates of EER and the youth population. Countries with sustained and substantial youth population growth might be expected to find considerable difficulty in accommodating an increased proportion of the age group in school. The problems of finance, construction of new buildings, and the training of teachers within relatively short periods may be expected to impose constraints on enrollment (cf. Simon and Pilarski 1979). Conversely, countries with more modest population growth over the medium-term would more likely be able to accept and accommodate increasing EER, especially if intervening short-term population increases had forced the creation of additional educational places, which subsequently became available for the smaller cohorts with higher EER.

In regard to teenagers, the results of regression analysis supported the hypothesis that EER growth responds inversely to population growth. The regression equation predicted that for each 1 percent differential between countries in the average annual compound population growth rate, a reduction was likely to result in average annual EER increase of 0.28 percentage points for males, and 0.16 percentage points for females (Table 3.7). This measure showed the expected greater effect on males, which arose because changes in female enrollment rates are influenced by a more varied set of circumstances. The regression accounted for 47 percent of the variation among countries in EER for teenage males and 24 percent for teenage females, a stronger relationship than was shown by the starting levels hypothesis. Given the limited number of countries in the analysis, the statistical significance of both results is satisfactory.

No country had a sufficiently high growth of teenage population to predict a negative change in enrollment rates. Because its teenage population growth was most rapid in the 1960–1975 period, Canada had the lowest predicted annual growth of teenage enrollment rates, still well above zero, at 0.68 percent. The New World countries, which had comparatively high teenage population increases, also tended to have the smallest growth of EER. Japan exhibited very little difference between actual and predicted EER for each sex, an indication of the strength of the explanatory power of the population variable, since very little residual was left to be explained by other factors. A similarly clearcut inverse relationship failed to emerge for the young adult group when EER changes were regressed on population growth. Due to the relatively low level of young adult EER in most countries, the anticipated negative relationship was suppressed by a variety of other labor market related factors.

When population growth over the 1960–1975 period and 1960 EER starting levels were considered together, as explanatory variables for the four age-sex groups, the stepwise regression supported the earlier bivariate regression results. The stepwise regression established the dominance of population growth as a negative influence on EER growth for teenagers, explaining almost 50 percent of the variation between countries for teenage males. The percentage of explained variation for teenage males rose by only 2 percentage points when the starting level was added as a second independent variable, after the population growth variable had been introduced. When the order was reversed, however, the explained variation increased by 29 percentage points, emphasizing the importance of population growth as an explanatory variable. Weaker relationships existed for other age-sex groups.

The third investigation relates EER to per capita GNP. First, enrollment rates in 1975 for each age-sex group were regressed on 1975 per capita GNP (in current prices and exchange rates). Supporting the hypothesis, the regression indicated, as expected, that differences in GNP levels among countries were positively related to EER levels, with 26 percent of cross-national variation explained for teenagers and 19 percent for young adults. In individual countries the teenage group showed closer conformity to the cross-national pattern than did young adults. For both age groups, Japan and the United States displayed considerably higher EER than GNP levels predicted, while Australia showed much lower EER. These results probably reflect the higher relative valuation placed on education in Japan and the US, and the relatively lower valuation accorded in Australia.

In a second regression with the same data, growth in EER over the period 1960–1975 was regressed on the rate of change in per capita GNP between 1960–1977. A weaker though still positive relationship resulted, explaining 13 percent of teenage cross-national variation and 9 percent for young adults. Thus the previous finding that teenage demographic changes were preeminent in explaining changes in EER in the medium-term is not altered by the introduction of the GNP growth variable.

These findings are confirmed by an OECD study over the period 1950–1970 of 19 countries, which includes most of our twelve (OECD 1972b). This study found support for the hypothesis that demand by teenagers and young adults for education — and then enrollment rates — increased as per capita income grew in the nation. The analysis also concluded that it was most likely that enrollment rates increased relatively slowly at low levels of per capita GNP, then increased more rapidly as per capita GNP rose, and eventually leveled off at comparatively high per capita GNP levels. The proportion of explained variation attributable to the per capita GNP variable was much higher in the OECD study than in our own, largely reflecting differences between the two samples. The OECD analysis also tested the null-hypothesis that time was an independent factor in changing preferences for education and increasing EER, once the influence of income was controlled. A strong independent time effect was shown for 20–24-year olds, but not for teenagers. The analysis concluded that the relationship between per capita GNP and EER had been stronger and more consistent for teenagers than for young adults (OECD 1972b). Another cross-national analysis of industrialized market economies found a high correlation between growth of enrollments and growth of GNP per capita (Kaser 1966). On the other hand, a British effort to link "annual growth in A levels and of staying on at school, against changes in real national income show no convincing links between them" (Layard, King, and Moser 1969, p. 33).

In addition to the type of explanatory factors analyzed in the previous section, differences among countries in the starting levels and rate of growth of EER can be explained by variations in the structure and practices of national education systems. Among the more important features are cross-national differences in the compulsory school-leaving age in 1945 and over the postwar period (*Table A3.4). The higher the compulsory age is above 15, the more the teenage category 15–19 is affected and the higher its EER should be. It also affects enrollment rates of the subsequent years. In some countries, changes in the compulsory education laws lag behind actual enrollment patterns, and the determining factor is the socially acceptable norm rather than the law. It has long been true in the United States that anything less than completion of high school is regarded as dropping out of school, although the normal age for completion is one or two years beyond the legal school-leaving age in the vast majority of states. Similarly, in Japan the leaving age is 15, but completion of high school at age 18 is now "at least culturally, semicompulsory" (Kato 1978, p. 35).

Enrollment rates may be higher in some countries than others because of the practice of requiring repetition of a whole year's work if there is failure in a single subject. The starting age and length of the different educational sequences also influence the EER of the two age groups. While in most countries the end of the teenage years chiefly involves entrance to higher education, in Germany completion of the full upper-secondary sequence occupies 19–20-year-olds. Whether school systems permit part-time studies or offer evening and correspondence courses has a differential effect on national EER. Similarly the presence and role of private schools, colleges, and universities influence EER.

The extent to which students complete a full educational sequence without interruptions and the speed with which they transfer from one level of education to another influence national EER differences, as do the dropout and transfer rates directly. Examination systems, their degree of difficulty and importance in the admission procedures for the next educational level also affect national EER.

Perhaps the most important factor for secondary school enrollment rates above compulsory age is the organizational differentiation of pupils in schools (Sørensen 1978, pp. 1–9). In countries which separate children into distinct schools and curricula at an early age, forcing irreversible decisions, the implications for enrollment rates after compulsory education are harsh (von Dohnanyi 1978). Thus, the leavers from the German *Hauptschule* (usually at age 15) and the *Realschule* (usually at age 16), who together constitute a substantial majority of the total in the age group, show very limited enrollment in further academic education and only a small amount in full-time vocational schooling (Kühlewind, Mertens, and Tessaring 1976).

In Japan, on the contrary, the comprehensive junior high school or middle school, which ends at age 15 and has virtually no dropouts, feeds directly into the senior high school. Rising from about 55 percent of junior high school graduates in 1959, the entrants to senior high school constituted close to 100 percent of JHS graduates by 1978. Minimal dropout rates in senior high school assure high enrollment rates through age 18 (Kato 1978). The comprehensive nature of the upper-secondary school in Japan, the United States, Sweden, and most provinces in Canada promotes higher rates of enrollment in colleges and universities than occurs in the countries with selective upper-secondary schools or complicated examination systems.

Although a comparative view indicates that the countries with selective and divided school systems have lower postcompulsory enrollment rates than other countries, the latter are not immune to the criticism that the grouping of students in classrooms, grades, tracks, ability groups, and other divisions, within ostensibly comprehensive school systems, restricts later educational opportunities and behavior and shapes social and economic outcomes. Investigating American primary and secondary schools, Sørensen concludes that "organizational differentiation creates career trajectories in an educational system, and thus structures educational opportunities. It may create different learning and social environments relevant for academic achievement and socialization. It presents a set of signals about the competencies and likely futures of students relevant for the decision making of teachers, parents, and the students themselves" (Sørensen 1978, p. 62).

Private costs of attending postcompulsory education are difficult to measure comparatively, but it is likely that differences in the net cost in relation to private net income plays some role in national differences in EER. In the same way, variations among nations in total government expenditures on postcompulsory education, including aid to students, is a factor; Table A3.5 provides some rough comparative data.

These variables do not exhaust the possible causes of cross-national differences in EER. Moreover, no effort has been made to capture the effects of such concepts as the national attitude toward education, although it surely plays a part.

Educational Attainment of Youth

Over the postwar period, substantial changes have occurred in the average number of years of education and the levels reached by the two youth age groups. At the same time, changes in the form and types of education have taken place, adding certain qualitative aspects to the pattern of extended duration of education. Both kinds of change in educational attainment over recent years have significantly contributed to altered educational perceptions and aspirations and consequently affected the labor force expectations and experience of youth. Moreover, in many countries the gap between the educational attainment of youth and of older cohorts is wider than it has been in the past, resulting in areas of potential difficulty for both younger and older labor force participants.

The expansion of enrollments throughout the postwar period has been accompanied by a rising average age of exit from formal education and a consequent increase in level of attainment. In 1957–1958 it was not uncommon for the age of exit from formal education to average around 16 years; the United States was exceptional in that it was 19. By 1974, the average was slightly over 18, a rise of almost two years. The range of average ages of exit in nine countries in 1974 was from 17.4 in Australia and New Zealand to 19.7 in the US (Denison 1967, Table 8-8; OECD 1977b).

Increased proportions of the youth population have attained the higher educational levels in many countries. In doing so they have significantly advanced their position in relation to the attainment achieved by older age groups. For example, Canadian 15–24-year olds, many of whom had not completed their education, displayed markedly higher educational attainment in 1977 than the same age group in 1961 (Table 3.9). Attainment data for those leaving the Canadian education system show similar trends. In 1966, 82 percent had left school at the primary or secondary level, and 18 percent at the tertiary level; by 1976, the proportions were 64 and 36 percent respectively (Canada 1978a). Comparison of the educational attainment of Canadian 15–24-year-olds with the 65 and older age group further emphasizes the effects of the postwar expansion of education and the widening of the generational gap. The difference in attainment between the two age groups in 1977 was particularly striking at the lower education levels, and was wider than had been the case in 1961.

Educational attainment of the American youth population, expressed as the attainment of the 25–29-year-old group, has likewise risen dramatically over the postwar period (Table 3.9). Comparison of U.S. younger persons (25–29) with an older age group (55 and older) showed, as in Canada, great generational disparity in

Table 3.9   Highest Level of Educational Attainment of the Population, by Selected Age Groups, Canada and the United States, 1947–1977

	Age	Highest Level of Attainment			Total
		Elementary	Secondary	Postsecondary	
			(percent)		
Canada					
1961	15–24	27	60	13	100
	65+	69	25	6	100
1977	15–24	7	68	25	100
	65+	56	31	13	100
United States					
1947	25–29	26	59	15	100
	55+	70	21	9	100
1975	25–29	6	53	41	100
	55+	40	43	17	100

Source: Canada: Statistics Canada, unpublished data; United States: Department of Commerce, Bureau of the Census, Statistical Abstract of the United States, 1950 and 1976 (Washington: GPO).

attainment that had widened between 1947 and 1979, particularly at the postsecondary level (US 1980a, Table 13). Similarly, the U.S. labor force aged 20–24 had a
reduction from 14 percent to 3 percent between 1959 and 1978 in the proportion attaining only elementary level. The proportion attaining higher education increased
over the period from 21 to 38 percent. Educational attainment by sex has risen along
similar paths over time in the U.S. labor force, although the proportion of
20–24-year-old males attaining no more than elementary education has remained
higher than that of females, while males attaining higher education has remained
slightly lower (US 1960–79b). The proportion of high school graduates in the U.S.
labor force rose from 43 to 73 percent from 1952 to 1977, while the proportion of
college graduates more than doubled in the same period, increasing from 8 to 17 percent (Freeman 1980c, p. 12). Inequalities persist according to economic status,
however. The lower the family income, the higher was the proportion of nonenrolled
youth in October 1977 who had less than four years of high school, according to unpublished BLS data on never married youth living at home.

Sweden shows similar time trends. In 1969, 89 percent of 20–24-year-old youth
had passed lower-secondary level examinations, and 11 percent had passed examinations at the upper-secondary level or above. By 1979, lower-secondary school was the
highest level of attainment of a smaller proportion, 73 percent of the 20–24-year-
olds, while 27 percent had attained upper-secondary school or above (Sweden
1969–1979). Results are affected by the fact that some in the 20–24 age group have
not completed their education.

Wide generational disparities are also evident in Sweden, when comparison is
made of the educational attainment of 20–24-year-olds and 65–74-year-olds. In 1975,
only 9 percent of the younger age group had completed less than 9 years of education, while the proportion for the older group was 73 percent; 16 percent of
20–24-year-olds reached the higher education level, compared with only 5 percent of
65–74-year-olds (Sweden 1978f, p. 22). A similar pattern, though less pronounced, is
shown by age-group comparisons in Japan and the Netherlands (Japan 1976a, p.
364; Netherlands 1977a, p. 95).

Flows from Education to the Labor Force

Obviously, the added years of education obtained by the youth cohort over the
postwar period have been reflected in a later age of entry to the full-time labor
market. A substantial proportion now enter the labor market expecting higher-level
entry positions than their counterparts of previous decades. In addition, prolonged
education in some countries has resulted in an increase in the proportion combining
education and paid work. Finally, in some countries it is suspected that some of
those with increased years of education have lower performance standards in the
basic subject than earlier cohorts.

A British estimate is that the average age of entry into employment has risen by
nearly three years in the past thirty years (Maclure 1979, pp. 2–3). Japanese entrants
to the labor force from junior high school (at age 15) have shrunk from 44.5 percent
of the total in 1965 to 12.3 percent in 1975, while the senior high school contingent
has risen from 44.9 percent of the total to 57.0 percent, and higher education
graduates tripled their share from 10.6 to 30.7 percent in the same decade (Japan
1976a). These trends have continued to the present, placing Japan in first rank
among countries in the level of education of new labor market entrants, but creating
absorption problems as a result.

Similarly, the flow from education into the Dutch labor force over the short time period 1965–1975 indicates a substantial aging of new entrants. The change was striking for both sexes but more so for females. In the initial year, 43.2 percent of the male entrants were younger than 17 years, but by 1975 only 10.0 percent were that age. Similarly, less than one-fourth were twenty years or older in 1965, while almost half were that age in 1975. Females, typically entering earlier than males, showed 56.8 percent younger than 17 in 1965 and only 12.9 by 1975. A doubling of the proportion who were over 20 from 1965 to 1975 brought the share of such new female entrants from 13.6 percent to 29.1 percent (Netherlands 1969–79).

Less dramatic change appears in Canadian estimates of potential labor force entrants from 1966 to 1975. These indicate that the most marked changes occurred in the share of those with some postsecondary education, but without a completed diploma or degree. In 1975 18.1 percent had this amount of education, compared with 5.8 percent in 1966. There was only a small change in those with completed postsecondary education. The proportions of potential labor market entrants having graduated from secondary school or less fell from 81.5 to 64.8 percent of the total (Canada 1978a, p. 45). Other countries with high starting levels or slowdown in EER growth also show the Canadian pattern.

The quantitative advance in educational attainment produced by demographic factors and the rise in EER has not been viewed as unmitigated progress. In many countries employers and other interested parties have complained that a certain portion of young people obtaining diplomas and other credentials from various levels of the educational system do not possess the knowledge and skills which should be exhibited by graduates of their level. A depreciation of the value of educational credentials has occurred in such situations, contributing an additional obstacle to the reconciliation of the labor market expectations of young people and the number and type of jobs offered to them.

The full implications of these educational attainment and flow patterns will appear in the chapters to follow on the youth labor force. Educational trends play a major role in the medium-term evolution of the size of the youth labor force and youth labor force participation rates.

Table A3.2 Enrollment Rates in Full-Time Education, by Age and Sex, in Eleven Countries, 1960–1975

| | Full-Time Enrollment Rates, 15-19 | | | | | | Full-Time Enrollment Rates 20-24 | | | | | |
| | Male | | | Female | | | Male | | | Female | | |
	1960	1970	1975	1960	1970	1975	1960	1970	1975	1960	1970	1975
				(as a percent of age-sex group)								
Australia	40.5	42.2	45.0	32.6	35.0	43.9	1.8	4.5	6.7	0.6	1.5	4.1
Canada	52.7	66.6	67.3	45.7	63.2	65.4	9.8	18.1	18.3	4.3	10.1	10.7
France	30.9	40.9	50.5	34.1	50.0	56.0	8.2	12.3	14.8	6.4	6.8	8.6
Germany	37.0	52.3	52.9	32.3	42.5	43.0	9.9	12.6	15.0	3.8	7.6	9.8
Italy	22.1	37.0	48.1	15.2	26.0	38.2	9.0	11.6	20.5	0.7	5.5	12.9
Japan	48.2	65.0	76.1	42.0	63.6	75.0	10.3	17.7	19.8	2.1	6.1	9.0
Netherlands	37.0	51.6	64.4	23.9	35.9	50.3	8.6	13.1	17.7	2.8	4.4	6.7
New Zealand	34.3	43.3	43.3	28.1	39.3	39.3	4.3	9.2	7.9	1.3	3.3	4.7
Sweden	36.1	57.7	58.3	37.7	54.4	55.6	17.8	16.8	14.1	13.1	15.3	14.6
United Kingdom	18.5	34.9	44.4	14.7	32.9	44.8	8.3	8.0	9.3	1.5	4.1	6.1
United States	68.7	75.4	72.1	59.4	73.4	71.9	17.0	26.6	24.4	7.2	12.9	18.8
Mean	38.7	51.5	56.6	33.3	46.9	53.0	9.5	13.7	15.3	4.0	7.1	9.6
Standard deviation	14.0	13.4	11.8	13.2	15.1	12.9	4.7	6.0	5.6	3.7	4.2	4.5

Source: OECD, Working Party of the Education Committee on Educational Statistics and Indicators, revised data, unpublished (Paris: OECD, March 1979).

Table A3.3 Enrollment Rates by Age, Sex, Income, and Living Arrangements, United States, October 1977

| | Youth never married and living at home (or at school) | | | | All other youth | | | |
| | 16-19 Years | | 20-24 Years | | 16-19 Years | | 20-24 Years | |
	Males	Females	Males	Females	Males	Females	Males	Females
Total number (000s)	7,582	6,721	4,218	2,967	592	1,583	5,039	6,956
As percentage of age-sex group	92.8	80.9	45.6	29.9	7.8	19.1	54.4	70.1
Income classes			Enrollment Rates (percent)					
Less than $5,000	64.2	68.8	25.9	34.8	34.9	25.3	31.4	24.0
$5,000-7,499	67.3	75.7	24.3	34.0	21.2	16.0	21.4	13.0
$7,500-9,999	68.9	74.0	31.9	35.3	18.4	14.7	17.3	12.3
$10,000-14,999	72.0	77.9	34.9	41.4	32.9	19.1	11.5	9.4
$15,000-24,999	77.1	79.6	36.6	43.2	51.0	32.8	13.7	10.4
$25,000 and over	85.5	86.1	54.1	59.2	52.6	60.0	17.5	14.2
All income classes[a]	74.7	78.7	38.5	44.1	30.4	22.7	18.6	13.7

[a] Includes some whose income level was not reported.

Source: U.S. Department of Labor, Bureau of Labor Statistics, unpublished data.

Table A3.5 Government Educational Expenditures, by Level of Education, in Twelve Countries, 1964-1979 (percentages)

	Government expenditure (all levels) on education as percent of GDP (gross domestic product)				Share of total government expenditure on education on			Government income transfers to households for educational participation as proportion of total government (all levels) expenditure on education	
	All education	Upper-secondary education	Higher education	Year	Upper-secondary education	Higher education	Year		Year
Australia	5.8	3.6a	1.8	(1976/7)	61.4a	30.3	(1976/7)	n.a.	
Canada	7.5	4.9a	2.1	(1974)	65.1a	28.6	(1974)	2.8	(1971)
France	4.9	2.3c	0.6	(1977)	48.2c	12.2	(1977)	2.5	(1977)
Germany	4.6	0.6	0.7	(1977)	13.9	14.6	(1977)	4.7	(1977)
Italy	4.8	1.0	0.5	(1977)	21.1	9.8	(1977)	1.5	(1977)
Japan	6.3f	1.1f	1.2f	(1976)	16.9	18.4	(1976)	n.a.	
Netherlands	7.2	0.6	1.3	(1977)	8.5	18.6	(1977)	3.9	(1977)
New Zealand	5.7	1.2c	1.8	(1976)	20.3	31.1	(1976)	n.a.	
Sweden	6.1	0.7	1.1	(1979)	11.4	18.2	(1979)	6.2	(1979)
Switzerland	3.6	2.7a	0.9	(1972)	76.1a	23.9	(1972)	n.a.	
United Kingdom	5.6	1.3	1.1	(1977)	23.5	19.8	(1977)	4.5	(1977)
United States	7.3f	4.7a,f	2.6f	(1977)	70.5a	20.1	(1978)	3.4	(1978)

Table A3.5 (continued)

	Share of total education transfers to households for students in			Loans as proportion of all educational transfers to households		Proportion of students receiving direct[f] government transfers			Average proportion of student income from government educational transfers	
	Upper-secondary education	Higher education	Year		Year	Upper-secondary education	Higher education	Year		Year
Australia	n.a.	n.a.		n.a.		20	58-76	(1974/5)	48[b]	(1974/5)
Canada	n.a.	n.a.		n.a.		n.a.	25	(1972/3)	29	(1964)
France	32.0[d]	24.4[d]	(1977)	n.a.		36-63	13-15	(1974/5)	25	(1974/5)
Germany	37.0[c]	63.0	(1977)	19.5	(1977)	25	45	(1974/5)	40	(1974/5)
Italy	0.7[e]	95.9[e]	(1977)	3.3	(1975)	2	10-15	(1968)	n.a.	
Japan	n.a.	n.a.		n.a.		n.a.	10	(1977)	13-30	(1974/5)
Netherlands	6.9	80.2	(1977)	41.5	(1977)	n.a.	38-50	(1974/5)	65	(1974/5)
New Zealand	n.a.	n.a.		n.a.		n.a.	n.a.		n.a.	
Sweden	n.a.	n.a.		n.a.		100	70	(1974/5)	60+	(1974/5)
Switzerland	n.a.	n.a.		n.a.		n.a.	n.a.		n.a.	
United Kingdom	0.0[g]	93.1[g]	(1977)	n.a.		1-10	90[h]	(1974/5)	54	(1974/5)
United States	n.a.	n.a.		n.a.		n.a.	10-25[i]	(1976/7)	21+	(1976/7)

[a] Primary and all secondary levels; [b] Excludes trainee teachers whose proportion was 76 percent; [c] All secondary levels; [d] 9 percent of total not itemized by level; [e] 3 percent of total not itemized by level; [f] As percent of GNP; [g] 7 percent of total not itemized by level; [h] Home students only; [i] Federal aid only; [j] Composed mainly of loans and grants. Excludes tuition exemption and cases where tuition costs have been abolished or are not charged. Also excludes indirect aid such as subsidized accommodation, meals, health, or insurance facilities (OECD 1978d).

Source: EC 1980c; OECD 1974a, 1976b, 1978e; Australia 1979a; Canada 1978b; Japan 1979a; Sweden 1979j; U.S. 1950–79.

4 Youth Labor Force Trends

In industrial countries, postwar labor supply trends, of which youth trends are a part, depict a long-run decline in the labor force participation rate (LFPR) and annual hours of work of adult men, a long-run increase for adult women, and a long-run plateau or slight decline in the total hours per year supplied by households. These postwar patterns continue prior trends, both for adults and youth (Long 1958).

The present chapter compares the twelve countries with regard to medium-term trends in the youth labor force in the quarter-century or so after the end of World War II. Relevant dimensions of the youth labor force for such a comparative discussion are influenced by the definitions adopted and the data chosen for analysis. Building on the preliminary discussion in Chapter 1 and referring to the appendix to this chapter for details (Appendix 4:1), we make a few observations here. This study regards all persons engaged in military service, whether voluntary or compulsory, as part of the population base and the labor force, in accordance with the procedures of the international agencies in collecting labor force data. To the extent that we have been able to obtain the necessary data, we have recomputed national labor force series to incorporate all military personnel (both volunteers and conscripts) in the population and labor force (Tables A4.1–A4.8). We have followed national practice in regard to persons in institutions in the national series, and international practice where international data are cited. The institutionalized population is small in every country, and few of its members would be in the labor force.

Our emphasis on the number of individuals in the labor force relegates hours of work during the week and weeks of work during the year to a position of secondary importance. The differences in hours worked between youth and other age groups within countries as well as cross-national differences in hours worked by youth are discussed in Chapter 5, as are related issues concerning the participation of students in the labor force. The present chapter does refer to the differential impact of student labor force participation rates (LFPR) upon overall trends in the youth labor force of various countries.

This study relies primarily on historical series of cross-national labor force data, either for single points in time during the year or as a yearly average. Such data not only relate most compatibly to the educational data, but they are most easily available for a cross-national study. Appendix 4:1 shows the difference between the single-date and the yearly average approaches for Australia and the United States. For a few countries, still another sort of cross-sectional series is available, based on the number of individuals who have been in the labor force at any time in a given year. The two series, shown for the US and Sweden in *Table A4.10, indicate the expected excess of the LFPR at any time of the year, but Sweden has a somewhat greater excess than the US in all age-sex groups.* Similar calculations for Australia in 1972 and 1978 indicate that the excess for young adults was about the same as in the US, but that Australian teenagers had only about half the excess of U.S. teenagers (Australia 1972–78; Australia 1971–80).

*Tables marked with an asterisk are not included in this volume, but may be obtained from the authors.

Gross flow data, derived from the cross-sectional monthly data, offer another perspective on the youth labor force, as the discussion in Chapter 1 indicated. Longitudinal surveys of individuals, appearing more widely in countries in recent years (Appendix 4:1), already offer an opportunity to check findings from the cross-sectional data and will provide more as time goes on. Still, such surveys are unlikely to soon form the basis of a cross-national study, given all the differences among countries and surveys.

The specific data for this chapter are drawn basically from two sources. Using national survey data, a complete set of basic labor force tables has been drawn up for the eight countries which conduct regular labor force surveys (Tables A4.1–A4.8). While differences in definitions and some internal discontinuities in data in the national series mar complete comparability among countries, these data are useful for indicating the turning points in national trends and year-to-year oscillations around the trend. In addition to the national series, considerable use is made of OECD data for 1950, 1960, 1970, and 1975, revised as of March 1979. These statistics were compiled by OECD from information supplied on a uniform basis by the individual countries in response to an OECD request. These benchmark data for all twelve countries can be compared to the educational data assembled from other sources by OECD at the same time. Appendix 4:1 describes the labor force data of the other international agencies and makes comparisons among different sources (Tables *B4.5, *B4.6). While differences exist among sources, and data from some countries probably will be revised by OECD as new national estimates become available, no major incompatibility has so far emerged.*

As in the education chapter, the youth group is here divided into two main components, teenagers and young adults. Teenagers are defined as 15 to 19 years of age, although 14 and 16 are the more appropriate lower cut-off points in several of our countries. Young adults are 20 up to 25 years of age, expressed as 20 to 24. A large proportion of teenagers are still in school, predominantly in secondary school, in all of the industrialized market economy countries. New labor force entrants form a sizeable proportion of the total teenage labor force. In contrast, a significantly lower proportion of young adults is enrolled in educational institutions, almost exclusively in higher education. The young adult labor force has relatively few new entrants, since a sizeable proportion has accumulated labor force experience, having entered the labor force as teenagers.

More important, the two age groups differ markedly in educational attainment, skill, and occupational composition. The proportion of school dropouts is smaller in the young adult labor force than among teenagers, and the 20–24-years-old labor force includes many more college graduates. A greater representation of persons who have acquired special skills through formal or on-the-job training is found among young adults. Finally, the marital and family status and living arrangements of members of the labor force drawn from these two age groups differ. Teenagers primarily reside with parents or other adults, while young adults are more likely to live apart, either married in their own households, or in some other arrangement. While no distinct line of separation between the two age groups can be drawn and significant divisions appear within the two groups, broad differences in regard to patterns of labor market entrance, attachment, and experience can be discerned between teenagers and young adults.

---

*Data we use differ slightly in some cases from those published by OECD in *Demographic Trends* 1950–1990, Paris, 1979.

Variations among countries in the characterization of the two youth groups reflect the average age of leaving school, trends in the prolongation of education, and the proportion entering and completing higher education. In the United States, for example, where education has been prolonged, many of the characteristics assigned to teenagers in other countries are applied to young adults, as in this recent statement: "Young adults do not have firmly established work patterns. The years between age 20 and 25 are dynamic, often providing a transition from teenage years and schooling to adulthood, career and marriage" (Leon 1978, p. 3). While certain other countries might use such a description in reference to recent university graduates, they would not characterize the whole age group in this way.

We are not concerned in this study with cyclical variations in the youth labor force or in LFPR, although we recognize that medium-term and cyclical trends are inter-related. For example, a Canadian analysis of factors affecting the LFPR of young people, based on annual data for 1954–1974, found support for the hypothesis that young people 14 to 19 years old "prefer the short-term benefits of available employment to future benefits from a better education" (Bertrand 1975, p. 10). This interpretation is not consistent with the observed medium-term trend in Canada of a rise in educational enrollment rates and decline in teenage LFPR. It is more easily understood either as a cyclical effect in which employment level fluctuations impact on EER, or as a response during a period when the relative benefits of prolonged education declined. The difficulty of separating the various strands appear in many analyses.

It is of course true that cyclical factors affect the significance of the starting and terminal years in data that rely on uniform reference years. Also, cross-national variations in the frequency and severity of cyclical fluctuations influence differentially the level and timing of individual and household decisions to supply labor to the youth labor market. Whenever and wherever the net effect is negative, it produces the "discouraged worker" effect. While our comparative discussion of the youth labor force in this and the next chapter do not deal with discouraged workers, they are studied in Chapter 6, which concerns those who are neither in school nor the labor force (NISLF). In the same way we have left to Chapter 6 the issue of the impact on youth labor force trends of government programs such as income transfers, since disincentive effects are uppermost in analysts' minds.

In the case of youth, as Chapter 3 indicated, educational enrollment trends have strong implications for labor force trends. In most of the twelve countries, a clear-cut choice between entering the labor force and undertaking additional education must be made, and such a choice is realistically open to at least a portion of each youth age group. A certain segment of young people elects to enter the labor market each year without consciously or unconsciously weighing any alternative. Whether driven by economic necessity, a dislike or lack of qualification for further study, or achievement of a high level of education, they choose to terminate formal education, in most cases making a lifetime decision. The remainder divide into two groups. The first rejects the labor market as a main activity at that point in their lives because their career and occupational goals and expectations dictate that they continue their education; the jobs available to them at their current educational levels are unacceptable for the long-term. The second group, falling between the other two, is in a position to weigh all the advantages and disadvantages of entering the labor force versus continuing their education, immediately and over a long period.

The groups described exist in all countries and have not changed over time. But the proportion of each age cohort that elects each choice has altered markedly in the postwar period. Thus the trend toward a prolongation of education on the average has indeed made enrollment trends and rates a key factor in youth labor force trends.

Nonetheless, the medium-term development of the youth labor force does not precisely coincide with the evolution of educational enrollments in some countries. This lack of congruency arises in part because some young people are double-counted when they are simultaneously in school and the labor force. By the standards used to measure labor force participation, students who work even a few hours or seek such jobs during the school year are counted as full labor force units, on a par with young people who work at or seek full-time jobs. To the extent that such duplication occurs and labor force data are collected during the school months, the following results may be observed:

Cross-national comparisons are affected because the phenomenon of working while in school ranges from very important to insignificant among the twelve countries.

Educational enrollments in some countries do not directly predict youth labor force trends.

It is necessary to analyze the enrolled and nonenrolled labor force separately, as will be done in Chapter 5.

Some inflation of the total size of the youth labor force appears in countries where the enrolled labor force is relatively large and works much shorter hours than the nonenrolled labor force.

Educational and labor force trends are not symmetrical for another reason. The existence of a residual group that is neither in school nor the labor force (NISLF) and changing trends in the relative size of that group, especially among females, affect the expected relationship between educational enrollments and labor force participation. Chapter 6 explores the NISLF population and its relation to youth labor force trends.

The remainder of this chapter addresses the three main aspects of the youth labor force: trends in its absolute size in the twelve countries, youth shares in the total labor force, and labor force participation rates (LFPR) over time and among countries. A special section deals with the components of change in the LFPR of young adult females. The chapter concludes with an analysis of some explanatory factors in the cross-national variation in youth LFPR trends.

Size of the Teenage Labor Force

The twelve countries divide into two groups in regard to trends in the size of the teenage labor force in the postwar period. Five countries (Canada, United States, Australia, New Zealand, and Switzerland) displayed an increase in size for each sex; six countries (Japan, Italy, France, Netherlands, Germany, and United Kingdom) indicated a decline for each sex; and one, Sweden, had a small drop for males and a small increase for females over the period 1950–1975 (Chart 4.1; Tables *A4.12, *A4.13). This bimodal distribution arises from divergence among countries in population trends as well as in LFPR trends, the two main components of change in the size of the youth labor force. In many countries demographic factors outweighed changes in LFPR in accounting for overall changes in labor force size, but in others the LFPR changes predominated; the relative weight and direction of the two components of change varied even within individual countries in the different subperiods.

The importance of the population component is shown by the high correlation of

Chart 4.1 Change in the Teenage (15-19 Years) Labor Force, by Sex, in Twelve Countries, 1950-1975

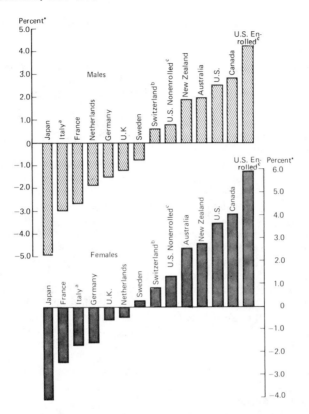

a 1960-75; b 1950-70; c Aged 16-19 years; *Average annual compound percent.

Source: Calculated from OECD, Manpower and Social Affairs Committee, Demographic Trends: Their Labour Market and Social Implications, Annex 2, unpublished revisions (Paris, 1979). Labor Force includes all military personnel; U.S. Department of Labor, Employment and Training Report of the President 1980, Table B-6 (Washington: GPO, 1980); Bureau of Labor Statistics, unpublished data.

country ranks for changes in teenage population and labor force size: $r_S = +.74$ for teenage males and $+.80$ for teenage females. In addition, we regressed average annual rates of change in teenage population on similar changes in labor force size 1950-1975. For teenage males in eleven of the countries (excluding Switzerland), the regression predicted that countries with population growth averaging under 1.8 percent would have, on average, a declining labor force size. A zero population growth rate would be associated with a 3.5 percent drop in labor force size. Population growth rates averaging over 1.8 percent would be associated with a rising size of labor force. The regression for teenage females indicated a systematically higher predicted value of labor force change for any value of population change.

Another way of measuring the impact of the two components of change is shown in *Table A4.11. It shows the size the U.S. youth labor force would have reached by 1975 if each of the two main components of change had, in turn, been frozen at the 1955 level. In all four age-sex groups and at all three time intervals, the influence of changes in population was clearly stronger than that of changes in LFPR; this is shown by the fact that the size of the hypothetical labor force is larger in the second column than in the third for each age-sex group (*Table A4.11). For both groups of females, the actual increase in labor force size exceeded either of the hypothetical totals at almost every reading, indicating the combined effect of rising population and LFPR. Actual labor force size for both groups of males was smaller than that predicted in the hypothetical size based on population change alone, evidence of a downward trend in male LFPR (*Table 4.2).

Records for the twelve countries on the size of the teenage labor force can be compared in three time frames: from the beginning to the end of the postwar period; over three subperiods, 1950-1960, 1960-1970, and 1970-1975; and through year-to-year changes. In 1950-1975, Canada, the United States, Australia, and New Zealand had the greatest expansion of the teenage labor force for each sex (Chart 4.1; *Table A4.13). These countries, but in a different order, also appear in Chapter 2 as the leaders in teenage population growth over the same period. Chart 4.1, which includes national data for the US on the growth in labor force size separately for enrolled and nonenrolled youth, indicates clearly that the surge of teenage labor force in the US was largely due to growth in LFPR among the enrolled. Canada's first place probably is due also to the rising contribution of students; Australia and New Zealand have less labor force participation by students than the North American countries but more than the European countries and Japan (see Chapter 5).

Using 1950 size as the base, the male teenage labor force in Canada had doubled by 1975, while, at the other extreme, the Japanese teenage male labor force had dwindled to almost one-fourth of its 1950 size. No other country approached Japan's situation; France's 1975 level was about 50 percent of its 1950 level, and the four other countries with a smaller 1975 than 1950 teenage male labor force ranged upward from France's figure. The dispersion was even greater for teenage females, ranging from a growth of 263 percent in Canada to a decrease of 65 percent in Japan (Tables *A4.12, *A4.13).

Changes in teenage labor force size in the subperiods confirm the basic pattern. The four leaders in overall growth showed consistent growth of the teenage labor force for each sex in the subperiods. There were differences in the growth rates, however. Canada and the United States showed increase at accelerating rates in the subperiods for each sex; for example, the average annual compound percentage change in the size of the Canadian teenage female labor force was 2.4 percent in the 1950s, then a comparatively high rate, rising to 8.4 percent in 1970-1975. Over the 1960s at least, Australia and New Zealand displayed decelerating rates of increase for both females and males (*Table A4.13).

Japan is the only country which had an accelerating rate of decline in all three subperiods in the size of both the male and female teenage labor force. Male teenagers experienced an average annual decline of 2.2 percent in the 1950s, rising to 4.4 percent in the 1960s and to 11.2 percent in the 1970-1975 period. Japanese teenage females show an even more significant acceleration of the rate of decline, from a modest 1.0 percent in the 1950s to an average annual 11.0 percent in the 1970s. If Italian data were as extensive, they probably would also show consistent decline in the three subperiods. Most other countries indicate some increase in the 1950s and later decline, at least for the males. In Sweden there was a pattern of increase-decline-increase, while in France decline was followed by increase in the 1960s with decline again in the 1970s (*Table A4.13).

Year-to-year changes in the size of the teenage labor force, as reported in the national data for eight countries, indicate a predominant direction of change (except for Sweden), but still make clear that there was considerable annual variation in the amount and direction of change (Tables A4.1–A4.8). None of the eight countries had a consistent pattern of annual increase or decrease over the entire period, although a full, albeit unreliable, series might show annual decrease for Italy from 1960 to 1978. Canada displayed almost constant increase from 1953 to 1979, especially for female teenagers. The trend in Australia was more mixed, particularly for females, although annual increases predominated over decreases in terms of both frequency and magnitude. Sweden's annual trend from 1963 to 1970 was clearly downward; thereafter it was mixed but primarily one of increase, especially for females. France had large increases at the beginning and end of the period 1963–1979, with substantial decreases in the intervening years. The German record was mixed from 1962 to 1966 and subsequently showed annual decline. In Japan, years of decline predominated over increase, both in number and size of the changes. American year-to-year change was primarily one of increase from 1948 to 1979, and displayed only a few negative years with changes of small magnitude after the early 1950s. Separate examination of the U.S. teenage enrolled and nonenrolled labor force reveals that the former had many more years of increase than the latter, indicating again how much of the U.S. growth is owing to participation by students (see Chapter 5). In several countries the growth or decline of the teenage labor force over a twelve-month period was substantial: France, Italy, Japan, Sweden and the United States had one or more years with a change exceeding 10 percent (Tables A4.1–A4.8).

Country ranks for change in teenage labor force size 1950–1975 were remarkably similar for each sex, with at most a two-place difference (Chart 4.1; Tables *A4.12; *A4.13). This similarity of trends for male and female teenagers in each country, also present in educational enrollment trends, suggests that national differences are important and consistent. At the same time, teenage females in every country demonstrated more growth, or less decline, in labor force size than corresponding teenage males; Germany is the one exception. In the United States and Canada, for example, the teenage female labor force grew by about 60 percentage points more than the male between 1950 and 1975. As expected, in the subperiods the size of the female teenage labor force, almost without exception, displayed more rapid increase or less rapid decline than the corresponding male labor force. Females made an outstanding contribution to the periods of growth and to the limitation of the decrease. In the 1950–1960 period the vast majority of the countries had an increasing teenage labor force for each sex. In the 1960s the number of countries with a growing teenage male labor force declined dramatically, while female trends changed in a similar direction but were less marked. Between 1970 and 1975, a larger number of countries revealed a declining female teenage labor force, but there was no further increase in the number of countries with a declining male teenage labor force. In the 1970–1975 period, four of the twelve countries had high rates of decline (over 3 percent) for each sex. The magnitude of variation among countries at points of time and over time in the size of the teenage labor force was more significant for teenage females than for males (*Table A4.13).

At the end of the period, the size of the teenage female labor force in most countries was more nearly equal to that of the male than it had been a quarter of a century earlier, while in Japan and the Netherlands there actually was a female excess (*Table A4.12). Since population growth was much the same for teenagers of each sex in every country, sex differences in labor force size are attributable to a greater rise or lesser fall in LFPR for females than for males. In turn, the faster female growth was facilitated by the presence of a greater margin for increase in the higher initial proportion of females neither in school nor the labor force (NISLF). By reductions in this category, the female labor force grew without restricting educational enrollments. Secular deline in NISLF, reviewed in Chapter 6, contributed to female advances in both labor force and educational enrollments.

In summary, the three time frames yield very similar trends in the size of the teenage labor force. The clearcut decline in Japan, Italy, France, the Netherlands, the United Kingdom, and Germany was due to demographic factors compounded by a rise in full-time enrollments in education, unaccompanied by much growth in the enrolled labor force. Sweden has occupied a middle ground with substantial modulations in trends, while Switzerland and the New World countries (Australia, New Zealand, Canada, and the United States) basically experienced upward teenage labor force patterns. Evidence presented thus far suggests important postwar cross-national differences in the size of the teenage labor force that limit the comparability of teenage unemployment rates. Further information on teenage shares of the total labor force and LFPR will enlarge on these international differences.

Teenage Share of the Labor Force

Medium-term trends in the absolute *size* of the teenage labor force, reviewed above, are indicators either of the changing number of entry jobs required to meet the needs of this age group or of the group's potential for assisting the economy in meeting labor shortages. Changes in the teenage *share* of the total labor force within countries over time and differences among countries at given points of time bear on the relative position of teenagers in the labor market, the age and sex composition of the total labor force, and its skill structure and quality (Anderson, J.M. 1978; Freeman and Medoff 1978; Freeman 1979b; Layard 1979; Welch 1979; Grant and Hamermesh 1980). The degree to which teenagers, as new entrants to the labor force or inexperienced workers, are substitutable for or complementary to older workers needs to be studied more fully in a number of countries.

At the outset (1950), the share of male teenagers in the male labor force, shown in Table 4.1, averaged 8.9 percent in eleven countries (Italy omitted), with the United States at the low end (6.7 percent) and Japan by far the highest (12.5 percent). When male teenagers are measured as a share of the total labor force of both sexes (*Table A4.14), country ranks are roughly the same, but there is less spread between the countries and more clustering around the 1950 average of 6.3 percent. In 1950, teenage females in eleven countries averaged 17.8 percent of the total female labor force, twice the male ratio (Table 4.1). In addition, teenage females displayed a much wider range in shares than males in 1950. Shares were arrayed from a low of 10.0 percent in the US up to 26.3 percent in the Netherlands; Australia and New Zealand also had very high teenage female shares, because these three countries had relatively high LFPR for unmarried females and comparatively low LFPR for married women. When teenage females are considered as a proportion of the total 1950 labor force of both sexes (*Table A4.14), the average share drops to 5.0 percent, 1.3 percentage points below the average male share. Reflecting the predominance of males in the labor force of each country, the teenage female shares of the total for both sexes range only from 6.4 percent in Japan to 2.9 percent in the US.

At the beginning of the postwar period there was a considerable dispersion among countries in teenage shares of the labor force, as well as differences in country ranks

Table 4.1 Share of Male and Female Teenagers (15–19) in Total Labor Force of Same Sex, in Twelve Countries, 1950–1975

	Males				Females			
	1950	1960	1970	1975	1950	1960	1970	1975
				(percent)				
Australia	8.5[a]	9.6	9.4	9.4	23.3[a]	24.4	18.2	16.1
Canada	8.1	7.7	8.5	9.9	18.9	15.5	13.2	14.2
France	9.6[a]	6.7	7.8	4.3	11.9[a]	9.9	10.5	5.4
Germany	10.5[a]	9.7	6.9	6.5	16.9[a]	15.2	11.1	9.2
Italy	n.a.	8.4	6.5	5.4	n.a.	15.0	12.1	9.8
Japan	12.5[a]	8.7	4.8	2.5	16.6[a]	12.8	7.6	4.3
Netherlands	10.0[a]	9.1	7.1	5.1	26.3[a]	28.7	24.4	15.4
New Zealand	8.5[a]	9.3	9.7	10.0	23.2[a]	26.3	22.3	21.4
Sweden	6.9[a]	7.1	5.1	5.5	13.6[a]	14.0	7.2	6.7
Switzerland	8.2[a]	8.3	7.2	n.a.	16.9[a]	16.7	12.2	n.a.
United Kingdom	8.6[a]	8.4	7.5	7.6	18.7[a]	15.8	12.2	11.8
United States	6.7	7.2	9.0	9.6	10.0	9.6	11.0	11.9
Mean	8.9	8.4	7.5	6.9	17.8	17.0	13.5	11.5
Standard deviation (STD)	1.7	1.0	1.6	2.6	5.0	6.2	5.4	5.1
Percent of countries within 1 STD of mean	73	58	67	55	55	58	67	73

[a] Total labor force data derived from stated labor force totals for all ages, less actual or estimated labor force participants under age 15.

Source: Calculated from OECD, Manpower and Social Affairs Committee, *Demographic Trends: Their Labour Market and Social Implications*, MAS(77)1, Annex 2, revisions March 1979 (Paris: OECD, 1979). Total labor force data derived by adding labor force data for five separate age groups 15 years and older. All military personnel are included.

and levels compared to teenage shares of population (see Chapter 2). Cross-national variations in the levels of educational enrollment rates (EER) are a major explanatory factor in the greater dispersion of teenage shares of the labor force than of population, but disparities across nations in the LFPR of other age groups, particularly among females, undoubtedly contributed as well. Country ranks for teenage labor force shares also varied considerably in 1950 for males and females; only two countries held the identical rank in each array. Given the considerable similarity for teenagers of each sex in country ranks in the size of the labor force, it appears that national differences in ranks by sex in the size of the labor force of the remaining age groups largely account for the variation by sex in country ranks for teenage shares in 1950, as shown in Table 4.1.

The significance of the size of the teenage share of the labor force in 1950 varied from country to country according to the postwar economic situation and the degree of substitutability and complementarity of young and older workers. Whether the group constituted a needed addition to the labor force or a problem in absorption depended as much on general economic circumstances as on the relative size of the teenage labor force. The high shares in Japan, Germany, and the Netherlands initially were a burden, given the postwar disorganization in these countries. On the other hand, the postwar labor force of the United States and Sweden probably could have absorbed an even higher share of teenagers.

An interpretation of changes in teenage shares of the labor force after 1950 must bear in mind starting levels, rates and direction of change, and alterations in the rate and composition of economic growth in individual countries. On average, the teenage male share declined in the 1950–1975 period, especially in the 1960–1970 and 1970–1975 subperiods, and the 1975 teenage male share of the male labor force averaged 2 percentage points lower than the 1950 mean. Yet the trend for individual countries was mixed, and over time there was a widening of cross-national differences, represented by the size of the standard deviation relative to the mean (Table 4.1). The following groups of countries emerge in a survey of trends in labor force shares to 1975–1980 (Tables 4.1, *A4.14, *A4.1a–A4.8a):

Five countries (Japan, France, the Netherlands, Germany, and Italy) displayed a sharp drop in the teenage male share over the postwar period. These countries also had marked declines in the size of the teenage labor force. In 1950–1975 Japan's male teenage share fell from 12.5 percent, the highest among the countries, to 2.5 percent, the lowest; this fact further explains reported labor shortages and negligible teenage unemployment. France, the Netherlands, and Italy experienced difficulties in absorbing teenagers by the 1970s, although the teenage labor force share was much smaller than it had been in 1950 and was smaller than in other countries. The prime cause was the failure of employment to grow as rapidly as it had previously.

Three countries, Sweden, Switzerland, and the United Kingdom, trended downward, but not strongly, and had much year-to-year variation in shares. Switzerland and the UK also were in the middle group in size of labor force change. Only Switzerland escaped problems of absorbing teenagers in the 1970s.

Teenage male shares in four countries – the United States, Australia, Canada, and New Zealand – trended slightly upward, with the most marked advance in the US (almost 3 percentage points). Demographic forces affecting all age groups, the growth in LFPR of students, and reduced LFPR of older men are among the most important explanations. Despite the fact that the US had the lowest teenage male share in 1950 and was exceeded by two other countries in 1975, the steady and pronounced upward movement, which overlaid American year-to-year variations, may account for the persistent American preoccupation from the 1960s with the absorption of the teenage labor force and the relatively high ratios of teenage to adult unemployment rates.

In Canada, Australia, and New Zealand, the buildup in the adult male labor force due to immigration tended to restrain the increase in the teenage share. Until the 1970s neither the Australian nor the New Zealand labor force had serious trouble in absorbing their teenage males, but Canada paralleled U.S. experience in youth unemployment rates, though not in unemployment ratios.

These findings hold equally for the teenage male share of the total labor force of both sexes (*Table A4.14). A zero-order correlation of the two ways of measuring the teenage male share of the labor force yielded a very close association ($r_s = +.87$ in 1950, rising to $+.98$ in 1975).

Year-to-year fluctuations in the teenage male share of the male labor force might be an important modifier of medium-term trends, since countries with large annual variations in shares might have experienced more absorption difficulties than others, especially where there was a general excess supply of teenagers. Five of the eight countries providing annual data had no more than a few tenths of a percent change in the male teenage share from one year to another. Over a 15 to 30-year period, the gap between a country's lowest and highest share was only 2 to 3 percentage points. France and Italy were exceptional in having a 5 percentage point gap between highest and lowest shares and quite large changes in the teenage male share from year to year, while Japan experienced variation in excess of 8 percentage points between highest and lowest share, but small year-to-year changes (Tables A4.1b–A4.8b).

The share of teenage females was strongly affected by the marked growth of the adult female labor force in many countries (*Table A4.17). From 1950 to 1975 the labor force share of teenage females declined in every country except the United States (Tables 4.1, A4.1c–A4.8c). In some countries the drop was most marked from 1970 to 1975, as in the French and Dutch cases, but other countries showed a steady erosion throughout the period. The mean share of teenage females dropped by over 6 percentage points from 1950 to 1975, but the standard deviation remained similar, an indication of continued dispersion of country shares. In 1975, teenage female shares ranged from 4.3 percent in Japan to 21.4 percent in New Zealand, a wider spread than the female age group displayed in 1950 or than males showed in 1975 (Table 4.1). When teenage females are measured as a share of the total labor force of both sexes, a reduction in the disparity among countries appears, and countries occupy somewhat different ranks (*Table A4.14). Year-to-year changes in teenage female shares and the spread between lowest and highest shares in individual countries were considerably wider than for teenage males. Of the eight countries providing annual data, all but two had a gap of about 5 percent or more between the lowest and highest shares. As a result, year-to-year changes in shares at times were over 3 percent in some countries, but on the whole changes tended to be less than 1 percent (Tables A4.1c–A4.8c).

In summary, cross-national differences in trends in the teenage share of the labor force as well as differences in level were noteworthy for each sex. Comparative assessment of teenage labor markets and youth unemployment should reckon with these differences.

Teenage Labor Force Participation Rates

The postwar trend in teenage LFPR (the proportion of an age group in the labor force, either as employed or unemployed) was predominantly downward for each sex. The mean LFPR for male teenagers in the twelve countries descended from 72.8 percent in 1950 to 44.6 percent in 1975, an annual average decline of 1.1 percentage points, while the mean LFPR for female teenagers declined somewhat less in the same period, from 59.1 percent in 1950 to 41.0 percent in 1975. While the mean declined in each subperiod, the drop for males was most marked in 1960–1970 and for females in 1970–1975. From 1950 to 1975, cross-national variation in male teenage LFPR increased, as shown by the simultaneous drop in the mean and rise in the standard deviation from 9.0 to 13.5; there was a great decline in LFPR in some countries which had previously been close to the mean (*Table 4.2). LFPR for teenage males was lower in 1975 than in 1950 in each country, although in three countries an upturn occurred between 1970 and 1975. Female cross-national variation tended to diminish slightly from 1950 to 1975, though rising from 1970 to 1975. Teenage female LFPR trends varied more than male in individual countries, since two countries displayed a higher female LFPR in 1975 than in 1950. As a result of these divergent patterns of LFPR change, the rank order of the countries in 1975 correlated weakly with their ranks in 1950 (r_s = + .21 for males and + .37 for females).

Combining OECD data for three points in time and year-to-year national data for

Chart 4.2   Teenage Labor Force Participation Rates, by Sex, in Eight Countries, 1950-1979

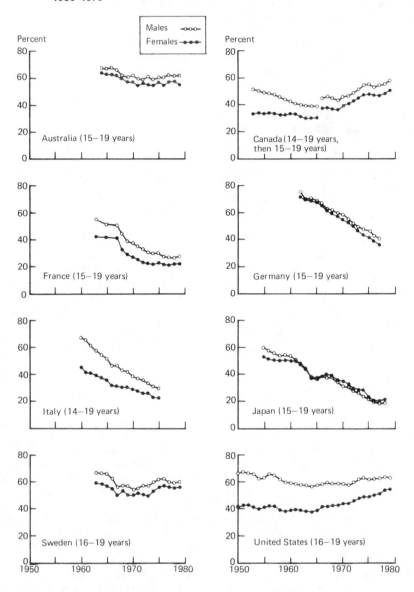

eight countries, we find the countries dividing into three groups, valid for each sex (*Tables 4.2, A4.1–A4.8; Charts 4.2, 4.3, 4.4):

Precipitous decline in teenage LFPR: France, Germany, Japan, and the Netherlands.

Chart 4.3   Male Labor Force Participation Rates, by Age, in Twelve Countries, 1960, 1970, and 1975

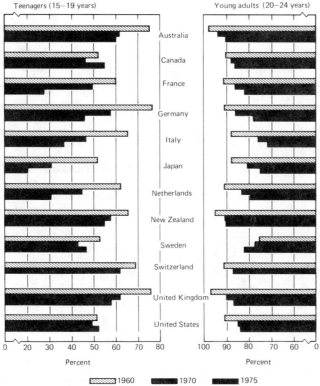

Source: Calculated from OECD, Manpower and Social Affairs Committee, Demographic Trends: Their Labour Market and Social Implications, Annex 2, unpublished revisions (Paris, 1979). Data base includes the institutionalized population and all military personnel. Labor force includes all military personnel. The LFPR scale in the chart is not the same for both age groups.

Moderate to strong decline in teenage LFPR: Australia, Italy, New Zealand, Switzerland, United Kingdom.

Decreasing and then rising teenage LFPR: Canada, Sweden, the United States.

Differences among the countries in LFPR trends for teenage males reflect international variations in the rate of growth of educational enrollment rates (EER), on the one hand, and in the growth of the LFPR of students, on the other. The three countries with a rising trend in LFPR — Canada, Sweden, and the United States — showed a growth in student LFPR, although they also experienced a slowdown in EER growth or even retrogression. Cross-national differences in female LFPR are explained in similar terms, except that the drop in EER growth was less noticeable, and as Chapter 6 discusses, teenage females in some countries expanded both LFPR and EER by reducing the proportion of the age group NISLF, mainly engaged in household activity. A later section presents the regression analyses of LFPR and EER.

Chart 4.4   Female Labor Force Participation Rates, by Age, in Twelve Countries, 1960, 1970, and 1975

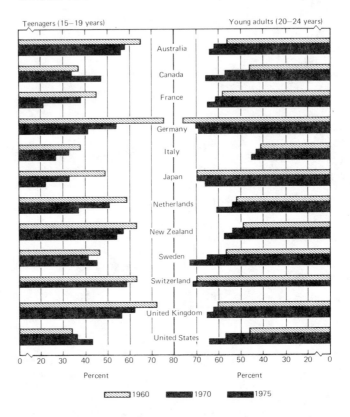

Source: Calculated from OECD, Manpower and Social Affairs Committee, <u>Demographic Trends: Their Labour Market and Social Implications</u>, Annex 2, unpublished revisions (Paris, 1979). Data base includes the institutionalized population and all military personnel. Labor force includes all military personnel.

A comparison of this three-fold grouping of countries for LFPR change over the period 1950–1975 with the bimodal distribution of countries for postwar change in the size of the teenage labor force reveals some similarity in relative position. The four countries which had the sharpest decline in LFPR also had an overall decrease in the size of the teenage labor force. Countries with strong growth in the size of the teenage labor force either had a moderate drop in LFPR or some years of decline followed by a leveling off or upturn. Less association appears between the classification of countries for teenage LFPR and for the share of the teenage labor force in the total labor force of each sex (or of both sexes). A relatively high LFPR for teenagers at any time did not mean that the teenage share of the labor force would be correspondingly high, nor did the two series necessarily move in the same direction.

At the outset the differential among the countries in teenage LFPR was substantial, ranging from a high of 84.7 percent in Germany and the United Kingdom down to 57.0 percent in the United States for males, and from 79.5 percent in the UK to

35.0 percent in the US for females (*Table 4.2). Significantly, countries with high as well as low 1950 LFPR appear in each of the three groups designated to represent trends over the 1950–1975 period. At a later point in the chapter we will present the results of regression analysis which deal with the influence of starting levels on subsequent changes in LFPR.

By 1975, the highest LFPR for teenage males was Australia's 59.7 percent, while the lowest was Japan's 20.4 percent; there was a gap of 25.0 percentage points between the highest rates in 1950 and 1975 and of 36.6 percentage points between the lowest rates in the same benchmark years. In 1975 females in the United Kingdom had the highest LFPR (56.7 percent), maintaining first place. The lowest female LFPR in 1975 appeared in France (21.3 percent), displacing the United States from its 1950 rank. The gap between the highest female LFPR in 1975 and 1950 was 22.8 percentage points, while for the lowest LFPR it was 13.7 percentage points (Chart 4.2). This was a considerably smaller difference than males had.

The three countries which displayed some rise in LFPR include two with high educational enrollment rates (US and Canada) and one with middle-level EER (Sweden). Though Swedish teenagers had only a modest upward movement in LFPR after reaching their low point, national data show Canadian teenagers of each sex with much higher LFPR in 1979 than in the initial postwar period (Chart 4.2; Tables A4.2b, c, A4.7b, c). American teenagers also registered a substantial rise, but only females actually had a higher LFPR in 1979 than in 1948 (Table A4.8b, c). If it were not for the possibility that full-time students could be in the labor force, all twelve countries probably would have displayed declining teenage LFPR over the whole postwar period, since the growth of EER in all countries, detailed in Chapter 3, would automatically have reduced LFPR especially for males.

Sex differences in LFPR trends are much less marked for teenagers than for young adults or other age groups. This is a result of the parallel EER trend for male and female teenagers and the dominant influence of EER on teenagers. Nevertheless, some variation between the sexes in LFPR trends can be observed over the postwar period. Starting levels were markedly different in 1950, with male LFPR on average 14 percentage points higher than female, and at least 20 percentage points higher in Canada, France, Italy, Sweden, and the United States. A gap of less than 10 percentage points appeared in Germany, New Zealand, Switzerland, and the United Kingdom, while Australia, Japan, and the Netherlands showed more than 10 percentage points difference. Despite these differences, a high r_S of +.81 was found between 1950 country ranks for males and females. Over time, sex differences in teenage LFPR have declined in almost every country (Chart 4.2). By 1975 the mean LFPR for teenage males exceeded that of females by only 3.6 percentage points, and a correlation of the rank order of countries for male and female LFPR yields an extremely close association ($r_S = +.96$). The male excess in LFPR dropped in every country from 1950 to 1975 except Germany, where it rose from 1.4 to 4.9 percentage points (Table 4.3). By 1975 female LFPR exceeded male in Japan and the Netherlands.

Similar calculations for sex differences in educational enrollment rates in 1960 and 1975 indicate that the male excess declined overall, although Germany, Italy, the Netherlands, and Sweden displayed a larger male advantage in EER in 1975 than in 1960. All other countries record a narrowing of the EER gap, and the advantage shown by French females in 1960 was even greater in 1975. Both in 1960 and in 1975, countries varied as to whether the male excess in LFPR was greater than their excess in EER. In 1975 teenage females in Australia, Canada, France, Italy, the United Kingdom, and the United States had more room to catch up in LFPR than in EER.

Table 4.3 Sex Differences in Labor Force Participation Rates and Educational Enrollment Rates, Teenagers (15-19), in Eleven Countries, 1960 and 1975

| | 1960 | | 1975 | |
| | Percentage point excess of male rates over female | | Percentage point excess of male rates over female | |
	Labor force participation (LFPR)	Educational enrollment (EER)	Labor force participation (LFPR)	Educational enrollment (EER)
Australia	11.1	7.9	3.5	1.1
Canada	15.1	7.0	8.2	1.9
France	15.5	-3.2	6.5	-5.5
Germany	1.4	4.7	4.9	9.9
Italy	26.9	6.9	10.1	9.9
Japan	3.6	6.2	-1.8	1.1
Netherlands	4.4	3.1	-6.2	14.1
New Zealand	2.3	6.2	1.1	4.0
Sweden	6.3	-1.6	2.1	2.7
United Kingdom	5.9	3.8	0.9	-0.4
United States	4.3	9.3	9.9	0.2

Source: Calculated from OECD, Manpower and Social Affairs Committee, *Demographic Trends: Their Labour Market and Social Implications*, Annex 2, unpublished revisions; Working Party of the Education Committee on Educational Statistics and Indicators, unpublished data (Paris, 1979).

In the remaining countries, the reverse was true (Table 4.3).

Perhaps the outstanding feature of teenage LFPR trends is the remarkably low levels reached in certain countries. For example, Japan's 1978 LFPR rate for males was 18.1 percent and for females 20.2 percent (Table A4.6 b,c). The Netherlands, Italy, and France displayed almost as low levels, reflecting the advance of EER without an accompanying growth in student LFPR. There are thus several countries where the teenage labor supply has been dwindling away because of LFPR trends, apart from the influence of population changes. Japan, with both factors at work, understandably had little teenage unemployment. Moreover, the particular recruiting system in Japan for new entrants to the labor market and the growth of export goods industries emphasized the need for inexperienced teenage workers, who have been hired at low wages relative to those of prime-age adults. Severe labor shortages were therefore reported in the booming 1960s.

In the same way, persistently high youth unemployment in North America can be better understood against a comparative view of teenage LFPR trends. The need to find more jobs for teenagers in Canada and the United States, already driven by strong demographic pressures, was reinforced after 1965 by the rising LFPR of the age group, attributable mainly to students. If the educational and financial situation of students in Canada and the US had more closely resembled that of Western European students, the growth of teenage LFPR in North America might have been less marked and the unemployment rate could have been reduced. In effect, more highly subsidized full-time studies might have partially replaced part-time labor force participation. It is clear that important divisions exist among the twelve countries in teenage LFPR trends. While EER trends are a key element, attention also must be paid to the need, propensity, and ability of students to combine studies with labor force participation. Chapter 5 will explore this subject further.

The foregoing comparative survey of trends in the size, shares, and LFPR of the teenage labor force that has broadly identified the central tendencies and place of individual countries in the array of industrialized nations will be followed by a similar discussion for young adults (20 to 24 years old).

Size of the Young Adult Labor Force

Unlike the teenage labor force, in which the countries essentially divided into two groups with half demonstrating growth and half decline, almost all countries displayed a rise in the size of the young adult labor force of each sex 1960-1975. Both Italy and Germany experienced a decrease in the size of the male young adult labor force, while Germany also showed a drop for young adult females. But all other countries registered positive gains (Chart 4.5; Tables *A4.12, *A4.15).

Data permit an examination of the size of the young adult labor force over the

Chart 4.5   Change in Young Adult (20-24) Labor Force, by Sex, in Twelve Countries, 1960-1975

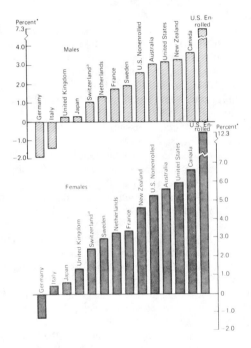

a 1960-1970; *Average annual compound percent.

Source: Calculated from OECD, Manpower and Social Affairs Committee, Demographic Trends: Their Labour Market and Social Implications, Annex 2, unpublished revisions (Paris, 1979). Labor Force includes all military personnel; U.S. Department of Labor, Employment and Training Report of the President 1980, Table B-6 (Washington: GPO, 1980); Bureau of Labor Statistics, unpublished data.

whole period 1960–1975, over the two shorter subperiods 1960–1970 and 1970–1975, and from year to year. Among our countries, most of which experienced substantial postwar economic growth, the young adult labor force in each nation grew more rapidly than the comparable teenage labor force in every case except for Canadian males. The difference in growth rates between the two age groups is striking in some countries: in 1975 the Japanese teenage labor force was only about one-third of its 1960 size, but the young adult labor force registered a modest increase over the same time span. Among countries, there was a wider spread in growth rates for young adult females than males (Tables A4.1–A4.8).

Countries had much the same relative position for the growth of the young adult labor force as they did for teenagers; the r_S was +.76 for males and +.80 for females. Canada, in first place, was eclipsed only by U.S.-enrolled youth, whose labor force reached a staggering average annual rate of increase−7.3 percent for males and 12.7 percent for females. Canada's 3.7 percent annual rate for males and 6.6 percent for females meant that its male labor force had grown by 72 percent and its female by 160 percent in the 15-year period. Generally, both males and females registered higher growth rates in the subperiod 1960–1970 than in 1970–1975. Germany and Italy were exceptions; in fact, Germany's earlier negative growth turned positive in the 1970s. Several countries displayed a positive change in the 1960s and a negative change in 1970–1975: these were Japan, the Netherlands (males), Sweden, and the United Kingdom.

Year-to-year records confirm a consistent expansion of the size of the young adult male labor force in Australia (1964–1979), although the rate of increase decelerated from 1972 (Table A4.1b). Records going back to 1953 highlight the importance of high growth for Canadian young adult males in the 1960s (Table A4.2b). American annual data, starting in 1948, are mostly positive, except for a steady decline in the size of the male young adult labor force in 1951–1957; the highest single year's growth occurred in 1966–1967, fully reflecting the effects of the Vietnam War, inasmuch as these data include military personnel (Table A4.8b). At the other extreme, Germany recorded only six years of growth out of 15 in the case of young adult males (Table A4.4b). Most of the other countries had mixed patterns of ups and downs. Repeating the teenage pattern, the array of countries by growth rates was much the same for each sex among young adults; New Zealand and Sweden were the only countries where either sex was as much as two places away from the rank of the other (Chart 4.5; *Table A4.15). A rank correlation yielded the extremely high r_S of +.95.

In spite of this similarity, sex differences within countries in labor force size are highly significant for young adults, contrary to the findings for teenagers. In most of the countries, the components of change in labor force size differed for young adult males and females. LFPR of young adult males, being high and relatively stable, would be expected to alter less than demographic change, making the latter the main component of change in postwar labor force size. Among young adult females, however, in several countries the size of the labor force would be expected to reflect as great or greater change in LFPR than in population. Regression analysis for each sex confirms that these relationships did exist in 1960–1975.

In every country, females recorded more growth in the size of the labor force than males over the period 1960–1975; the differences between the sexes exceeded that shown for teenagers. Canada and the United States had the largest gaps between male and female growth rates 1960–1975, while the smallest gaps appeared in Japan and Germany. In every country except Germany, the growth rate of females exceeded that of males in the subperiod 1960-1970, in some cases by a wide margin. But the female advantage over males was even greater in 1970-1975, except in Japan where the decline in the size of the female labor force exceeded that of the male (Tables *A4.12, *A4.15). Year-to-year patterns for females in most countries displayed a larger number of growth years and somewhat higher growth rates, especially in the latter years, than those displayed by males. Occasionally, sharp differences appear for males and females in specific years. For example, in 1964-1965 and 1966-1967, when Australian young adult males recorded a 4.6 percent growth in their labor force, Australian females recorded 12 and 15 percent, respectively. In France, males indicated a rise of 20 percent in 1968, while females showed a 48 percent increase; even if these unusually high rates are statistical artifacts, the gap between the sexes appears to be real.

Even more than teenage females, young adult women had a margin for growth in those who were not in school or the labor force (NISLF). It was thus possible for the size of the labor force and the number enrolled to increase simultaneously for these females. At the end of the period, the female young adult labor force generally was closer in size to that of the male than it had been fifteen years earlier (*Table A4.12).

When trends in the size of the labor force of the two youth age groups are considered as an entity, it is clear that growth in the young adult labor force 1960-1975 wholly or partially offset the declining size of the teenage labor force in France, the Netherlands, Sweden, the United Kingdom, and Japan. In Germany, alone of the countries, the fall in the size of the young adult labor force in each sex accompanied a similar drop for teenagers; Italy had this situation for males only. All other countries experienced a mushrooming of the whole youth labor force due to growth in each age group and for both sexes.

Young Adult Share of the Labor Force

Young adults 20 to 24 years old constitute an important part of the labor force quantitatively and qualitatively, and their share of the labor force frequently is greater than their share of the working-age population. The share of young adult males was measured against a total male labor force in which LFPR was shrinking, while young adult females confronted the opposite situation (Cain 1977). The numbers in the total labor force of each sex were rising in most countries, however, due to demographic factors (*Table A4.17). Indeed, as the baby boom cohorts aged they contributed to the size of the total labor force, adding an element of autocorrelation. By 1975 only the first waves of the postwar boom in births had moved out of the youth age groups.

On average, young adult males constituted 11.0 percent of the total male labor force in 1960, the first year for which comparable data are available for the twelve countries. This mean exceeded that of teenage males by 2.6 percentage points (Tables 4.4, 4.1). The highest share in 1960 was found among German young adult males and the lowest among Swedes, with a difference between the two of 5.7 percentage points. By 1975 the mean had advanced only to 12.0 percent, and the country shares ranged from New Zealand's 14.3 percent to Italy's 9.9 percent. From 1960 to 1975, the rise in shares was greatest in the United States, from 10.3 to 14.1 percent (Table 4.4). Germany's decline from 1960 to 1970 and Japan's drop in the first half of the 1970s were sharp. When young adult males are measured as a proportion of the total labor force of both sexes, the range among countries is narrower in all years and the ranks of countries vary somewhat (*Table A4.16). For most purposes the share of

Table 4.4   Share of Male and Female Young Adults (20–24) in Total Labor Force of Same Sex, in Twelve Countries, 1950–1975

	Males				Females			
	1950	1960	1970	1975	1950	1960	1970	1975
				(percent)				
Australia	n.a.	10.8	13.9	13.4	n.a.	16.4	18.9	17.7
Canada	12.5	11.2	14.0	14.1	24.6	16.5	19.6	18.8
France	12.1[a]	10.3	13.2	12.5	12.1[a]	13.1	16.5	16.9
Germany	11.5[a]	13.5	9.6	10.1	16.1[a]	17.8	13.2	14.8
Italy	n.a.	12.4	10.7	9.9	n.a.	17.3	16.2	15.5
Japan	n.a.	12.4	13.9	10.6	n.a.	15.8	18.8	15.1
Netherlands	n.a.	11.4	14.1	12.7	n.a.	22.5	27.5	24.3
New Zealand	n.a.	11.3	13.8	14.3	n.a.	17.1	19.2	19.5
Sweden	9.1[a]	7.8	10.9	10.0	16.1[a]	13.6	13.6	11.6
Switzerland	n.a.	10.9	10.9	n.a.	n.a.	18.2	16.8	n.a.
United Kingdom	n.a.	10.1	11.9	10.8	n.a.	12.7	13.5	12.7
United States	11.4	10.3	13.4	14.1	14.5	11.0	15.4	16.3
Mean	11.3	11.0	12.5	12.0	16.7	16.0	17.4	16.7
Standard deviation (STD)	1.4	1.4	1.6	1.7	4.7	3.1	3.9	3.5
Percent of countries within 1 STD of mean	80	83	83	45	60	75	83	73

[a] Total labor force data derived from stated labor force totals for all ages, less actual or estimated labor force participants under age 15.

Source: Calculated from OECD, Manpower and Social Affairs Committee, *Demographic Trends: Their Labour Market and Social Implications*, MAS(77)1, Annex 2, revisions March 1979 (Paris: OECD, 1979). Total labor force data derived by adding labor force data for five separate age groups 15 years and older. All military personnel are included.

the same sex labor force is most significant and useful.

Changes in shares in the main subperiods primarily consisted of declines from 1950 to 1960 (based on five countries), rises from 1960 to 1970 (based on twelve countries) and drops from 1970 to 1975 (based on eleven countries). No country had a continuously rising share for the young adult male labor force from 1950 to 1975; but Canada, the US and New Zealand exhibited this trend from 1960 to 1975. Only Italy showed a constant decline from 1960 to 1975 (Table 4.4). Year-to-year data confirm the trends of the countries which had a decided direction (Tables A4.1b–A4.8b). Other countries tended to have modulating movements without a predominant direction. In each of the eight countries with annual data, the spread between the lowest and highest annual share of young adult males did not exceed 6 percentage points, and year-to-year changes tended to be under 1 percentage point above or below the previous years' share.

The countries showing an upward direction and the greatest amount of increase in young adult male shares also were those most likely to have above-average shares in the 1960s and 1970s. This evidence suggests that, other things being equal, young adult males would have relatively greater potential labor market problems in the US, Canada, New Zealand, and Australia than in the other countries. At the same time, countries with labor shortages in the 1960s, such as Germany, were hindered by the decline in the young adult male share of the male labor force.

Young adult women had a similar pattern to young adult males in shares of the female labor force. Starting in 1960 with a mean share of 16.0 percent, 1 percentage point lower than the teenage female share, by 1975 young adult females advanced only to a mean of 16.7 percent; this was 5.2 percentage points above the teenage female share in 1975 (Tables 4.4, 4.1). In 1960 young adult women in the Netherlands displayed the highest share (22.5 percent) and those in the United States the lowest share (11.0 percent), duplicating the high and low ranks for teenage females in 1960. By 1975 the Netherlands still was highest (24.3 percent), a reminder of the slow enlargement of the adult female labor force and Dutch society's strong resistance to work by married women. Sweden was lowest with 11.6 percent. The gap between highest and lowest shares, greater than for males, had actually widened between 1960 and 1975. When females are measured in relation to the total labor force for both sexes, their share declines greatly (*Table A4.16).

Over the entire period 1950–1975, only France demonstrated consistent growth in the young adult female share, while the United States and New Zealand showed it for 1960–1975. Sweden had steadily declining shares 1950–1975 and Italy the same from 1960 to 1975; Switzerland's 1960–1970 data moved downward, contrary to the direction for most of the countries. In six countries the typical pattern was up-down for the 1960–1975 period, with Germany reversing the sequence. Particularly large changes in shares (more than 4.5 percent) appeared in France (1950–75), Canada (1950–60), Germany (1960–70), the Netherlands (1960–70), Sweden (1950–75), and the US (1960–75), as Table 4.4 shows.

Young adult female shares were more volatile than those of males, although directions were much the same for each sex in individual countries. In most countries, increases in the total female labor force were strikingly higher than in the total male labor force (*Table A4.17). Gains in the labor force size of young adult females were set against the gains of other age groups of females for whom LFPR had begun to rise earlier. Year-to-year changes in young adult female shares, shown in eight country tables, have a greater amplitude than the male shares, as might be expected (Tables A4.1c–A4.8c). Cross-national differences in the female shares have much the same impact as was described for males.

Young Adult Labor Force Participation Rates

While young adult males followed the pattern of teenagers of both sexes in showing a decline in LFPR, the decrease was modest compared to that exhibited by teenagers, and the level of male young adult LFPR remained relatively high. Young adult females, however, diverge from all other youth groups in establishing an overall increase in LFPR 1960–1975, as well as a rise in nine of the eleven individual countries (*Table 4.5; Charts 4.6, 4.3, 4.4). LFPR of young adult females approached more closely those of males in many countries by the end of the measurement period. The disparate experience of the two sexes sets the young adults apart from the teenagers and marks the situation of young adult females as special. For this reason a more detailed review will be made below of factors influencing trends in the LFPR of 20-24-year-old women, such as cross-national differences in fertility and marriage rates and changing attitudes.

Initial LFPR levels for males in 1960 indicate that nine countries had LFPR of over 90 percent and a mean for all countries of 90.5 percent (*Table 4.5). Sweden had a surprisingly low LFPR of 75.0 percent, which may be an underestimate,

Chart 4.6   Young Adult Labor Force Participation Rates, by Sex, in Eight Countries, 1950–1979

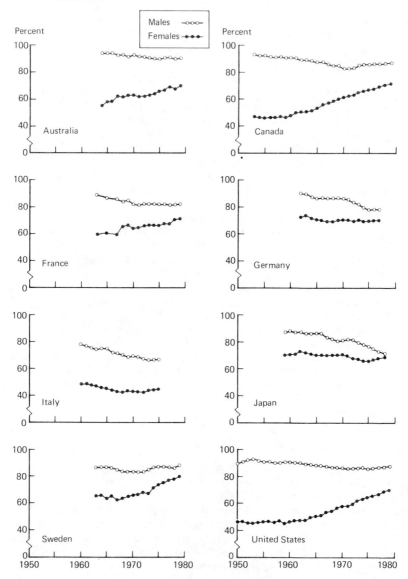

judging from national data 1963–1979, although these are on a slightly different base, tending to elevate LFPR slightly (Table A4.7b). Italy and Japan fall just below the mean, while Australia and the United Kingdom, with 97.0 percent or more, clearly have the highest LFPR, closely followed by New Zealand.

All countries except Sweden displayed a decrease in young adult male LFPR from

1960 to 1975; the mean dropped to 82.8 percent, 7.7 percentage points under the 1960 level (*Table 4.5). The correlation between 1960 and 1975 ranks of countries was $r_S = +.68$, higher than for teenagers. Greatest change 1960–1975 was shown in Germany, the Netherlands, Japan, and Italy, each of which had a drop in LFPR of 10 percentage points or more. Faster rising EER in these countries account for the more pronounced change in LFPR. A later section presents regression results for LFPR and EER. In Sweden the explanations of the divergent path are a leveling-off or decline in EER for males in the 20 to 24 age group and a sharp rise, induced by official policy, in the proportion of students in higher education aged 25 years or more. Year-to-year data indicate alternations of rising and declining LFPR (Table A4.7b). Several of the countries with relatively small decreases in male LFPR had offsets to the rise in EER in the form of increased labor force participation by students.

In most countries the change in LFPR proceeded fairly regularly in the subperiods. New Zealand was unusual in showing a drop 1960–1970 and a slight rise 1970–1975. Country dispersion was somewhat greater in 1975 than in 1970 or 1960, measured by standard deviation in relation to the mean. The highest LFPR in 1975, in New Zealand, was 91.7 percent, and the lowest, 72.1 percent, appeared in Italy, a gap of 19.6 percentage points (*Table 4.5). Year-to-year data for eight countries confirm the general trends but indicate that minor ups and downs occurred even in the midst of pronounced downward trends in seven countries and a milder upward movement in Sweden.

A comparison of trends in the LFPR of young adult and teenage males shows that the 1960 country ranks correlated modestly ($r_S = +.53$). On average, the magnitude of decline in LFPR 1960–1975 was significantly smaller for 20–24-year-old males than for the 15–19 group. By 1975 the mean young adult male LFPR was nearly twice that of teenage males, and the excess of young adult over teenage LFPR reached 38.2 percentage points, having been 26.9 percentage points in 1960. Rank correlation for LFPR of the two age groups in 1975 was high ($r_S = +.86$), however.

In most countries the declining LFPR for young adult males contrasts with the rising size of the labor force of this group and fluctuating shares of the total male labor force. In terms of labor market outcomes for youth, the size of the young adult male labor force and its share of the total male labor force at any given time are more significant than LFPR. In policy terms, however, the levels and potential change in LFPR are of great importance.

Due to rises in female LFPR and declines in male LFPR, the gap between the sexes narrowed perceptibly 1950–1975. In 1960 the mean for young adult females was 56.5 percent, 34 percentage points below the male. The rank order correlation of countries for male and female LFPR in both 1960 and 1975 shows no association, an indication that the national factors influencing the LFPR of young adult females operated in a different fashion from those which governed LFPR of young adult males. By 1975, young adult female mean LFPR reached 63.4 percent, a rise of almost 7 percentage points, and the spread between the sexes fell to 19.4 percentage points.

The array of countries also changed considerably. In 1960 Germany, Japan, and Switzerland led in LFPR for young adult females; the first two were the only countries to show a decrease in LFPR over the 1960–1975 period. In 1960 the lowest female LFPR was Italy's 40.9 percent; but Canada, the United States, New Zealand, Australia, and the Netherlands also were below the mean (*Table 4.5). All of these countries and the remaining countries as well showed consistent LFPR increase to 1975, when first place was taken by Swedish women who registered an LFPR that was about 9 percentage points below that of males. Canada and the US also recorded a gain of 15 percentage points or more in LFPR 1960–1975. Germany was in second place in 1975, in spite of the downward movement of its LFPR since 1960. Last place was again taken by Italy (45.3 percent), the only country with a 1975 rate under 50 percent. Year-to-year data for Australia, Canada, France, Sweden, and the US not only indicate the persistence of the upward movement to 1975, but also demonstrate a strong continuation of the trend from 1975 to 1979. LFPR also began to rise in the two countries which had a decline in the earlier period; this turnabout in Japan and Germany for young adult females may signify the start of an upward trend, observed earlier in other countries (Tables A4.1c–A4.8c).

Country dispersion decreased considerably by 1975, although the gap between the highest and lowest LFPR for young adult females remained very large. Germany's LFPR in 1960 exceeded Sweden's first place rate in 1975. The rank order correlation between 1960 and 1975 country ranks was not strong for young adult female LFPR ($r_s = +.55$). Moreover, in 1975 the rank order of countries for young adult female LFPR showed almost no correlation with rank order for teenage female LFPR ($r_s = +.06$). Young adult female LFPR, which had been 2.5 percentage points above that of teenage females in 1960, showed an excess of 22.4 percentage points by 1975.

Clearly, the rising LFPR of young adult females constitutes a special case. The labor participation behavior of young adult females resembles that of older females more than it does that of teenage females, chiefly because the proportion of young adult females in education is much smaller and the NISLF rate is much higher than for teenagers. While the level of educational attendance and the growth in EER of young adult females differentiates them from the next-older female cohorts, labor force participation rates and patterns of change are fairly similar. A more detailed review of young adult female trends follows, stressing the components of change.

The Female Revolution:
Labor Force Participation Rates of Young Adult Women

Much has changed in the world since Martin Luther confidently asserted:

> Men have broad and large chests, and small narrow hips, and are more understanding than women, who have but small and narrow chests, and broad hips, to the end that they should remain at home, sit still, keep house, and bear and bring up children.

Postwar trends in marriage rates, age-specific fertility, and LFPR of married women and mothers disclose how far women have come over the centuries from Luther's model, which was not fully operative even in his own time. Change in female LFPR in the past century has gradually shifted the bulk of women's labor force participation from the family farm, workshop, or business into paid employment. In the postwar period the rise in female LFPR specifically represents a combination of larger numbers of women in the labor force at any time; more weeks of participation by women during the year; more years of participation by women over their life cycle due to briefer interruptions in connection with marriage, births, and child-rearing; and more part-time work by women.

These postwar developments among wives and mothers tended to affect the older age groups first in most countries. If the movement into the labor force of married women and mothers in the 25–54 age group was strong enough, it might even displace married young adult women from their traditional first or second rank in female LFPR by age group. As the labor force behavior of young adult women who were wives and mothers began to emulate that of the older female cohorts, the 20–24-year-olds regained or achieved first place in many countries. Rising LFPR of wives and mothers added to the young adults' strong LFPR, which was based on a relatively large share of unmarried women, whose LFPR was traditionally high, and an existing higher LFPR of married women in this age group than in older cohorts, because the former have a larger share of women with no children.

A comparison of postwar LFPR of young adult females to those of other age groups indicates a consistent excess in LFPR for 20–24-year-old women over women 15 years and older. As shown in Table 4.6, all ten countries had such an excess at each reading in the postwar period; the amount of the excess varied among countries and over time, but generally was over 15 percentage points. In five countries the amount of the excess tended to rise over time, while in four others it fell; in Germany, with data on only two points in time, there was no trend.

It is clear from Table 4.6 that the postwar rise in LFPR of young adult females, detailed in the previous section, was not mainly due to alteration in the LFPR of un-married women. Moreover, the share of separated, divorced, and widowed women is too small to account for much of the change (Table 4.6). Instead one must look to the changed share and behavior of married women and mothers for the sources of the increase in LFPR of young adult females. For this purpose we have presented data for ten countries that cover trends in the postwar period in marriage and fertil-ity rates of 20–24-year-old females and the share of the age group of both sexes in the working-age population. LFPR over time by marital and maternal status also are of-fered (Table 4.6). Data which facilitate disaggregation of sources of change in the LFPR of 20–24-year-old females have been drawn primarily from periodic censuses of population. Therefore, the ten countries for which we have collected information are represented by different years. An effort has been made, however, to present three readings for each country, covering a sufficient time span to reveal trends.

Changes over time in the proportion of the age group who are married or are mothers would influence the LFPR by a compositional effect, while changes over time in the propensity of wives and mothers to enter the labor force have a participa-tion effect. The two types of change can operate singly, in combination, or in op-posite directions. Clearly, the greatest gains in young adult female LFPR would occur in countries with simultaneous trends toward a declining share of wives and mothers in the population of the age-sex group and a rising LFPR for the remaining wives and mothers. In the following review of the evidence on marriage and fertility rates and the LFPR of wives and mothers, we hypothesize that maternal status has been much more important than marital status in LFPR of 20–24-year-old women.

It is apparent from Table 4.6 that the ten countries vary in both the levels and the trends in postwar marriage rates for 20–24-year-old females. In no country was over half of the age group married at each point in time, but in seven of the countries the rate in many years reached 50 percent or more, and the lowest rate was over 40 per-cent. In Japan the marriage rate was under one-third and dropped only slightly in twenty years, making changes in the relatively high LFPR of the age-sex group mostly a function of the rate for unmarried women and of changes in EER. Sweden's precipitous drop in the marriage rate may be partly an artifact of current reports that Swedish young people do not enter legal marriage until a child is planned or con-ceived. Along with the United States and Canada, these two countries were the only ones to show a decided increase in the nonmarried share of the population, providing a compositional element in their rising LFPR. In the other countries, the marriage rate increased, in some cases by a considerable magnitude. This tended to restrain

purposes, may be omitted from the present discussion and treated as similar to Japanese female teenagers. The low percentage who are married and the tendency of the marriage rate to decline gives married women's LFPR a low weight in the overall LFPR of the age group. Among single women, who traditionally have had a very high LFPR compared to other countries, LFPR has been reduced by rising educational enrollments and the decline of family farming, which engaged a high proportion of all women in the labor force. The small upturn of LFPR in all female age groups since 1974 has been explained as a combination of short- and long-term factors (*Japan Labor Bulletin* c). These trends may soon result in a catching-up to other countries, but as long as young adult females have such low marriage and fertility rates, they are unlikely to show the dramatic changes that appear in countries where wives and mothers have formed a larger share of the age group.

The magnitude of the contribution of the composition and participation effects to total change in the LFPR of young adult females in ten countries is shown in Table 4.7; it takes into account change in the shares and LFPR of each marital subgroup. In the longest time period measured in each country and in most subperiods, the net effect of changed participation rates for each subgroup dominated over the effect of changes in the marital composition of the age group. For most countries the two effects operated in opposite directions, but the participation effect was the stronger; Great Britain was the one exception. Further analysis confirms that in all cases, change in the LFPR of married women was the most important factor in the participation effect. Thus, we can conclude that in the postwar period and especially since 1960, the greater propensity to work of wives and women who were separated, divorced, or widowed has been a far more important explanation than postponement or rejection of marriage, which increased in only four countries.

These results imply profound changes in social attitudes and lifestyles in all countries. But as Table 4.6 indicates, a wide gap still exists between the LFPR of married and nonmarried young adult females in most countries, and among nations the LFPR for married females is widely dispersed. Much room remains for a further narrowing of differences according to marital status, if the Swedish results may be used as a baseline of potential direction and level.

Even more striking than the increased LFPR of wives and former wives is the growth in LFPR of mothers who are 20 to 24 years old; because of the age of the mothers, almost all of their children would be under school attendance age. Trends in age-specific fertility rates and their association with changes in LFPR offer one approach to this subject. Fertility rates for the 20–24-year group are a proxy for a more exact distribution of young adult females by the number and age of their children, and are used because of the difficulty of obtaining suitable data for the ten countries. As Table 4.6 indicates, fertility rates for young adult females varied considerably among the ten countries; for example, it ranged from 110.0 in the Netherlands to 200.5 in the United States in 1947. Among countries, the association has not been close at any point between the precise level of fertility rates and the LFPR for the age group or for married women (Table 4.6).

An outstanding aspect of the rise in the LFPR of married women 20 to 24 has been its occurrence without great change in age-specific fertility rates. For example, Table 4.6 demonstrates that in France, an age-specific fertility rate of 136.9 per thousand in 1946 was associated with an LFPR of 39.2 percent for married 20–24-year-old females, while a fertility rate of 127.0 in 1975 matched a LFPR of 62.3 percent. While in most countries the LFPR of married women 20–24 rose as age-group fertility rates declined, representative years in Table 4.6 show that high years for fertili-

Table 4.7 Components of Change in Labor Force Participation Rates, Young Adult Females, in Ten Countries, 1946–1978

	Period	Participation effect[a]	Composition effect[a]	Net change in LFPR	Contribution to change in LFPR[a,b]		Average annual change in LFPR
		(percentage points)			Participation effect (percent)	Composition effect	(percent)
Australia	1947–1971	+17.2	−7.8	+9.4	+182.9	−82.9	+0.41
	1947–1961	+9.6	−7.7	+1.9	+507.0	−407.0	+0.14
	1961–1976	+8.9	−1.4	+7.5	+119.0	−19.0	+0.75
Canada	1961–1976	+16.3	+1.8	+18.1	+89.9	+10.1	+1.21
	1961–1971	+12.5	+1.2	+13.7	+91.4	+8.6	+1.37
	1971–1976	+3.9	+0.5	+4.4	+89.1	+10.9	+0.88
France	1946–1975	+6.9	−0.6	+6.3	+110.2	−10.2	+0.22
Germany	1962–1976	−2.0	−0.7	−2.7	+72.7	+27.3	−0.19
Great Britain	1951–1971	+0.1	−5.5	−5.4	−1.5	+101.5	−0.54
	1972–1977	+2.9	+1.1	+4.0	+72.1	+27.9	+0.80
Japan	1955–1975	−3.2	+0.9	−2.3	+138.4	−38.4	−0.12
Netherlands	1960–1971	+10.6	−7.9	+2.7	+392.6	−292.6	+0.25
New Zealand	1951–1976	+12.2	−6.2	+6.0	+203.2	−103.2	+0.24
	1951–1961	+3.2	−6.2	−3.0	−106.9	+206.9	−0.30
	1961–1976	+10.3	−1.3	+9.0	+114.1	−14.1	+0.60
Sweden	1962–1978	+8.5	+6.0	+14.5	+58.8	+41.2	+0.91
	1962–1970	+0.3	+0.8	+1.1	+23.6	+76.4	+0.14
	1970–1978	+10.0	+2.2	+12.2	+82.1	+17.9	+1.53
United States	1959–1978	+15.9	+5.5	+21.3	+74.4	+25.6	+1.12
	1950–1960	+3.2	−1.2	+2.0	+161.5	−61.5	+0.20

[a]Methodology follows E. M. Kitagawa, "Components of a Difference Between Two Rates," American Statistical Association Journal, 50 (1955).
[b]Participation effect and composition effect total to 100.0.

Source: Table 4.6.

ty, mostly in the 1960s, did not interrupt the sharp rise in LFPR for married women in Australia, France, Great Britain, New Zealand, and the United States. Thus, as fertility rates for American women 20–24 rose annually from 193 per thousand in 1948 to a postwar peak of 258 in 1960, the LFPR for this group fluctuated annually within a narrow range around 46 percent (Table A4.8c). In other words, there was no dampening effect on LFPR from rising fertility rates. On the other hand, the drop in U.S. fertility rates for this age group after 1960 was accompanied by a rise in married female LFPR, as was true in most other countries.

Additional evidence on the relation between motherhood and LFPR for females under 25 is provided by Table 4.8, in which LFPR data for six countries are presented for women with and without children. Although the data clearly show similar trends in individual countries, LFPR levels cannot be compared cross-

Table 4.8   Labor Force Participation Rates of Women Younger than 25, by Presence of Children, in Six Countries, 1959-1978

| | | Labor force participation rate of women | | | Women without children |
	Year	Without children	With children	Total	(as a percent of all women younger than 25)
		(percent)			
Canada[a]	1971[b]	75.9	30.6	50.5	43.9
	1976[b]	78.0	36.5	58.5	52.3
	(1976)	(79.5)	(36.5)	(68.0)	(72.7)
Sweden[a,c]	1963	81.3	33.6	64.9	65.5
	1967	75.1	41.7	62.4	62.1
	1971	73.1	52.9	65.8	63.9
	1978	82.1	66.2	77.7	71.2
Great Britain	1972[d]	86.0	18.3	61.6	64.0
	1976[e]	69.0	24.0	59.0	77.6
France[f]	1962[g]	63.9	28.6	43.7	42.7
	1975[h]	79.8	48.5	61.4	41.2
Netherlands[b,g,i]	1971	56.9	8.1	31.1	52.9
United States[b]	1959[e]	58.2	20.6	32.7	32.2
	1966[e]	63.5	26.2	39.4	35.3
	1967[j]	62.4	28.2	41.5	34.3
	1970[j]	66.6	34.9	47.1	38.5
	1978[j]	75.5	43.5	58.0	45.3

[a] Women 20–24 years old.
[b] Ever married women.
[c] Children less than 7 years of age.
[d] Women 18–24 years old.
[e] Women 14–24 years old.
[f] Married women living with husbands.
[g] Women less than 25 years old.
[h] 15–24 years old.
[i] Children less than 21 years of age.
[j] Women 16–24 years old.

Source: Canada, France, Netherlands: Census data; Sweden SCB (Statistiska Centralbyrån), Arbetskraftsundersökningen, Årsmedeltal, Råtabeller [Labor Force Survey, Annual Averages, Raw Tables], 1963-1978, Table 1 (Stockholm: SCB, Annual); Great Britain: OPCS (Office of Population Censuses and Surveys), General Household Survey, 1972, Table 3.2; 1977, Table 6.2 (London: HMSO, 1975 and 1979); United States: Marital Status and Family Characteristics of the Labor Force, Special Labor Force Reports, nos. 2, 7, 80, 94, 130 and 219 (Washington: GPO).

nationally because data vary as to the minimum age of the young women, coverage of all women or only the ever-married, and precise definitions of the category "without children." Nevertheless, several conclusions about the six countries can be drawn which probably also apply to most of the countries for which data were not available.

1. An increasing share of the whole age group of ever-married women in this age group was childless over time. Thus over 50 percent of ever married women 20–24 years old had no children in Canada (1976) and the Netherlands (1971), while slightly lower proportions were shown in France (1975) and the United States (1978). In Sweden, Great Britain, and Canada, over 70 percent of the whole age group had no children (Table 4.8). Whether births were delayed to an older age or rejected entirely, the implications for LFPR were significant.

2. In each country there was a substantial gap between the LFPR of women with and without children, but the difference tended to decline over time. The narrowing of the gap occurred chiefly because of the almost uninterrupted rise in the LFPR of 20–24-year-old women with children who, for example, reached the surprisingly high LFPR of 66.2 percent in Sweden in 1978 (Table 4.8). The ready availability of part-time work in Sweden undoubtedly has been a factor in the high level and rapid increase of LFPR of mothers of young children.

3. In each of the five countries, greater dissimilarity in LFPR has been shown between childless women and mothers aged less than 25 than between single and married young adult women (Tables 4.6, 4.8).

4. LFPR for all childless young adult women, without regard to marital status, was the same or higher than LFPR for single young adult women, whether or not they had children, in Canada in 1976 and Sweden in 1978; these are the only countries in which the data refer to an identical age group for each category (Tables 4.6, 4.8).

5. Young mothers who were single, separated, divorced, or widowed tended to have higher LFPR than married women, but there are several exceptions. Government policy toward families, availability of child care and welfare benefits, public attitudes toward unmarried mothers, and educational and socioeconomic differences among the young women are likely to influence the LFPR of the various subgroups. In France, the 1975 census, distinguishing between nonmarried women who were heads of households and married women living with their husbands, reported an LFPR for 15–24-year-old women with two children of 71.0 percent for the former and only 27.0 percent for the latter. LFPR for the same age group with three or more children were, respectively, 43.0 and 10.5 percent (Deville 1977; France 1979d). In the same year, 20–24-year-old Swedish single mothers of two children had an LFPR of 29.8 percent, about the same as similar married women, but much less than the 48.0 percent of separated, divorced, and widowed women. As indicated, however, French nonmarried young mothers of two children clearly had a much higher LFPR than Swedish. In the United States in 1978, the labor force survey indicated that 20–24-year-old mothers whose children were under six years of age had a lower LFPR when they were never married than when they were ever married. In the small share of cases where children were older, 6 to 17 years, the never married had the higher LFPR, 66.7 percent, compared with the ever married rate of 58.3 percent.

6. Information for young women in France, Sweden, and the US indicates that the number and age of children substantially affects LFPR, but the magnitude of the impact has been shrinking over time as dramatic increases in LFPR have occurred among young women with preschool children as well as those with several young

children. For example, French women under 25 with two children under six years of age increased their LFPR from 16.0 percent to 26.8 percent from 1962 to 1975 (France 1979d).

7. National attitudes are reflected in the LFPR of both young women with children and those without, and the size of the gap between each group's LFPR. For example, LFPR has been markedly lower and the gap between the two female categories has been wider in the Netherlands than in the United States, France, and Great Britain (Table 4.8). Moreover, 1971 Dutch census data indicate that the number and age of children were not significant factors in LFPR, since the presence of any children was in itself so inhibiting to labor market participation.

8. It is unclear whether rising LFPR hold down fertility, declining fertility rates lead to increases in LFPR, or both are determined simultaneously by other forces. Japanese experience suggests that, in an unfavorable labor market climate, a persistent decline in fertility can occur without a rise in the LFPR of wives or mothers. In most of the countries, however, there is an association between fertility and LFPR trends, although the existence or direction of causality cannot be established indisputably.

9. Canadian data for 1976 indicate little difference in LFPR between all women and ever married women when separate LFPR rates are computed for women with and without children. The large difference in total LFPR between all and ever married women 20–24 is mainly due to the weight of each group in its total (Table 4.8). This is further evidence that, for this age group at least, marital status may be almost irrelevant in LFPR variation, in the face of the larger LFPR differences between women with and without children, disregarding marital status (Tables 4.6, 4.8). It suggests that the focus of recent theoretical and empirical analysis of the changing role of women in the labor force, which has concentrated on wives, might well shift to mothers, especially in regard to the younger cohorts whose lifetime LFPR patterns probably are set by their early experience.

The foregoing focus on marital and maternal status as supply-side explanatory forces in the LFPR of young adult women should not obscure the importance of several other supply-side factors that have received recent attention, especially in microanalysis. Among these are educational attainment of women, occupation of husband, income of husband or family, amount of time devoted to household work, socioeconomic position, religion, area of residence, and availability and type of public programs affecting mothers and dependent children (Mincer 1962; Cain 1966; Spencer and Featherstone 1970; Gronau 1973; Mincer and Polachek 1974; Skoulas 1974; Gramm 1975; Standing 1976; Bednarzik and Klein 1977; Deville 1977; Greenhalgh 1977; Huet 1977; McNabb 1977; Heckman 1978; Smith, R.E. 1979a, 1979b).

Education is one of the most complex of these factors affecting the 20 to 24 age group. To the extent that young women are still enrolled in educational institutions, their LFPR and marital and fertility rates are restrained; but to the extent that their educational attainment is thereby likely to exceed that of other females, they will have higher LFPR in the long run, accompanied by lower marital and fertility rates.

Differences on the demand side among countries and over time within countries also play a significant role in explanations of trends and levels of female LFPR. Among the factors cited most frequently in recent studies are changes in: real earnings of females, female earnings relative to male, the composition of employment as regards service and part-time jobs, regional and urban differences in quantity and type of jobs available and unemployment levels (Leicester 1978; Lloyd and Niemi 1978; Nakamura, Nakamura, and Cullen 1979).

Noneconomic factors receive attention when trends in female LFPR are analyzed. Many kinds of change are significant, such as social attitudes and mores about work by women outside the home, women's personal aspirations, family goals concerning the education of children, home ownership and retirement, and husbands' attitudes toward participation in household tasks and child care.

Explanations of the postwar explosion in female LFPR, of which the young adult age group is a part, for the most part emphasize a secular movement in which economic or social factors, or some combination of the two, account for change thus far and presage a continuation of the trend, possibly in intensified form (Butz and Ward 1979; Smith, R.E. 1979a). Sharp disagreement with this interpretation of soaring female LFPR has been offered by two Americans, who have written separately and together that the US has experienced a temporary and reversible phenomenon as part of a long-swing cycle (Easterlin 1973, 1978; Wachter 1977; Easterlin, Wachter, and Wachter 1978, 1979). No final judgment can be made about this interpretation of American experience until much more time has elapsed. Nonetheless, a cross-national perspective throws doubt on the general validity of the theory, inasmuch as other countries (Australia and New Zealand) experienced the same demographic boom identified by Easterlin and Wachter as responsible in the US for the prolonged surge in female LFPR, yet did not encounter the American drop in marital rates or decline in relative earnings of young men, and still had a rise in female LFPR. Moreover, other countries (Sweden, Great Britain) with a comparatively small demographic increase have experienced the decline in marriage rates and surge in female LFPR.

On balance, our review of young adult women leads to the expectation that the current cohorts in all industrialized countries will have a greater labor force attachment throughout their lives than their predecessors had, and that later cohorts will display even greater attachment. This revolution is likely to reach into Japan and the Netherlands, judging by the latest reports from those countries. Thus, the separate analysis of young adult women, apart from their male contemporaries and teenagers of both sexes, probably will become more firmly established, and explanations of trends in youth LFPR, to which we turn now, will continue to apply weakly, if at all, to young adult females.

Explanatory Factors in
Youth Labor Force Participation Trends

Among the variables likely to have some or great explanatory power over medium-term trends in youth LFPR and cross-national differences in LFPR trends are: educational enrollment rates (EER), the proportion of students also in the labor force, the size of the youth population, youth share of the working-age population, youth share of the total labor force, LFPR starting levels, real earnings of youth, earnings of youth relative to other age groups, trend level of youth unemployment rates, trend share of youth in total unemployment, trend level of prime-age male unemployment rates, proportion of youth population that is not in school or the labor force (NISLF) and want to work, and net incentive or disincentive effects of government programs. Some of these variables are more important than others; some are redundant or intercorrelated; some lack suitable data over the required time period on a comparable basis for the twelve countries. The last five variables, which are marginal factors to medium-terms trends in LFPR, are likely to be more significant in an explanation of trends in NISLF rates because the proportion neither in school nor in the labor force is quite small compared to LFPR. Therefore, consideration of these last factors is deferred to Chapter 6.

Because changes in EER capture trends in major underlying social and economic factors, we deemed EER a crucial variable. Moreover, it has been our hypothesis that medium-term trends in LFPR are highly influenced by changes in EER, especially for males, since these two activities constitute the main alternatives in their nonleisure time. The relationship would also be expected to obtain for females, if one held constant the proportion neither in school nor in the labor force (NISLF); in our calculations the NISLF group is not controlled. To the extent that individuals combine EER and LFPR, the reciprocal relation is undermined. As Chapter 5 will show, such combinations are more highly developed in some countries than others and are more prevalent among teenagers than young adults.

Regression analysis for eleven countries confirms that changes in EER and LFPR 1960–1975 are closely and negatively related for three of the four sex-age groups. As expected, the two male youth groups had higher zero-order negative correlating coefficients than teenage females (Table 4.9). Males 20–24 show the strongest inverse correlation between changes in EER and LFPR, followed by teenage males and teenage females. Young adult females 20–24 are more prone to choose among several alternatives than the other age-sex groups. Therefore, only a small negative association appears between change in EER 1960–1975 and change in LFPR 1960–1975 for young adult females. In short, the expected negative correlation between EER and LFPR is suppressed for this age-sex group by a positive indirect link due to the importance of the NISLF (not in school or the labor force) alternative for young adult females and the fact that both educational enrollments and labor force participation can simultaneously increase or decrease by a diminution or expansion of the NISLF group. In fact, an increase in EER in this age group, which includes many who will complete tertiary education programs, may directly lead to a rise in LFPR, since female LFPR is positively correlated with level of education completed.

In understanding differences among countries in medium-term trends of youth LFPR, we placed great significance on cross-national variation in the growth rates of

Table 4.9   Correlation between Educational Enrollment Rates (EER) and Labor Force Participation Rates (LFPR) in Eleven Countries, 1960–1975.

	Zero-order correlation coefficients between average annual percentage point change in EER and LFPR 1960–1975
Males 15–19	−0.59
Females 15–19	−0.30
Males 20–24	−0.77
Females 20–24	−0.07

Source: Calculated from OECD, Working Party of the Education Committee on Educational Statistics and Indicators, unpublished revisions; Manpower and Social Affairs Committee, *Demographic Trends: Their Labour Market and Social Implications*, Annex 2, unpublished revisions (Paris: OECD, March 1979). Labor force includes all military personnel.

the size of the youth population and in the levels of starting LFPR. In regard to the first variable, we hypothesized that the higher the medium-term population growth trend for an age-sex group in a given country, the more marked would be the LFPR increase, or the less marked would be the LFPR decline, according to the trend in the individual country. The rationale was that strong and persistent population growth in the medium term would work through EER to restrict the growth of EER, because of limitations in the capacity of educational institutions combined with failure of the public authorities to approve expenditures. Although the proportion of an age-group desiring to enroll in schools might respond positively to the relative size of the cohort, thus exceeding the trend level in EER, the actual EER would be below the trend level because of restricted educational places. Therefore, the cohort would be forced to increase their LFPR or NISLF rate. We further hypothesized that the main effect of sustained youth population increase would be to increase LFPR (or reduce its rate of decline).

Our hypothesis for the youth groups, especially for males, rejects the more general formulation that does not distinguish among age groups. According to this version, LFPR may be influenced by changes in the rate of population growth when the latter is not consistent with the demand for labor. If demographic trends cause the increase in the size of the labor force to lag behind the rising demand for labor, LFPR will tend to increase, and if demographic trends cause the size of the labor force to be greater than the economy requires, the LFPR will tend to fall (Durand 1960). Because of the special relation of the youth groups to the educational alternative and our related hypothesis that the share of young people who are NISLF will not rise markedly when there is a fast-growing youth population or an increasing youth share of the working-age population, we do not accept this LFPR theory.

Instead we expect that LFPR decisions by young people will be fairly independent of the level of labor market demand in the medium term, although short-run fluctuations are influential. A later discussion on the relation of medium-term trends in youth earnings to LFPR elaborates on this subject. Still another issue is the impact of generational crowding or thinning on labor force participation behavior and other youth alternatives, when demand-side influences are controlled. At this point, we are testing cross-national medium-term trends in population growth as an influence on LFPR trends, without controlling for demand-side effects.

In regard to the second variable, starting levels of LFPR, cross-national variations were expected to have a negative relationship to change in LFPR because of the previously cited "regression to the mean" and the fact that LFPR cannot exceed 100 percent or decline below 0. The results support the hypothesis that the lower the starting level of LFPR, the higher the LFPR growth or the smaller the decline.

Stepwise multiple regression has been applied to the influence of population growth and LFPR starting levels on changes in LFPR. OECD data for eleven countries provide the dependent variable, the average annual percentage point change in LFPR (1950–1975 for the two teenage groups and 1960–1975 for the two young adult groups). The two independent variables are the average annual compound percentage change in population for the relevant age-sex group in 1950–1975 or 1960–1975 and the starting levels of LFPR for the given age-sex group in 1950 or 1960.

Both hypotheses are borne out in the expected direction. Each of the independent variables displays a strong effect on cross-national variation in LFPR change, regardless of which variable is entered first. The increment of explained variation is somewhat higher when the population variable is entered second, however, except in the case of 20–24-year-old males (Table 4.10). The multiple regression indicates that the observed impact of each variable is not diminished by controlling for the other, implying that the effects are additive. The explanatory power of the two variables (and associated unmeasured variables) is impressive. In three of the four age groups, 72 to 76 percent of cross-national variation is accounted for, while even for males 20-24, over 50 percent is explained by the two independent variables together (Table 4.10). All eight of the multiple regression slope parameters are significant at the 0.10

Table 4.10   Relationship between Changes in Labor Force Participation Rates, Starting LFPR Levels, and Youth Population Growth, by Age and Sex, in Eleven Countries, 1950-1975

Subgroup	Dependent variable	Independent variables		Variation accounted for by independent variables (R^2)
		Δ POP[a]	Starting LFPR level[b]	
				(percent)
Males 15-19	Δ LFPR/year[c] (1950-1975)	+0.43** (0.30)[d]		68.0
			-0.03** (0.02)[d]	25.0
		+0.39****** (0.09)[d]	-0.02** (0.01)[d]	74.4
Females 15-19	ΔLFPR/year[c] (1950-1975)	+0.40* (0.34)[d]		57.8
			-0.03* (0.03)[d]	46.2
		+0.36****** (0.09)[d]	-0.02**** (0.01)[d]	77.0
Males 20-24	Δ LFPR/year[c] (1960-1975)	+0.11 (0.23)[d]		17.6
			-0.04** (0.05)[d]	26.0
		+0.09** (0.06)[d]	-0.04**** (0.02)[d]	53.1
Females 20-24	Δ LFPR/year[c] (1960-1975)	+0.25* (0.22)[d]		56.0
			-0.04* (0.04)[d]	53.6
		+0.17***** (0.06)[d]	-0.03**** (0.01)[d]	72.1

[a] Average annual compound percentage rate of growth of 15-19-(20-24) years-old population. Computations are based on the 1950-1975 and 1960-1975 periods for teenagers and young adults, respectively.
[b] LFPR in 1950 and 1960 for teenagers and young adults, respectively.
[c] Average annual percentage point change in LFPR (linear estimation).
[d] Standard error of the estimate of the slope:

    *Significant at the 0.25 level.
    **Significant at the 0.10 level.
    ***Significant at the 0.05 level.
    ****Significant at the 0.025 level.
    *****Significant at the 0.01 level.
    ******Significant at the 0.005 level.

Source: Calculated from OECD, Manpower and Social Affairs Committee, *Demographic Trends: Their Labour Market and Social Implications* Annex 2, unpublished revisions (Paris, 1979).

level or better, a considerable achievement with a small sample size. Finally, the two variables together and singly account for considerably more of cross-national variation in LFPR than they did for EER, suggesting that national institutional arrangements and differences have relatively greater importance for educational enrollment rates than for labor force participation rates (see Chapter 3).

The strength of the population factor is shown by the fact that young people in the New World nations, which had relatively larger cohorts reaching labor market entrance age than countries with slower youth population growth (e.g., Japan and Italy), also had a relatively greater tendency to enter the labor force, other things being equal. The relatively greater growth of LFPR in these countries could be partially explained by the rising proportion of enrolled youth who also participated in the labor force. In turn, a pattern of simultaneous educational and labor force activity may be influenced by the demographic trends. That is to say, the baby boom may in part explain a rise in the propensity to combine school and work in certain countries.

LFPR starting levels also were highly significant as an explanatory factor. All parameters are negative as expected, and for both age groups the male and female effects are of the same magnitude (Table 4.10). Unlike the population variable, the starting level is a somewhat stronger factor for young adults than for teenagers. Predicted values for individual countries, computed from the cross-national multiple regression equation (Table 4.11), give the average annual percentage point change in LFPR expected in each country. When these predicted values are compared to actual values, the resulting residuals disclose the country differences unexplained by the two chosen variables and identify the individual countries which deviate most from the cross-national pattern. Positive residuals indicate that the actual increase in

Table 4.11   Country Deviations from 1950–1975 Changes in Labor Force Participation Rates Predicted by Cross-National Regressions on LFPR Levels 1950 and Compound Growth Rate of Population 1950–1975, by Sex, in Eleven Countries

Sex	Males	Females	Males	Females
Age	15–19 years old		20–24 years old[a]	
	(average annual percentage points)			
Australia	−0.17	−0.14	+0.23	−0.06
Canada	+0.14	+0.14	+0.07	+0.21
France	−0.52	−0.54	−0.13	−0.10
Germany	+0.09	−0.11	−0.08	+0.01
Italy	n.a.	n.a.	−0.47	−0.22
Japan	−0.07	0.00	−0.33	−0.32
Netherlands	−0.43	−0.13	−0.26	−0.09
New Zealand	−0.12	−0.11	+0.36	−0.39
Sweden	+0.32	+0.50	+0.42	+0.72
United Kingdom	+0.49	+0.52	+0.26	+0.13
United States	+0.28	+0.17	−0.06	+0.13

[a] All data refer to 1960–1975.

Note: Actual minus predicted values equal residuals. Multiple regression parameters utilized to derive residual series are given in Table 4.10

Source: Calculated from OECD, Manpower and Social Affairs Committee, Demographic Trends: Their Labour Market and Social Implications, Annex 2, unpublished revisions (Paris, 1979).

LFPR was greater or the decline was lower than was predicted, while negative residuals show the reverse (Table 4.11).The largest positive residuals were shown by Sweden and the United Kingdom, which had positive residuals in all four age-sex groups. New Zealand young adult males also had a large positive residual. Large negative residuals appeared for young adult males in Italy and the Netherlands, young adult females in New Zealand and Japan, male teenagers in the Netherlands, and French teenagers of each sex. Trends much stronger than the average that had been predicted point to explanatory factors in each country apart from population change and LFPR starting levels. In the case of Sweden, for example, deliberate efforts by the government to hold down enrollments in higher education, encouragement of a waiting period in the labor force before entering higher education, and an effective policy to increase the proportion of older students (over 25) have contributed to higher than predicted LFPR in all four age-sex groups. For other countries, different explanations, stemming either from the education or labor force side, and perhaps of a less public nature, would be relevant; further investigation is required.

The influence of trends in earnings on LFPR has been a central theme in theoretical and empirical analysis of the labor force, whether earnings have been the earnings of the group in question, real or nominal, or relative earnings (that is, the earnings of a stated group as a ratio of the earnings of a reference group, such as prime-age workers). In the case of secondary workers, among whom youth are an important part, the hypothesis has been that LFPR responded positively to rises either in group earnings or in relative earnings (Wachter 1972). Recent studies on female LFPR have regarded changes in earnings as a prime factor in explaining trends.

Empirical evidence on youth earnings and LFPR in the postwar period raise questions about the applicability to youth of the postulated earnings-LFPR nexus, inasmuch as the direction of causality may be the reverse of what is suggested by the theory. It may be that youth LFPR influences trends in earnings rather than the opposite. Moreover, youth LFPR may operate on earnings trends by way of changes in cohort size due to demographic factors. The unifying element is the influence on youth LFPR decisions of the alternative of investing in their future and life-time earnings and status through additional education and training.

Earnings patterns in the twelve countries varied between those with a decided postwar rise in real earnings of youth (or relative earnings of youth to adults) to countries with a decline in both indices. In Australia, Great Britain, Japan, the Netherlands, and Sweden, postwar male youth earnings rose relative to a reference group (OECD 1978i). Data on full-time, private, nonmanagerial employees in Australia show that males younger than 21, excluding those who received adult rates (estimated at 18 percent in May 1975), earned 45 percent of adult male weekly earnings in 1965; by 1976 it had risen to 54 percent (Australia 1979a, pp. 615–17). A British calculation for manual workers in all industries of average hourly earnings of males under 21 as a percent of all male hourly earnings 1948–1976 revealed a climb from just over 45 percent to almost 61 percent (Layard 1979, Tables 5,6, Chart 2). Swedish hourly wage ratios in manufacturing and mining for males under 18 to adult males range from 59 percent in 1965 to 68 percent in 1976 (Wadensjö 1978, Table 7). By another measure of the same industries, the index number of average hourly earnings (1939 = 100) rose by mid-1978 to 4,054 for youth of both sexes, but only to 2,461 for adult males and 3,481 for adult females (Sweden 1979i, Table f). Unpublished Dutch data show weekly earnings of 16–18-year-old males in industry and services as

40.1 percent of those of 16–64-year-old males in 1972, rising to 43.7 percent by 1978. In Japan, the monthly cash contract earnings of under 18 males soared from 28.6 percent of earnings of all males to 44.5 percent in 1975 (Japan 1958–1980).

This uniform trend in earnings was associated with variation among the countries in LFPR trends; while all had a downward trend in LFPR at first, it was sharper among some countries than others, and Sweden had an upturn in LFPR toward the latter part of the period. In any case, the expected general upward movement of LFPR as a response to rising earnings is not evident in any of these countries. Indeed, the case that declining LFPR tended to increase the demand for young people and hence raised their relative earnings seems easier to sustain. It also is of interest that these countries range from those with a very strong baby boom (Australia) to those with a generally declining youth population (Japan). Apparently, changing size of cohort was not associated in any consistent way with changes in relative youth earnings.

Contrary to most countries, the trend in youth earnings in the United States has been downward. A comparison of male weekly wages 1967–1975 of new entrants (less than five years of work experience) with those of peak earners (23–27 years of work experience) indicated a decline in the ratio for all educational levels. The ratio fell from .56 to .48 for those with eight to eleven years of schooling and from .65 to .55 for those with twelve years of schooling (i.e., high school graduates). Among the college-educated, the ratio dropped from .59 to .55 for those with one to three years of education, and from .63 to .54 for those with four or more years (Welch 1979). Another analysis of the U.S. males measured change between 1967 and 1977 for males with twelve years and 16 years of education, comparing 18–24-year-olds with 45–54-year-olds (Freeman 1979b). This study found an especially large impact on college graduates compared to only a modest impact on high school graduates; this implies a higher rate of substitutability or complementarity of younger for older workers among less educated groups. Neither of these studies investigated the impact of the less favorable earnings ratios on youth LFPR, since they were concerned with the impact of the baby boom cohorts and the changed age structure of the labor force on earnings.

While much more collection and analysis of data is required on youth earnings in themselves and as a factor in medium-term trends in LFPR, preliminary investigation lends support to our emphasis on trends in educational enrollment rates as a fundamental explanatory factor in youth LFPR, especially of males.

Summary

A downward movement of LFPR of teenage females and both age groups of males occurred in most countries in the postwar period. Young adult females had a sufficiently different record to warrant a separate investigation of the remarkable rise in LFPR of young wives and mothers. Among teenagers, an upward trend in LFPR in Canada, the United States, and Sweden after the mid-1960s is attributed to a leveling out of EER and a growth in LFPR among students. The latter factor also served to restrain the drop in young adult male LFPR and bolstered rising young adult female LFPR in some countries.

As a share of the total labor force of the same sex, teenagers displayed diverse trends in the various countries, with greater change among the females. Rising shares in the US and Canada, though from lower levels than in other countries, probably are associated with labor market pressures and youth unemployment problems.

Young adults' shares for males had a spread of about 5 percentage points and experienced the most general rise in the 1960s. Young adult female shares were more volatile than those of males, reflecting in most cases a rise in LFPR of the total female labor force as well as the young adult group. In regard to change in the size of the teenage labor force, countries divided into those which had postwar growth and those which exhibited postwar decline. Young adults demonstrated growth in most countries. Demographic developments were an important component of change in the size of the youth labor force, but in some countries changes in LFPR were of equal or greater significance.

Explanatory factors in cross-national trends and differences in LFPR revealed a close association between trends in EER, population growth trends, and LFPR starting rates. We found that trends in earnings did not behave as a stimulant to LFPR in the expected way, regarding youth as secondary workers. Instead, the human capital explanation of young people's LFPR was closer to the mark.

This chapter has treated each member of the labor force as a full unit, regardless of how many hours per week or weeks per year were spent in the labor force. To the extent that data permit, Chapter 5 will modify these results by reporting on cross-national differences in the work patterns of youth, youth hours versus those of adults, and participation of students in the labor force.

Appendix Tables A4.1b–A4.9c

Table A4.1b Labor Force, Annual Change, Participation Rates, and Share of Youth, Males, by Age, Australia, August 1964–1979

| Year | 15 and older | | | Civilian Labor Force 15–19 | | | | 20–24 | | | |
	Number (000s)	Year-to-year change	Participation rate (percent)	Number (000s)	Year-to-year change	As percent of 15 and older (percent)	Participation rate (percent)	Number (000s)	Year-to-year change	As percent of 15 and older (percent)	Participation rate (percent)
1964[a]	3,252	—	83.9	335	—	10.3	67.7	367	—	11.3	94.0
1965[a]	3,320	2.1	83.8	340	1.5	10.2	66.3	384	4.6	11.6	93.6
1966	3,405	2.6	84.0	347	2.1	10.2	66.6	404	5.2	11.9	93.7
1967	3,453	1.4	83.5	339	-2.3	9.8	64.7	420	4.0	12.2	92.2
1968	3,514	1.8	83.2	327	-3.5	9.3	61.5	450	7.1	12.8	92.5
1969	3,581	1.9	82.7	327	0.0	9.1	60.3	468	4.0	13.1	91.8
1970	3,684	2.9	83.1	334	2.1	9.1	61.2	492	5.1	13.4	92.3
1971	3,757	2.0	82.5	333	-0.3	8.9	59.4	512	4.1	13.6	91.5
1972	3,833	1.8	82.5	331	-0.6	8.6	58.5	510	-0.4	13.3	91.7
1973	3,891	1.5	82.1	351	6.0	9.0	60.5	512	0.4	13.2	90.9
1974	3,915	0.6	81.0	344	-2.0	8.8	58.3	513	0.2	13.1	90.0
1975	3,959	1.1	80.5	364	5.8	9.2	60.0	517	0.8	13.1	90.1
1976	3,993	0.9	80.0	374	2.7	9.4	60.2	522	1.0	13.1	90.8
1977	4,057	1.6	79.8	394	5.3	9.7	62.1	529	1.3	13.0	91.2
1978	4,054	-0.1	78.3	399	1.3	9.8	61.1	531	0.4	13.1	89.6
1979	4,101	1.2	77.8	402	0.8	9.8	61.4	547	3.0	13.3	90.3

[a] Not strictly comparable to data for 1966–1979.

Source: Australian Bureau of Statistics. The labor force survey sample includes the institutionalized population.

Table A4.1c Labor Force, Annual Change, Participation Rates, and Share of Youth, Females, by Age, Australia, August 1964–1979

	Civilian Labor Force										
	15 and older			15–19				20–24			
Year	Number	Year-to-year change	Participation rate	Number	Year-to-year change	As percent of 15 and older	Participation rate	Number	Year-to-year change	As percent of 15 and older	Participation rate
	(000s)		(percent)	(000s)		(percent)		(000s)		(percent)	(percent)
1964[a]	1,289	—	33.0	305	—	23.7	64.1	207	—	16.1	54.9
1965[a]	1,363	5.7	34.1	313	2.6	23.0	63.2	232	12.1	17.0	58.1
1966	1,498	9.9	36.3	327	4.5	21.8	63.0	248	6.9	16.6	58.2
1967	1,567	4.6	37.2	315	-3.7	20.1	61.1	285	14.9	18.2	61.6
1968	1,623	3.6	37.7	313	-0.6	19.3	59.6	299	4.9	18.4	60.6
1969	1,681	3.6	38.1	302	-3.5	18.0	56.6	323	8.0	19.2	62.8
1970	1,789	6.4	39.6	311	3.0	17.4	57.0	336	4.0	18.8	62.5
1971	1,852	3.5	40.0	307	-1.3	16.6	54.7	342	1.8	18.5	61.0
1972	1,921	3.7	40.6	320	4.2	16.7	56.2	345	1.0	18.0	61.7
1973	1,998	4.0	41.4	317	-0.9	15.9	55.0	350	1.4	17.5	62.0
1974	2,081	4.2	42.2	321	1.3	15.4	54.5	366	4.6	17.6	63.8
1975	2,160	3.8	43.0	343	6.9	15.9	57.3	378	3.3	17.5	65.3
1976	2,198	1.8	43.0	334	-2.6	15.2	54.7	385	1.9	17.5	66.4
1977	2,298	4.5	44.2	360	7.8	15.7	57.6	404	4.9	17.6	68.7
1978	2,312	0.6	43.5	360	0.0	15.6	57.5	399	-1.2	17.3	67.2
1979	2,315	0.1	42.9	346	-3.9	14.9	55.0	417	4.5	18.0	69.2

[a]Not strictly comparable to data for 1966–1979.

Source: Australian Bureau of Statistics. The labor force survey sample includes the institutionalized population.

Table A4.2b Labor Force, Annual Change, Participation Rates, and Share of Youth, Males, by Age, Canada, 1953–1979

Year	14 and older or 15 and older[a]			Civilian Labor Force 14-19 or 15-19[a]				20-24			
	Number	Year-to-year change	Participation rate	Number	Year-to-year change	As percent of 15 and older	Participation rate	Number	Year-to-year change	As percent of 15 and older	Participation rate
	(000s)		(percent)	(000s)		(percent)		(000s)		(percent)	
1953[b]	4,206	—	82.9	332	—	7.9	51.7	473	—	11.2	92.9
1954[b]	4,263	1.4	82.2	330	-0.6	7.7	50.2	472	-0.2	11.1	92.0
1955[b]	4,341	1.8	82.1	327	-0.9	7.5	48.6	475	0.6	10.9	92.2
1956	4,437	2.2	82.2	333	1.8	7.5	48.1	476	0.2	10.7	91.7
1957	4,573	3.1	82.3	348	4.5	7.6	47.8	489	2.7	10.7	91.4
1958	4,641	1.5	81.7	349	0.3	7.5	45.6	496	1.4	10.7	91.7
1959	4,687	1.0	81.0	350	0.3	7.5	43.6	495	-0.2	10.6	91.0
1960	4,754	1.4	80.7	359	2.6	7.6	42.8	498	0.6	10.5	91.2
1961	4,782	0.6	79.8	353	-1.7	7.4	40.3	499	0.2	10.4	90.7
1962	4,819	0.8	79.1	367	4.0	7.6	39.6	499	*	10.4	88.6
1963	4,879	1.2	78.5	386	5.2	7.9	39.2	519	4.0	10.6	88.7
1964	4,961	1.7	78.1	398	3.1	8.0	38.3	547	5.4	11.0	88.2
1965	5,065	2.1	77.9	420	5.5	8.3	38.7	578	5.7	11.4	87.6
1966[c]	5,147	—	79.8	401	—	7.8	44.5	609	—	11.8	87.4
1967	5,261	2.2	79.3	415	3.5	7.9	44.7	648	6.4	12.3	86.1
1968	5,354	1.8	78.6	420	1.2	7.8	44.0	680	4.9	12.6	84.4
1969	5,465	2.1	78.3	421	0.2	7.7	42.8	713	4.9	13.0	84.3
1970	5,571	1.9	77.8	460[c]	—	8.3	45.0	730[c]	—	13.1	82.7
1971	5,667	1.7	77.3	479	4.1	8.5	45.4	753	3.2	13.3	82.8
1972	5,797	2.3	77.5	521	8.8	9.0	48.2	769	2.1	13.3	83.4
1973	5,973	3.0	78.2	568	9.0	9.5	51.5	798	3.8	13.4	84.6
1974	6,163	3.2	78.7	613	7.9	9.9	54.5	837	4.9	13.6	85.5
1975	6,294	2.1	78.4	625	2.0	9.9	54.6	860	2.7	13.7	85.0
1976	6,369	1.2	77.6	614	-1.8	9.6	52.6	884	2.8	13.9	85.1
1977	6,505	2.1	77.6	638	3.9	9.8	54.0	910	2.9	14.0	85.2
1978	6,650	2.2	77.9	651	2.0	9.8	54.8	941	3.4	14.2	85.8
1979	6,799	2.2	78.4	678	4.1	10.0	57.2	968	2.9	14.2	86.4

[a] Figures for 1953–1965 begin at age 14. Figures for 1966–1979 begin at age 15.
[b] Figures for 1953–1955 not comparable with those for 1956–1965 or later years.
[c] Figures for 1966–1979 not comparable with earlier years. Data for 15–19 and 20–24 age groups for 1966–1969 have not been revised separately on the same basis as those for 15 and older.

Note: Asterisk * signifies less than plus or minus 0.05 percent.

Source: Statistics Canada, Labour Force Survey Division, *Historical Labour Force Statistics – Actual Data, Seasonal Factors, Seasonally Adjusted Data 1978* (Ottawa: Statistics Canada, 1979); *The Labour Force December 1979*, Table 56 (Ottawa: Statistics Canada, 1979) unpublished data. The labor force survey sample excludes the institutionalized population.

Table A4.2c Labor Force, Annual Change, Participation Rates, and Share of Youth, Females, by Age, Canada, 1953-1979

| | 14 and older or 15 and older[a] | | | Civilian Labor Force | | | | | | | |
| | | | | 14-19 or 15-19[a] | | | | 20-24 | | | |
Year	Number	Year-to-year change	Participation rate	Number	Year-to-year change	As percent of 15 and older	Participation rate	Number	Year-to-year change	As percent of 15 and older	Participation rate
	(000s)		(percent)	(000s)		(percent)		(000s)		(percent)	
1953b	1,191	—	23.4	213	—	17.9	33.2	257	—	21.6	47.2
1954b	1,231	3.4	23.7	221	3.8	18.0	33.6	255	−0.8	20.7	46.6
1955b	1,269	3.1	23.9	222	0.5	17.5	32.9	254	−0.4	20.0	46.3
1956	1,346	6.1	24.9	235	5.9	17.5	33.9	260	2.4	19.3	47.1
1957	1,435	6.6	25.8	239	1.7	16.7	33.1	262	0.8	18.3	46.5
1958	1,496	4.3	26.2	242	1.3	16.2	32.1	271	3.4	18.1	47.4
1959	1,554	3.9	26.7	253	4.5	16.3	32.1	268	−1.1	17.2	46.5
1960	1,657	6.6	27.9	268	5.9	16.2	32.6	279	4.1	16.8	47.9
1961	1,739	4.9	28.7	278	3.7	16.0	32.3	287	2.9	16.5	48.7
1962	1,797	3.3	29.0	280	0.7	15.6	30.9	300	4.5	16.7	49.7
1963	1,870	4.1	29.6	286	2.1	15.3	29.9	314	4.7	16.8	50.3
1964	1,972	5.5	30.5	301	5.2	15.3	29.9	331	5.4	16.8	51.0
1965	2,076	5.3	31.3	318	5.6	15.3	30.2	357	8.5	17.2	52.6
1966c	2,226	—	35.4	330	—	14.8	36.9	407	—	18.3	55.8
1967	2,346	5.4	36.5	337	2.1	14.3	37.0	446	9.6	18.9	56.8
1968	2,485	5.9	37.1	338	0.3	13.7	36.2	487	9.2	19.8	58.6
1969	2,597	4.5	38.0	345	2.1	13.4	35.9	518	6.4	20.1	59.5
1970	2,824	8.7	38.3	391c	—	13.8	39.3	549c	—	19.4	60.7
1971	2,972	5.2	39.4	415	6.1	14.0	40.4	582	6.0	19.6	62.3
1972	3,101	4.3	40.2	442	6.5	14.3	42.0	590	1.4	19.0	62.8
1973	3,303	6.5	41.9	481	8.8	14.6	44.8	621	5.3	18.8	64.8
1974	3,477	5.3	43.0	520	8.1	15.0	47.5	648	4.3	18.6	65.4
1975	3,680	5.8	44.4	528	1.5	14.3	47.4	689	6.3	18.7	67.0
1976	3,837	4.3	45.2	531	0.6	13.8	47.0	712	3.3	18.6	67.4
1977	3,994	4.1	46.0	532	0.2	13.3	46.6	745	4.6	18.7	68.9
1978	4,232	6.0	47.8	550	3.4	13.0	48.0	775	4.0	18.3	70.3
1979	4,408	4.2	48.9	581	5.6	13.2	50.8	798	3.0	18.1	71.3

a Figures for 1953-1965 begin at age 14. Figures for 1966-1979 begin at age 15.
b Figures for 1953-1955 not comparable with those for 1956-65 or later years.
c Figures for 1966-1979 not comparable with earlier years. Data for 15-19 and 20-24 age groups for 1966-1969 have not been revised separately on the same basis as those for 15 and older.

Source: Statistics Canada, Labour Force Survey Division, *Historical Labour Force Statistics – Actual Data, Seasonal Factors, Seasonally Adjusted Data 1978* (Ottawa: Statistics Canada, 1979); *The Labour Force December 1979*, Table 56 (Ottawa: Statistics Canada, 1979); unpublished data. The labor force survey sample excludes the institutionalized population.

Table A4.3b Labor Force, Annual Change, Participation Rates, and Share of Youth, Males, by Age, France, March 1963–1979

	15 and older			Total Labor Force[b]								
				15-19				20-24			
Year[a]	Number	Year-to-year change	Participation rate	Number	Year-to-year change	As percent of 15 and older	Participation rate	Number	Year-to-year change	As percent of 15 and older	Participation rate
	(000s)		(percent)	(000s)		(percent)		(000s)		(percent)	
1963[c]	13,041	—	79.3	1,017	—	7.8	55.6	1,153	—	8.8	89.3
1965[c]	13,110	0.5[d]	77.3	1,083	6.5[d]	8.3	51.5	1,108	-3.9[d]	8.5	87.1
1967[c]	13,035	-0.6[d]	75.4	1,139	5.2[d]	8.7	50.0	1,243	12.2[d]	9.5	85.7
1968	13,165	1.0	75.3	906	-20.5	6.9	43.6	1,494	20.2	11.3	84.0
1969	13,205	0.3	74.6	788	-13.0	6.0	38.0	1,572	5.2	11.9	84.2
1970	13,259	0.4	73.6	769	-2.4	5.8	36.9	1,667	6.0	12.6	81.4
1971	13,300	0.3	73.1	721	-6.2	5.4	34.8	1,657	-0.6	12.5	81.1
1972	13,244	-0.4	72.6	666	-7.6	5.0	32.3	1,660	0.2	12.5	81.8
1973	13,240	*	72.3	617	-7.4	4.7	29.8	1,622	-2.3	12.3	82.7
1974	13,309	0.5	71.7	612	-0.8	4.6	29.3	1,596	-1.6	12.0	82.3
1975	13,649	2.6	71.8	583	-4.7	4.3	29.7	1,660	4.0	12.2	81.3
1976	13,676	0.2	71.7	544	-6.7	4.0	27.5	1,630	-1.8	11.9	81.7
1977	13,636	-0.3	71.2	542	-0.4	4.0	27.2	1,608	-1.3	11.8	81.0
1978[c]	13,471	-1.2	71.9	477	-12.0	3.5	27.1	1,390	-13.6	10.3	81.6
1979[c]	13,576	0.8	71.8	491	2.9	3.6	27.7	1,384	-0.4	10.2	81.6

[a] 1964 and 1966 not available.
[b] Includes all voluntary military and conscripts younger than 24.
[c] Excludes military conscripts.
[d] Entries for 1965 and 1967 show change over a two-year period.

Note: Asterisk * signifies less than plus or minus 0.05 percent.

Source: INSEE [Institut national de la statistique et des études économiques]. *Enquête sur l'emploi de Mars* [March Labor Force Survey], Résultats détaillés [detailed results]. 1978 and 1979. Les collections de l'insée (Paris: IN, 1979, 1980) unpublished data. The labor force survey sample includes the institutionalized population.

Table A4.3c Labor Force, Annual Change, Participation Rates, and Share of Youth, Females, by Age, France, March 1963-1979

	Total Labor Force[b]											
	15 and older			15-19				20-24			
Year[a]	Number	Year-to-year change	Participation rate	Number	Year-to-year change	As percent of 15 and older	Participation rate	Number	Year-to-year change	As percent of 15 and older	Participation rate
	(000s)	(percent)		(000s)		(percent)		(000s)		(percent)	
1963	6,780	—	37.2	756	—	11.2	42.8	767	—	11.3	59.1
1965	6,964	2.7c	37.4	837	10.7c	12.0	41.9	739	-3.7c	10.6	60.0
1967	7,126	2.3c	37.5	875	4.5c	12.3	41.1	810	9.6c	11.4	59.0
1968	7,462	4.7	38.7	656	-25.0	8.8	32.8	1,183	46.0	15.9	64.8
1969	7,599	1.8	39.0	573	-12.7	7.5	28.9	1,266	7.0	16.7	65.9
1970	7,712	1.5	38.9	543	-5.2	7.0	27.4	1,343	6.1	17.4	63.9
1971	7,698	-0.2	38.6	486	-10.5	6.3	24.4	1,337	-0.4	17.4	64.0
1972	7,832	1.7	39.1	466	-4.1	5.9	23.3	1,315	-1.6	16.8	65.1
1973	7,985	2.0	39.6	457	-1.9	5.7	22.6	1,292	-1.7	16.2	65.2
1974	8,146	2.0	40.2	434	-5.0	5.3	21.8	1,295	0.2	15.9	65.8
1975	8,308	2.0	40.8	440	1.4	5.3	23.0	1,326	2.4	16.0	65.7
1976	8,457	1.8	41.2	412	-6.4	4.9	21.3	1,350	1.8	16.0	67.3
1977	8,717	3.1	42.1	412	*	4.7	20.9	1,360	0.7	15.6	67.5
1978	8,933	2.5	44.6	381	-7.5	4.3	21.8	1,374	1.0	15.4	70.7
1979	9,192	2.9	45.4	391	2.6	4.3	22.5	1,380	0.4	15.0	71.1

a 1964 and 1966 not available.
b Includes voluntary military, if any.
c Entries for 1965 and 1967 show change over a two-year period.

Note: Asterisk * signifies less than plus or minus 0.05 percent.

Source: INSEE (Institut national de la statistique et des études économiques), *Enquête sur l'emploi de Mars* [March Labor Force Survey], Résultats détaillés [detailed results]. 1978 and 1979. Les collections de l'inséé (Paris: IN, 1979, 1980) unpublished data. The labor force survey sample includes the institutionalized population.

Table A4.4b Labor Force, Annual Change, Participation Rates, and Share of Youth, Males, by Age, F.R. Germany, 1962-1977

| | 15 and older | | | Total Labor Force[a] 15-19 | | | | 20-24 | | | |
| | Number | Year-to-year change | Participation rate | Number | Year-to-year change | As percent of 15 and older | Participation rate | Number | Year-to-year change | As percent of 15 and older | Participation rate |
Year	(000s)	(percent)	(percent)	(000s)	(percent)	(percent)	(percent)	(000s)	(percent)	(percent)	(percent)
1962	16,872	—	82.7	1,348	—	8.0	74.9	2,230	—	13.2	90.3
1963	16,996	0.7	82.6	1,229	-8.8	7.2	69.4	2,160	-3.1	12.7	89.7
1964	17,036	0.2	82.1	1,227	-0.2	7.2	69.6	2,025	-6.3	11.9	87.8
1965	17,156	0.7	81.7	1,251	2.0	7.3	68.2	1,844	-8.9	10.7	86.6
1966	17,189	0.2	81.3	1,282	2.5	7.5	66.6	1,671	-9.4	9.7	86.7
1967	16,895	-1.7	80.3	1,217	-5.1	7.2	62.1	1,547	-7.4	9.2	86.2
1968	16,784	-0.7	79.8	1,207	-0.8	7.2	60.8	1,522	-1.6	9.1	86.8
1969	16,951	1.0	79.6	1,198	-0.7	7.1	59.5	1,555	2.2	9.2	86.7
1970	17,172	1.3	79.3	1,183	-1.3	6.9	57.9	1,644	5.7	9.6	86.3
1971	17,226	0.3	78.2	1,128	-4.6	6.5	54.0	1,764	7.3	10.2	85.2
1972	17,175	-0.3	77.1	1,104	-2.1	6.4	51.6	1,779	0.9	10.4	83.2
1973	17,121	-0.3	76.0	1,065	-3.5	6.2	48.3	1,778	-0.1	10.4	81.5
1974	16,906	-1.3	74.5	1,062	-0.3	6.3	46.8	1,731	-2.7	10.2	79.5
1975	16,580	-1.9	73.1	1,070	0.8	6.5	46.1	1,670	-3.5	10.1	78.0
1976	16,379	-1.2	72.1	994	-7.1	6.1	41.7	1,671	0.1	10.2	78.3
1977	16,268	-0.7	71.1	981	-1.3	6.0	40.0	1,693	1.3	10.4	78.0

[a] Includes voluntary military and conscripts.

Source: Der Bundesminister für Arbeit–und Sozialordnung, Arbeits-und Sozial-statistik (Hauptergebnisse, 1979), p. 23. The labor force survey sample includes the institutionalized population.

Table A4.4c Labor Force, Annual Change, Participation Rates, and Share of Youth, Females, by Age, F.R. Germany, 1962–1977

Year	15 and older			Total Labor Force[a]							
				15–19				20–24			
	Number	Year-to-year change	Participation rate	Number	Year-to-year change	As percent of 15 and older	Participation rate	Number	Year-to-year change	As percent of 15 and older	Participation rate
	(000s)	(percent)		(000s)		(percent)		(000s)		(percent)	
1962	9,792	—	40.9	1,247	—	12.7	72.4	1,681	—	17.2	72.0
1963	9,845	0.5	40.9	1,178	-5.5	12.0	69.4	1,655	-1.5	16.8	72.9
1964	9,795	-0.5	40.4	1,171	-0.6	12.0	69.2	1,562	-5.6	15.9	71.7
1965	9,805	0.1	40.2	1,190	1.6	12.1	68.0	1,421	-9.0	14.5	70.4
1966	9,719	-0.9	39.6	1,201	0.9	12.4	65.6	1,291	-9.1	13.2	69.8
1967	9,501	-2.2	38.7	1,151	-4.2	12.1	61.6	1,209	-6.4	12.7	68.7
1968	9,493	-0.1	38.6	1,126	-2.2	11.9	59.5	1,191	-1.5	12.5	68.8
1969	9,570	0.8	38.7	1,101	-2.2	11.5	57.3	1,218	2.3	12.7	69.6
1970	9,631	0.6	38.6	1,066	-3.2	11.1	54.6	1,270	4.3	13.8	69.8
1971	9,670	0.4	38.4	1,040	-2.4	10.8	52.4	1,366	7.6	14.1	69.6
1972	9,712	0.4	38.3	1,028	-1.2	10.6	50.6	1,407	2.9	14.5	69.1
1973	9,851	1.4	38.5	963	-6.3	9.8	46.1	1,453	3.3	14.7	69.6
1974	9,878	0.3	38.4	923	-4.2	9.4	43.1	1,460	0.5	14.8	69.2
1975	9,818	-0.6	38.0	905	-2.0	9.2	41.2	1,451	-0.6	14.8	69.1
1976	9,770	-0.5	37.7	867	-4.2	8.9	38.3	1,449	-0.1	14.8	69.3
1977	9,806	0.4	37.6	831	-4.2	8.5	35.7	1,468	1.3	15.0	69.6

[a] Includes voluntary military, if any.

Source: Der Bundesminister für Arbeit-und Socialordnung, Arbeits-und Sozial-statistik (Hauptergebnisse, 1979), p. 23. The labor force survey sample includes the institutionalized population.

Table A4.5b Labor Force, Annual Change, Participation Rates, and Share of Youth, Males, by Age, Italy, 1960–1978

| | 14 and older | | | Total Labor Force[a] | | | | | | | |
| | | | | 14–19 | | | | 20–24 | | | |
Year	Number	Year-to-year change	Participation rate	Number	Year-to-year change	As percent of 15 and older	Participation rate	Number	Year-to-year change	As percent of 15 and older	Participation rate
	(000s)	(percent)	(percent)	(000s)	(percent)	(percent)	(percent)	(000s)	(percent)	(percent)	(percent)
1960	14,553	—	80.9	1,486	—	10.2	67.1	1,412	—	9.7	77.4
1961	14,448	-0.7	80.1	1,438	-3.2	10.0	64.4	1,383	-2.1	9.6	76.5
1962	14,315	-0.9	78.7	1,386	-3.6	9.7	60.4	1,337	-3.3	9.3	75.3
1963	14,248	-0.5	77.4	1,314	-5.2	9.2	56.5	1,293	-3.3	9.1	74.0
1964	14,474	1.6	77.0	1,278	-2.7	8.8	54.0	1,276	-1.3	8.8	75.0
1965	14,410	-0.4	76.0	1,268	-0.8	8.8	51.6	1,253	-1.8	8.7	74.6
1966	14,168	-1.7	74.4	1,089	-14.1	7.7	46.1	1,190	-5.0	8.4	71.8
1967	14,297	0.9	74.4	1,075	-1.3	7.5	46.2	1,245	4.6	8.7	71.6
1968	14,215	-0.6	73.4	983	-8.6	6.9	43.1	1,235	-0.8	8.7	69.1
1969	14,019	-1.4	72.5	934	-5.0	6.7	41.3	1,248	1.1	8.9	68.5
1970	14,070	0.4	71.8	857	-8.2	6.1	38.0	1,312	5.1	9.3	68.7
1971	14,018	-0.4	71.4	828	-3.4	5.9	36.6	1,318	0.5	9.4	68.3
1972	13,918	-0.7	70.2	808	-2.4	5.8	35.5	1,275	-3.3	9.2	67.7
1973	13,901	-0.1	69.4	770	-4.7	5.5	32.8	1,197	-6.1	8.6	66.1
1974	14,028	0.9	69.1	746	-3.1	5.3	30.6	1,190	-0.6	8.5	66.1
1975	14,114	0.6	68.8	715	-4.2	5.1	28.9	1,196	0.5	8.5	66.7
1976	14,134	0.1	68.6	697	-2.5	4.9	28.1	1,160	-3.0	8.2	65.5
1977b	14,666	n.a.	54.1	862	n.a.	5.9	n.a.	1,258	n.a.	8.6	n.a.
1978	14,734	0.5	54.1	840	-2.6	5.7	32.1	1,293	2.8	8.8	70.6

a Includes voluntary military but excludes conscripts.
b Labor force survey methods and labor force definitions were revised from 1977. Data prior to 1977 are therefore not directly comparable to those for 1977 and after. The revised survey from 1977 identified an undercounting of the labor force and participation rates prior to 1977.

Source: Instituto Centrale di Statistica (ISTAT), Annuario di Statistiche del Lavoro 1971, 1976, 1978, 1979 (Rome: 1972, 1977, 1979, 1980). The labor force survey sample excludes the institutionalized population.

Table A4.5c Labor Force, Annual Change, Participation Rates, and Share of Youth, Females, by Age, Italy, 1960–1978

	15 and older			Total Labor Force[a]							
				14–19				20–24			
Year	Number	Year-to-year change	Participation rate	Number	Year-to-year change	As percent of 15 and older	Participation rate	Number	Year-to-year change	As percent of 15 and older	Participation rate
	(000s)	(percent)		(000s)		(percent)		(000s)		(percent)	
1960	6,148	—	31.5	999	—	16.2	45.2	909	—	14.8	48.0
1961	6,198	0.8	31.4	1,000	0.1	16.1	41.7	913	0.4	14.7	48.4
1962	6,066	-2.1	30.4	982	-1.8	16.2	40.8	892	-2.3	14.7	47.7
1963	5,792	-4.5	28.8	916	-6.7	15.8	38.9	855	-4.1	14.8	46.9
1964	5,629	-2.8	27.7	875	-4.5	15.5	37.3	811	-5.1	14.4	45.1
1965	5,491	-2.5	26.7	868	-0.8	15.8	35.7	756	-6.8	13.8	44.5
1966	5,228	-4.8	25.3	751	-13.5	14.4	31.9	731	-3.3	14.0	43.2
1967	5,228	*	25.3	721	-4.0	13.8	31.5	764	4.5	14.6	43.1
1968	5,269	0.8	25.2	688	-4.6	13.1	30.9	781	2.2	14.8	42.7
1969	5,247	-0.4	25.1	696	1.2	13.3	30.9	826	5.8	15.7	43.8
1970	5,232	-0.3	24.8	640	-8.0	12.2	28.8	847	2.5	16.2	43.2
1971	5,236	0.1	24.7	611	-4.5	11.7	27.3	855	0.9	16.3	43.1
1972	5,110	-2.4	23.9	582	-4.7	11.4	26.1	794	-7.1	15.5	42.0
1973	5,267	3.1	24.3	578	-0.7	11.0	25.5	786	-1.0	14.9	43.8
1974	5,430	3.1	24.8	538	-6.9	9.9	22.8	797	1.4	14.7	44.0
1975	5,536	2.0	25.0	537	-0.2	9.7	22.2	802	0.6	14.5	44.2
1976	5,724	3.4	25.7	531	-1.1	9.3	21.7	843	5.2	14.7	45.7
1977b	6,943	n.a.	24.4	738	n.a.	10.6	n.a.	1,013	n.a.	14.6	n.a.
1978	6,997	0.8	24.5	720	-2.4	10.3	28.0	1,031	1.8	14.7	54.2

[a] Includes voluntary military, if any.

b Labor force survey methods and labor force definitions were revised from 1977. Data prior to 1977 are therefore not directly comparable to those for 1977 and after. The revised survey from 1977 identified an undercounting of the labor force and participation rates prior to 1977.

Note: Asterisk * signifies less than plus or minus 0.05 percent.

Source: Instituto Centrale di Statistica (ISTAT), Annuario di Statistiche del Lavoro 1971, 1976, 1978, 1979 (Rome: 1972, 1977, 1979, 1980). The labor force survey sample excludes the institutionalized population.

Table A4.6b Labor Force, Annual Change, Participation Rates, and Share of Youth, Males, by Age, Japan, 1955–1979

| | Total Labor Force[a] | | | | | | | | | | |
| | 15 and older | | | 15–19 | | | | 20–24 | | | |
Year	Number (000s)	Year-to-year change	Participation rate (percent)	Number (000s)	Year-to-year change	As percent of 15 and older (percent)	Participation rate	Number (000s)	Year-to-year change	As percent of 15 and older (percent)	Participation rate
1955[b]	24,550	—	85.9	2,580	—	10.5	59.7	—	—	—	—
1956	25,040	2.0	85.8	2,510	-2.7	10.0	57.0	—	—	—	—
1957	25,650	2.4	86.0	2,430	-3.2	9.5	55.7	—	—	—	—
1958	25,860	0.8	85.1	2,450	0.8	9.5	53.6	—	—	—	—
1959	26,250	1.5	84.6	2,470	0.8	9.4	53.6	3,360	—	12.8	87.0
1960	26,730	1.8	84.8	2,340	-5.3	8.8	52.7	3,250	-3.3	12.2	87.8
1961	27,090	1.3	84.9	2,150	-8.1	7.9	51.1	3,290	1.2	12.1	86.8
1962	27,530	1.6	84.3	2,160	0.5	7.8	46.7	3,770	14.6	13.7	87.1
1963	27,910	1.4	83.1	2,080	-3.7	7.5	42.4	3,840	1.9	13.8	86.1
1964	28,310	1.4	82.1	1,940	-6.7	6.9	37.3	4,000	4.2	14.1	85.8
1965	28,840	1.9	82.1	2,010	3.6	7.0	36.3	4,000	0.0	13.9	85.8
1966	29,420	2.0	81.7	2,220	10.4	7.6	37.9	3,830	-4.3	13.0	85.7
1967	29,920	1.7	81.6	2,090	-5.9	7.0	36.9	3,720	-2.9	12.4	83.6
1968	30,580	2.2	82.1	1,980	-5.3	6.5	37.0	3,910	5.1	12.8	82.2
1969	30,910	1.1	81.9	1,690	-14.6	5.5	33.7	4,050	3.6	13.1	80.4
1970	31,290	1.2	81.8	1,480	-12.4	4.7	31.4	4,340	7.2	13.9	80.7
1971	31,820	1.7	82.2	1,370	-7.4	4.3	30.7	4,650	7.1	14.6	81.3
1972	32,170	1.1	82.1	1,160	-15.3	3.6	27.4	4,460	-4.1	13.9	81.1
1973[b]	32,550	1.2	82.1	1,040	-10.3	3.2	25.3	4,090	-8.3	12.6	79.4
1973[c]	32,790		82.1	1,050		3.2	25.2	4,130		12.6	79.6
1974	33,110	1.0	81.7	970	-7.6	2.9	23.5	3,780	-8.5	11.4	77.6
1975	33,360	0.8	81.3	830	-14.4	2.5	20.4	3,510	-7.1	10.5	76.1
1976	33,680	1.0	81.1	770	-7.2	2.3	19.2	3,290	-6.3	9.8	74.9
1977	33,810	0.4	80.5	740	-3.9	2.2	18.2	3,050	-7.3	9.0	72.3
1978	34,060	0.7	80.3	740	0.0	2.2	18.1	2,930	-3.9	8.6	71.6
1979	34,370	0.9	80.2	740	0.0	2.2	18.0	2,840	-3.1	8.3	70.1

a Includes all military.
b Excludes Okinawa 1955–1973.
c Includes Okinawa 1973–1979.

Source: Japan, Office of the Prime Minister, Bureau of Statistics, Annual Report on the Labor Force Survey, 1969, 1970, 1979. The labor force survey sample includes the institutionalized population.

Table A4.6c Labor Force, Annual Change, Participation Rates, and Share of Youth, Females, by Age, Japan, 1955-1979

	15 and older			Total Labor Force[a]							
				15-19				20-24			
Year	Number	Year-to-year change	Participation rate	Number	Year-to-year change	As percent of 15 and older	Participation rate	Number	Year-to-year change	As percent of 15 and older	Participation rate
	(000s)		(percent)	(000s)		(percent)		(000s)		(percent)	
1955b	17,400	—	56.7	2,220	—	12.8	53.0	—	—	—	—
1956	17,650	1.4	56.4	2,160	-2.7	12.2	51.7	—	—	—	—
1957	17,980	1.9	56.3	2,210	2.3	12.3	51.0	—	—	—	—
1958	18,020	0.2	55.4	2,220	0.5	12.3	49.9	2,760	—	15.3	70.1
1959	18,080	0.3	54.5	2,230	0.5	12.3	49.6	2,770	0.4	15.1	70.8
1960	18,380	1.7	54.5	2,190	-1.8	11.9	49.0	2,900	4.7	15.6	70.9
1961	18,540	0.9	54.3	2,100	-4.1	11.3	49.3	3,170	9.3	17.0	72.5
1962	18,610	0.4	53.4	2,100	0.0	11.3	46.8	3,200	0.9	17.2	71.9
1963	18,620	0.1	52.0	2,000	-4.8	10.7	41.9	3,280	2.5	17.5	70.7
1964	18,780	0.9	51.1	1,880	-6.0	10.0	37.4	3,250	-0.9	17.1	70.2
1965	19,030	1.3	50.6	1,910	1.6	10.0	35.8	3,100	-4.6	15.9	70.1
1966	19,490	2.4	50.9	2,140	12.0	11.0	38.0	3,130	1.0	15.7	70.0
1967	19,910	2.2	51.2	2,140	0.0	10.8	38.8	3,320	6.1	16.6	70.1
1968	20,030	0.6	50.7	1,990	-7.0	9.9	38.1	3,500	5.4	17.4	70.6
1969	20,070	0.2	50.1	1,700	-14.6	8.5	35.0	3,740	6.9	18.5	69.2
1970	20,240	0.8	49.9	1,530	-10.0	7.6	33.6	3,880	3.7	19.4	67.3
1971	20,050	-0.9	48.8	1,370	-10.5	6.8	31.7	3,670	-5.4	18.5	67.1
1972	19,820	-1.1	47.7	1,170	-14.6	5.9	28.5	3,470	-5.4	17.1	67.0
1973b	20,340	2.6	48.3	1,120	-4.3	5.5	28.1	3,500	0.9	17.1	65.8
1973c	20,470	—	48.2	1,130	—	5.5	28.0	3,500	—	17.1	65.9
1974	19,990	-2.3	46.6	950	-15.5	4.8	23.9	3,190	-8.9	16.0	66.5
1975	19,870	-0.6	45.8	850	-10.5	4.3	21.9	3,010	-5.6	15.2	67.9
1976	20,100	1.2	45.8	740	-12.9	3.7	19.2	2,870	-4.7	14.3	68.3
1977	20,700	3.0	46.7	770	4.1	3.7	19.9	2,790	-2.8	13.7	67.9
1978	21,250	2.7	47.4	790	2.6	3.7	20.2	2,730	-2.2	12.8	68.3
1979	21,600	1.6	47.6	730	-7.6	3.4	18.6	2,760	1.1	12.8	69.9

a Includes all military, if any.
b Excludes Okinawa 1955-1973.
c Includes Okinawa 1973-1979.

Source: Japan, Office of the Prime Minister, Bureau of Statistics, Annual Report on the Labor Force Survey, 1969, 1970, 1979. The labor force survey sample includes the institutionalized population.

Table A4.7b Labor Force, Annual Change, Participation Rates, and Share of Youth, Males, by Age, Sweden, 1963-1979

| | 16-74 | | | Total Labor Force[a] 16-19 | | | | 20-24 | | | |
Year	Number (000s)	Year-to-year change	Participation rate (percent)	Number (000s)	Year-to-year change	As percent of 16-74 (percent)	Participation rate	Number (000s)	Year-to-year change	As percent of 16-74 (percent)	Participation rate
1963	2,375	—	86.2	177	—	7.5	67.0	230	—	9.7	86.8
1964	2,379	0.2	85.5	175	-1.1	7.4	66.3	246	6.9	10.3	86.9
1965	2,393	0.6	85.0	171	-2.3	7.1	65.8	263	6.9	11.0	86.5
1966	2,404	0.5	84.4	157	-8.2	6.5	61.8	278	5.7	11.6	85.5
1967	2,389	-1.2	83.2	137	-12.7	5.7	55.9	284	2.2	11.9	84.3
1968	2,391	0.1	83.0	135	-1.5	5.6	57.2	283	-0.4	11.8	83.5
1969	2,387	-0.2	82.3	130	-3.7	5.4	56.3	284	0.4	11.9	83.8
1970[b]	2,399	0.5	81.7	125	-3.8	5.2	54.6	282	-0.7	11.8	83.7
1970[c]	2,393	0.3	81.5	125	-3.8	5.2	54.6	281	-1.1	11.7	83.4
1971	2,398	0.2	81.2	125	0.0	5.2	55.3	275	-2.1	11.5	83.1
1972	2,381	-0.7	80.6	126	0.8	5.3	56.5	263	-4.4	11.0	83.2
1973	2,371	-0.4	80.3	125	-0.8	5.3	56.3	255	-3.0	10.8	84.2
1974	2,378	0.3	80.5	133	6.4	5.6	60.2	252	-1.2	10.6	86.0
1975	2,394	0.7	80.7	136	2.3	5.7	61.5	252	0.0	10.5	87.5
1976	2,386	-0.3	80.1	136	0.0	5.7	62.1	250	-0.8	10.5	87.4
1977	2,367	-0.8	79.2	130	-4.4	5.5	59.6	250	0.0	10.6	87.1
1978	2,365	-0.1	78.9	128	-1.5	5.4	58.7	247	-1.2	10.4	86.7
1979	2,379	0.6	79.1	132	3.1	5.5	60.0	250	1.2	10.5	88.0

[a] Includes voluntary military and all conscripts.
[b] 1963-1970 quarterly averages.
[c] 1970-1979 monthly averages.

Source: Central Bureau of Statistics (SCB), *Arbetskraftsundersökningen, Årsmedeltal* (Stockholm: SCB, annual). The labor force survey sample includes the institutionalized population.

Table A4.7c   Labor Force, Annual Change, Participation Rates, and Share of Youth, Females, by Age, Sweden, 1963–1979

Year	16-74 Number (000s)	16-74 Year-to-year change	16-74 Participation rate (percent)	Total Labor Force[a] — 16-19 Number (000s)	16-19 Year-to-year change	16-19 As percent of 16-74 (percent)	16-19 Participation rate (percent)	20-24 Number (000s)	20-24 Year-to-year change	20-24 As percent of 16-74 (percent)	20-24 Participation rate (percent)
1963	1,373	—	49.4	151	—	11.0	59.6	165	—	12.0	64.9
1964	1,368	-0.4	48.8	149	-1.3	10.9	59.0	178	7.9	13.0	65.7
1965	1,378	0.7	48.7	142	-4.7	10.3	57.0	184	3.4	13.4	63.6
1966	1,416	2.8	49.6	133	-6.3	9.4	54.7	198	7.6	14.0	64.6
1967	1,410	-0.4	49.1	120	-9.8	8.5	50.9	199	0.5	14.1	62.4
1968	1,457	3.3	50.5	122	1.7	8.4	54.0	206	3.5	14.1	63.6
1969	1,494	2.5	51.5	112	-8.2	7.5	50.6	209	1.5	14.0	64.4
1970[b]	1,549	3.7	52.9	112	0.0	7.2	50.9	207	-1.0	13.4	64.3
1970[c]	1,546	3.5	52.8	112	0.0	7.2	50.9	210	0.5	13.6	65.2
1971	1,590	2.8	54.0	113	0.9	7.1	51.9	209	-0.5	13.1	65.8
1972	1,615	1.6	54.7	108	-4.4	6.7	50.4	207	-1.0	12.8	68.0
1973	1,629	0.9	55.2	105	-2.8	6.4	49.8	198	-4.3	12.2	67.6
1974	1,688	3.6	57.1	112	6.7	6.6	53.4	201	1.5	11.9	71.1
1975	1,756	4.0	59.2	118	5.4	6.7	56.2	204	1.5	11.6	73.7
1976	1,787	1.8	60.0	120	1.7	6.7	57.4	207	1.5	11.6	75.5
1977	1,824	2.1	61.1	116	-3.3	6.4	56.1	211	1.9	11.6	77.1
1978	1,863	2.1	62.2	115	-0.9	6.2	55.5	212	0.5	11.4	77.6
1979	1,909	2.5	63.5	119	3.5	6.2	56.5	218	2.8	11.4	79.9

a Includes voluntary military, if any.
b 1963–1970 quarterly averages.
c 1970–1979 monthly averages.

Source: Central Bureau of Statistics (SCB), *Arbetskraftsundersökningen, Årsmedeltal* (Stockholm: SCB, annual). The labor force survey sample includes the institutionalized population.

Table A4.8b Labor Force, Annual Change, Participation Rates, and Share of Youth, Males, by Age, United States, 1948–1979

Year	16 and older			Total Labor Force[a]							
				16–19				20–24			
	Total labor force (000s)	Year-to-year change	Participation rate (percent)	Total labor force (000s)	Year-to-year change	As percent of 16 and older (percent)	Participation rate (percent)	Total labor force (000s)	Year-to-year change	As percent of 16 and older (percent)	Participation rate (percent)
1948	44,729	—	87.0	3,002	—	6.7	67.0	5,117	—	11.4	85.7
1949	45,097	0.8	86.9	2,899	-3.4	6.4	66.4	5,198	1.6	11.5	87.8
1950	45,446	0.8	86.8	2,821	-2.7	6.2	65.9	5,224	0.5	11.5	89.1
1951	46,063	1.4	87.3	2,865	1.6	6.2	67.5	5,267	0.8	11.4	91.1
1952	46,416	0.8	87.2	2,812	-1.8	6.1	65.9	5,223	-0.8	11.3	92.1
1953	47,131	1.5	86.9	2,777	-1.2	5.9	64.9	5,084	-2.7	10.8	92.2
1954	47,275	0.3	86.4	2,726	-1.8	5.8	62.2	4,959	-2.5	10.5	91.5
1955	47,488	0.5	86.2	2,812	3.2	5.9	63.0	4,851	-2.2	10.2	90.8
1956	47,914	0.9	86.3	2,947	4.8	6.2	65.0	4,814	-0.8	10.0	89.8
1957	47,964	0.1	85.5	2,985	1.3	6.2	64.2	4,781	-0.7	10.0	89.5
1958	48,126	0.3	85.0	2,951	-1.1	6.1	61.3	4,849	1.4	10.1	90.1
1959	48,405	0.6	84.5	3,042	3.1	6.3	59.7	4,987	2.8	10.3	90.2
1960[b]	48,870	1.0	84.0	3,184	4.7	6.5	59.4	5,089	2.0	10.4	89.8
1961	49,193	0.7	83.6	3,229	1.4	6.6	58.1	5,187	1.9	10.5	89.1
1962	49,395	0.4	82.8	3,252	0.7	6.6	57.7	5,275	1.6	10.7	88.3
1963	49,835	0.9	82.2	3,406	4.7	6.8	56.8	5,471	3.8	11.0	88.0
1964	50,387	1.1	81.9	3,575	5.0	7.1	56.1	5,704	4.3	11.3	88.0
1965	50,946	1.1	81.5	3,831	7.2	7.5	56.7	5,926	3.9	11.6	87.9
1966	51,560	1.2	81.4	4,123	7.6	8.0	58.1	6,139	3.6	11.9	87.5
1967	52,398	1.6	81.5	4,214	2.2	8.0	59.2	6,546	6.6	12.5	86.5
1968	53,030	1.2	81.2	4,195	-0.5	7.9	58.3	6,788	3.7	12.8	86.8
1969	53,688	1.2	80.9	4,282	2.1	8.0	58.3	7,088	4.4	13.2	86.6
1970	54,343	1.2	80.6	4,395	2.6	8.1	58.4	7,378	4.1	13.6	85.7
1971	54,797	0.8	80.0	4,489	2.1	8.2	58.0	7,608	3.1	13.9	85.9
1972	55,671	1.6	79.7	4,791	6.1	8.6	59.9	7,795	2.5	14.0	86.8
1973	56,479	1.5	79.5	5,039	5.2	8.6	61.6	8,021	2.9	14.2	87.3
1974	57,349	1.5	79.4	5,189	3.0	9.0	62.5	8,105	1.0	14.1	85.9
1975	57,706	0.6	78.5	5,127	-1.2	8.9	60.9	8,186	1.0	14.2	86.4
1976	58,397	1.2	78.1	5,178	1.0	8.9	61.0	8,421	2.9	14.4	86.7
1977	59,469	1.8	78.3	5,315	2.6	8.9	62.5	8,623	2.4	14.5	87.1
1978	60,535	1.8	78.4	5,383	1.3	8.9	63.5	8,811	2.2	14.6	87.6
1979	61,466	1.5	78.4	5,309	-1.4	8.6	63.0	8,983	2.0	14.6	87.6

[a] Includes voluntary military all years and conscripts 1948–1973.
[b] From 1960, includes Alaska and Hawaii.

Source: U.S. Department of Labor, Employment and Training Report of the President 1979, Tables A-2 and A-12 (Washington: GPO, 1979); unpublished data. The labor force survey sample excludes the institutionalized population.

Table A4.8c   Labor Force, Annual Change, Participation Rates, and Share of Youth, Females, by Age, United States, 1948–1979

	16 and older			Total Labor Force[a] 16–19				20–24			
Year	Total labor force (000s)	Year-to-year change	Participation rate (percent)	Total labor force (000s)	Year-to-year change	As percent of 16 and older (percent)	Participation rate	Total labor force (000s)	Year-to-year change	As percent of 16 and older (percent)	Participation rate
1948	17,351	—	32.7	1,835	—	10.6	42.0	2,721	—	15.7	45.3
1949	17,806	2.6	33.2	1,813	-1.2	10.2	42.4	2,662	-2.2	15.0	45.0
1950	18,412	3.4	33.9	1,714	-5.5	9.3	41.0	2,681	0.7	14.6	46.1
1951	19,054	3.5	34.7	1,763	2.9	9.3	42.5	2,670	-0.4	14.0	46.6
1952	19,314	1.4	34.8	1,758	-0.3	9.1	42.4	2,519	-5.7	13.0	44.8
1953	19,429	0.6	34.5	1,713	-2.6	8.8	40.8	2,447	-2.9	12.6	44.5
1954	19,718	1.5	34.6	1,688	-1.5	8.6	39.5	2,441	-0.2	12.4	45.3
1955	20,584	4.4	35.7	1,729	2.4	8.4	40.7	2,458	0.7	11.9	46.0
1956	21,495	4.4	36.9	1,868	8.0	8.7	42.3	2,467	0.7	11.5	46.4
1957	21,765	1.3	36.9	1,866	-0.1	8.6	41.1	2,453	-0.6	11.3	46.0
1958	22,149	1.8	37.1	1,838	-1.5	8.3	39.1	2,510	2.3	11.3	46.4
1959	22,516	1.7	37.2	1,902	3.5	8.4	38.2	2,484	-1.0	11.0	45.2
1960b	23,272	3.4	37.8	2,062	8.2	8.9	39.4	2,590	4.3	10.7	46.2
1961	23,838	2.4	38.1	2,148	4.2	9.0	39.7	2,708	4.6	11.4	47.1
1962	24,047	0.9	38.0	2,152	0.2	8.9	39.1	2,814	3.9	11.7	47.4
1963	24,736	2.9	38.3	2,238	4.0	9.0	38.0	2,970	5.5	12.0	47.6
1964	25,443	2.9	38.7	2,321	3.7	9.1	37.1	3,220	8.4	12.7	49.5
1965	26,232	3.1	39.3	2,519	8.5	9.6	38.1	3,375	4.8	12.9	50.0
1966	27,333	4.2	40.3	2,880	14.3	10.5	41.5	3,601	6.7	13.2	51.5
1967	28,395	3.9	41.2	2,897	0.6	10.2	41.7	3,981	10.6	14.0	53.4
1968	29,242	3.0	41.6	2,948	1.8	10.1	42.0	4,251	6.8	14.5	54.6
1969	30,551	4.5	42.7	3,109	5.5	10.2	43.3	4,615	8.6	15.1	56.8
1970	31,560	3.3	43.4	3,250	4.5	10.3	44.0	4,893	6.0	15.5	57.8
1971	32,132	1.8	43.4	3,301	1.6	10.3	43.5	5,090	4.0	15.8	57.8
1972	33,320	3.7	43.9	3,576	8.3	10.7	45.9	5,337	4.9	16.0	59.1
1973	34,561	3.7	44.7	3,809	6.6	11.0	47.9	5,618	5.3	16.3	61.2
1974	35,892	3.9	45.7	4,005	5.1	11.2	49.3	5,867	4.4	16.3	63.2
1975	37,087	3.3	46.4	4,059	1.3	10.9	49.3	6,116	4.2	16.5	64.3
1976	38,520	3.9	47.4	4,159	2.5	10.8	50.1	6,339	3.6	16.5	65.2
1977	40,067	4.0	48.5	4,286	3.1	10.7	51.5	6,619	4.4	16.5	66.7
1978	42,002	4.8	50.1	4,482	4.6	10.7	54.0	6,926	4.6	16.5	68.5
1979	43,531	3.6	51.1	4,504	0.5	10.3	54.6	7,100	2.5	16.3	69.3

a Includes voluntary military.
b From 1960, includes Alaska and Hawaii.

Source: U.S. Department of Labor, Employment and Training Report of the President 1979, Tables A-2 and A-12 (Washington: GPO, 1979); unpublished data. The labor force survey sample excludes the institutionalized population.

Table A4.9b Labor Force, Annual Change, Participation Rates, and Share of Youth, Males, by Age, in Four Countries, 1950–1975

	Total Labor Force							
	15 and older		15–19			20–24		
Country and year	Number	Participation rate	Number	As percent of 15 and older	Participation rate	Number	As percent of 15 and older	Participation rate
	(000s)	(percent)	(000s)	(percent)	(percent)	(000s)	(percent)	(percent)
Netherlands								
1950	2,971	84.3	297	10.0	71.7	n.a.	n.a.	n.a.
1960	3,256	82.3	297	9.1	63.5	372	11.4	90.7
1970	3,592	76.6	255	7.1	44.8	506	14.1	83.2
1975	3,609	71.7	185	5.1	30.9	458	12.7	79.4
New Zealand								
1950	574	84.2	49	8.5	71.0	n.a.	n.a.	n.a.
1960	654	82.3	61	9.3	65.6	74	11.3	94.9
1970	774	81.6	75	9.7	58.1	107	13.8	91.5
1975	846	78.9	85	10.0	55.6	121	14.3	91.7
Switzerland								
1950	1,513	88.8	124	8.2	73.8	n.a.	n.a.	n.a.
1960	1,756	87.3	146	8.3	69.2	191	10.9	91.0
1970	1,952	76.3	141	7.2	62.7	213	10.9	87.7
1975	n.a.	n.a.	n.a.	n.a.	n.a.	n.a.	n.a.	n.a.
United Kingdom								
1950	15,899	85.5	1,370	8.6	84.7	n.a.	n.a.	n.a.
1960	16,487	85.9	1,392	8.4	76.3	1,673	10.1	97.0
1970	16,365	81.7	1,224	7.5	62.1	1,951	11.9	90.6
1975	16,075	78.1	1,225	7.6	57.6	1,739	10.8	87.7

Source: OECD, Manpower and Social Affairs Committee, *Demographic Trends: Their Labour Market and Social Implications,* unpublished revisions, 1979. Data base includes the institutionalized population.

Table A4.9c Labor Force, Annual Change, Participation Rates, and Share of Youth, Females, by Age, in Four Countries, 1950–1975

Country and year	15 and older		Total Labor Force					
			15–19			20–24		
	Number	Participation rate	Number	As percent of 15 and older	Participation rate	Number	As percent of 15 and older	Participation rate
	(000s)	(percent)	(000s)	(percent)	(percent)	(000s)	(percent)	(percent)
Netherlands								
1950	917	26.3	241	26.3	60.7	n.a.	n.a.	n.a.
1960	919	22.5	264	28.7	59.1	207	22.5	52.3
1970	1,137	23.7	277	24.4	51.1	313	27.5	54.3
1975	1,383	26.8	213	15.4	37.2	336	24.3	60.8
New Zealand								
1950	177	26.0	41	23.2	63.1	n.a.	n.a.	n.a.
1960	217	27.1	57	26.3	63.3	37	17.1	49.3
1970	323	33.3	72	22.3	57.6	62	19.2	53.9
1975	369	33.9	79	21.4	54.5	72	19.5	57.6
Switzerland								
1950	640	33.7	108	16.9	63.9	n.a.	n.a.	n.a.
1960	753	35.2	126	16.7	63.3	137	18.2	69.9
1970	1,038	46.3	127	12.2	58.3	174	16.8	71.3
1975	n.a.	n.a.	n.a.	n.a.	n.a.	n.a.	n.a.	n.a.
United Kingdom								
1950	7,056	34.4	1,319	18.7	79.5	n.a.	n.a.	n.a.
1960	8,015	37.9	1,268	15.8	72.0	1,015	12.7	60.4
1970	9,578	43.3	1,168	12.2	62.3	1,293	13.5	61.6
1975	9,720	43.5	1,143	11.8	56.7	1,239	12.7	65.4

Source: OECD, Manpower and Social Affairs Committee, Demographic Trends: Their Labour Market and Social Implications, unpublished revisions, 1979. Data base includes the institutionalized population.

Appendix 4:1   Sources of Youth Labor Force Data:
The Situation at the End of 1979

National Labor Force Surveys

Eight of the twelve countries included in this study have conducted regular labor force surveys during the postwar period.* Initiated by the United States in 1940, the modern labor force survey, conforming closely to U.S. concepts, spread to Canada, Japan, Sweden and Australia. Germany, France, and Italy have also developed and conducted labor force surveys which vary from, but are comparable to, those of the other five countries.

Results from the eight national series are presented in Appendix Tables A4.1-A4.8, separately for two youth age groups and each sex. The German national series (Table A4.4) consists of averages of monthly data constructed by the Federal Statistical Office from the once-yearly labor force survey included in the *Microzensus*, modified by statistics on persons employed and unemployed, developed by the social insurance system and the Federal Institute for Employment. An additional Japanese series used in this study is the triennial survey on the employment status of the population, which yields types of information not available from the monthly labor force survey.

Regular national labor force survey data in a continuous series are not available for four of the countries, and other sources have been used. New Zealand and Switzerland do not conduct labor force surveys. The Netherlands labor force survey, conducted in conjunction with the European Communities biennial survey in each member country, began in a systematic fashion in 1973. The British annual General Household Survey, which was initiated in 1971, contains labor force data; they are questionable because of the small sample size and have age breaks that do not entirely match those adopted in this study.

Discontinuities in Data

Most of the labor force surveys have had changes or discontinuities in their series (Table B4.1). In Australia, estimates have been placed on a consistent basis from August 1966 onward. Labor force survey data for 1964 and 1965 have not been revised and thus are not directly comparable. Also, in February 1978 a revised questionnaire and new sample were introduced, and a monthly survey replaced the quarterly one. At the same time population benchmarks were revised, based on the 1976 population census and earlier censuses and a revised method of measuring overseas net migration.

Australian data in this study (Table A4.1) are for August of each year rather than annual averages, since the detailed revised estimates for 1966-1977 are for that month only. A comparison in selected years of the August labor force figures with a less reliable and unpublished annual average computed by the Australian Bureau of Statistics indicates relatively small differences between the two sets of figures for the two youth groups (Table B4.2).

Several breaks occur in the Canadian monthly labor force series (Table A4.2). Data for 1953-1955, 1956-1965, 1966-1970, and 1970-1978 are internally consistent

*This section draws heavily on US 1978a. List of references appears at end of Appendix 4:1.

Table B4.1 Labor Force Survey Characteristics in Eight Countries

	Australia	Canada	France	Germany	Italy	Japan	Sweden	United States
1. Year originated in present form	1964	1952[a]	1960	1957	1959	1947	1962	1947[b]
2. Data collection agency	ABS[c]	Statistics Canada	INSEE[c]	Federal Statistical Office	ISTAT[c]	Bureau of Statistics OPM[c]	SCB[c]	Bureau of the Census
3. Frequency of surveys (current)	Monthly (quarterly to 1977)	Monthly[a]	Bi-annual[d]	Annual[e]	Quarterly	Monthly	Monthly (quarterly to 1977)	Monthly
4. Number sampled currently	30,000 dwellings	56,000 households	55-60,000 households	230,000 households	83,000 households	33,000 households	22,000 persons	56,000 households
5. Percentage sampled	0.66% of total population	0.8% of households	0.33% of households	1.0% of households	(n.a.)	0.1% of population 15+	0.4% of population 16+	0.1% of population 16+
6. Rotation of sample—rate of change	1/8 per month	1/6 per month	1/3 per year	1/4 per year	1/2 per quarter	1/8 per month	1/8 per month	1/4 per month
7. Response rate	About 95%	90-95%	Over 94%	98-99%	97%	100% usually	98% (1970) 93% (1975)	96%
8. Cost of 1977 survey (1977 US dollars)	$5.0 million	$8.2 million	$1.2 million (1975 survey)	$4.2 millon	$2.3 million	$1.9 million	$2.1 million	$9.5 million

[a] First conducted in 1945 as a quarterly survey.

[b] First conducted in 1940 on a monthly basis by the Works Progress Administration.

[c] Agency abbreviations are as follows:
ABS: Australian Bureau of Statistics.
INSEE: Institut national de la statistique et des études économiques.
ISTAT: Instituto Centrale di Statistica.
OPM: Office of the Prime Minister.
SCB: Statistiska Centralbyrän.

[d] Between 1960 and 1967, the survey was conducted in October and March of alternate years except in 1961 when no survey was taken. From 1968 to 1976 a new series of labor force surveys was conducted annually each March. From 1977 onwards the survey has been conducted twice a year, in March and October. March survey is used in this study.

[e] While the main (one percent) sample has been conducted in April or May of each year, between 1957 and 1975 three other quarterly surveys were also conducted each year, on a 0.1 percent level. See text on German data used in this study.

Sources: See References at end of Appendix.

Table B4.2   Differences in Youth Labor Force Totals, Australia, 1967–1979

Year	15–19 both sexes		20–24 both sexes	
	August	Annual average	August	Annual average
	(000s)		(000s)	
1967	654	654	705	706
1970	644	647	827	828
1975	707	714	895	904
1979	748	787	964	967

but have limitations when used as a continuous series. A change in the minimum age (from 14 to 15) in 1966 affects continuity also. Table A4.2 gives alternative 1970 figures, showing the small difference between the 1966–1970 and 1970–1978 series. The French survey has been taken no more than twice a year, in March and October, and the more continuous series for March is used in this study (Table A4.3). March seasonal patterns differ from those in October, especially for young persons newly entering the labor market and returning to school. In 1968, a census year, a new sampling technique was introduced, resulting in changes in the reported labor force. No linkage has been established between the pre- and post-1968 surveys. German survey definitions have remained unchanged over time, and despite some minor methodological changes, survey data have been consistent (Jusenius and von Rabenau 1979).

Italian survey methods were revised and definitions of unemployment sharpened in 1964 and 1977, which affected the numbers in the labor force reported in the quarterly survey. Although the 1977 survey indicated that the size of the labor force had been significantly understated in prior years, official data show no break in the series (Table A4.5). The Japanese survey method was changed in 1967 from partial to complete self-enumeration. At the same time the survey format was amended, but Japanese authorities retrospectively revised the survey results on the basis of the new survey in order to maintain consistency. The Swedish sample was enlarged in 1970, at the same time as the survey was changed from a quarterly to a monthly basis (Table A4.7). Two separate reports are available for 1970 that show the different results from the quarterly and monthly data. While most countries revise population and labor force estimates after completion of a population census, Swedish labor force reports contain monthly population adjustments according to independent projections.

The U.S. Current Population Survey redefined its measures of employment and unemployment in 1967 as a result of the findings of the Gordon Committee. Since the differences between the old and new monthly series were relatively small, historical data were not revised to take account of such changes (Table A4.8). For all practical purposes, the U.S. labor force totals constitute a consistent series, although some analysts consider that there is a break in the employment and unemployment totals.

Three of the eight surveys have been monthly for all or most of the time; two converted to monthly from quarterly in 1970 or later; one has remained quarterly; one has been annual but also has been estimated on a monthly basis; and one has fluctuated, but is now conducted twice yearly (Table B4.1). The United States has the longest series, going back to 1947. The shortest, for Australia, begins in 1964.

Geographic Coverage

The geographic area covered in labor force surveys may contain minor exclusions, such as Canada's omission of its northern territories and Indian reservations. Other countries may not include all outlying islands. As long as the geographic size of a country remains unchanged, these omissions concern a very small part of the population and do not affect trends. When the US accepted Alaska and Hawaii as states, the labor force survey for 1960 showed an increase in both population and labor force; the latter rose by 300,000. Japan's inclusion of Okinawa, after it was returned from U.S. occupation, made no appreciable difference in the two alternative figures for 1973 (Table A4.6).

Definition of Population

Surveys in Australia, Canada, and the United States are based on the civilian population and labor force, while the other five countries include the military forces, usually by adding in independently derived official estimates. Military forces posted outside the country may be counted, but except for the US this has not been a major category in the period covered by the national labor force survey data. The triennial Japanese Employment Status Survey is based on the civilian population, unlike the Japanese monthly survey. The US publishes a series on total population and labor force that includes all military forces. Since no age breaks are given, our adjustments have been made from unpublished data (Table A4.8).

Civilian population is usually defined as those civilians who are resident in the country, although temporary absentees may be included. Italy has surveyed only in-area population since 1972. Daily border-crossers are excluded in most countries, and France also omits those who live in mobile homes, because it samples designated areas of the country rather than the entire nation. Foreign nationals are included if they otherwise qualify, and some countries produce separate information on the foreign population and labor force.

The population base in some countries specifically includes dormitories, lodgings, and other communal dwellings. Hotels and other places of transient residence are generally omitted. Australia, France, Germany, Japan, and Sweden include institutionalized persons, either through direct investigation or by adding in numbers derived from other sources. The Japanese triennial Employment Status Survey excludes the institutionalized, unlike the labor force survey. The other countries exclude the institutional population. The precise kinds of institutions covered vary from country to country, but long-term hospital and sanitoria patients, residents of homes for the aged and residential educational institutions, and inmates of prisons and detention homes usually are covered.

Age limits are set for the sampled population in accordance with labor force concepts. The minimum age has risen over the years in most countries as compulsory schooling and child labor laws have been altered. At present the minimum age is 14 in Italy, 16 in Sweden and the United States, and 15 in the other five nations. Continuous data on 14–15-year-olds have been collected in Sweden and the US and are published separately. All surveys produce data on the two age groups, teenagers and young adults (20 to 24 years old). There is no upper age limit set in any of the surveys except Sweden, where the limit is 74.

Labor Force Sampling

Labor force sample surveys are conducted by national statistical agencies, which also are responsible for other types of data collection (Table B4.1). In some cases, survey analysis is left to another agency; for example, in the United States, the Department of Labor's Bureau of Labor Statistics analyzes data collected by the Department of Commerce's Bureau of the Census. In many countries, changes in the size and character of the sample have been made at intervals in order to improve its reliability. The number sampled is defined in terms of households or persons.

Currently, the proportion of the population surveyed ranges from 0.1 percent of those of working age in Japan (monthly labor force survey) and the US to 1.0 percent of households in Germany and in the Japanese triennial Employment Status Survey. The labor force survey sample is rotated in each country. In most countries, the selected household or person, or institution where included, remains in the sample for a limited time. The proportion of the sample replaced in each survey varies between one-half and one-eighth. In all eight countries the response rate to labor force surveys is over 90 percent. The Japanese monthly survey practices self-enumeration. The household receives a questionnaire to complete and return by mail; the high response rate reflects the literacy and conformity of the population. Similarly, the enumerators for the Japanese Employment Status Survey leave the questionnaire with the household and call later to collect the completed schedule. In other countries, data are collected by telephone or personal interview. In many cases, one person in the household, often the adult female, answers the questions for all members, but Sweden contacts the individuals directly by telephone. In the United States the sample is chosen by address or housing unit and not by name. Questions are not directed to a particular family but to whoever resides in the designated house or apartment. Therefore, some discontinuity arises if families move while they are in the sample. Possible bias is being studied as a result of the report of the National Commission on Employment and Unemployment Statistics.

The United States plans to conduct a study of the biases in the measurement of labor force status that arise from the use of a single household respondent for all members, disaggregating the effects on the labor force by age and sex (Stein 1980, p. 14). Differences between the results of the cross-sectional monthly labor force survey and longitudinal surveys of youth have been attributed to the fact that, in the former, the female adult in the household and, in the latter, the youth themselves gave the response (Borus, Mott, and Nestel 1978; Freeman and Medoff 1979). Nevertheless, the current versus retrospective aspects also play a role (Hills and Thompson 1980).

Surveys are conducted at fixed times of the month, quarter, or year, and the questions commonly relate to the personal characteristics of the population, labor force status, jobseeking activity, employment experience, and hours of work. While some labor force surveys are highly detailed, others ask basic questions only. The results of the sample surveys are extrapolated to reflect the full size of the population. France supplements the labor force numbers to cover omitted groups; recently this category has added about 500,000 to the labor force.

In some countries, special or supplementary questions are added to surveys and are repeated each year in a given month, providing additional information about employment or unemployment experience, earnings, school enrollment status, and related matters. If the special questions in the labor force survey refer retrospectively to the respondents' work history, a longitudinal element is added that enriches the cross-sectional data.

Labor Force Definitions

The definitions and concepts employed in labor force surveys for the most part conform to those recommended by the Eighth International Conference of Labor Statisticians organized by the International Labor Office (ILO) in 1954. Since 1974, France has published the results of its own survey, together with the results that would be obtained if ILO concepts and definitions were used. These two sets of statistics accompany a third — the results according to the concepts and definitions of the French Census.

Inclusions and Exclusions from the Labor Force

Institutionalized. Institutionalized persons are usually excluded from the labor force, but a question might arise in the relation to prisoners on work release schemes.

Military. Among the five countries which include military personnel in the labor force, Japan (monthly labor force survey) and Germany count all military as in the labor force and employed. France and Italy include only volunteers or career military in the labor force and exclude all conscripts. Sweden counts as in the labor force those conscripts who are temporarily absent from a job because of conscription, as well as all career military. Thus, Swedish conscripts who were previously in school, unemployed, or not in school or the labor force (NISLF) are excluded from the labor force; those who left a job immediately before undertaking national service are counted as in the labor force and employed.

As far as possible, the tables presented in this study have treated *all* military as part of the employed labor force, in accordance with the practice of international agencies. This applies to countries which include some or all of the military in their official labor force series, as well as countries which use a civilian population and labor force. All text and appendix tables indicate whether a total (including military) or civilian population and labor force base has been used. In the case of the United States, most of the data in this study have been converted to a total population and labor force base, adding in Department of Defense statistics on total military personnel, whether stationed in the US or abroad. This procedure conforms to the recommendation by the National Commission on Employment and Unemployment Statistics that all armed forces stationed in the US should be included as employed members of the labor force in national labor force statistics and employment/population ratios (US 1979b). The Secretary of Labor accepted this recommendation, but said that it might be reconsidered if there were a shift from an all-volunteer to a conscription system (Stein 1980).

Employment and unemployment. Following the ILO concepts, in all surveys the labor force is the sum of the numbers employed and unemployed. Employment chiefly covers those persons who performed any work as paid employees or as self-employed (at least one hour's work for pay or profit in Japan and Sweden) during a one-week reference period. The Japanese triennial Employment Status Survey defines persons as with or without a job; numbers of hours worked are not used as a criterion, unlike the monthly labor force survey. In accordance with such standard definitions, paid part-time workers are included in the labor force, irrespective of the number of hours worked. The data in the eight country surveys usually identify full-time and part-time workers, but countries vary as to the weekly number of hours that distinguish full-time from part-time status. In the United States and Sweden, 35 hours or more constitutes full-time work. Further subdivisions of part-time workers by hours worked reflect the data needs of individual countries and rarely are the same between any two countries. In response to the recommendation of the National Commission on Employment and Unemployment Statistics, the U.S. survey will determine the usual hours worked for all employed persons and the reasons for working fewer hours. Unemployed persons will be asked whether they are looking for 35 hours or more of work or less than 35 hours, instead of the earlier "full-time" and "part-time" (Stein 1980, p. 13).

ILO definitions specify that unpaid family workers should be included in the labor force as employed if they work for one-third or more of normal working hours. Australia, France, Sweden, and the United States specify a minimum of 15 hours worked during the reference week, while the other four countries include unpaid family workers if they did any work at all during the week. Youth, especially females, are affected by these differences in coverage.

Unemployment refers to those who, during the reference week, were without a job and were available for and seeking work for pay or profit. All countries specify active jobseeking as a criterion for unemployment status, although not all labor force surveys define what active jobseeking entails, or within what time period such activity must be demonstrated. In general, however, active seeking covers registration at a public or private employment office; meeting prospective employers; checking with friends or relatives; placing or answering advertisements; looking at factory and employment service notice boards; writing letters of application, or as in Japan, awaiting the results of previous job applications; or being on a union or professional register.

Persons on lay-off are treated as unemployed in some countries and employed in others. Where they are considered unemployed, they are not required to conduct job search, thus constituting an exception to the general rule. Under some circumstances such persons may become "out of the labor force." The next section contains additional details on persons on lay-off.

ILO defines the reference period for jobseeking activities by the unemployed as one week, but only five of the eight countries specify any reference period in which the unemployed must have made active job search efforts in order to be included in the labor force. Only Japan applies the one-week period. In Australia, Canada, and the United States, it is a more-inclusive four weeks, while Sweden uses a still easier 60-day period. France, Germany, and Italy do not specify a fixed period, accepting job search at any time as evidence of unemployment and labor force membership. All countries except France and Germany specify that persons without jobs and seeking work must also be available for work, usually within the reference week, in order to be included in the labor force. Neither the Italian nor Swedish survey includes questions that verify availability within the reference week, although Sweden raises the question in regard to students. The Japanese monthly survey requires availability but specifies no time period. Japan's triennial Employment Status Survey records separately persons without a job and those seeking work, although no criteria of active job search or availability are specified.

The effect of a short reference period, such as Japan's, is to reduce the number recorded as unemployed and to increase persons out of the labor force compared with countries which have longer reference periods, or, as in France, Germany, and Italy, no designated period during which job search must have occurred. An availability requirement within the reference week tends to reduce the unemployment total, and hence the labor force, less than an availability requirement without a time specification, but more than in a country with no mention of availability. In particular, French and German students, looking to work after the end of the term, may be counted as unemployed during periods when they are unavailable to take a job. To exclude this spurious unemployment, some countries do not count students seeking jobs as unemployed if there is no test of availability for work. In the German May 1977 survey, persons not currently available comprised 15 percent of the total unemployed and 30 percent of the unemployed under age 20 (Jusenius and von Rabenau 1979).

In Australia, persons stating that they were looking for work but who took no active steps to find jobs or would have been unable to start work in the survey period for reasons other than their own illness or injury are classified as not in the labor force (Australia 1979, p. 1). Such persons, however, are not included among discouraged jobseekers. The Australian definition prevents students and others who may be looking for future jobs from being counted in the current labor force.

Discouraged Workers. Following ILO concepts, most countries exclude from the labor force those who say they want to work but who do not search for jobs because they believe that no work is available. This group, called discouraged workers or jobseekers, must give only one reason for not searching. Separate data are collected in the surveys of all eight countries; Canada, France, and Germany initiated their series from 1977 (Petrie 1978). Since the French labor force survey does not require the unemployed to show active jobseeking or current availability for inclusion in the labor force, some who would be discouraged workers elsewhere may be included. The German *Microzensus* counts in the labor force all who consider themselves unemployed, whether or not they are seeking work, so that discouraged workers may also be included in the labor force (Jusenius and von Rabenau 1979). The French, Dutch, and Italian, as well as the European Communities, labor force surveys use a concept of "marginal activity." Included in the labor force are the "marginally employed"—those principally inactive but who performed some work in the reference week—and the "marginally unemployed," those who do not consider themselves as unemployed but rather as out of the labor force, and who performed no work but sought work in the reference week.

A Canadian study has aptly characterized the treatment of discouraged workers and others who assert that they want to work but who are not currently engaged in active job search as "without question, the most controversial element of the labour force measurement process" (Canada 1980a, p. 5). The report goes on:

> In essence, this debate reduces to a concern over the appropriate choice of definitions to be used in distinguishing between those persons who are to be classified as unemployed and those who are to be regarded as not in the labor force.

In the United States, after much discussion, the National Commission on Employment and Unemployment Statistics recommended, and the Department of Labor accepted on an interim basis, that discouraged workers would continue to be excluded from the labor force, but that the CPS would begin to collect and tabulate monthly data on the group. A final decision will be made after an evaluation of the new data, which will include new definitions of discouraged workers reflecting job search in the last six months, current availability, and the desire for work (Stein 1980, p. 13).

Treatment of Specific Groups. Labor force surveys vary as to the inclusion of specific groups in the labor force and their distribution between the employed and unemployed.

Students. ILO labor force definitions do not make special provision for those who are enrolled as full-time students or whose chief activity is studying, which implies that they should be treated in the same way as the rest of the population. Most countries follow this convention, so that students with jobs also are members of the labor force if their employment meets the requirements of the survey; in some countries they are placed in special categories. Full-time students seeking jobs during the school term are excluded from the labor force in some countries.

Canada excludes full-time students who declare that they are seeking full-time work on availability grounds, although some individuals actually do work and study full-time. Swedish full-time students seeking work when school is in session are not in practice counted as in the labor force, because their availability for work is in question. France, on the other hand, includes in the labor force "marginally unemployed" students—those who sought work in the reference week, although they considered themselves out of the labor force.

When attempts are made to separate the in-school labor force from the out-of-school labor force and to establish comparable categories across countries, various difficulties emerge in the data. First, only a few countries regularly publish labor force data that separate the enrolled from the nonenrolled. Australia began to publish monthly data in September 1978 and Canada in April 1980, following special studies (Canada 1977b). Unpublished Canadian data on the labor force activity of full-time students is available from 1975 to April 1980 on a monthly or annual basis. In November 1975 a special tabulation was run in Canada to discover how closely the answers to the regular labor force survey questions on school attendance matched those to a supplementary question on enrollment status. The unpublished results show a high degree of overlap, but also some inconsistencies that prevent school attendance status from being substituted for school enrollment status. In Table B4.3, showing the two youth age groups, the boxed numbers represent the responses that appear to be consistent.

An American annual series on the labor force status of enrolled and nonenrolled youth goes back to 1947 and is based on the supplementary question in the October labor force survey. U.S. monthly labor force surveys also have collected, but not published, monthly data on those whose major activity in the reference week is given as attending school. Those who also worked or sought work are counted in the labor force. The published October survey data classify youth by enrollment status, but otherwise count labor force participation by the same standards. Although most analysts have preferred the October data, results from the two types of data are reported to be similar (Ragan 1977, p. 131). A comparison of March with October data indicates that there are small but important differences (Feldstein and Ellwood, 1979). The National Longitudinal Survey of Young Men found that of 841 recorded as enrolled full-time in 1970, only 678 reported school as their major activity (letter from Steven C. Myers, November 15, 1978).

New questions in the American survey, tested in 1980, will provide a published monthly series on the school enrollment status of all 16–24-year-olds, ascertaining whether school attendance is on a full- or part-time basis (Stein 1980, p. 13).

Table B4.3 Youth Labor Force Activity by School Attendance and Enrollment Status, Canada, November 1975

Attendance status	Not enrolled	Enrollment Status		Total
		Enrolled full-time	Enrolled part-time	
		15–19 years		
Major activity: school	16	1,493	9	1,519
Secondary activity: school	···	26	15	42
Did not go to school	712	9	15	736
Total	730	1,528	39	2,297
		20–24 years		
Major activity: school	···	338	8	348
Secondary activity: school	···	12	44	58
Did not go to school	1,714	5	54	1,773
Total	1,716	356	106	2,178

French student labor force data, without an age distribution, can be obtained by adding together March data on marginally employed students and marginally unemployed students. Japan's triennial Employment Status Survey gives July information on those who are in school and the labor force. Sweden cannot directly calculate students in the labor force; but estimates are made from information on weekly hours of work by age, from the differences in educational enrollments according to the educational authorities that count all students, and from the labor force survey that counts only students who are not employed.

Other issues of comparability within and between countries involve whether "students" include only the full-time enrolled or part-time as well, and the time of year of the survey. In the United States, both full-time and part-time students are counted as enrolled. Published data in the *Employment and Training Report of the President* (US 1979b) do not distinguish between the two, but the Special Labor Force Reports on Students, Graduates and Dropouts (US 1960–79a) offer separate data on part-time students. Other countries usually ask individuals to identify themselves as students without specific identification as full-time or part-time, but imply that full-time students are sought.

Data on student labor force activity should be drawn from time periods when school is in session. During vacation periods many students are not reported as students and are either in the labor force or NISLF (not in school or the labor force). Annual averages of monthly data therefore are misleading about the size of the student labor force and fail to distinguish vacation workers from school year workers. In the US, large differences are shown in the civilian youth labor force as reported in October data that adds enrolled and nonenrolled, and as derived from averaging monthly data which do not distinguish students (*Table B4.4).

Trainees. Trainees in ordinary employment who receive wages are counted as employed in all countries' surveys. Australia excludes trainee teachers specifically; presumably they are unpaid. The German *Microzensus* specifies that the trainee must be in the workplace or attending a special training workshop. In the United States, paid trainees attending educational institutions full-time, including trade school trainees and those in private establishments, are excluded from the labor force. Seekers of paid traineeships are counted as unemployed in all countries.

Apprentices. Paid apprentices with an employment contract are counted as employed. Persons seeking paid apprenticeships are considered as unemployed in all countries except Germany, where the individual must also be registered as seeking jobs other than apprenticeships in order to be counted as unemployed (Lenhardt 1979, p. 182).

Waiting to report to work. ILO definitions label those persons unemployed who have obtained a job but are waiting to report at a later date. This convention is followed by all countries except Germany and Japan, where such persons are treated as out of the labor force. The Canadian and the U.S. surveys, however, specify that employment must be taken up within a certain period — four weeks and thirty days, respectively; if longer, such persons are excluded from the labor force.

Temporarily ill. Persons temporarily absent from work because of illness are counted as employed in all countries; however, the Australian survey specifies a limit of four weeks' absence, while Japan requires paid absence for inclusion in the labor force. Temporarily ill unemployed persons are included in the labor force, although the Japanese survey requires the illness to be sufficiently minor that the respondent is still available for work.

Other temporary absence from work. Those absent from work due to labor dispute, vacation, or leave entitlement, or inclement weather are counted as employed, though Australia specifies a four-week limit to absence. In Japan such absence must be paid for inclusion in the labor force.

Temporarily laid off. Those on temporary lay-off from work are called unemployed and included in the labor force in ILO definitions. Nevertheless, they are counted as employed in France, Germany, and Italy. In Japan and Sweden they are employed if they continue to be paid, as usually is the case; others are unemployed, provided that they search for jobs. In Australia, if workers are laid-off for less than four weeks and the cause is bad weather or plant breakdown, they continue as employed. All on temporary lay-off are counted as unemployed in the United States and in Canada, if laid-off for less than six months, or, if longer, when job search and availability criteria are met. Those on temporary lay-off are excluded from the labor force in Australia and Canada if the lay-off continues beyond four weeks and six months, respectively, and no job search is made; and in Japan where the lay-off is unpaid and there is no job search (Petrie 1978).

American unemployment totals would be increased more than those of the other countries as a result of the definitions and treatment of temporary lay-offs. To the extent that such lay-offs are larger relative to other types of unemployment in the US than in the other countries, this may be an important source of difference in comparative unemployment rates.

Persons in government training or employment programs. Special government employment programs may change the labor force status of individuals, drawing some into the labor force and removing others from it. For the most part, persons in government job creation or work experience programs who are paid are considered employed and thus are included in the labor force, as they would be if they remained unemployed. In some countries, however, those who are engaged in job creation schemes remain on the unemployed rolls. In the United States it has been decided, as a result of the recommendation of the National Commission on Employment and Unemployment Statistics, that persons in work experience programs should be counted as employed rather than unemployed (Stein 1980, p. 13). In a variety of training programs, participants who may previously have been in the labor force as unemployed are not considered either employed or unemployed, and are thus out of the labor force. Sweden, for example, considers all persons admitted to government-financed, full-time, labor market training programs as part of the educational system and hence not in the labor force. As a result of the recommendation of the U.S. National Commission on Employment and Unemployment Statistics, American participants in government training programs in institutions will be counted as out of the labor force rather than unemployed, provided that they are not actively seeking work (Stein 1980, p. 13). In still other cases, such as sheltered workshop programs for the handicapped, participants previously considered not in the labor force continue to be counted in the same manner.

Unrecorded or illegal labor force. A category of increasing importance in a number of countries, and one which creates a substantial margin of error in employment estimates, consists of citizens and aliens whose income and work status, or lack of residence and/or work permits, result in false recording or complete omission from labor force surveys. Citizens who benefit from certain government income programs, which do not permit work or heavily tax earnings, may in fact work but not report it. They may be counted as out of the labor force when they are in fact in it. Illegal or undocumented aliens are likely to be omitted from the labor force survey sample, but if they are included, their responses might depend on whether or not they hold counterfeit papers (such as social security cards or green cards in the US). A degree of undercounting of employment is likely in most industrialized countries. Even Italy, a source of labor for northern Europe, has a substantial amount of unrecorded employment by foreigners who lack residence and work permits (Pettenati 1979).

National Censuses of Population

As an alternative or supplementary source of demographic and labor force data, the results from population censuses are used at various points in this study. Censuses are conducted less frequently than labor force surveys, usually contain far more detailed information, and have been carried out over a longer time period than labor force surveys. Provided that census methods, definitions, and concepts are consistent or are adjusted from one census to another, longer historical series and trends can be developed (Long 1958). Moreover, in the absence of a frequent and regular labor force survey, as is the case in four of our countries, the census is the chief or only national source of information. There has been, however, a recent movement against the taking of censuses in a number of countries on the grounds of invasion of privacy, high cost, and the possibility of obtaining the same information as effectively and more cheaply by carefully controlled anonymous samples.

Certain methodological problems in the census arise from the fact that the collection of labor force data is not as central a purpose for the census as it is to the labor force survey. Concepts of economic activity not only differ between the census and labor force surveys in individual countries, but some censuses do not inquire into economic activity with reference to a specified time period. Both the ILO and UN have recommended that *current* economic activity should be measured in censuses.

Problems also arise if the census survey week is not at the same time of year each time a census is taken, or if the enumeration week in a given census is not the same for all persons, since the reference week for employment data will not be uniform and, for some, may pertain to a holiday period. With the exception of Sweden and the United States, population censuses generally classify young people as students or as in the labor force and do not permit a joint status, unlike labor force surveys. Thus, if a census survey period falls during the long school vacation or is unusual in relation to the school-attendance and work patterns of young people, it may show an unusually high proportion of new school-leavers to be neither in school nor the labor force.

It is possible that a census may miss parts of the population, just as a labor force survey may do in its sample design. Census postenumeration surveys in some countries indicate significant undercounting of parts of the population, resulting from missed dwellings or missed or undernumerated individuals in identified dwellings. The U.S. censuses of 1960 and 1970 are estimated to have "missed" 3.1 and 2.5 percent, respectively, of the total true population; the undercount was proportionately greater for males and nonwhites of both sexes in both years and was higher for 20–24-year-olds than for the 15–19 age group. It was estimated that the census of 1970 missed 8.7 percent of nonwhites aged 20–24 (Johnston and Wetzel 1969; US 1974). The labor force status of the undercount group of males in the U.S. 1960 census was similar to those enumerated, although the rate of nonparticipation in the labor force was somewhat larger for the undercount group (Klein 1970). Similarly, in Great Britain and Australia postenumeration surveys identified a net undercount of about 1.7 percent of the population in the 1966 census of Great Britain, and of 2.7 percent in the 1976 Australian census (GB 1968a; Australia 1979). The United States made strong efforts to improve collection techniques in order to reduce the undercount group in the 1980 census (Herriot 1979). Unfortunately, all information in the initial months after the census date of April 1, 1980, indicate a continuing problem of underenumeration.

Less complete coverage of the total labor force may result from the fact that censuses obtain information through self-enumeration, while most labor force surveys use personal interview or telephone calls, or both. Detailed census economic activity questions, unlike the basic demographic questions, tend to be answered by a sample of households rather than the whole population, but a census sample is far larger than that used in labor force surveys. Evidence from U.S. postenumeration surveys indicates that census data identify fewer persons in the labor force than do labor force surveys (Johnston and Wetzel 1969; US 1974), but an analysis for 1970 showed significant differences only for youth, with progressively smaller gaps as older age groups were surveyed (US 1975a). The 1950 undercount in the U.S. census for certain age groups was attributed in part to the use of inexperienced temporary census enumerators (Long 1958).

In Japan, which uses self-enumeration both for the census and the monthly labor force survey, this factor should not be a cause of differences in numbers in the labor force. Nevertheless, while census population data, taken in October, corresponded closely to the population count in the October labor force survey for the two youth groups, teenage labor force data were substantially different (over 14 percent higher in the census); the number recorded in the census as not in the labor force was about 8 percent lower for both teenagers and young adults.

New Zealand, which has no regular labor force survey, relies on its census at five-year intervals. Analyses of differences between the census total of unemployment and the unemployment register at the employment service have shown that unemployment in the census has a broader definition. However, the relation between the numbers reported in the two systems has altered since 1967, when rising unemployment first appeared, which indicates that definitional differences do not constitute the whole explanation of the divergence between the two series (New Zealand 1979).

Comparability between census and labor force survey definitions and concepts is of particular interest in the countries where each source of data is well developed. In spite of the fact that the same official agency usually is directly involved in conducting both the census and labor force survey, there are several differences in definition and concept. Such differences are now described for France, Sweden, and the United States, in which both kinds of survey are important, and Great Britain, where the census is the chief source.

France

The French census, carried out every seven years by INSEE, provides the conceptual and definitional framework for the labor force survey. Postwar censuses have been held in 1947, 1954, 1962 (delayed from 1961), 1968, and 1975. Both the census and the labor force survey base their results on the total population, including the military forces and the institutional population, but the labor force survey excludes from its direct sampling certain portions of the population who are enumerated in the census. Certain categories are designated as inactive by the census, while the labor force survey probes into their "marginal" economic activity and status; for example, students, housewives, and the retired are listed as marginally employed or marginally unemployed.

In order to quantify the differences between the census and the labor force survey, official sources give some results of the latter as they would be on census definitions. In 1977 the census definitions produced lower labor force participation rates and numbers in the labor force for all age groups than the labor force survey definitions. For the 15–19 age group, participation rates under labor force survey definitions were 30 percent for males and 25 percent for females, compared with 27 and 21 percent respectively under census definitions. For the 20–24-year-olds, labor force participation rates were 83 percent for males and 72 percent for females under labor force survey definitions, compared with 81 and 68 percent respectively under census definitions (France 1978a). The census has not adopted the broader ILO labor force concepts introduced into the labor force survey since 1974. These include questions on availability for work and active jobseeking to qualify as unemployed.

Sweden

The Swedish population census has been held at five-yearly intervals since 1930, with the exception of 1955. In 1960 it was changed and combined with the housing census, resulting in some discontinuity with earlier census data on the labor force (Sweden 1974a). Recent censuses also are not entirely comparable in definitions. The census differs from the labor force survey both in methodology and definitions (Sweden 1977c). The census gives separate numbers for those whose labor force status is unknown, while the labor force survey compensates for sample nonresponse by weighting the respondents in the sample, as is common in other countries. The questions asked by the census and the labor force survey differ both in number, format, and data coding methods. In addition, the census groups individuals according to their year of birth, that is, their age at the end of the year. The labor force survey reports the age of respondents at the time of interview. While the census of 1975 defined the economically active to exclude all military conscripts, the labor force survey included those conscripted from employment. The census of 1975 included (as economically active) unpaid family workers who worked for any number of hours in the reference week (although in certain primary industries—farming, forestry, and fishing, for example—a minimum work week of 16 hours was required), while the labor force survey stipulates that all unpaid family workers needed a minimum of 15 hours of work to qualify as in the labor force. Sweden annually converts its averaged labor force data for the months of September, October, and November to the numbers that would prevail if census definitions and concepts were applied to labor force results (Sweden 1974a, 1977b).

United States

The employment status concepts in the 1970 census differ from those of the 1960 and 1950 censuses, mainly as a result of revised official government concepts of employment and unemployment, instituted in 1967, which likewise affected the labor force survey, called the Current Population Survey (CPS). Census labor force definitions and concepts are considered to be generally comparable with those of the CPS, although variations in enumeration and processing techniques cause some differences. Definitions of the labor force and school enrollment are the same in the census and the CPS, but the census reference week has not been uniform throughout the nation. As a result, the census gives student status to all who were enrolled in school within the previous two months. On the other hand, the CPS, using a standard reference week, includes as students those enrolled within that weekly period. Direct comparison between census and CPS data of labor force participation rates for each sex and for 1950, 1960, and 1970 shows that the census has lower rates, mostly accounted for by lower rates of employment; unemployment rates are very similar (US 1973b).

Great Britain

The British census, unlike population censuses in most other countries, has been a major source of postwar labor force data. The British full census has been held every ten years up to 1971. An additional 10 percent sample census was taken in 1966, but it was skipped in 1976 because of the cost.

British census labor force definitions are similar to the ILO, although some differences occur in the allocation of persons between the employed and unemployed categories. Moreover, it is possible that some ill persons are counted as unemployed in the British census because of misinterpretation of the census questionnaire. Such persons would be excluded from the labor force in other countries' surveys (US 1978a).

The principal labor force groups have been defined fairly consistently over time in the census. The 1961 census defined the unemployed as those economically active persons who were out of employment in the reference week but who intended and expected to work again. The 1966 census counted the unemployed group as the registered unemployed, those not registered but seeking work, those unable to seek work due to temporary ill-health, and those waiting to start work at a later date. In 1971, the unemployed were categorized as persons out of employment seeking work, those unable to seek work due to temporary ill-health, and those waiting to start work at a later date.

A comparison of census concepts and definitions with those of the General Household Survey instituted in 1971, which provides too small a sample for a satisfactory labor force survey, shows that the census covers the entire population, including all armed forces and the institutionalized population, while the GHS sample represents the civilian, noninstitutionalized population. The census requires information referring to a specific week, while the GHS is a continuous inquiry whose results are given in annual average form. The GHS youth age groups differ slightly from those in the census. While comparisons of GHS annual data and census-based mid-year estimates indicate that the GHS provides good overall coverage of household population, there are indications that youth aged 15 to 24, as well as students, are underrepresented to some extent (US 1978a).

The census treats full-time students as economically inactive and out of the labor force even if they worked part time in reference week, whereas the GHS began by counting anyone who worked in reference week as employed and in the labor force. From 1972, however, the GHS also excluded full-time students from the labor force. Asking more probing questions on labor force status, the GHS is more likely to identify the actively jobseeking unemployed. The GHS also enumerates numbers of nonactive jobseekers. As a result of these various differences, 1971 census data show more economically inactive and unemployed than the GHS, while census employment estimates are lower.

International Agencies

Comparability of cross-national labor force data has been advanced by the efforts of international agencies, especially the OECD, ILO, and the European Communities. In addition, the U.S. Bureau of Labor Statistics has adjusted data for eight foreign countries to American definitions and plans to add additional countries. Since the U.S. definitions are very close to the international standards set by the ILO in 1954, these modified data increase comparability (OECD 1976c; US 1978a; *Table B4.6).

Organization for Economic Cooperation and Development (OECD)

OECD data and projections for 1950–1990 were produced in 1978–1979 for the Manpower and Social Affairs Committee. This work was initiated in 1976 when the Committee agreed that its program should include the collection of demographic and labor profiles for a study of social and manpower policies. A first questionnaire was sent to OECD member countries during 1976, requesting actual population and labor force data for 1970 and 1975 and projections for 1980, 1985, and 1990. Initial responses to the questionnaire and subsequent revisions of data by countries form the basis of the OECD statistics for 1970–1990. Where countries failed to provide adequate data or submitted statistics that appeared inconsistent with other OECD sources or national data, the OECD Secretariat relied on the latter as well as supplementary sources, such as the United Nations Demographic Yearbooks and the Yearbooks of the International Labor Office. These latter sources were extensively used for the 1950 and 1960 calculations, while extrapolation and interpolation were additionally used by the Secretariat in order to establish data for uniform age groupings not necessarily provided by national data (OECD 1978c).

Adjustments to national data made by the OECD provide a more comparable series than can be obtained from the separate national sources. OECD requested that countries base all labor force data on mid-year population totals. These were to include the institutionalized population, the volunteer and conscript military forces (including those stationed abroad), diplomats abroad, and other residents temporarily overseas, contrary to the practice in some national labor force surveys. All OECD data were to be adjusted to consistent geographic boundaries. The OECD provided respondent countries with standard labor force definitions based on those developed by the United Nations and International Labor Office and asked that these be taken into account as far as possible. Nevertheless, the OECD data reflect the current employment and unemployment definitions used by individual countries, on the assumption that the variations are minor. An OECD committee continues to work for greater standardization among countries in these definitions.

OECD data, in comparison to the eight national labor force surveys, offer a uniform 15 to 19-year age group, and provide data on population, labor force, and labor force participation rates for each country. Moreover, labor force data by age group are available from OECD for four of our countries with no suitable labor force survey. The fact that OECD data have been extended back to 1950 is a further advantage, since only U.S. data, among the eight national sources, are available so far back. However, problems arose for the OECD Secretariat in compiling labor force data and participation rates for age groups, and the process necessitated the use of different sources to compute the total labor force and the separate age groups. Due to the use of different sources, discrepancies resulted between the stated totals and the totals derived by adding separate age groups (*Table B4.5). In our study, OECD labor force data for separate age groups rather than the stated totals have been used. In some cases, however, OECD stated totals provided the base for estimates of the youth age groups in years when separate age groups were not given.

International Labor Office (ILO)

A pioneer in comparative labor force statistics, ILO has presented information annually for more than a hundred countries in its *Yearbook*, and data and projections for the years 1950–2000 in a special study (ILO 1977). ILO data are obtained from national sources, including population censuses and labor force surveys. ILO, unlike OECD, attempts to adjust for differing concepts and definitions employed by countries in gathering national data. In addition, ILO, in common with OECD, uses standardized age group and geographical boundaries, includes the armed forces and institutionalized persons, and adjusts data to mid-year estimates.

*Table B4.6 compares labor force data for 1960 and 1970 for the 20–24-year-old age group from OECD, ILO, national sources, and the U.S. Bureau of Labor Statistics (based on U.S. definitions). The differences among the series are not great, and the directions of change for each source between 1960 and 1970 are all the same. These conclusions would not hold if annual changes and a longer time period, including projections, were considered, or if the teenage group were added and each sex were considered separately. While the record among countries has been mixed, aggregate OECD data have conformed rather more closely to national data than have ILO data. In addition, OECD data provide more frequent intervals, and 1975 data are actual rather than estimated or provisional.

European Communities Labor Force Survey (EC)

The EC survey was first conducted in 1960 among the original six member states: Belgium, France, Germany, Italy, Luxembourg, and the Netherlands. The next survey was carried out in 1968 (and excluded Luxembourg). Thereafter, the survey was conducted annually to 1971, without participation by the Netherlands. From 1973, with the admission into the EC of Denmark, Ireland, and the United Kingdom, the survey has been conducted biennially (excepting Denmark and Ireland in 1973).

Unlike the OECD and ILO, EC survey concepts have been determined in advance and handed down to member countries; to the extent that the definitions and procedures have been observed, all results in a given year are comparable. Prior to 1973, definitions and questions were changed in each survey, impairing comparability over time, but the three biennial surveys from 1973 through 1977 had the same definitions and questions (EC 1975-78). Despite the use of standardized definitions among member states, the EC labor force survey does not claim perfect comparability between countries, due to the different timing of reference weeks and methods of enumeration, grossing up of results, and other minor differences. Results from the 1979 survey were not available by early 1980.

EC survey data are collected by national statistical agencies, which also select the sample. The country sample size in 1977 varied between 10,000 households in Luxembourg; 30,000 to 50,000 households in Belgium, Denmark, Ireland, and the Netherlands; and 60,000 to 100,000 households in France, Germany, Italy, and the United Kingdom. The biennial survey is conducted in all countries during the spring months (in 1977, between March and June), although the exact period in which it is carried out over these months differs among countries. In most countries the survey period falls within the school term. While France, Germany, and Italy utilize existing national labor force samples to derive the relevant data, the remaining six countries have had to initiate surveys; these may result in a spinoff of new national series, perhaps at more frequent intervals than every two years.

Data are collected for the youth groups aged 14-19 years and 20-24 years. The starting age of 14 was adopted because of its relevance to Italy, but 15 or 16 would be more appropriate for other member countries. It would be desirable to collect additional information based on 15-19 or 16-19 years, according to the situation in individual countries. In defining the labor force, the employed are regarded as those with a "principal occupation," that is, normally or usually engaged in a gainful activity and working any hours at all in this activity during the reference week. The unemployed must be seeking paid employment to be counted, though no period is specified in which active jobseeking must have taken place. A question on availability for work was introduced for the first time in the 1977 survey.

The biennial EC survey is based on the noninstitutional total population, including all military forces. Military volunteers or career personnel are included in the labor force, but conscripts are excluded. Students working part time are excluded from the labor force, as are persons who declare that they are primarily economically inactive but have a temporary or occasional occupation, and persons who are seeking or have obtained a job to begin at a later date. In comparison, ILO definitions include in the labor force both students with employment and those seeking or having a job to begin at a later date. In EC surveys, as in ILO data, unpaid family workers are included in the labor force if they work for at least 14 hours in the reference week, as are employed persons temporarily absent from work because of illness, labor dispute, leave entitlement, or inclement weather, and those temporarily laid-off (EC 1975–78d).

National Longitudinal Surveys

Longitudinal survey data, based on at least two and usually a series of observations over time on the same group of young people from a given age or educational cohort, provide information about individual changes in status over time, behavioral responses, and developmental process within youth cohorts. By periodically re-cording the status and activities of the same group of individuals, it becomes possible to trace and provide explanations of labor force behavior and the flows among labor force categories during the year and from year to year. Such surveys also provide alternative cross-sectional, "moment-in-time" data, which can be compared with labor force survey and census data (Kalachek 1978, 1979; Sproat 1979).

Longitudinal surveys or panel studies have several advantages for research on youth labor markets and efforts to evaluate public policy. They can reveal the extent to which particular labor market experiences are concentrated on small groups of young people. They enable account to be taken of how much influence earlier ex-periences, decisions, and views have on current outcomes. Finally, they can attempt to control for individual differences, called heterogeneity, so that process, or state dependence, can be observed, the relative weight of heterogeneity and state dependence can be measured, and suitable public policies can be devised in light of the findings.

Longitudinal surveys should be distinguished from retrospective surveys. The lat-ter obtain information by asking questions about past history and depend entirely on recollection. This is a less reliable, although less expensive, source of information than current questioning, in which recollection is required only back to the previous survey, except perhaps in the initial questionnaire. It also is possible to obtain a longitudinal series for a limited time period from an adaptation of the cross-sectional labor force survey, in which the responses of a fixed group of households or in-dividuals are tallied over the period they remained in the sample. Response error is a problem, as is attrition from the sample. One advantage of this procedure over the regular longitudinal survey is the much greater frequency of information on labor force status; monthly rather than yearly, biennial, or even less frequent reports are obtained, albeit on a more narrow range of subjects. Like all surveys involving reinterviews, response inconsistency occurs. In this study we utilize the Swedish con-version of cross-sectional labor force survey data to gain a perspective on the youth labor force not yet available for any other country. Population censuses also can be used longitudinally by following the labor market history of the same individuals at different intervals of their lives, through a matching of individual responses to various censuses. All these methods are supplementary rather than competitive with longitudinal or panel surveys (Kalachek 1979, annex).

Longitudinal surveys of young people have become increasingly common, and several of the countries in this study currently are conducting longitudinal surveys of young people from which labor force data and trends can be extracted. In some countries, surveys are undertaken of a given age group, while in other countries the sample is constituted from those at stipulated educational levels. Surveys may be started infrequently and run on for many years, or they may be undertaken for each year's new cohort on a short-run basis, covering fewer subjects and obtaining less detailed information.

United States

Two longitudinal surveys of youth which stress labor market activity have provided information for a substantial time period. They are the National Longitudinal Survey (NLS) on youth, under the aegis of the Bureau of the Census and the Center for Human Resource Research at the Ohio State University, and the National Longitudinal Study of the high school class of 1972 of the National Center for Education Statistics (NCES) of the U.S. Department of Education, formerly DHEW. There also have been other longitudinal surveys of youth, such as Project Talent, which originated in the educational sector and yielded relatively little labor force information.

In addition, several other longitudinal studies are currently underway in the United States, some of which contain youth labor force information. The Panel Study of Income Dynamics (ID), conducted at the University of Michigan, yields family labor market information, income data, and economic, social, and attitudinal characteristics. The Continuous Work History Sample (CWHS), based on social security tax records, covers population, employment, and wage data. The Continuous Longitudinal Manpower Survey (CLMS), initiated by the Employment and Training Administration, is designed to follow and evaluate the later work experience of participants in programs under the Comprehensive Employment and Training Act (CETA). The Continuous Wage and Benefit History Study (CWBH), established by the Unemployment Insurance Service and other sections of the Department of Labor, provides data on U.I. benefit claimants and recipients by a variety of characteristics (Kalachek 1978).

The present study draws on the NLS and NCES youth surveys. The original NLS surveys cover two youth groups: males aged 14–24 in 1966 and females aged 14–24 in 1968, both of which will be followed to 1981. Each national sample had over 5,000 individuals at the start and was drawn from households in the CPS (Current Population Survey) sample. Both youth groups were reinterviewed annually over a five-year period, with further information obtained biennially by telephone and a tenth-year personal interview, followed by telephone surveys in alternate years and a final personal interview. In both cases, black youth was deliberately oversampled to enable adequate racial analysis. Questions dealt with labor market characteristics and experience, personal attitudes, education, and family background. The NLS and CPS surveys are similar in their methods, definitions, and questions, but the NLS questions are more detailed and probing. CPS interviewers have been used to collect data on the NLS youth cohorts, but they spend more time on each NLS interview than they do on the CPS interview for an entire household. Results are published in two series: *Career Thresholds* for young men (US 1970–79) and *Years for Decision* for young women (US 1971–81). In addition a vast amount of academic research has utilized NLS tapes (CHRR 1979; Kalachek 1979, pp. 8–14).

An extension of the NLS was undertaken in 1979, when a new cohort of youth aged 14 to 21 was interviewed during the first three months of the year, for the first of five annual surveys. The cohorts contain 11,500 civilians and 1,300 military personnel; earlier studies had been limited to civilians only. Both males and females are included, with an overrepresentation of blacks, Hispanics, and economically disadvantaged whites. The new NLS cohort will be questioned in detail on additional areas to aid in the evaluation of new government programs for disadvantaged youth and vocational education; to offer separate information on Hispanic youth; to provide further information on the economic, social, and psychological factors affecting youth in the labor market; and to assess the change in the educational and labor market experiences of youth by comparison with earlier NLS cohorts.

The NCES study of the high school class of 1972 is a stratified national probability sample of over 20,000 twelfth-grade students. The national sample was based on 1,200 schools, with 18 students selected from each. Schools with students from low-income backgrounds and high proportions of minority youth were deliberately oversampled. The extensive base-year survey was conducted at the schools in the spring of 1972, with over 18,000 respondents. Students answered questions on family background, education, job experience, attitudes, and plans. They were tested on verbal and nonverbal abilities. Full high school records and counselor responses to a questionnaire were collected. Follow-up surveys have been conducted annually or biennially by mail and telephone, collecting data on the subsequent educational and vocational patterns of high school seniors, their work and military experience, attitudes, and aspirations. Such information can be related to prior educational experiences and personal characteristics. Data have been published in a number of volumes (US 1976–79). New longitudinal surveys of the classes of 1980 and 1982 are planned.

Great Britain

The National Survey of Health and Development, based at the Medical Research Council unit at the London School of Economics, conducted a national longitudinal study of more than 5,000 young people born in one week in March 1946 and selected to overrepresent middle-class and agricultural families. The cohort was followed from birth to over age 30, mostly every two years. Information was collected on family situation, educational ability and attainments, health, and other personal characteristics. Ability tests and teachers' opinions were secured at age 15. Of the original sample of more than 5,000, more than 4,000 remained by the time they reached age 18. Data were collected by a series of interviews or questionnaires on the occupational history from age 15 onward. Labor force information concerned technical education, training, the choice of a first job, subsequent jobs, job changes, and unemployment. The transition from school to work and the occupational progress of the sample also were followed, as well as the effect of early work experience on later labor force behavior. Relatively little has been published about the educational and labor market experience of the cohort (Cherry 1976; Douglas and Cherry 1977). The major report, unpublished, deals with the labor market experience of those who left school before age 18 (MRC 1971).

A further longitudinal study — the National Child Development Study (NCDS), run by the National Children's Bureau — originated in the 1958 British Perinatal Mortality Survey, whose aim was to investigate the effects of a variety of factors on abnormality or mortality among babies. A sample of 17,000 born in a single week in 1958 was used. When the cohort reached age six in 1964, it was decided that data should be obtained on educational development, thus marking the beginning of the NCDS. The first follow-up was carried out in 1965 and the second in 1969, at age 11. In 1974, at age 16 during the final year of compulsory schooling, the third follow-up gathered information on health, family characteristics, educational performance, attitudes toward school and society, and expectations about education and employment (Fogelman 1976).

A briefer longitudinal survey of a more limited population was initiated in 1967 by the Social Survey Division of the Office of Population Censuses and Surveys. It followed 1,700 15- and 16-year-old boys from schools in ten areas of England and Wales for 18 to 20 months while they prepared to leave school, made the transition to work, and had their initial employment experiences. Much valuable information was obtained, but only the first volume on the preparatory period was published (Thomas and Wetherell 1974). The draft manuscript of the second volume, tentatively titled *Starting Work and After*, offers much detail on important aspects of early labor market experience, some of which has been cited in Reubens (1977a).

France

A longitudinal study of the entry into working life and subsequent labor market experience of a cohort of youth born in 1955 — *L'entrée des jeunes dans la vie active: la génération 1955* — was undertaken by the CEE (Center for Employment Studies) in Paris. The original sample was constituted in 1971, during the last year of compulsory education, and drawn from a variety of institutions in four *départements*, representing separate geographical areas and believed to be reasonably representative of the range in the nation. The initial survey was conducted by mail in early 1972, in the year following the end of compulsory education, with the aim of collecting current information on activities and a retrospective account of the previous year of transition between school and work for those who left school. The questionnaires, seeking information on family socioeconomic and professional status, education history and expectations, personal economic status and employment experience, methods of obtaining employment, earnings, hours, and conditions of work, were returned by almost 6,000 respondents. A first follow-up survey was conducted in 1974, three years after the end of compulsory schooling, to which over 3,500 responded, and another in 1976, to which over 2,500 replied. These follow-up studies sought further additional information on marital status, mobility, job changes, and unemployment experience (Rousselet et al. 1975; Faguer, Dossou, and Kandel 1977; Faguer 1980).

Several longitudinal surveys are being conducted by CEREQ (Center for Study and Research in Occupational and Educational Qualifications). As part of a project on *L'observatoire national des entrées dans la vie active* (The National Observation of the Entrance to Working Life), information is gathered each year on samples of individuals who left specified types and levels of vocational and academic education in a given school year. The first interviews took place in 1976 of those who left various types of education in 1974–1975. These were followed by additional cohorts in 1977, 1978, and 1979 from other educational levels. Each cohort was to be reinterviewed at four-year intervals into the mid-1980s. As one group of cohorts is reinterviewed, a new set of cohorts from the same educational levels is established and interviewed, to show the effects of different dates of entry. Information collected includes economic activity and status; job search processes, duration, and mobility; unemployment rates and first job search data; type of employment, by occupation and industry; earnings; and the process of the transition from school to work (France 1976–79). Full results are published in a number of volumes (France 1977–79, 1978–79), and many others are in preparation. A data base comprised of pooled data from the 1976–1979 cohorts is planned (France 1980a, 1980b).

Sweden

Since the mid-1960s the Statistiska Centralbyrån (the Central Bureau of Statistics) has conducted a series of longitudinal surveys giving information on the labor market experience and status of successive cohorts who have left the education system at various levels. Questionnaires asking information on students' plans for further studies and economic activity are collected at the time of graduation, and surveys at intervals are undertaken to obtain information on economic activity, education, employment and unemployment, occupations, and earnings. Attitudes and plans are also canvassed. Some cohorts are followed for only six months after leaving school, and none are followed for more than three to four years. Results are published in a series that contains separate volumes for graduates from each educational level above compulsory education and for specialized types of courses; at times summary volumes are issued to review the experience of successive cohorts (Sweden 1972–79, 1974–79, 1975–79).

Germany

Under sponsorship of the Federal Ministry of Education and Science, the IAB (Institute for Labor Market and Careers Research) of the BA (Federal Employment Institute) recently initiated a longitudinal study of youth in the transition from school to work. Data are collected on personal characteristics and attitudes, and educational and labor market intentions and experience. Two samples of young people were selected carefully from all over Germany. The first sample contained 60,000 young people, mostly 15 to 16 years old, in their ninth year of general education, and constituted 6 percent of all in the ninth year (Saterdag and Stegmann 1980). The second sample consisted of 30,000 school-leavers from the lower-secondary level in 1975/76 and 1976/77, according to the school type, plus those who left these schools without diplomas or completion of courses (Germany 1977).

A basic survey of the first sample was undertaken in May and June 1977, with a 78 percent response rate. Foreign youth constituted only 1.7 percent of the total sample, too small a proportion to be representative of the total of 15–16-year-old foreign youth. Initial findings have been published, and it is expected that the sample will be followed at intervals at least until they are 20 years old (Saterdag and Kraft 1979).

For the second sample, the basic survey was begun in the summer of 1977, followed by a questionnaire in the fourth quarter of 1977. The sample was questioned again in 1980. The initial response rate ranged from 69 to 87 percent, according to school type. Lowest response rates were found among those who left the basic school, the *Hauptschule*, without a certificate. First results concerning the relation of the school-leavers to apprenticeship and further education have been published (Stegmann and Holzbauer 1978).

Methodological Issues in Surveys

If a longitudinal or panel survey of youth is to yield rich results, it must be carefully planned to start at an early enough point in the life of the youth, ask a full range of questions without using up the good will of the respondent, tap sources of information other than the respondent, last long enough to cover changing experience, and have a large enough sample so that analysis can center on particular years of age or educational levels at a given time without pooling data. And with all this, successive cohorts are needed to answer new questions and to allow the measurement of the impact of different times.

More than cross-sectional surveys that rotate samples and can adjust the size and composition of samples, longitudinal surveys are liable to exhibit sample bias over time, which is not easily corrected. The source of bias is the attrition of some of the sample due to nonresponse, emigration, death, or institutionalization, or military service if only civilians are followed. In the case of the large attrition rate for young men in the American National Longitudinal Survey (NLS) based on civilian population, military service was the main factor (Parnes 1972). Between 1966 and 1971, there was an attrition rate of 24 percent for young males, which was accounted for by 10 percent of the sample entering the armed forces, 8 percent by refusals and "disappearance," and 6 percent due to institutionalization, death, and temporary absence from home. The noninterview rate was higher than average for blacks and high school dropouts in particular (US 1970–79, VI). At the time of the tenth year survey in 1976, 29 percent of the young men and 24 percent of the young women in the original sample no longer responded (CHRR 1979, p. 1). In general, attrition is more likely among those with poor employment records. One study by NLS analysts claims that such attrition is no more substantial in the NLS than in the U.S. Current Population Survey in which the sample is rotated (Borus, Mott, and Nestel 1978).

The longitudinal survey deals with individuals rather than households, and some analysts have wondered whether longitudinal surveys do not underrepresent, more than cross-sectional surveys, the long-time unemployed and similar youth (Corcoran 1979; Ellwood 1979). Such young people may be uninterested in the multiyear commitment of a longitudinal survey. In household surveys, the time in the sample is relatively brief. Moreover, longitudinal surveys collect retrospective data, which is subject to errors of memory, while household surveys obtain current information. Differences in findings are attributed in large part to this factor (Hills 1980, p. 24).

Longitudinal data also may differ substantially from other labor market sources because of survey timing. Longitudinal information tends to be compiled over a period of several weeks or months, with the survey reference week usually occurring prior to the week in which the interview takes place. Labor force survey and census data usually refer to specific weeks and are more prone to seasonal factors that affect the results.

References (see full citations at the end of the book).

National Labor Force Surveys

Official national sources
  Australia 1978a, 1979a
  Canada 1976c, 1977b, 1979c
  France 1978a
  Germany 1963–78, 1978b
  GB 1973–79a
  Italy 1961–80, 1978
  Japan 1956–80
  Sweden 1963–79, 1977b, 1977c
  US 1976b, 1978a, 1979c
International agency sources
  EC 1975–78d
  ILO 1977c
  OECD 1976–77, 1976c
Other
  Cain 1978
  Jusenius and von Rabenau 1979
  Macredie and Petrie 1976b
  McCarthy 1978
  Petrie 1978

National Censuses of Population

Official national sources
  France 1971
  GB 1966, 1968a, 1975
  Sweden 1974a, 1977b
  US 1973b, 1975a, 1978a
Other
  Long 1958

International Agencies

EC 1975–78, d
ILO 1977
OECD 1978c

National Longitudinal Surveys

United States
Official national sources
  US 1970–79, 1971–80, 1976–79
Other
  Bielby et al. 1977
  Borus et al. 1978
  CHRR 1979
  Hills and Thompson 1980
  Kalachek 1978, 1979
  Parnes 1972, 1975
  Sproat 1979
Great Britain
Other
  Fogelman 1976
  MRC 1971
France
Official national sources
  France 1976–79, 1977–79, 1978–79, 1980a, 1980b
Other
  Faguer et al. 1977, 1980
  Rousselet et al. 1975a
Sweden
Official national sources
  Sweden 1972–79, 1974–79, 1975–79
Germany
Official national sources
  Germany 1977
Other
  Saterdag and Kraft 1979
  Saterdag and Stegmann 1980
  Stegmann and Holzbauer 1978

5 Patterns of Labor Force Participation

Analysts of labor force participation rates and trends have routinely acknowledged the incomplete view of the labor supply resulting from a simple head count that ignores the total number of hours offered on the labor market. A rise in the size of the labor force, if accompanied by a decline in the average number of hours or weeks worked, can mean an actual decrease in the total work hours available to the economy. The omission of hours and weeks of work as a modifier of numbers in the labor force also distorts the relative position of groups. There are substantial differences in total hours offered by groups, defined by such variables as school enrollment status, marital and maternal status, age, sex, race, educational attainment, and place of residence. Allowance for total hours of work can alter the absolute and relative size of the labor force, calculated as full-time equivalents.

No group's labor force participation is more subject to misrepresentation through a simple count of heads than young people who are enrolled in school and simultaneously work or seek jobs. Full-time students who participate in the labor force are likely to work and seek fewer hours per week and fewer weeks per year than nonenrolled youth. In weighting each youth equally, as long as the minimum conditions for labor force participation are met, the official statistics raise measurement issues in regard to the labor force, and they may misrepresent the extent and nature of youth unemployment. As a consequence, youth program and policy implications may vary according to the way young people are counted. Cross-national comparisons are affected.

This chapter therefore examines trends within countries and variations among countries both in the proportion of the youth labor force that is enrolled in school and in the hours and weeks worked by students and nonstudents. We also investigate differences between male and female youth as a whole, since young females more frequently are in the part-time and part-year labor force than their male counterparts, which distorts youth labor force comparisons within and between countries. Finally, since it is alleged that out-of-school youth in some countries work fewer hours per year than adult members of the labor force, age group comparisons or weekly hours and weeks of labor force participation during the year are in order.

While it is not possible at present to compute "full-time equivalents" in the youth labor force, this chapter presents the available information on the subjects mentioned above. Due to the form of the data and the nature of the subject, there is more information about the employed than the unemployed portion of the labor force. This is a limitation, to the extent that the two subgroups differ significantly in regard to hours and weeks in the labor force. Numerically, however, the employed so dominate the labor force that little distortion results from citing information only about them.

Students in the Labor Force

Considerable variation among countries exists in the propensity of full-time students to work or seek work during the academic year and in vacation periods. The comparative situation cannot be described with precision because of definitional and data problems (Appendix 4:1). Although, in principle, each country which conducts a labor force survey should be able to obtain separate information about students who work, the subject is not equally well reported in all countries. If labor force activity by students is relatively rare in a country or tends to occur in a limited time period or occupational setting, the household members who report to the survey may omit or understate such work or job search. They also may deliberately conceal such information if allowances or benefits of various kinds might be adversely affected. Some labor force surveys face a special difficulty. If they are set up so that students who work are counted in the labor force but are not identified separately, as in the Swedish labor force survey, then the LFPR of the enrolled and nonenrolled can only be estimated. This is done by the rough method of comparing total educational enrollment data produced by the education authorities with the number reported by the labor force survey as out of the labor force because of studies; the balance is considered a measure of the number of students who also work. This procedure is particularly unsatisfactory in the summer months when many who are enrolled are not so reported because they are on vacation. Whatever difficulties appear in labor force surveys are compounded in countries which estimate labor force from other sources, such as social insurance records. Some countries deliberately exclude students from estimates of the labor force.

National definitions cause further problems of comparability. As Appendix 4:1 explains, two definitions, "enrolled in school" or "school was major activity in the survey week," are used to count students; each yields a slightly different total. We prefer the enrollment concept, provided that full-time students are distinguished from part-time. Some part-time students, who attend school in the evenings or on one or two days a week as part of a formal program, such as apprenticeship, should not be counted as students for labor force purposes. Exclusions of certain types of school from the data also complicate comparisons; both the United States and Australia have had such limitations on their coverage of students, since the US treats students in trade and business schools as out of the labor force and Australian data on teenagers do not cover those enrolled in postsecondary institutions.

It also is problematical whether students in educational programs that require a paid or unpaid work experience, such as practice teaching, should be counted as student workers. Although we would prefer to limit the present discussion to student labor force participation which is not directly due to an educational program, some data include these cases. In the same way, special government job programs for some young people in school, such as the United States has provided under YEDPA, probably should be excluded because parallel programs do not exist elsewhere; however, we do not know to what extent household members report such youth activity in the U.S. labor force survey. Some countries do not count students who are seeking jobs while they are attending school, including in the labor force only students who actually hold jobs (Appendix 4:1). Finally, the lower cutoff age for teenagers in this study, based on legal school-leaving and child labor laws, apparently results in the omission of labor force activity by youngsters under the cutoff age.

Whatever solutions are adopted for the aforementioned problems, it remains undesirable to use annual average data to determine student labor force participation rates or share of the youth labor force. An annual measure is likely to understate student labor force activity, as stated in connection with Sweden's data method, because of the usual treatment of students as nonstudents during the vacation months (Canada 1977b). An annual measure also adds together heavy activity during vacation periods and more limited participation during the academic term. Fragmentary information suggests that there is no large overlap between students who are in the labor force in vacation periods and those who work during the school period. A 1976 Swedish survey of upper-secondary school students who were completing the three- or four-year program found that about two-thirds of the students who worked during vacation periods did not work in term-time. All who worked during the term also worked in vacation periods, however, and formed a core of year-round workers whose hours varied according to the academic calendar (Sweden 1979c).

A somewhat different pattern was found in the United States in a special survey in 1969 (Perrella 1971). As in Sweden, almost 70 percent of enrolled students aged 16 to 21 who worked during the summer were not in the enrolled labor force in October 1969; the remaining 30 percent who had been summer workers accounted for 40 percent of all term-time student workers. This means that 60 percent of the American student workers recorded in October had not worked in the previous summer vacation period, while in Sweden all term-time workers also were in the summer labor force. The large number of students who are only in the vacation work force suggests that we should consider the vacation and term-time student labor force separately.

Vacation Period Labor Force Activity

In most countries, students who take jobs or seek employment during the various vacation periods, but especially in the long summer break, are a familiar aspect of the labor force scene. While few countries possess complete information about the extent of this activity, there are some indications of its incidence. In Sweden the same study of upper-secondary school students (ages 18–20) revealed that 94 percent had worked during vacations; of these, 54 percent reported that they worked only in the summer vacations, while 40 percent worked both in the summer and other holiday periods. Male and female patterns were comparable (Sweden 1979c). A similar 1976 Swedish inquiry among pupils (aged 15 and 16) who completed the last year of the basic school but did not proceed directly to upper-secondary school found that almost 60 percent had worked during vacations; of these, under 40 percent worked only in summer vacations, while 19 percent worked both in the summers and other holidays. Among the 24 Swedish counties, the proportion of pupils who worked during vacations ranged from 74 percent to 27 percent (Sweden 1979b).

In Canada a count of student summer workers has been made in recent years through supplementary labor force surveys that identify full-time students in March and ask them questions about plans to be enrolled in the fall term. The September survey then covers the summer labor force experience of those previously identified as students. In September 1975, for example, students with jobs constituted 19 percent of all employed 14 to 24-year-olds; information is not available on their proportion of all students in the age group. Further Canadian information is derived from a survey by the Department of Manpower and Immigration in 1970. It found that 83 percent of female and 93 percent of male community college students wanted summer jobs; for university students the respective percentages were 88 and 92. Moreover, among the small proportion of students who did not seek summer work, some did not search because they believed there were no jobs.

In the United States, a full-scale study of students and summer jobs in 1969 was undertaken through a supplementary survey of a sample of 12.1 million 16 to

21-year-olds who were enrolled in school in October 1969. Almost 80 percent, or over 9.5 million students worked or sought work during the summer, ranging from 91.1 percent of 18–19-year-old Negro and other males to 69.2 percent of 16–17-year-old white females (*Table 5.1).* Subsequent information about U.S. students who work during the summer months has been less complete and has been calculated as a net inflow. For example, a net expansion of about 4.3 million in the youth labor force (16–24 years old) between April and July 1978 included 2.9 million students net who entered the labor force for temporary jobs and 815,000 students net who were in the labor force in April and remained in over the summer. These net figures are not comparable to the 1969 study.

Another approach has been through gross flows analysis. Restricting the discussion to teenagers, it was estimated that almost three million teenagers entered the U.S. labor market in June in the late 1970s, either as summer workers or new entrants. At the same time about one million others who worked or sought jobs during the school year left the labor force, for all or part of the vacation period. When school resumed in September, the teenage labor force declined by the withdrawal of two million summer workers at the same time that about one million others newly entered the labor force (Smith and Vanski 1978a). Clark and Summers (1979b) made estimates for 1968-1976 from average stocks and flows. LFPR of 16–19-year-old males was almost 40 percent higher in July than the annual average. About three-fourths of summer labor force entrances are attributed to the desire of graduates and students for jobs, rather than to fluctuations in employment opportunities. During August and September, about one-third of the teenage population exits from the labor force, mostly to return to school. An important factor in the summer work pattern of American teenagers is deliberate creation of summer jobs financed by the federal government. Clark and Summers estimated that some 600,000 summer jobs were provided, on average, by federal programs each summer 1968-1976, accounting for 20 percent of the 3 million teenagers entering the labor market each summer. Just how entrenched student summer work is in the United States is conveyed by a recent survey in a newspaper article called "The Winter Hunt for a Summer Job" (*NY Times* m). A number of student-oriented publications are devoted to summer job opportunities, and a pamphlet is issued by the federal government on available summer jobs in government agencies.

As a Southern Hemisphere nation, Australia's summer vacation period begins in December and lasts into February. Over the period August 1978–January 1980, enrolled teenage males were, on average, 12.4 percent of the teenage male labor force, but they constituted 15.2 percent in December 1978 and 16.0 percent in December 1979, in both cases the highest proportion registered in each year. At the same time, the enrolled share of the male population fell, as would be expected. For enrolled teenage females, whose average share August 1978–January 1980 was 14.7 percent, the 1978 high was 16.9 percent in December, preceded by almost as high proportions in October and November. Thus, LFPR of both nonenrolled and enrolled young people rose in December, responding both to the entrance of school-leavers to the full-time labor market and the increased summer labor force activity of the remaining enrolled students (Table 5.2).

During the 1960s when Germany faced extreme labor shortages, recruitment of students for temporary summer jobs increased rapidly. In July 1969, 400,000 students were hired, an increase of 45 percent over the prior year, while over one-

---

*Tables marked with an asterisk are not included in this volume, but may be obtained from the authors.

Table 5.2 Teenage Labor Force Participation Rates and Share of Labor Force, by Enrollment Status and Sex, Australia, August 1978–May 1980

| | Both sexes | | Males | | | | Females | | | |
| | Labor force participation rate (percent) | | Enrolled[a] as a percent of teenage | | Labor force participation rate (percent) | | Enrolled[a] as a percent of teenage | | Labor force participation rate (percent) | |
Date	Enrolled[a]	Nonenrolled	Civilian population	Civilian labor force	Enrolled[a]	Nonenrolled	Civilian population	Civilian labor force	Enrolled[a]	Nonenrolled
1978 August	20.2	84.8	38.9	11.5	18.3	89.5	38.8	14.9	22.1	80.0
September	20.1	84.1	40.4	12.9	19.3	88.3	40.1	14.9	20.1	79.6
October	21.1	84.7	41.2	13.6	20.2	89.5	41.9	16.6	22.1	79.6
November	20.0	84.7	41.3	12.8	18.4	88.0	42.7	16.5	21.6	81.1
December	31.2	86.2	34.2	15.2	31.1	90.1	34.8	16.9	31.2	82.1
1979 January	26.6	84.8	32.3	12.8	27.1	88.6	33.0	13.7	26.1	80.8
February	20.1	85.0	32.4	9.4	19.2	88.9	33.6	11.6	21.0	80.8
March	19.8	84.3	33.5	10.1	19.6	88.1	34.3	11.5	20.0	80.4
April	20.8	84.1	34.2	10.1	19.1	88.9	35.5	13.5	22.4	79.0
May	20.4	83.2	35.2	10.3	18.6	88.0	36.2	13.9	22.2	78.0
June	19.0	83.6	36.7	9.5	16.0	88.3	38.3	14.7	21.9	78.7
July	19.7	83.2	37.7	10.6	17.2	88.0	39.5	15.5	22.1	78.0
August	20.0	83.2	38.2	11.3	21.8	88.2	40.7	16.1	18.1	77.7
September	23.2	85.1	39.7	13.8	21.7	89.5	41.3	17.7	24.7	80.4
October	22.1	84.8	41.1	13.7	20.4	89.6	42.0	17.7	23.8	79.7
November	23.4	84.6	41.2	14.5	21.5	88.9	41.6	15.0	25.4	80.1
December	32.2	86.5	34.5	16.0	32.9	91.0	34.5	12.7	31.5	81.8
1980 January	28.1	85.0	33.3	14.5	30.0	88.2	32.0	10.8	26.0	81.7
February	20.5	85.8	33.0	10.0	20.5	90.5	31.8	10.6	20.6	81.0
March	21.0	84.5	33.8	10.0	19.3	88.4	33.5	12.5	22.8	80.6
April	21.4	83.9	34.6	11.0	20.2	86.7	34.9	13.1	22.7	81.0
May	24.6	85.0	35.0	12.2	23.0	89.5	35.6	15.4	26.3	80.2

[a] Enrolled in secondary schools only. Excludes primary education and higher education.

Source: ABS (Australian Bureau of Statistics), *The Labour Force* (Canberra, monthly); *Employment Status of Teenagers* (Canberra, October 1978).

fourth of university students held summer jobs in 1967. By the 1970s more students sought summer jobs because of their need for income, since rapid cost rises affected even students receiving government grants. Rising from 45 percent in 1969, about 60 percent of students in universities held summer jobs in the summer of 1973. Due to the recession, the 1976 share fell to about 50 percent, but a large number of students stated that they had looked unsuccessfully for work or had been offered inadequate pay. In 1980, about half the students worked during the summer (Germany 1970–80 g,h). A survey conducted in the Lombardy region of Italy in 1975–1976 showed that 30 percent of pupils in lower-secondary school held vacation jobs; the range was from 15 percent in Milan province to 60 percent in Sondrio province (Council of Europe 1977–80). A much earlier British survey (late 1950s) disclosed that only 8 percent of boys in grammar and technical school and 9 percent of such girls worked in the school holidays, with still smaller proportions in the modern and all-age schools where leavers were overwhelmingly 15 years of age (GB 1959, p. 32). A number of other countries acknowledge substantial labor force activity by students during vacations but do not provide statistics.

University and other higher education students are more likely to enter the vacation labor market than younger students. Summer jobs usually entail longer hours than in-term jobs. Employment connected with tourism, recreation, and seasonal holidays appear to rank high. In some countries a large share of student summer jobs are as replacements for vacationing regular workers, but these opportunities are far more limited in countries, such as France and Sweden, where many places of work close down for a month or more because of the simultaneous vacation periods of most of the staff. Countries with a relatively high proportion of small family businesses or farms absorb high proportions of students, including those under the legal working age. An American source book on summer jobs identified vacancies in restaurants, resorts, hotels, camps, construction and roadwork, farming, house painting, mother's helpers, hospitals, supermarkets, department stores, factories and door-to-door sales (NY Times m).

In general, students accept summer jobs in occupations and under conditions that are quite removed from their expectations about their jobs after leaving school. On a visit to a Swedish Employment Service office a few years ago, one of the authors heard a young woman student request a summer job on a construction gang. When she was offered a job as a nurse's aide instead, she replied with some dismay: "But I am a medical student!" Of course, a small proportion of student summer workers not only hold the same job during the school term, possibly with shorter hours, but they also may take the same or a similar job with the same firm upon completing school. The lower the age and academic credentials on leaving school, the more likely that this pattern will appear.

Information on Canadian community college and university students in 1969 and 1970 suggests that in many cases their summer jobs were at a fairly low occupational level, but that a fair number of the jobs were related to studies. University males most often had nonagricultural laborer jobs, followed by professional and technical and service occupations. Clerical, service, and sales jobs occupied 67 percent of the university females; over 60 percent of community college females also were in these fields. Community college males had about the same proportion as university males in nonagricultural labor, but a smaller proportion in professional, administrative, and technical jobs. Summer jobs were overwhelmingly in private industry for both sexes in both types of higher education. University students had superior earnings from jobs in the public sector, as did females in community colleges; but community college males made their highest earnings in private industry. In the majority of cases, earnings were higher when jobs were related to studies. Earnings and savings were greater for university than community college students and for males than females (Canada 1971).

In the American study of student summer work in 1969, the occupational distribution in the summer jobs followed typical sex, age, and racial patterns for young people of that age. Earnings varied by age, sex, race, occupation, industry, hours and weeks worked, and the rate of pay. Almost half of 20–21-year-old white males earned over $1000, but under 1 percent of 16–17-year-old white females reached this sum. Generally, males earned more than females and black males earned less than white, although there was no great difference between black and white women (Perrella 1971; *Table 5.1).

Whether students in summer jobs work as many hours and weeks as out-of-school youth of the same age is not easily established. The Canadian college and university students had fewer weeks of work in 1969 and 1970 than they desired; the great majority of male university students worked for 9 weeks or more, while most females fell within the 5 to 16-week span. Community college students had somewhat shorter work duration (Canada 1971). In the American study of summer work in 1969 by the 6.1 million students who worked only in the three-month summer period, a full-time work week (35 to 40 hours) was most common for the oldest group, and for males; about one-third of the students worked fewer hours because they could not find full-time jobs. Two-thirds or more of the two older groups worked for 9 weeks or more (*Table 5.1).

Pending information to the contrary, it can be assumed that the hours and weeks of work in vacation periods are not markedly dissimilar for students and nonstudents. Therefore LFPR need little or no adjustment on account of differences in hours and weeks of summer work by students. Countries with a relatively high EER and a high LFPR of students will experience a greater seasonal surge in the youth labor force than other countries; however, such movements will be captured in annual averages of youth LFPR. More complicated adjustments may be required for students who are in the labor force during the academic year, if their hours and weeks diverge from those of out-of-school youth. As a first step we consider levels and trends in student labor force activity during the school year.

Labor Force Activity During the School Year

Until the 1960s in most of the twelve countries, a combination of school and work would have been suspect as a legacy of child labor (Roberts 1967, p. 134). Full-time attendance in school was only slowly achieved by a reduction in the hours worked by children; in some cases, work continued to occupy more of the child's time than school (Gibb 1907; Thomas 1945). Social reformers and educators regarded employment while attending school as a correlate of poverty or parental neglect. In Britain, legislation was enacted permitting only limited work during the term by school children above a certain age, usually a year or two before the legal school-leaving age. During the 1930s when many local authorities in Britain permitted 13-year-olds to work a certain number of hours per week, it was estimated that in England and Wales 7 percent of those under 14, then the legal leaving age, and 11 percent in Scotland held jobs (Jewkes and Jewkes 1938, pp. 25, 144–47). As late as 1950 an American survey found that 8 percent of school children 10 to 13 years old worked during the school term: 60 percent were in paid jobs and the remainder performed unpaid family work of 15 hours or more per week (Long 1958, p. 391). At any point, accurate Italian records would have shown far more.

This aspect of combining school and work has not disappeared completely in any of the twelve nations, and it continues to be quite important in Italy. It is surprising to find that 14–15-year-olds, who no longer are included in the regular labor force count but are listed separately in Sweden and the United States, have fairly substantial LFPR; a portion is of course explained by summer jobs (US 1979b; Sweden 1963–79a). Italy, though, is only marginally better off than many developing nations in regard to child labor during the school year (Mendelievich 1979, p. 568).

As labor force activity in the school term has become more common and has involved older and middle-class youth, as well as poor youngsters below the legal school-leaving age, working schoolchildren have recently become the less conspicuous part of student labor force activity in the industrialized countries. In no country has the phenomenon been prominent for a long period of time. A tradition has long existed in the United States that it is respectable, even praiseworthy, to work one's way through school. But the numbers involved were not large, and as Bowen and Finegan (1969, p. 474) observed about pre-World War II teenagers, "attending school and holding a market job were almost exclusive activities." Long (1958, p. 423) remarked that "it has never been common for a boy to work his way through high school or college in Great Britain (or in any European country)," offering a contrast to the US.

In the postwar period, Americans and Canadians became more familiar with substantial student labor force activity of a regular type, going beyond the deliveryboy/baby-sitting/lawn-mowing variety. According to the 1940 census, 4 percent of 16-year-old in-school males and 1 percent of similar females held jobs in the survey week. Thirty years later, these figures had risen to 27 and 16 percent respectively. Male American students are estimated to have comprised 1 percent or less of the total male labor force in 1940, 2.5 percent after World War II, and over 6 percent of the males employed in nonagricultural industries around 1977 (Owen 1978, p. 32). Even if this estimate includes summer jobs, a significant growth of the student labor force is indicated. Canadian students in the labor force in the mid-1970s were estimated at 8 percent of the total labor force in the period January–April and September–December (Canada 1977b, p. 8). By contrast, in the mid-1960s European students seeking part-time jobs were said to be the exception rather than the rule. Moreover, such part-time work as existed was not well adapted to the needs of students, who were reported to be taking casual jobs instead (Hallaire 1968, p. 34). If this indeed was an accurate representation of student labor force activity during the term, it has changed considerably since that time in many European countries (OECD 1979c). A lag in measurement capability may conceal some of the European growth in student LFPR.

Upward trends in student LFPR, as observed in the United States up to 1965, were attributed to the increased fraction of college students from lower and middle-income families; the growth of part-time jobs, especially those calling for fewer than 15 hours per week; the associated growth in service industries; greater managerial sophistication in using part-time workers; and a rising proportion of married students in the total. As offsetting factors that tended to hold back the rise in student LFPR, the analysts noted the decline in agricultural employment, the relatively slow growth of predominantly male industries, greater competition for part-time jobs among the rising proportion of students, high levels of unemployment in the economy, and an upward trend in relative wages of teenage males (Bowen and

Finegan 1969, pp. 472–75). Several of these may have been peculiar to the United States.

A consideration of the growth since 1965 in student LFPR during the term in the United States and other countries suggests several additional forces that may have fostered a rise in student LFPR. In families with several children reaching postcompulsory school age in rapid succession, a micro aspect of the baby boom, the burden of financing full-time education for so many at one time led to combinations of education and work for youth from socioeconomic groups that might have had less of this activity in earlier periods. In the US it was found that siblings' work patterns while in school influenced younger brothers and sisters (Rees and Gray 1979). Although this factor applied much more to some countries than others, an almost universal phenomenon was the sharp rise in out-of-pocket costs of higher education, due to inflation and the fact that governmental aid to students tended to lag behind rises in such costs.

In spite of common causes of the upward trend in student LFPR, differences among countries in levels of student labor force activity continued. A review of available data for individual countries follows.

Measures of Student LFPR

An ad hoc method of estimating the extent to which young people combine school and work consists of adding together educational enrollment and labor force participation rates for a given age group (*Table A5.1). The excess over 100 may indicate that individuals are in both categories, but it also may result from incompatible and nonadditive data. Totals under 100 do not mean that no persons combine school and work, since a certain portion of the age group, especially females, is neither in school nor the labor force (NISLF).

When a country maintains a series on the enrolled and nonenrolled youth population and labor force, as the United States does through its supplementary questions to the October Current Population Survey (CPS), it is possible to derive a consistent total activity rate that reflects the student labor force by showing rates over 100 percent. Thus, teenage males in the US showed a clear rising trend from 1965 to 1977, as the total activity rate moved from 123.8 to 128.7. Young adult males, however, were fairly static at about 110. As stated previously, these readings should be adjusted for the NISLF proportion before they are read as the student LFPR.

In any event, this method is less satisfactory for most countries than direct inquiries into the labor force activity of students during the academic year, either through special studies of students or labor force survey data. The former, whose findings we present first, do not always distinguish clearly between students who were working at the time of the inquiry and students who had worked at some time during their school years. As might be expected, each country also selected particular educational levels for investigation.

Several national surveys have provided information on the work experience of British pupils at the end of compulsory school. For this group there has not been much change from the mid-1950s to the mid-1970s. A report issued in 1959 noted that about 55 percent of boys and 22 percent of girls had held paid part-time jobs before they left compulsory school, which then ended at 15 (Great Britain 1959, vol. 2, p. 30). A 1966 survey of 15-year-old school-leavers revealed that 42 percent of the boys and 20 percent of the girls had paid employment for at least two hours a week outside the home (Great Britain 1968, p. 139). In the 1974 national survey of 16-year-olds, 49 percent of pupils of both sexes in the final year of compulsory school had worked during the term (Fogelman 1976, Ch. 4). Many of these were delivery or baby-sitting jobs with brief hours.

Swedish 1976 surveys of students at two educational levels showed that in the last year of the compulsory school, only about 20 percent of the students who did not proceed to upper-secondary school had worked during the school year; the fraction was almost identical for boys and girls (Sweden 1979b, Table 3.1). This comparatively low proportion was sustained in a survey of older students who had completed the three- or four-year upper-secondary course. Only about one-third of both males and females (ages 18 to 20) had worked at any time during their upper-secondary schooling (Sweden 1979c, Table 4:2).

A December 1971 questionnaire to students in the last three years of American high schools found that 49 percent of all boys and 35 percent of all girls were working, and that 35 percent of 10th graders, 39 percent of 11th graders and 54 percent of 12th graders worked currently (Purdue Opinion Panel 1972, p. 3a). In March 1973 a similar sample showed 56 percent of boys and 45 percent of girls at work; 41 percent of 10th graders, 50 percent of 11th graders and 61 percent of 12th graders worked currently (Purdue Opinion Panel 1973, p. 15a). Such a large increase in employment rates in a period of 15 months can be due to one or more of the following causes: sampling variations, seasonal differences between the December and March surveys, cyclical improvement in the youth job market, and the upward trend in student LFPR visible from the mid-1960s.

Official Japanese records show those transferring from one level of education to another on a full-time and part-time basis and include data on those who will be attending school and working. From 1955 to 1979, students entering senior high school, about 15 years old, show a declining proportion in part-time schooling as well as a shrinking fraction who work while attending school. While only some 7.5 percent were "also working" in 1955, the proportion dropped to 1.2 percent by 1979. A similar trend was exhibited by those entering higher education, mostly 18 years old. Their LFPR dropped from around 6 percent in 1955 to 1.6 percent in 1979 (Japan 1976a, pp. 248-49, 261-63; 1979a, pp. 86, 90-92). There is no evidence that the method of recordkeeping changed. According to a Ministry of Education survey, about one-fifth of Japanese college and university students are said to have part-time jobs during the term, mostly as tutors to younger children for thirty to fifty hours a month. The 15 percent of university students who work full-time during the academic year may largely consist of the nominally registered who do not attend classes or complete their degrees (Kato 1978, pp. 13, 46-47). Thus, Japanese students who work participate in the regular labor market to a minor extent.

French information primarily concerns students in specific fields in higher education. As of September 1976, 40 percent of those who recently left the science faculties had held jobs entailing ten hours of work or more per week in their last year. The data include some in jobs, such as practice teaching, which are part of the educational program, some who are technically enrolled but do not attend classes, and students working for advanced degrees; many students were over 25 years old. Of those who worked, three-fourths of the men and two-thirds of the women worked more than thirty hours a week. The economic activity rate in the last year of education rose so rapidly for females from 1970 to 1975 that it exceeded that of males, holding constant age and level of education. The LFPR of these women increased twice as rapidly as that of all women in the age group 20-29 (France 1978-79a, pp. 48-52). German university students showed a marked rise over time in the proportion who worked consistently or frequently during the academic year. In 1963 about 8 percent were said to hold such jobs, while by the mid-1970s it was 20 to 25 percent (Germany 1970–80, g,h). These survey results are merely suggestive of levels and trends; they will be supplemented below by broader statistical data.

Personal Factors in Student Labor Force Activity

Individual and family characteristics that foster or hinder participation in the labor force during the school term can be isolated in cross-sectional country studies or data. Bowen and Finegan have done the most thorough analysis, using the U.S. 1960 census results for urban areas in cross-sectional fashion and considering in turn the effects of age by single years, family income (excluding students' earnings), presence of parents and living arrangements, type of school attended and education, and occupation and employment status of the head of the household. Each analysis controlled for the other variables (Bowen and Finegan 1969, pp. 381–401).

With a rise in age of a single year, Bowen and Finegan found that student LFPR increased for boys and girls 14–17 and females 18–24, but not males 18–24; the unadjusted LFPR by single years of age did not differ significantly from adjusted LFPR, which controlled for the other variables. American longitudinal studies of males indicated that, as the particular in-school cohort aged, it became a smaller fraction of its age group and its LFPR rose (US 1970–79, vol. 6, p. 10; Meyer and Wise 1979). Swedish follow-up surveys of those leaving compulsory school from 1970 to 1978 revealed that a fairly level proportion (10 to 11 percent of both sexes) combined school and work, while a Swedish cross-sectional survey of a narrower age range disclosed that 16-year-old students had a higher LFPR than those who were 15 or younger or 17 and older (Sweden 1979e, p. 29; 1979b, p. 4). In a British analysis of a similar age group, boys in grammar and technical schools showed a declining LFPR with an advance in the age at which they left school; for girls the situation was reversed (GB 1959, p. 31). Japanese census data for 1960, 1970, and 1975 depict a fairly consistent decline in student LFPR for each sex with every year of age. A special study drawn from the Canadian Census of 1971 and limited to never married youth living at home demonstrated for each sex a rise in student LFPR with each year of age from 15 to 21 and then a drop to 24 (Canada 1978c, Chart 7). Available data thus show no central tendency in student LFPR by single years of age. More uniform and recent studies across countries, separately for each sex, are required, but it is probable that national and temporal differences would persist.

Relationships between family income and the LFPR of students were analyzed by Bowen and Finegan in terms of several direct and indirect indicators: total family income less the earnings of the student, the number and age of siblings, whether students live away at school or at home, whether the school attended is private or public, and the ratio of college teachers to college students as an index of the cost of attending the institution. Both the adjusted and unadjusted LFPR in 1960 of 14–17-year-old students varied irregularly with family income, excluding that of students. Family income was divided into $1,000 intervals: from under $1,000 to $11,000, followed by three intervals, with the top income class $25,000 or more. Apart from a distinct decline in LFPR at $15,000 or more, the results are inconclusive (Bowen and Finegan 1969, pp. 386–88). British data in the mid-1950s for LFPR of students who were mostly under 15 years of age indicated that father's income had little effect on boys' LFPR except for diminishing it in the top income class. Among girls, however, the LFPR tended to rise slightly as father's income increased, quite regularly for girls attending modern and all-age schools and less so for those in grammar and technical schools (GB 1959, Table 13). The reasons given by boys and girls for working part-time may account for the lack of a strong relationship between LFPR and father's income. Under 10 percent of each sex in the two main types of school worked to help at home; most youngsters used earnings as pocket money, to buy a specific object, or for vacations (GB 1959, Table 13c). Another British study showed a much smaller proportion of upper middle-class children than others having part-time jobs (Roberts 1967, p. 131).

More comprehensive information was provided by unpublished data from the U.S. October 1977 Current Population Survey, which divided the enrolled population by age, sex, living arrangements, and average annual household income, including the earnings of employed students. As Table 5.3 demonstrates, never married enrolled youth living at home or away at school tended to show rising LFPR as household income increased, up to the $25,000 and over level, at which point there was a decline in LFPR in all four age-sex groups. Teenagers, a significant fraction of whom live at home, had the clearest progression of LFPR as household income ascended. The LFPR of never married students in households with under $5,000 a year was 15 to 27 percentage points below that of youth from families in the $15,000–$24,999 bracket.

Somewhat the same progression of LFPR with rising income was shown by enrolled young adults who lived on their own or were married, but their LFPR levels were much higher than those of their never married counterparts living at home, as would be expected. Too few teenagers were in the "all other youth" category to attach much significance to the irregularity of their LFPR by income class (Table 5.3). A comparison of the LFPR of never married enrolled and nonenrolled youth by income class points to a lower propensity of youth from poorer families to be in the labor force whether or not they are in school; this observation is equally valid for whites and blacks (Table A7.5). These findings on the relation between household income and student LFPR, running counter to economic theory, are not reported in another American study, based on a smaller sample and dealing with college students only (Myers 1977). If the BLS findings are accurate, a significant socioeconomic pattern is present. As Chapter 3 indicates, full-time enrollment rates are higher as household income climbs up to $25,000. And among this larger enrolled proportion in the higher income classes, student LFPR is relatively greater, thus giving these income classes a highly disproportionate share of part-time or student labor market. This is a significant point to consider in youth employment policy.

The extent to which student earnings are correctly or completely reported in the CPS and the relation of such earnings to the size of total household income is not known. It might be expected that households that contain student workers would have higher average incomes than similar families without student workers. As indicated by Table 7.6, among never married enrolled youth living at home, average annual household income in all four age-sex groups was higher where there was an employed student than where the student was unemployed or out of the labor force. It is not clear, however, that student earnings were the major factor in these income differences.

It is possible that enrolled, never married, living at home students work during the term primarily to meet their own financial requirements and that very little of their income is contributed to the household. This view is supported by an inquiry in March 1973 among American students in the last three years of high school, which disclosed that in all three years students divided relatively evenly into three groups:

Table 5.3 Civilian Labor Force Participation Rates of Youth by Enrollment Status, Age, Sex, Living Arrangements, and Annual Household Income, United States, October 1977

Enrolled

	Never married youth living at home (or at school)				All other youth			
	16-19		20-24		16-19		20-24	
	Male	Female	Male	Female	Male	Female	Male	Female
Total in labor force (000s)	2,575	2,170	745	623	111	176	672	623
Income class	Labor force participation rates							
	(percent)							
All classes[a]	45.5	41.0	45.9	47.6	61.7	48.9	71.8	65.3
Less than $5,000	30.4	21.9	30.3	36.3	73.8	51.9	59.5	53.3
$5,000-7,499	35.7	32.9	29.5	38.5	44.8	38.5	74.3	68.3
$7,500-9,999	40.6	36.7	47.2	48.3	71.4	53.6	76.2	65.5
$10,000-14,999	48.2	41.9	40.3	50.9	75.0	60.0	85.9	67.3
$15,000-24,999	52.6	48.4	52.1	51.6	65.4	50.0	81.5	85.0
$25,000 and more	46.2	20.7	48.1	49.3	36.4	25.0	45.5	90.0

Nonenrolled

	16-19		20-24		16-19		20-24	
	Male	Female	Male	Female	Male	Female	Male	Female
Total in labor force (000s)	1,730	1,140	2,356	1,426	397	690	4,026	3,992
Income class	Labor force participation rates							
	(percent)							
All classes[a]	90.0	79.7	90.8	86.0	96.6	56.4	98.1	66.5
Less than $5,000	80.2	49.4	79.1	60.7	95.0	55.5	95.5	60.6
$5,000-7,499	85.1	63.8	84.8	76.8	94.4	52.9	97.8	66.4
$7,500-9,999	87.9	76.3	87.9	76.4	100.0[b]	57.4	97.5	63.6
$10,000-14,999	91.0	84.8	93.2	86.4	100.0[b]	60.0	98.6	65.6
$15,000-24,999	92.3	91.3	94.7	94.8	100.0[b]	61.0	99.3	74.3
$25,000 and more	97.1	92.1	95.2	95.4	75.0	100.0	100.0	78.5

[a] Includes those whose income was not reported.
[b] Not in the labor force total is less than 1,000.

Source: U.S. Department of Labor, Bureau of Labor Statistics, unpublished tables from October 1977 Current Population Survey.

those who saved most of their earnings, those who spent about half and saved the rest, and those who spent most of their earnings (Purdue Opinion Panel 1973, p. 15a). While the Special Labor Force Reports on youth of the Bureau of Labor Statistics usually cite financial need in the family as a cause of student LFPR, the distribution by income class and evidence on how students use their earnings raise questions that require further investigation. In several other countries – Japan, France and Germany, for example – it has been noted that some middle-class university and college students work in term-time in order to gain psychological independence from their families (Kato 1978; France 1978–79a). Most students in higher education who work are nevertheless assumed to need the income to meet living expenses for themselves or newly formed families. As further information is collected on the motives of students in seeking jobs and their disposition of earnings, new evaluations can be made of the significance of the in-school unemployment rate compared to that of out-of-school youth.

Bowen and Finegan measured the 1960 LFPR of American 14–17-year-old students by family characteristics: presence of parents, schooling of family head, and employment of family head. Enrolled teenagers from broken homes were more likely to be in the labor force than those living with parents; the differential was particularly apparent when all other variables were controlled (Bowen and Finegan 1969, pp. 396–97). American data for October 1977 on living arrangements of teenagers show the same relationship, without controlling for other variables (Table 5.3); additional unpublished data for the same date confirm this relation for whites and blacks separately.

The labor force status of U.S. enrolled teenagers bore no consistent relationship to the educational attainment of the family head (Bowen and Finegan 1969, p. 397). According to the same source, some student subsets who lived in families where the head was unemployed had higher adjusted LFPR than those where the head was employed, but the differentials were not statistically significant at the 10 percent level except for 14–17-year-old males, whose adjusted LFPR gave an unexpected result; it was 10 percentage points lower for boys with unemployed than employed fathers (Bowen and Finegan 1969, pp. 399–400). A similar effect was observed in the Canadian 1971 census among never married young people (under 25) living at home. Although these data do not deal separately with the enrolled, it is interesting that the Canadian interpretation was that children tend to mirror the family head's labor force status (Canada 1978c, Table 11).

Another interesting relationship concerns the interface between student LFPR and school grades. The direction of causality is not clear, since those who are least able academically may be most prone to work, rather than that working reduces grades. Cross-national differences in the demands of academic work also are related to the findings on this subject. A Swedish survey indicated that those who never worked during the (three- or four-year) upper-secondary course had the highest grade point averages, followed respectively by those who worked weekends only, those who worked weekdays only, and, in lowest position, those who worked in both time periods (Sweden 1979c, p. 18). In the highest scholastic group, among boys who left Glasgow schools at the earliest age, a lower percent worked while in school than in the group as a whole (Ferguson and Cunnison 1951, pp. 77–78). A French study of university students in the science faculties had adverse findings about the impact on academic performance of simultaneous employment (France 1978–79a). Working while in school was associated with a lower rate of taking certifying examinations in a London area survey (Roberts 1967, p. 135).

An American study of 10th and 11th graders in Orange County, California, found that those with jobs during the school term obtained significantly lower grade point averages than others. The authors concluded that the lower GPA (grade point averages) were "a consequence of working, rather than a factor explaining differential selection into the work force, since job seekers and non-seekers do not differ from each other in GPA" (Greenberger and Steinberg 1979, p. 15). Grades suffered most among student-workers who were academically less able and who worked 25 hours or more a week. Although in theory employed students might reduce their leisure hours in order to maintain study hours, such a practice was not evidenced (Greenberger and Steinberg 1979). A totally different perspective was adopted by Italian officials who evaluated work while in school: not against potentially better grades, but against potential delinquency and loitering on the streets, in the absence of part-time jobs (Council of Europe 1977–80).

In an American survey of high school students (16 tô 18 years old) course grades (below average, average, above average, excellent) were matched to whether or not students currently worked and how many hours per week they worked in December 1971. Without any separation by sex or school year, the findings were that excellent students had the highest LFPR (50 percent), followed by below average, above average, and average students (40 percent). Positions were altered when the number of hours worked entered the picture, however. One-fifth of below average students but only 4 to 8 percent of the other three categories worked as much as 26 to 40 hours a week. Similarly, the proportion working few hours (under 6 hours a week) was highest for excellent students (17 percent), 10 to 11 percent for average and above average, and only 6 percent for below average students (Purdue Opinion Panel 1972, p. 3a). While other countries measure academic performance in relation to whether students worked or did not work, American analysis stresses number of hours worked.

Another perspective on academic performance and student LFPR is gained by considering the type of course or school. A Swedish survey of upper-secondary students in the three- and four-year course found a range in LFPR of 26 to 39 percent, according to the type of major subject, or "line," as it is called. Those in the natural science line, which is very demanding academically and strongly associated with entrance to higher education, had the lowest LFPR, while the highest LFPR were shown by those in the economics line (Sweden 1979c, Table 4:3). Follow-up data on U.S. males in the high school class of 1972 who continued their education confirmed that the type of postsecondary education undertaken was related to the proportion participating in the labor force during the academic year. Those enrolled in two-year colleges had an LFPR of 57.3 percent in October 1972, nearly twice as high as that of four-year-college enrollees (29.6 percent) and considerably higher than the 46.1 percent LFPR of students in vocational-technical schools. These relationships persisted in subsequent years (US 1977d).

Student LFPR and Share of the Youth Labor Force

For purposes of weighing the relative importance of the student labor force in various countries, we need information on student labor force activity that can be compared with the LFPR of nonstudents or of the whole youth labor force. Calculations of the student share of the youth labor force add to the picture, since they make allowance for cross-national differences in the proportion of the age group that is enrolled. Special tabulations from labor force surveys or censuses provide the basic information on student LFPR and are available for only a few countries.

Although nominally described as a teenage inquiry, the Australian survey, which began in August 1978 on a monthly basis, effectively concerns 15–17-year-olds, since the survey results for teenage students apply only to those enrolled in regular secondary schools, which few 18- or 19-year-olds attend. Due to the exclusion of trade and business schools and all higher education, teenagers who attend these institutions are recorded in the nonstudent population, thus reducing both the LFPR and the enrolled share of the teenage labor force compared to measures used in other countries. Table 5.2 shows that, in the school months, teenage Australian male students generally constituted 10 to 11 percent of the teenage male labor force and had a LFPR of 16 to 23 percent, compared to a LFPR of 87 to 90 percent for nonstudent teenage males; to the extent that students in higher education are out of the labor force, they depress the teenage nonstudent LFPR. Enrolled teenage females have constituted 12 to 18 percent of the teenage female labor force, with a slightly rising trend over the past two years. Enrolled female LFPR has exceeded that of males, while nonenrolled female LFPR has been lower than that of corresponding males.

Monthly data on the student population and labor force in Australia fluctuate considerably, throwing doubt on data of countries whose readings are for one time of year only. Australian youth appear to move frequently between enrolled and nonenrolled status, according to the monthly data, and students also make many entrances and exits from the labor force. There appears to be as much monthly variation in LFPR for the enrolled over the course of a year as might be expected over several years, measured by annual averages.

Information for the four age-sex groups in Japan can be drawn from censuses or the triennial Employment Status Survey. Table 5.4 presents student LFPR from the latter source and employed students as a share of the youth labor force from the

Table 5.4 Student LFPR and Employed Students' Share of the Youth Labor Force, by Age and Sex, Japan, 1959–1975

Year	Labor force participation rates of students				Employed students as a share of youth labor force			
	Males		Females		Males		Females	
	15–19	20–24	15–19	20–24	15–19	20–24	15–19	20–24
	(percent)				(percent)			
1959	9.3[a]	22.9[a]	7.6[a]	18.2[a]	—	—	—	—
1960	—	—	—	—	2.6	0.3	1.6	0.1
1962	7.0	17.1	6.6	15.4	—	—	—	—
1965	6.5	17.4	6.0	14.9	—	—	—	—
1968	9.5	22.0	8.8	21.3	—	—	—	—
1970	—	—	—	—	7.4	2.5	6.3	1.3
1971	8.2	22.1	7.1	20.7	—	—	—	—
1975	—	—	—	—	7.4	2.5	7.5	1.5

[a] Estimated.

Sources: LFPR: Japan. Office of the Prime Minister. Bureau of Statistics. Employment Status Survey, 1962–1977. Tokyo, 1968–1978; Share: Japan. Office of the Prime Minister. Bureau of Statistics. 1960 Population Census of Japan, vol. 2, pt. 3, table 1; 1970 Population Census of Japan, vol. 5, pt. 1, div. 1, table 15; 1975 Population Census of Japan, vol. 5, pt. 1, div. 1, table 4. Tokyo, 1962, 1973, 1978.

census. All data were collected at a time when school was in session. The results reflect the meager labor force activity of students and their small share of the youth labor force. Even the relatively low student LFPR shown in Table 5.4 may exaggerate the actual situation, since Japanese student LFPR are constructed by adding together the very small number of students actually holding jobs with the much larger number of students recorded as "wanting to work." For example, among enrolled young adults in 1971, 7.3 percent of males and 6.9 percent of females actually held jobs, while 14.8 percent of males and 13.8 percent of females "wanted to work." The number unemployed thus was about twice as large as the number employed, a relationship unknown in other countries. No definite trends are shown in student LFPR, but the proportion of employed students in the youth labor force has tended to rise from 1960 to 1975, reflecting higher EER. The annual labor force survey, giving data for 15 to 24-year-olds and both sexes, also shows a rising share of employed students in the total of employed youth.

British official estimates of student LFPR have been rare, since official policy has been to exclude students from calculations of the working population. An estimate for 1966 dealt with students who were in the labor force at some time during the year. Including summer work, male teenagers indicated an LFPR of 15 percent, female teenagers 25 percent, young adult males 50 percent, and females 60 percent (GB 1969–80c, pp. 214–15; 1969–80d, p. 425).

The rise in part-time work by youth during the school months over a period of years has been interpreted in Sweden as a rise in student LFPR (Sweden 1976a, pp. 29, 34; 1978e). A method of calculating student LFPR has been to subtract from the number of young people enrolled in school (according to the education authorities) the number of youth in school (as recorded by the labor force survey). For each age-sex group a figure is obtained which, if the two series are entirely compatible, would represent students in the labor force. This is a less satisfactory method than a direct measure of the enrolled LFPR through the labor force survey, but it permits some estimates. In 1978, 20.1 percent of 16–19-year-olds and 12.7 percent of 20–24-year-olds appeared to be combining education and work, although some part-time students may have been included in the educational statistics and the labor force survey. It is possible that the official data do not record all student part-time work, since the follow-up surveys of Swedish students cited earlier and general opinion in Sweden suggest that student LFPR is quite widespread.

While Canadian data on student LFPR are drawn from diverse sources and are not continuous or fully comparable from year to year, they establish that Canada's student LFPR are among the highest. One of the earliest measures was derived from the 1971 census (Canada 1978c, pp. 22–25). Confined to never married, full-time students living at home, these LFPR may be somewhat high, especially for the older age group, inasmuch as the census period (late May and early June) coincided with the beginning of vacation periods in higher education. Therefore, some summer labor force activity may be mixed with the LFPR we are seeking to establish. The results show an LFPR of 37.4 percent for 15–19-year-old males who are full-time students, compared to 69.4 percent for those who are not full-time; the latter group includes part-time students and nonenrolled. For teenage females, the respective LFPR were 27.9 and 59.6 percent, while for young adult males (20 to 24) it was 71.6 and 87.3 percent, and for young adult females 60.5 and 82.3 percent (Canada 1978c, p. 24). Thus, the LFPR of full-time young adult students were almost twice as high as those of teenagers in full-time school attendance.

A subsequent calculation for November 1972, based on the labor force survey, gave data for the 14 to 24 age group as a whole with no sex breakdown, and divided them into out-of-school and in-school. LFPR for out-of-school youth was 81.4 percent against 19.8 percent for students; the student share of the youth labor force was 20.9 percent (Canada 1976a, p. 77). Considerably lower student LFPR are shown for October 1966–1973 (*Table 5.5; Gendreau 1974). Later analysis indicated that these estimates, based on an indirect method of interpreting labor force survey results, understated the number of students (Canada 1977b, p. 7). In addition, students in the Gendreau study included those enrolled in training courses run by the Department of Manpower and Immigration and those in private trade schools and business colleges; both categories are excluded in the enrollment data of the United States and other countries. The Gendreau study (1974) shows clearly that student LFPR was rising as nonstudent LFPR declined. Other studies of the youth labor force confirmed that students, especially younger teenagers, were increasing their LFPR in the first part of the 1970s (Canada 1976d, pp. 12–13). The teenage labor force as a whole showed a rising trend 1966–1974 as did young adult females, but young adult males exhibited a slight decline (Table A4.2b, c).

A special study of the labor force activities and characteristics of Canadian students in the period January 1975 to April 1977 arose out of a revised labor force survey questionnaire designed to collect more extensive and accurate information on student labor force activity (Canada 1977b). Students included in the results are those who were enrolled (before January 1977) during the reference week or attended school (January–April 1977) in the reference week. School was defined as an institution which offered credits to be applied toward a certificate, degree, or diploma, and a question was asked about full-time and part-time attendance. Data were given only for students, and the age group analyzed was 15 years and over, although most students would fall in the 15–24-year category, the age groups with which we are immediately concerned.

These Canadian data document the seasonal variations in the student population and LFPR that were noted for Australia, as well as a division into full-time and part-time students and student labor force. Among full-time students, who constituted about five-eighths of the total student population during the academic year, monthly LFPR generally ranged from 25 to 30 percent in the January 1975–April 1977 period (omitting vacation months), while the LFPR of part-time students varied slightly around 85 percent (Canada 1977b, Table 1). U.S. full-time college students aged 16 to 24 had an October LFPR of 40 to 43 percent in 1975–1977, while part-time students' LFPR reached 85 to 90 percent (US 1960–77; 1960–79a). American college students therefore show slightly higher LFPR, regardless of the division into full-time and part-time students.

Canadian monthly data on full-time students, 15–24 years old, who were in the labor force began to be published from March 1980 in *The Labour Force*, an official journal. Taken together with earlier unpublished annual and monthly data for 1975–1979, a series can be constructed which is not directly comparable to *Table 5.5. Bearing in mind that Canadian annual data understate student LFPR because those not attending school in the summer months are regarded as nonenrolled, Table 5.6 indicates no trend in average annual student LFPR or in the student share of the labor force from 1975 to 1978, although 1979 generally moves upward as do LFPR for the whole age group (Tables A4.2b, c). Census LFPR results for 1971 are conspicuously higher than rates in the labor force survey for 1975–1980; the former probably is less reliable. Although Canadian definitions are more restrictive, student shares of the youth labor force are higher in Canada than shares shown in Japan

Table 5.6   Full-Time Student LFPR and Student Share of the Youth Labor Force, by Age and Sex, Canada, 1975–1980

	Labor force participation rate of students				Student share of labor force of same age			
	15–19		20–24		15–19		20–24	
	Male	Female	Male	Female	Male	Female	Male	Female
	(percent)				(percent)			
1975	32.1	27.2	28.9	27.7	32.8	30.9	4.9	3.8
1976	29.7	27.7	27.4	29.8	30.9	31.8	4.4	4.1
1977	30.4	26.8	24.5	29.8	30.3	30.6	3.7	4.2
1978	30.4	27.8	25.0	26.7	29.5	30.7	3.4	3.5
1979	33.5	30.9	28.0	28.6	30.7	32.4	3.9	3.6
April 1980	35.5	33.0	25.8	31.5				
May 1980	35.3	31.7	30.9	28.7				
June 1980	38.3	32.5	27.2	30.5				

Source: Canada, Statistics Canada, Labour Force Survey Division, unpublished data; The Labour Force, March 1980–July 1980.

(Tables 5.6, 5.4). Comparisons with Australia are inappropriate because the recorded enrolled are chiefly 15 to 17 years old, as explained earlier. It now remains to judge Canada against the U.S. record.

American data on the LFPR of enrolled and nonenrolled youth are available as an annual series, going back to 1947, based only on data for October (which is close to the beginning of a new school year and may not be fully representative of all the school months in regard to enrolled population and labor force, as recent monthly data for Australia and Canada suggest). A further limitation of the U.S. data is the inclusion of part-time and full-time students in the main series; some separation of the two is possible in higher education for recent years. Despite these flaws, the American data offer the best opportunity to view the development of student LFPR.

Dividing young people into three age groups (16 and 17, 18 and 19, 20 to 24) which are particularly relevant to U.S. educational sequences, Chart 5.1 and Tables A5.2–A5.5 present information on the annual trends in educational enrollment rates, LFPR for the enrolled and nonenrolled, and the enrolled share of the labor force of the same age. A separate table is provided on the 16 to 19-year group to facilitate comparisons with other countries (*Table A5.4). In the youngest group, 16 to 17 years, the share of the population who were enrolled in school rose from around 70 percent in the late 1940s to 90 percent by the late 1970s for each sex, while the enrolled share of the 16–17-year-old labor force rapidly reached 50 percent around 1950 and thereafter soared to 85 percent, growing faster than EER. In other words, American high school students aged 16 and 17 completely dominate the labor market of that age group, with no difference between the sexes. As Chart 5.1 demonstrates, the LFPR of nonenrolled males in this age group has dropped considerably over the years, from close to 90 percent to under 80 percent, while enrolled males moved up from about 30 percent to 45 to 46 percent. Enrolled females 16 and 17 more than doubled their LFPR, while their nonenrolled counterparts showed mostly decline to 1968 and then some rise; in 1979 only 10 percentage points separated the two groups' LFPR, which in the immediate postwar years had been 30

Source: U.S. Department of Labor, Employment and Training Report of the President 1980, Table B-6 (Washington: GPO, 1980); Bureau of Labor Statistics, unpublished data for 1979; 1947-1952 data for 18-19-year-olds furnished by Professor J. D. Mattila; Department of Defense unpublished data on military enlistments (volunteer and conscripted) as of October of each year. Data include all military and exclude the institutionalized population.

to 40 percentage points apart. The relatively high LFPR of American 16-17-year-old students are confirmed when they are compared with Australian rates for 15-19-year-old secondary school students, who in practice are mostly 15 to 17 years old (Tables 5.2, A5.2).

The next age group, 18 and 19, also exhibited a substantial expansion in the enrolled fraction of the age group until 1968 for males and 1976 for females (Table A5.3). Shares of the enrolled in the 18-19-year labor force mirrored the EER, but grew much more rapidly, quadrupling from 1947 to the high point (1968 for males, 1977 for females). The subsequent decline in the enrolled share of the labor force was mostly due to a drop in relative numbers, since the LFPR of enrolled males and females maintained a more vigorous growth than that of the nonenrolled, as Chart 5.1 indicates. By the end of the period, almost half of all students 18 and 19 were in the labor force, and they accounted for over one-fourth of the male labor force and about one-third of the female labor force in that age group.

For comparative purposes, the U.S. data on 16–19-year-olds may be consulted (*Table A5.4). With two-thirds of the American teenage group enrolled, over half of all labor force participants counted as students; with a student LFPR of almost 45 percent, American student labor force activity in 1979 was ahead of that in Canada, though allowance should be made for the Canadian restriction to full-time students.

Young adult males in the US began the postwar period with a comparatively high enrollment rate but a small enrolled share of the labor force (Table A5.5). The latter rose to 14 percent by 1979 which, with the female share of 17 percent, gave the US greater student representation in the young adult labor force than Australia, Japan, Canada, Sweden, or Great Britain displayed. Enrolled LFPR in this age group more than doubled in the US, while nonenrolled male LFPR dropped off a few percentage points. Nonenrolled female LFPR advanced substantially though somewhat less rapidly than enrolled LFPR (Chart 5.1; Table A5.5).

Although the bases for such comparisons could be much improved and amplified, it appears certain that the US and Canada are near the top of a list of countries in regard to student labor force activity and that Japan is close to the bottom. The implication of these results is that the nominal size and growth of the U.S. and Canadian youth labor force should be reduced on the ground that students are likely to work fewer hours per week and year than nonstudents. The next step therefore is to review what is known about hours of work of students and nonstudents within and across countries.

Hours and Weeks Worked by Enrollment Status

Since full-time students who are in the labor force during the school term span a wide age group and hold jobs that range from casual to full time employment, differences in hours and weeks worked are to be expected by age, educational level, sex, country, and historical time period. In addition to those who actually worked, account should be taken of the desired hours of work of students who sought work unsuccessfully. Direct surveys of students' jobs during the term usually make a distinction between weekend jobs and jobs that are performed before and after school hours. A few surveys, wise to the actual practices of some young people, inquire about jobs held *during* school hours. A survey among American 17-year-olds discovered that as many as 7 percent had worked at a paid job during school hours, 62 percent had jobs before or after school hours, and 64 percent had weekend jobs in 1973–1974 (Mitchell 1977, Table 9).

In a Swedish survey of 15–16-year-olds who were in the final year of compulsory school in 1976 and did not proceed to upper-secondary school, of those who worked during the last year of school, 37 percent of boys and 55 percent of girls held jobs during weekends, 47 percent of boys and 35 percent of girls were employed during the week, and 16 percent of boys and 10 percent of girls worked both in the school week and at weekends. Among those who worked at weekends, the average was 7.9 hours for boys and 8.5 for girls. Three-fourths of the females and over four-fifths of the males who worked weekends averaged less than 11 hours per week, and only 6 percent of males and 8 percent of females had as many as 16 to 20 hours a week; none worked more. Work during the week averaged 9.8 hours for each sex. Slightly higher proportions than for weekend workers were in the 11 to 20 hours category; 1.7 percent of males and 3.6 percent of females worked 21 hours or more (Sweden 1979b, Tables 3.1, 3.4, 3.5).

A similar Swedish inquiry among selected terminal upper-secondary students in 1976 (18 and 19 years old), found that about one-third of all students worked during the term. Of those who worked, about three-fourths worked only at weekends, about 15 percent worked during the week, and 10 percent had jobs both at weekends and during the week. On average, they worked 8 hours a week. Jobs that took 10 to 19 hours a week accounted for 29 percent of the student workers, while those working 20 hours or more constituted 6 percent of the total who worked (Sweden 1979c, Tables 4.2, 5.1). A British survey in the late 1950s of school-leavers (15–18 years old) who held jobs indicated that about one-fourth of the boys worked over 10 hours per week, while a majority of the girls worked 10 hours per week or less (GB 1959, p. 32).

American inquiries in the early 1970s revealed larger proportions with long working hours than either the Swedish or British surveys. In December 1971, U.S. male students in the 10th to 12th grades (16–18 years old) reported that of those who held jobs currently, almost half worked 16 hours or more a week, including about 20 percent who worked 26 to 40 hours a week. Those working 16 to 40 hours were mostly in grade 12 with below average course grades and doubts about completing high school. Girls and younger boys worked shorter average hours (Purdue Opinion Panel 1972, pp. 6, 3a). A similar poll in March 1973 indicated that about one-fourth of the boys and 15 percent of the girls worked 26 to 40 hours a week, and another fourth of the boys and 30 percent of the girls worked 16 to 25 hours a week, on average (Purdue Opinion Panel 1973, p. 15a).

This type of evidence suggests that American enrolled youth work longer hours during the school term than their counterparts elsewhere. It also appears that a larger proportion of American enrolled youth who have worked at any time, including summers, have held full-time jobs; in March 1973 over one-third of boys and 17 percent of girls in grades 10, 11 and 12 (ages 16 to 18) who had worked at some time had held full-time jobs (Purdue Opinion Panel 1973, p. 11a).

Moreover, it appears that these longer hours of American students are not a recent phenomenon. An overall review of the hours worked by male American students in nonagricultural industries from 1948 to 1975 disclosed that the average workweek had lengthened by four hours, but the actual workweek probably was unchanged if allowance is made for an advance in the average age of students and the dropping of 14–15-year-olds from statistics in the later years (Owen 1978, p. 34). However, the U.S. census reported increases from 1960 to 1970 in the proportion of enrolled youth of 16, 17, and 18 who worked 15 to 34 hours per week. This change implies a lengthening of the average workweek of younger students; nonenrolled youth did not show the same relative increase in the 35 hours and more category (Table 5.7). Since census data do not refer to the entire youth group, Owen's overall conclusion, based on other data, may still be valid.

Enrolled and Nonenrolled Hours per Week

Next we consider data generated by labor force surveys on the hours per week of the students by age group and sex. Australia, Canada, and the United States provide separate information on students who worked or sought work by the number of hours per week or by a part-time–full-time dichotomy. These data for students can be compared with parallel information for nonstudents or the whole youth labor force.

Australia made a detailed inquiry into the weekly hours of employed teenagers by enrollment status in connection with the launching of a new monthly series on the

Table 5.7 Distribution of Hours Worked by Employed Youth (16-18 Years), by School Enrollment Status, Single Years of Age, and Sex, United States, March 1960 and 1970

			\multicolumn{6}{c}{Number of hours worked per week}
			1-14	15-34	35+	1-14	15-34	35+
				Enrolled			Nonenrolled	
Age	Sex	Year	\multicolumn{3}{c}{(percent)}	\multicolumn{3}{c}{(percent)}
16	Male	1960	55.9	36.1	8.0	17.2	24.4	58.4
		1970	44.2	45.1	10.7	12.7	27.0	60.3
16	Female	1960	65.9	27.9	6.2	19.3	22.1	58.6
		1970	54.2	37.7	8.1	13.8	29.1	57.1
17	Male	1960	47.7	41.7	10.6	13.9	22.4	63.7
		1970	34.9	51.7	13.4	8.6	23.9	67.5
17	Female	1960	57.8	33.8	8.4	16.2	19.7	64.1
		1970	44.4	47.3	8.3	11.1	27.4	61.5
18	Male	1960	38.6	38.0	23.4	6.9	14.4	78.7
		1970	28.9	48.8	22.3	4.2	16.0	79.8
18	Female	1960	46.0	28.9	25.1	5.7	10.8	83.5
		1970	40.3	43.8	15.9	4.6	17.7	77.7

Note: Hours worked in the reference week in 1970 may have been affected by the holiday in that week.

Source: U.S. Department of Commerce. Bureau of the Census. *Census of Population 1960.* United States Summary, Detailed Characteristics, Table 197. Washington: GPO, 1963; *Census of Population 1970.* United States Summary. Detailed Characteristics, Table 217.

student labor force in August 1978, a winter month. Teenage students, mostly 15 to 17 years old due to the restrictive definition of "in school" for survey purposes, worked on average 8.1 hours (males) and 7.2 hours (females). By contrast, teenage nonstudents, who include the whole age range, had an average workweek of 37.4 hours (males) and 34.9 hours (females)(Australia 1978, Tables 10,11). Thus, the ratio of in-school and out-of-school hours was more than 4 to 1. Among teenagers of both sexes seeking jobs, almost all of those who were out of school wanted full-time work; only some 4 to 7 percent per month registered for part-time jobs (less than 35 hours per week) in 1978-1980. More variable monthly proportions were indicated by the student jobseekers, even confining the discussion to the school term. In the first months of the school year, two-thirds to almost three-fourths of students wanting jobs signed up for part-time work, but by the latter months the proportion was closer to 50 to 60 percent (Australia 1974-80).

As a reflection of the increased proportions of students in the labor force, a decline in both age groups in the proportion of all Australian youth in full-time jobs has been observed for some time, with a more pronounced drop among teenagers. By 1979, only 83.4 percent of employed male teenagers and 74.5 percent of females were in full-time jobs, contrasting with 91.3 percent and 93.0 percent respectively in 1970 (Australia 1971-80). In spite of the fact that the Australian in- and out-of-school groups have differences in age composition that accentuate the shorter average hours of the students, it appears that the Australian category of teenage nonstudents, which includes students in higher education, work a fairly full week, with 69.4 percent of the teenage males and 57.4 percent of the females having a workweek of 40 hours or more in August 1978 (Australia 1978, Tables 10,11). More information is needed on teenage students in higher education, but the hours of Australian students, taking them as 16–17-year-olds, appear to be low compared to American, Canadian, and Swedish students of similar ages. Australian nonstudents appear to work as long or longer weekly hours than similar youth in the other three countries.

A special Canadian study of the labor force activities of students provides data on employed and unemployed students by full-time (35 hours or more) and part-time status (Canada 1977b). This information can be compared with data on the whole labor force. In October 1976, for example, 80.9 percent of 15–24-year-old employed males and 74.9 percent of females were in full-time jobs (Canada 1976–80). In the same month, only about 10 percent of full-time male students of the same age and 8 percent of such females were employed full time. On the other hand, 78.1 percent of male part-time students and 94.3 percent of female part-time students were employed full time. Among student jobseekers 15 years and over, 22.1 percent of both sexes were looking for full-time jobs in October 1976; unemployed part-time students (17,000 out of 58,000) mostly wanted full-time jobs (Canada 1977b, Tables 2, 3). It is therefore clear that full-time students diverge sharply in hours worked and sought from both part-time students and nonstudents. Part-time students, however, a minority of the student population, appear to work at full-time jobs more often than the whole youth labor force.

Because of the importance of the student labor force in the United States, fuller information over a longer time period is available than for other countries. The data presented on hours of work for enrolled and nonenrolled youth refer to all students, whether or not full time. Yet even at the higher education level where part-time enrollment is most prevalent, as recently as 1977 only about 15 percent of 16–24-year-olds in college or graduate school were part-time students. Therefore, the results for a division between enrolled and nonenrolled are significant. The Current Population Survey for October offers data showing in-school and out-of-school youth by the number of hours per week actually worked in nonagricultural industries. While this measure is not identical to the number of hours offered on the labor market, it may be assumed that the ratio of desired hours to actual hours is not significantly different for in- and out-of-school employed youth. A similar assumption may be made about the desired hours of in- and out-of-school unemployed youth. October data reflect a high level of school enrollments, close to the annual peak, and thus may not give the average annual division of the youth population between school and nonschool status, apart from questions about the accuracy of CPS classifications. On the other hand, October data probably capture reasonably well the numbers combining school and work during the school year. CPS data on enrollment status, labor force participation, and hours of work do not agree with comparable information drawn from other sources, such as the census or National Longitudinal Surveys.

CPS data for October 1967 and 1977, showing the relation of enrollment status to hours of work, disaggregated by four age groups and by sex, are revealing (Table 5.8). A sharp difference in working hours between enrolled and nonenrolled youth appears in each age group, in each sex, and in both 1967 and 1977. In every case, enrolled youth worked fewer hours than nonenrolled, and the younger the age group, the wider was the gap between the enrolled and nonenrolled. Average weekly hours increased with age, regardless of school status or sex. Females generally worked fewer hours than males of the same age and school status. In most of the age

Table 5.8   Distribution of Hours Worked by Employed Youth, Nonagricultural Industries, by School Enrollment Status, Age, and Sex, United States, October 1967 and 1977

		Number of hours per week					Number of hours per week				
		Enrolled				Average hours worked	Nonenrolled				Average hours worked
	Year	1-14	15-21	22-34	35+		1-14	15-21	22-34	35+	
		(percent)[a]					(percent)[a]				
16–17 Male	1967	47.4	28.6	18.7	5.4	16.1	8.1	6.9	18.8	66.2	35.7
	1977	35.9	35.4	21.0	7.7	18.1	6.5	6.0	22.4	65.2	37.1
16–17 Female	1967	63.6	23.8	9.3	3.4	12.7	7.5	14.4	15.1	63.0	33.7
	1977	40.9	38.6	15.5	5.0	16.2	10.1	14.1	22.6	53.3	31.2
18–19 Male	1967	33.5	29.2	22.2	15.1	20.6	3.7	4.2	11.1	81.0	40.4
	1977	27.9	29.3	21.3	21.5	22.6	2.9	4.4	15.5	77.0	39.0
18–19 Female	1967	39.9	24.7	15.7	19.7	19.8	4.9	4.9	15.8	74.4	36.3
	1977	35.4	32.2	19.5	13.1	19.5	5.2	6.6	20.5	67.7	35.5
20–21 Male	1967	31.9	21.7	18.2	28.2	23.9	1.7	2.6	10.4	85.3	42.3
	1977	22.1	24.7	23.4	30.0	26.0	2.8	2.8	12.6	81.8	40.8
20–21 Female	1967	36.9	24.4	12.9	25.8	21.2	3.6	4.0	14.7	77.7	37.3
	1977	28.0	36.5	18.2	17.5	20.9	4.3	5.1	17.4	73.3	36.7
22–24 Male	1967	15.4	14.9	15.2	54.5	32.4	0.7	1.4	7.4	90.8	43.8
	1977	15.6	18.3	19.5	46.6	31.2	1.5	1.7	9.4	87.4	42.9
22–24 Female	1967	20.1	14.7	13.6	51.6	30.1	2.9	6.2	13.5	77.4	37.5
	1977	14.4	21.5	18.3	45.6	29.6	3.4	5.1	19.6	71.9	37.1

[a] May not add to 100 percent because of rounding.

Source: U.S. Department of Labor, Bureau of Labor Statistics, unpublished data.

groups, the gap between enrolled and nonenrolled females was smaller than between similar groups of males. From 1967 to 1977, average hours of work were more likely to increase in the in-school than the out-of-school groups; this was most marked among the younger males. Where reductions in average hours occurred from 1967 to 1977, the drop was small.

The October CPS data on hours show significant differences among the age groups. Among the enrolled 16–17-year-olds, over one-third of the boys and two-fifths of the girls worked fewer than 15 hours a week in 1977. These were higher proportions than were found for the enrolled in any other age group and were consistent with work on weekends only or on daily newspaper delivery routes, for example. Long hours of work also were recorded for some 16–17-year-olds engaged in full-time studies. In 1967 almost one-fourth of the boys and one-eighth of the girls worked 22 hours or more per week, and there was a rise from 1967 to 1977 in these proportions among boys and girls alike (Table 5.8).

Nonenrolled 16–17-year-olds were mostly dropouts. Although employed 16–17-year-olds were composed of relatively fewer full-time workers than the nonenrolled in other age groups, two-thirds of the boys (down slightly from 1967) and over half of the girls (down substantially from 1967) reported workweeks of 35 hours or more in 1977; some undoubtedly were less fully employed than they wished to be. The average number of work hours of out-of-school 16–17-year-olds, males and females alike, was twice that of the respective in-school group in 1977 (Table 5.8).

Many in the 18–19-year-old population had completed high school. Of those who were employed in nonagricultural industries in 1977, two-thirds of the males (up from 61.2 percent in 1967) and almost two-thirds of the females (down from 74.1 percent in 1967) were not enrolled. While the nonenrolled of each sex constituted a larger share of those who worked than of the age group as a whole, there was a conspicuous increase in the share of jobs held by the in-school group over the decade 1967–1977. Since the age group's enrollment ratios did not change much, the increase is attributable to pressures on young people to earn while they attended school. Thus, the proportion of enrolled boys who worked 35 or more hours rose from 15.1 percent to 21.5 percent during the ten years. The three other age-sex groups among 18–19-year-olds showed a decline in full-time and overtime workers, but an increase in the 15 to 34 hours category. Enrolled males worked more hours on average in 1977 than in 1967, but all of the other 18–19-year-olds showed a slight decrease in average hours in the decade. Average hours worked by the nonenrolled were almost twice those of the enrolled in this age group in 1967 and 1977 (Table 5.8).

The 20–21 year-old group was heavily nonenrolled. While full-time workers predominated in both sexes among the nonenrolled, males had the greater commitment to full or overtime work. Among the nonenrolled, the proportion in the 35 hours and more category declined from 1967 to 1977 for each sex, and gains were registered in each of the remaining hours categories. Enrolled 20–21-year-olds, some of whom were attending junior college or college on a part-time basis or at night, had a relatively high share of full-time workers, rising over the decade in the case of males and falling in the case of females. A decline in the proportion working less than 15 hours over the ten-year period suggests the same financial pressures as on other youth in school, since the enrolled, more than the nonenrolled, can set their own hours. The gap between the average hours of the enrolled and nonenrolled in this age group was somewhat smaller than for the 18–19-year-olds (Table 5.8).

The final youth group, aged 22 to 24, was mainly in the labor market or in household activity in 1977 and included many college graduates. Displaying a heavier commitment to a workweek of 35 hours or more than any other age group, both the enrolled and nonenrolled were most likely to be full-time workers in 1967 and 1977. There still were marked differences between nonenrolled and enrolled in the distribution of hours in both years, especially in the 1 to 14-hours category. In the decade 1967–1977, a distinct tendency appeared among enrolled and nonenrolled to work fewer hours. The work week of less than 35 hours increased at the expense of 35 hours and over, except that enrolled females showed a distinctly lower proportion in the 1 to 14-hours class as well (Table 5.8). For the older age groups, trends do not agree with those shown in Table 5.7 from the U.S. census for the 16–18-year-olds.

Important differences between age-sex groups emerge from these comparisons, in addition to the overriding disparity between the in- and out-of-school youth. All of the nonenrolled, except for 16–17-year-old females, had average hours above full time, measured by the standard of 35 hours per week. Among the enrolled, however, no group's average hours reached the full-time standard, and only three averages were more than 30 hours a week (Table 5.8). Average hours are somewhat misleading for the oldest enrolled youth, however, since over half of males and females worked 35 hours or more in 1967 (Table 5.8).

Having set forth the CPS data, the differences between the CPS and NLS data on hours may now be cited. The comparison between the CPS and NLS data covers male 16–21-year-olds for 1967 and 1968 and female 16–21-year-olds for 1968, 1969, and 1970, with supplementary data available for 1966 for males in and out of school and 1968 for females in school. Showing about 25 percent more employed young men and 10 percent more employed young women than the CPS, the NLS surveys also displayed a different distribution of hours during the survey week, with more part-time workers, mostly among the youngest age group, and more workers employed overtime, mostly among the 18–21-year-olds. Mean hours tended to be somewhat higher in NLS surveys, especially for males (US 1970–79, I, Table 4.7; US 1971–81, I, Table 3.8). This finding of more hours worked in NLS than CPS data is consistent with other differences between the two data sets, which have been discussed elsewhere in this book (Borus, Mott, and Nestel 1978; Freeman and Medoff 1979; Hills and Thompson 1980). Despite differences between the surveys, there is agreement on the basic issue of the influence of school status on hours worked and on the age and sex differences among the enrolled and nonenrolled.

When the worktime of American enrolled and nonenrolled youth is divided into a part-time or full-time pattern, information is available for additional subsets of the youth population. From the annual Special Labor Force Reports on *Students, Graduates and Dropouts in the Labor Market*, it can be established that enrolled unemployed youth desired full-time jobs to about the same extent as the employed students. Among the nonenrolled, however, a higher proportion of unemployed than employed youth appear as full-time workers; this may represent enforced part-time work by the employed rather than differences between the two groups in work commitment. Longitudinal evidence from the survey of the American high school class of 1972 provides further information. As Table 5.9 demonstrates, part-time white male students are more often employed in full-time work than full-time students at each separate postsecondary educational level. In successive years the fraction in full-time jobs tends to rise for the cohort, affecting both full-time and part-time students and reversed only by adverse economic conditions, as indicated in the variable unemployment rates in Table 5.9.

The assumption that part-time work by youth largely represents the work patterns

Table 5.9 Labor Force Participation History of Enrolled Segment of High School Class of 1972, White Males, United States, October 1972-1976

School status	Percent in full-time work					Percent in part-time work				
	1972	1973	1974	1975	1976	1972	1973	1974	1975	1976
Full-time										
Vocational technical	24.0	25.6	28.8	33.8	36.0	31.8	31.7	26.9	22.5	19.0
Two-year college	14.2	17.5	14.2	27.4	20.7	45.2	45.7	49.1	36.5	29.6
Four-year college	5.1	6.5	4.5	6.4	8.5	26.5	30.9	37.7	41.2	44.8
Other	26.9	21.2	15.2	20.0	30.1	26.9	3.0	12.1	11.7	19.2
Part-time										
Vocational technical	74.3	79.8	74.2	90.3	78.3	12.9	13.2	10.9	4.3	3.3
Two-year college	47.9	60.6	66.5	68.9	71.0	35.7	23.9	18.5	12.4	13.5
Four-year college	37.3	42.4	53.2	50.3	52.4	30.5	36.1	23.8	26.7	29.5
Other	62.0	58.8	57.1	48.2	53.3	13.9	9.8	7.1	3.7	13.3

School status	Percent looking for work				
	1972	1973	1974	1975	1976
Full-time					
Vocational technical	7.8	8.2	2.3	7.8	11.0
Two-year college	7.3	8.1	3.8	7.9	11.9
Four-year-college	4.4	6.5	1.0	2.8	5.6
Other	4.3	0.0	9.1	0.0	2.7
Part-time					
Vocational technical	5.7	0.8	0.8	1.1	4.2
Two-year college	1.4	3.0	3.4	3.6	4.0
Four-year college	6.8	2.9	1.4	4.7	4.8
Other	2.5	0.0	2.4	3.7	10.0

Note: Survey dates are October of each year.

Source: Adapted from R. H. Meyer and D. A. Wise, *High School Preparation and Early Labor Force Experience*, National Bureau of Economic Research Working Paper no. 342 (Cambridge, Mass., 1979), Appendix Tables A1-A5.

of students can be checked from Swedish and Canadian surveys. A Swedish analysis of the reasons for working part time of 16–24-year-olds in 1977 found that 64.7 percent of such males and 22.8 percent of females attributed it to student status (Sweden 1978a, Table 15). If females 16 to 19 had been separated out, they would show a higher proportion than females 16 to 24. Also, if only the school months had been tallied, instead of an annual monthly average, all proportions would have been larger.

Another Swedish analysis, which used the cross-sectional labor force survey in a longitudinal fashion, found that part-time jobs occured most frequently among male and female teenagers whose labor market status over the 1975–1977 period was characterized by movement in and out of the labor force, such as would be the case with students. Teenagers who were in the labor force over the entire period had the lowest fraction employed in part-time work, while those who were in the labor force and left it or were out of it and then entered tended to have slightly higher proportions with part-time work. Male young adults show the same pattern, but the record for young adult females is complicated by the fact that movement in and out of the labor force and part-time jobs are as much influenced by household responsibilities as studies (Sweden 1979a, Table 6.4).

A Canadian analysis of part-time employment of 15–24-year-olds in 1976, defining part-time work as less than 30 hours a week at one or more jobs and including those who were involuntarily part-time workers, asked respondents the reason for working part time. Some 78 percent of the males and 62 percent of the females chose "going to school." The report stated that a large share of these youthful part-time workers were high school students with jobs during the school year (Canada 1977a). Since the vacation months are counted for this age group, there may be some understatement of the weight of students in the part-time workforce.

Adjusting the Youth Labor Force

Having examined direct and indirect data which establish that the student labor force works fewer hours than the nonstudent, we next consider how national youth labor force data should be adjusted. Bowen and Finegan made such an adjustment for the 1960 American census data, which they analyzed, deriving an index of labor supply for the enrolled that modified the adjusted LFPR by taking account of adjusted mean hours worked (Bowen and Finegan 1969, p. 385, Table 12-2). As expected, the younger the students, the greater the difference between LFPR and the index of labor supply. A similar exercise was not performed for the nonenrolled, however, nor for youth as a whole.

CPS data for American youth in Table 5.8 can be translated into rough full-time equivalents for both enrolled and nonenrolled, using the BLS definition of a full-time week as 35 hours (Table 5.10). If a full-time equivalent measure of employment is applied for 1977, 16–17-year-old enrolled employment declines by more than half. The 18–19- and 20–21-year-old enrolled females drop by 40 to 44 percent on the full-time measure, and the corresponding males decline by 35 and 26 percent respectively. Only 22–24-year-old males and females would suffer a loss of as little as 10 to 15 percent. On the whole, the younger enrolled groups moved closer to full-time work from 1967 to 1977, while the older groups were mostly stable or slightly on the decline in the ratio of full-time equivalents to the number employed. By the same standard, all of the nonenrolled, except for 16–17-year-old females, gained when full-time equivalent measures were applied. Males in the oldest group added almost

Table 5.10   Employed Youth in Nonagricultural Industries and Full-Time Equivalents, by School Enrollment Status, Age, and Sex, United States, October 1967 and 1977

| | Enrolled | | | | | | Nonenrolled | | | | | | | | |
| | Number employed (000s) | | Full-time equivalents (FTE) (000s) | | Ratio of FTE to number employed | | Number employed (000s) | | Full-time equivalents (FTE) (000s) | | Ratio of FTE to number employed | | Nonenrolled share of total FTE | |
	1967	1977	1967	1977	1967	1977	1967	1977	1967	1977	1967	1977	1967	1977
16–17 Males	986	1301	454	673	.46	.52	160	201	163	213	1.02	1.06	26.4	24.0
16–17 Females	719	1120	261	518	.36	.46	146	198	141	177	.96	.89	35.1	25.5
18–19 Males	537	734	316	474	.59	.65	899	1469	1038	1637	1.15	1.11	76.7	77.5
18–19 Females	376	693	213	386	.57	.56	1073	1278	1113	1296	1.04	1.01	83.9	77.1
20–21 Males	429	535	293	397	.68	.74	1130	1876	1366	2187	1.21	1.17	82.3	84.6
20–21 Females	271	521	164	311	.60	.60	1336	1731	1424	1815	1.07	1.05	89.7	85.4
22–24 Males	402	584	372	521	.92	.89	2508	3558	3139	4361	1.25	1.23	89.4	89.3
22–24 Females	184	492	158	416	.86	.85	1835	2960	1966	3138	1.07	1.06	92.6	88.3

Note: Full-time work is defined as 35 hours or more per week.

Source: U.S. Department of Labor, Bureau of Labor Statistics, unpublished data.

25 percent to their total employment. The 1977 ratios were lower than the 1967 in seven of the eight age-sex groups, however, rising slightly only for 16–17-year-old males.

All of the measures are brought together when the nonenrolled share of the number employed is compared to its share of the full-time equivalents. In the youngest age group, 16–17, the share of the enrolled declined sharply when the full-time equivalent measure was applied. A lesser impact was exerted on the 18–19 and 20–21 year groups, and the 22–24 year group was barely affected. Over the decade the nonenrolled share of the full-time equivalents tended to decline slightly, reflecting the increased labor force participation and longer working hours of students. But the use of the conventional employment measure continued to exaggerate the labor force contribution of the enrolled (Table 5.10).

An application of the findings on the distribution of·the hours of youth employment to youth unemployment suggests that the unemployment situation of American enrolled 16–17-year-olds in particular should be disaggregated according to the number of hours of work sought, since this is the age group with the largest proportion enrolled and the highest youth unemployment rate. Such a procedure might be used equally well for 18–19 and 20–21-year-olds in school. The foregoing review of hours of work reinforces earlier conclusions, based on studies of unemployment rates, that analyses of youth should proceed by separating the age groups more finely than into teenagers and young adults, and that the in-school, out-of-school division is essential.

Weeks of Work in the Year

Thus far, differences between the hours of enrolled and nonenrolled have been judged entirely on the basis of weekly hours reported at a particular time of the year. It is equally important to compare the weeks of work throughout the year for enrolled and nonenrolled youth. Only American data are available, and they are questionable in that the previous years' work experience was classified according to school attendance status in March of the survey year. To the extent that those who were students in March had not been students in the previous year or had been students only in part of the year, the March classifications are misleading. However, the results for 16–21-year-olds conform fairly well to expectations, so that the classification problem may not be serious.

Annual records for 1967–1978 indicate that male and female students who worked full time during the previous year constituted about 35 percent of all males and 25–30 percent of all females who worked, and that over the years around 60–70 percent of these full-time male student workers held jobs for 1–13 weeks. These findings point to vacation periods as the primary time for full-time work by students. Among the almost two-thirds of males and three-fourths of female students who worked part time annually 1967–1978, the 1–13 weeks category again had the largest proportion; but a majority worked over 14 weeks of the year, with an even distribution between the three intervals, 14–26 weeks, 27–49 weeks, 50–52 weeks (US 1964–79, Table A-1A).

Indirect evidence on the effects of school status in the United States can be obtained from disaggregating teenage part-time workers into 16–17- and 18–19-year-olds and then dividing the two groups of part-time workers into part-year (under 27 weeks) and full time. As would be expected, 16–17-year olds, the vast majority of whom are enrolled, contain a high proportion who work for less than 27 weeks a year at part-time jobs (less than 35 hours a week); in 1977 it was 46.0 percent for males and 53.4 percent for females. Ten years earlier the respective percentages had been 38.3 and 50.9. Among 18–19-year-olds, far fewer followed this pattern: 18.7 percent of males and 27.1 percent of females. In 1967 it had been 18.3 percent for males and 22.1 percent for females (US 1964–79, Table A).

American work experience surveys have asked respondents the major reason for part-year work. Results confirm that for two-thirds to three-fourths of male teenagers and only slightly fewer females, school attendance during all or part of the year was the primary cause. Among young male adults, school was cited as a major cause in 30–40 percent of the cases, while for females school was the major reason in about one-third or less of the cases (US 1964–79). (It is likely that Australian young people, for example, would report much lower proportions because the end of the school year coincides more closely with the end of the calendar year, educational enrollment rates have been lower and relatively fewer enrolled young people have been in the labor force).

Over the ten-year period, the proportion of enrolled males working part time in the United States increased slightly and of these, the share working 50–52 weeks dropped somewhat. Enrolled females showed an even stronger rise in the proportion working part time but they also had a small growth in the share of the part-timers who worked either 50–52 or 27–49 weeks. Since, over the decade, there was a decline in the proportion of enrolled males who worked at all in the previous year (from more than 70 percent to around 63 percent), this record for 16–21-year-olds signifies a diminution in enrolled male labor force activity (US 1964–79, Table A-1A). While enrolled female trends are less marked, these data do not present a picture of rising labor force activity, as is shown by LFPR in Chart 5.1.

Nonenrolled American males and females 16–21 years old had little variation over the 1967–1978 period in the proportion (about 90 percent for males and 73 percent for females) who worked at some time in the previous year. Yet each sex experienced a sharp decline during the decade in the proportion who worked full time; it dropped from 82.7 to 74.1 percent for males and from 82.8 to 65.0 percent for females. A similar decline occurred in the 1967–1978 period for each sex in the percent of full-time workers who were employed for 50 to 52 weeks. Among the increasing proportion of the employed working part time, the distribution of weeks of work did not change much (US 1964–79, Table A-1A).

Despite these trends, the two groups remained distinct in work experience. As expected, in each year the nonenrolled were predominantly full-year workers, in contrast to the enrolled who were primarily vacation period workers. Although the trend from 1967–1978 suggests a general retreat from full-time jobs among all American youth, there continued to be a large gap between the enrolled and nonenrolled in the proportion working full time and full year. It is expected that these general findings would appear if more detailed and controlled U.S. data were available and if other countries generated similar information by enrollment status.

Summary

Persistent differences between the hours and weeks of work of enrolled and nonenrolled employed youth indicate that this variable should enter into calculations of the size of the youth labor force, nationally and cross-nationally. Improvements are needed in the method of recording enrollment status so that part-time students can be clearly distinguished. Additional, comparable surveys of hours of work, by identically defined enrollment status, are required for several school months. Special adjustments must be made for student working hours in the vacation months, after surveys establish the patterns. Finally, once weekly work hours enter as a variable in estimates of the size of the youth labor force, it becomes relevant to add questions on the number of weeks worked per year. Data on this aspect by age, already available from some labor force surveys, can be improved by adding questions on the annual work history according to enrollment status.

An obvious implication of a change in the method of counting youth is its applicability to other age-sex groups in which voluntary part-time work is important. The trends for adult women in the labor force and employment would show a less steep rise if they were converted to full-time equivalents, since part-time work has increased more rapidly than full-time work among women in most countries. The total effect of taking account of weekly work hours and number of weeks of work would be to augment the labor force and employment shares of adult males in the prime working ages. To the extent that measurement is concerned with the amount of labor supply to the economy as well as the behavior of individuals in the labor market, work hours and weeks are relevant.

Our review of student and nonstudent hours, LFPR and weeks of work, as far as the data go, establishes that the greatest reduction would occur in the U.S. youth labor force if a standard adjustment were applied in all countries for the number of students in the labor force. Still, if such a cross-national adjustment also took account of differences between the student and nonstudent labor force in regard to hours and weeks of work, the relative amount of adjustment for the US would diminish and it would increase for other countries. This would be due to the observed tendency of American students to work relatively more hours (and probably weeks) than those in other countries and the propensity of American nonenrolled to work the same or rather less than other youth.

Whether student LFPR or hours and weeks of work are at issue, it is clear that substantial cross-national variations have existed and continue to exist. In an effort to understand and verify these differences, we turn next to the explanatory factors.

Factors in Cross-National Differences in Student Labor Force Participation Rates

Observed cross-national differences in the proportion of the youth labor force that simultaneously attends an educational institution are only slightly attributable to variations in the methods and practices of national or international labor force surveys. These are real differences which must be examined in terms of the size and circumstances of the student body in each country, on the one hand, and the character and organization of the employment opportunities open to youth, on the other.

One of the most important factors in divergent student LFPR is the size of the postcompulsory student population relative to the remainder of young people in the age group. When in-school youth become a majority or close to a majority, implying a comparatively high age of leaving full-time education or a well-developed part-time education sector, the educational system may undergo reorganization tending toward reduced hours spent in school and limited homework. These developments have facilitated extensive labor force activity on the part of American and Canadian youth, for example, compared to those European countries which have long school days, heavy homework, demanding examinations, and an educational division of pupils by ability and planned destination. The situation in Japan is somewhat mixed in that the highly competitive and hard-working life of students from the youngest ages changes once entrance is obtained to university, according to a professor in a prestigious Japanese university (Kato 1978). Social attitudes toward student workers also are an influence. Student LFPR in the United States has become acceptable in all strata of society, including the wealthiest communities, because the ethos of the society and peer pressures lend support. Thus, a report on American high school student part-time work in Connecticut observed that parents in Greenwich, one of the highest-income towns in the nation, now permitted their children to work where once they would not have approved (*NY Times* n). In other countries, different traditions, a lack of social acceptability, the demands of schooling, limits or outright prohibition on student work if the government contributes to costs—these and related forces hold down the supply of student labor.

Another factor is the ratio of total out-of-pocket educational expenditures of the family *for all family members* to family income without the earnings of students. It is not sufficient for this purpose to compute cross-nationally the contributions of government toward tuition and living costs or the availability of loans. These are important, but they must be seen in terms of the levels of GNP and family income. We also consider the presence of several siblings in a family, close in age to one another, which undoubtedly put pressures during the 1960s and 1970s on families in such countries as the United States, Canada, Australia, and New Zealand, which were absent or minimal elsewhere. In spite of the importance we attach to this factor, we must acknowledge that Japanese experience appears to belie its significance. The Japanese passion for education and the low accompanying labor force activity of students exist alongside high private costs of education relative to family income, due to a large private postsecondary educational sector and comparatively low government contributions to such students. In other countries, however, there appears to be a connection between the net costs of education and students' desire to work. A modifying influence may be exerted by differences among nations in the socioeconomic composition of higher education students. Student bodies which are drawn very disproportionately from the upper income level classes also may have large government contribution to educational costs, thus combining two causes of a low student LFPR. As we have shown in Chapter 3, U.S. higher education enrollments are widely diffused throughout the population, and there is a relatively high private contribution to education costs, which probably explains part of the high LFPR of students and their long hours of work.

A more elusive element is the role of young people's desire for financial and personal independence from parents and intercountry differences in this regard. For example, unmarried Dutch youth appear to live at home and attract various government family allowances to a much more advanced age than youth in other countries, but further study is required on this matter. An associated question is the effect on student LFPR of the standards of consumption and the spending habits of the youth of individual countries. Until we know more about the disposition of student earnings and the extent to which such earnings make individuals able or unable to remain enrolled, one of the key components of cross-national differences in student LFPR will be a matter of guesswork.

Available data on student LFPR and their hours and weeks of work reflect not only the demand of students for jobs while they attend classes, but also the supply of suitable jobs. The latter consist primarily of part-time jobs. Because the growth of service sector employment, in absolute and relative terms, has gone hand-in-hand with the development of part-time schedules in shops and offices, job opportunities for students have been most plentiful in the US and Canada, countries with the earliest and greatest development of service employment. A further incentive to organizing certain kinds of youth jobs around part-time schedules has arisen in these same countries, where a high proportion of the age group is enrolled. In order to employ any youth at all, or to recruit the more able youth, employers have had to arrange jobs to fit school hours.

In the United States, the fast food industry is the most frequently cited example, since streamlined organization makes it possible to operate such enterprises with minimal full-time supervision and a rotating staff of teenagers who are in school. An advantage of operating in this fashion is that part-time students, like most part-time workers in all countries, are paid somewhat less per hour than comparable full-time workers and do not qualify for many of the fringe and social benefits available to full-time workers. Given sufficient part-time openings, young people are not completely overshadowed by adult women and retired people seeking part-time work and certain kinds of jobs become the preserve of student workers. Undoubtedly, if Japanese service employment continues to grow rapidly and industrial employment does not, an increased number of part-time jobs for students will become available. Competition with older females may for a time restrict student opportunities, but eventually Japan should catch up to other nations, just as those other countries are likely to reach current U.S. levels in time.

Although we have discussed the demand for jobs and the supply for students separately, as in all other questions of supply and demand, it is likely that an interaction between the two also operates. This will result in a rising trend of student LFPR and longer average workweeks and weeks of work in the year as students progress from casual or vacation period workers to a regular part of the workforce and become an important element in the part-time labor force.

Hours and Weeks Worked by Male and Female Youth

Statistics on youth labor force size and youth LFPR by sex tend to understate male numbers and rates, or overstate female numbers and rates, to the extent that the actual labor supply for young females consists of fewer hours and weeks of work than that offered by young males. All of the tables presented in this chapter, which contain data on hours or weeks by age and sex, reflect the tendency of females to work and seek work for fewer hours per year than similar males. Our data are not complete enough to rank the twelve countries according to the amount of adjustment required to take account of male-female differences in hours and weeks in the labor force. It also would be relevant to discover whether involuntary part-time, part-year work is more prevalent among females than males and whether countries vary on this point. Further collection and analysis of data are required.

Table 5.10 affords the best opportunity to consider the differences in the United States between the two sexes in hours worked per week; for a complete accounting one would want similar data for the entire year or perhaps a succession of years, as well as information on those seeking jobs. The columns of Table 5.10 that show the ratio of full-time equivalents (FTE) to the number employed in nonagricultural industries in the US in 1967 and 1977, separately for the enrolled and nonenrolled, clearly point to a smaller reduction for males than females among the enrolled and a larger excess for males than females among the nonenrolled. In fact, among the nonenrolled, 16–17-year-old females are the only group to show no excess of FTE over actual hours. The male-female differential is greater for the nonenrolled than the enrolled, implying that student workers of each sex have greater similarity in patterns of hours and weeks than nonstudents.

Hours and Weeks Worked by Youth and Adults

A comparison of hours worked by young people with those of other age groups should begin by taking account of the striking differences among countries in the length of the usual workweek as well as in the total hours worked per year. In 1975, among the nine member countries of the European Communities, average total hours worked in the year by manual workers in all industries ranged from 1,521 in Italy to 2,051 in Ireland (EC 1979a). Another comparison of the net yearly hours of production workers in manufacturing in 1978 showed Japan in the lead with 2,146 hours, followed by the United Kingdom and the United States with 1,957 and 1,934 respectively. France was next with 1,799, while Germany was last with 1,728 hours (*Japan Labor Bulletin* d). These national patterns should influence the internal age distribution.

It is commonly assumed that out-of-school young people, especially teenagers, supply a total number of hours to the labor market which is disproportionately small compared to the youth share of the labor force. Data to test this proposition suffer from the defect that in most countries they include the hours worked or sought by students during the academic year. It is, of course, desirable to exclude students in the labor force from all calculations which compare youth to older workers. John Owen has done this for the United States and discovered that, contrary to the impression that young people tended to work fewer hours in the postwar period, male nonstudents exhibited no real trend in hours from 1948 to 1977, on both an adjusted and unadjusted basis. In this respect they closely resembled other age groups, which also tended to show a leveling off in the historical decline in worktime (Owen 1978, 1979).

The issue of whether youth work fewer hours per year than adults can be addressed through direct measures of average hours, which are scarce, or less direct evidence on part-time and part-year work. It appears that in five European countries, the youth share of the part-time labor force often was no smaller than its share of the full-time and part-time labor force together (Table 5.11). This finding would be consistent with an American study of 20–24-year-olds, which found that out-of-school males worked about as many hours as prime-age males in 1967, single females worked slightly less than prime-age single females, and married young adult women worked more than prime-age married women, after standardizing for differences in number and age of children (Garfinkel and Masters 1974).

Youth are underrepresented in overtime work in the United States, however. Measures by age group and sex of those who worked more than 41 hours a week in the US in 1978 and 1979 indicate that, for each sex, smaller fractions of teenagers and young adults than of prime-age workers (25–54) had overtime hours (Stamas 1979, 1980). There also is evidence that, among American workers normally on a full-time work schedule, younger workers tend to lose more working hours due to illness, injury, and other causes than prime-age workers. Annual American studies since 1973 consistently show 16–19-year-olds with higher percentages of absent workers and aggregate time lost than 20–24-year-olds or 25–54-year-olds; the latter in turn have lower rates than young adults (Hedges 1973, 1977; Taylor 1979).

Similarly, cross-sectional information for three countries—Australia, Sweden, and the United States—on part-year labor force participation by age clearly indicates

Table 5.11 Youth Share of Part-Time and Total Labor Force in Five Countries, 1975

	Part-time males		All occupied males		Part-time females		All occupied females	
	14-19	20-24	14-19	20-24	14-19	20-24	14-19	20-24
			(percent)					
France	8.0	10.4	3.9	10.4	1.9	6.5	4.6	15.8
Germany	2.4	3.1	6.2	7.9	0.5	4.1	9.1	13.9
Italy	5.3	7.4	3.7	7.5	4.5	7.1	7.4	14.0
Netherlands	7.6	9.4	3.5	10.3	2.5	13.4	13.1	27.3
United Kingdom	1.9	3.4	4.9	10.3	0.4	2.9	6.8	12.2

Source: European Communities, *Working Conditions in the Community*, Titles I/4, III/6 (Luxembourg: Eurostat, 1975).

Table 5.12   Persons in Labor Force at Some Time During the Year Who Were in Labor
Force for Less than 26 Weeks, Australia, Sweden, and United States,
1967-1978

	Year	Teenagers (15-19)		Young adults (20-24)		Adults (45-54)	
		Male	Female	Male	Female	Male	Female
		(percent)					
Australia[a]	1972	31.7	30.4	6.9	17.3	0.7	13.1
	1978	24.1	28.4	6.6	8.4	0.0	8.6
Sweden	1967[b]	53.3[c]	52.8	26.9	28.4	2.6	12.8
	1974[a]	50.5[d]	52.9	24.6	26.0	1.3	8.2
	1978[a]	54.2[d]	54.2	22.0	18.5	0.6	4.8
United States[b,d]	1967	56.6	62.6	25.7	36.0	3.4	15.8
	1974	49.4	55.4	23.3	30.8	4.2	14.8
	1977	55.4	56.9	25.1	30.9	5.1	15.9

[a] Base is in labor force at any time in the year.
[b] Base is employed at any time in the year.
[c] 14-19 years old.
[d] 16-19 years old.

Source: Australian Bureau of Statistics (ABS), *Labour Force Experience* 1972, 1978
(Canberra: ABS, biennial); Arbetsmarknadsstyrelsen (AMS), Meddelanden från
Utredningsbyrån [Reports from the Research Bureau] no. 1969:11, 1976: 12
(Stockholm, 1969, 1976); Arbetsmarknadsstyrelsen (AMS), *Årssysselsättningen 1978
och Utbildningsnivån Februari 1979* [Work Experience in 1978 and Educational Level
in February 1979]. (Solna, 1979); Department of Labor, Bureau of Labor Statistics,
Work Experience of the Population, Special Labor Force Reports 107, 181, 224
(Washington: GPO, 1969, 1975, 1979).

that adults (45-54 years old) have a much lower proportion in the labor force (or
working) less than 26 weeks a year (Table 5.12). It is, however, difficult to calculate
how much of the age difference between adults and the two youth groups or between
young adults and teenagers is attributable to entrance to the labor market in mid-
year after leaving school or to working while enrolled. Longitudinal studies of out-
of-school youth in the US, however, which find a decreased number of weeks out of
the labor force with increased age suggest that American youth or some segments of
it have somewhat weaker attachment than their elders (Corcoran 1979; Ellwood
1979; Meyer and Wise 1979). Such data are lacking for other countries.

Considerably more information is required to determine whether apparently
diverse national patterns in regard to the hours of out-of-school youth and adults are
indeed substantiated when consistent definitions and measures of actual hours are
applied. It seems, however, that some countries require practically no adjustment of
the male labor force by age in order to take account of differences in hours supplied
by out-of-school youth and adults. On the other hand, countries such as the US,
Canada, and Sweden may find their out-of-school male youth labor force
overstated, relative to their own adult groups and to other countries' youth.

Because adult females tend to have higher proportions on part-time and/or part-
year schedules than out-of-school teenage and young adult females, the labor force
size of the latter is likely to be somewhat of an understatement of the hours contributed by out-of-school female youth relative to adult females. Of course, the addition of the student labor force to the youth group would alter all of the relationships

for both sexes. It is interesting that the countries which seem to require the greatest amount of adjustment of the out-of-school youth labor force to take care of differences among age groups in hours and weeks of work (or job search) also are those which have relatively large proportions of students in the labor force. It is possible that the nature of youth jobs for the remainder becomes transformed when a large fraction of the age group combines labor force participation and full-time school attendance.

Youth Share of Adverse Hours and Workplaces

Data on hours and weeks worked by out-of-school youth versus older age groups do not capture other elements of jobs that relate to hours and that may in part explain youth's shorter hours. If young people are assigned disproportionately to evening, night, Sunday, and holiday work or to shift-work, they may be inclined to curtail their total hours. Similarly, if young people are more exposed than other age groups to noisy, unhygienic, dangerous workplaces and to strenuous, dirty, fast-paced, monotonous, or risky jobs, there may be repercussions on the total number of hours worked. Table 5.13 presents 1975 data for five European Communities countries on the youth share of shift, night, Sunday and holiday work compared to the youth share of the total labor force. Teenagers of each sex in each country had a disproportionately small share of the disliked work schedules, but young adult males in France and Italy and young adult females in all five countries had disproportionate shares of one or more of such work schedules. An American CPS report reveals disproportionate evening and night shift working among young, full-time, wage and salary workers (employed for 35 hours per week or more). The distribution of workers who usually work full time on day shifts in May 1977 indicated that 82 percent of all men, but only 73 percent of 16–19-year males and 78 percent of 20–24-year males, were on the full-time day shifts. For females, the overall percent was 87, while it was 80 percent for 16–19-year females and 86 percent for 20–24-year females. Thus, relatively more of the young full-time workers, whether enrolled or not, than of the other age groups were likely to be assigned evening and night shifts. Subsequent information for May 1978 confirmed the results (Hedges and Sekscenski 1979, Table 2).

The remainder of Table 5.13 concerns undesirable working conditions. Male teenagers and young adults in the three countries with such data—Germany, the Netherlands, and the United Kingdom—showed a disproportionate share in one or more type of unfavorable workplace, while teenage females had no such cases and only Dutch young adult females had a markedly higher proportion in risky workplaces than they had in the total labor force. A Swedish inquiry into the work environment disclosed that young workers, aged 16–24, were more likely than other age groups to have physical strain, dirty work, and fast-paced and monotonous tasks on their jobs, and, with the 25–34-year group, to have the most noise and greatest risk of accident in their work. Only in psychological strain were the youth rated in less than first place (Sweden 1979f, p. 28).

We are not prepared to draw direct conclusions about the relation between the adverse conditions just described, which affect youth in some countries, and youth nonstudent hours of work over the year compared to adult hours. Many other factors should be considered, such as the availability of overtime work to those with greatest seniority, in reckoning the balance between the age groups. While efforts should be made to expand the data base on nonstudent hours, information also should be collected in these ancillary aspects of the work situation.

Table 5.13   Youth with Adverse Hours and Working Conditions, by Age and Sex, in Five Countries, 1975

	Share of youth group in total labor force[a] (14 and older)	Shift work	Night work	Sunday and holiday work	Work in noisy place	Work in unhygenic place	Work in place with risks
	(Youth as a percent of all 14 years and older)						
Males 14–19							
France	4.1	2.4	1.7	2.3	n.a.	n.a.	n.a.
Germany	6.4	3.4	1.8	2.0	5.8	8.0	6.7
Italy	4.3	2.7[b]	1.3	2.2	n.a.	n.a.	n.a.
Netherlands	3.7	n.a.	1.4	1.5	4.0	4.2	4.1
United Kingdom	5.2	1.9	1.5	2.0	4.8	6.7	5.1
Females 14–19							
France	5.3	4.6	2.1	3.2	n.a.	n.a.	n.a.
Germany	8.6	8.1	2.8	4.2	5.4	4.2	8.4
Italy	8.4	7.9[b]	3.0	3.7	n.a.	n.a.	n.a.
Netherlands	13.5	n.a.	9.6	9.6	12.2	9.0	13.4
United Kingdom	7.1	5.9	3.3	4.1	6.8	5.8	6.3
Males 20–24							
France	10.7	12.7	9.0	7.3	n.a.	n.a.	n.a.
Germany	8.1	7.9	7.2	6.7	7.2	8.3	8.0
Italy	8.1	8.8[b]	6.0	5.9	n.a.	n.a.	n.a.
Netherlands	10.7	n.a.	8.8	7.5	10.6	11.4	11.4
United Kingdom	10.6	9.6	8.8	8.3	10.6	12.5	10.2
Females 20–24							
France	16.1	21.3	10.9	10.0	n.a.	n.a.	n.a.
Germany	14.0	17.0	10.8	9.2	13.0	9.8	13.1
Italy	15.1	19.7[b]	11.8	8.6	n.a.	n.a.	n.a.
Netherlands	27.3	n.a.	38.5	24.9	25.3	26.4	31.0
United Kingdom	12.4	16.1	14.6	11.1	12.7	11.8	11.8

[a] European Communities, Statistical Commission, *Labour Force Sample Survey 1975*, Tables II/1; II/3 (Luxembourg: Eurostat, 1976).
[b] In industry only.

Source: European Communities, Statistical Commission, *Working Conditions in the Community 1975*, Tables I/4; III/6; IV/4; V/5; VI/5, VII/5; VIII/5.

Summary

Students comprise varying proportions of the youth population in different countries, and the proportion of students who are simultaneously in the labor force also varies cross-nationally. Therefore, comparisons among countries of the size of the youth labor force and of youth LFPR, as presented in Chapter 4, do not present a full picture, to the extent that students may participate in the labor force more in some countries than others and students everywhere tend to work fewer hours per week and year than nonstudents.

Our investigation of student LFPR and the student share of the youth labor force revealed that the countries with the most substantial growth in the youth labor force in the postwar period had the highest enrollment rates and student LFPR. Although inadequate data complicate the comparison, the United States appears to be the clear leader in student LFPR; Canada also has relatively high levels of student LFPR, and Japan has low levels. Based simply on student LFPR, a substantial downward adjustment of U.S. and Canadian youth LFPR might be indicated, if full-time equivalents were used as the measure. Still, the introduction of data on student and nonstudent hours of work for the few countries where these are available suggest that the long hours worked by American students, in relation to students in other countries and American nonstudents, somewhat offset the large share they constitute of the youth labor force. Canadian and Swedish data confirm that a large fraction of all part-time workers in the youth groups are students.

Despite the limitations of the data, it is obvious that trends within countries and cross-national comparisons of the youth labor force should be modified to take account of students in the labor force and differences among countries in the number of hours per week and per year of students and nonstudents. Similar conclusions follow from an investigation of the differences in hours offered on the labor market by male and female youth. Precise adjustments cannot be computed on the basis of currently available data, but it is clear that male-female differentials in LFPR for youth do not convey the full extent of the labor supply gap between the sexes.

In computing the youth share of the total labor force and comparing this statistic among countries, some bias may intrude to the extent that nonstudent youth work fewer hours than adults. Handicapped by the difficulty of controlling for students in the data, we have presented available cross-country data on hours and weeks of work by youth and adults in various countries and the somewhat conflicting conclusions they produce. A consideration of some qualitative elements allows a comparison of work hours of youth and adults. Youth in some countries bear a disproportionate share of unpleasant jobs and work at unsociable hours. These circumstances might have a bearing on youth hours of work, where youth can exercise a choice.

Table A5.2 Enrolled Proportion of 16-17-Year-Old Total Population and Total Labor Force, and Labor Force Participation Rates by Enrollment Status, by Sex, United States, October 1947-1979

	Males				Females			
	Enrolled population as percent of total population	Enrolled labor force as percent of total labor force	Labor force participation rate Enrolled	Labor force participation rate Nonenrolled	Enrolled population as percent of total population	Enrolled labor force as percent of total labor force	Labor force participation rate Enrolled	Labor force participation rate Nonenrolled
	(percent)							
1947	67.6	35.9	26.8	91.8	67.5	38.3	17.0	56.8
1948	72.1	45.1	31.6	92.0	70.3	45.5	19.9	56.4
1949	70.8	41.2	27.5	88.0	68.2	47.1	21.5	51.8
1950	72.8	51.2	37.4	89.3	68.8	49.3	22.5	53.3
1951	74.7	53.9	39.6	84.4	75.5	59.7	25.8	52.7
1952	73.9	50.2	35.7	90.2	73.4	51.2	21.7	57.0
1953	74.6	49.3	29.0	87.7	72.9	49.0	17.9	49.9
1954	78.9	58.2	31.2	86.7	75.2	63.0	23.8	42.1
1955	78.9	60.8	37.3	89.9	73.8	56.1	21.4	47.3
1956	77.3	58.5	36.0	87.1	76.9	64.2	26.8	49.6
1957	80.2	63.0	36.2	85.9	78.1	68.3	26.6	44.1
1958	82.2	66.1	33.5	86.1	77.3	62.6	22.4	45.7
1959	83.4	67.2	34.0	82.1	81.0	69.1	23.5	44.7
1960	83.1	66.2	31.8	83.6	80.6	64.9	22.6	50.8
1961	82.8	65.7	32.0	79.8	82.4	65.5	20.7	50.9
1962	85.5	70.5	33.7	79.3	81.6	70.3	23.1	43.2
1963	88.0	75.3	32.5	81.0	84.6	75.2	23.8	43.8
1964	88.5	76.6	37.2	75.9	85.6	76.1	22.7	42.6
1965	87.0	75.0	38.5	83.0	86.9	80.0	26.0	42.9
1966	88.7	79.7	40.9	76.7	87.1	80.5	27.1	44.1
1967	90.2	82.7	39.4	77.6	86.7	80.8	27.8	43.0
1968	91.0	84.5	40.8	73.4	88.7	85.2	28.5	38.9
1969	90.8	83.3	38.9	80.6	87.7	84.1	33.4	45.3
1970	90.6	82.7	40.2	77.8	88.6	86.4	33.5	41.1
1971	91.1	84.4	40.1	75.6	88.7	84.7	31.3	44.4
1972	89.4	81.3	44.2	77.6	87.6	83.4	33.5	47.0
1973	88.5	81.1	43.4	79.4	87.1	84.1	38.0	48.9
1974	87.7	79.5	41.7	79.8	87.1	83.1	39.2	53.6
1975	90.0	82.9	42.8	77.4	87.2	84.8	38.9	47.7
1976	89.8	83.3	45.6	75.5	87.7	85.3	37.3	45.9
1977	89.2	83.0	46.6	77.5	87.7	83.4	39.1	55.3
1978	89.0	83.8	45.8	73.1	88.7	85.3	43.4	58.9
1979	90.5	85.8		75.5	87.6	85.1	43.5	53.6

Source: U.S. Department of Labor, *Employment and Training Report of the President 1980,* Table B-6 (Washington: GPO, 1980); Bureau of Labor Statistics, unpublished data for 1979; 1947-1952 derived from data furnished by Professor J. D. Mattila; Department of Defense unpublished data on military enlistments (volunteer and conscripted) as of October of each year. Data include all military and exclude the institutionalized population.

Table A5.3 Enrolled Proportion of 18-19-Year-Old Total Population and Total Labor Force, and Labor Force Participation Rates by Enrollment Status, by Sex, United States, October 1947-1979

(percent)

	Males				Females			
	Enrolled population as percent of total population	Enrolled labor force as percent of total labor force	Labor force participation rate Enrolled	Labor force participation rate Nonenrolled	Enrolled population as percent of total population	Enrolled labor force as percent of total labor force	Labor force participation rate Enrolled	Labor force participation rate Nonenrolled
1947	25.2	8.2	25.4	95.2	18.5	7.3	21.2	61.0
1948	29.9	11.0	27.9	96.4	20.3	5.9	14.4	58.8
1949	26.5	9.4	27.5	95.9	19.9	9.1	24.4	60.8
1950	31.1	14.4	36.0	96.6	24.3	12.8	27.7	60.8
1951	25.2	10.1	32.2	96.5	21.2	11.3	28.6	60.7
1952	29.2	12.0	31.4	95.1	22.0	7.3	16.9	60.6
1953	30.3	12.6	32.1	97.0	25.8	9.0	17.8	62.4
1954	33.6	13.1	27.4	92.2	25.3	11.6	23.4	60.7
1955	34.4	19.3	43.9	96.3	22.4	11.6	28.1	62.0
1956	36.1	19.2	39.4	93.6	27.3	14.4	27.1	60.6
1957	33.9	17.1	38.3	95.1	28.0	14.3	26.6	61.8
1958	38.6	18.5	34.4	95.1	29.4	18.1	31.6	59.5
1959	38.4	19.1	35.9	94.7	29.1	17.0	28.7	57.6
1960	41.3	20.7	34.9	94.5	29.9	16.5	27.9	60.4
1961	41.8	20.2	32.6	92.5	28.6	16.6	30.1	60.3
1962	41.6	21.8	34.9	88.9	33.6	15.1	21.8	61.9
1963	42.7	22.3	36.7	95.3	32.2	18.2	28.7	61.5
1964	42.9	22.4	36.0	94.2	33.6	17.4	25.2	60.4
1965	50.4	28.4	36.2	92.8	37.7	21.7	29.0	63.4
1966	50.9	29.9	37.5	91.3	37.7	24.3	33.5	63.0
1967	46.2	27.3	40.1	91.9	40.2	24.7	31.2	63.8
1968	53.4	35.1	42.9	90.9	41.1	26.0	31.8	63.1
1969	52.6	34.7	43.5	91.0	41.7	28.4	36.7	66.1
1970	49.4	31.1	41.2	89.1	41.5	29.5	37.7	63.8
1971	51.0	33.1	43.1	90.4	43.3	31.5	37.0	61.4
1972	47.1	30.7	45.4	91.3	41.7	28.7	37.0	65.7
1973	44.1	28.2	45.5	91.4	38.0	26.0	38.1	66.5
1974	42.2	26.2	44.5	91.2	40.5	28.0	39.5	69.4
1975	46.1	28.0	42.0	92.5	43.9	32.4	41.1	67.2
1976	44.7	28.7	45.0	90.4	44.2	33.0	43.8	70.4
1977	45.1	29.3	46.6	92.7	43.8	33.6	45.6	70.4
1978	44.8	29.6	48.3	93.1	42.8	32.3	45.7	71.7
1979	43.9	26.7	42.3	90.9	43.2	32.0	45.9	74.1

Source: U.S. Department of Labor, *Employment and Training Report of the President 1980*, Table B-6 (Washington: GPO, 1980); Bureau of Labor Statistics, unpublished data for 1979; Department of Defense unpublished data on military enlistments (volunteer and conscripted) as of October of each year. Data include all military and exclude the institutionalized population.

Table A5.5 Enrolled Proportion of 20-24-Year-Old Total Population and Total Labor Force, and Labor Force Participation Rates by Enrollment Status, by Sex, United States, October 1947-1979

(percent)

	Males				Females			
	Enrolled population as percent of total population	Enrolled labor force as percent of total labor force	Labor force participation rate Enrolled	Labor force participation rate Nonenrolled	Enrolled population as percent of total population	Enrolled labor force as percent of total labor force	Labor force participation rate Enrolled	Labor force participation rate Nonenrolled
1947	15.8	—	—	—	3.9	—	—	—
1948	15.1	4.7	26.8	96.7	3.4	1.8	—	46.0
1949	14.0	5.0	31.2	95.7	3.7	2.6	—	47.1
1950	12.5	5.1	36.0	96.1	4.6	3.1	23.3	49.6
1951	10.5	4.6	40.5	98.0	4.3	3.0	33.5	47.5
1952	11.2	3.4	27.3	96.2	4.9	3.2	32.5	46.4
1953	11.6	3.5	25.9	97.7	6.3	3.7	32.8	46.4
1954	12.5	5.5	39.1	96.2	6.0	4.6	29.9	48.5
1955	12.9	5.9	41.7	97.8	6.1	5.3	26.6	48.8
1956	15.7	8.1	46.0	97.3	6.8	6.7	36.6	49.6
1957	16.8	8.7	46.3	97.3	8.2	8.5	42.0	45.7
1958	16.8	9.3	49.4	97.2	8.2	5.8	48.9	48.3
1959	16.0	8.9	49.9	97.5	7.2	6.8	47.6	46.9
1960	16.5	8.2	44.2	97.7	7.1	6.3	45.3	46.8
1961	17.0	9.5	49.5	96.8	7.4	7.1	40.6	48.5
1962	19.7	11.8	52.8	97.0	8.3	8.3	40.3	49.9
1963	21.7	12.5	49.9	96.7	9.1	8.1	45.3	49.4
1964	20.4	11.2	48.0	97.2	10.3	8.2	38.4	51.9
1965	22.9	13.0	49.0	97.1	10.9	9.2	37.8	51.9
1966	23.5	12.7	46.7	98.3	11.8	9.4	39.6	53.7
1967	24.4	14.1	49.5	97.3	12.4	12.1	39.0	55.4
1968	23.5	14.1	51.2	95.9	15.0	11.2	43.7	57.2
1969	25.0	15.2	51.7	96.6	14.3	13.6	43.6	58.8
1970	23.9	14.3	51.2	95.9	15.9	13.0	49.0	60.1
1971	24.8	15.4	52.5	95.2	15.1	12.7	50.5	60.8
1972	24.6	15.4	53.2	95.7	15.7	13.2	47.4	62.8
1973	22.8	14.5	54.7	95.2	16.0	13.5	49.9	64.6
1974	23.5	15.1	55.5	95.9	16.7	15.1	50.3	65.9
1975	24.3	14.8	51.2	94.2	17.3	15.9	56.2	66.8
1976	24.0	15.7	55.7	94.8	18.6	17.0	55.1	68.6
1977	24.0	15.2	54.0	95.3	20.7	16.6	54.0	70.1
1978	22.5	14.4	55.3	95.2	19.9	16.2	58.4	72.3
1979	21.6	14.4	57.7	94.9	20.0	16.5	56.9	72.3

Source: U.S. Department of Labor, *Employment and Training Report of the President 1980*, Table B-6 (Washington: GPO, 1980); Bureau of Labor Statistics, unpublished data for 1979; Department of Defense unpublished data on military enlistments (volunteer and conscripted) as of October of each year. Data include all military and exclude the institutional population.

6 Young People Not in School or the Labor Force

Just as national levels and trends in educational enrollments and differences among countries in educational enrollment rates may affect comparative trends in the youth labor force, so may levels and trends in the remainder of the youth population, the part which is not in school or the labor force (NISLF). Although changes in the size of the NISLF group have less influence on the size of the youth labor force than is exerted by educational enrollments, NISLF merits attention as one of the major alternative statuses for youth.

There are additional reasons for examining the NISLF youth population in a cross-national context. If a country's NISLF rate exceeds that of comparable countries or if selected groups within a country have conspicuously higher proportions NISLF than the national average, there is reason to investigate the causes. Also, if some NISLF youth claim that they want to work or attend school, the question arises whether there is concealed unemployment, adverse conditions or discrimination in the labor market, or blocked access to education. Finally, if a number of out-of-school youth offer unacceptable explanations or no reasons for being NISLF or for making frequent entrances to and exits from the labor force, further examination is warranted to check for weak attachment to the labor force or possible social pathology. In particular, designers of educational and labor market programs for youth need to be aware of the size, composition, and needs of the NISLF group, since portions of the group, as well as some in school but out of the labor force, may qualify for and participate in programs actually designed for unemployed youth. This leads to an unintended increase in the size of the youth labor force and a disappointingly small impact on enumerated unemployment.

From the perspective of a labor force survey, NISLF status requires no disaggregation. NISLF youth appear to be a single group, defined negatively as out-of-school youth who were not employed and were not seeking paid work during the survey week. But the NISLF group is in fact diverse and heterogeneous and has a rationale apart from its relation to the labor market. NISLF status requires further disaggregation, as Chapter 1 discussed. A classification scheme for NISLF, which retains the central theme of the relationship to the labor force, takes the following form, starting with those farthest from the labor force:

1. Do not want a job at present.
   a. Not able to work.
   b. Able to work.
2. Want a job but not available and not searching for a job.
   a. Personal reasons.
   b. Labor market reasons.
3. Want a job, available to work, but not searching for a job.
   a. Personal reasons.
   b. Labor market reasons.

The addition of availability as a factor distinguishing between two groups which say they want to work has been adopted in Canada and is urged by critics of the U.S. procedures (Finegan 1978, pp. 83–95).

These main categories correspond roughly to Holt's suggestion that the NISLF population might be divided into "not in the labor force" and "temporarily withdrawn from the labor force" (Clark and Summers 1979a, p. 72). But a temporal distinction such as Holt proposes may be even more troublesome than one between wanting and not wanting a job, and available and not available, at the time of the survey. Of course, borderline cases cause classification problems in all systems. For example, an NISLF youth who was on drugs might be classified as ill or disabled and be assigned to either 1a or 2a. In some cases, 1b or 2b might be chosen as the proper category.

Despite the obvious difficulties attending a classification based on subjective judgment and the inherent possibilities of overlap and error, these proposed subdivisions are much more revealing about the composition of the NISLF group than a blanket category "not in the labor force." This point is reinforced when one describes the NISLF population in terms of their own activities and reasons for being NISLF. Those who do not want jobs consist of out-of-school youth who have elected nonmarket work (usually in the home), institutionalized youth (an excluded category in some national surveys), and youth whose illness, disability, or other circumstances cause them to defer, reject, or be denied access to the labor market permanently or for a period of some length. In addition, some youth are NISLF because they are waiting for some event, such as marriage or entrance to an educational program. Finally, some youth say that they do not want to work for miscellaneous or unstated reasons. Some of the possible explanations are the custom that unmarried females remain at home, absence of an economic need to work, a desire to pursue interests apart from school and work, income from illicit sources and activities, or reliance on governmental transfer payments. Those who are NISLF because they do not want to work may change their minds or the precipitating circumstances may alter, but within a given year they are unlikely to move repeatedly between nonparticipation and participation in the labor force or education.

Among those who express a desire to work but have not searched for jobs, some offer the same reasons that others gave for not wanting a job: illness, household responsibilities, etc. There also are some who give vague or no reasons. Without detailed investigation it is not possible to determine how this last group differs from their counterparts who say that they do not want jobs. A portion, as the later discussion details, are waiting for certain events in the labor market and are ambiguously called "not in the labor force." They account for some of the mysterious rapid movement in and out of the labor force observed by analysts of gross flows in the youth labor market (Denton 1973; Smith 1974, 1975; Smith and Holt 1974; Denton, Feaver, and Robb 1976; Clark and Summers 1978b, 1979b; Smith and Vanski 1978).

Those who are NISLF and do not fit any of the above descriptions are called discouraged workers or jobseekers. They are out-of-school young people who said that they wanted to work but did not search during the survey period because they believed that it would be fruitless, due to personal factors, such as their own qualifications and employers' requirements and prejudices, or such labor market reasons as the unavailability of suitable jobs at desired pay rates in given locations. It is, of course, difficult to verify that the expressed desire for work is genuine, but the citation of labor market reasons for not seeking employment distinguishes this subgroup from all other NISLF.

Because of the great diversity in each country's NISLF population, the lack of a labor force orientation on the part of many in the NISLF group, and the evidence, to be presented below, that discouraged workers and indeed the entire group wanting to work among NISLF youth constitute a minority of total NISLF numbers, we accept NISLF as a separate and distinct category, not to be added to the unemployed to form a new category called "nonemployed." At the same time we recognize that there may be little to distinguish some of the youth unemployed from some who are not in the labor force and that a certain portion of youth frequently change their status from in the labor force to not in the labor force without necessarily altering their actual labor market position.

The remainder of this chapter is devoted to an exploration of the size, nature, and trends of the NISLF group in a number of countries and a consideration of explanatory factors. Differences in NISLF rates among countries would be anticipated because of cross-national variations in the basic circumstances and institutions which influence overall NISLF rates. Some of those basic factors would be:

the incidence of illness, disability, and handicaps among youth;

public attitudes and programs to bring disabled or handicapped youth into the labor force;

levels and trends in marriage rates and fertility of women younger than 25 years of age;

acceptance by society and families of labor force participation by married women and mothers;

strength of the work ethic;

presence of institutions, such as apprenticeship or the lifetime employment system, which provide employment security for some new entrants to the labor force;

youth unemployment rates and ratios as they affect the number wanting to work but not looking for jobs;

distribution of young people among various educational attainment levels;

distribution of young people by geographic region, size, and type of place of residence;

employment security systems which protect established employees and are adverse to new entrants;

the net results of all relevant government programs affecting youth as between those which favor enrollments in education or participation in the labor force, on the one hand, and those which favor remaining out of school and the counted labor force, on the other hand;

level of affluence of the society;

opportunities to obtain income without working; and

opportunities for and incidence of socially deviant behavior.

In addition, the incidence of NISLF varies among youth groups within a country, as Chapter 7 demonstrates for the United States. Therefore, differences among countries in NISLF rates could be attributable in part to such variables as:

homogeneity of the youth population;

degree of equality of household income distribution after taxes and income transfers;

amount of variation in educational attainment of youth by racial, ethnic or religious divisions; and

amount of variation in youth residential patterns by racial, ethnic or religious divisions.

Finally, data and measurement variations, described below, might have important effects on recorded differences among countries in NISLF rates. These might, in fact, overwhelm all other influences. It also is quite possible that the net effect of all the potential factors cited above will be to cancel each other and produce relatively small differences in NISLF rates for males. Females, on the other hand, are expected, on the basis of the earlier chapters, to show common trends in NISLF rates but continuing wide differences among countries.

Dimensions of Not in School or the Labor Force

Comparisons across nations are based as far as possible on data for a time of year in each country when schools are in session. Annual averages that include vacation months tend to escalate NISLF rates because some young people who continue in student status after the vacation period are reported as out-of-school during the vacation, and would also be NISLF if they did not seek or have a job (Appendix 6:1).

Where possible, national NISLF data have been adjusted to include all of the armed forces and institutionalized persons in the population base. Members of the armed forces, including military conscripts, are regarded as in the labor force, contrary to the practice in some countries. *Table A6.1 shows the effect of using the total instead of the civilian population as a base for male NISLF rates in the United States.* Inclusion of the U.S. military in the population base, especially in the Vietnam years, decreases NISLF rates. For example in 1968, a peak military year, 20-24-year-old males would have had a 4.0 percent NISLF rate using the civilian population base, but only 3.1 percent using the total population including the military.

In most countries certain portions of NISLF youth with weak societal attachment may be missed in surveys and censuses. This is likely to occur more frequently for such youth than for those who are clearly in school or the labor force. Such undercounting may be more prevalent in the countries which already have relatively high proportions of NISLF youth in the age group.

On the whole, countries agree reasonably well on the classifications that qualify as not in school or the labor force. NISLF status is fairly easy to establish on the educational side, although countries differ in their treatment of part-time educational enrollees in their official enrollment statistics. In addition, some forms of education/training, even if full time, are not counted as part of the regular educational system; in the US for example, those attending business and other proprietary schools have been treated as NISLF in the labor force survey. Furthermore, the truancy rate is so high at certain schools and actual attendance of classes so irregular that the in-school designation may be misleading for a proportion of young people. While these problems have been observed in American inner-city schools in particular, they have also been noted elsewhere.

Differences among countries that affect the definition of the labor force also have a bearing on the comparability of the NISLF statistics. Young people who assist in a family business as unpaid workers may be excluded from the labor force if they work less than a stipulated number of hours per week. Nevertheless, differences among

*Tables marked with an asterisk are not included in this volume, but may be obtained from the authors.

countries in this definition, as well as in the size of the category itself, are a minor influence on cross-national variations in the size of the NISLF group. Similarly, in some countries the labor force may include young unemployed whose efforts to find work are the same or minimally greater than those of youth in other countries who regard themselves as outside the labor force. These differences do not invalidate a direct comparison of NISLF rates among countries. Moreover, an examination of labor force survey and census methods indicates sufficient similarity to justify cross-national analysis.

Several types of data cast light on the NISLF category. Cross-sectional, moment-in-time information comes from labor force surveys or censuses; some countries provide data from both. Longitudinal surveys of a retrospective or current type can be used both cross-sectionally and longitudinally to reveal the dimensions of the NISLF population. Cross-sectional data from labor force surveys and censuses provide the bulk of our information.

Cross-Sectional Results

Although the absolute number of young people classified as NISLF is in large part a function of the absolute size of the population, a factor which varies widely from tiny New Zealand to the populous United States, there is some interest in the absolute numbers of NISLF youth at different points in time for the four age-sex groups (*Table 6.1). Country ranks in the number of NISLF youth in each age-sex group are close but not identical. These ranks also correlate closely with country ranks in the size of the youth population. Over time, male numbers have risen in most countries while female numbers have declined, especially among the young adults.

Within an age group the ratio of male to female NISLF numbers has varied considerably among the countries and over time within countries. Japan's 1977 teenage ratio was barely in excess of 1:1, a low ratio at that time. In 1959 the ratio had been over 1:3.5, still low in comparison to Sweden's ratio of almost 1:5 in 1963 or the American ratio in excess of 1:9 in 1955. As expected, the young adult male-female ratios were even larger at the outset, but dropped more sharply over time than those of the teenagers. Sweden, whose 1979 ratio of slightly over 1:3 for young adult males to females is probably as low as any of the countries would have shown if 1979 data had been available for all countries, had had a ratio of 1:13.3 in 1963. The U.S. ratio was 1:24.7 in 1955 and 1:5.6 in 1979.

Greater comparability among the countries can be achieved by controlling for differences in size of population and computing the NISLF rates, that is, the proportion of NISLF youth for each age-sex group in each country. NISLF rates can be computed by taking the population of the age-sex group as the base (Method A) or by taking only those who are out of school (Method B). The latter method controls for differences among countries in the level of educational enrollment rates (EER) and in the rate of change in EER. Results from the two methods would be expected to differ significantly for teenagers, because their EER levels are sufficiently high in several countries to reduce the denominator substantially and thus increase NISLF rates under Method B. In policy terms it might be said that NISLF rates derived from Method B reveal the existence and extent of a potential social problem more fully and precisely than calculations based on the whole age group. Yet, to the degree that trends in NISLF are a joint effect of EER and LFPR trends, it may be useful to have a series using the age-group population, as in Method A. Alternatively, if NISLF is regarded primarily as a relationship to the labor force, the out-of-school series in Method B may be preferred. Table 6.2a shows, side by side, the results of the two methods for males of each age group, while Table 6.2b does the same for females. NISLF rates are presented for nine countries over a period of years according to the availability of data; for six countries data are drawn from labor force surveys, and for three countries from periodic population censuses.

As Tables 6.2a and 6.2b indicate, the variation among countries in NISLF rates by either method is greater for females than males. Both groups of females show such large cross-national differences, whichever calculation method is used, that it may be assumed that the factors influencing female activity in and out of the household dominate all other variables in inter-country differences. The country ranks for female NISLF rates are consistent with what is known about EER and LFPR for these groups, and with national attitudes.

Among teenage girls, the United States, Canada, and the Netherlands have relatively high NISLF rates. The US and Canada are conspicuously high when NISLF rates are computed as a proportion of the out-of-school population. Low NISLF rates for teenage females were found in Japan, Sweden, and France. The NISLF rates of teenage females are unusual in the exceptionally high rates shown by the US and the low rates of Japan. Under Method A, the US shows a range of from over 10 percent to more than 21 percent in a 25-year period. Only the Netherlands, with 16 percent in 1961, has as much as 10 percent in any year. Japan has rates of less than 5 percent after the 1962 entry of 5.4 percent, and dips to 1.9 percent in 1977. Converting the rates by Method B raises the U.S. range from 30 percent to 44 percent and removes some of the regularity in the long-run decline of NISLF rates. Canada edges up with rates greater than 22 percent by Method B, while Sweden displaces Japan in the lowest rank. The rate in the highest country has been about four times that of the lowest in recent years. Italy's estimate by Method A of 32 percent for teenage females in 1975 also places it in the high group, but, as in the case of males, some may be engaged in "black labor" (de Francesco 1978; Pettenati 1979). In the nine member countries of the European Communities, NISLF rates for females aged 14–24 dropped from 1973 to 1977 in each country, and averaged 14.6 percent in 1975 and 12.8 percent in 1977 (Table 6.2c).

NISLF 1971 rates for teenage females in seven countries ranged from 3.2 to 13.9 percent (Method A) and from 9.1 to 41.7 percent (Method B). Even more than for teenage males, controlling for EER levels in Method B raised teenage female NISLF rates; the 1971 rates were tripled or more by Method B, and similar effects were shown in other years. Overall, the highest NISLF rates were shown by young adult females. Method A gave a range of 18.9 to 42.9 percent in 1971, while Method B yielded a span of 22.2 to 43.8 percent; for this group, controlling for EER differences had little impact.

Young adult females in New Zealand, the Netherlands, Australia, and Great Britain had high NISLF rates by both methods, while Sweden, France, and Japan are the low countries, with exceptionally low rates for Swedish young adult females in recent years. Sweden's low percentage of NISLF females, less than 10 percent for both youth groups by 1979, reflects low marriage and child-bearing rates in the relevant age groups, growing opportunities for female employment (especially part-time), official support for working women, and the equality movement. The French situation is attributable in part to the educational patterns of females and to expansion of employment in the service sector, but unpaid family labor on farms and in small businesses still plays a role for this age group. Japan, the most traditional of the

Table 6.2a Males Not in School or the Total Labor Force, by Age, in Nine Countries, 1955-1979

	Australia[a,b] (Aug)	Canada[b] (Oct)	France[c] (Mar)	Japan[b] (Jul)	Sweden[c,d] (Nov)	United States[d] (Oct)	Great[e] Britain (Apr)	Netherlands[a] (May) (Censuses)	New Zealand[a] (Mar)
			(Labor force surveys)						
				Teenage (15-19) Males					
			(percent of total noninstitutional population) (Method A)						
1955						2.3			
1956						3.5			
1957						3.0			
1958						2.7			
1959				2.0		3.1			
1960						3.0		2.1	
1961						3.9	1.8		
1962				2.0		4.8			
1963					1.8	2.5			
1964					1.0	3.0			
1965				2.2	2.2	2.9			
1966					1.0	3.5	3.4		
1967					1.9	3.3			
1968				1.8	1.3	3.3			
1969					2.0	3.0			
1970					2.0	3.8			
1971	1.9			2.1	2.1	3.4	1.7	2.3[f]	1.4
1972	1.9				3.5	3.5			
1973	2.1				3.7	3.6			
1974	2.3			2.3	2.5	3.8			
1975	2.1	3.4	1.7		1.6	3.2			
1976	1.9	4.1	1.7		1.2	3.9			1.4
1977	2.5	4.1	2.1	1.6	1.8	3.2			
1978		4.3	1.9		1.9	3.4			
1979					0.5	3.9			
				Young adult (20-24) Males					
1955						2.0			
1956						2.3			
1957						2.2			
1958						2.3			
1959				2.2		2.1			
1960						1.9		1.3	
1961						2.7	1.3		
1962				1.7		2.4			
1963					1.9	2.6			
1964					2.4	2.2			
1965				1.7	2.1	2.2			
1966					2.7	1.3	1.5		0.5
1967					1.9	2.0			
1968				1.4	1.4	3.1			
1969					2.4	2.5			
1970					3.2	3.1			
1971	2.3			1.5	2.7	3.6	1.2	3.6[f]	1.3
1972	2.7				3.2	3.3			
1973	2.8				2.4	3.7			
1974	3.2			1.6	2.2	3.1			
1975	3.2	3.6	3.5		1.8	4.4			
1976	3.2	4.0	3.2		2.3	4.0			1.7
1977	3.1	4.5	2.8	1.8	2.7	3.5			
1978		3.7	4.0		2.4	3.7			
1979					2.5	4.0			

[a] Includes institutionalized population

[b] Based on civilian population and labor force; excludes military forces.

[c] Includes institutionalized population. Total population and labor force include military conscripts and volunteers.

[d] Aged 16-19.

[e] Includes institutionalized population; the British Census was taken in April, during or soon after a school-leaving period. This may inflate proportions in school or the labor force for the 15-year-old school-leavers.

[f] Netherlands 1971 census was taken in February.

Source: Australia. ABS (Australian Bureau of Statistics), unpublished annual statistics.
   Canada. Statistics Canada, Labour Force Survey Division, unpublished annual statistics.
   France. INSEE (institut national de la statistique et des études économiques). Enquêtes sur l'emploi 1975-1976 [Labor Force Surveys, 1975-1976], Résultats détaillés. Table PT 01. Les collections de l'insée, no. 265, Série D57 (Paris: IN, May 1978); INSEE, Enquête sur l'emploi de Mars 1977 [Labor Force Survey, March 1977], Résultats détaillés, Table PT 01. Les collections de l'insée, no. 250, Série D53 (Paris: IN, March 1978); INSEE, Enquête sur l'emploi de Mars 1978 [Labor Force Survey, March 1978], Résultats détaillés, Table PT 01: Les collections de l'insée, no. 287, Série D61 (Paris:

Table 6.2a (continued)

	Australia[a,b] (Aug)	Canada[b] (Oct)	France[c] (Mar)	Japan[b] (Jul)	Sweden[c,d] (Nov)	United States[d] (Oct)	Great[e] Britain (Apr)	Netherlands[a] (May) (Censuses)	New Zealand[a] (Mar)
			(Labor force surveys)						
	Teenage (15–19) Males								
	(percent of total out-of-school noninstitutional population) (Method B)								
1955						5.3			
1956						8.2			
1957						7.1			
1958						7.1			
1959				4.1		8.3			
1960						8.1		3.2	
1961						10.4	2.3		
1962				4.5		13.0			
1963					2.8	7.5			
1964					1.5	9.5			
1965				6.4	3.3	9.3			
1966					1.7	11.4	4.6		
1967					3.6	10.3			
1968				4.9	2.3	12.1			
1969					3.8	10.7			
1970					3.7	12.8			
1971	3.1			6.7	3.8	11.9	2.7	5.4[f]	2.4
1972	3.2				6.0	11.1			
1973	3.4				6.4	10.7			
1974	3.8			9.6	4.1	10.9			
1975	3.4	10.6	5.4		2.7	9.9			
1976	3.1	12.6	5.7		2.1	11.9			2.5
1977	3.8	12.0	7.2	8.1	3.1	9.8			
1978		11.7	6.8		3.2	10.2			
1979					0.9	11.7			
	Young adult (20–24) Males								
1955						2.2			
1956						2.7			
1957						2.7			
1958						2.8			
1959				2.4		2.5			
1960						2.3		1.5	
1961						3.2	1.4		
1962				1.9		3.0			
1963					2.2	3.3			
1964					2.8	2.8			
1965				2.0	2.4	2.9			
1966					3.2	1.7	1.6		0.7
1967					2.3	2.7			
1968				1.7	1.6	4.1			
1969					2.8	3.4			
1970					3.7	4.1			
1971	2.5			1.8	3.3	4.8	1.3	4.2[f]	1.5
1972	2.8				3.7	4.3			
1973	3.0				2.8	4.8			
1974	3.5			2.0	2.5	4.1			
1975	3.5	4.7	4.1		2.0	5.8			
1976	3.4	5.2	3.7		2.6	5.2			1.9
1977	3.3	5.8	3.3	2.5	3.1	4.7			
1978		4.6	4.8		2.8	4.8			
1979					2.8	5.6			

IN, January 1979); INSEE, unpublished annual statistics.

Japan. Office of the Prime Minister. Bureau of Statistics. *Employment Status Survey. All Japan.* 1959: estimated from Tables I–1 and II–2; 1962: Tables I–1 and II–8; 1965: Tables 1 and 28; 1968: Tables 1 and 28; 1971: Tables 1 and 39; 1974: Tables 2 and 31; 1977: Tables 2 and 31. Tokyo, triennial.

Sweden. SCB (Statistiska Centralbyrån), *Arbetskraftsundersökningen*, Råtabeller [Labor Force Survey, Raw Tables] (Stockholm, monthly).

U.S. Department of Labor, *Employment and Training Report of the President 1979*, Table B–6 (Washington: GPO, 1979); U.S. Department of Labor, Bureau of Labor Statistics, unpublished data.

Great Britain. General Register Office, *Census 1961, Summary Tables*, Table 32 (London: HMSO, 1966); *Sample Census 1966. Economic Activity Tables*, Part I, Tables 1 and 3 (London: HMSO, 1968); Office of Population Censuses and Surveys, *Census 1971: Economic Activity*, Part II, Tables 3 and 5 ((London HMSO, 1975).

Netherlands. CBS (Centraal Bureau Voor de Statistiek), *Algemene Volkstelling 1960* [General Population Census 1960] Vol. 8, Part a (Voorburg: CBS); *Algemene Volkstelling 1971* [General Population Census 1971] (Voorburg: CBS); unpublished data.

New Zealand. Department of Statistics, *Population Census*, 1966, 1971, 1976 (Wellington: Department of Statistics, quinquennial); unpublished data.

Table 6.2b   Females Not in School or the Total Labor Force, by Age, in Nine Countries, 1955–1979

	Australia[a] (Aug)	Canada (Oct)	France[a] (Mar) (Labor force surveys)	Japan (Jul)	Sweden[a,d] (Nov)	United States[d] (Oct)	Great[e] Britain (Apr)	Netherlands[a] (May) (Censuses)	New Zealand[a] (Mar)
			Teenage (15–19) Females						
				(percent of total noninstitutional population) (Method A)					
1955						21.5			
1956						20.1			
1957						19.8			
1958						20.1			
1959				7.4		19.6			
1960						18.2		16.0	
1961						18.6	6.6		
1962				5.4		17.9			
1963					9.2	16.6			
1964					9.8	16.4			
1965				4.7	8.4	15.0			
1966					8.5	15.3	8.2		
1967					9.6	14.6			
1968				3.6	6.7	14.2			
1969					7.1	13.1			
1970					6.8	13.7			
1971	8.1			3.2	6.3	13.9	7.5	9.3[f]	7.6
1972	8.0				7.9	13.2			
1973	7.7				8.5	13.6			
1974	8.3			2.9	5.2	12.1			
1975	7.2	8.0	3.8		4.2	12.6			
1976	6.9	8.5	3.7		4.5	11.7			7.9
1977	6.3	7.9	3.3	1.9	3.7	11.2			
1978		8.6	3.5		3.5	10.5			
1979					4.3	10.4			
			Young adult (20–24) Females						
1955						48.2			
1956						47.1			
1957						49.9			
1958						48.1			
1959				25.9		49.4			
1960						49.4		44.6	
1961						47.4	35.1		
1962				23.7		45.7			
1963					26.5	45.5			
1964					25.1	42.9			
1965				24.9	27.7	42.5			
1966					25.9	40.6	34.6		45.8
1967					23.3	37.6			
1968				21.3	22.4	36.7			
1969					21.4	34.8			
1970					19.3	33.9			
1971	35.8			22.7	18.9	33.1	34.2	39.7[f]	42.9
1972	34.8				17.6	31.3			
1973	34.2				17.0	29.6			
1974	32.0			23.4	15.9	28.3			
1975	30.4	25.7	17.5		13.8	27.1			
1976	29.1	25.8	16.5		12.7	25.1			38.0
1977	26.9	23.3	16.4	17.4	12.1	24.1			
1978		22.0	16.0		10.8	22.5			
1979					8.8	22.3			

[a] Includes institutionalized population

[b] Based on civilian population and labor force; excludes military forces.

[c] Includes institutionalized population. Total population and labor force include military conscripts and volunteers.

[d] Aged 16–19.

[e] Includes institutionalized population; the British Census was taken in April, during or soon after a school-leaving period. This may inflate proportions in school or the labor force for the 15-year-old school-leavers.

[f] Netherlands 1971 census was taken in February.

Source: Australia. ABS (Australian Bureau of Statistics), unpublished annual statistics.
   Canada. Statistics Canada, Labour Force Survey Division, unpublished annual statistics.
   France. INSEE (institut national de la statistique et des études économiques). Enquêtes sur l'emploi 1975–1976 [Labor Force Surveys, 1975–1976], Résultats détaillés. Table PT 01. Les collections de l'inseé, no. 265, Série D57 (Paris: IN, May 1978); INSEE, Enquête sur l'emploi de Mars 1977 [Labor Force Survey, March 1977], Résultats détaillés, Table PT 01. Les collections de l'inseé, no. 250, Série D53 (Paris: IN, March 1978); INSEE, Enquête sur l'emploi de Mars 1978 [Labor Force Survey, March 1978], Résultats détaillés, Table PT 01: Les collections de l'inseé, no. 287, Série D61 (Paris:

Table 6.2b (continued)

Teenage (15–19) Females

	Australia[a,b] (Aug)	Canada (Oct)	France[a] (Mar)	Japan (Jul)	Sweden[a,d] (Nov)	United States[d] (Oct)	Great[e] Britain (Apr)	Netherlands[a] (May) (Censuses)	New Zealand[a] (Mar)
			(Labor force surveys)						
	(percent of total out-of-school noninstitutional population) (Method B)								
1955						41.9			
1956						42.2			
1957						42.6			
1958						44.2			
1959				13.3		45.6			
1960						41.9		21.2	
1961						41.7	8.6		
1962				10.6		42.4			
1963					13.8	42.4			
1964					15.2	43.5			
1965				11.8	12.8	40.4			
1966					13.7	40.2	11.0		
1967					15.8	40.2			
1968				8.5	11.2	41.1			
1969					12.4	37.8			
1970					11.3	40.2			
1971	12.9			9.1	11.1	41.7	11.7	15.7[f]	11.8
1972	12.5				14.2	37.8			
1973	12.3				14.8	36.7			
1974	13.3			10.4	8.5	33.6			
1975	11.1	22.6	14.0		7.0	36.6			
1976	11.2	24.9	14.4		7.4	34.2			13.3
1977	9.8	23.5	13.2	8.6	6.1	32.5			
1978		23.1	15.4		6.2	30.5			
1979					7.4	29.7			

Young adult (20–24) Females

	Australia[a,b] (Aug)	Canada (Oct)	France[a] (Mar)	Japan (Jul)	Sweden[a,d] (Nov)	United States[d] (Oct)	Great[e] Britain (Apr)	Netherlands[a] (May)	New Zealand[a] (Mar)
1955						51.4			
1956						50.5			
1957						54.4			
1958						51.9			
1959				27.1		53.2			
1960						53.3		45.8	
1961						51.6	36.0		
1962				24.8		50.2			
1963					29.2	50.7			
1964					27.6	48.2			
1965				26.5	30.2	48.2			
1966					29.9	46.4	35.9		46.3
1967					26.6	44.6			
1968				23.8	25.6	42.9			
1969					24.6	41.4			
1970					23.1	40.0			
1971	36.9			24.4	22.2	39.3	36.2	41.7[f]	43.8
1972	36.1				20.4	37.3			
1973	35.5				19.8	35.5			
1974	33.4			25.5	18.6	34.2			
1975	31.8	30.4	20.7		16.3	33.4			
1976	30.5	30.8	19.3		14.3	31.7			39.3
1977	28.2	28.4	19.2	19.4	13.8	30.1			
1978		25.4	19.0		12.3	27.9			
1979					9.9	28.0			

IN, January 1979); INSEE, unpublished annual statistics.

Japan. Office of the Prime Minister. Bureau of Statistics. *Employment Status Survey. All Japan.* 1959: estimated from Tables I-1 and II-2; 1962: Tables I-1 and II-8; 1965: Tables 1 and 28; 1968: Tables 1 and 28; 1971: Tables 1 and 39; 1974: Tables 2 and 31; 1977: Tables 2 and 31. Tokyo, triennial.

Sweden. SCB (Statistiska Centralbyrån), *Arbetskraftsundersökningen*, Råtabeller [Labor Force Survey, Raw Tables] (Stockholm, monthly).

U.S. Department of Labor, *Employment and Training Report of the President 1979*, Table B-6 (Washington: GPO, 1979); U.S. Department of Labor, Bureau of Labor Statistics, unpublished data.

Great Britain. General Register Office, *Census 1961, Summary Tables*, Table 32 (London: HMSO, 1966); *Sample Census 1966. Economic Activity Tables*, Part I, Tables 1 and 3 (London: HMSO, 1968); Office of Population Censuses and Surveys, *Census 1971: Economic Activity*, Part II, Tables 3 and 5 (London: HMSO, 1975).

Netherlands. CBS (Centraal Bureau Voor de Statistiek), *Algemene Volkstelling 1960* [General Population Census 1960] Vol. 8, Part a (Voorburg: CBS); *Algemene Volkstelling 1971* [General Population Census 1971] (Voorburg: CBS); unpublished data.

New Zealand. Department of Statistics, *Population Census*, 1966, 1971, 1976 (Wellington: Department of Statistics, quinquennial); unpublished data.

Table 6.2c   Young People (14–24 Years Old) Not in School or the Total Labor Force, in Nine European Communities Countries, 1973, 1975, and 1977

	Males			Females		
	1973	1975	1977	1973	1975	1977
	(percent of total noninstitutional population)					
Belgium	0.9	0.8	0.7	12.5	10.3	8.1
Denmark	n.a.	18.8[a]	1.0	n.a.	23.5[a]	4.3
France	1.5	2.6	2.3	11.5	10.9	10.0
Germany	2.2	15.8[a]	2.3	12.1	10.7	9.4
Ireland	n.a.	1.0	1.0	n.a.	12.0	10.6
Italy	2.6	2.4	3.3	26.6	22.5	21.9
Luxembourg	0.0	0.3	0.5	14.9	12.3	11.0
Netherlands	0.9	1.0	1.0	16.4	14.0	11.1
United Kingdom	2.1	1.3	1.2	17.4	14.1	13.5
Average	n.a.	2.4	2.2	n.a.	14.6	12.8

[a] These rates appear to have been calculated on different standard than similar ones for 1973 and 1977 and probably should be disregarded.

Source: European Communities, Statistical Office, *Labor Force Sample Survey 1973, 1975, 1977*, Table II, 6 (Luxembourg: Eurostat, 1980).

countries in its role assignments to women, probably is in the group with low NISLF rates, mainly because the age of marriage has been somewhat later than in other countries and fertility rates have dropped rapidly. Since unmarried females have access to education and jobs, the NISLF rate can be lower than in other countries, even though a relatively high proportion of Japanese married females are NISLF.

The economies of New Zealand and Australia still are heavily dependent on primary production and extractive industries, in which males predominate. Each country also has a reputation as "a man's country," which translates into limited acceptance of women in the labor force. At the slightest sign of labor market difficulty, suggestions are likely to be heard that it would be helpful if married females left the labor force and returned to their homes. While Australia's NISLF rate for young adult females is not much higher than the U.S. rate, New Zealand must have a considerable drop in its rate in order to reach the levels of NISLF in the US and Canada. The Netherlands has had a low NISLF for unmarried females and a very high rate for married women. Since the Dutch marriage age was high and the birth rate was, until recently, the highest in western Europe, NISLF rates for young adults were second only to New Zealand. In recent years changes have occurred, and the 1981 Dutch census is likely to show a sharp decline.

Under both calculation methods, NISLF rates of young adult males had a relatively small spread among countries in 1971, ranging from 1.2 to 3.6 percent by Method A and 1.3 to 4.8 percent by Method B in a year when data for seven countries were recorded (Table 6.2a). These NISLF rates for young adult males exhibit consistent inter-country differences in which Canada, the United States, and France are on the high side, and Great Britain, New Zealand, and Japan are on the low side. Countries whose data were obtained from censuses seem to run lower than those drawn from labor force surveys. Controlling for EER raises Japan's rate somewhat more than those of the other two countries, but at 2.5 percent Japan is still outstandingly low; six countries have higher rates in the most recent available data.

Teenage males have NISLF rates very like those of young adult males when Method A is used, but under Method B the level and range for teenage males rise far beyond those of young adult males. Thus, in 1971 Method A yields a range for teenagers of 1.4 to 3.4 percent, while Method B produces a span of 2.4 to 11.9 percent. The highest teenage male rates are shown in Canada and the United States; Japan, among the lowest in Method A, rises to third highest when Method B is used because of Japan's rapidly shrinking out-of-school population. Under Method B, the U.S. rate was twice that of Japan's in 1959, but was barely higher in 1977. Great Britain, New Zealand, and the Netherlands were at the low end for male teenagers. The fact that the rates for the latter group of countries were derived from census returns in the absence of labor force surveys may have an effect. Yet, in the comparison of census and labor force survey results for the US (*Table A6.2), the census yielded higher NISLF rates than the labor force survey (Bowen and Finegan 1969, pp. 406-8).

Indirect evidence for Italy suggests that an even higher proportion of their male teenage population was in the NISLF group than in the US and Canada (Method A in Table 6.2a). In 1975, 11 percent of Italian males (14-19 years old) were counted as NISLF (de Francesco 1978). Allowance must be made for overstatement, however, since a considerable number of young people are hired by employers without being officially entered on the payroll. Known as "black labor," this type of worker is used by employers to evade the heavy social security taxes. Youth working in this fashion are not reported as employed, but some may continue to be regarded as unemployed rather than NISLF (Fuà 1977; Frey 1978; Pettenati 1979). Data for nine member countries of the European Communities for the age group 14-24 show an average male NISLF rate in 1975 and 1977 of over 2 percent and a narrow range among nations. As for the females in EC countries, Italian rates usually were highest (Table 6.2c). EC labor force survey definitions tend to elevate NISLF rates for youth compared to other surveys (Appendix 4:1).

Contrary to hypotheses that associate the level of male NISLF rates positively with such variables as immaturity, living at home, never married status, lower educational attainment, and less work experience, and which predict that teenage rates will be higher than young adult, in several countries young adults usually had higher rates than teenage males (Table 6.2a, Method A). Nevertheless, teenage male rates were higher than those of young adults in all countries under Method B, based on the out-of-school population.

If NISLF rates are adjusted for the absence of institutionalized persons in some country surveys, rates might rise by 1 percent (Tables 6.7, 6.8; NY Times c). This would widen the gap between the United States and Canada, and other countries. Also, Australia, Canada, and Japan would have slightly lower male NISLF proportions if their military forces were included, since these three countries had fairly small proportions of the age group in the military.

There may be considerable monthly variation in NISLF rates. The Australian Bureau of Statistics began a new breakdown of the teenage population in August 1978, which permits the construction of a monthly series of NISLF rates. The new Australian data indicate how widely NISLF rates can fluctuate from month to month. From August 1978 to January 1980, by Method B, male teenagers showed a low monthly NISLF rate of 9.0 percent and a high of 12.4 percent, while female teenagers ranged from 17.9 to 21.6 percent (Australia 1971-80). The data are limited in that educational enrollments beyond the secondary level are not recorded, so that the size of the NISLF population is artificially inflated and the newly computed NISLF rates are higher than they would be according to data used in Tables 6.2a and 6.2b.

Female trends in NISLF rates are far more marked than male. In countries with a sufficiently long time series, females in both age groups showed a distinct downward trend in NISLF rates by both methods, with a stronger decline for young adults than teenagers (Table 6.2b). As later detail demonstrates (Table 6.11), reductions in the fraction of NISLF females due to household responsibilities, accompanied by increased labor force participation and educational enrollments, explain the female trends in general. Associated declines in marriage rates for the age groups, lower fertility rates, and increased social acceptance of female activity outside of the home occurred in all twelve countries, but at varying rates and from differing starting levels.

Among teenage females several countries showed a halving or more of NISLF rates by Methods A and B from the initial year listed to the last data year. Since data are sparse and irregular, direct comparisons of inter-country trends are difficult. Yet Japan's steep decline in NISLF rates altered its ratio to the U.S. rate from 1:2.6 in 1959 to 1:5.9 in 1977 (Method A), and from 1:3.4 in 1959 to 1:3.8 in 1977 (Method B). For young adult females, 1965 and 1977 data for Japan, Sweden, and the US indicate the pace of the decline in different countries. In 1965, Japan was lowest with an NISLF rate of 24.9 percent, followed by Sweden with 27.7 percent, and the US with the much higher 42.5 percent. By 1977 Sweden was lowest with 12.1 percent, Japan had 17.4 percent, and the US was down to 24.1 percent. Although the percentage point difference between countries had narrowed from 1965 to 1977, the ratio between Japan, the lowest of the three, and the US had risen. It would be desirable to discuss all female NISLF rates disaggregated by marital status and/or presence and age of children; however, relevant data were discovered for only a few countries and are presented below.

Male NISLF rates, on the whole, show no trends (Table 6.2a). To the extent that trends are visible, they appear only under Method B and chiefly for teenagers in Japan and the US, which are among the few countries with a long time series. The rising trend in these two countries prompts two related explanations. The first is that as the out-of-school base population shrank sharply, absolutely or relatively, due to the rise of EER in this age group, the proportion NISLF automatically rose, since the absolute or relative number NISLF was at some stable or irreducible level. This explanation can be accepted by itself, or jointly with a second line of reasoning. It assumes that very high EER for teenagers, such as the US, Canada and Japan attained, may leave a residual disadvantaged group of out-of-school teenage youth with low educational attainment, deteriorated labor market prospects, and a greater propensity to be NISLF than is the case in countries where most of the age group leaves school at 16 or 17. Japan has a small group leaving school early, but they are reported to enter work easily. Moreover, the Japanese description of themselves as a nation of workaholics, with an interesting economic rationale, surely would have consequences for the behavior of young people and even more for their attitudes (Koshiro 1978–79).

The United States and Canada offer much supporting evidence about a disadvantaged residual group. Reports from Sweden also confirm the deterioration of labor market prospects for those who leave school at 16 or fail to complete an additional course. Since Sweden also is a country with a rising EER for teenagers, although more particularly for the 16–18 age group, a trend in teenage male NISLF rates similar to that for Japan and the US might have been expected. The absence of a definite Swedish trend by Methods A or B may reflect the highly organized labor market and the absorption of potentially NISLF youth into Swedish manpower programs, which have been relatively large compared to those of other countries at all times and especially in recent periods of rising youth unemployment. Interpretations of changing NISLF rates in all the countries should allow for cyclical variations from year to year, and the impact in particular periods of especially large cohorts of young people, due to demographic trends.

As expected, NISLF rates of young adult males were less apt to be affected by changes in the calculation method, since EER in this age group still concerns a relatively small part of the total population and thus does not differ significantly from the out-of-school population. The absence of distinct trends, such as the teenagers exhibited, supports the view of a minimum level of NISLF. Moreover, it also would be expected that the residual group, formed in the teenage years, would be considerably diminished by the time young adulthood was reached.

Despite the strong downward trend for females and weaker upward movement in some male rates, females in every country had higher NISLF rates than comparable males at the latest reading. The remaining gap between the sexes is attributable to the way in which society distributes responsibility for nonmarket work in the home, and to the larger proportion of females than males in these age groups who are married or in other relationships leading to nonmarket work, rather than education or paid labor force participation. By Method A, Italy, Australia, Canada, the United States, and Great Britain had the largest gap between the sexes for teenagers. In the 1950s, the proportion of American NISLF female teenagers exceeded that of their male counterparts by 15 percentage points, and it continued to be more than 10 percentage points well into the 1970s. Sweden, France, and Japan had the smallest spread between the two sexes. Among young adults, the differences between males and females were considerable; Sweden had the least disparity, followed by France. As a consequence of the social forces impinging on current female behavior, whether married or not, no country can be said to have reached an irreducible minimum of NISLF females.

In summary, among the nine countries, the US and Canada consistently have the highest or close to the highest NISLF rates for three of the age-sex groups, using both calculation methods. The exception is among young adult females where Australia, New Zealand, the Netherlands, and Great Britain exceeded American and Canadian rates in most years. Consistently low rates for all age-sex groups were shown by Sweden by both calculation methods, although Sweden was not necessarily the lowest or next-to-lowest country in each category and in each time period. Japan also ranks among the countries with low NISLF rates for all groups, except that Method B altered its standing for teenage males. Great Britain and New Zealand had low rates for males only.

Although the cross-sectional information discussed above provides the main data on levels and trends in NISLF rates, longitudinal studies offer some supplementary information and an opportunity to check country estimates derived from cross-sectional sources.

Longitudinal Studies

Several American studies of out-of-school youth have estimated weeks of nonparticipation in the labor force in a year and have derived a NISLF rate in terms of total number of weeks, rather than in terms of the proportion of individuals. An analysis of follow-up data on males in the U.S. high school class of 1972 indicated that the NISLF rate was about three times as high when the out-of-school population was the base (Method B) as when the age-group population (Method A) was used (Meyer and Wise 1979). This is consistent with the results shown in Table 6.2a.

Drawing on the data bank of the National Longitudinal Surveys, two parallel studies were conducted, one of young out-of-school civilian males and one of females; all had less than 14 years of completed education. The out-of-school males had a 13.9 percent NISLF rate, while the females had a 32.2 percent rate. During the first year out of school, 40 percent of the males and 62 percent of the females spent some time out of the labor force. Males who spent any time out of the labor force averaged 18 weeks in NISLF status, while similar females averaged 27 weeks (Corcoran 1979; Ellwood 1979).

Cross-sectional results can be compared directly to longitudinal findings when data from the latter are used cross-sectionally. Such a comparison can be made from three different types of American data (*Table A6.2). The labor force survey (Current Population Survey of CPS) shows substantially lower NISLF rates for males than the 1960 or 1970 census. But the CPS records higher male rates than the NLS results for selected years. For females, the census and CPS results are quite compatible, while the NLS again has lower rates. The tendency of U.S. longitudinal data to show lower NISLF rates, higher LFPR rates, lower unemployment rates, and higher employment rates than CPS results has been established in a number of comparisons (Borus et al. 1978; Corcoran 1979; Ellwood 1979; Meyer and Wise 1979; *NY Times* k).

Ellwood and Corcoran stated that the NLS sample was less likely than the CPS to include or retain those who were long-term unemployed or NISLF. Freeman and Medoff (1979) found that the lower NISLF rates in the NLS surveys might result from the source of the information: in the NLS it is the young person directly involved, while in the CPS, it is the respondent for the household, usually the housewife. By an ingenious matching of responses of sons and mothers, both of whom were in their respective NLS samples, Freeman and Medoff (1979) determined that mothers were more likely to report NISLF status for their sons than the sons did in their independent responses.

Another perspective on the possible reasons for lower NISLF rates in U.S. longitudinal surveys has been offered by Hills and Thompson (1980, p. 24). Although their comment is on unemployment rates, it applies to NISLF rates as well. Without completely resolving the puzzle of the lower rates from longitudinal than from cross-sectional surveys, Hills and Thompson find them "to result in part from an undercount which occurs when respondents are asked about unemployment retrospectively, rather than reporting for a survey week only." In other words, cross-sectional rates may be more accurate.

This finding and the reasoning behind it may also apply to other countries in regard to NISLF rates. One French longitudinal survey produced a smaller NISLF proportion than the cross-sectional labor force survey results (Rousselet et al. 1975). Another source is a single follow-up of all who had left the French educational system in each year from 1972 to 1977. The annual survey, some months after leaving school, showed higher proportions in the NISLF category than showed in the labor force survey data in Tables 6.2a and 6.2b. The age groups and enumeration methods are not strictly comparable, however (France 1977–79b, p. 23). The 1975 French census indicates lower male NISLF rates than the labor force survey but slightly higher female rates (France 1979d). Follow-up studies by the Swedish Central

Statistical Bureau of those leaving various levels of education are difficult to compare directly with the age groups of the labor force survey, but the NISLF rates appear to be compatible. It may be significant that Swedish surveys, including the cross-sectional labor force survey, query the individuals concerned rather than members of the household. Moreover, the follow-up period is brief, requiring little retrospection (Sweden 1974c, Tables 129–133; Sweden 1977d, Tables 137–144; Sweden 1978f, Tables 6.36, 6.37, 6.39, 15.38–15.42).

This review of the sparse longitudinal evidence raises no serious doubts about the validity of the NISLF rates derived from cross-sectional sources. From the evidence in Table 6.2a, the proportion of young men who abstain from the two main pursuits of their age group—education and labor force participation—does not constitute a large segment of the age group in any country, even by Method B. NISLF status and trends in it should have only a minor effect on the potential male youth labor supply, in contrast to educational enrollment rates that have trended sharply upward since the end of the war. If there is an irreducible percentage of NISLF youth, perhaps 1 to 3 percent of the age group, then a few countries, notably the United States, Canada, and Italy, tend to have NISLF rates higher than that level. Nevertheless, cross-national differences are not large.

A different situation prevails for females, since considerable potential for enlarging the female labor supply out of the NISLF category still exists, and cross-national differences in rates remain wide. From another perspective, teenage male NISLF rates computed on the basis of the out-of-school population also indicate substantial differences in NISLF rates across countries. No single hypothesis can be framed, but even multiple explanations require additional information. The chapter goes on to discuss the incidence of NISLF status, its persistence and consequences, and reasons for being NISLF.

Incidence of Not in School or the Labor Force

Within countries, NISLF rates for youth vary according to age, marital status, socioeconomic position, household income, type of education, level of educational attainment, and place of residence. Differences according to race are discussed in Chapter 7. Insufficient information about the incidence of NISLF is at hand to draw conclusions about its impact on cross-national differences in NISLF rates, but some of the findings are suggestive.

Age

The earlier separation between the two major age groups conceals patterns of individual years of age (or two-year groups). Cross-sectional and longitudinal data for various time periods in France, Great Britain, Sweden, and the United States indicate, as expected, that an increasing proportion of females is likely to be NISLF with successive years of age. For example, the French census of 1975 shows, by single years of age, a steady rise from 6.4 percent NISLF, for 17-year-old females, up to 25.7 percent NISLF, for 24 year-old females (France 1979d, Table 10). Given the overriding importance of household responsibilities as the reason for female NISLF, both cross-sectional and longitudinal surveys show the same positive correlation between increased age and a rising NISLF proportion.

Male age patterns are less clear in cross-sectional data; this appears in adjusted

U.S. 1960 census data (Bowen and Finegan 1969, pp. 408–11). British males show a stable proportion for single years of age, except for the two youngest groups, 15 and 16, whose higher NISLF proportions are associated with the taking of the census during, or soon after, a school-leaving period (GB 1968a, 1975). In labor force surveys, American 18–19-year-old males generally have the highest NISLF proportions among the youth groups, but the 1970 census indicated that the NISLF rate for 20–21-year-olds exceeded that for 18–19-year-olds, reversing the position in the census of 1960 (US 1963, 1973). The NISLF rate for French males neatly descends for single years of age, according to the 1975 census. Among 17–19-year-olds, the rate dropped from 3.5 percent for 17-year-olds to 2.9 percent for 19-year-olds, while for the 20–24 group the rate went down from 3.1 percent for 20-year-olds to 2.4 percent for 24-year-olds (France 1979d, Table 10).

Cross-sectional age data on out-of-school youth are sometimes interpreted as if they reveal the independent effects of aging on NISLF rates. Nevertheless, changes in the educational attainment composition of cross-sectional out-of-school age groups make such readings unreliable. Unadjusted longitudinal data for a cohort of males also present difficulties, since they tend to mix the effects of aging itself with those of additional educational/training and work experience. They also include the effects of changing labor market circumstances. Moreover, if a longitudinal survey drops young men from the sample when they enter military service and also picks up returned servicemen, the validity of both the base population and the NISLF numbers comes into question unless data adjustments are made, as was particularly the case for the American NLS survey of young men in the 1960s.

Nevertheless, longitudinal results are the most suitable for examining the effects of aging on male NISLF rates. Data from the American NLS of out-of-school males for 1966 through 1971 make it possible to trace five cohorts of young men who were, respectively, 14–15, 16–17, 18–19, 20–21, and 22–24 in 1966. These unpublished results lend no credence to the view that increasing age reduces the proportion NISLF, but the data have not been controlled for the various factors mentioned above. A study that used a small pooled NLS sample of young men, who left school in 1965, 1966 or 1967 with less than 13 years of completed education, found that their NISLF rate dropped regularly in the first four out-of-school years from 13.9 percent to 5 percent (measured as the average number of weeks out of the labor force in a year, divided by 52). Similarly, although 40 percent of the sample spent time out of the labor force during the first year out of school, the proportion dropped in each year thereafter and was 24.1 percent in the fourth year. According to the author, declining proportions in successive years may be due to a reluctance on the part of older young men to acknowledge time out of the labor force (Ellwood 1979). Based on a five-year follow-up of the high school class of 1972, still another study shows a drop in NISLF rates from October 1972 to October 1974 and then a slight rise to October 1976 (Meyer and Wise 1979). This probably reflects adverse economic conditions which offset the tendency of aging to reduce male NISLF rates.

Living Arrangements

As expected, British and Swedish census data confirm that marriage greatly increases the probability that females will be NISLF, while for males the reverse is true but less strongly (Table 6.3). Well over half of married British females, in both age groups at

Table 6.3 Young People Not in School or the Civilian Labor Force, by Age, Sex, and Marital Status, Great Britain 1961, 1966, and 1971, and Sweden 1970 and 1975

	Males	Females	
	20–24	15–19	20–24
	(as percent of civilian population)		
Great Britain			
1961 census: Total	1.4	6.6	35.1
Married	0.6	58.0	58.1
Nonmarried	1.7	3.2	4.7
1966 census: Total	n.a.	8.2	34.6
Married	n.a.	56.2	56.1
Nonmarried	n.a.	4.1	4.7
1971 census: Total	n.a.	7.5	34.2
Married	n.a.	57.7	53.3
Nonmarried	n.a.	2.7	5.7
	20–24	16–19	20–24
Sweden[a]			
1970 census: Total	14.8	6.6	23.6
Single	16.7	5.4	9.5
Married	4.8	56.6	45.8
Divorced	6.9	*	22.2
1975 census: Total	13.8	9.0	19.1
Single	14.5	8.5	13.1
Married	5.8	45.7	39.1
Divorced	7.3	*	20.3

[a] Percentages of the total population whose economic activity status is known. Includes volunteer and conscripted military forces. The unemployed are counted as not in the labor force. These census results are not comparable to Swedish labor force survey data, cited in other tables.

Note: Asterisk indicates less than 0.05 percent.

Source: Great Britain. General Register Office. *Census 1961, Summary Tables*, Table 33. London: HMSO, 1966; *Sample Census 1966, Economic Activity Tables*, Part I, Tables 1 and 3. London: HMSO, 1968; Office of Population Censuses and Surveys. *Census 1971, Economic Activity*, Part II, Tables 3 and 5. London: HMSO, 1975. Population data include institutionalized persons.
Sweden. SCB (Statistiska Centralbyrån). *Folk-och Bostadsräkningen 1970.* [Population and Housing Census 1970], Vol. 10, Table 1. Stockholm: SCB, 1974. Population data include institutionalized persons.

all three censuses, and of married Swedish teenagers in 1970 were neither in school nor the labor force, whereas the proportion for nonmarried females in both age groups was less than 6 percent in Britain and less than 15 percent in Sweden. Due to large differences between the two countries and between the two age groups in the percent of the population which is married, the countries vary in the effects of marital status on overall NISLF rates. French longitudinal data reveal that the NISLF group is disproportionately composed of women with children (Faguer, Dossou, and Kandel 1977b).

A related matter concerns the effects on NISLF status of living with parents or other head of household versus living apart, possibly in a new family headed by a young person (Bowen and Finegan 1969, pp. 411–13; Hill 1978). The proportion of all teenagers living at home is far higher than the proportion of all young adults. According to an unpublished tabulation for October 1977 of the U.S. Current Population Survey, within each age-sex group, the proportion living at home also varies according to household income; as family income increases, never married youth living at home comprise a rising share of each age-sex group.

These unpublished U.S. data also indicate that male NISLF youth, especially young adults, are disproportionately found among the never married living at home, but the reverse is true for females. Thus, 92.8 percent of all teenage males and 93.2 percent of NISLF teenage males were never married and living at home; this is only a slight difference. For young adult males, however, the respective rates were 45.6 percent and 74.1 percent, a significant excess of NISLF youth living at home. In the case of teenage females, 80.9 percent of the age group but only 48.3 percent of NISLF teenage females were never married and living at home. Young adult females showed 29.9 percent never married and at home, but only 10.4 percent of the NISLF group were in that position.

As demonstrated, the situation for the two sexes varies and requires separate analysis in regard to the effects of living at home; some age differences within each sex emerge as well. NISLF status for young adult males may be strongly associated with physical or mental handicaps that prevent schooling or labor force participation, encourage an unmarried state, and lead to remaining in the parental home in disproportionate numbers. Certainly young male adults who lived on their own had a much lower NISLF rate than those who lived at home (1.9 percent against 8.5 percent, based on the out-of-school civilian population). Male teenagers living at home had a 9.9 percent NISLF rate, while those living on their own had a 3.4 percent rate (Table A6.3). These differentials suggest that parental support of various kinds may make it possible for youth living at home to be NISLF, while their equivalents on their own are less able to do so. On the other hand, the composition of the two groups may differ in significant ways that more readily explain the gap in NISLF rates. Individuals least prone to NISLF may be overrepresented among those living away from home.

Females would be expected to have higher NISLF rates when they were out of the parental home than when living there as never married, because of the effects of marriage and child raising. Teenage females living at home had an NISLF rate of 20.3 percent, less than half the 43.6 percent rate of the one-fifth no longer at home; rates are based on the out-of-school population. Much the same relationship held for young adult females: 14.0 percent NISLF at home against 33.3 percent for the 70 percent living away from home (Table A6.3). Financial support from others than parents probably is of equal or greater importance for females. In fact, in the lowest income class, never married females living at home had higher NISLF rates than those living away from home, an unusual situation not duplicated in the other income classes. It is possible that payments from AFDC (Aid to Families with Dependent Children) that are made to unmarried females with children (or to the grandmother of the children) account for a portion of the high NISLF rate reported for females living at home in the lowest income classes; all such persons do not respond "unemployed" in the CPS survey, as legally provided (Devens 1979). Never married teenage and young adult males living at home have considerably higher NISLF rates at each income level than males living on their own (Table A6.3).

Socioeconomic Status and Household Income

Limited socioeconomic data suggest a slightly negative relation between this variable and NISLF status. Analysis of the U.S. high school class of 1972, divided into four quartiles according to a computed index of socioeconomic status, showed that NISLF homemakers (but not other NISLF youth) were disproportionately of low socioeconomic status (Bowen and Finegan 1969, p. 415; US 1976a, 1977a, 1978a). French longitudinal data display a small NISLF proportion in 1972 at age 16–17, but those from families of lower occupational status were more prone to be NISLF (Rousselet 1975, Tables 56, 57, 58).

Some analysts consider that national affluence may account for a higher overall NISLF rate than in countries with lower GNP per capita (Layard 1979, pp. 6–7). Parents in the United States, for example, are seen as willing to support nonenrolled young people who are not looking for work (Feldstein and Ellwood 1979, pp. 11–14). National affluence can be hypothesized to elevate NISLF rates above those of poorer nations in more than one way. In the first model, parents in the higher-income groups would subsidize out-of-school youth in periods of self-development and experimentation with life styles. In this case, NISLF rates for youth would be expected to rise as family income rose. This model assumes that NISLF largely consists of youth who are able to work but do not wish to.

In another model, NISLF rates might be highest among youth from the poorest families, in the relatively rich countries, because the society would offer opportunities to exist without working, either through illegal activities or government transfer payments which were high relative to earnings from available jobs (Wachter 1980, pp. 45–46, 56). It is assumed that the ratio of social benefits to earnings rises as national per-capita GNP levels rise, an assumption that holds when comparisons are made between less developed and more developed nations but is questionable within the group of twelve industrialized nations in the study.

An alternative hypothesis is that a wide spread in household incomes within a country fosters high NISLF rates among youth from the lowest income groups, partly through low educational attainment which is related to the level of family income, and partly through other social and economic effects of low incomes.

Significant cross-sectional information is available for the US on the relation between household income and NISLF rates for the four age-sex groups of youth. Unpublished data, drawn from the CPS survey of October 1977, divide the youth population into never married youth living at home, and other household members (which former category includes all youth who have left home as well as married, separated, divorced, or widowed young people residing with parents or a substitute).

A tendency for NISLF rates to drop markedly as household income increases appeared clearly for all four age-sex groups of the never married youth living at home and fairly clearly for all other youth, except teenage males (Table A6.3). Females, never married and living at home, showed a much sharper decline in NISLF rates with rising household income than did other females, probably because the child-care or other home duties of the latter overwhelmed the income effect. A suggestion that a very small, monied leisure class of youth may exist arises from a NISLF rate of 25 percent for the few teenage males who lived away from home and reported incomes of $25,000 or more. Overall, however, the data do not support the view of Layard (1979) that indulgent middle-class parents are responsible for relatively higher NISLF rates for young males in the United States than in Great Britain.

If the national affluence hypothesis is rejected in its simplistic form, it does not follow that there is no relation between levels of national affluence and NISLF rates. One version, bypassing the cross-sectional evidence, would hypothesize that as families became more affluent in their own life cycle they would tend to indulge their children, permitting them to spend some time in NISLF status. This interpretation, however, does not fit our view of NISLF as largely a response to pressures rather than a free choice of leisure time. It also is difficult to reconcile such a view with exceptionally high NISLF rates in the very poorest households.

The disproportionate share of poor youth in the NISLF category is indicated by an income comparison between all youth and NISLF youth, taking the never married at home and all others as two separate groups. Accepting an annual income of less than $7500 per household as an indicator of poverty, 19.1 percent to 29.9 percent of never married youth living at home in the four age-sex groups fell below this income cut-off. But among NISLF youth, the range in poverty was from 38.2 percent to 48.9 percent, almost twice as high. Teenage males displayed the lowest proportion of youth in poverty households, while the highest shares were shown by all young adult females and NISLF teenage females.

Turning to the category "all other youth," the proportion in the group ranged from 35.6 percent for young adult females to 54.7 percent for teenage males. Among NISLF youth, the poverty span was from 36.4 percent for young adult females to 85.6 percent for teenage males. Since NISLF males are found disproportionately among never married youth living at home, the poverty disparities between the age group and NISLF youth are most significant for the never married living at home. Moreover, NISLF youth living at home came from households with lower incomes, on average, than out-of-school unemployed youth living at home, as the data in Table 6.4 demonstrate. All household income data include earnings and other income of youth, to the extent that these are reported.

While a less clear picture emerges for "all other" NISLF youth, the expected excess of household income of NISLF youth compared to nonenrolled unemployed youth occurs in only two of the eight age-sex groupings: teenage males and young adult females. In fact, whatever their living arrangements, average household income was highest for the categories of youth farthest removed from NISLF, namely, the enrolled, the nonenrolled employed, and the enrolled employed.

Since relatively more NISLF never married youth come from lower-income households than unemployed or employed youth, the puzzle is why and how the families least able to support idle youth do so. One possible explanation is that the

Table 6.4   Annual Household Income of Youth, by Living Arrangements, Labor Force Status, Age, and Sex, United States, October 1977

	Never married youth at home			All other youth		
Sex–Age Group	All	NISLF	Nonenrolled unemployed	All	NISLF	Nonenrolled unemployed
Male 16–19	$16,366	$8,621	$11,245	$6,642	$6,853	$3,593
Female 16–19	$16,156	$6,818	$11,249	$6,656	$6,582	$5,920
Male 20–24	$16,837	$8,485	$11,237	$8,738	$5,830	$6,541
Female 20–24	$16,563	$8,036	$11,287	$8,832	$8,689	$6,840

Source: U.S. Department of Labor, Bureau of Labor Statistics, unpublished data.

conditions that hinder labor force participation have a greater prevalence among the poorest households in which never married youth live. Data are not presently available to test that hypothesis in regard to illness and disability, but it is known that motherhood at an early age and large numbers of children are found in lower income households containing never married females.

Educational Attainment

Level of educational attainment or completed years of education in France, Sweden, and the United States consistently appear to be negatively related to NISLF proportions, for each sex and at various levels of education. Bowen and Finegan (1969, pp. 413–15) used the U.S. 1960 census 1/1000 sample for urban areas which they adjusted for the effects of color, age, other family income, family status, family size, and the family head's schooling and labor force status; they found the expected relation stronger for females than males and for persons 18–24 than 14–17. In the US, the annual survey of high school graduates and dropouts usually shows that a much higher proportion of the latter than the former are NISLF. Another American study, dealing with a poverty population, found that in 1977–1978, 14 percent of a sample of black youth who left school after eighth grade were NISLF, compared with 7 percent who left after tenth grade and 4.5 percent who attained eleventh grade. White youth had a similar pattern (MDRC 1979). Hills and Thompson (1980, p. 22) found for the US that the average number of weeks out of the labor force in the first two years after leaving school was negatively related to educational attainment, with high school dropouts showing by far the largest amount of time NISLF, while college leavers (not graduates) displayed a record only slightly better than that of high school graduates.

From the U.S. household income data for October 1977, NISLF rates can be calculated for those who had completed less than four years of high school (Table A6.3). Rates are shown as a proportion of the out-of-school civilian population with less than four years of high school, and as a proportion of all NISLF youth of similar age, sex, and living arrangements. Clearly, low educational attainment is associated with NISLF status and may foster it. Among all age-sex groups, NISLF youth with less than four years of high school constituted a higher proportion of all youth with less than four years of high school than NISLF youth as a whole did of the out-of-school youth population as a whole. For never married youth living at home, the 20–24-year-old female NISLF rate was 14.0 percent for the population as a whole, and 43.4 percent for those with less than four years of high school. While less marked differences according to education characterized youth living away from home, the disadvantage of those with minimal educational attainment appears.

It also is clear that a high proportion of all NISLF youth have less than four years of high school (Table A6.3). Teenagers of each sex and both types of living arrangement show proportions in excess of 60 percent. Young adults living at home fall in the 43 to 45 percent range, while those on their own have the lowest shares, 24.7 percent for the very small number of NISLF males, and 34.3 percent for females 20–24; the latter presumably are most prone to be engaged in child care, especially in the lowest income groups.

NISLF rates by educational attainment and household income are available. Without such a control, it appears that poverty breeds a propensity to inactivity, as represented by the higher NISLF rates of poor youth. The effect may be via a positive association between relative poverty and low educational attainment, however. The measures in Table A6.3 indicate that the incidence of NISLF is highest for youth both in the lowest income classes and with less than four years of high school. Thus, NISLF rates for females with less than four years of high school were 71.9 percent for never married females living in households with incomes under $5,000, but only 20 percent for similar females from families with $25,000 and more a year; rates are based on the out-of-school population with less than four years of high school. In the same way, in each age-sex group, two-thirds or more of NISLF youth, never married and living in households with under $5,000 income, had completed less than four years of high school, while in the highest income class, the range was from one-third downward (Table A6.3). Thus a combined effect appears in which youth from lower income levels tend to have lower educational attainment, and youth with lower educational attainment and lower household incomes tend to have higher NISLF rates than others. Changing the income distribution might reduce NISLF rates in the lowest income classes, both directly and via raising educational attainment.

In addition to demonstrating that the higher the educational attainment level, the lower the NISLF proportion, French and Swedish studies show that the type of education is important in NISLF rates. Follow-up studies indicate that occupationally oriented courses at secondary and tertiary level result in lower NISLF proportions than terminal general academic courses (France 1977a, 1976-79b, p. 5, 1976-79c, p. 5, 1977-79b, p. 25, 1978-79a, pp. 58-59; Sweden 1974c, 1977d, 1978f). This would be a likely finding in most European countries, but American assessments are less favorable, in keeping with a more critical appraisal of existing vocational education, especially at the high school level (Grasso and Shea 1979; Meyer and Wise 1979). Follow-up data on the U.S. high school class of 1972 disclosed that relatively fewer students who followed an academic program in high school (compared to a general, vocational, or technical program) were NISLF (US 1976-79). At the first survey in October 1972, only 3.6 percent of those who had been in the academic curriculum at high school were NISLF, compared to 12.0 percent of the vocational and 12.3 percent of the general curriculum students (Creech et al. 1977, Table 3.1).

Geographic differences in NISLF proportions appear in data for France and the United States, but it is not clear that the differences are statistically significant or whether there are explanations for the variations affecting each sex (France 1978-79b, p. 30; US 1976-79).

Obviously, much more information is needed for many countries on the incidence of NISLF status. It would be particularly useful to see whether the differences in NISLF rates revealed for the US according to household income obtain elsewhere and are as wide as in the US. Equality of income distribution might prove to be an important correlate of a low national NISLF rate, especially for males.

Persistence of Not in School or the Labor Force Status

Theoretical and empirical considerations suggest that, just as more employment during earlier periods tends to increase current labor force participation of individuals, NISLF status in one period may foster persistence in a later period (Clark and Summers 1979c). Methodologically, the issue is to control for the effects of personal characteristics that relate to NISLF status (heterogeneity) so that one can isolate the impact of the early NISLF experience on later labor force experience (state dependence). Only a few studies, mostly for the United States, address the issue whether those who are NISLF when they leave school tend to continue in that status for a few years. Similarly, it is not clear whether year after year the NISLF group consists mainly of the same individuals or is primarily made up of new members.

The limited longitudinal evidence does not carry the story beyond the first few years after leaving school. In the US, Hills and Thompson (1980, p. 22) found that the average number of weeks NISLF was lower in the second full year out of school than in the first, for a sample of young males drawn from the NLS. Since average number of weeks of unemployment did not behave in the same way, but rather rose in response to prevailing economic conditions, there is indirect support for our view of the unemployed and NISLF as two distinct groups, albeit some overlap occurs.

Average weeks NISLF, cited by Hills and Thompson, do not describe the distribution for individuals. Other U.S. studies which do this for individuals show a persistence effect but of varying intensity. Stevenson (1978), controlling for heterogeneity less rigorously than others, found that NISLF youth of both sexes at ages 16–19 were more likely to be in that status at ages 23–26 than nonenrolled teenagers who had been in the labor force or enrolled in school. The relationship was particularly strong for males. Ellwood (1979), studying a subsample of males drawn from the same survey, concluded that the probability that an out-of-school male would be NISLF in a given year was much higher if he had been NISLF in the preceding year. No long run effect was found on those who were NISLF at a young age, however; the NISLF rate decreased each year in the four years of the survey. Corcoran (1979), matching Ellwood's study with an analysis of females, found the same relationship as Ellwood had from one year to another in NISLF probability. Unlike males, however, the proportion of NISLF females and the average period out of the labor force rose over the four years, reflecting the increased pressures of household responsibilities.

Also studying males, Meyer and Wise drew on another longitudinal sample consisting mostly of high school graduates, including those who continued in additional education. They applied a method which measured labor force status each October, instead of throughout the year and found "almost no relationship . . . between weeks worked during the first year and weeks worked four years later" (1979, p. 88). Utilizing CPS micro-records, another U.S. study established the 1977 status of those who had been out of the labor force a year earlier. For all ages, less than 20 percent of those out of the labor force in 1976 were in it in 1977. Data for those aged 16–24, without a sex breakdown and including the in-school population, indicate that almost 60 percent of 1976 nonparticipants were in the labor force in 1977 (Job 1979, Table 1). If the NISLF youth population could be examined separately, the proportion might be considerably lower.

Information for other countries is sparse and tends to consist of comparisons of labor force status in successive years, following up those who were out of the labor force in the initial year. This type of analysis omits the intervening experience, which may vary from the once-a-year readings. Japanese data for a series of two-year periods, covering NISLF persons in all age groups, indicate that in each two-year period, very high proportions of males and females were NISLF during the survey week in the second year if they had been NISLF in the survey week of the previous year (Table 6.5). Additional longitudinal surveys and studies are needed to establish the persistence patterns of NISLF status.

Similar French data for the youth groups show that those who were NISLF in one

Table 6.5   Population Not in School or the Civilian Labor Force in Survey Period in One Year Who Were in That Status in Survey Period in the Following Year, 15 Years and Over, by Sex, Japan, 1958–1971

	Not in school or civilian labor force[a] in second survey	
	(as percent of those not in school or the labor force in first year)	
Years	Males	Females
1958–1959	88.3	97.5
1961–1962	88.7	96.8
1964–1965	89.7	96.6
1967–1968	91.4	96.2
1970–1971	91.2	96.1

[a] Includes a small number whose status is more properly described as "seeking work."

Source: Japan, Office of the Prime Minister, Bureau of Statistics. *Employment Status Survey*, All Japan. 1959: Table III–1; 1962: Table III–1; 1965: Table 37; 1968: Table 40; 1971: Table 44. Population data exclude institutionalized persons.

year were highly likely to be in the same category in the next year (France 1978a, 1978b, 1979a). A French longitudinal survey of 16-year-olds who no longer were in school supports the view of a small, immobile NISLF group. In 1972, the initial year, less than 1.0 percent of the sample was NISLF. Fewer than half of these responded to the 1974 follow-up, but 32 percent of them still were NISLF (Faguer et al. 1977a, p. 244). In the third follow-up in 1976, nonparticipation among the group, now 20–21 years old, had risen, possibly for cyclical reasons (Faguer, Dossou, and Kandel 1977b).

Some of the longitudinal surveys that follow a cohort for ten years or more from its exit from school have the capability of enlarging our knowledge about the persistence of NISLF status. Such surveys exist in Great Britain and the United States.

Whatever the reason for NISLF status, some who have been NISLF, even for a long period of time, do eventually enter or reenter education or the labor force. The impact of early periods of nonparticipation on later labor market success has been measured in several recent American studies. Although most utilize periods of nonemployment, a combination of time unemployed and time out of the labor force, it is likely that the findings would be much the same for NISLF time alone. The adverse effects of early nonemployment are felt in later years, chiefly through lower wage rates than otherwise might have been earned (Antos and Mellow 1979; Corcoran 1979; Ellwood 1979; Meyer and Wise 1979). More longitudinal research is needed in the US and other countries, distinguishing between those who were predominantly NISLF and others, in order to devise policies that take account of lifetime labor force patterns. Even if a majority of NISLF youth at any one time are not able or interested in participating in education or employment, the chances are that many will change with time, a consideration of particular importance for females.

Reasons for Not in
School or the Labor Force Status

Several countries offer data drawn from special questions in the labor force survey on the reasons for NISLF status. In some countries, data for all members of the household are based on the response of one person, usually the adult female (Appendix 4:1). Regardless of who answers the survey questions, caveats must be entered about subjective responses on labor force status. A certain amount of concealment, confusion, or projection is to be anticipated, especially if the respondent is not the subject. Females who spend precisely the same amount of time on household duties may give entirely different reasons for being NISLF. It also is difficult for individuals to choose a single explanation for behavior, when in fact a mix of reasons may be more accurate. Not only does the form of the question influence the reply, but the state of the economy also molds the answers. Young people who have sought work unsuccessfully or have moved in and out of certain types of unattractive jobs may appear to have little interest in job search. Unfavorable opportunity structures may lead to adaptations in value systems, which produce a seemingly weak attachment to the labor market, rather than the reverse—that some individuals or groups autonomously lack strong work motivation.

The difficulties are compounded when cross-national comparisons are attempted. Studies underway in the United States and elsewhere of the use of time by NISLF youth may provide more objective information on the division of waking hours for such purposes as constructive self-development, nonmarket work, enforced or deliberate idleness, substitutes for market work (such as illicit activity), socializing, and other activities. Such records may even suggest the extent of reporting error published in the labor force surveys. Studies also are needed on the influence of peers and family, among others, in relation to the social acceptability of NISLF status and the impact on behavior.

Despite these limitations, the results on the reasons for NISLF for the countries with such data are fairly consistent as well as useful. The leading reasons given for NISLF status are illness and disability, household responsibilities, and an amorphous "other reasons" category that includes discouraged workers, defined as those who did not search for jobs because they believed work was not available.

Illness and Disability

Among the standard and unquestioned reasons for NISLF status is illness or disability, which results in short-term or prolonged absence from job search or even rejection by the labor market. Since the incidence of illness and disability among young people does not vary greatly among the industrialized countries, the proportion of ill and disabled youth who are NISLF in each country is determined by the development and availability of medical, psychological, and rehabilitation services; the buoyancy of the economy; the extent of job creation for the group; and general social attitudes. Our immediate interest lies in another question, however. Of all youth who are NISLF, what percentage are in that status because of illness or disability? Data for several countries suggest that, on average, 15 to 25 percent of NISLF males claim illness or disability as the reason for NISLF status. In countries where the institutionalized population is not counted in the labor force survey, and includes some who are ill or disabled, the proportions would be somewhat higher, if

Table 6.6 Young People Not in School or the Civilian Noninstitutional Labor Force, by Desire for Work, Reasons Not Looking, Age, and Sex, United States 1970–1978, Japan 1959–1977, and Sweden 1975–1979

	United States[a] (4th quarter) 1970–1978 average Males		Japan[a] (July) 1959–1977 average Males		Sweden[b] (November) 1975–1979 average Males	
	16–19	20–24	15–19 (percent)	20–24	16–19	20–24
Number not in school or labor force (000)	257.9	298.2	91.7	75.0	31.0	66.6
Percentage not in school or labor force	3.3 (100.0)	3.5 (100.0)	2.0 (100.0)	1.7 (100.0)	1.6 (100.0)	2.4 (100.0)
Of which:						
Wanting a job	1.0 (30.3)	1.1 (31.4)	0.4 (20.0)	0.5 (29.4)	0.5 (30.6)	0.2 (8.8)
Reason not looking:						
—ill, disabled	0.1 (3.0)	0.2 (5.7)	n.a. (n.a.)	n.a. (n.a.)	0.1 (5.6)	0.1 (4.4)
—household duties	* (—)	* (—)	0.1 (5.0)	* (—)	0.0 (0.0)	0.0 (0.0)
—discouraged	0.5 (15.2)	0.4 (11.4)	n.a. (n.a.)	n.a. (n.a.)	0.4 (22.2)	0.1 (4.4)
—other	0.4 (12.1)	0.5 (14.3)	0.3 (15.0)	0.5 (29.4)	* (2.8)	* (1.5)
Not wanting a job	2.3 (69.7)	2.4 (68.6)	1.6 (80.0)	1.2 (70.6)	1.1 (69.4)	2.2 (91.2)
Reason not looking:						
—ill, disabled	0.4 (12.1)	0.7 (20.0)	n.a. (n.a.)	n.a. (n.a.)	n.a. (n.a.)	n.a. (n.a.)
—household duties	0.2 (6.1)	0.1 (2.9)	0.6 (30.0)	0.2 (11.8)	n.a. (n.a.)	n.a. (n.a.)
—other	1.7 (51.5)	1.6 (45.7)	1.0 (50.0)	1.0 (58.8)	n.a. (n.a.)	n.a. (n.a.)

	Females		Females		Females	
	16–19	20–24	15–19	20–24	16–19	20–24
Number not in school or labor force (000)	908.0	2,628.8	188.0	1,050.4	84.8	317.4
Percentage not in school or labor force	11.3 (100.0)	28.3 (100.0)	4.2 (100.0)	22.8 (100.0)	4.2 (100.0)	11.4 (100.0)
Of which:	(percent)					
Wanting a job	2.3 (20.4)	4.4 (15.5)	1.1 (26.2)	6.2 (27.2)	0.8 (18.4)	1.2 (10.9)
Of which:						
Reason not looking:						
—ill, disabled	0.1 (0.9)	0.3 (1.1)	n.a. (n.a.)	n.a. (n.a.)	0.1 (2.3)	0.1 (1.0)
—household duties	0.9 (8.0)	2.1 (7.4)	0.8 (19.0)	5.7 (25.0)	0.1 (2.3)	0.5 (4.8)
—discouraged	0.6 (5.3)	0.9 (3.2)	n.a. (n.a.)	n.a. (n.a.)	0.5 (12.6)	0.5 (4.5)
—other	0.7 (6.2)	1.1 (3.9)	0.3 (7.1)	0.5 (2.2)	0.1 (1.1)	0.1 (0.6)
Not wanting a job	9.0 (79.6)	23.9 (84.5)	3.1 (73.8)	16.6 (72.8)	3.4 (81.6)	10.2 (85.1)
Reason not looking:						
—ill, disabled	0.3 (2.7)	0.7 (2.5)	n.a. (n.a.)	n.a. (n.a.)	n.a. (n.a.)	n.a. (n.a.)
—household duties	7.3 (64.6)	22.1 (78.1)	2.1 (50.0)	15.0 (65.8)	n.a. (n.a.)	n.a. (n.a.)
—other	1.4 (12.4)	1.1 (3.9)	1.0 (23.8)	1.6 (7.0)	n.a. (n.a.)	n.a. (n.a.)

a Based on civilian noninstitutional population.
b Based on total population including institutionalized persons.

Note: Asterisk * signifies less than 0.05 percent.

Sources: U.S. Department of Labor, Bureau of Labor Statistics, *Employment and Earnings* Jan. 1972, Tables 2 and 4; Jan. 1975, Table A–50; Jan. 1977, Table A–53; January 1979, Table A–54 (Washington: GPO, monthly). U.S. Department of Labor, Bureau of Labor Statistics, unpublished data.
Japan, Office of the Prime Minister, Bureau of Statistics, *Employment Status Survey,* All Japan. 1959: Tables I–1 and II–2; 1962: Tables I–1 and II–8; 1965: Tables 1 and 28; 1968: Tables 1 and 28; 1971: Tables 1 and 39; 1974: Tables 2 and 31 (Tokyo, triennial).
Sweden, SCB (Statistiska Centralbyrån). *Arbetskraftsundersökningen,* Råtabeller [Labor Force Survey, Raw Tables] (Stockholm, monthly).

Table 6.7   Young People Not in School or Total Labor Force by Age, Sex, and Reason, Sweden, November 1963–1979 (average)

	Not in school or total labor force	Household duties	Reasons Institutionalized	Unable to work	Other
			(average annual percent)		
Males 16–19	2.0	0.1	0.3	0.3	1.3
	(100.0)	(5.0)	(15.0)	(15.0)	(65.0)
Males 20–24	2.4	0.1	0.6	0.3	1.4
	(100.0)	(4.2)	(25.0)	(12.5)	(58.3)
Females 16–19	6.7	4.1	0.2	0.3	2.1
	(100.0)	(61.2)	(3.0)	(4.5)	(31.3)
Females 20–24	18.7	16.7	0.2	0.3	1.5
	(100.0)	(89.3)	(1.1)	(1.6)	(8.0)

Source: Sweden, SCB (Statistiska Centralbyrån), *Arbetskraftsundersökningen*, Råtabeller [Labor Force Surveys, Raw Tables] (Stockholm, monthly). Population data include volunteer and conscripted military forces and institutionalized persons.

Table 6.8   Young People Not In School or the Civilian Labor Force, by Age, Sex, and Reason, Australia, August 1971–1977 (average)

	Not in school or civilian labor force	Illness/ disabled	Reasons Institutionalized	Other
	(average annual percent)			
Males 15–19	2.1[a]		0.9	1.2
	(100.0)		(42.9)	(57.1)
Males 20–24	2.9[a]	0.3	0.9	1.7
	(100.0)	(10.3)	(31.0)	(58.6)
Females 15–19	7.5[a]		0.5	7.0
	(100.0)		(6.7)	(93.3)
Females 20–24	31.9[a]		0.4	31.5
	(100.0)		(1.3)	(98.7)

[a] As percent of same age–sex group civilian population.

Source: Australia, ABS (Australian Bureau of Statistics), unpublished data. Population data include institutionalized persons.

Table 6.9   Young People (16–17 Years Old) Not in School or Civilian
Labor Force, by Sex and Reason, France, Spring 1972

	Males	Females
Percent not in school or civilian labor force	0.6	1.3

Distribution by reason of those who responded to questions
asking reasons for being out of school and labor force:

Not in school or civilian labor	(percent)	
force because of	100.0	100.0
Ill health	26.3	15.8
Household duties	0.0	29.8
Discouraged unemployed	0.0	8.8
Other	73.7	45.6
Of which:		
refuse to work	(10.5)	(1.8)
no need to work	(10.5)	(8.8)
transitional	(52.6)	(35.1)
Of which:		
awaiting training/education	(42.1)	(21.1)
awaiting marriage	(0.0)	(14.0)
awaiting conscription	(10.5)	(0.0)

Source: J. Rousselet, J. P. Faguer, I. Kandel, and F. Dossou, "L'entrée
des jeunes dans la vie active: la génération 1955" [The Entrance of
Young People into Working Life: The Generation of 1955]. Les jeunes
et l'emploi. Cahiers du centre d'études de l'emploi, no. 7 (Paris: Presses
Universitaires de France, 1975), pp. 201, 202, 236. Population data
exclude volunteer and conscripted military forces and institutionalized
persons.

such persons were added. For females, the illness and disability share is not large and
does not vary much among the countries (Tables 6.6–6.9).

Household Responsibilities

Nonmarket work, mainly in the household, is another standard and accepted reason
for NISLF status. An Australian list of possible reasons for being NISLF includes
such items as the ill health of another person; inability to find child care; children
thought too young; a preference for looking after children; disapproval by the person's spouse; and no necessity to work (Australia 1979a, p. 1). These reasons can be
subsumed under household duties, but in each country the list will have its own emphasis.

Considerable variation appears in the proportions of NISLF males and females
claiming this reason, as Table 6.10 demonstrates. The high and mystifying Japanese
male rates may reflect the inclusion as household duties of activities in workshops
and businesses, conducted in the home, a still prevalent feature of Japanese life.
Japanese men are known not to participate to any great extent in household duties as
they are understood elsewhere. In any case, there is no reason to believe that the
suprising data are the result of survey methods or processing techniques special to
Japan.

Relatively little female nonparticipation in school or the labor force remains to be

Table 6.10   NISLF Youth Claiming Household Duties in Selected Countries

	Males		Females	
	Teenage	Young Adult	Teenage	Young Adult
	(percent)			
France (16–17-year-olds)	0.0	—	29.8	—
Japan	35.0	11.8	69.0	90.8
Sweden	5.0	4.2	61.2	89.3
United States	6.1	2.9	72.6	85.5

Source: Tables 6.6, 6.7, 6.9.

explained after illness, disability, and household duties are counted. The small residual percentage may nevertheless refer to large numbers of women, because total female NISLF in each age group is much larger than male in every country.

Within an age group, females, subdivided by other statuses, may show differences in the percent citing household responsibilities as a factor in NISLF. A British study suggests that female NISLF due to household responsibilities varies according to educational attainment. Thus, among a sample of 19 and 20-year-old females, 23 percent of those who had left school at 15 were NISLF because of home duties, while only 6 percent of those who had left at 16 and 3 percent of those who left at 17 or 18 cited this reason (GB 1968b). Marital status does not cause much variation in the proportion citing household duties, according to Swedish data which are available for 1975-1979, separately for married women, unmarried women, and women with children under seven years of age. For the 20-24-year-old NISLF group, household duties were overwhelmingly the cause of inactivity in each of the above subgroups. It made little difference whether the labor force survey data were for November or for the annual average (Sweden 1963-79 a,b).

One of the striking features about female household responsibilities as a factor in NISLF is their time trend (Table 6.11). As in total female NISLF proportions, the percentage of an age group reporting household responsibilities as the reason for NISLF status has shown a remarkable decline in the three countries for which a data series is available (Table 6.11). In Japan, Sweden, and the US, the decline in the proportions claiming household duties accounts for a great deal of the decrease in aggregate female NISLF rates, and at times the decline associated with household duties exceeds the overall drop.

Other Reasons

The reasons discussed thus far do not account for the majority of males and also leave substantial numbers of females in each country in an amorphous "other reasons" category, which unfortunately dominates the statistics in all of the cross-sectional surveys; these surveys would benefit from an enlarged number of possible responses. In particular, it would be desirable to isolate those NISLF youth who do not wish to work at survey time because of a variety of acceptable and understandable reasons unrelated to the labor market. Among such causes would be waiting for various events, such as admission to an educational institution, a forthcoming mar-

Table 6.11 Young Females Not in School or the Civilian Labor Force Citing Household Responsibilities as the Main Reason, by Age, United States, Sweden, and Japan, 1959-1979

	United States (4th Quarter)				Sweden (November)				Japan (July)			
	Proportion of age group not in school or labor force		Proportion of age group citing household responsibilities		Proportion of age group not in school or labor force		Proportion of age group citing household responsibilities		Proportion of age group not in school or labor force		Proportion of age group citing household responsibilities	
	16-19	20-24	16-19	20-24	16-19	20-24	16-19	20-24	15-19	20-24	15-19	20-24
	(percent)											
1959									7.4	25.9	5.4	24.2
1962									5.4	23.7	4.0	21.4
1965					8.4	27.7	6.2	25.3	4.7	24.9	3.5	22.7
1968	11.7	36.2	9.0	32.5	6.7	22.4	4.0	20.6	3.6	21.3	2.2	19.1
1969	12.1	34.8	8.7	31.7	7.1	21.4	4.8	18.6				
1970	12.3	33.9	9.7	30.7	6.8	19.3	4.1	16.9				
1971	11.8	33.3	8.7	29.0	6.3	18.9	4.9	16.1	3.2	22.7	2.2	20.6
1972	11.5	31.2	8.6	27.3	7.9	17.6	4.3	15.9				
1973	12.5	29.9	9.0	26.4	8.5	17.0	4.3	14.4				
1974	11.5	27.5	7.7	23.5	5.2	15.9	3.6	14.0	2.9	23.4	1.9	21.3
1975	10.9	27.9	8.0	23.6	4.2	13.8	2.5	12.6				
1976	11.3	24.3	7.9	20.0	4.5	12.7	2.0	11.1				
1977	10.0	24.2	7.0	19.9	3.7	12.1	1.9	8.9	1.9	17.4	1.0	15.2
1978	10.3	22.1	6.9	17.9	3.5	10.8	1.5	8.1				
1979	9.2	21.9	5.3	18.0	4.3	8.8	1.9	7.6				

Source: U.S. Department of Labor, Bureau of Labor Statistics, *Employment and Earnings*, Jan. 1972, Tables 2 and 4; Jan. 1975, Table A-50; Jan. 1977, Table A-53; Jan. 1979, Table A-54 (Washington: GPO, monthly). U.S. Department of Labor, Bureau of Labor Statistics, unpublished data. Population data exclude institutionalized persons.

Sweden, SCB (Statistiska Centralbyrån), *Arbetskraftsundersökningen*, Råtabeller. [Labor Force Survey, Raw Tables] (Stockholm, monthly). Population data include institutionalized persons.

Japan, Office of the Prime Minister, Bureau of Statistics, *Employment Status Survey*, All Japan. 1959: estimated from Tables I-1 and II-2; 1962: Tables I-1 and II-2; 1962: Tables I-1 and II-8; 1965: Tables 1 and 28; 1968: Tables 1 and 28; 1971: Tables 1 and 39; 1974: Tables 2 and 31; 1977: Tables 2 and 31 (Tokyo, triennial). Population data exclude institutionalized persons.

riage, or a change of residence. Those who have just left school and intend to enter the labor market may spend some intervening time on vacation or in a waiting period. A small group of young people do not enter the labor force because their personal or family economic position does not permit them to work. Girls in some countries and in some classes are expected to remain at home until they marry.

A perspective on non–labor market reasons for being out of the labor force is provided by a monthly Canadian series and a quarterly U.S. series on the reasons for leaving the last job. Data for males and females 15–24 years old in Canada indicate that non–labor market reasons predominate among the total not in the labor force. To begin with, those who have never worked, mostly students, and those who have not worked in the past five years, mostly housewives, account for more than one-third of males and even more females, in typical months. Second, the residual flow from employment or unemployment to not in the labor force is largely explained by entrance or return to education, household duties, or illness. Only a small part of the flow is attributable to losing a job or being laid off. Moreover, even if the entire category "other reasons" for leaving a job is interpreted as having a labor force association, a dubious assumption, the sum of those dismissed or laid off and "other reasons" still constitutes a small part of the total, especially for females (Canada 1980b).

U.S. quarterly data for males and females 16–24 years old and not in the labor force in the last quarters of 1978 and 1979 also indicate that non–labor market reasons account for the vast majority of those currently not in the labor force. Among both males and females, over one-third had never worked or last worked five or more years ago, as in Canada. If to this is added those who last worked one to five years before and those who left a job during the previous twelve months in order to return to school, fulfill household responsibilities, or because of poor health or disability, only about 10 percent of the males and less than that proportion of the females left the labor force for direct labor market reasons. Again, adding those who left for other reasons would at most double the percentages, on the assumption that all giving "other reasons" actually had labor force-related reasons (US 1971–80f).

Canadian and American findings on this issue are remarkably similar, and neither country shows much variation over time. To be sure, the separation of in-school and out-of-school youth into two data series might show that a large part of out-of-school NISLF males have labor market reasons for leaving the last job. There then would be increased interest in discovering why they abandoned job search. Further guidance to the possible composition of "other reasons" may be obtained from the detailed French longitudinal survey (Table 6.9). While the proportions in the French results are of limited significance because coverage was confined to 16–17-year-olds, it appears that over half of French NISLF males and one-third of the females were in a transitional state, awaiting developments outside the civilian labor market. Among those in the "other reasons" category are a few who choose not to work. The French survey indicates that some young people are willing to declare this attitude openly (Table 6.9).

There also is a residual group of alienated, delinquent, or rebellious young people who do not regularly participate in the regular labor market. American evidence indicates that some of these may be fully employed in the illicit or irregular economy, but officially they are counted as NISLF, if indeed they are counted adequately or at all (Anderson, E. 1980). These portions of the NISLF group may be regarded as a social problem, in part caused by labor market inadequacies or deficiencies.

In connection with the large proportion who offer "other reasons" for NISLF or say they do not wish to work, the question arises whether government policies or programs tend to encourage NISLF status, and whether they are responsible for adding any large number of NISLF youth in the various countries. Analysts have documented the difficulties of testing the assumed effects of actual and hypothetical income support programs on labor force status (Cain and Watts 1973, Ch. 9; Borjas and Heckman 1978; Keeley et al. 1978; Ehrenberg 1979a, b). Most analysts deal with the effects on labor supply of programs that have relatively little impact on youth. They also tend to analyze a single program, such as unemployment insurance benefits or disability benefits. Even in this type of analysis, separate, and possibly opposite, effects may be due, on the one hand, to the desire to qualify for coverage in an insurance-type program and, on the other hand, to the opportunity to draw benefits. To become eligible to apply for work-related unemployment or disability benefits, for example, a young worker might remain in the labor force for a longer period than otherwise. On the other hand, if a program permits a certain amount of work without a reduction in benefits, it may simply reduce hours of work.

Withdrawal from the labor force or failure to enter it upon receipt of income support is most probable under programs, such as public assistance, that do not require the recipient to be available for work or that penalize recipients who have earnings. A shift from employed to unemployed status is more likely than a move out of the labor force under programs, such as unemployment insurance, that test availability for work and reduce or eliminate benefits if paid work is accepted. Under some income transfer programs there may be movement from out-of-labor force status to unemployed status. Prolongation of unemployed status more than increased incidence is the prevailing finding in the large number of studies of the impact of unemployment insurance (Spindler and Maki 1975; Hamermesh 1977, 1978; Cain 1978, p. 39; Grubel 1978; Donaldson 1979, pp. 12–23; Solon 1979; Hills and Thompson 1980, pp. 2–3).

Conclusions about particular programs confront a distinction between the behavioral and reporting effects of income transfers. The financial support offered by government might cause a young person to leave or not enter the labor force, but if receipt of the payment is contingent on registering as unemployed, such a person would be counted as in the labor force. If all persons qualifying for such programs initially were out of the labor force (OLF), an unlikely situation, they would constitute a spurious addition to the labor force, to the extent that they actually registered as unemployed, reported themselves as such to the Current Population Survey, and did not seek or obtain employment (Cain 1978; Clark and Summers 1978c; Devens 1979). If, on the other hand, recipients initially were in the labor force, then to the extent that they remain employed or unemployed rather than become OLF because of the reporting requirement, there is no diminution in the size of the labor force.

Three caveats must be entered on this point. Participation in the labor force is not the only alternative to living on an income transfer. It is possible that young mothers would find other means of financial support if public assistance were not available, rather than enter the labor force. Second, the registration requirement may apply only at the time of coming on the program or at infrequent intervals, as in the U.S. Food Stamp and Assistance to Families with Dependent Children (AFDC) programs. Although these programs have required registration as unemployed since 1973, a Current Population Survey question about the March 1976 labor force status of teenagers (16–19) of both sexes who received AFDC in 1975 indicated that only a third were reported as in the labor force, against 51.3 percent for all other teenagers. Similarly, teenage recipients of food stamps in the United States had a 49.4 percent labor force participation rate (LFPR) in August 1976, compared to an LFPR of 65.7

percent for all other teenagers (Devens 1979). On this evidence, the reporting requirement has not been as significant as the behavioral effect in determining labor force status.

Third, but exceptionally, even recipients of income support where both a regular test of availability for work and an unemployment registration are required, as in unemployment insurance benefits, may be reported as out of the labor force in labor force surveys or longitudinal surveys. This occurs most frequently in countries whose employment service lists relatively few suitable vacancies, rendering the work test inoperative. It also is produced by an attitude that unemployment benefits are an earned right, suitably used during a period of leisure and stock-taking rather than active job search. Young people in some countries are prone to take such a view, if they are not offered alternatives by the authorities. A desire for a solid block of leisure time may be strong in the US, for example, because paid vacations are short compared to those in Western Europe. A willingness to trade income for leisure time of this kind has been reported (Best 1980). Some of these youth might be reported as discouraged workers, a subdivision of the out-of-the-labor-force contingent.

No such divergence between program records and labor force statistics arises when the main source of such data is social insurance statistics or unemployment registrations, as in Great Britain. Not only would all young recipients of unemployment insurance automatically be included in the labor force, but so would young people who had never worked before, mostly new school-leavers, who registered as a condition of receiving means-tested supplementary benefits, available from age 16. Supplementary benefits in part provide unemployment assistance, among others to those who have not qualified for unemployment insurance. An official British report notes "a growing realization of the availability of supplementary benefits to school-leavers registering for employment" (GB 1969–80f, p. 503). Perhaps it is the availability of such a "safety-net" income transfer program, absent in the United States and some other countries, which leads official British opinion to discern only a small number of discouraged workers in the United Kingdom (GB 1969–80f, p. 501). Unofficial British views might be less sanguine on this point, but it is clear that British youth have more opportunity to be counted in the labor force than American because of the statistical system and the type of benefits available to unemployed youth.

A study of American youth employment used, as a variable, whether the household received income in 1975 from transfer payments. The analysts found that early in the study "a few of these variables showed significant negative effects on some measures of youth employment. However, they did not remain significant in the presence of the other variables included in the final model" (Rees and Gray 1979, p. 6). A comparison of income transfers available to British and American youth suggests that British youth have more access and higher levels of income support than American youth (Layard 1979). Yet British male youth have lower NISLF rates (Tables 6.2a, 6.2b).

Certain young people, prone to NISLF status and potentially unresponsive to alternative government programs which favor education or labor force participation, may be tipped into the NISLF category or induced to remain there by income transfers. Those countries which pay welfare benefits to single mothers without requiring registration as unemployed offer a relevant program. Such programs as the French payments to families, which may encourage women to remain at home, and disability benefits, particularly in Sweden and the Netherlands which make payments to young people such as drug addicts, may add individuals to NISLF ranks who, in other countries, would not be in that category.

All of the difficulties in interpreting the impacts of particular programs are compounded when the issue is broadened to the net effect of all relevant income transfer programs. Necessary as this next step is, it also raises questions about whether other government activities should not also be assessed. Young people's labor force status is affected by government action in regard to education and by special youth employment programs. These programs have national time trends and variations among countries which may, added to the effects of income support programs, produce different impacts on the size of the youth labor force than the income transfer programs alone. In general, a case can be made for a wider view that would assess the effects on labor supply decisions of taxation, housing and rent subsidies, education, and similar government activities (Lampman 1979; Rosen, H.S. 1979).

A U.S. estimate for 1978, which omitted public education, similar programs, and all relevant taxes but included the impact of eight social insurance programs and seven income assistance programs, found a 3 percent decline in total hours supplied to the labor force from 1950 (Danziger, Haveman, and Plotnick 1980). Lampman (1979), counting the effects of public education and similar programs as well as the taxes required to finance these plus all income support programs, estimated that there would have been 7.3 million more full-time equivalents in the U.S. labor force and 1.0 million more 18–24-year-old full-time participants in 1976 if the level of social welfare benefits had been maintained at 1950 rates (Lampman 1979, pp. 143–44). In appended criticism, Hamermesh correctly pointed out that Lampman's interpretation of enrollment rate trends and schooling subsidies missed the complementary possibilities of a rise in both enrollments and part-time labor force participation. On this and other grounds, it is clear that there is no agreement at present on the methodology or numerical results of efforts to calculate the impact of government programs (Lampman 1979, pp. 149–54).

It appears desirable to omit deliberate public support to education and similar constructive programs, although technically these also tend to reduce the labor force. In most countries it is likely that the unintended effects of government expenditure on education and manpower training and income support for young people has, on balance, reduced the youth labor force, although the net impact of the various types of income support offered to young people probably has enlarged the youth labor force slightly by increasing and prolonging unemployment. Youth employment measures which are not solely income transfers probably show more upward trend in expenditures since 1960 than income support programs. To a large extent, youth employment programs simply move young people from unemployed to employed, but they also tend to increase the youth labor force in some countries by a small amount because youth employment programs may lead to counting in the labor force young people who previously were out of the labor force, often because they were enrolled in educational institutions.

A great deal more research must be done before any comparative conclusions can be drawn about the unintended impact of programs which favor NISLF status. A preliminary judgment, based simply on the absence or presence of the required type of income transfer program in various countries, does not support the view that comparatively high male NISLF rates in the United States, Canada, and Italy can be attributed to the unintended increase in NISLF generated by such programs. The US, in particular, has fewer such programs covering youth than most other countries.

A certain portion of those giving "other reasons" for being NISLF are known to be involved in labor market events. This is a group for whom the distinction between being in and out of the labor force is unclear; their movement between statuses from one survey month to another is attributable to the artificial definitional boundaries on unemployment. Data for some countries document the main situations which affect youth of this type. First, out-of-school youth who made job search efforts during a survey period may be waiting for responses from employers and so are counted as not in the labor force (NILF). A Canadian survey in March 1979, directed only to those out of the labor force who said they wanted to work and were available, found that 17.9 percent of the 15–24-year-old males and 11.1 percent of the 15–24-year-old females gave this as the reason for not searching in the reference week. A larger share of this male age group than of two older groups cited this reason (Canada 1980a, p. 28). Youth waiting to be inducted into the armed forces are a subdivision of this group in countries with compulsory military service.

A second situation where NILF status may appear briefly between periods of being counted in the labor force affects young people who have been unemployed, have found jobs due to start in the future, and have discontinued job search. If the waiting period is longer than stipulated (usually 30 days), the person is moved from unemployed status to not in the labor force. An Australian survey in March 1979 of those NILF who wanted to work found that 3.3 percent of 15–24-year-olds were in this position (Australia 1979a, p. 3). The Canadian survey also found such a category (Canada 1980a, p. 19).

As a variant of the above, those on lay-off or others who expect to return to a former employer and do not engage in or terminate job search may be moved to the NILF category. Regulations regarding the treatment of persons on lay-off in the labor force survey vary among countries (Appendix 4:1). In countries where lay-off is regarded as unemployment for a given period (usually about 30 days) without job search, the person goes to NILF status if job search is not undertaken after that period elapses. This is the situation in Canada where waiting for recall by employers was a cause for not searching for work in the March 1979 reference week for 18.0 percent of males 15–24 years old and 10.3 percent of similar females; all were among NILF who wanted to work and were available. Males and females in the two older age groups had even higher proportions in this category, as would be expected given job tenure patterns in relation to age (Canada 1980a, p. 28). In other countries job search may be required throughout the lay-off period, placing some young people in the NILF category until they are recalled or give up hope and search for a new employer.

The Canadian surveys indicate that a high proportion of NILF wanting to work and available for work expect to work for their last employer. Over half of males 15–24 who expected to work in the next six months in the 1978 and 1979 surveys said that they expected to work for their last employer; for females 15–24 it was 38.1 percent in March 1978 and 30.2 percent in March 1979. Moreover, of this group expecting to work for the same employer in the next six months, 50.6 percent of the males and 55.4 percent of the females had looked for work in the year preceding March 1979 (Canada 1980a, pp. 28, 40–41; 1979a, p. 33).

Whether or not all of these expectations are realistic, part of the NILF for "other reasons" shows relationships to the labor force as its primary situation. Further information is needed about this group. It should be noted that the Canadian and Australian percentages cited here would be considerably reduced if the base of calculations were all NISLF youth instead of those who wanted to work.

American data for NILF persons of all ages suggest that a large share of those who give "other reasons" may be only temporarily NILF (Flaim 1969). Persons of all ages who gave "other reasons" for NILF status in 1976 were more likely to be in the labor force in 1977 than those who cited home responsibilities, ill health, disability, retirement, or old age in 1976 (Job 1979). It is not clear whether the same findings would obtain for NISLF youth.

Although the identification of NISLF youth by the reasons for being in that status is only partially satisfactory because of the large "other" category, the information can be used in combination with evidence about the desire to work.

Desire to Work

Do Not Wish to Work

A sure separation of NISLF youth from the active portions of the youth population can be made by accepting at face value declarations by NISLF youth that they do not wish to work. It remains possible, of course, that in each country a certain portion of youth not wanting to work offers unsatisfactory reasons for that position from the social viewpoint. Upon further investigation, some youth who say they do not want to work may have been led to take that position due to availability of transfer income. Others may have immediate or long-run labor market problems, deriving from personal or societal factors.

Showing considerable consistency over many years, from two-thirds to greater than 90 percent of NISLF youth, in three diverse countries for which comparable data are available, affirm that they do not wish to work (Tables 6.6, 6.12). Australian and Canadian data for recent years reinforce such a conclusion, although the form of the data do not permit direct comparison with Japan, Sweden, and the United States (Australia 1979a; Canada 1979a, 1980a). The Canadian survey is important because almost two-thirds of the responses were from the individuals directly concerned.

The proportion of NISLF youth not wanting to work, relating to different time periods in the three countries, is shown in Table 6.12.

Table 6.12   NISLF Youth Not Wanting to Work, Japan, Sweden, and United States

	Males		Females	
	Teenage	Young Adult	Teenage	Young Adult
	(percent)			
Japan	80.0	70.6	73.8	72.8
Sweden	69.4	91.2	81.6	85.1
United States	69.7	68.6	79.6	84.5

Source: Table 6.6.

The proportion of NISLF youth not wanting to work was highest in Sweden in three of the four age-sex categories; for male teenagers Sweden had the lowest proportion. Japan had the lowest proportions for both groups of females and the highest for male teenagers. The US was in the middle position, except for young adult males where it was lowest. Interpretation of these differences among the countries is only slightly assisted by the reasons for not wanting to work, since "other reasons" dominate the male side. Among the females, as expected, household duties explain the vast majority of the cases.

Those not wanting to work do not constitute a very large share of their age group.

They were 2.3 and 2.4 percent respectively of the male age groups in the US, 1.6 and 1.2 percent in Japan, and 1.1 and 2.2 percent in Sweden. Thus, the relatively low share of U.S. NISLF youth which does not want to work is somewhat offset by the higher proportion NISLF youth comprise of the age-group compared to the other countries. Among females the US is highest again, showing 9.0 and 23.9 percent, Japan has 3.1 and 16.6 percent, and Sweden the low proportions of 3.4 and 10.2 percent (Table 6.6). By this measure U.S. youth are somewhat more prone to not want to work than Japanese or Swedish. For males the cross-national differences come to at most about 1 percent of the age group, possibly an insignificant amount, but one involving a large number of individuals. For females, the cross-national differences appear to be substantial. They are unsurprising in regard to Sweden, but somewhat unexpected in the relative positions taken by the US and Japan. The U.S. NISLF rates cited in Table 6.6 are computed from a different data base than the rates in Tables 6.2a and 6.2b. Rates in Table 6.6 are slightly lower and less accurate than those in 6.2a and 6.2b.

To the extent that a country's NISLF youth constitute a relatively small percent of the sex-age group or of the out-of-school population, those NISLF not wanting to work might be expected to be a high proportion of all NISLF. This is the case for Swedish young adult males and females. If the proportions are calculated for 1977, using the out-of-school teenage population instead of the whole age group, Japanese rates come closer to those for the US and Sweden's rates decline relatively to the others. For teenage males the NISLF rates in Table 6.6 are increased fivefold in Japan, threefold in the US and 1 3/4 times in Sweden. The rates for teenage females rise by 4.5 times in Japan, almost threefold in the US and 1.65 times in Sweden.

In spite of a high proportion of NISLF youth who say that they do not want to work at a given time, many may feel this way only temporarily. Information on American NILF 16–24-year-olds, including all in school, indicate that over half of the males and under half of the females questioned in the last quarter of 1978 and 1979 intended to seek work in the next twelve months (US 1971–80f). These very substantial proportions would be reduced if students were eliminated from the numerator and denominator, to accord with our concept of NISLF.

Another American survey was made of the labor force participation in the first half of 1977 of those (all ages and including in-school youth) who were NILF in the first six months of 1976. Of those who said in 1976 that they did not want a job, 31 percent were in the labor force in 1977; this compared to a LFPR of 46 percent for those who said in 1976 that they did want to work (Job 1979). These results suggest that subjective views on the desire to work are, at best, fair guides to subsequent behavior. Nevertheless, at any particular time it is likely that the majority of NISLF youth has non-labor market reasons for not wanting to work. Even if data could be adjusted for the dubious cases, in most countries more NISLF youth would not want to work than would desire jobs at any given time.

Want to Work

Attention turns now to those NISLF youth who say that they *do* want to work but have not searched. Discouraged workers, to be discussed more fully in the next section, are one part of the group which wants to work. The remainder consists of youth who have not searched for personal reasons, such as illness or household duties. The main reason given for wanting or not wanting to work should not be interpreted as the only reason, however. Among those wanting to work, a considerable portion may have combinations of personal and labor market reasons for not seeking work, although the form of the survey may cause a single choice to be made (Appendix 4:1; Canada 1980a, pp. 7–8). The entire group is of social concern to the extent that disguised unemployment or weak societal and labor market attachment may be present.

Some believe that even the small proportions claiming a desire to work may be an overstatement. A Canadian study of persons not in the labor force succinctly stated the problems of testing the desire to work:

> Even when the question is addressed directly to survey respondents . . . major difficulties in the interpretation of the resulting data follow from the fundamental vagueness of the "want work" question. If the terms of employment were ideal from each individual's point of view, there are probably very few persons among those presently classified as not in the labor force who would not "want" such ideal work. However, remembering that the unemployment estimates are designed to measure the unutilized supply of labor in response to existing terms of employment, the question is inevitably raised as to whether those persons who claim to "want work" are in fact prepared to accept existing wage rates and other terms of employment. Indeed, in the absence of any activity serving to obtain information about possibly available jobs, one could question whether the survey respondent is even aware of the terms of employment currently being offered (Canada 1979a, p. 8).

After the second annual survey, the analysts commented that "the apparent stability of the 1978 and 1979 results suggests that either response variance is in fact lower than expected or its distribution is such that its effects tend to cancel over sufficiently large numbers of respondents" (Canada 1980a, p. 20). The "want to work" issue remains unsettled, since others contest the division between the unemployed and those wanting to work as artificial and unwarranted, because the current availability, and prior and subsequent labor market records, of those wanting to work are not very different from those of the unemployed (Finegan 1978, pp. 83–95).

Those youth who say they want to work but have not searched for jobs constitute a minority of NISLF youth, a miniscule part of the total age group, and a small share of the out-of-school population. NISLF youth who say that they want to work comprise from 8.8 to 31.4 percent of all NISLF youth in Japan, Sweden, and the United States (Table 6.5). Australian calculations in March 1979 show 19.6 percent of male NILF teenagers, 20.6 percent of female NILF teenagers, 29.9 percent of male NILF young adults, and 27.4 percent of female NILF young adults as wanting to work (Australia 1974–80, March 1979; Australia 1979a). Direct comparisons cannot be made with the other countries because students are included in Australia.

A somewhat different cross-national picture emerges when NISLF youth who want to work are taken as a percentage of their age group. To begin with, very small percentages are involved. The proportion of both groups of the male youth population and of female teenagers wanting to work is over twice as high in the US as it is in Japan and Sweden, however (Table 6.6). The ratio would be still higher if U.S. rates were derived from the October survey. For young adult females wanting to work, the highest share of the age group is found in Japan (6.2 percent), followed by the US (4.4 percent), with Sweden last at 1.2 percent. The high Japanese proportion reflects the restrictive female social role combined with limited labor market acceptance of married females and relatively few part-time jobs; the Swedish case is the opposite on each count, with the US somewhere in between. Australian rates for March 1979 are 6.8 percent for teenage males and 8.5 percent for teenage females, both much higher rates than in the other three countries. Young adult males in Australia showed 1.9 percent and young adult females 8.4 percent, also higher than in the other countries.

When the out-of-school population serves as the base of calculations for teenagers, the proportions wanting to work but not searching for jobs not only increase, but the relative standing of the countries changes somewhat. Applying the 1977 NISLF rates given in Tables 6.2a and 6.2b to the distribution in Table 6.6, the percentage of the out-of-school teenage population wanting to work, but not searching, would be as follows:

	Male	Female
Japan	2.0	5.0
Sweden	0.9	1.2
United States	3.1	6.7
Australia	10.3	12.9

Australian rates are for March 1979 and may slightly overstate the out-of-school population and include students among those wanting to work; both tend to raise the Australian rates. Probably Australia would remain in first place, followed by the US. The outstanding change from using an out-of-school population base is the relative advance in Japanese rates and the reduction in Swedish. Both trends in enrollment rates and the especially strong labor market measures for youth in Sweden account for the changes from the rates when the whole age group is the base.

Those who said that they wanted to work were queried about the reasons for not searching for jobs in Canada and Australia in March 1979; these results can be added to the information for other countries in Table 6.6. More than three-fourths of Australian male teenagers who did not search for jobs, although they wanted to work, cited personal reasons. More than four-fifths of young male adults in Australia also were in this situation (Australia, 1979a, p. 3). Among male Canadians 15–24 years old who wanted to work and were available, personal and family reasons were so insignificant they were not recorded (Canada 1980a, p. 28). Among American males wanting to work, about 10 percent of teenagers and more than 18 percent of young adults gave personal reasons. One-fourth of Japanese teenage males and an insignificant share of young adult males had such reasons. In Sweden, personal and family reasons accounted for about 20 percent of the male teenagers and about 50 percent of the young adult males who said they wanted to work (Table 6.6). Among American teenage females wanting to work, 43.5 percent had personal or family reasons, compared to 84.6 percent in Australia, 72.7 percent in Japan, and 25.0 percent in Sweden. Young adult females in the United States had such reasons in 54.5 percent of the cases, against 84.7 percent in Australia, 91.9 percent in Japan, and about 50 percent in Sweden (Table 6.6).

The wide range among the five countries for both males and females may be due in part to differences in definitions and survey procedures in the various countries and the inherent difficulty of separating personal from labor market reasons; the results for males may not be interpretable at present. While the range for females also is substantial, it is not inconsistent with what is known about attitudes toward women in the respective labor markets. Results for Canadian females are remarkably low, however, and may be due to the specification "available for work" and the earlier elimination from the group of all who gave "other reasons." The official exclusion of those who answered "studies" brings the Canadian survey into accord with the modifications introduced for Japan, Sweden, and the US, in order to have the data refer to the NISLF population. Since Australian data have not been so modified, the results should be treated guardedly.

Questions about their prior work records, job search efforts, and expectations about future job search and employment have been used to measure the sincerity of youth who claim to want to work but who are currently not searching for jobs. Canadian data are most complete (Canada 1980a). Of 15–24-year-old NILF Canadian males who wanted to work, were available, but had not looked for work in 1978 and 1979, about 80 percent had worked in the previous twelve months and more than 58 percent had searched for jobs. For females of the same age, more than 58 percent had worked and the same proportion had searched in both years. Moreover, better than half of the males 15–24 years old and slightly fewer of the females 15–24 years old who had worked during the previous year also had looked for work during the previous six months. The job search record was even better for the minority who had not worked in the prior year. Also, more than three-fourths of males and more than three-fifths of females 15–24 years old who wanted to work and were available in 1978 and 1979 expected to find work within six months. Asked about their reasons for ceasing active job search, about one-third of males and females 15–24 who had looked for work in the previous twelve months cited the belief that no work was available. Next in importance as a specific reason for both young males and females was waiting for replies to job applications. It is significant that females in this age group did not cite household responsibilities.

On this evidence, the group wanting to work and available for work had a reasonable claim to labor market attachment, although not as strong as that of Canadians 25 and older. Unpublished data for the United States collected in September–October 1978 refer to teenagers only, with so few in the sample that the results must be treated with great caution. While a direct comparison with the Canadian age bracket of 15–24 also adds difficulties, it appears that American youth wanting to work had a somewhat looser attachment to the labor force than Canadian youth who both wanted to work and were available.

Somewhat more detailed and reliable information for Americans of all ages who wanted to work indicates that similar Canadians who wanted to work and were available had stronger work records and intentions. Canadians aged 15 years and older who wanted to work, were available, but had not searched in March 1978 and March 1979 (constituting 3.9 percent and 4.2 percent respectively of all NILF) showed a much higher rate of having worked during the previous twelve months than Americans 16 years and older who wanted a job but had not searched (constituting 8.9 percent of all NILF in September–October 1978). The Canadian rates in the two years were 66.6 and 63.8 percent against the U.S. 43.1 percent (Hamel 1979, p. 59; Canada 1980a, pp. 30–31). The proportion of Canadians who had searched for a job in the previous twelve months also greatly exceeded that in the US: 60.5 percent (March 1978) and 70.4 percent (March 1979) in Canada versus 25.3 percent in the US. Similarly, Canadians who worked during the past twelve months had higher rates of job search than a similar American group. Finally, only 13.4 and 17.6 percent of the Canadian group had neither worked in the year prior to 1978 or 1979 nor searched for work in the previous 6 months. In the US, 42.9 percent had neither worked nor searched in the previous twelve months.

It is difficult to say how much of the difference is accounted for by the Canadian designation of "available for work" in their survey. Although the 1978 definition accords with the U.S. "want a job now," the 1979 definition on which all data are based considers "going to school" and "other reasons" for not being able to search as part of the *not* available group (Canada 1980a, pp. 11–12). Overall, Canadian results lead to more positive conclusions about the group wanting work than is usual in the US. The Canadian survey declares:

> The 1979 survey confirmed the observation from the 1978 survey that a very high percentage of those who "want" and are available for work but who are not seeking it have had recent labor market experience through holding a job in the past year or looking for work in the past six months, and that two thirds of the target population expected to again be part of the labour force by securing a job within six months of the survey. These characteristics demonstrate that such persons in fact do contribute to the changes in the employment and unemployment totals estimated by the monthly Labour Force Survey (Canada 1980a, p. 21).

Information for additional countries is needed to check whether the Canadian situation is typical. Meanwhile, credence may be given to the expressed desire to work, and validity may be attached to the division in the NISLF population in most countries between a relatively small group who say that they want to work and a larger group who affirm that they do not want to work.

Discouraged Workers

Within the group of NISLF youth who want to work, greatest attention is usually paid to those called discouraged workers. They believe that no jobs are available to them and offer this as the sole reason for not searching for employment. In the Swedish, Australian, and American surveys, labor market reasons for being discouraged are distinguished from personal factors. Inevitably, there are classification difficulties and problems of accuracy in the personal responses (Finegan 1978, pp. 4-7, 19). Canada's labor force survey identifies as discouraged workers only those who are such for labor force reasons, e.g., believe no work available (in area or suited to skills) and who did not look for work in the survey week but did look in the past six months.

Discouraged workers, especially in the youth groups, are a much disputed category, treated as an extension of the unemployed by some and by others as pretenders who really do not wish to work. After much discussion about the possible inclusion of discouraged workers in the regular count of unemployment, the U.S. National Commission on Employment and Unemployment Statistics decided against such a change in 1979. The validity of current job search as a test of unemployed status was upheld. Other countries continue to use the same criterion.

The problems surrounding the status of the discouraged are well put by an official Canadian survey:

> when respondents report that they "want work" but are not seeking in the belief that no jobs are available, the question can arise as to the soundness of that belief. In small labour markets . . . the respondent frequently can maintain an in-depth knowledge of the labour market without gathering information through job search. However, in larger more complex labour markets, such as those in which most Canadians are now located, this knowledge can only come from at least some minimal job search activity.

> The very fact that these persons have actively sought work in the past demonstrates that their labour markets are of sufficient size and complexity that active job search was considered necessary. . . . Accordingly, although they say that they "want" work, their belief that no work is available must be based on historical information gained through job search in the past. As a result, their in-

terest in finding work may be questionable since they are in effect declaring that they feel that further job search is not worth the trouble in light of what they see as the probability of finding a job (Canada 1979a, p. 9; see also Finegan 1978, pp. 45–47).

On the other side of the argument, many persons who have dealt directly with those youth most likely to be reported as discouraged workers believe that they would respond favorably and quickly to job offers on current terms. Frequent rejection by employers and unfavorable experience in briefly held jobs tend to produce genuine disaffection or discouragement, which may lead to withdrawal from job search and even antisocial behavior. On the other hand, certain types of youth and socioeconomic settings may stimulate behavior that leads to discouraged status.

One of the reasons for rejecting the discouraged as part of the unemployed count in the United States has been evidence of a sparse work record (Finegan 1978). To aid in its decisions on the issue, the National Commission on Employment and Unemployment Statistics had a special question attached to the September–October 1978 CPS Survey. It inquired into the prior job search activity and work record of discouraged U.S. workers. Unpublished data for teenagers, based on too small a sample to yield statistically reliable results, indicate that 68 percent of male discouraged workers and 47 percent of female had searched for jobs during the previous three months. Their search rates were considerably higher than those of teenagers who wanted a job now or of all NILF teenagers. Discouraged teenagers were more likely to have searched for a job in the past twelve months if they had not worked than if they had worked at some time during the year.

Published results for U.S. discouraged workers 16 years and older of both sexes show that 44.2 percent (52.4 percent of those discouraged for job-market reasons and 23.7 percent for personal reasons) had looked for work during the previous twelve months (Hamel 1979). About 40 percent of the U.S. discouraged had search activity within the past six months, and 34 percent within the prior three-month period. Discouraged workers had far higher rates of search activity than those who wanted a job now or the total not in the labor force. Job market factors affected discouraged men and women fairly evenly, but personal factors had a considerably greater negative effect on the job search activity of females than of males (Hamel 1979). The Australian job search rate of discouraged workers 15–64 years old in March 1979 (40.5 percent) was slightly lower than in the US (Australia 1979a, p. 7).

Some unpublished data of low statistical reliability, for American discouraged teenagers of both sexes, show that over 58 percent had worked in the twelve months prior to September–October 1978. These rates were higher than those for NILF teenagers and similar to those of NILF teenagers who wanted to work. The employment record of discouraged workers of all ages in the previous twelve months can be compared for the US and Australia. In March 1979 the percentage of discouraged Australians 15–64 years old who had worked at all during the past 12 months was 15.5 for all persons, 14.9 percent for married persons, 13.3 percent for females, and 14.1 percent for married females (Australia 1979a, p. 7). U.S. rates for 16 years and older for September–October 1978 show that 33.2 percent of all discouraged, 36.9 percent of the discouraged for job market reasons, and 23.7 percent of discouraged for personal reasons worked during the prior twelve months. The overall American rate was over twice as high as the corresponding Australian rate.

Interestingly, the employment rate for discouraged Americans was lower than that for the entire group of Americans who wanted a job now, of which the discouraged are a part; the respective rates were 33.2 and 43.1 percent. The discouraged, however, had somewhat higher rates than all who wanted a job now when the categories were "worked or searched" and "worked and searched" (Hamel 1979, p. 59). These data lend support to critics of the official data who maintain that the differences between the discouraged and others who want to work are exaggerated and that behavior cannot be inferred from questions on attitudes (Finegan 1978, pp. 83–95).

American analysis indicates that discouraged workers, those who want a job now, and the total not in the labor force were more likely to have searched for work in the past twelve months if they had not worked than if they had worked during that period (Hamel 1979, Table 2). Australian discouraged, on the other hand, were more likely to have looked for work in the twelve months preceding March 1979 if they had held a job in that period (Australia 1979a, p. 7). Canadian evidence, which is for those who wanted to work and were available, shows that in March 1978 those who had worked had slightly lower job search rates than those who had not, as in the US, but the reverse situation prevailed in Canada in March 1979 (Canada 1980a). Apparently, repeated surveys are needed to take account of changes in behavior as well as the effects of cyclical movements. The data just reviewed on the job search and employment records of discouraged workers are scanty, but they suggest that this group is even less remote from the labor market than other NISLF who want to work.

No matter what method is used to measure discouraged youth, their relative numerical importance is not great; the smaller the base, of course, the larger the share accounted for by discouraged youth. Japan has no separate data referring to discouragement, possibly because of its extremely low youth unemployment rates. In spite of the small percentage of youth involved, a large number of individuals are affected. Moreover, of all the subgroups in NISLF status, discouraged youth are the most suitable to be assisted to obtain jobs or to improve their situation via the labor market. The following review summarizes data on discouraged NISLF youth as proportions of those NISLF wanting to work and NISLF youth as a whole, and, then, of the age group population and the appropriate out-of-school population.

As a proportion of NISLF youth who want to work, itself a minority of the NISLF category, discouraged youth do not comprise the majority in most countries having data on this category. For U.S. males and females of both age groups, the proportion is one-half or less. Swedish shares are higher: 80 percent for teenage males, 62.5 percent for teenage females, 50 percent for young adult males, and 41.7 percent for young adult females (Table 6.6). Canadian data, which are for 15–24-year-olds, indicate that in March 1979 discouraged males constituted 24.4 percent and females 31.3 percent of the total in their age group who wanted to work and were available (Canada 1980a, Table 2). Australian discouraged teenagers of both sexes comprised only 7.8 percent of all teenagers who wanted to work in March 1979 (Australia 1979a, p. 3). France's longitudinal survey of 16–17-year-olds showed no discouraged males (Table 6.9). Especially in Sweden, reduction of the number of discouraged youth would impact on the proportion of NISLF wanting to work.

In the United States, discouraged males constituted 15.2 percent of teenage and 11.4 percent of young adult NISLF males, as an average of fourth-quarter data for 1970–1978 (Table 6.6). It has been argued that the American CPS understates the number of discouraged workers compared to results from econometric analyses (Wool 1978, pp. 57–61). Sweden's comparable survey, started only in 1975, shows an average of 22.2 percent of NISLF male teenagers and 4.4 percent of NISLF young adult males as discouraged in November 1975–1979. The Swedish teenage rate is higher than the U.S., while the young adult rate is lower.

Discouraged female workers comprise a surprisingly large percentage of NISLF, given the share attributable to household duties. In the US, 5.3 percent of NISLF female teenagers and 3.2 percent of 20–24-year-old females were discouraged workers, compared to 12.6 and 4.5 percent, respectively, for Swedish female teenagers and young adults (Table 6.6). French girls of 16–17 showed 8.8 percent discouraged (Table 6.9). Translated into numbers of individuals, discouragement affects somewhat more young females than males. This is illustrated also by Australian data. The 6,000 discouraged Australian females in both age groups in March 1979 were a larger number than the total shown for males in both age groups, but the female discouraged constituted a much smaller proportion of the 103,700 NILF females who wanted to work than the males did of their 56,300 total (Australia 1979a, p. 3).

Turning to a still larger base, the population of the age group, Australian male teenagers constituted 0.7 percent of the age group, somewhat more than U.S. and Swedish male teenagers. Australian discouraged female teenagers made up 0.5 percent of the age group, quite close to the proportion in the US and Sweden (Table 6.6; Australia 1979a). When the out-of-school population is used as the base for teenage NISLF rates, the share attributable to the discouraged rises more in the US than it does in Sweden or Australia because of differences among the countries in the level and trend in educational enrollment rates.

The relation between the proportion of discouraged youth in the out-of-school population and the out-of-school youth unemployment rate has not been established firmly, but it is reasonable to hypothesize a positive relation. American analyses of discouraged workers point to a positive cyclical relationship between unemployment rates and the number of discouraged workers (Flaim 1973; Finegan 1978; Ondeck 1978; Wool 1978). The relation is even closer when the variable is changed to the number citing job market factors, rather than the total discouraged or those citing personal factors, for discouragement (Table 6.13; Finegan 1978, pp. 28–29). Canadian surveys in 1978 and 1979 have detected a cyclical relationship between unemployment and the numbers wanting and available to work (Canada 1980a).

Somewhat more detailed information on young discouraged workers has been collected in the United States (Table 6.13). Comparison of 1968 and 1978 annual average data shows that in both years, when a higher percentage of females than males was NISLF, a greater proportion of females did not seek work because they cited themselves as discouraged, with the exception of female teenagers in 1978. Among those who were NISLF, the proportion of young discouraged workers was higher in 1978 than in 1968 with the exception of teenage females, although overall a lower proportion of young females was NISLF in 1978 than in 1968.

American detailed inquiries into the reasons people have felt discouraged about their job prospects were first conducted in the 1960s. In 1966 the reasons cited by discouraged workers of all ages were: believe they are too old or too young; could not find or did not believe any job available; lack necessary schooling, training, skills or experience; no means of transportation; language difficulties; pay too low; and racial discrimination (Stein 1967). Subsequent surveys have provided reasons by age. Youth in general, but particularly 20–24-year-olds, were reported as citing labor market factors more frequently than personal factors in explaining their discouragement. This pattern was even more pronounced in 1978 than it had been in 1968; it should be noted that a change in CPS procedure in 1970 slightly reduced the numbers of workers counted as discouraged due to personal factors. The main job market factor cited was the belief that a job could not be found, and in 1978 a

Table 6.13   Young Discouraged Workers, by Age, Sex, and Reason, United States, 1968 and 1978

	Males				Females			
	1968		1978		1968		1978	
	16-19	20-24	16-19	20-24	16-19	20-24	16-19	20-24
	(000)	(000)	(000)	(000)	(000)	(000)	(000)	(000)
				(annual averages)				
Total number not in school or civilian labor force	489	239	599	419	1328	2953	1291	2441
Percent not in school or labor force[a]	7.3	3.9	7.1	4.1	18.9	38.0	15.6	24.2
Total number of NISLF discouraged workers	43	10	71	44	67	46	59	76
Percentage discouraged workers[a]	0.6	0.2	0.8	0.4	1.0	0.6	0.7	0.8
Percent discouraged workers[b]	8.8	4.2	11.9	10.5	5.0	1.6	4.6	3.1
Unemployment rate of age-sex group	11.6	5.1	15.7	9.1	14.0	6.7	17.0	10.1
				(percent)				
Total reasons for NISLF discouragement	100.0	100.0	100.0	100.0	100.0	100.0	100.0	100.0
Personal factors								
Employers think too young/old	30.2	*	12.7	2.3	25.4	*	15.3	1.3
Lack of education or training	16.3	10.0	12.7	9.1	16.4	19.6	8.5	14.5
Other personal handicap	7.0	10.0	1.4	13.6	4.5	10.9	3.4	6.6
Job-market factors								
Could not find job	27.9	40.0	50.7	45.5	32.8	26.1	55.9	53.9
Thinks no job available	18.6	40.0	22.5	29.5	20.9	43.5	16.9	23.7

[a] As percent of civilian noninstitutional population.
[b] As percent of number not in school or labor force.

Note: Asterisk * signifies less than 0.05 percent.

Source: U.S. Department of Labor, Bureau of Labor Statistics, Employment and Earnings, Jan. 1969, Table A-1 and A-6; Jan. 1979, Tables 3, 15 and 41 (Washington: GPO, monthly), P. O. Flaim, "Persons Not in the Labor Force: Who They Are and Why They Don't Work," Monthly Labor Review, July 1969.

greater proportion cited this reason than in 1968. All other explanations declined in importance in 1978 compared with 1968 (Table 6.13).

Summary

An overview of this chapter on youth not in school or the labor force (NISLF) notes the following main points:

At any given time under existing circumstances, a large part of NISLF youth, a majority of females, and possibly a majority of males are NISLF because neither school nor the labor market is relevant for them.

A part of NISLF youth can be considered an indistinguishable extension of a segment of the youth unemployed. This small portion of NISLF youth, composed of discouraged workers and others who want to work but have ceased job search, has the greatest potential for absorption into the labor market through deliberate efforts and revised definitional and statistical procedures in surveys.

Every country has the potential of moving some males who "want to work," and even some who "do not want to work," into the labor force proper. In part, such a movement might occur through statistical redefinitions and more careful questioning of behavior; in part, it might come from a more robust youth labor market and more successful youth employment programs. A decline in the proportion of female NISLF who do not want to work is almost a foregone conclusion, on the basis of past trends.

Knowledge gained in this chapter suggests the inadvisability of analyzing the out-of-school unemployed and NISLF youth as a single entity, called "jobless" or "nonemployed." Even pending additional information on NISLF for more countries based on finer breakdowns and definitions, more uniform definitions in national surveys, and more explicit reasons for NISLF status, the consistency of findings from such diverse countries as Japan, Sweden, and the US argues against the combining of these categories.

Females of both age groups and in all countries show much clearer patterns and trends than males. Reduced time devoted to household responsibilities has decreased female NISLF rates and probably will continue to do so, regardless of other influences. Explanations of cross-national differences for females largely revolve around the differences in practice and attitudes in regard to the post-compulsory education and labor force participation of married women and mothers. The cross-national spread in NISLF rates is wide and is likely to remain so.

Cross-national differences in male NISLF rates are not large and suggest that there is an irreducible minimum of NISLF. No clearcut explanation of inter-country differences was found. In the countries where a somewhat elevated proportion of the age group is NISLF — the U.S., Canada and Italy — some common features appear: high youth unemployment rates and marked geographic, income level, and educational attainment differences among youth groups. National affluence does not appear to be a valid explanation of differences, but it has not been fully tested.

The net effect of all relevant governmental programs does not appear to swell NISLF ranks beyond the level that would exist in the absence of such programs. Programs which might tend toward an increase in the number NISLF probably are more than offset by governmental programs which on the one hand, foster educational enrollments and, on the other, encourage participation in the labor force by enforcing registration as unemployed as a prerequisite for remaining in a program. Evidence within countries, let alone comparisons among countries, is sparse, but it does not permit the conclusion that any substantial part of the NISLF group, which offers no reason for NISLF status or says it does not want a job, is influenced by governmental income transfers to themselves or their families or by tax policies. Indeed, the countries in which such policies are most highly developed do not have as high NISLF rates as other countries.

The absence of a definite upward trend in the proportion of all males in each age group which is NISLF is indirect confirmation that there has been no net effect from all of the forces acting on these rates, including government programs. It is possible that a slightly downward trend has not appeared in some countries, however, because of the net effects of government programs. Further exploration and explanations also are required of the tendency of NISLF rates to rise over time when the out-of-school population base is used.

Table A6.3 Youth Not in School or the Civilian Labor Force, by Age, Sex, Household Income, and Educational Attainment, United States, October 1977

	NISLF as a percent of out-of-school civilian population				Never married youth living at home							
					NISLF with less than 4 years of high school as a percent of all NISLF				NISLF with less than 4 years of high school as a percent of out-of-school civilian population with less than 4 years of high school			
	16–19		20–24		16–19		20–24		16–19		20–24	
Income class	Male	Female	Male	Female	Male	Female	Male	Female	Male	Female	Male	Female
					(percent)							
All classes[a]	9.9	20.3	8.5	14.0	62.8	61.7	44.5	43.8	15.2	46.1	17.3	43.4
Less than $5,000	19.4	50.0	20.9	40.7	76.7	77.1	66.0	67.2	22.0	71.9	26.3	68.3
$5,000–7,499	14.9	36.9	15.2	23.2	83.3	66.1	73.0	51.2	22.5	51.3	26.0	37.0
$7,500–9,999	13.3	23.7	12.1	23.6	69.6	67.9	39.1	34.6	17.6	39.6	15.0	56.3
$10,000–14,999	9.0	15.2	6.5	13.6	55.6	52.3	58.6	54.8	12.3	31.9	16.8	46.0
$15,000–24,999	7.3	8.7	5.1	5.2	40.5	44.1	15.8	16.7	10.7	27.8	6.0	11.2
$25,000 and more	2.9	7.9	4.8	4.6	33.3	23.1	*	*	4.9	20.0	*	*
					All other youth							
All classes[a]	3.4	43.6	1.9	33.3	78.6	66.2	24.7	34.3	5.9	68.1	2.1	53.0
Less than $5,000	5.0	44.5	4.5	39.4	50.0	77.6	31.0	55.2	4.8	67.8	3.6	55.9
$5,000–7,499	5.6	47.1	2.2	33.6	100.0	67.4	26.7	47.4	12.2	58.8	1.8	58.2
$7,500–9,999	*	42.6	2.5	36.4	*	59.4	6.7	35.7	*	65.1	0.7	57.9
$10,000–14,999	*	40.0	0.8	34.4	*	51.3	11.1	21.3	*	49.4	0.7	48.9
$15,000–24,999	*	39.0	0.7	25.7	*	46.9	9.5	15.0	*	57.7	3.1	40.4
$25,000 and more	25.0	*	*	21.5	100.0	*	*	10.3	100.0	*	*	40.0

[a] Includes income not reported.

Note: Asterisk * indicates less than 1,000 NISLF youth.

Source: U.S. Department of Labor, Bureau of Labor Statistics, unpublished tables from October 1977 Current Population Survey.

Appendix 6:1. Annual versus Monthly NISLF Data

Labor force survey data on NISLF in Chapter 6 deliberately present a month or quarter when school is in session rather than average annual data, because the latter tend to overstate the category not in school or the labor force. Differences resulting from using annual averages instead of monthly data are shown for selected years for Sweden and the United States (*Table B6.1). NISLF rates have been computed on the basis of total population and the total labor force. Comparisons of the Swedish November data and U.S. October data with the respective annual averages indicate that the most pronounced differences in the NISLF proportions appear for teenagers, as would be expected. For teenage males in both countries, annual averages run 4 to 5 percent higher than monthly data, and for teenage females, the difference is 5 to 6 percent in most years. The discrepancy between the sources is smaller for 20–24-year-olds. When disaggregated by reason for NISLF status, both Swedish and U.S. annual average data show a greater proportion than the monthly data as NISLF for "other" reasons (that is, other than household duties, institutionalization, and ill health or disability). Since U.S. fourth-quarter data, cited in Tables 6.6 and 6.11, closely resemble the October levels in Tables 6.2a and 6.2b, it is probable that the summer vacation factor is mainly responsible for the higher annual averages.

7 Racial, Ethnic, and Religious Minorities

While the primary purpose of this book is to study the postwar youth labor force as a whole in a cross-national setting, the subject has been disaggregated in the preceding chapters, to the extent that separate analyses by sex have appeared and some attention has been given to geographical variation. The present chapter deals with another aspect of youth differentiation within and among countries, which is of great importance in current and emerging social policy. This issue is the position of youth from racial, ethnic, or other minority groups in the society, especially their demographic, education, and labor force experience as it differs from majority youth patterns. These subgroups may consist entirely of the children of recent arrivals, including some children born abroad and others born in the host country. Alternatively, the subgroups also may include young people whose forebears settled as early or earlier than the majority population.

The size of these groups at present and their anticipated growth in the future would be enough reason for social interest, especially in countries which have been accustomed to a homogeneous population. But the discovery that some racial, ethnic, or religious subgroups of youth are disadvantaged compared to majority youth provides additional cause for public attention on grounds of both equity and efficiency. On the one hand, the issue is important because the educational, social, and economic handicaps of these subgroups result in an inferior labor market position for individuals. On the other hand, if there is a labor shortage, the quantitative and qualitative contribution of such subgroups to the youth labor force may be smaller than is possible or desirable.

Whatever the basis for concern, an increasing number of countries have or will soon recognize the distinctive problems of minority youth groups, and it is safe to guess that the issue will not soon be resolved. The subject is suited to cross-national study, inasmuch as certain consistent patterns appear from nation to nation, regardless of the size or origins of the subgroups. Moreover, the special programs adopted in various countries to ameliorate the situation have common elements and potential transferability.

The recency and degree of interest among countries in the youth subgroups are related to the historical background in each case. Countries which have long had resident minority groups in major population centers, as in the case of blacks in the United States, have tended to become concerned sooner and more deeply than those whose minority groups have been primarily in remote areas, as in the case of Eskimos and Indians in Canada, Lapps in northern Scandinavia, Aborigines in Australia, or Maoris in New Zealand. These latter countries, however, have usually become concerned earlier than those which have come to the problem primarily through a postwar inflow of foreign workers to meet labor shortages, as was true of most of northern Europe.

Most of this last group of countries were slow to accept that a problem existed. At first they thought that no children would be produced by the "guest" workers whose stay was to be brief. As the length of stay increased and families entered as permanent residents or intermarriages occurred, it was expected that the locally born children would soon be indistinguishable from native children of the same socioeconomic class, provided they were educated similarly. This has proved not to be the case, since most of these children are subject to special or additional problems beyond those affecting the lowest socioeconomic groups in which the subgroups are disproportionately represented.

In most countries, matters are complicated by the fact that there are multiple youth subgroups that vary in origins, characteristics, and legal status. Adding to groups already present, countries acquired foreign populations during the postwar period in three main ways, outside the normal immigration process. These were: granting settlement rights to natives of former colonies and territories (France, United Kingdom, the Netherlands) or to political refugees (Sweden, US); permitting importation of foreign workers on short, renewable contracts (West Germany, France, Switzerland) or as potentially permanent residents (Sweden, Australia, and Canada); and making agreements for unrestricted mobility among groups of nations (e.g., members of the European Community or the Nordic nations). In addition, the US has had two important sources of Hispanic inflow in the special relation with Puerto Rico and the entrance of undocumented aliens from Mexico and other parts of Latin America.

As a result of the complex sources of subgroups with potential problems, it often has been difficult for policymakers to see the points of similarity among the disadvantaged youth groups from divergent backgrounds. At the same time, all subgroups clearly have not been equally disadvantaged. Indeed, youth in some groups have exhibited no differences from the majority youth population. Not only may the various subgroups require varied types of assistance, but they may actually compete with one another in the youth labor force. These aspects partially explain why the required information on subgroups is only now being sought officially, as yet in a limited fashion.

Another reason for the paucity of relevant data is the nature of academic research interests. Social science research in most market-oriented countries has dealt primarily with socioeconomic classes and categories; relatively little attention has been given thus far to minority groups, either within or outside this framework. As the research community extends its interests to the subgroups, it may be expected that a new literature will grow up, either independent of or integrated into the existing socioeconomic framework. The US has been exceptional in its early attention to racial subgroups, both in official and nonofficial data collection, and analysis. Nevertheless, American absorption with issues of racial discrimination has led to much research strictly along purely racial lines, often without a subdivision of these populations along appropriate socioeconomic lines.

American analyses of data on racial minorities often assume a specious homogeneity in racial populations, since significant internal socioeconomic differences have been omitted. When efforts are made to incorporate variables other than race, the latter's explanatory significance diminishes in importance. For example, in a recent analysis of out-of-school teenage males in the United States, differences in socioeconomic, educational, and demographic factors accounted for 50 percent of the racial difference (Feldstein and Ellwood 1979). Yet, the extent to which these other differences also are race related remains an open issue. These findings should be borne in mind in evaluating the striking differences between the majority and minority youth groups which are detailed below; they should not be attributed entirely to inherent racial factors.

As early as the US was in its concern about black youth and its extensive documentation of the group's adverse position, it was tardy in coming to realize the distinct and serious problems affecting various other subgroups, lumped together for the time being as Hispanic youth. It is likely that these groups, which will form a larger part of the youth population in coming decades than blacks, will constitute a high priority for U.S. youth policy. It is therefore unfortunate that there is relatively little data on these youth groups, especially by their component national elements. Historical series are particularly lacking (Newman 1978; Cardenas 1979). The new youth sample in the National Longitudinal Survey at Ohio State University will afford an opportunity to study this group in depth, starting with 1979 interviews.

Given the wealth of data on U.S. black youth and the scarcity of information on other subgroups, the demographic, educational, and labor force position of black youth will be described below as a model of what might be sought for other subgroups in the US and, with variations, in the other countries. Following a fairly extended treatment of U.S. black youth, some discussion of the situation in other countries will be offered, recognizing the importance of the issues, the limited data, and the need for additional data and research.

U.S. Black Youth

The development of the black youth labor force since the end of World War II will be compared with that of white youth. Following the approach used in the rest of the book, the situation of black youth will be developed by surveying the demographic trends, developments in education enrollment rates and attainment, the position of black youth in the armed services and in the civilian labor force, the LFPR of students, and NISLF youth. Comparisons with the remainder of the black population, with white youth, and with the remainder of the white population will be made where relevant. Qualitative as well as quantitative aspects will be weighed.

A more rapid postwar increase in the number of black than white potential youth entrants to the labor force would be a relatively greater source of hardship to black youth, given their initial less favorable position in the youth labor market. The main elements of that less favorable position were higher unemployment rates, lower earnings, and a more restricted choice of jobs due to discrimination and less adequate preparation. If the flow of black youth into the civilian labor force was more rapid than that of white youth due to the net effects of demographic forces, educational trends, recruitment practice in the armed forces, racial differences in LFPR of students, and a greater propensity to be neither in school nor in the labor force, then a relative worsening of the position of black youth, largely originating on the supply side, could be posited. In the absence of offsetting factors on the demand side, black youth would suffer disproportionately.

In fact, all of the factors are not expected to behave in this way. Demographic factors would be expected to cause an increase in the number of black youth available to enter the labor market in excess of the effects of the baby boom on whites. Reinforcement of the pressure of numbers would be anticipated from the racial composition of the armed forces until the voluntary services were instituted; thereafter the armed forces would be expected to serve as a safety valve for the potential black civilian labor force. Another offset to the rise in relative numbers could be anticipated from educational trends and the lower LFPR of black students; this latter aspect might, however, be evidence of an unsatisfactory labor market situation for black youth rather than a useful withholding of labor supply (Iden 1980, p. 14).

The final offset to the pressure of black numbers on the civilian labor force would be expected to appear in the form of higher black than white NISLF rates. However, to the extent that relatively more blacks than whites are not in school or the labor force for reasons associated with their inferior overall economic or social position, this numerical relief to the potentially larger black labor force must be regarded as part of the problem, rather than an element of the solution. It was this discovery that black youth unemployment rates did not tell the whole story of disadvantagement because they omitted the lower black LFPR (the effect of higher NISLF rates) that led to analysis of the nonemployed or jobless, a total of the unemployed and the NISLF. As Chapter 6 has explained, these two categories should not be added together or analyzed as one phenomenon, although it is entirely correct to regard a portion of the excess black NISLF as closely related to a portion of black youth unemployment.

American data sources refer alternately to "blacks," "nonwhites," and "blacks and other races." While all three categories have distinct and separate definitions, the preponderance of blacks in each series permits the extraction of the major trends for the black youth labor force from several data series, each of which may have a slightly different coverage. Accordingly, "black" will frequently be used below when cited data are for "nonwhites" or "blacks and other races."

Demographic Pressures

Demographic developments which influenced the postwar youth labor supply in the United States ensured a faster growth of the potential black youth labor force than of the white. In a postwar economy which rarely exhibited a strong demand for the available supply of young workers, especially blacks, and in which there has been racial discrimination in the labor market and geographic maldistribution of population and jobs, the demographic element added another pressure.

American blacks had a more intense and prolonged baby boom than the total American population. Black fertility patterns, however, have been consistent with those of U.S. whites when educational levels are standardized (Johnson 1979). Compared to American whites, the death rates of black infants, children, and young people have been higher and slightly offset their higher birth rates (Table 2.4). As a result of these demographic developments, young black people who reached labor market entrance age since the end of World War II constituted a larger and a faster growing share of their total age group than had their elders (Table 7.1). They also consistently accounted for a higher proportion of the minority population of working-age (15–64) than white youth did of the white working-age population (*Table A7.1).*

The 15–19-year black group as a proportion of the all races 15–19 age group increased from 11.8 percent in 1945 to 12.7 percent in 1955, dropped back to 11.8 percent by 1962, and afterwards advanced annually to a high in 1980 of over four percentage points above the low registered in 1945 and 1962. The 20–24-year group escalated slowly from 1945 to 1962 and then experienced a slight decline in 1967. In the next decade a steady rise brought the share to 15.1 percent by 1980. In each year the shares of the two youth groups exceeded the share of the 15–64 group, with a widening margin appearing from the 1960s onward. Moreover, projections to 1990, shown in Table 7.1, and involving only those already born indicate that there will be

---

*Tables marked with an asterisk are not included in this volume, but may be obtained from the authors.

Table 7.1 Population by Race and Age, Both Sexes, United States, 1945-1990

	15-64 All races	15-64 Black and other races		15-19 All races	15-19 Black and other races		20-24 All races	20-24 Black and other races	
			Percent of all races			Percent of all races			Percent of all races
	(000)	(000)	races	(000)	(000)	races	(000)	(000)	races
Actual									
1945	94,856	9,572	10.1	11,669	1,374	11.8	12,036	1,330	11.1
1946	95,473	9,651	10.1	11,378	1,365	12.0	12,004	1,321	11.0
1947	96,277	9,734	10.1	11,308	1,356	12.0	11,814	1,307	11.1
1948	97,085	9,832	10.1	11,072	1,336	12.1	11,794	1,315	11.1
1949	97,891	9,911	10.1	10,870	1,315	12.1	11,700	1,315	11.2
1950	98,877	10,168	10.3	10,675	1,330	12.5	11,680	1,351	11.6
1951	99,574	10,281	10.3	10,557	1,333	12.6	11,552	1,335	11.6
1952	100,263	10,396	10.4	10,535	1,335	12.7	11,350	1,327	11.7
1953	100,925	10,517	10.4	10,684	1,350	12.6	11,062	1,321	11.9
1954	101,669	10,652	10.5	10,894	1,371	12.6	10,832	1,316	12.1
1955	102,455	10,795	10.5	11,039	1,397	12.7	10,714	1,313	12.3
1956	103,394	10,944	10.6	11,340	1,434	12.6	10,616	1,311	12.3
1957	104,433	11,109	10.6	11,798	1,487	12.6	10,603	1,308	12.3
1958	105,702	11,281	10.7	12,501	1,542	12.3	10,756	1,317	12.2
1959	106,843	11,456	10.7	13,019	1,591	12.2	10,969	1,332	12.1
1960	107,919	11,626	10.8	13,442	1,630	12.1	11,134	1,358	12.2
1961	109,048	11,816	10.8	13,759	1,664	12.1	11,483	1,410	12.3
1962	111,177	12,078	10.9	14,950	1,766	11.8	11,959	1,471	12.3
1963	112,999	12,347	10.9	15,509	1,862	12.0	12,714	1,539	12.1
1964	114,815	12,644	11.0	16,250	1,988	12.2	13,269	1,604	12.1
1965	116,601	12,944	11.1	17,027	2,119	12.4	13,746	1,664	12.1
1966	118,547	13,281	11.2	17,962	2,286	12.7	14,050	1,697	12.1
1967	120,583	13,635	11.3	17,948	2,380	13.3	15,248	1,800	11.8
1968	122,656	14,008	11.4	18,303	2,484	13.6	15,786	1,898	12.0
1969	124,737	14,403	11.5	18,756	2,589	13.8	16,480	2,023	12.3
1970	126,909	14,853	11.7	19,315	2,707	14.0	17,184	2,154	12.5
1971	129,036	15,280	11.8	19,724	2,799	14.2	18,089	2,313	12.8
1972	131,260	15,738	12.0	20,184	2,914	14.4	18,033	2,396	13.3
1973	133,388	16,181	12.1	20,554	3,010	14.6	18,345	2,487	13.6
1974	135,479	16,642	12.3	20,826	3,098	14.9	18,741	2,578	13.8
1975	137,525	17,143	12.5	21,015	3,175	15.1	19,229	2,692	14.0
1976	139,679	17,628	12.6	21,214	3,240	15.3	19,629	2,791	14.2
1977	141,718	18,114	12.8	21,168	3,274	15.5	20,073	2,906	14.5
1978	143,792	18,644	13.0	21,074	3,312	15.7	20,461	3,012	14.7
1979	145,714	19,139	13.1	20,918	3,330	15.9	20,726	3,100	15.0
Projected									
1980	147,317	19,536	13.3	20,609	3,337	16.2	20,918	3,162	15.1
1985	153,945	21,656	14.1	18,007	3,164	17.6	20,510	3,325	16.2
1990	158,495	23,657	14.9	16,777	3,229	19.2	17,953	3,165	17.6

Note: Total population, including institutionalized persons and armed forces, as of July 1.

Source: U.S. Department of Commerce, Bureau of the Census, *Estimates of the Population of the United States, By Single Years of Age, Color and Sex, 1900 to 1959.* Series P-25, No. 311, 1965; *Estimates of the Population of the United States, By Age, Sex and Race: April 1, 1960 to July 1, 1973.* Series P-25, No. 519, 1974; *Estimates of the Population of the United States By Age, Sex, and Race: 1970-1977.* Series P-25, No. 721, 1978; *Projections of the Population of the United States; 1977 to 2050.* Series P-25 (Washington: GPO, 1965-1978), unpublished data. All races data differ from U.N. data for US, cited in Chapter 2.

another advance in the share of the 15–19 black group (to 19.2 percent) and almost as substantial an increase for the 20–24 year black group (to 17.6 percent). This is a potent element to reckon with in devising policies for black youth in the coming decade.

Little attention has been given to another aspect—the possible labor market competition that minority young people have faced from their own elders, especially as successive cohorts have constituted an ever-rising share of the minority working-age population (15–64). While white youth have also been in this position, black youth have been affected more strongly (*Table A7.1). It is arguable that youth and older workers do not compete extensively for jobs and that competition for jobs among age groups does not actually follow strict racial lines. But to the degree that age-overlapping and racially segregated labor markets do exist, the postwar demographic developments indicate a black youth disadvantage.

Residential patterns have intensified the differential demographic trends. Whatever part of the country they live in, blacks and especially black youth have been more concentrated in central cities and less in suburbs and nonmetropolitan areas than whites. In 1977 54.1 percent of blacks but only 22.1 percent of whites lived in central cities, while the situation was reversed for the suburbs: 43.3 percent for whites and 20.8 percent for blacks (Swinton 1979, pp. 21–22). Inner cities and poverty areas have even greater concentrations of black youth (Mangum and Seninger 1978, pp. 9, 14–23). In 1977, 48.4 percent of black teenagers lived in poverty areas, of which 26.3 percent resided in the poverty areas of central cities. By contrast, only 14.4 percent of white teenagers lived in poverty areas, of which a mere 2.5 percent were in central cities (Swinton 1979, pp. 21–25). Since many central cities and particularly inner cities or poverty areas have lost large numbers of jobs and offer a restricted labor market for youth, this geographical distribution of black youth, coupled with their rising share both of their own age group and of the older black population, presents a more adverse situation than is signalled by the overall demographic trends.

Educational Enrollments

Educational enrollment patterns have provided some offset to the demographic pressures on the labor supply, insofar as black enrollment rates have risen more rapidly than white since the end of World War II (Mare and Winship 1980). As is true for all young people, additional postcompulsory education for black youth temporarily has limited or eliminated labor force participation, but simultaneously has elevated qualifications and aspirations. More rapidly rising black than white educational enrollment rates (EER) explain in part the decline in black labor force participation rates and employment/population ratios, since those enrolled in school consistently have lower labor force participation rates than the nonenrolled. A contrary influence on black LFPR from increased EER also has been present, inasmuch as a more educated black out-of-school population would tend to have higher LFPR, since LFPR vary with educational level (US 1975–80e). Since most of this effect appears after age 25, it is not captured in our data. On the whole, the depressing effect of EER on LFPR probably was the stronger influence.

It is possible that the pressure of numbers was a factor causing black youth to increase their EER faster than whites. When the potential youth labor supply increases without a corresponding expansion of demand, education becomes an attractive alternative either to unemployment or to a reduction in relative earnings. Moreover, the opportunity cost of further schooling would be low under such circumstances. In this particular case, not only were there no obstacles in the form of limited numbers of educational places, as in some countries, but there were many positive incentives to blacks—beyond those offered to whites—to continue their schooling. Thus, the more rapid rise of black than white EER may reflect an adjustment to demographic pressures, a relatively unfavorable employment situation, special programs to encourage college entrance, new types of schools, financial assistance, remedial programs, rising expectations of minority youth, higher educational requirements of desirable central-city jobs, and the impact on educational aspirations of antidiscrimination employment programs.

Over the years, EER by race not only showed a steady reduction in the racial differential, but for some age-sex groups, black EER have actually surpassed white rates in recent years (Table 7.2). While EER for 14 and 15-year-olds of both races (not shown in the table) have altered little over time, remaining mostly over 95 percent, those for 16 and 17-year-olds of each sex have increased sharply since 1960, converging on white rates. Since 1976 EER for black, 16–17-year males actually surpassed the white rates. Also, the gap between the two sexes has narrowed for 16–17-year-olds in each race, so that the whole range in 1979 was from a low of 87.1 percent for black females to a high of 94.6 percent for black males. If these EER were standardized for family, income, and socioeconomic characteristics, they would show even more progress in black EER, judging by the results for an earlier period (Bowen and Finegan 1969, pp. 416–17).

Unpublished data from the Current Population Survey for October 1977 permit a comparison of enrollment rates, based on civilian population, by race and household income, for never married teenagers living at home (or away at school). Both races show the expected rise of EER as family income increases. In several categories, black EER exceed those of whites, especially in the lower income classes where blacks are disproportionately represented (Table 7.3). A higher proportion of black than white teenagers is likely to be never married and living at home (in every income class, for each age-sex group), according to the unpublished data. Since EER are higher for the never married living at home than for other youth, a larger proportion of black than white youth is covered by these higher EER. Teenage enrollment rates presented in Table 7.3 are not far from the EER for all teenagers, regardless of living arrangements, but a majority of young adult females of both races and white young adult males live on their own. Therefore, their enrollment rates cited in Table 7.3 refer only to a part of the young adult population. Nevertheless, the propensity to be enrolled is much higher for young adults living at home than for other youth who are, as males, more heavily in the labor force, and, as females, more engaged in household duties than their never married counterparts living with parents. It should be borne in mind in interpreting racial differences, whether in EER or in other variables associated with identical income classes, that the size of the households and number of persons sharing a given income probably are larger for blacks than whites at each income level.

Some caveats are in order about all officially recorded increases in black EER, since they may somewhat overstate black educational progress through high school. The enrollment data in the October Current Population Survey include anyone who had been enrolled at any time during the current term or school year in day or night school, thus covering some part-time students and some who had already dropped out. Furthermore, EER for inner-city schools record many young people, disproportionately from minority populations, who infrequently attend classes or are persis-

Table 7.2 Enrollment Rates, by Race, Age, and Sex, United States, October 1960–1979

	16–17				18–19			
	Black		White		Black		White	
	Male	Female	Male	Female	Male	Female	Male	Female
	(percent of relevant civilian noninstitutional population)							
Year								
1960[a]	79.1	74.7	85.2	81.4	36.9	32.2	49.5	29.7
1964	84.3	80.6	90.4	86.1	39.9	31.7	52.4	33.7
1965	82.2	85.6	88.6	87.0	47.5	32.5	56.6	38.3
1966	87.4	83.1	90.3	87.6	46.3	30.3	59.0	38.6
1967	86.7	81.6	91.4	87.4	48.6	34.0	57.2	41.0
1968	88.5	84.3	92.1	89.4	53.1	38.6	61.5	41.3
1969	87.4	84.3	92.2	88.2	49.5	40.1	60.9	41.8
1970	85.4	85.9	92.2	89.0	41.3	38.9	55.6	41.8
1971	90.0	88.4	92.0	88.9	50.7	43.1	55.9	43.2
1972	88.9	90.1	90.4	87.3	47.7	38.7	51.5	41.9
1973	89.0	86.4	89.4	87.3	43.5	32.8	48.4	38.7
1974	90.1	84.2	88.2	87.6	46.1	42.1	45.5	39.9
1975	88.2	85.6	91.0	87.5	49.9	44.7	49.6	43.5
1976	90.9	87.0	90.6	87.7	54.9	46.4	46.9	44.0
1977	92.5	89.1	89.5	87.4	50.5	46.3	47.7	43.4
1978	92.8	89.6	88.9	88.4	50.5	42.4	47.2	42.7
1979	94.0	87.1	90.3	87.7	48.0	45.4	46.1	43.0

[a] 1960 data for blacks include "other races."

Source: U.S. Department of Commerce, Bureau of the Census, *School Enrollment—Social and Economic Characteristics of Students*, Series P–20 (Washington: GPO, annual).

tent truants. Because the rules in regard to state financial support to schools often are based on enrollments and attendance, schools have an incentive to retain absent students on the rolls for as long as possible. EER also fail to convey that a disproportionate number of blacks are overage in grade. In 1975, for example, almost half of the enrolled blacks 18–19 years old were in classes below college level, in contrast to only 18 percent of whites (US 1946–79 no. 294, Table 6). Similar results for 8 to 17-year-olds are shown for 1970–1977 (US 1975–80e, Tables 2.7, 2.8). Blacks still are relatively numerous among school dropouts; the sample drawn for the follow-up study of the high school class of 1972 revealed that the attrition rate for black males from kindergarten through twelfth grade had been higher than for the total (Peng, Stafford, and Talbert 1977, p. 11). Black girls have been more prone to drop out of high school than white girls. Childbearing is less disruptive to the education of black than white females, however (Hoeppner 1978; Mott and Shaw 1978; Waite and Moore 1978; Moore et al. 1979).

If official EER possibly exaggerate the educational advance of black secondary school students, an even greater overstatement of progress results from differences in the quality of education in various parts of the country. The relative inferiority of education in parts of the South and in the poverty areas of central cities is well known. It is chiefly borne by minority youth and impairs both their competence and credentials. The separation of high school students by curriculum, which influences academic performance and determines future educational and labor market careers, also is unfavorable to blacks; only one-fourth of blacks were in the preferred

Table 7.2 (continued)

| | 20-21 | | | | 22-24 | | | |
| | Black | | White | | Black | | White | |
Year	Male	Female	Male	Female	Male	Female	Male	Female
	(percent of relevant civilian noninstitutional population)							
1960[a]	13.7	10.4	29.2	13.5	6.3	2.8	16.3	3.5
1964	14.2	13.7	36.6	20.3	3.8	3.8	17.7	4.5
1965	18.5	8.0	39.9	20.9	4.3	7.8	23.3	6.3
1966	14.4	9.3	44.9	22.3	9.1	3.6	23.0	6.6
1967	24.5	18.5	46.9	25.6	9.0	5.6	22.0	7.5
1968	23.4	14.5	47.8	22.3	7.5	8.3	21.9	8.2
1969	28.4	19.6	48.9	25.8	10.7	6.9	24.2	9.4
1970	27.8	18.9	45.0	24.1	9.6	6.7	22.6	9.7
1971	31.3	24.1	39.7	27.0	12.9	10.1	24.6	8.1
1972	27.1	17.9	38.4	27.5	18.4	8.5	21.6	8.9
1973	24.5	17.3	35.7	27.4	13.9	11.1	19.6	9.9
1974	27.1	20.1	35.0	26.6	16.0	9.0	19.2	11.4
1975	28.7	25.8	36.3	27.5	14.7	13.8	20.5	12.2
1976	28.0	28.4	34.2	30.9	18.7	14.5	20.4	13.7
1977	31.0	28.2	34.7	29.0	18.5	12.6	19.4	13.3
1978	25.2	26.0	32.0	27.4	14.7	15.2	19.2	13.0
1979	26.9	30.0	32.2	30.0	14.6	15.3	17.6	13.9

academic program in the high school class of 1972, compared to half of the white students (Peng, Stafford, and Talbert 1977, p. 11). The awarding of high school diplomas for mere attendance became routine in some places, especially inner cities, leading the labor market to discount the value of the diploma and its bearer. In coming years, the smaller numbers in high school classes and the implementation of competency examinations may improve the situation. But thus far, quantitative achievement has outstripped the qualitative element in the high schools attended by a large part of minority youth.

EER of those 18–24 years old, which exclude students in trade or business schools, primarily reflect normal postsecondary education. Table 7.2, based on the civilian rather than the total population, indicates substantial gains in EER from 1960 to 1979 for all groups except white males, whose peak rates occurred in 1965–1971. If enrollment rates were calculated on a population base which included those in military service, male EER would drop even more, especially in the Vietnam years. The decrease would be greater for white than black males until 1973, and the reverse thereafter. By 1979 black progress was such that black EER exceeded or were the same as white rates for all but males 20–21 and 22–24. The most impressive increase was that of 22–24-year-old black females who, starting with 2.8 percent enrolled in 1960, showed an almost sixfold increase over 20 years (Table 7.2). A slackening of growth or even a decline in EER began in the 1970s; among 18–24-year-olds, only four age-sex-race groups out of twelve had higher rates in 1979 than in 1976; three of these groups were black.

Table 7.3   Enrollment Rates by Race, Age, Sex, and Household Income, United States, October 1977

Household income classes	Males 16-19		Females 16-19		Males 20-24		Females 20-24	
	Black	White	Black	White	Black	White	Black	White
				(percent)				
All[a]	76.3	74.2	76.4	79.0	32.6	39.6	35.4	45.8
Less than $5,000	65.3	61.8	71.9	66.1	27.8	23.5	36.2	32.5
$5,000-7,499	79.9	61.5	76.1	75.5	29.9	19.7	27.9	38.0
$7,500-9,999	78.3	65.5	77.1	72.8	39.0	29.2	31.5	35.5
$10,000-14,999	81.2	70.5	81.2	77.2	35.7	35.0	30.4	33.4
$15,000-24,999	83.5	76.5	74.4	79.7	41.7	35.9	39.8	43.2
$25,000 and more	87.2	85.4	82.6	86.3	32.4	54.7	65.0	58.5

[a] Includes some whose income was not reported.

Source: U.S. Department of Labor, Bureau of Labor Statistics, unpublished data.

Table 7.4   High School Graduates Entering College in the Year of
Graduation, by Race and National Origin, United
States, 1962–1979

Year	Total	Whites	Blacks	Spanish origin
		(percent)		
1962	49	51	34	n.a.
1963	45	46	38	n.a.
1964	48	49	39	n.a.
1965	51	52	43	n.a.
1966	50	52	32	n.a.
1967	52	53	42	n.a.
1968	55	57	46	n.a.
1969	54	55	37	n.a.
1970	52	52	48	n.a.
1971	53	54	47	n.a.
1972	49	49	48	45
1973	47	48	35	54
1974	48	47	51	47
1975	51	51	46	58
1976	49	49	48	53
1977	51	51	50	51
1978	50	50	46	43
1979	48	48	46	45

Source: U.S. Department of Labor, Bureau of Labor Statistics, *Students, Graduates and Dropouts in the Labor Market*, Special Labor Force Report no. 200, Table 4; no. 215, Table 3 (Washington: GPO, 1977, 1978); BLS, unpublished data.

Although never married young adults living at home constitute a minority of their age group, the EER for 20–24-year-olds from the unpublished October 1977 CPS survey, cited above, indicate how much household income influences EER for both races. Overall, 1977 EER were higher for 18–24-year-old blacks than whites in low- and middle-income families (US 1975–80d).

If EER for blacks and whites have reached a plateau, temporarily or for the longer run, they have done so at a time when racial differences have been much reduced. This is also shown by the proportion of June high school graduates of both sexes who were enrolled in college in October of the same year. Although the percentage has been roughly similar for the three main racial-ethnic groups since 1974 (Table 7.4), the black percentage rose sharply from 1962 to 1968 and with a few exceptions remained high thereafter, while the white percentage was at about the same level in 1979 as it had been in 1964. In the decade of the 1970s, the racial gap in educational attainment of 25–34-year-olds was cut in half. By 1979, 86 percent of whites and 73 percent of blacks had completed high school, while 25 percent of whites and about 13 percent of blacks had completed four or more years of college (US 1980a, p. 10).

The substantial increase in black enrollments above secondary level has not been reflected in the number of recipients of college and university degrees, however. Although blacks constituted 12.4 percent of the appropriate age group, they earned only 6.4 percent of the bachelor's degrees and even lower proportions of the master's, doctor's and first professional degrees in 1975–1976. Hispanic, American Indian, and Alaskan native youth were equally underrepresented, but Asian

Americans were overrepresented at every level, exceeding the white ratios (US 1975–80e, Table 6.5).

Rapid increase of postsecondary education in the minority groups is partially explained by special programs and financial aid and the growth of the two-year college, which provides a truncated, occupationally oriented education and is disproportionately attended by minority groups (Peng, Stafford, and Talbert 1977, p. 12; *NY Times* a). Expansion of the occupations which require a postsecondary credential, taken together with the factors cited above in reference to minority high school students, also have stimulated minority college enrollments. On balance, current near equality in EER has erased the racial differences which much earlier made it likely that labor force participation rates of black youth would exceed those of whites (Long 1958, pp. 148–49).

As in secondary education, doubts about the quality of some minority postsecondary education modify the finding of quantitative progress and unfavorably affect the equality of educational opportunity, as well as educational and labor market outcomes. The labor market position of blacks relative to whites has not improved as much as the closing of the gap in EER and educational attainment would suggest, on the assumption that level of education is related to labor market outcomes. Whatever measure is used—be it labor force participation rates, employment/ population ratios, unemployment rates, occupational prestige rankings, or earnings—young blacks with the same nominal educational attainment as whites have inferior labor market outcomes. In 1977, out-of-school blacks with four years or more of college had an unemployment rate of 15.1 percent, compared to the white rate of 5.7 percent (Swinton 1979, p. 20).

While the most educated black youth have made the most progress and have the narrowest differentials with whites on all indicators, the gap for others is still substantial. The causes of the gap are uncertain and debated. Recent analyses of the subjects and courses elected by black students in higher education suggests that their choices are less geared to labor market demand and financial rewards than those of white students (*NY Times* g). Others consider that racial discrimination accounts for much of the differential in labor market experience. Still others believe that comparisons of the races by years of education are meaningless because of qualitative differences in education and in the competence of the products of education by race. Finally, the optimists, observing the closing of the educational gap in recent years, offer the hope that it is only a matter of time until racial equality is reached in the labor market for those with identical years of educational achievement. Further study of this imperfectly understood racial differential is desirable in its own right and because it can perhaps prepare those in other countries whose faith in the instant benefits of educational equality has not yet been shaken.

Armed Forces

Trends in the black youth labor force and comparisons with whites deal separately with the armed forces and the civilian youth labor force because of changes in racial representation in the military in the postwar period, as well as the utilization by blacks in particular of enlistment in the armed forces as an alternative to unemployment or low wages.

While the white share of population in the armed forces exceeded the black until 1973, thereafter, with the introduction of the voluntary military service, the position was reversed in each age group (Table 7.5). Black dependence on the armed forces as

Table 7.5 Male Youth in the Armed Forces, by Race and Age, United States, 1964–1978

| | 18–19 | | 20–24 | |
	White	Black and other	White	Black and other
Year	(percent of relevant total noninstitutional population)			
1964	16.8	10.0	15.2	10.5
1966	11.5	7.5	19.5	14.4
1968	14.5	9.2	22.5	17.2
1970	10.2	7.3	20.2	15.6
1972	7.7	7.6	12.2	11.5
1974	7.7	10.2	8.8	11.4
1976	7.3	8.5	7.2	11.3
1978	6.2	9.4	6.7	11.5

Note: Data are annual averages.

Source: U.S. Department of Labor. Bureau of Labor Statistics, unpublished data.

an alternative to civilian labor force activity was greater than white in recent years when the relative employment of young blacks has worsened (Bowers 1979; Newman 1979; Swinton 1979; Freeman 1980b; Iden 1980; Wachter 1980). Without heavy black enlistment in the armed forces, unemployment rates and NISLF rates would have been still larger. The decline in the size of the armed forces since 1969 has been offset more for blacks than whites. Black teenagers maintained their share of population while black young adults had a decline from the peak, possibly contributing to their adverse position in the 1970s.

Illustrating in another way that the change from military conscription to an all-volunteer service in 1973 initiated a distinctly new and more favorable period for the black share of the armed forces, Table 7.6 shows, by age group, the black youth share of the total armed forces set beside the black share of the youth population. Prior to 1973, black males were consistently underrepresented in the armed forces and as a consequence had a relatively larger civilian population than whites. Because black male educational enrollment rates also were generally lower than white in this period, the added black civilian population had to be absorbed either in the labor force or in the NISLF category. Since 1973 the black share of the total armed forces in each age group, rising rapidly, has exceeded the black share of the relevant population. Furthermore, within the armed forces the balance of numbers between teenagers and young adults moved in favor of the teenagers. With a higher proportion of the black youth population than the white in the armed forces since 1973, the relative pressure on the black civilian labor force has been somewhat reduced, reinforcing the effects of the rise in black male educational enrollment rates which have caught up to and in some cases overtaken white male rates.

Civilian Labor Force

Since the 1950s the black male youth civilian labor force has increased, but less rapidly than white. This racial differential in labor force growth together with a

Table 7.6   Black and Other Races in Armed Forces as a Share of Total Armed Forces, by Age, United States, 1963–1979

Year	Males 18–19 Years Old		Both sexes 15–19	Males 20–24 Years Old		Both sexes 20–24
	Total in armed forces (annual average)	Share black and other of armed forces	Share black and other of all races civilian noninstitutional population[a]	Total in armed forces (annual average)	Share black and other of armed forces	Share black and other of all races civilian noninstitutional population[a]
	(000)	(percent)		(000)	(percent)	
1963	447	7.4	12.0	956	7.8	12.1
1964	449	7.6	12.2	950	8.1	12.1
1965	388	8.2	12.4	1032	8.5	12.1
1966	393	7.9	12.7	1318	8.8	12.1
1967	543	7.7	13.3	1502	9.0	11.8
1968	488	8.6	13.6	1718	9.1	12.0
1969	381	10.8	13.8	1807	9.8	12.3
1970	358	9.8	14.0	1670	9.7	12.5
1971	300	11.3	14.2	1414	10.5	12.8
1972	301	13.3	14.4	1100	11.6	13.3
1973	332	16.0	14.6	942	13.8	13.6
1974	328	17.7	14.9	853	16.1	13.8
1975	329	18.2	15.1	788	18.4	14.0
1976	317	16.4	15.3	755	19.5	14.2
1977	300	18.0	15.5	746	20.2	14.5
1978	282	20.9	15.7	748	21.5	14.7
1979	263	23.6	15.9	744	23.5	15.0

[a] As of July 1.

Source: U.S. Department of Labor, Bureau of Labor Statistics, unpublished data; Table 7.1.

widening excess of black over white youth unemployment rates may explain the finding of Freeman (1979a, 1980b) that the relative earnings of employed black male youth have been maintained while those of whites have fallen sharply. The increase in employment shown by white male youth was not duplicated by blacks. All young females show absolute labor force growth and a narrowing gap between themselves and comparable males. Black teenage females exhibited a less decided and strong upward movement than whites, while for young adults the situation was reversed (Table *A4.8a,b,c; *A7.2, A7.3, A7.4). Looking at the relative position, the black teenage share of the black working-age population was much larger than its share of the total black labor force (both sexes) and compares unfavorably with similar white shares, although these also show a considerable gap. On the other hand, black young adults of both sexes had a larger share of the black labor force than of the black working-age population and were better off in this regard than their white counterparts (Chart 7.1). In addition, black teenagers of both sexes had a lower share of their age group's labor force than of its population. But for young adults of both sexes, the black share of the youth labor force generally exceeded the black share of the population for the age group. These cross-sectional data for a specific historical period suggest a decided improvement in the labor market position for blacks as they age and leave the teenage period. A separation of data for the two sexes and

Chart 7.1   Youth Shares of Total Population (15–64) and Youth Shares of Civilian Labor Force (16 and older), by Race, Both Sexes, United States, 1945–1979

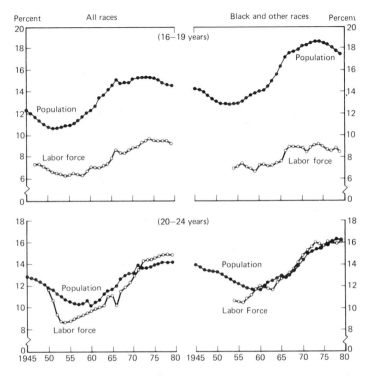

Source: Table 7.1; U.S. Department of Labor, Employment and Training Report of the President 1980, Tables A-3, A-4 and A-5 (Washington: GPO, 1980).

longitudinal information produce little advantage for the older black male youth, however, especially in recent years.

An overview of the postwar period can be obtained by a racial analysis of the components of change in the absolute youth labor force. Calculating the percentage change in the size of the youth labor force in five distinct five-year periods, Table 7.7 shows the allocation of that percentage change between two crucial factors, namely, changes in the size of population and changes in LFPR. In four of the five time periods, the size of the youth labor force grew in all eight age-sex-race groups, but more vigorously for all races than for blacks and others.

Only in the 1950–1955 period were there any declines in the size of the labor force. Reflecting the demands of the Korean War and demographic factors, all groups except teenage females showed a decrease in 1950–1955. Young adult males had a drop of more than 30 percent in 1950–1955, to which a decline in LFPR contributed very little and population change a great deal. In all of the succeeding periods, teenage males had positive labor force growth, ranging from a low of 9.0 percent for blacks and others in 1970–1975 to a high of 21.9 percent for all races in 1960–1965. Population growth was the overwhelming explanation, since LFPR declined for six of the eight separate entries (Table 7.7).

Table 7.7 Components of Change in the Youth Civilian Labor Force, by Race, Age, and Sex, United States, 1950–1975

	15–19						20–24					
	Change in labor force numbers		Attributable to:				Change in labor force numbers		Attributable to:			
			Population change		Change in labor force participation rate				Population change		Change in labor force participation rate	
Years	Male	Female	Male	Female	Male	Female	Male	Female	Male	Female	Male	Female
						(percent)						
1950–1955												
All Races	-5.4	0.7	1.5	2.7	-6.9	-2.0	-30.5	-8.6	-29.2	-8.4	-1.3	-0.2
Black & other	n.a.	n.a.	n.a.	n.a.	n.a.	n.a.	n.a.	n.a.	n.a.	n.a.	n.a.	n.a.
1955–1960												
All races	17.6	19.2	22.1	20.2	-4.5	-1.0	28.0	5.5	26.5	5.1	1.5	0.4
Black & other	12.8	17.0	18.0	16.7	-5.2	0.3	34.6	14.7	34.0	10.1	0.6	4.6
1960–1965												
All races	21.9	22.3	25.8	25.5	-3.9	-3.2	18.7	30.4	21.2	21.7	-2.5	8.7
Black & other	12.7	15.5	21.5	24.1	-8.8	-8.6	8.9	29.0	9.3	15.0	-0.4	14.0
1965–1970												
All races	17.9	29.0	13.4	12.2	4.5	16.8	16.7	44.9	19.5	27.8	-2.8	17.1
Black & other	14.3	42.7	21.4	25.7	-7.1	17.0	18.1	38.3	24.5	33.6	-6.4	4.7
1970–1975												
All races	18.9	24.6	13.2	12.3	5.7	12.3	29.6	24.5	28.0	12.7	1.6	11.8
Black & other	9.0	26.5	16.7	21.9	-7.7	4.6	19.6	22.9	25.2	25.4	-5.6	-2.5

Note: The method used in this calculation provides for allocation of the interaction between the terms.

Source: Tables *A2.6, *A2.7, A7.3, A7.4; U.S. Department of Labor, *Employment and Training Report of the President*, 1979, Tables A–3 and A–4 (Washington: GPO, 1979).

Teenage females, recording stronger labor force growth than teenage males, showed the black females ahead in recent years. Population growth again was the more important factor, but both racial groups also recorded substantial advances in LFPR. In fact, in 1965–1970 the rise for teenage females of all races was due more to growth in LFPR than in population, the only such instance in the entire period for all groups. Among young adults (20–24) in both racial groups, females displayed larger LFPR growth for the most part than males and almost none of the negative LFPR influence that males showed, in five of the eight entries. For both age groups, the changes in LFPR were a greater drag on black than white male labor force growth and less of a stimulus for black than white females in most cases (Table 7.7).

Trends in LFPR for blacks and whites also can be considered separately. Lower black youth labor force participation rates (LFPR) are a postwar phenomenon, since the record from 1890 to 1950 showed black youth rates greater than white at each censal count (Long 1958, pp. 149, 252). Black migration out of the rural South and detachment from agriculture probably account for much of the decline. The advantage of rural areas for black youth persists to the present day. In 1977 black teenagers living in the nonmetropolitan areas had higher LFPR than those living in central cities or suburbs (Swinton 1979, Table 14).

In the postwar period, the level of LFPR for each youth age-sex group was lower for blacks than for all races (Chart 7.2), but the gap between male and female LFPR was substantially narrowed for blacks as well as whites. Teenage LFPR exhibit greater racial divergence than those of young adults. Starting at a lower level, black female teenagers had less growth in LFPR since 1965 than whites. Since 1960, 20–24-year-old females of both races experienced considerable growth in LFPR; but while whites moved ahead briskly throughout, blacks advanced little between 1965 and 1975, showing a rise thereafter. Racial differences in the levels and trends of LFPR of males are striking. While for all of the male groups LFPR in the last years was lower than in the initial years, the two black groups displayed no sign of the upward turn shown in the mid-1960s by the white groups, which was particularly marked among white teenagers.

Important racial variations emerge when the LFPR of students are separated from those of out-of-school youth. In the case of white males, the overall rise in LFPR since the mid-1960s has been mainly attributable to the surge in the LFPR of the enrolled, who constituted a rising proportion of the age group until recently. For the white male nonenrolled, LFPR dropped over the thirty-year period in both youth age groups, most markedly among 16–17-year-old dropouts, who increasingly constituted a residual disadvantaged group as their contemporaries remained in full-time education. An overall decline in black male LFPR occurred because black enrolled males, an even faster-growing percentage of all black males in the age group during most of the period than was the case for white male enrolled, increased their LFPR much less than whites. It was not enough to offset the sharp decline, especially among teenagers, in the LFPR of the black nonenrolled.

Although the racial gap was less pronounced than among males, females also showed an enrollment effect. White females as a whole had striking gains in LFPR, particularly large for enrolled teenagers and 22–24-year-olds and for nonenrolled 20–21-year-olds. Black females had a more mixed picture. Black enrolled females had declines in LFPR for 16–17-year-olds but level or rising rates for the enrolled in other age groups. Among black out-of-school females, LFPR for 18–19-year-olds did not change much, fluctuating between 55 and 60 percent over most of the period;

Chart 7.2   Youth Participation Rates in Civilian Labor Force, by Race, Age, and Sex, United States, 1950–1979

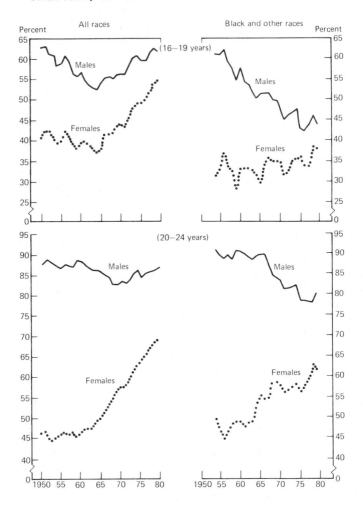

Source: U.S. Department of Labor, Employment and Training Report of the President 1980, Tables A-3, A-4 and A-5 (Washington: GPO, 1980).

but the 20–24-year-old group showed a substantial long-run rise in LFPR, marked by considerable year-to-year variation.

Unpublished data from a special survey in October 1977 indicated that the overall LFPR of black enrolled never married youth living at home in four age-sex groups was much lower than that of similar white enrolled. Black males in the highest family income bracket, $25,000 and over, had higher LFPR than similar white males, however; comparable black females remained well below the whites (Table A7.5). With some exceptions, notably white females aged 20–24, the LFPR of students in both races tended to rise as family income increased, up to $25,000. The possibility of failure to report labor force activity among those enrolled in school and living at home should be considered, especially in the lowest income classes. But it is likely that substantially fewer black than white students were in the labor force at every income level, after all possible adjustments. There is a puzzle here, especially when comparison is made with the LFPR of enrolled youth living on their own (Table A7.5).

Youth living on their own who were enrolled in school formed a disproportionately small share of all enrolled, since living with parents or other older household head increased the chance that a young person would be enrolled. Of those whites who were enrolled and living on their own, the LFPR tended to rise with household income up to $25,000, whereupon the LFPR fell off sharply except for females 20–24. Apparently for the other three age-sex groups, a household income of $25,000 or over greatly diminished the need to work while attending school. Black enrolled youth living on their own had more erratic LFPR patterns according to household income, but the whole group generally matched white LFPR rates fairly closely, with some classes showing LFPR of 100 percent (Table A7.5).

The average family income of black enrolled youth who were not in the labor force was, in almost every case, markedly lower than that of their black counterparts who were in school and in the labor force, whether employed or unemployed. In the case of white enrolled youth, the differences were small between the family incomes of those not in the labor force, those who were employed and those who were unemployed, but the last group had slightly lower incomes. In all categories white family incomes averaged at least twice that of black. Youth living on their own had much lower incomes than their counterparts living with parents (Table A7.6). *Table A7.1 indicates slightly different relationships for nonenrolled youth in regard to average family income.

Nonenrolled, never married, black youth living at home showed a tendency to have higher LFPR as their family income rose, but the LFPR levels were lower than those of corresponding whites (Table A7.8). As in the case of whites, the LFPR of nonenrolled blacks were much higher than the LFPR of black enrolled youth. Again, there is the puzzle that while nonenrolled black LFPR behave in the same general way as nonenrolled white as household income rises, at each income level white LFPR is much higher. It is mysterious enough that such regularity should exist between income levels and LFPR and that it should run counter to the commonsense expectation that the poorer the household, the higher the LFPR of its nonenrolled youth. But there is no easy explanation for the consistently lower black LFPR. The same considerations apply to the discussion below on the higher black NISLF rates. The puzzle is compounded because white and black nonenrolled youth living on their own had quite similar LFPR overall and by income levels; in several cases the black rates were higher (Table A7.8). Young adults living on their own were the majority of the age group for both whites and blacks, giving more importance to the similarity of their LFPR among the nonenrolled. There almost is a suggestion that a black household head or the extended family is more willing to tolerate low LFPR than a white unit. Further investigation of these differences is needed together with the matching findings on NISLF, discussed below.

In seeking explanations of the divergent movements of LFPR of black and white youth in the postwar period, one may first cite the benign causes. A reduction in black LFPR would have been expected because of the pace of increase in black EER. It is also possible that the tendency of the LFPR of the black enrolled students to fall or rise much less than comparable white LFPR may be partially due to relatively plentiful financial aid to black students and other inducements to concentrate on schoolwork, reducing their need or ability to work while at school. However, to the extent that black students remained out of the labor force because they felt that jobs were not available, they were disadvantaged versus whites (Bowen and Finegan 1969, pp. 401–6; Iden 1980, p. 14).

The persistent racial gap in the LFPR of male nonenrolled and the strong downward trend for black males compared to the mild white decline, as well as the lesser difference between white and black females, suggest a variety of explanatory factors. Geographic difference in residence patterns between the races have been unfavorable to blacks in regard to gaining basic skills and finding attractive employment possibilities. The observed lower LFPR in these areas weigh more heavily in black national averages than in white because of the geographic distribution of the respective populations.

Family structure and income are variables that relate positively to the LFPR of young people, whether enrolled or nonenrolled, although the influence may be partially through educational attainment as affected by parental attainment and household income. Given the much lower average black family income, and the fact that more individuals may share a given income among blacks, it is possible that the lower level of black LFPR is explained in part by income differences between the races.

Finally, a series of factors—high unemployment, discouragement, alternative sources of income—may depress black youth LFPR by swelling the group which is neither in school nor in the labor force (NISLF).

Not in School or the Labor Force

Bearing in mind the general discussion in Chapter 6 of the difficulties of establishing the boundaries between those who are unemployed, those who want to work but are not searching, and those who do not want to work, official data on racial differences in NISLF rates are bound to be disturbing. A higher proportion of black than white youth consistently are not in school or the labor force (NISLF). This finding in both cross-sectional and longitudinal surveys raises serious questions about the excess black proportion. The analysis in the preceding chapter shows that some out-of-school youth always will be out of the labor force, for understandable and acceptable reasons. It is possible that the proportion of the black youth population that has been NISLF for such acceptable reasons as serious illness, handicaps, or household responsibilities runs higher than for whites. Other aspects of demographic composition and family income also may tend to raise black NISLF rates. To obtain racial equality in the incidence of these conditions requires a range of social policies beyond the purview of labor market policy.

Part of the NISLF group of each race is in that status for labor market reasons. Some NISLF youth are identifiable as discouraged workers or youth suffering from extended unemployment (Clark and Summers 1979a) or as youth with a weak attachment to the labor market (Feldstein and Ellwood 1979). Therefore, if a larger percentage of black male youth than white is regularly counted as NISLF and if the female differential is not largely attributable to home duties, it is a matter for social concern, especially since the previous chapter indicated that the overall American proportion in this category has been large compared to other countries (Bowen and Finegan 1969, pp. 416–18).

Black male youth, divided into three age groups, have regularly had a higher

Table 7.8   Young Males Not in School or the Total Labor Force, by Race and Age, United States, October 1964–1978

Year		16–17	18–19	20–24
		(percent of relevant total noninstitutional population)		
1964	White	2.4	3.1	2.0
	Black and other	5.9	5.2	4.6
1966	White	2.3	3.9	1.1
	Black and other	5.2	7.1	2.9
1968	White	2.0	4.1	2.9
	Black and other	4.9	5.8	4.4
1970	White	1.6	4.4	2.6
	Black and other	5.5	12.6	6.6
1972	White	2.3	˙4.0	2.8
	Black and other	3.1	8.8	6.5
1974	White	2.4	5.0	2.8
	Black and other	2.7	6.1	5.4
1976	White	2.2	4.5	3.0
	Black and other	4.0	9.9	10.3
1978	White	2.9	3.0	3.1
	Black and other	3.4	8.9	7.9

Source: U.S. Department of Labor, Bureau of Labor Statistics, *Employment of School Age Youth*, Special Labor Force Reports; *Students, Graduates and Dropouts in the Labor Market*, Special Labor Force Reports (Washington: GPO, annual); BLS unpublished data.

NISLF proportion than similar white males; these cross-sectional calculations use total population as the base, including members of the armed forces as part of the labor force (Table 7.8). NISLF rates for 18–19-year-olds and 20–24-year-olds in each racial group often were higher than for 16–17-year-olds, especially in more recent years. Over time, the margin between the two races widened for 18–19 and 20–24-year-old males. In contrast, the racial gap narrowed for the 16–17 year-olds because the black NISLF percentage declined over the years with the rise in EER, while the white NISLF proportion remained more or less stable. Significantly, the proportion of black NISLF youth increased markedly in the two older age groups, but NISLF rates for white youth in these age groups show variability over time rather than any clear trend (Table 7.8; Bowers, N. 1979, pp. 6–9; Young 1979, pp. 35–36). This development reflects a worsened labor market position over time for older black males vis-à-vis whites of the same age, as well as versus younger blacks. Employment/population ratios describe the same changes, in part caused by demographic trends. In longitudinal surveys showing the percentage of a sample with time out of the labor force in a given year, black youth also exceed white, but the racial gap is somewhat smaller than in cross-sectional surveys such as the CPS (Appendix 7:1; Adams and Mangum 1978; Borus, Mott, and Nestel 1978; Meyer and Wise 1979; MDRC 1979).

When the out-of-school population is the base for calculating the NISLF rate, much wider differentials appear between the races. For example, in the CPS survey for October 1976, white teenage males had a NISLF rate of 11.5 percent while non-whites had 27.8 percent (Feldstein and Ellwood 1979, p. 20). Since EER for teenage males were virtually the same for the two races at this time, one cannot accept the explanation that a residual disadvantaged NISLF group with weak labor force attachment is left when EER rise relatively high. This explanation fails to explain the much higher nonwhite NISLF rate, unless there are substantial differences in composition of the racial residual groups.

The reasons for being NISLF are available from the CPS survey for male youth in each race. They show a dominance of the miscellaneous "other reasons" in all cases. This unhelpful finding merely confirms that neither household responsibility nor physical or mental inability to work has been cited by respondents to the labor force survey as a major cause for male abstention from both labor force and educational participation, although black male youth have been more likely than white to report these two specific, inhibiting reasons. Objections may be offered to analyses based on responses to questionnaires, especially if the respondents are family members rather than the individual concerned, and if the nature of the questions is to place the onus on the individual, thus absolving the economy and society of differential treatment among racial groups. Still, such series are useful for the consistent differences and trends they reveal. It would therefore be desirable to include a greater number and variety of reasons in statistics disaggregated by age, sex, and race.

As was expected, larger proportions of females than males in each racial group are likely to be NISLF, due to the females' greater household responsibilities. Lower white female NISLF rates probably are associated with lower fertility rates. Like white females, black females show a distinct and unbroken downward trend over time in the NISLF proportion (Table 7.9). The rate of decrease has been roughly similar for 16–17-year-old females of each race, but among 18–19 and 20–24-year-old females, the white rate of decrease has been sharper. Among the youngest females (16–17) in both racial groups, the drop in the NISLF proportion is largely attributable to the decreasing share citing household responsibilities, with a greater drop in the black than the white proportion. At present, "other" reasons outweigh household responsibilities for both races. In the 18–19-year group, household responsibilities, though falling sharply for both groups, continue to be a more important explanation than "other" reasons, which have constituted a rising proportion of the explanation for both racial groups, especially for blacks.

Females 20–24 years old of both races who are NISLF attribute their status almost entirely to the pressure of household responsibilities. Until 1972, the proportion of NISLF black females in this age group was smaller than the proportion of whites, reflecting the historically greater commitment to the labor force of black women (Long 1958). The slight reversal of position from 1972 onward is due to a more rapid increase of blacks in the "other reasons" category and a more rapid drop in the percentage of whites in the "household responsibilities" category. For both races and all age groups, Table 7.9 indirectly points to the movement of females from non-market work at home to paid employment, job search, and additional education, confirming the direct evidence in earlier chapters.

Reasons for being NISLF, according to the respondents to the CPS survey, are available from an additional series that consolidates the two youth age groups and two sexes but gives separate annual average data by race. This series, published in *Employment and Earnings*, reveals that for the majority of young people in both racial groups who were NISLF, a lack of suitable jobs was not a major reason. While the "discouraged worker" phenomenon appears not to be a major factor for either racial group, it has been more important for blacks than whites. Annual averages may understate the share of the discouraged, however, since many of the in-school population who take the summer period as vacation are recorded as NISLF in the CPS survey when they should in fact be regarded as in school.

Over four-fifths of 16–24-year-old whites who were NISLF in 1978 did not want

Table 7.9 Young Females Not in School or the Labor Force, by Race, Age, and Reason, United States, 1962–1978

Year		16-17			18-19			20-24		
		Total all reasons	Household responsibilities	All other reasons	Total all reasons	Household responsibilities	All other reasons	Total all reasons	Household responsibilities	All other reasons
		(percent of civilian noninstitutional population)								
1962	White	20.4	10.0	10.4	25.0	21.2	3.8	48.3	47.0	1.3
	Black and other	26.8	15.0	11.8	35.2	29.8	5.4	47.3	45.0	2.3
1964	White	18.8	7.9	10.9	25.7	20.9	4.8	45.5	43.8	1.7
	Black and other	23.5	11.3	12.2	33.7	28.3	5.4	41.7	39.3	2.4
1966	White	17.3	6.7	10.6	22.3	17.8	4.5	43.1	41.2	1.9
	Black and other	21.3	10.1	11.2	29.7	25.5	4.2	39.6	39.0	0.6
1968	White	16.4	6.7	9.7	20.7	15.8	4.9	38.8	36.9	1.9
	Black and other	20.2	10.3	9.9	29.1	22.4	6.7	35.8	33.1	2.7
1970	White	16.1	6.5	9.6	21.1	16.3	4.8	35.8	33.6	2.2
	Black and other	18.6	8.3	10.3	28.8	22.0	6.8	35.3	32.4	2.9
1972	White	15.4	6.4	9.0	19.9	15.3	4.6	33.8	31.9	1.9
	Black and other	18.6	8.9	9.7	27.9	21.4	6.5	34.4	31.1	3.3
1974	White	15.0	5.9	9.1	19.5	14.5	5.0	29.3	27.0	2.3
	Black and other	18.8	8.4	10.4	29.6	22.1	7.5	34.0	29.8	4.2
1976	White	14.5	5.4	9.1	17.6	12.7	4.9	26.6	24.0	2.6
	Black and other	18.0	6.2	11.8	26.0	17.0	9.0	32.7	27.8	4.9
1978	White	13.0	5.0	7.9	16.2	11.4	4.8	23.7	20.8	2.9
	Black and other	17.0	6.9	10.1	25.2	16.2	9.0	27.8	23.1	4.7

Note: Data are annual averages.

Source: U.S. Department of Labor, Bureau of Labor Statistics, unpublished data.

jobs (because of illness, disability, household responsibilities, or other reasons). Less than 4 percent wanted a job but did not search because they thought they could not find work; they met the definition of discouraged workers. The remainder, 13.8 percent, wanted a job but did not search for the same set of reasons that kept the majority from wanting a job. Among the 16–24-year-old blacks who were NISLF, under two-thirds, less than the white percentage, did not wish to work at that time for the usual list of reasons. Some 12.6 percent were discouraged workers; this was more than three times the white proportion. The remaining 24.6 percent, almost twice the white percentage, desired jobs but did not search because of illness, disability, household responsibilities, or other reasons.

These 1978 results by race are similar to those for earlier years, which show higher proportions of black than of white youth wanting to work but feeling discouraged or facing circumstances which prevent job search (US 1971–80e, Table 40; Wool 1978, pp. 51–55). The association between high levels of reported youth unemployment and relatively large proportions of young people who want to work or are discouraged, reported earlier in the cross-national analysis, appears to hold also for the American racial analysis.

Over and above the effects of an unfavorable opportunity structure, some authors claim that racial differences in the NISLF percentages may be explained in part by the disproportionate involvement of black youth in situations that have been called "dysfunctional life styles" (Mangum and Seninger 1978, Chap. 4). Inadequate family structure and role models, crowded and deteriorated housing, poverty-stricken neighborhoods, poor health, high rates of crime, drug and alcohol addiction, and unemployment among local populations – all may be deterrents to strong labor force attachment. They also may lead employers to attach labels to whole groups (Osterman 1978, 1979).

Some youth activities are counterproductive for labor force participation. Acquisition of a police record interferes with career development. School failure and drug or alcohol addiction foster adverse attitudes toward work. Early child-bearing, in or out of wedlock, discourages girls from pursuing education or seeking jobs. Those who engage in hustling or illicit street crime, often beginning at an early age before "regular" jobs are available, may never develop a taste for such jobs, displaying an impeccable economic calculus of effort and reward. These realities, more relevant to inner-city minority youth than to others, may explain a part of the excess proportion of NISLF blacks (Twentieth Century Fund 1971; Friedlander 1972; Bullock 1973; Mangum and Seninger 1978; Mott and Shaw 1978; Newsweek 1978; Standing 1978, pp. 123–34, 126–37; Anderson, E. 1980).

Educational attainment differences by race may play a role in NISLF rate divergence. An analysis of nonemployment rates in 1976 indicates that at each educational level, black rates were higher than white for male teenagers and young adults (Feldstein and Ellwood 1979). Holding educational attainment constant, both blacks and whites showed decreased nonemployment in the 20–24-year group, but the disadvantage of dropouts continued for whites and blacks. This finding has been interpreted as a warning that those in both races with weak academic achievement will continue to have labor market problems as they age.

The usual cross-sectional finding is that NISLF rates for males decline with age. This is due in part at least to changes in the educational composition of the out-of-school group. The 16–17-year-olds are largely high school dropouts, while in the 18–19-year group, high school graduates predominate; the educational composition of the 20–24 year group is enriched by the addition of two-year and four-year college graduates plus college dropouts. What is attributed to aging by itself may reflect increased average educational attainment and the propensity of each race to show lower NISLF rates with rising educational attainment, irrespective of age (Feldstein and Ellwood 1979). Yet cross-sectional data over time in Table 7.8 suggest that even the assumed cross-sectional aging effect is absent, since the older groups do not have the lowest NISLF rates at all times. Longitudinal surveys which show decreases in NISLF with age may be reflecting increased education as well as maturation (MDRC 1979, p. 103; Meyer and Wise 1979).

To what extent do higher black than white male NISLF rates reflect greater tolerance among blacks for such status? One also wonders how differences in the proportions of youth living with and apart from their elders influence racial differences in NISLF rates. If living away from the family is assumed to foster economic independence, then it would be expected that the race with the higher proportion living at home would have a factor tending to increase its NISLF rate. This discussion can be seen as another aspect of social differences in the LFPR of the nonenrolled.

According to unpublished BLS data for October 1977, black never married youth living at home constituted a higher proportion than similar whites of their respective populations. Never married black male teenagers living at home constituted 95.1 percent, while similar white males made up 92.5 percent of the respective age group. For teenage females, the black percentage was 87.4 percent and the white 79.8. Similar differences characterize young adults. For males, never married blacks living at home accounted for 56.2 percent of the total age group, while for whites it was 44.1 percent. Black never married females living at home registered 42.5 percent, but for the same group of whites it was only 27.9 percent. Blacks as well as whites in each age-sex group showed a strong tendency for the proportion never married and living at home to increase as the level of family income rose. Most extreme was the situation for young adult females. In families with less than $5,000 annual income, 7.7 percent of white and 29.5 percent of black 20–24-year-old females were never married and living at home. But at $25,000 or more annual income, the white share rose to 75.1 and the black to 87.0 percent.

Some of the racial divergence in youth NISLF rates may be explained by racial differences in family income and in income structure. Unpublished CPS data for October 1977 make clear that NISLF youth in both races come from considerably lower income families, on average, than the other nonenrolled categories (the employed and the unemployed) or than all youth (including the enrolled) (Tables A7.6, A7.7). In every case, the income levels of black youth are much lower than those of whites. The situation is the same for the "all other youth" category, which covers youth living away from home and even married youth living at home. The "all other youth" category is minor for teenagers of both races, but is very important for all young adults because it includes a majority of the whites and black females and a substantial share of black males (Tables A7.6, A7.7).

As further evidence that the less families seem able to finance inactivity, the higher is the NISLF rate, Table 7.10 indicates a fairly consistent pattern of declining NISLF rates as income rises for both races in all age-sex groups, especially among the never married youth living at home. In all age-sex groups, average black NISLF rates exceed white for never married youth living at home. NISLF rates for teenagers living on their own are very similar for the two races, but refer to relatively few young people. This category is far more significant for young adults. Young male adults living on their own had lower overall NISLF rates for blacks than whites; cases are too

Table 7.10 NISLF Youth as a Percent of Civilian Youth Population, by Race, Age, Sex, Living Arrangements, and Household Income, United States, October 1977

Never married youth living at home

	16–19 Years				20–24 Years			
	White		Black		White		Black	
Income classes	Male	Female	Male	Female	Male	Female	Male	Female
	(percent)							
All classes[a]	2.2	3.3	4.7	9.5	4.5	5.3	10.0	8.0
Less than $5,000	6.0	16.7	8.4	14.6	13.1	21.7	17.9	8.4
$5,000–7,499	4.7	6.2	5.4	14.2	14.1	8.0	7.7	11.7
$7,500–9,999	4.7	6.6	2.5	4.2	6.6	10.0	15.3	9.9
$10,000–14,999	2.4	3.3	3.5	4.0	2.9	7.3	9.6	6.7
$15,000–24,999	1.7	1.6	1.4	4.0	3.4	3.0	1.4	2.7
$25,000 and more	0.4	1.1	*	*	2.3	2.0	*	*
	All other youth							
	(percent)							
All classes[a]	2.2	33.7	0	34.7	1.2	21.1	4.4	33.3
Less than $5,000	3.8	33.0	0	34.9	2.1	26.5	9.2	40.8
$5,000–7,499	3.3	40.0	0	37.5	2.0	29.4	*	30.7
$7,500–9,999	*	37.2	0	*	1.3	32.4	11.8	22.4
$10,000–14,999	*	33.0	0	25.0	0.7	31.3	*	29.9
$15,000–24,999	*	25.2	0	28.6	0.6	22.9	*	19.3
$25,000 and more	11.8	0	0	*	0	17.3	*	*

[a] Includes income not reported.

Note: Asterisk * indicates less than 1,000 NISLF youth.

Source: U.S. Depatment of Labor. Bureau of Labor Statistics, unpublished tables from the October 1977 Current Population Survey.

limited to analyze blacks by income class. Young adult black females had higher overall NISLF rates than whites, as well as higher rates in the significant lowest income classes, but lower rates in the income classes beginning at $7,500 per year (Table 7.10).

A comparison of the NISLF rates of male youth living at home and those living on their own shows that white teenagers have the same overall rate, but for the other three race-age groups, those living on their own have considerably lower rates, as expected. Comparisons across the individual income classes are not valid because of the small number of NISLF youth living on their own, especially for blacks. Females of both age groups and races, never married and living at home, have much lower NISLF rates and a steeper decline as household income rises than females living away from home. Many of the latter are involved in child care. NISLF rates decline equally for both races for females living away from the parental home, but less markedly in all cases than for never married females living at home (Table 7.10).

Higher black than white NISLF rates at the same income levels also raise the possibility of other explanatory factors, such as variations in educational attainment at different income levels, which may be as or more responsible for NISLF rate differences by income than the income differences themselves. Chapter 6 demonstrated for all U.S. youth that the lower the educational attainment level, the greater the propensity to NISLF status. Thus it is not surprising to find that among never married NISLF teenagers living at home, a majority in both races, in all income classes, and in both sexes had completed less than four years of high school (Table 7.11). For the age group as a whole a majority had completed high school. Overall, black teenage NISLF males had a higher proportion without four years of high school than similar whites, but for females the racial situation was reversed. While the proportions with less than four years of high school among NISLF youth declined quite regularly as income rose for white teenagers of both sexes, for blacks no clear trend was visible (Table 7.11).

Among never married NISLF young adults living at home, well under half of the whites, but about half of black females and two-thirds of males, had not completed four years of high school (Table 7.11). Moreover, the white proportions with less than four years of high school tended to drop with a rise in family income, though not so regularly as for white teenagers. But the black proportions moved irregularly, suggesting that NISLF never married youth living at home who had not completed four years of high school were an important part of the total NISLF group at virtually all income levels.

Among the relatively smaller male NISLF population living on their own, white teenagers who had not completed four years of high school constituted a larger share of their NISLF group than was true of NISLF white teenage males living at home. In all other age-race groups, NISLF males living on their own had much lower proportions whose educational attainment did not reach high school graduation than those living at home. The lower overall NISLF rates of the males living away from home is apparently less associated with low educational attainment than is true for those living at home. Also, black NISLF teenage and young adult males living away from home were less prone than similar whites to have low educational attainment, judging by the proportions of NISLF not completing four years of high school.

NISLF females living at home had lower proportions with less than four years of high school than those living on their own in the case of all age-race groups except white young adults. Black female NISLF fractions with low school attainment were higher than white in both age groups for those living on their own. The association

Table 7.11   NISLF Youth with Less than Four Years of High School as a Percent of All NISLF Youth, by Race, Age, Sex, Living Arrangements, and Household Income, United States, October 1977

Never married youth living at home

| | 16-19 Years | | | | 20-24 Years | | | |
| | White | | Black | | White | | Black | |
Income classes	Male	Female	Male	Female	Male	Female	Male	Female
				(percent)				
All classes[a]	58.9	62.9	75.0	57.7	36.7	38.9	65.5	49.5
Less than $5,000	84.2	81.4	70.8	71.0	75.0	72.2	59.3	62.5
$5,000–7,499	85.0	80.8	90.0	56.3	71.4	75.0	77.8	41.4
$7,500–9,999	75.0	69.6	33.3	50.0	14.3	54.5	77.8	23.1
$10,000–14,999	51.7	50.0	66.7	62.5	56.3	56.7	72.7	50.0
$15,000–24,999	40.0	48.3	100.0	*	16.2	9.5	*	50.0
$25,000 and more	33.3	23.1	*	*	*	*	*	*
				All other youth				
				(percent)				
All classes[a]	75.0	65.8	0	70.6	26.7	32.1	10.0	50.4
Less than $5,000	50.0	75.9	0	82.7	43.8	13.7	15.4	62.3
$5,000–7,499	100.0	67.5	0	75.0	26.7	47.3	*	47.6
$7,500–9,999	*	60.3	0	*	11.1	36.0	*	47.1
$10,000–14,999	*	49.3	0	100.0	11.1	20.5	*	30.4
$15,000–24,999	*	48.3	0	50.0	50.0	15.3	*	18.2
$25,000 and more	100.0	0	0	*	0	11.4	*	*

[a] Includes income not reported.

Note: Asterisk * indicates less than 1,000 NISLF youth.

Source: U.S. Depatment of Labor. Bureau of Labor Statistics, unpublished tables from the October 1977 Current Population Survey.

between low educational attainment, low household income, early child-bearing, and NISLF status implied in these data could usefully be explored further and in other national settings.

Evidence from the unpublished data for October 1977 suggests that the persistently higher black than white NISLF rates are due to a greater propensity of black male youth to live at home, the higher proportions of black youth who do not complete four years of high school, and the greater concentration of black youth in poverty families. Further investigation is required of racial differences in size of families and composition; the relation between marital status, living at home and NISLF; and other psycho-social aspects of attitudes toward NISLF status. Other questions needing study are racial differences in the way NISLF youth spend their time, the structure of families at various income levels, and divergent behavior of male and female youth.

Feldstein and Ellwood (1979, pp. 22–25) adjusted nonemployment rates (nonenrolled unemployment + NISLF) for teenage boys in October 1976 so that they represented 48 nonoverlapping subgroups of whites and nonwhites with identical age, schooling, and family income. Using this information, they calculated how much of the overall racial difference in nonemployment rates was due to demographic composition and how much was due to racial differences in nonemployment rates in the 48 subgroups. Application of the white demographic composition to nonwhites results in a decline in the nonwhite nonemployment rate from 57.1 to 46.9 percent, a 33 percent decrease in the racial gap in nonemployment rates. But application of the nonwhite weights to white nonemployment rates raised the white rate from 25.9 to 32.5 percent, leaving a large gap to the 57.1 percent rate of nonwhites. Even limited demographic factors thus account for a considerable part of the racial difference, but changing the weight is more important for the non-whites.

It has been suggested that welfare and other income maintenance payments, disproportionately received by young black women and by black families, encourage NISLF status by such young women and by young family members (because payments to the family are reduced by the amount of the earnings of all members). Although anecdotal evidence is plentiful and theorists affirm it (Cain 1977, p. 13), no clear-cut evidence exists that the availability of government transfer payments accounts for the higher NISLF rates of black young mothers (Mott 1978; Bowers, N. 1979, p. 10; Ehrenberg 1979a,b). To the extent that those receiving welfare payments are required to register as unemployed, the recipients are counted in the labor force and are not NISLF. Moreover, the WIN program for welfare mothers has financed a return to school for some young female AFDC recipients, again reducing the impact on the number in the NISLF category.

Two caveats should be entered about young males. First, a limited deterrence to labor force participation does arise from the terms of welfare payments, which increase the total family allowance for a family member enrolled in school up to a stipulated cut-off age. This, however, requires enrollment in school and is not an encouragement to NISLF status. Second, in order to avoid a reduction of the welfare payment by amounts earned, out-of-school youth living in welfare families may hold jobs but fail to report earnings. Since many adult welfare recipients are known to be working "off the books," it seems probable that young people in such families do the same. Therefore, the actual increase in NISLF persons attributable to income transfers may be smaller than the reported increase (Clark and Summers 1978c).

The salient question may be whether official surveys can or do sample this group adequately. The omissions may more than offset concealed labor force activity among those actually sampled. It is possible that racial differences in NISLF rates are even larger than our tables show. But in any case, the persistence of higher black than white NISLF rates in social records and the generally higher U.S. rates compared with other countries require more explanation than has yet been furnished.

In summary, the black youth population and labor force faced multiple disadvantages in the postwar period. Black youth cohorts grew faster than white cohorts, due to higher birth rates. According to the vigor and expansiveness of the economy, such growth might have provided a potential source of needed additional labor, or it could produce a social problem. In American circumstances, the latter effect has been more noticeable. Demographic differences have been intensified by the geographic distribution of population and the lower family incomes of blacks. Until recent years, black educational enrollment rates and participation in the armed forces were relatively lower than white, albeit EER increased more rapidly for blacks than whites. In addition, while the black civilian labor force grew, labor force participation rates for black males declined over the whole period, and the racial gap widened in recent years as white participation rates rose because of the labor force activity of students.

Taken together with the fact that black youth have held a disproportionately small share of employment, resulting in a widened racial disparity in youth unemployment rates, the adverse trend in LFPR for black males intensifies racial disadvantage in the youth labor market. Part of the explanation, namely the relative rise of black educational enrollments, may relieve anxiety, but the more important category of NISLF, neither in school nor in the labor force, continues to show marked racial differences, indicative of social malaise. Given the unavoidable demographic pressures in the next decade and the limited potential of further offsets via educational enrollment rates, the chief hope for redress in the balance lies in a change in the relative racial-ethnic demand for young workers which would favor black youth. An equally adverse situation confronts Hispanic youth, whose fast-rising numbers may shift the emphasis in public policy from blacks to another minority group, with the potential of even larger accretions from legal and illegal immigration (*NY Times* i). Moreover, the geographical location of minority youth is likely to intensify youth labor market problems in the 1980s, offsetting the relief from smaller numbers of white youth.

Western Europe

As new cohorts of children have been born of immigrant parents in the host country, the issue of minority status has replaced that of being foreign-born, and is independent of legal status. The expected superiority in education and labor market status of immigrant youth who were mostly or entirely educated in the new country over immigrant youth who were born and educated elsewhere has not emerged. Moreover, the former group plus other minority youth have remained unequal to native-born, majority youth in important respects. In the years of full employment, problems were not revealed because young foreigners' labor force participation rates equaled or exceeded those of native youth, while their unemployment was negligible. After the recession began in 1974-1975, many countries displayed a reduced tolerance of foreigners and an unwillingness to provide them access to the labor market (*Guardian* a). Among the measures adopted were restrictions on or prohibition of new residence and work permits, inducements to immigrant workers to return home, and related programs. Nevertheless, at the end of the decade the residual foreign population was large, settled more or less permanently, and more prolific than the natives. As countries contemplated their prospective labor needs in the 1980s and the low level of native birth rates, some began to see positive benefits from their foreign populations (OECD 1980a, p. 25). Increasingly, the chief flow of foreign labor comes from those already admitted to the country as wives or children of earlier immigrants. In Belgium such persons obtained 62.4 percent of new work permits in 1978, compared to 48.7 percent in 1973. Over four-fifths of French admissions to employment in 1978 were of persons already in the country, against 22.5 percent for this group in 1973 (OECD 1980b, p. 22).

As the less favorable economic circumstances of the 1970s turned attention to youth in general, the adverse position of minority youth groups, especially those with distinctive racial, cultural, or religious characteristics, aroused attention in several countries. They began to acknowledge that problems with minority youth were likely to arise for the foreseeable future. Some commentators have pointed to American conditions as a model to avoid. The prospect is that an increasing number of countries will regard such young people as minorities who require particular attention and special programs in order to ensure adequate education and participation in the youth labor market. An impetus to undertake such programs has come from the Council of Social Affairs Ministers of the European Communities, which adopted a directive in June 1977 on the adaptation of school structures and curricula to meet the specific educational needs of immigrant children. While the directive applies in a binding manner only to the children of nationals from one member country who are employed in another member country, the intention of the Community is that equivalent measures should be established on behalf of children of nonmember countries. Other international agencies, such as the Council of Europe, UNESCO, and OECD, have lent support to EEC efforts, although only EEC has authority to issue directives to member countries.

Demographic Factors

In European countries the children of recent immigrants are the most conspicuous current problem group. The difficulty is partly a matter of the unexpectedly large number of such children. Because of family reunification, which brought a continued inflow of children of immigrants and the relatively high birth rates of the immigrant group, their share of the population did not decrease as expected when the recession caused some to return home and restrictions were placed on new entrants. Both the youth share and the locally born share of the foreign population have risen (Castro-Almeida 1979). Finally, the foreign share of all births has increased, influencing the current and next generation that will enter the schools and eventually the labor market.

In the mid-1970s, the foreign share of the population, including naturalized persons and children born of foreign parents, was 4 to 9 percent in Australia, Great Britain, Sweden, Germany, France, Belgium, and the Netherlands, and as much as 15.8 percent in Switzerland (Table 7.12). The youth share tends to be higher in the foreign population than in the total population. From 40 to 50 percent of the foreign population in France, Sweden, Switzerland, Germany, and Belgium consisted of young people under 25; in these five countries there were 3.8 million youth under 25, according to the OECD survey (1980 b). They accounted for 6.6 percent of all youth under 25 in France, the lowest of the five countries, and as much as 15.3 percent in Belgium.

Immigrants and their children constitute 14.7 percent of a Swedish population of

Table 7.12   Foreign Share of Total Population, Births, and Employment, in Eight Countries, 1975

	Total population	Foreign[a] share of Births	Employment
		(percent)	
Australia	4.2	8.4	4.3
Belgium	8.5	16.8	8.9
France	7.8	9.7	10.9
Germany	6.6	16.0	9.7
Great Britain	5.8	11.9	7.4
Netherlands	2.7	4.6	5.5
Sweden	5.5	9.0	6.2
Switzerland	15.8	29.5	19.8

[a] Includes naturalized persons and children born of foreign parents (one or both).

Source: Germany, Institut für Arbeitsmarkt-und Berufsforschung der Bundesanstalt für Arbeit. *International Labour Market: Employment Patterns and Trends in the Federal Republic of Germany and in other Countries.* Quint.AB9 (Nürnberg: IAB, 1978), pp. 40–41.

8.5 million (*NY Times* j). Of the 1.25 million immigrants, about 425,000 were foreign nationals, 300,000 were immigrants with acquired Swedish citizenship, and 300,000 were citizens whose parents were immigrants. Some thirty ethnic minorities and 130 nationalities are represented in the country (Blomqvist 1980). According to Swedish law, children are born with the parents' nationality, so that successive generations of foreigners can be born on Swedish soil, unlike the American situation in which birth in the United States confers automatic citizenship. Naturalization is relatively easy in Sweden.

Between October 1976 and January 1979, France had a net decline of about 50,000 in the foreign working-population, due to an excess of departures over arrivals (admitted or authorized). But this was more than offset by 65,000 births to resident foreigners and the entrance of 45,000 family members. The total population called foreign remained about the same, however, because of 25,000 deaths and naturalization proceedings for about 50,000 (ILO 1975–80, 1/80, p. 108).

In Germany the combined effects of the return home of workers and the freeze on new labor recruitment abroad resulted in a 25 percent drop in foreign workers, a decline of 663,000 from September 1973 to 1978. The actual drop in the foreign population was only 180,000 between 1974 and 1977, however; in 1977–1978 the total increased slightly. The entrance of the dependents of foreigners who remained in Germany and new births to them, although declining absolutely after 1974, offset the decline in the number of foreign workers. Thus, between 1974 and 1978 the number of foreign children under the age of 16 rose by 24 percent, partially in response to a change in the German legislation on family allowances. By 1978 there was a resumption of the inflow of foreign workers (1978–79 net 53,000). In a single year, 1978–1979, net foreign population rose by 4 percent, and females constituted 42 percent of the total. Foreign children under 16 increased by more than 10 percent in 1978–1979. As a result, the absolute number of foreigners was higher in 1979 than it had been at the peak in 1973–1974, and their proportion of the total population once more was at a high point (Germany 1975–80b, p. 7; Spies 1978; Tippelt 1978). At the end of September 1979, half of all foreigners in Germany had been in the country for more than eight years, and 32 percent claimed residence for more than ten years. Almost half of the foreign children under 16 living in Germany had been born there (Germany *INPS* d; Germany *BAS* d,e). Similar evidence comes from Great Britain; over 40 percent of all nonwhites resident in 1979 were born in Great Britain, and the proportion among young people would be even higher (*NY Times* b).

In virtually every European country the foreign share of total births has exceeded their share of population, at times by more than two to one (Table 7.12). In part, this high birth rate for foreigners is due to a lower age composition compared to the native population, and in part to differences in fertility rates. Foreign women in France had 60 percent more births on average than French women in 1968 (Castro-Almeida 1979, n.5). One in four births in Sweden has close immigrant connections; by the year 2000 it is expected to be one in two (Blomqvist 1980, p. 3). In Germany 14.4 percent of all births in 1976 were to foreigners who constituted 6.4 percent of the total population (Castro-Almeida 1979, p. 764; Germany *INPS* d, p. 9). In England and Wales babies born to mothers with a birthplace outside the United Kingdom constituted 11.5 percent of all births in 1973 and 13.1 percent in 1978; both proportions are higher than the share of the non-British population in the total (*New Society* 1).

Variations in birth rates among the different foreign groups have been significant. In Germany, one out of two foreign births has been to Turks, although they accounted for only 30.6 percent of the foreign population in 1979. In England and Wales from 1971 to 1975, live births to women from the Asian subcontinent rose from 2.8 to 3.4 percent, and from the African continent and other countries (mainly Malta, Gibraltar, Cyprus, and Hong Kong) from 1.4 to 2.0 percent of all live births; while the West Indian share dropped from 1.6 to 1.3 percent (GB 1978b, Table 3.16). Because of the concentration of the foreign population in a few urban centers, in some German central cities 50 percent or more of all births have been to non-Germans. In Greater London in 1978, 35 percent of all births were to women who were born overseas, and in some boroughs it was almost two-thirds (*New Society* 1; *American Educator* 1978; *NY Times* b). Similarly, in 1978 one-third of children born in Rotterdam, the Netherlands' largest city, were not of Dutch nationality; it is estimated that in thirty years one-half of Rotterdam's population will be of Turkish or Moroccan origin (*Europe* 1979). Demographic trends and residential patterns produce some schools with a majority or large share of foreign pupils.

Education, Vocational Training, and Labor Force

Immediate evidence of the educational problem appears in data on nonattendance of school by foreign children. In 1974 a report for the United Nations estimated that 300,000 foreign children of school age in countries of immigration in Western Europe were receiving no education; two million such children were attending compulsory school. Moreover, the noncompletion or failure rate has been higher for foreign children who do attend school than for native children. Only 20 percent of foreign children attending compulsory school in France were able to proceed immediately to the next higher level (Courbin 1978). A disproportionate number are assigned to special schools or classes, designed for those with mental or physical handicaps and behavioral problems. Often, language difficulties are the actual cause. The educational experience of West Indian youth in Great Britain also shows the same patterns, in spite of some limited contrary evidence (Driver 1980; *New Society* j, m). Foreign youth also are underrepresented in the secondary schools which lead to tertiary education and in tertiary education itself (EC 1977d).

Explanations of the poorer educational participation and performance of foreign youth born in the receiving country stress the language problem, social and cultural differences, the lack of teachers specially trained to deal with such youth, sparse use of bilingual instruction, the socioeconomic background of the foreign families in which adults may be illiterate in their native tongue, the tension between preparing such youth to live in the host society and to return to the parents' homeland, low participation of foreign parents in school matters, the desire of foreign parents to educate their children in their native language only, and conflicts between family values and those imparted in school by peers and teachers.

Foreign youth of the second and third generation also receive less vocational education and training than native youth. They tend to be concentrated in short educational cycles and training for occupations where foreign workers are substantially represented; often the training courses, especially those offered to foreign girls, are not designed to meet the needs of an industrialized society (OECD 1980b). Foreign youth participation in the special French youth unemployment programs was somewhat smaller than their share of the youth labor force (Castro-Almeida 1979). In Switzerland where the vast majority of school-leavers enter apprenticeship, only a minority of the foreign school-leavers (who are in turn a smaller proportion of the foreign youth population than is true of their native counterparts) achieve this highly regarded training form, and they do not obtain a proportionate share of the better apprenticeships.

Young people under 25 comprised a relatively large share of the foreign labor force in five countries OECD studied at the end of the 1970s – 14.3 percent in France and Switzerland, to 22.6 percent in Belgium, with Germany and Sweden in the middle. As a share of all young people (under 25) in the labor force, young foreigners constituted from 5.8 percent (France and Germany) to a high share of 9.9 percent in Switzerland (OECD 1980b, p. 19). Labor force participation rates for youth of each sex (up to 25 years) were lower for foreigners than for nationals in all five countries (except for French males), but foreigners 25 years old and older had higher LFPR than nationals in each country for each sex, except in the case of French females. This difference in LFPR between the two age groups is critical and points to absorption problems for the second and third generations.

The gap between national and foreign youth in LFPR is generally greater for females than males in the five countries and is particularly marked for females in Belgium, France, and Switzerland, while among males Swiss foreign youth show the most conspicuous deficit in LFPR (OECD 1980b, p. 20). In England, relatively high EER for West Indian youth (16–24 years old) account for lower LFPR than white youth of the same age display (Barber 1980, p. 843). Late entrance to British schools and repetition account for much of the excess EER, however. Many countries report higher unemployment rates for foreign than native youth, although trends for each group move together. Because of their inferior record in compulsory schooling and lower rate of participation in vocational education and training, foreign youth hold a relatively high proportion of unskilled, low-paid and temporary jobs, especially in occupations already penetrated by foreign workers. West Indian youth, whether born in the United Kingdom or not, tend to be disproportionately in all levels of manual jobs, compared to whites and all foreign groups except youth from Pakistan and Bangladesh (Barber, 1980).

These general observations are extended in reports on West Germany and Sweden.

Germany: Education and Labor Force

In Germany, where immigrants have become an important political issue, a commissioner for integration of foreigners was appointed in 1978 by the Federal government. The "integration deficit" suffered by the immigrant children of the second and third generation has been measured and a goal has been set of equal opportunity with German children in education, vocational training, and the labor market (Germany 1975–80b; Germany *BAS* d; Germany *INPS* d).

In the school year 1978–1979, more than half-a-million foreign pupils were attending German schools, a 14-fold increase since 1965–1966. Over two-fifths (41.3 percent) were from Turkey and another 35 percent were from Italy, Greece, and Yugoslavia; Spain and Portugal contributed 8.7 percent together. The proportion of foreign pupils at *Sonderschule* (remedial schools) increased from 2.5 percent in 1972–1973 to 4.3 percent in 1978–1979 (Germany *INPS* e).

The spillover of demographic factors to the educational system produces some schools with a majority of foreign pupils. German primary schools in the 1980s expect an average of 15 to 20 percent foreign pupils, with up to 50 percent in school districts in built-up areas. The foreign share of those leaving German compulsory school, 5.4 percent in 1978, probably will rise to over 15 percent by 1989 and will be much higher in some areas (Germany *INPS* d).

Foreign children in Germany who are subject to the compulsory education laws have complied much less fully than German children. About 20 percent of foreign children up to age 15 or 16 were not attending full-time schools in 1979, and the absence rate has been as high as 25 percent in some states. They also were overrepresented in the special schools for those with learning handicaps. The required part-time school attendance to 18 years of age met with even less compliance; in 1977–1978 about 55 percent of eligible foreign youth were estimated not to be enrolled, in part because employers would not hire these youths if they had to be absent from work in order to attend school for one day a week.

Foreign children who do attend compulsory school perform poorly, often because of language difficulties. In 1978 only 41 percent of the foreign pupils but 82 percent of German pupils completed the *Hauptschule* (main school) with a final certificate. Lacking such a certificate, access to secondary school is limited. In 1977–1978 only 12.6 percent of foreign children in the age group were in the secondary schools that provide entrance to higher education and the better apprenticeships. While this was an improvement on the 1970–1971 rate of 5 percent, it was well below the rate of 50 percent for German youth (Germany *PIB* a; Germany *INPS* a,d; Germany 1975–80a; *Position* a; Tippelt 1978).

Although foreign parents are often said to be less ambitious than German in regard to their children's education, a survey among foreign parents revealed that aspirations of both groups were not dissimilar. Three-fifths of the foreign parents wanted their children to attend school beyond compulsory education, one-fourth desired them to complete an apprenticeship, and only 3 percent believed that they should go to work after compulsory school. That the facts depart markedly from these wishes is due in part to economic necessity in the foreign households and in part to language, cultural, and religious differences and adjustment problems among the young people (Tippelt 1978).

Because of their low enrollment rate and poor record of completing compulsory school with a certificate, foreign youth are underrepresented in the apprenticeship system, which is highly regarded in Germany as continuing education-training, as an alternative to full-time school, as a good bridge between school and work, and as a route to skilled worker status. The proportion of all apprenticeships held by children of foreign workers is still less than 5 percent; in 1976 it was 2.3 percent and disproportionate to their share of all out-of-school youth. Although the vast majority of German teenagers (15–18) who were not in full-time general education were either in apprenticeship or at full-time vocational schools, only 25 percent of such foreign youth were in these activities in 1976–1977 (Germany *INPS* d; Germany 1975–80c; *Position* a). The alternative followed by foreign youth is to become young workers, filling unskilled and temporary jobs. This residual category consists of around 190,000 youth (6.2 percent of the 15–18 age group in 1978). Foreign youth are disproportionately represented, as are females, whether foreign or German.

As a reaction to the recession, Germany imposed restrictions on residence permits and work permits at the Federal and State level, which blocked employment opportunities for some young foreigners, including school-leavers seeking work for the first time. The Federal rule provided that a migrant worker's child who arrived in Germany from a country outside the European Communities after December 1974 was not entitled to obtain a work permit, thus banning employment where a work permit was required as well as the use of the employment service. Because of the various measures to deny foreign youth work permits, it was estimated in 1976 that there were actually about 100,000 unemployed foreign teenagers rather than the 7,000 reported by the official statistics. In order to favor German youth at a time of rising unemployment, the youth labor force had been artificially reduced by the various residence and federal work permit regulations (Tippelt 1978).

The situation was eased when the effective date of the ban on work permits was changed to cover youth entering the country after January 1977. Following a reduction in youth unemployment and responding to pressure from employer's associations in the hotel and restaurant field, the Federal government in March 1979 decided that young people who had entered the country on or after January 1, 1977, could obtain a one-year, renewable, work permit for a specific job, after a two-year waiting period, if they displayed a good knowledge of the German language and nation. Enrollment in a six-months or longer course could reduce the waiting period. Five-year general work permits could be issued to young migrants with one parent in regular work for five years. Between April 1979 and January 1980, about 6,500 foreign workers' children received work permits under these provisions (Germany *BAS* a,b,c,d).

In reviewing the education situation of foreign youth in 1978–1979, the Federal education minister declared that the main objective of educational policy for foreign youth should be to provide them with the educational preparation that would enable them to enter apprenticeships or full-time vocational education. He opposed separate classes for foreign children at German schools because these only accentuated the language problem and intensified the difficulties of obtaining an apprenticeship (Germany *INPS* d).

In December 1979, the Minister of Labor and Social Order announced the formation of a coordinating body for the social integration of foreign children and youth. Consisting of private and public officials, it included representatives of the trade union federation, the national employers' federation, the churches, the private and religious social service agencies, the federation of local governments, the Federal Institute for Employment (BA), labor divisions of State governments, the political parties in the *Bundestag,* and the relevant Federal agencies (Germany *BAS* f). The Minister of Education and Science followed with a full program (Germany 1975–80 b,c). The cooperative organization of the Federal and State education authorities for planning and research and the Conference of State Ministers of Education (KMK) also have been active in the programs to offer foreign youth equal opportunities.

In early 1980 the Federal cabinet enunciated a policy to integrate foreigners and especially foreign youth into German life, further building on earlier policies that established model projects, Federally financed in part. The thirty model programs and pilot schemes include such items as TV programs, special courses, bilingual instruction on film, the teaching of the German language at as early an age as possible, action to ensure attendance in compulsory education, the development of remedial educational facilities, and the improvement of career guidance and preparation for work. A new program was initiated in 1980 to assist entrance to apprenticeship. In addition, the states offer projects (Germany *BAS* a,b,c,d,e,f; Germany 1975–80 b, pp. 26–40, c; Germany *INPS* d,e).

Sweden: Education and Labor Force

Sweden's immigrant or minority youth requiring special educational consideration can be divided into two main groups. The first consists of native Lapps, Finns native to the north of Sweden, and gypsies; special educational provision is made for each. The second is comprised of immigrants or children born of immigrants. Finns are the most numerous immigrant group under the free access granted by the Nordic Common Market. Part of the Finnish immigrant population residing in Sweden is Swedish-speaking from birth, since Swedish is the major second language in Finland and is particularly prevalent as a first language in the western part of Finland. The rest of the second group consists of youth born in countries outside of Sweden or born in Sweden with one or both parents of foreign origin and a native tongue other than Swedish. Finnish and Swedish-speaking Finnish immigrants comprised almost three-fifths of the total non-Swedish children in the compulsory school in 1978, followed by Yugoslav, German, and Danish children respectively (Sweden 1978h, p. 12).

The actual diversity of the Swedish population, which usually is thought of as homogeneous, is revealed by the number of languages, other than Swedish, spoken in the homes of pupils in the compulsory school. A 1978 tabulation lists Arabic, six Assyrian languages, Czech, Danish, Dutch, English, Estonian, Finnish, French, German, Greek, Hungarian, Icelandic, Italian, Norwegian, Polish, Portuguese, Spanish, Turkish, and still other languages (which accounted for 5.8 percent of the foreign pupils) (Sweden 1978h, p. 12). A count at a later date would add Vietnamese as a separate entry. In 1978, immigrant pupils in the compulsory school constituted 8.5 percent of the total number of pupils, but in twelve communes they exceeded 20 percent of the total and in one they constituted a majority. The total number of immigrant pupils rose from 62,778 in 1975 to 88,313 in 1978 and is still increasing.

Progression from the Swedish compulsory school (*Grundskole*) at about age 16 to the upper-secondary comprehensive school (*Gymnasieskole*) is of particular importance because the latter is the vehicle both for education leading to entrance to higher education and for a mixture of academic and occupational courses, mainly one to two years in length, leading to entrance to the full-time labor force. In the fall of 1977, there were 7,283 immigrant pupils enrolled in the final year of compulsory school, and a year later 5,075 immigrant pupils, or 69.7 percent, entered the upper-secondary school. The transfer rate for Swedes was around 85 percent for the enrollment of 100,276 pupils in the final year of compulsory school. Transfer rates to upper-secondary school among the immigrant pupils were highest for those whose native tongue was English, Norwegian, Estonian, Swedish, Hungarian, and German; these rates were over 80 percent. The lowest rates were shown by Turks, Danes, Arabs, and Finns. Females had higher transfer rates than males among both the immigrant pupils (74 to 66 percent) and the total Swedish enrollment (85 to 84 percent). Compared to the previous year, the overall transfer rate of immigrant pupils rose by 3 percent to 70 percent, while that for Swedish people increased by 6 percent to 85 percent. Although the statistics are presented as transfer rates, they are in fact a comparison of enrollments, not a match of individuals. Since some of the entrants to upper-secondary school came from other types of school and from those who had completed compulsory school in earlier years, the rates are not precise. They do, however, indicate the magnitude of difference between immigrant and other pupils (Sweden 1978h, pp. 32–36).

In 1978, 5.5 percent of the total enrollment in the upper-secondary school consisted of immigrants, a lower proportion than in the compulsory school or in the youth population. Moreover, immigrant youth opted for the shortest, most vocational courses; they constituted 6.0 percent of those in one-year courses, 5.2 percent in the two-year courses, 5.0 percent in the three-year courses, and 3.1 percent in the four-year courses (Sweden 1978h, p. 25). An official of the National Immigration and Naturalization Board attributed this educational pattern to the desire of the young immigrants, molded by their parents' wishes and behavior, to enter work early in order to contribute to the family's upkeep. Others are forced to leave school early because their knowledge of Swedish (and in some courses, English) is inadequate for further studies (Blomqvist 1980, p. 5).

Early entrance to the labor market with poor educational credentials and a limited knowledge of Swedish confines the immigrant youth to a narrow selection of low-level jobs, and produces higher unemployment rates than for Swedish youth and a disproportionately low participation in government manpower training and other programs. Even immigrants with a higher education find it difficult to obtain more skilled jobs, however, with the exception of specialists who were recruited because of shortages in Sweden (Blomqvist 1980, p. 3).

Sweden has long had governmental agencies dedicated to equality of opportunity and freedom of choice for immigrants as well as cooperation between immigrants and Swedes. The National Immigration and Naturalization Board, a quasi-public agency under the Ministry of Labor which was organized in 1969, has responsibility for applications for residence permits, visas, and citizenship, as well as policy and coordination of action on immigrant issues. There also is a newer Swedish Commission on Prejudice and Discrimination. Reliance on voluntary action is nevertheless strong, and few complaints of discrimination are passed on to the police for investigation and punitive action. Moreover, such cases usually involve admission to restaurants and hotels, rather than job discrimination, which is considered to be rife (Evans 1980; NY Times j). In spite of strong government efforts to smooth the absorption of immigrants, it has been observed that racism and resentment against immigrants is sharper than it was in boom periods. Some maintain that labor shortages should have been met by drawing Swedish women and handicapped into the labor force instead of importing workers. Against this background, the main Swedish approach is an education-information effort to reduce the xenophobia of the Swedish population. Attempts to improve the labor force status of immigrant youth are largely part of the overall attack on youth unemployment, which some Swedish authorities consider inadequate to the problem (Blomqvist 1980, p. 5). It is held that a separate campaign to improve the educational participation and performance of immigrant youth is an important part of the approach to the problem.

Educational philosophy in regard to immigrant children has undergone a radical change since its initial formulation five to ten years ago. Because Sweden has not used the "guest worker" approach but instead offered potential citizenship to all with valid work permits, permanent settlement was expected. Therefore, it seemed necessary that immigrants' children should learn Swedish as quickly as possible and make it their first language in order to get on in Swedish society. If they wished, they could learn their parents' mother tongue later on (Blomqvist 1980, p. 4).

Research and practical experience showed that this approach was unsatisfactory. Many immigrant children were placed in day nurseries from the age of one, as were Swedish children, so that their mothers could work. Such immigrant children did not obtain a proper grasp of Swedish, nor did they learn their parents' languages adequately; they developed a "double semi-lingualism" (Blomqvist 1980, p. 4). A home-language reform movement established some tentative steps toward bilingual instruction. Pupils in the preschool, initially at six years of age and later at five, up to and including the final year of upper-secondary school were entitled to request auxiliary lessons in the Swedish language and/or subject study outside of class in their mother tongue. In 1978, 44 percent of the immigrant pupils in the compulsory school were judged in need of auxiliary Swedish lessons, and 31.5 percent actually received them. Around 16 percent of all immigrant pupils received subject study assistance in their mother tongue. Over 40 percent participated in optional language study in their native tongue, and another 4,000 pupils expressed a desire to participate. Around 14 percent of the upper-secondary school immigrant pupils were reported to need auxiliary tuition in Swedish or subject study in the mother tongue, but only 300 of the 11,500 took part in such courses. Some may have met the need by taking their native tongue as a foreign language elective within the normal curriculum (Sweden 1978h, pp. 37–38).

A program developed by the National Board of Education late in 1979 suggested the areas in which further improvement was desirable. It was recommended that local education authorities make educational guidance and language instruction in the native tongue compulsory for those who need it in the preschool and compulsory school. Schools should offer instruction in any native language if pupils and their parents desire it. Preschool should end with a diagnosis of the pupils' language needs. The teaching of Swedish as a foreign language and the teaching of English should be improved. Evaluation of the instruction given to immigrant children should be continuous and the needs of immigrants should have a greater place in the construction of the curriculum.

At upper-secondary level, it was recommended that immigrant students should be able to carry a reduced program from the first term so that they can study their native language. Certain immigrant students should be excused from the general requirement of English as a prerequisite for entry to particular lines of study. English should be offered as a third foreign language for immigrant pupils. Curricula for certain courses should be changed to include compulsory instruction in the home language, and new courses should be introduced to fit particular strengths of the immigrants, for example interpreter training, international commercial correspondence, and international legal studies.

Teacher training in languages should emphasize the need for bilingual instruction. Such courses should rate equally with other courses and home language teachers should be eligible for administrative posts in the school system. Basic training should be introduced for teachers of Swedish as a foreign language. All teacher trainees should receive more information on the culture and background of immigrants and on inter-group attitudes and relations. Countries of emigration should be approached for joint ventures in the production of teaching materials and aids. Possibly a national center for immigrant and minority teaching aids should be established. The National Board of Education proposed a long-term plan for information activity, in cooperation with immigrant organizations and other government authorities (Council of Europe 1977–80, 3/79, pp. 32–33).

The National Immigration and Naturalization Board, convinced that it is necessary for immigrant children to learn their mother tongue first, has been proposing measures to deal with preschool children. They would like to see all preschool immigrant and minority children, who are not cared for at home, placed in proper day nurseries with bilingual staff. But the shortage of day nurseries makes this an impractical solution since "it would be impossible and unfortunate to give priority to immigrant children in view of the resentment this would cause among Swedish parents on the waiting list" (Blomqvist 1980, p. 4). Therefore, as a temporary measure it is proposed that housewives of each cultural and linguistic group should be mobilized and trained for six months and then be established as registered child care agents for small groups of children of the same background.

The Board also found that the amount of time devoted in the first years of the compulsory school to lessons in the mother tongue was inadequate; it praised experimental programs which teach completely or partly in the immigrant children's own language for a year or two, after which the children transfer to Swedish-speaking classes on a part-time and then full-time basis. Such classes may be difficult to organize in communities with few immigrant children or large numbers of different immigrant groups with small numbers in each. But the general principle is now accepted that "immigrant children with a basic knowledge of their own language find it easier to learn Swedish" (Blomqvist 1980, p. 5).

Canada, New Zealand, Australia

Native populations form significant minorities in Canada, New Zealand, and Australia, as they do in the United States and Sweden. Canada's Eskimos and Indians, New Zealand's Maoris, and Australia's Aborigines present the same mix of problems, reflecting the isolation of part of the group, and the difficulty felt by the rest of the group in assimilating; both groups are poor compared to the majority population. In recent years all of the countries have mounted special programs concerned with the education and labor force status of youth.

New Zealand is unusual in that it has a postwar quinquennial census series for the native minority population, which consists chiefly of Maoris. This series enables comparisons to be made of the youth population and labor force. Postwar teenage population growth in New Zealand reflected one of the strongest postwar baby booms experienced by any country, as Chapter 2 demonstrated. As a consequence, the teenage share of the total population aged 15 years or older rose from 9.5 percent in 1951 to 13.7 percent in 1976. Maori teenagers started out in 1951 as 19.7 percent of Maori population 15 years and older, more than double the national share. There was little change in the Maori share from 1951 until 1966, except for a drop in 1961. The 1971 and 1976 censuses then registered a rise in the share to 20.5 and 22.4 percent, respectively. While still well ahead of the whole teenage group in population share, the Maori teenagers had less of a baby boom and a more recent and concentrated one than other New Zealand youth.

Labor force participation rates started out much lower for Maori teenagers than for the whole teenage group, nor have the two groups shown the same trends. As a result of the increase in educational enrollment rates (EER) for New Zealand youth, both male and female teenage labor force participation rates (LFPR) dropped sharply from 1951 to 1976. Maori LFPR, on the other hand, have been rising over time. Thus, by 1976 male Maori teenagers had a higher LFPR than all teenage males, although in 1951 their LFPR had been 10 percent less—61.2 percent against the overall teenage LFPR of 71.4 percent. Among teenage females, Maori LFPR in 1951 was 39.0 percent, while it was 64.5 percent for all races. The LFPR for all teenage girls dropped to 51.1 percent by 1976, but the Maori girls showed a rise to 57.0 percent in 1971 and then a drop in the recession to 48.4 percent in 1976—each a reverse movement to that of the whole teenage population. Maori teenagers also constituted a far higher share of the Maori labor force than all teenagers did of the total labor force, giving the Maoris a disadvantage of numbers on top of their locational, educational, and training handicaps, over and above the effects of discrimination.

The New Zealand censuses record a somewhat smaller racial gap for young adults. The all-races, young adult share of the population 15 years and older fluctuated around 10 percent and rose only to 12 percent in 1971, stabilizing through 1976. Young adult Maoris mostly comprised about 16.5 percent of the population 15 years and older, dipping down to 15 percent in 1966. LFPR for young adult males of both groups have been very similar—well over 90 percent. The all-races group had a slight decline from 1951 to 1976, however, representing increased full-time education, while the Maori LFPR fluctuated but trended slightly upward. Both female groups followed their elders by showing rising LFPR over the quarter-century and especially since 1966. Yet a 20 percentage point gap in LFPR continued between the all-races, young adult females and the Maoris. The Maoris were advancing, but not catching up rapidly. As in the case of male teenagers, Maori young adults constituted a larger share of the male Maori labor force than did all-races, young male adults of the male labor force. Female shares were almost the same for the two groups.

Australian investigations of Aboriginal students in schools throughout the country revealed that their performance has been 15 to 20 percent lower than the Australian average and even lower in the Northern Territory schools. This record restricts their entrance to postsecondary education and labor market opportunities. Their access to education is limited by rural location, culture, and economic factors as well. The 1971 census reported that one-fourth of the Aboriginal population had never attended school, that just a third had completed primary education, and only 2 percent had reached the tenth year of education or higher. Lack of basic and advanced general and technical education limits many Aboriginals to seasonal work or unskilled labor and very high unemployment rates relative to Australian youth. A symposium on Youth Unemployment in 1977 declared:

Unemployment of Aborigines . . . is merely one of the problems interlocked in patterns of multiple causation facing Aborigines. The basic reason is race prejudice and habitual discrimination . . . For services other than those specially provided . . . the Aboriginal still stands at the end of Australian queques [sic] or with his file at the bottom of the heap. Even the educated Aboriginal youth is more likely to get no further than the leading place in the Aboriginal queque [sic] for jobs.

Race prejudice of white Australians has for generations held up "on the fringe" Aboriginal attempts to join the work force in towns and cities . . . When statistics of employment are available, they illustrate a set of conditions quite beyond those applicable to non-Aborigines (Australia 1979a, pp. 637–38).

Canada's Indian youth are representative of native populations in other countries which live partly in their own separate settlements or reservations and partly intermixed with the majority population. A recent report of the Canadian Ministry of Indian and Northern Affairs reviewed the past twenty years and found that, despite improvements, wide disparities between the Indian and white societies persist. The EER of the total Canadian population of high school age is 12 percentage points higher than that of the comparable Indian population. An increased proportion of young people living off the reservations has been accompanied by lower LFPR, higher unemployment, and greater dependence on welfare than was the case twenty years earlier (*NY Times* h).

One of the complaints of the Canadian Indian organizations is that disproportionate attention is given to the French minority in Canadian governmental allocations of funds for programs. This highlights the complexity of the Canadian situation, in which a substantial portion of the long-settled French population regard themselves as an oppressed minority, sometimes referring to themselves as "white niggers" to draw the analogy with the United States. Moreover, postwar Canadian immigration policy has opened the doors to permanent immigrants with occupational skills from a vast number of countries, and a pending second generation problem akin to that in Europe seems inevitable. Toronto and Montreal, in particular, are centers of immigrant settlement. Australia also has imported workers from southern Europe, who come as permanent settlers. They have crowded into the centers of the largest cities, especially Sydney, and it is already clear that their children have education, training, and employment problems of a special kind and intensity. Various programs have been launched nationally and locally, but they are not as advanced as those in Sweden and Germany.

Although the detail offered for U.S. black youth has been duplicated here for no other country, and while the U.S. situation cannot be fully understood in the absence of a complete report on Hispanic youth (with all of its subdivisions) and on native Indian youth, it still can be suggested that countries have much to learn from one another in regard to minority youth. The tension between a policy of assimilation and attempts at bicultural and bilingual policies has been visible everywhere. Comparisons of views and programs and the evolution of policy, as was traced in Sweden, can be helpful to those countries which lag behind in facing the educational and other problems of their minority native or second generation immigrant youth. Equally, those countries which see their own experience as unique and tend to overemphasize local political aspects can broaden their viewpoint by considering the basic similarity in situation and experience among countries. Finally, the diverse programs launched to date suggest that satisfactory solutions are still a long way off for all countries and that the underlying problems are complex and resistant to treatment. Continuing surveys are needed to measure the progress toward equality and to fill the remaining gaps.

Table A7.3   Black and Other Races in Civilian Labor Force, Annual Change, Participation Rates, and Share of Youth, by Age, Males, United States, 1954-1979

Civilian labor force (excludes institutional population)

Year	16 and older Number (000s)	16 and older Year-to-year change	16 and older Participation rate (percent)	16-19 Number (000s)	16-19 Year-to-year change	16-19 As percent of 16 and older (percent)	16-19 Participation rate	20-24 Number (000s)	20-24 Year-to-year change	20-24 As percent of 16 and older (percent)	20-24 Participation rate
1954	4203	—	85.2	305	—	7.3	61.2	396	—	9.4	91.1
1955	4279	1.8	85.0	313	2.6	7.3	60.9	419	5.8	9.8	89.7
1956	4359	1.9	85.1	321	2.2	7.4	61.8	450	7.4	10.3	88.9
1957	4376	0.4	84.3	311	-3.1	7.1	59.0	473	5.1	10.8	89.6
1958	4442	1.5	84.0	313	0.6	7.0	57.4	493	4.2	11.1	88.7
1959	4490	1.1	83.4	310	-1.0	6.9	54.2	532	10.1	11.8	90.8
1960	4645	3.5	83.0	353	13.9	7.6	57.5	564	6.0	12.1	90.4
1961	4666	0.5	82.2	343	-2.8	7.4	54.3	575	2.0	12.3	89.7
1962	4668	*	80.8	337	-1.7	7.2	53.5	553	-3.8	11.8	89.3
1963	4725	1.3	80.2	344	2.1	7.3	51.5	558	0.9	11.8	88.6
1964	4785	1.3	80.0	359	4.4	7.5	50.1	588	5.4	12.3	89.4
1965	4855	1.5	79.6	398	10.9	8.2	51.3	614	4.4	12.6	89.8
1966	4899	0.9	79.0	431	8.3	8.8	51.4	620	1.0	12.7	89.9
1967	4945	0.9	78.5	443	1.9	9.0	51.0	628	1.3	12.7	87.2
1968	4979	0.7	77.6	445	0.5	8.9	49.7	639	1.8	12.8	85.0
1969	5036	1.1	76.9	458	2.9	9.1	49.6	667	4.4	13.2	84.4
1970	5182	2.9	76.5	455	-0.7	8.9	47.2	725	8.7	14.0	83.5
1971	5220	0.7	74.9	447	-1.8	8.6	44.7	772	6.5	14.8	81.5
1972	5335	2.2	73.7	488	9.2	9.1	46.0	804	4.1	15.1	81.5
1973	5555	4.1	73.8	506	3.7	9.1	46.3	874	8.7	15.3	81.8
1974	5700	2.6	73.3	532	5.1	9.3	47.2	871	-0.3	15.3	82.1
1975	5734	0.6	71.5	496	-6.8	8.7	42.7	867	-0.5	15.1	78.4
1976	5853	2.1	70.7	504	1.6	8.6	42.1	908	4.7	15.1	78.4
1977	6028	3.0	71.0	524	4.0	8.7	43.4	934	2.9	15.5	78.2
1978	6284	4.2	72.1	553	5.5	8.8	45.4	963	3.1	15.3	78.0
1979	6443	2.5	71.9	539	-2.5	8.4	43.9	1013	5.2	15.7	80.1

Note: Asterisk * indicates less than plus or minus 0.05 percent.

Source: U.S. Department of Labor, *Employment and Training Report of the President* 1980, Tables A-3, A-4 and A-5 (Washington: GPO, 1980).

Table A7.4 Black and Other Races in Civilian Labor Force, Annual Change, Participation Rates, and Share of Youth, by Age, Females, United States, 1954–1979

Civilian labor force (excludes institutional population)

Year	16 and older			16-19				20-24			
	Number (000s)	Year-to-year change	Participation rate (percent)	Number (000s)	Year-to-year change	As percent of 16 and older (percent)	Participation rate	Number (000s)	Year-to-year change	As percent of 16 and older (percent)	Participation rate
1954	2621	—	46.1	169	—	6.4	31.0	326	—	12.4	49.6
1955	2663	1.6	46.1	182	7.7	6.8	32.7	307	-5.8	11.5	46.7
1956	2768	3.9	47.3	206	13.2	7.4	36.3	297	-3.3	10.7	44.9
1957	2812	1.6	47.2	193	-6.3	6.9	33.2	311	4.7	11.1	46.6
1958	2905	3.3	48.0	191	-1.0	6.6	32.0	328	5.5	11.3	48.3
1959	2928	0.8	47.7	173	-9.4	5.9	28.1	338	3.0	11.5	48.8
1960	3069	4.8	48.2	213	23.1	6.9	32.8	352	4.1	11.5	48.8
1961	3136	2.2	48.3	220	3.3	7.0	32.9	353	0.3	11.3	47.7
1962	3195	1.9	48.0	224	1.8	7.0	33.0	364	3.1	11.4	48.6
1963	3279	2.6	48.1	235	4.9	7.2	32.5	377	3.6	11.5	49.2
1964	3384	3.2	48.5	242	3.0	7.2	31.1	424	12.5	12.5	53.6
1965	3464	2.4	48.6	246	1.7	7.1	29.5	454	7.1	13.1	55.2
1966	3597	3.8	49.3	298	21.1	8.3	33.4	466	2.6	13.0	54.5
1967	3704	3.0	49.5	329	10.4	8.9	35.3	497	6.7	13.4	54.9
1968	3780	2.1	49.3	335	1.8	8.9	34.8	558	12.3	14.8	58.4
1969	3918	3.7	49.8	344	2.7	8.8	34.6	598	7.2	15.3	58.6
1970	4015	2.5	49.5	351	2.0	8.7	34.1	628	5.0	15.6	57.7
1971	4102	2.1	49.2	333	-5.1	8.1	31.2	649	3.3	15.8	56.0
1972	4249	3.6	48.7	361	8.4	8.5	32.2	682	5.1	16.1	56.7
1973	4470	5.2	49.1	403	11.6	9.0	34.4	734	7.6	16.4	57.5
1974	4633	3.6	49.1	414	2.7	8.9	35.0	768	4.6	16.6	58.2
1975	4795	3.5	49.2	444	7.2	9.3	35.6	772	0.5	16.1	56.2
1976	5044	5.2	50.2	427	-3.8	8.5	33.5	823	6.6	16.3	57.9
1977	5266	4.4	50.9	434	1.6	8.2	33.7	874	6.2	16.1	59.4
1978	5679	7.8	53.3	497	14.5	8.8	38.1	954	9.2	16.8	62.8
1979	5863	3.2	53.5	497	0.0	8.5	38.0	962	0.8	16.4	61.6

Source: U.S. Department of Labor, *Employment and Training Report of the President* 1980, Tables A–3, A–4 and A–5 (Washington: GPO, 1980).

Table A7.5 Labor Force Participation Rates of Enrolled Youth, by Race, Age, Sex, Living Arrangements, and Household Income, United States, October 1977

	Never married enrolled youth living at home (or at school)				All other enrolled youth			
	16-19 Years		20-24 Years		16-19 Years		20-24 Years	
	Male	Female	Male	Female	Male	Female	Male	Female
Total number enrolled								
White (000)	4,780	4,425	1,404	1,078	140	312	821	828
Black (000)	777	776	189	193	29	44	72	94
	Labor force participation rates (enrolled)							
	Whites							
Income classes (annual)	(percent)				(percent)			
All classes[a]	48.9	44.7	47.1	51.4	65.0	51.3	73.8	66.2
Less than $5,000	41.8	32.4	34.9	63.0	73.9	52.8	62.0	52.1
$5,000–7,499	39.2	40.1	38.5	52.6	61.9	44.7	78.1	68.6
$7,500–9,999	45.5	40.9	53.2	51.3	72.7	55.6	74.6	63.4
$10,000–14,999	52.0	45.3	44.6	55.1	73.9	58.1	86.7	71.4
$15,000–24,999	54.9	49.9	52.1	53.5	73.9	54.1	83.7	84.7
$25,000 and more	46.3	44.7	47.5	49.9	22.2	26.1	52.6	88.9
	Blacks							
	(percent)				(percent)			
All classes[a]	27.2	19.6	27.0	27.5	55.2	38.6	75.0	65.5
Less than $5,000	19.8	12.8	26.2	23.5	83.3	50.0	66.7	65.5
$5,000–7,499	29.3	19.2	11.4	16.1	0.0[b]	20.0	70.8	53.3
$7,500–9,999	24.8	21.6	34.8	41.2	66.7	0.0[b]	83.3	76.5
$10,000–14,999	29.0	25.0	19.5	29.0	100.0[c]	100.0[c]	100.0[c]	44.4
$15,000–24,999	24.1	29.0	36.7	32.4	0.0[b]	0.0[b]	50.0	100.0
$25,000 and more	50.0	26.3	54.5	38.5	100.0[c]	0.0[b,c]	0.0[b]	100.0[c]

[a] Includes those whose income was not reported.
[b] Employed or unemployed total is less than 1,000.
[c] Not in labor force total is less than 1,000.

Source: U.S. Department of Labor, Bureau of Labor Statistics, unpublished tables from October 1977 Current Population Survey.

Table A7.6   Labor Market Status and Household Income of Enrolled Youth by Age, Sex, Race, and Living Arrangements, United States, October 1977

Sex-age group	Never married enrolled youth living at home (or at school) — Not in labor force, Number (000s)	Household income ($)	Employed, Number (000s)	Household income ($)	Unemployed, Number (000s)	Household income ($)	All other enrolled youth — Not in labor force, Number (000s)	Household income ($)	Employed, Number (000s)	Household income ($)	Unemployed, Number (000s)	Household income ($)
Males 16–19	3,085	16,383	2,186	17,424	389	13,940	84	6,695	96	5,823	15	8,431
Females 16–19	3,120	13,906	1,817	17,311	353	13,698	184	6,646	132	5,887	44	5,899
Males 20–24	879	17,697	678	22,549	67	17,429	264	5,644	625	8,153	47	4,520
Females 20–24	685	17,346	569	17,850	54	17,317	331	5,692	578	8,410	45	5,817
Whites												
Males 16–19	2,441	17,032	2,035	17,629	304	16,761	49	8,296	78	6,692	13	8,781
Females 16–19	2,446	16,857	1,701	17,484	278	16,368	152	6,853	120	6,583	40	8,053
Males 20–24	743	22,912	611	22,942	50	22,664	215	5,702	569	8,211	37	3,641
Females 20–24	524	22,745	516	22,098	38	17,977	280	5,604	513	8,575	35	5,925
Blacks												
Males 16–19	566	8,121	130	8,880	81	8,396	13	6,795	14	4,576	2	560
Females 16–19	624	6,872	86	11,612	66	6,942	27	2,742	12	4,655	5	3,542
Males 20–24	138	8,333	38	8,902	13	11,933	18	6,721	44	8,112	10	5,644
Females 20–24	140	8,062	37	11,539	16	13,239	29	6,709	46	6,982	9	5,785

Source: United States Department of Labor, Bureau of Labor Statistics, unpublished tables from the October 1977 Current Population Survey.

Table A7.7 Household Income of Nonenrolled Youth, by Race, Age, Sex, and Living Arrangements, United States, October 1977

Never married youth living at home

| | Enrolled and nonenrolled youth | | Enrolled and nonenrolled youth | | Nonenrolled youth | | | | | |
| | | | | | NISLF | | Employed | | Unemployed | |
Sex–age group	White	Black	White	Black	White	Black	White	Black	White	Black
	(000s)				(average annual household income in $)					
Male 16–19	6,440	1,018	$16,940	$6,992	$11,630	$4,924	$16,007	$ 6,716	$13,006	$5,580
Female 16–19	5,598	1,016	16,844	6,922	8,704	5,686	16,691	11,725	11,943	6,827
Male 20–24	3,547	580	17,501	8,103	11,520	5,935	17,112	8,307	13,293	6,673
Female 20–24	2,355	545	17,442	8,160	11,748	5,778	17,196	11,279	13,542	6,780

All other youth

| | Enrolled and nonenrolled youth | | Nonenrolled youth | | | | | |
| | | | NISLF | | Employed | | Unemployed | |
Sex–age group	White	Black	White	Black	White	Black	White	Black
	(000s)		(average annual household income in $)					
Male 16–19	525	53	$ 6,712	$4,975	$ 8,296	n.a.	$ 6,739	$ 3,713	$ 3,556	$5,636
Female 16–19	1,413	147	6,759	3,715	6,682	$3,655	6,583	4,770	6,819	4,542
Male 20–24	4,502	451	8,886	6,708	6,551	4,596	11,177	6,787	6,719	4,938
Female 20–24	6,082	738	11,077	5,564	8,946	4,565	11,477	6,661	8,482	4,534

Source: U.S. Department of Labor, Bureau of Labor Statistics, unpublished tables from October 1977 Current Population Survey.

Table A7.8 Labor Force Participation Rates of Nonenrolled Youth, by Race, Age, Sex, Living Arrangements, Educational Attainment, and Household Income, United States, October 1977

| | Never married nonenrolled living at home | | | | All other nonenrolled youth | | | |
| | 16-19 Years | | 20-24 Years | | 16-19 Years | | 20-24 Years | |
	Male	Female	Male	Female	Male	Female	Male	Female
Total number nonenrolled								
White (000s)	1,660	1,173	2,143	1,277	386	1,102	3,680	5,254
Black (000s)	241	240	391	352	24	104	378	654
	Labor force participation rates (nonenrolled)							
	Whites							
Income classes (annual)	(percent)				(percent)			
All classes[a]	91.5	84.1	92.6	90.1	96.9	56.8	98.5	67.1
Less than $5,000	52.6	51.1	83.0	67.9	94.5	56.3	96.8	63.2
$5,000-7,499	87.8	74.8	82.4	87.2	96.0	53.7	97.4	66.2
$7,500-9,999	86.4	75.5	90.7	84.3	100.0[b]	55.8	98.4	63.1
$10,000-14,999	92.0	85.4	95.5	87.1	100.0[b,c]	59.2	99.2	65.7
$15,000-24,999	92.7	91.9	94.7	94.8	100.0[b]	67.8	99.3	74.4
$25,000 and more	97.0	91.8	94.9	95.3	75.0[c]	100.0[b]	100.0[b]	80.0
	Blacks							
	(percent)				(percent)			
All classes[a]	80.1	59.2	85.2	70.5	100.0	51.0	94.7	62.4
Less than $5,000	76.0	46.6	75.2	55.6	100.0	39.6	89.8	55.2
$5,000-7,499	70.3	40.7	87.8	62.5	100.0	42.9	100.0[b]	65.9
$7,500-9,999	84.6	77.3	75.0	67.6	100.0	100.0[b]	85.0	70.7
$10,000-14,999	75.0	81.6	85.1	83.1	100.0	71.4	100.0[b]	66.7
$15,000-24,999	91.3	87.5	97.6	91.1	100.0	33.3	100.0[b]	77.6
$25,000 and more	80.0	100.0[b]	100.0[b]	85.7	100.0	0.0[b,c]	100.0[b]	100.0

[a] Includes those whose income was not reported.
[b] Not in labor force total is less than 1,000.
[c] Employed and unemployed total each is less than 1,000.

Source: U.S. Department of Labor, Bureau of Labor Statistics, unpublished tables from October 1977 Current Population Survey.

Appendix 7:1 Longitudinal NISLF Rates

Unpublished NISLF rates from the National Longitudinal Survey of Young Men and Young Women are presented in Table B7.1. A comparison of the NISLF rates in Table B7.1 with those in text Tables 7.8 and 7.9 for the age groups 16–17 and 18–19 indicates that the rates from the longitudinal source are lower for each race and that the racial differential is smaller in the longitudinal source, in almost every case. It should be noted also that NISLF rates for males from CPS data as given in Table 7.8 have been adjusted to a total population base, thus yielding slightly lower NISLF proportions than would a civilian population base, which the unpublished longitudinal data use. Therefore, the fact that the NLS rates are lower than those from the CPS is additionally noteworthy.

Table B7.1 NISLF Youth, by Race, Age, and Sex, United States, 1966-1972

	16-17		18-19		20-21	
	White	Black	White	Black	White	Black
	Males					
	(as percent of civilian noninstitutional population)					
1966	1.3	2.9	3.0	4.0	1.4	4.2
1968	1.8	2.7	3.1	3.6	2.7	4.3
1970	n.a.	n.a.	4.7	6.0	4.2	7.6
	Females					
	(as percent of civilian noninstitutional population)					
1968	5.1	10.4	18.9	19.7	26.8	44.2
1970	4.5	13.6	19.1	24.3	22.1	27.8
1972	n.a.	n.a.	16.9	29.4	23.5	29.0

Source: Center for Human Resource Research, Ohio State University. National Longitudinal Survey, Male Youth and Female Youth, unpublished weighted data. Males are surveyed October-December and females are surveyed January-March.

8 Prospects 1980–1995

Auguste Comte's dictum "to know is to be able to foresee, to foresee is to be able to do" is an apt reminder of the motivation for engaging in as hazardous an occupation as forecasting. If it is close to the mark, a forecast for the next 15 years of the trend in the youth population and labor force can be an important aid for planners and policymakers.

The decision to cast demographic, educational, and labor force projections to 1995 for most of the twelve countries, giving the whole study a span of a half-century, was reinforced by several circumstances. First, virtually all who will enter the labor force up to 1995 had been born by 1979, since the usual minimum entry age is likely to be 16 by 1995. There is thus a fair amount of certainty about the population projections, assuming the accuracy of current population counts and barring large-scale wars, other major catastrophes, or net migration patterns grossly divergent from those projected in Table 2.5. Some demographic uncertainty surrounds young females, however, inasmuch as both their marriage and fertility rates to 1995 and their impact on EER and LFPR are difficult to predict. Implicit assumptions about these matters are incorporated in national educational and labor force projections for females.

Second, since many of the twelve countries included in this study responded to the request by OECD that they provide national projections of labor force and LFPR from 1975 to 1990 according to uniform definitions and specifications, projections are available that are consistent with OECD data used in earlier chapters.* Moreover, national projections are available to fill blanks in the OECD projections and to validate them. Such national projections also assist in establishing the underlying assumptions made by different countries for the period ahead. Finally, this is an opportunity to compare our findings and their implications for the future with the results of national projections of the youth labor force.

Both in terms of the flow of events and the availability of data, the years from 1975 to 1980 represent a transition period from the historical past to the projected future. Within this half-decade, several turning points in medium-term trends may be observed. Therefore, both 1975 and 1980 or intermediate years are cited as base years on occasion. In some countries and series 1975 data are historical, and in some they are projected.

Population Projections

As a prime determinant of the size of the youth labor force, the projected youth population from 1975–1980 to 1995 is fairly reliably established from hard data on births through 1979 (*Table A2.1).† In most of the twelve countries the size of the youth population will follow a decidedly different trend from that shown previously, especially if 1960 marks the beginning of the period (*Table A2.6). Those countries

---

*Projections published by OECD in *Demographic Trends 1950–1990*, Paris, 1979, differ slightly in some cases from the unpublished revised data of March 1979 which we use here.
†Tables marked with an asterisk are not included in this volume, but may be obtained from the authors.

Chart 8.1 Actual and Projected Index of Population Change, Teenagers (15-19 Years), in Twelve Countries, 1950-1990

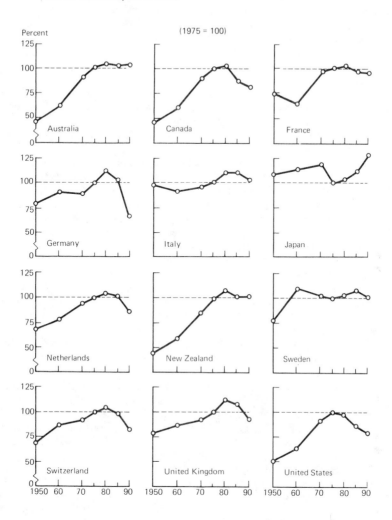

Source: OECD, Manpower and Social Affairs Committee, Demographic Trends: Their Labour Market and Social Implications, Annex 2, unpublished revisions (Paris, 1979).

which predominantly had larger teenage cohorts each year from the 1960s, or earlier, up to the late 1970s or into the 1980s will show a reverse pattern of diminishing teenage cohorts from the peak year through all or most of the years to 1995 (Charts 8.1, A8.1; *Table 8.1). While the decline will not be steady or unreversed and differences among countries will appear, a general downward movement will occur in Canada, France, Germany, Italy, the Netherlands, Switzerland, the United States, and the United Kingdom in the size of teenage population (US 1965-78; Netherlands 1976a; GB 1978c; Canada 1979b; France 1979b; Germany 1979; OECD 1979b).

The change in situation from the earlier period, extreme in the case of Canada and the United States, will not affect Australia and New Zealand, which were among the leaders in the sustained postwar baby boom (*Table A2.1). Because their high level of births persisted through the 1970s, Australia and New Zealand are likely to experience a continuation of annually expanding teenage cohorts to the end of the century and perhaps beyond (New Zealand 1978b).

The two remaining countries, Japan and Sweden, will have a reversal of pattern, but in the opposite direction from the first large group of countries. Japan's decided decline in the size of the teenage population began in 1967, reached bottom in 1975, and then started to climb, giving Japan the only genuine teenage population boom in the period to 1995. Sweden, showing a drop in teenage population from 1963, began a modest rising trend in 1977, which will last through 1995 with oscillations (Sweden 1977b; OECD 1979a).

The divergence in prospects among these twelve countries is indicated in the fact that Germany's 1990 teenage population is likely to be 30 percent lower than its 1975 level, while Japan's may be almost 30 percent higher. While the German figure is somewhat affected by counting only German nationals, both the US and Canada also show a substantial drop in teenage population (Charts 8.1, A8.1; Germany 1980a). Some countries which will experience a decline in teenage numbers from 1980 will nevertheless have a larger total in 1990 or 1995 than they had in 1975; Italy is one such case. Projections for Japan, the Netherlands, and New Zealand to 1990, as developed by OECD, contain no assumptions about net migration. Japan's situation is not much affected, judging by past trends; the omission of migration assumptions probably understates the growth in New Zealand and is more difficult to assess in the Netherlands. The general expectation of OECD is that future trends in net migration will be less significant than in the recent past.

Following five years behind teenagers, the young adult population (20–24 years old) exhibits later turning points and fewer countries whose 1990 or 1995 young adult population will be below the 1975 level. Among the nine countries examined, the US, Japan, and France will have fewer young adults in 1990 than in 1975; Canada, the Netherlands, and Sweden will show small increases in the same time period; and New Zealand, the UK, and Italy will experience substantial increases ranging from 17.1 to 15.4 percent (*Table 8.1; Charts 8.2, A8.2). Within the 15-year time span, only Italy shows an increase in each five-year period. The other countries—Canada, UK, the Netherlands, and New Zealand—have at least one period of decline, often after two periods of rise (Netherlands 1976a; New Zealand 1978b). The U.S. decline of more than 6 percent from 1975 to 1990 is the largest and is likely to continue through 1995 (US 1965–78). National projections for Sweden, France, and the UK (whose turning point is 1987), also show 1995 totals lower than those for 1990 (Sweden 1977f; France 1978c, 1979b; GB 1978c). In addition, births data for Canada, Germany, and Italy indicate a declining 20–24-year-old population from 1990 through 1995 (excluding migration effects).

Several countries whose overall youth population will decline, promising easier accommodation in educational institutions and in the labor force, will simultaneously face a continuing increase in the number of minority or immigrant youth or at least a rising share of such youth in the total. As Chapter 7 suggested, it would be wise to develop separate projection series, with and without net migration assumptions, for the special groups of youth in order to understand and plan for these subdivisions whose educational and labor force problems diverge from those of the majority.

The countries which confront sustained increases in the size of youth cohorts from 1975–1980 to 1995 will be in a less favorable position than the countries where numbers are generally declining, to the extent that pressures are placed on the educa-

Chart 8.2   Actual and Projected Index of Population Change, Young Adults (20-24 Years), in Twelve Countries, 1950-1990

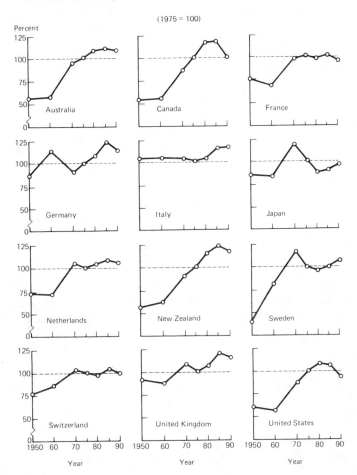

Source: OECD, Manpower and Social Affairs Committee, Demographic Trends: Their Labour Market and Social Implications, Annex 2, unpublished revisions (Paris, 1979). Projections include migration assumptions.

tional systems and other age-specific activities. Young people will face competition with their peers which earlier or later cohorts may not confront. Whether such added numbers of youth are a burden or a blessing to the economy depends on youth and other participation rates (LFPR), the rate of economic expansion, the level of employability of the young people, the organization and structure of the job market, and the degree of reliance on foreign workers or permanent immigrants in the event of labor shortages. Some indication of the complexity of the issues and the diversity of opinion is conveyed in discussions of the future, to the end of the century and beyond, of the youth cohorts in the United States that derive from the postwar baby boom (Easterlin 1973, 1978; Wachter 1976, 1977; Easterlin, Wachter, and Wachter

1978; US 1978e; Freeman 1979b; Welch 1979; Russell 1980).

At present writing, the four countries most likely to experience rising numbers of youth — Australia, New Zealand, Japan, and Sweden — are not short of young workers with the educational and skill qualifications currently required by the labor market. The situation may well change as the period advances, but present medium-term economic forecasts are not promising. Seen simply from the supply side, Australia and New Zealand would be expected to have greater persistence of high youth unemployment than Canada and the United States.

Since the absolute size of a youth cohort may be incongruent with the number of available entry level jobs, in countries where cohorts of youth are shrinking in size, some advantage may accrue to those who follow larger cohorts. But in a great many activities, including the labor market, there may be competition across age groups. What counts then is the relative size of the teenage cohort compared to that of young adults, the 25-34-year group, and even the entire working-age population. Projected trends in the size of the working-age population and in the shares of teenagers and young adults in the larger group therefore constitute an important aspect for individual countries and for comparisons among nations.

Considering projections for nine countries from 1975 to 1990, only Japan is likely to show a distinctly higher share of teenagers by 1990 than in 1975, reversing a long-run trend of declining shares to 1975 in Japan (Tables 8.2, A2.8). Italy, Sweden, and the United Kingdom project some rise in the teenage share, followed by declines. Five countries — Canada, France, the Netherlands, New Zealand, and the US — show steady decline in shares from 1975. In 1990, teenage shares of the working-age population in nine countries are projected to range from 9.9 percent in Canada to 13.0 percent in New Zealand, with six countries falling between 10.3 and 11.2 percent. This compares with a 1975 range of 10.2 percent in Sweden to 15.7 percent in New Zealand, with four countries between 10.2 and 11.8 percent (Table 8.2). New Zealand, and probably Australia, will have the highest teenage shares to 1995, due in part to substantial growth of the teenage population. Despite its projected increase in teenage population, Sweden's teenage share will remain one of the lowest among the countries. These population shares are not the same as projected labor force shares, which are discussed below.

Trends in the shares of 20-24-year-olds are less consistent. While six countries — Canada, France, Japan, the Netherlands, New Zealand, and the US — have lower shares in 1990 than in 1975, only France shows a steady decline in each five-year interval. According to national data for 1990-1995, in both youth age groups the share of the working-age population will decline further in six countries (US 1965-78; Netherlands 1976a; Sweden 1977f; GB 1978c; New Zealand 1978b; France 1979b). In 1990 the young adult shares of the working-age population are projected to range from 10.3 percent in Japan to 12.9 percent in New Zealand, with five countries falling between 11.2 and 11.7 percent, a smaller spread than for teenagers. The 1975 shares for young adults ranged from 10.7 percent in Sweden to 14.3 percent in Canada, with six countries showing over 12 percent. Japan's rising absolute number of young adults in the projection period is associated with lower shares than in the other eight countries in 1980, 1985, and 1990, and Sweden also is at the low end in the population shares. New Zealand (and Australia) will have large shares of young adults throughout the projection period compared to other countries, although after 1985 a declining trend is projected (Table 8.2).

These projections of youth shares of population should be weighed simultaneously with the demographic trends for each age group, since both the absolute numbers of

young people and their relative position vis-à-vis other age groups are important guides to national policy. Comparative interpretations of possible changes in educational enrollment and the youth labor market in the period ahead require careful consideration of the demographic differences among countries.

Labor Force Projections

Far less certainty attaches to projections of the youth labor force than to the youth population projections that were solidly based on births already registered. All practitioners acknowledge that projections based on extrapolations of current trends must make tenuous and arbitrary assumptions. When projections prove to be close to the mark, as often as not it is due to compensating errors rather than accurate estimation. This is not surprising, given the many variables that are included in overall trends and the propensity of these variables to alter over time.

Extrapolations of current trends are the mainstay of projections, whether they refer to population, educational enrollments, or labor force size and participation rates. Differences in results may appear in several projections for an identical subject and time period. These are due to variations in the conditions prevailing in the starting and terminal years of the base period, the length of time covered in the estimation period for deriving trends, the functional form chosen for estimation, and the extrapolation procedures adopted. Because of the uncertainties, labor force and educational projectors in several countries are beginning to copy the established procedure in population projections, in which three or four different projections are produced, based on varying assumptions about the course of the main components. For example, New Zealand's alternative projections of labor force size from 1979 to 1985 are based on a single labor force participation rate for each group, derived from the 1961-1976 trend, but use three variants of net annual migration (New Zealand 1978b, Table 6). These do not have strong effects on youth, since the 1985 teenage male labor force varies only slightly, from 78,600 to 79,400, under the three migration assumptions. A later section cites other efforts at alternative labor force projections. No matter how hard the estimators try to give equal validity to all of their alternative projections, users tend to choose the projection that falls in the middle.

Bearing these general limitations in mind, youth labor force projections to 1995 can be examined directly, using the OECD series and national estimates which extend or revise projections. There is no need to proceed through an independent examination of educational enrollment projections, since the extrapolation of labor force trends incorporates the influence of trends in educational enrollment rates and tactily assumes that both trends will continue as reflected in prior LFPR. It is, however, useful to compare independent labor force projections and educational enrollment projections for specific groups and countries as a test of consistency. The two sets of estimators are not known to consult one another or even to use each other's products. Labor force projections usually are made for the entire labor force, subdivided into conventional age groups; special information for particular age groups, such as projected EER, does not commonly enter into the calculations. Although projections of educational enrollments and EER are made for a more limited age group, they are subject to all of the estimating difficulties that plague labor force projections.

An overview of the official projections of the youth labor force to 1990–1995 for nine countries shows many nations with a smaller youth labor force than in the period 1960–1975, except for young adult females who show a rise in seven countries.

In most countries there will be more pronounced changes in labor force size for male teenagers than for young adult males, while young adult females will have greater change in labor force size than teenage females. Among teenage and young adult females, in many countries the projected change in labor force size exceeds that in population size.

Projections of youth labor force participation rates to 1995 largely reveal belief in the persistence of trends observed from the 1960s to 1975–1979. Most countries foresee a continuing surge in the LFPR of young adult females, a sustained decline in LFPR in both male age groups and among teenage females due mainly to increased EER, and a further convergence of male and female LFPR, leading in a few countries to female LFPR that will surpass male rates. In the years ahead, youth will have declining shares of the total labor force in most countries, contrasting with the pre-1975 experience of long periods of rising youth shares (Table A2.8). Implicit in generally lower LFPR of youth is a continued rise in educational enrollment rates and levels of educational attainment. In some countries, the increased LFPR of enrolled students assumed in the projection of earlier trends may offset a decline in LFPR among the nonenrolled. Changes in the youth shares of the total labor force (15–64), for the most part reflect downward movement in numbers on the youth side and upward movement in the 25–64 group, reflecting the maturation of earlier baby boom cohorts.

Labor Force Size

Most of the countries project that their teenage labor force will be smaller in 1990 and 1995 than it was in 1975. Up to 1990 only Sweden projects a rise in labor force size (3.8 percent) for males; for females, Sweden has a substantial increase, and New Zealand and the United States have slight increases. Italy, the Netherlands, and Canada indicate the largest declines for each sex, ranging from one-third to more than half in the 1975–1990 period (*Table 8.1; Chart A8.3; GB 1969–80d; Sweden 1976b; France 1978c; New Zealand 1978b).

The drop in the male and female teenage labor force exceeds the age group's decline in population in Canada, France, the Netherlands, and the United Kingdom. In Italy and Japan for both sexes and in New Zealand for males, a decrease in teenage labor force numbers will accompany a rise in the age group's population. American male teenagers have a smaller decline in labor force than in population, and females actually show a small rise in labor force against a drop in population. Teenage females in New Zealand also have an increase in the projected labor force, although smaller than the rise in population. In Sweden, both sexes have increases in labor force in excess of population growth. In six of the nine countries, the female labor force will decline more slowly or grow more rapidly than the male. Only Canada, Italy, and the UK project a larger drop in the size of the teenage female than the male labor force to 1990, and the Canadian difference between the sexes is small (*Table 8.1; Chart A8.3).

The 20–24-year group is projected to show less departure to 1995 from the labor force size reached in the pre-1975 period than will teenagers. This trend arises in part because young adults display the effects of demographic trends in births five years later than teenagers, on average, and because young adult females are projected to have a sharper increase in LFPR than teenage females. For young adults the projected sex differences from 1975 to 1990 are striking. In seven countries, the female labor force will show increases of 11 to 30 percent; declines will occur only in Canada and Japan. On the other hand, the male labor force is projected to increase only in four countries and by no more than 5 to 15 percent (*Table 8.1; Chart A8.3). The drop in the male labor force to 1990 will persist as France, New Zealand, and Sweden show further declines to 1995 (Sweden 1976b; France 1978c; New Zealand 1978b).

Among young adult males the largest relative growth in labor force size to 1990 is projected for the United Kingdom, and the largest decline is shown for Japan. Young adult females in Italy show the greatest rise and those in Japan the greatest decrease. Japan's youth labor force in both age groups and sexes will diminish, but more substantially for young adults. Sweden is the only country where a rise is projected for each age-sex group (*Table 8.1; Chart A8.3). Change in labor force size was projected to exceed change in population size for young adult males in France and Japan; in Canada and the Netherlands the population change is positive and the labor force change is negative. For females 20–24, as expected, predicted labor force change surpasses population change in all countries except New Zealand; in France and the United States positive labor force growth accompanies negative population change (*Table 8.1, Chart A8.2).

The impact on the nation and the specific cohorts of young people of changes in numbers in the labor force is, as was stated earlier, complex and varies with circumstances in each country at the time. A possibility not contemplated in the projections is that the youth labor force might in fact be larger or smaller than projected, because of cyclical events in the particular years selected for forecasts. It also is possible that the year-to-year variations in the size of a cohort may affect the proportion entering the labor force.

Youth Shares of the Labor Force

Generally declining labor force numbers for the 15–19-year group contrast with rising numbers in the 25–64-year labor force, due to a continued inflow of women and maturation of large youth cohorts. Therefore, steadily declining shares of the total labor force are projected for teenagers in seven of the eight countries for which data are available (Table 8.2). Sweden is the exception, showing a stable share between 1975 and 1980, an increase between 1980 and 1985, and a decline to 1990; this results in a lower share than in 1975. National data for New Zealand and Sweden indicate projected declines in teenage labor force shares continuing after 1990, through 1995 (Sweden 1976b; New Zealand 1978b).

In terms of shares of the total labor force, the 20–24-year-old group is projected to show generally downward trends, though not to the extent of the younger age group (Table 8.2). Of the eight countries for which data are available, France, Japan, and the Netherlands show steadily falling shares over the whole period. New Zealand and the United States display falling shares after 1980, as do Italy and the United Kingdom after 1985. Sweden shows the young adult share rising after 1980 to 1990. Swedish national data project a declining share from 1990 to 1995; national data for France and New Zealand do likewise (Sweden 1976b; France 1978c; New Zealand 1978b).

The range of teenage shares of the labor force in 1990 is expected to be from 3.3 percent in France to 10.6 percent in New Zealand, a narrower range than in 1975 when Japan's 3.3 percent was the lowest and New Zealand's 13.8 percent the highest. It is noteworthy that the spread among countries in teenage shares of the labor force is wider than for teenage shares of the population in both 1990 and 1975. Labor force shares are smaller than population shares, as expected. Aging of the labor force is of concern in several countries, especially Japan.

Among young adults, the 1990 range of labor force shares will be from 11.0 percent to 14.5 percent, while the 1975 range was from 9.0 percent to 16.3 percent. The spread in labor force shares was somewhat wider than in population shares, but not markedly so. In the 1990 projections six out of seven countries show higher young adult shares of the labor force than of the working-age population. In 1975, eight of the nine countries were in this position, providing evidence of the importance of this age group in the labor force.

The significance of rising or falling youth shares in the labor force in particular countries and of low or high shares in cross-national comparisons cannot be established without reference to more specific institutional and economic circumstances in each country at a given time. In principle, a large or increasing share of teenagers or young workers in the labor force implies a dilution of the labor force with inexperienced workers and a reduction in average productivity; this has been alleged to be one cause of the slow-down in productivity growth in the United States in the 1970s.

On the other hand, Germany has treated its expected large cohorts of school-leavers in the early 1980s as a great asset to the economy, to be trained for skilled work through the apprenticeship system and held in reserve for a later period in the 1980s when the number of teenagers will drop and shortages of skilled workers are expected to be severe. Recognizing that this line of argument is a convenient rationale for expansion of the number of apprenticeship places to absorb the current large outflow from the basic schools, one who has interviewed German business leaders and trade unionists knows that the fear of future labor shortage is sincerely felt. Whether Germans would have the same attitudes if their youth shares were as high as those in, say, New Zealand is open to question. Yet it appears, on balance, that rational reactions to impending changes in youth shares of the labor force are shaped primarily by such specific factors as the existence of institutional arrangements to absorb and train new entrants and a perceived need in the economy for young workers.

Labor Force Participation Rates

According to OECD data for eight countries, LFPR for teenage males in 1990 are likely to range from 17.7 percent in the Netherlands to 56.9 percent in the United Kingdom. Japan's rate, not estimated here, would be even lower than the Netherlands. Most countries' LFPR will fall in the 45- to 57-percent interval in 1990 (Charts 8.3, A8.1). Compared to 1975 LFPR for teenage males, the 1990 rates are somewhat lower; in 1975 the UK had the highest LFPR for teenage males (57.6 percent), while Japan was lowest with 20.4 percent. The absolute level of LFPR for male teenagers in the nine countries will range as widely in 1990 as it did at any time from 1945 to 1975. The countries are polarized between a majority with a projected 1990 LFPR of 45 percent or more and four in the low range—two just over 20 percent (France and Italy) and two under 20 percent (Netherlands and Japan). If the three missing countries were added, Australia and Switzerland would join the majority with relatively high LFPR, while Germany might fall at or just below the lower limit. Most countries project a decline in male teenage LFPR. Projections of LFPR of less than 19 percent in Japan and the Netherlands imply extraordinarily high EER with little labor force participation by enrolled students, since they do not project a trend increase in NISLF teenage males. Only the United States and Sweden indicate

Chart 8.3   Projected Labor Force Participation Rates, by Age and Sex, in Nine Countries, 1975-1990

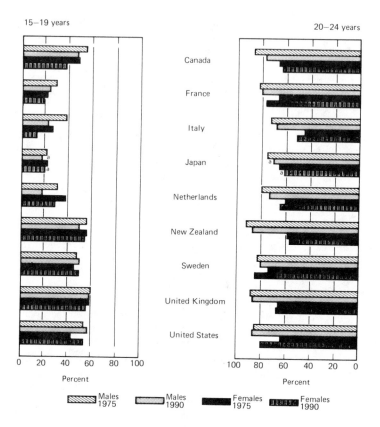

15—19 years   20—24 years

Canada
France
Italy
Japan
Netherlands
New Zealand
Sweden
United Kingdom
United States

0   20   40   60   80   100   100   80   60   40   20   0

Percent   Percent

Males 1975   Males 1990   Females 1975   Females 1990

ᵃ1985.

Source: Charts A8.1, A8.2.

a rise in LFPR for teenage males during the whole projection period (Charts 8.3, A8.1). In the earlier historical period, no country had as prolonged a period of rise in LFPR for this age group as is now projected in the US and Sweden; it reflects the rising LFPR of students in the base period.

LFPR for teenage females follow similar paths and are around the same level as those of males; much the same countries tend to appear as the high and low nations. In 1990, the range for teenage females should be from 13.1 percent in Italy to 54.8 percent in the United Kingdom. Higher rates prevailed in 1975, when the range was from 21.2 percent in France to 56.7 percent in the UK. There is the same polarization of countries as with males. The majority of countries have LFPR for teenage females of 45 percent or more during most of the projection period and would be joined by Australia, Germany, and Switzerland. Japan, France, and Italy are around 20 percent or lower, while the Netherlands is in a middle ground of around 30 percent (Charts 8.3, A8.1).

Trends from 1975 to 1990 and beyond are mostly downward, in some cases by striking proportions. Only Sweden and the US show a rise throughout the projection period, a reflection of rising female LFPR and combinations of education and labor force participation. In the other countries an assumed rise in EER, extrapolated from earlier periods, is chiefly responsible for the decline in LFPR.

Convergence of teenage male and female LFPR, apparent before 1975, is expected to continue. In 1975 females had higher LFPR than males in Japan and the Netherlands; projections to 1990 widen the female excess. In these countries, the higher EER of males and acceptance that unmarried females will enter the labor market account for the higher female LFPR. In New Zealand, teenage female LFPR will surpass male in 1980 and thereafter, according to OECD data, but not according to national projections (New Zealand 1978b). The OECD definition of teenagers (15–19 years old) does not fit the labor market situation in Sweden and the US, given a legal school-leaving age of 16; but even by the OECD definition, Swedish female teenagers will have a higher LFPR than males by 1990. At that time, U.S. teenage female LFPR will be only two percentage points below male LFPR (Charts 8.3, A8.1).

LFPR for males 20–24 years old have a narrower range among the countries than those for teenagers and are projected to change less from 1975 to 1990 (Charts 8.3, A8.2). In 1990, the range would be from a low of 68.3 percent in Italy (subject to the questions about accuracy and coverage) to a high of 86.9 percent in New Zealand. In 1975 the males ranged from 72.1 percent in Italy to 91.3 percent in New Zealand (Charts 8.3, A8.2). The relatively narrow range among the countries at any point in time, the small changes over time, and the stability in country ranks are evidence of the high degree of commitment to the labor market and the limited potential for expanding EER in this age-sex group.

Females aged 20–24 also show less dispersion in 1990 than teenagers, but in a number of countries young adult females show the strongest projected growth of any sex-age group. The female range in 1990 will be from 51.4 percent in Italy to 84.3 percent in Sweden. Compared to the range of 1975 LFPR for females, the 1990 LFPR range is expected to be somewhat higher. In 1975 the low was 45.3 percent in Italy and the high 73.7 percent in Sweden; the LFPR for the other countries clustered around 65 percent in 1975. The low and high countries are identical in both years (Charts 8.3, A8.2). New Zealand national data (1978b) display rather higher participation rates for 20–24-year-old females than do OECD; the difference between sources is projected to rise to 10 percent in 1985–1986.

Trends in labor force participation rates for young adults by sex will diverge even more in the projection period than in the pre-1975 period. The general trend of male LFPR is downward, with six of the nine countries projecting steady decrease and two indicating mixed decline. Only the United States has a rise between 1975 and 1990. Sweden increases to 1985 and then drops back below the 1975 level. Females, however, have steadily rising LFPR in five countries, and recovery after drops in two others. National data confirm and extend these trends to 1995 (GB 1969–80d; France 1978c; New Zealand 1978b; Sweden 1978g). In France, Italy, Sweden, and the US, young adult female LFPR rates are projected to be at least five percentage points higher in 1990 than they were in 1975, while the Netherlands and the UK have smaller increases. Rising LFPR for young adult females do not imply reductions in EER, since the residual NISLF rates are sufficiently high to permit the expansion of both LFPR and EER, while female NISLF rates decline. Canada, Japan, and New Zealand will show a drop in LFPR, reflecting anticipated growth in EER for young adult females, a possibly static position of the NISLF group, and residual obstacles to the absorption of married women in the labor market.

As a consequence of these projected trends, a catch-up of young adult female LFPR to male LFPR is predicted in the 1975-1990 period; rates for this age group were widely separated by sex in the pre-1975 period, unlike those of teenagers. In five countries—Canada, France, Italy, the Netherlands and the US—female LFPR will move much closer to male rates, and in Sweden they will exceed male rates by 1990. The remaining three countries—Japan, New Zealand, and the UK—also show some narrowing of the gap in rates between the sexes (Charts 8.3, A8.2).

Having examined the main features of the OECD projection data, we briefly present some alternative national projections before considering the reliability of the projected LFPR.

Alternative LFPR Projections

Projections for a given time period may change significantly if the projectors have opportunities to issue revisions. Reviewing the most recent developments and in some cases incorporating the newly accumulated experience, the projectors arrive at new numbers and rates. Thus, in some countries more recent LFPR projections have been issued, which differ from those supplied to the OECD. An example of a revision of an official projection of LFPR is Sweden's 1977 alteration of its 1975 projections. For males, for example, the projections made in 1975 showed no change from 1975 to 1985 in LFPR rates, but those made in 1977 and extending only to 1983 showed a marked drop in LFPR from 1975. In the same way, the 1977 projection for Swedish women 20-24 modified the 1975 projection by showing a continued rise in LFPR to 1983 for those with no children under seven years of age, instead of an unchanged rate from 1975, and a less steep rise than was projected in 1975 for those with children under seven years of age (Sweden 1978g).

Sweden also has developed a more complex set of three alternative projections of LFPR to year 2025, in which assumptions about fertility, unemployment rates, and LFPR are varied. Designated O-alternative, trend-alternative and maximum-alternative, the three paths show considerable spread for the youth groups (Table 8.3).

Apart from the differences shown for the youth groups in the three alternatives, the Swedish procedures indicate an unwillingness to make projections far into the future. In the low O-alternative, rates remain unchanged after 1983. In the other two alternatives, no change occurs after 2000, and all youth age-sex groups have identical projected LFPR rates of 70 percent after 2000, under the maximum-alternative. The trend-alternative projection, showing a slight increase in teenage LFPR to 1995,

Table 8.3   Projections of Youth Labor Force Participation Rates, Sweden, 1983-2025

Age-sex groups	Actual 1978	O-alternative 1983-2025	Trend-alternative 1995	Trend-alternative 2000-2025	Maximum-alternative 1995	Maximum-alternative 2000-2025
			(percent)			
16-19 male	55.0	54.1	56.2	56.4	65.3	70.0
16-19 female	55.5	56.4	56.4	56.4	66.0	70.0
20-24 male	82.9	86.1	86.1	86.1	74.7	70.0
20-24 female	77.6	82.9	85.8	86.1	73.8	70.0

Source: Arbetskraftsresurserna 1977-2025 [Labour Force Resources 1977-2025], unpublished (Stockholm: SCB).

displays greatest similarity to OECD projections of teenage Swedish LFPR to 1990, although LFPR levels shown by the two sources are somewhat divergent as a result of different age groupings (15–19 years for the OECD and 16–19 for national data). While the trend-alternative LFPR projection also matches the OECD projection for Swedish young adult females, Swedish national projections show greater projected growth for young adult males (with the exception of the marked decline over the period in the maximum-alternative) than the OECD projections (Sweden 1978g; OECD 1979a).

Uncertainty that a single set of LFPR projections can be made with confidence has led other countries to offer a series of alternative LFPR projections—usually low, medium, and high—based on different assumptions about trends in the crucial variables. Development of such alternative LFPR projections copies procedures commonly used in population projections. In 1978 the U.S. Bureau of Labor Statistics for the first time offered three alternative paths for LFPR to 1990 (Flaim and Fullerton 1978). Covering five separate age-sex groups and two racial groups, these alternative LFPR are based on a population already born; the only variant is in the assumptions about the course of LFPR. The three U.S. alternatives show markedly different projected LFPR for the youth groups. Female teenagers, the most affected group, have a projected 1990 total LFPR ranging from 57.0 percent to 69.0 percent. Young adult women, projected to have a greater increase in LFPR than any other youth group under each of the three alternatives, show a 1990 range of 75.4 to 85.3 percent (Flaim and Fullerton 1978). OECD projections of U.S. teenage LFPR show increases over the period comparable to the intermediate national projection for both sexes. Exact comparison of projections for teenagers is hampered, however, by the use of different age groups: 15–19 years by the OECD, 16–19 by the national source. For young adults of both sexes, the OECD projections and the national intermediate projections are directly comparable from 1980 to 1990 (Flaim and Fullerton 1978; OECD 1979a).

Accepting the OECD projections of LFPR as a reasonable cross-national data bank, one can verify them in two main ways. The first is to compare them with educational enrollment rate projections. The second is to discuss limiting factors and potential changes in trends in important variables which may affect LFPR, drawing on the discussion in earlier chapters. Both approaches are methods of checking on projections based on extrapolations of trends.

Consistency of LFPR and EER Projections

The sum of independently derived projections of LFPR and of full-time EER for male youth should be reasonably close to 100 percent. A total under 100 percent allows for the NISLF proportion, while the LFPR of students can raise the total over 100 percent through double counting. If the totals are out of line, reason may exist to question either the projected LFPR or EER or both. In the case of males, the sum of LFPR and full-time EER should exceed 95 percent in all countries, except Italy, based on what is known about NISLF. A total in excess of 135 percent would be suspicious, since it would imply that a higher proportion of enrolled students were in the labor force than are shown in historical data for the United States, probably the country where this phenomenon is most highly developed. In addition, incompatible totals of projections of LFPR and EER also are possible for technical reasons, such as the time of year in which trend data were collected, or definitional peculiarities which result in under- or overcounting in one or both categories. However, it is unlikely that major discrepancies would be caused by these factors.

Projected LFPR and full-time EER for 1975 and 1980 can be established for nine countries, according to information they provided to OECD. Total activity rates have been derived, and it is these which suggest error if they fall much below or greatly exceed 100 percent. Limiting the examination to males, the total of projected LFPR and full-time EER for teenage males in 1975 and 1980 is thoroughly unsatisfactory only in France, because such a large residual is left; both LFPR and EER appear to be at fault. The direction of change from 1975 to 1980 in New Zealand and Canada is surprising, inasmuch as an increase in the total would be expected, representing a rising trend in LFPR of enrolled students. Italian increases in projected full-time EER from 1975 to 1980 for all teenagers seem unrealistically large for a five-year period, and the decline in LFPR may be overstated. Young adult male totals are over 95 percent in all countries in 1975 and 1980; this was set as the acceptable level. The drop from 1975 to 1980 in total activity rates in Canada, France, and New Zealand is surprising on the same ground as was given for teenagers. Still, if, as in Sweden, other countries move increasingly toward more substantial higher education enrollment for those older than 25, declines in total activity rates of the youth groups may be expected (*Table 8.4).

Because the proportion of enrolled students is so much greater among teenage males than young adult males, the latter would be expected to have a smaller excess over 100 percent than the former. This would not occur only if the percent of the age group enrolled and in the labor force was larger for young adults than teenagers. In all countries with activity rates of over 100 percent — Canada, Sweden, the UK and the US — teenagers do have higher total activity rates than young adults.

Without investigating comparable female total activity rates, it can be said that the examination of male rates above indicates that OECD projected LFPR, with the stated exceptions, are generally congruent with OECD projected EER and offer reasonable total activity rates. Additional evidence on projected full-time EER, available from published and unpublished national sources for the same years covered by OECD as well as for later years, displays the expected differences in levels and trends. But on the whole, these results of the extrapolation process validate the LFPR projections discussed earlier (US 1972, 1978g; New Zealand 1976; Sweden 1977e, 1978d; Canada 1978a, 1979b; Great Britain 1978d; Harrisson 1978; Harrisson and Hersleb 1978; Germany 1979; McGill 1979; Netherlands 1979). This does not guarantee accuracy in the projections, however. Verifications of forecasts against actual developments reveal significant differences. The amount of error in the projections usually is proportionate to the distance they look into the future, leading to suggestions that frequent revisions should be made in projections. It also is urged that evaluations should be conducted of prior forecasts. We therefore accept as inevitable that further national projections of youth LFPR and EER to 1995 and OECD revisions of their basic documents will alter the projected rates and trends we have presented here.

Modification of Extrapolated Trends

As a closing contribution to this look into the future, we discuss some of the factors observed in our historical study that may behave in a sufficiently different fashion in the years ahead to modify projections of LFPR derived from extrapolation of earlier trends. A consideration of the variables affecting both EER and youth LFPR and the earlier analysis of differences among countries in their level and trends suggests that the introduction of such factors into the calculations might alter the projections. Some countries' estimates and some age-sex groups would be more affected than others by such a procedure, which in any case is only suggestive.

On the education side, the following possible departures from earlier trends may serve as modifiers of LFPR extrapolations that implicitly assume a continuation of prior EER trends. The list, beginning with factors which may dampen the future growth of EER, is not presented in order of importance or general applicability across countries:

Direct and indirect costs of education to the individual will be much higher than earlier.

Public financial support will level off or decline.

Part-time enrollments will be much larger than prior trend.

Delays beyond the trend will occur in completion of education.

Students older than 25 years of age will comprise a much larger share of the total.

As high EER are approached, the prior expansion rate cannot continue because progression rates (from grade to grade) respond less to changes in family background factors in postsecondary than in secondary education (Mare 1977b).

Relative oversupply at more advanced educational levels beyond the trend may discourage a rise in enrollments or in EER at those educational levels.

On the other side there are fewer factors that might stimulate the growth of EER beyond the trend and hence reduce LFPR more than the extrapolation shows:

Developments in the economy may call for higher levels of educational attainment among young people than trends forecast.

A more rapid catch-up than indicated by trend may occur in the EER of groups, such as females, minorities, young people of low socioeconomic background or family income, or in geographic areas with low EER. As far as females are concerned, the relatively large proportions NISLF permit increases in both LFPR and EER. Therefore, this point is of limited significance.

Compulsory education laws may advance the school-leaving age, raising EER. This also is a point with limited impact. Most countries are not considering increases in the compulsory age and some have discussed reductions. Moreover, in the countries where such a rise is underway or contemplated—Belgium, the Netherlands, Germany, Denmark, Luxembourg—the legal enactment may have little impact on EER if voluntary EER have already risen to nearly 100 percent for the affected age group.

On balance, therefore, possible changes in EER beyond the trend seem to be directed more toward factors that would decrease rather than increase extrapolated EER. Countries in which EER had not grown strongly throughout the estimation period would be less affected than others by the departures from trend specified here. Also, some developments that dampen growth of EER are more likely to take root in certain countries than in others. But it appears that the anticipated decline in teenage LFPR to extremely low rates in Japan and the Netherlands (Italian and French estimates are suspect) may be excessive, since it is largely based on the extremely strong growth of EER through the 1970s. Factors that began to temper EER growth in other countries had not yet affected Japan and the Netherlands. Revised projections, using early 1980s experience, may result in a slower decline or leveling off of LFPR in these countries and perhaps in others.

Some factors that affect LFPR directly may change beyond trend lines. The most important is the increased tendency of students to be in the labor force during term time and vacations, and, second, the greater recording of such activity as LFPR in national surveys. Persistence of inflation, smaller government loans and grants to students (relative to direct and indirect costs of education), a trend toward living away from parents, and similar factors may increase LFPR beyond current projections.

Finally, reliance on past trends may seriously underestimate future teenage and young adult female LFPR in many countries (Smith 1979a). In particular, the age group 20-24 may confound the projectors, as happened with females in other age groups earlier. Whether or not inflation continues surely will be a factor, since it contributes to two-earner families. Most serious underestimation of future, young adult, female LFPR is likely to occur in countries such as Japan, the Netherlands, Italy, New Zealand, and Australia, where tradition and the employment structure have not favored work by married women. On the other hand, a return to earlier marriages, a larger number of children per family, and relatively fewer female-headed households might moderate the rise so that even the projections of trends would be overstated (Easterlin 1978; Easterlin, Wachter and Wachter 1979).

A scenario of a quite different kind emerges from forecasts that 80 percent or more of all new households formed in the United States between 1975 and 1990 will not be nuclear families and that women's commitment to work is a revolution whose end is not yet in sight (Smith, R.E. 1979a; Masnick and Bane 1980).

Predictions of the youth labor force also can be affected by unexpected developments on the demand side, which also tend to be experienced unevenly in various countries. Such situations as a sudden rise in energy prices, a marked strengthening of job security programs for established workers, or a cyclical upturn or downturn toward the end of the period might cause the actual youth labor force to diverge from that projected for 1995.

Despite the modifications in projected youth LFPR that might result from inclusion of the variables we have found to be important historically, and allowing for unforeseen or short-run conditions which may affect the projections, several basic conclusions remain. Substantial differences will continue among countries to the end of the century in youth population, labor force size and shares, and LFPR. Most countries will face a different quantitative situation in regard to these factors in the future than in the postwar period. The potential for qualitative mismatch between young people's qualifications and aspirations and employment opportunities is likely to widen in most countries.

Chart A8.1 Teenage Population, Labor Force, and Labor Force Participation Rates, by Sex, in Nine Countries, 1975–1990

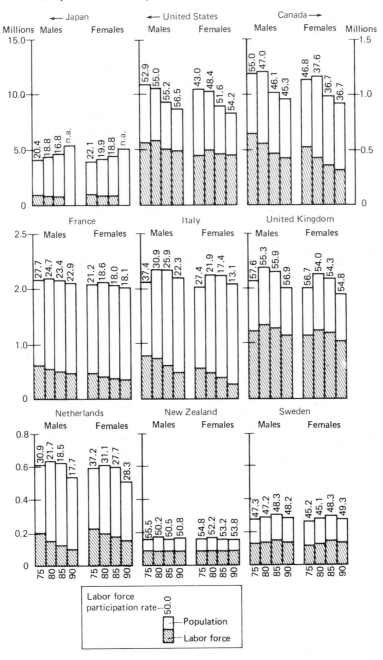

Note: Arrows indicate which scale applies to each country.

Source: OECD, Manpower and Social Affairs Committee, Demographic Trends: Their Labour Market and Social Implications, Annex 2, unpublished revisions (Paris, 1979).

Chart A8.2 Young Adult Population, Labor Force, and Labor Force Participation Rates, by Sex, in Nine Countries, 1975–1990

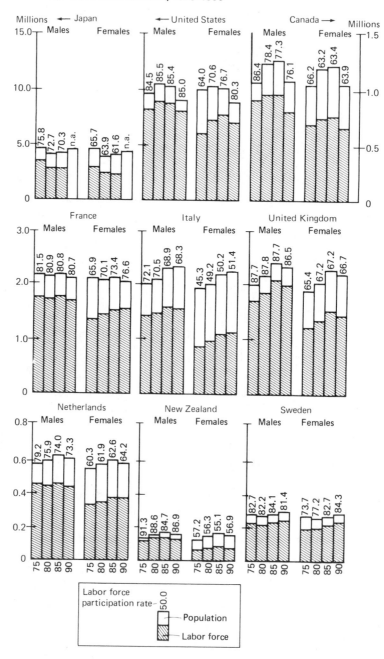

Note: Arrows indicate which scale applies to each country.

Source: OECD, Manpower and Social Affairs Committee, <u>Demographic Trends: Their Labour Market and Social Implications</u>, Annex 2, unpublished revisions (Paris, 1979).

Chart A8.3   Projected Change in Labor Force, by Age and Sex, in Nine Countries, 1975-1990

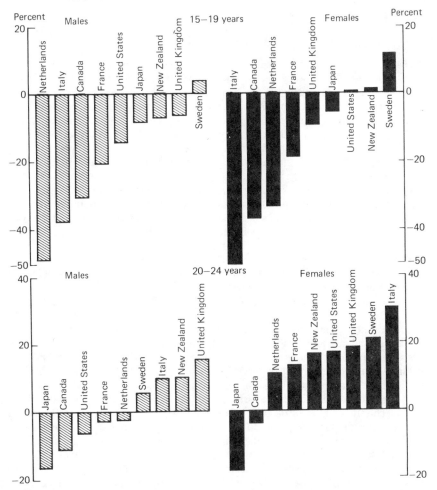

Source: OECD, Manpower and Social Affairs Committee, Demographic Trends: Their Labour Market and Social Implications, Annex 2, unpublished revisions (Paris, 1979).

9 Findings and Implications

As we examined medium-term trends in the youth labor force over the postwar half-century 1945–1995 in twelve industrialized market economy countries (Australia, Canada, France, Germany, Italy, Japan, Netherlands, New Zealand, Sweden, Switzerland, the United Kingdom, and the United States), we became aware that comparisons among actual and projected developments in these countries did not merely reveal the anticipated cross-national variation. While this aspect, of course, proved to be important, two additional features emerged. The first was that some similarities were detected among countries which were not previously established as common patterns.

One example of this is our finding, presented in Chapter 1, that gross flows in and out of the labor force are substantial and comparable in several countries, and that such changes exceed movements between employment and unemployment and vice versa. Another example is the evidence presented in Chapter 6 that, in a large number of countries, similar proportions of males in the youth age groups have been neither in school nor the labor force. Nothing is more important in comparative research than to discover that relationships previously deemed unique in individual countries are in fact shared experience.

Our second observation was that some of the actual similarities in trends may be obscured by a time lag in the development process. Relationships that appear to vary fundamentally among countries may reflect nothing more than a slower historical evolution in some countries. This may apply, for example, to changes in the distribution of employment among the primary, secondary, and tertiary sectors and particularly to the development of service employment and part-time jobs, which are so closely related to the participation of students in the labor force. Chapter 5's report of marked differences in the various countries in labor force activity by students may be chiefly a matter of delayed emergence of suitable circumstances. There is a confirmation of this interpretation in a report in the October 1980 *Japan Labor Bulletin* that recent structural changes in the labor market have kept the unemployment rate from declining as might have been expected with the current high economic growth rate. Two structural changes were identified and both are relevant to us: a sharp increase in the female labor force, catching up to developments in other countries (Chapter 4), and the appearance of youth, who previously tended to be either full-time students or full-time workers, in the part-time labor market. The latter development is consistent with the potential growth in student LFPR, discussed in Chapter 5.

We do not espouse a theory of historical inevitability, but we have been struck by the regularity with which certain types of developments spread from one industrialized country to another, albeit with time lags. This implies that, in certain aspects relevant to the youth labor force, conditions and responses observed in the United States may be a signal to other countries that similar developments will appear in their own nations. Such developments, however, may be insufficient to induce all the effects observed in the most advanced country. Institutional forces, some of which can be deliberately controlled, can modify the extent to which one nation's experience will be repeated in another. Nor should the process be seen as one of catching up to the leader, since the leader also is not standing still, and technological, organizational, and social transformations continue to alter the relationships which influence youth labor market trends. While it is true that limits exist on possible change in some variables (for example, the rise of educational enrollment rates or the decline of youth labor force participation rates, since these are bounded by 0 and 100 percent), it is unlikely that the narrowing of inter-country differences over time will result in uniformity at some future date. Nonetheless, trends toward convergence may be more significant than existing differences. This awareness of time lags among countries in economic and social development assisted us in interpreting data either as signifying basic differences among countries or as compatible trends.

In light of these general conclusions, we proceed to sum up what we have learned more specifically and then to identify the subjects that most need further data and research on a national and comparative basis. The concluding section considers the implications of our findings, bearing in mind that our subject has been medium-term trends and that our emphasis has been on supply-side variables.

Main Findings

Medium-term trends from 1945 to 1995 in the size of the youth labor force and labor force participation rates and cross-national differences in these factors are strongly influenced by the chief supply-side factors, demographic and educational enrollment rate trends. These forces overwhelm the influence of shorter-term labor market fluctuations, while some medium-term factors on the demand side are captured, at least in part, by changes in educational enrollment rates.

Sheer numbers of young people and changes in those numbers were found to be a significant element in medium-term trends and projections in the youth labor force and labor force participation rates. Population changes were identified as an influence on changes in youth labor force participation rates and educational enrollment rates and an important explanatory factor in differences among countries in LFPR and EER (Chapters 3 and 4). The record for the twelve countries of births, deaths, and migration since 1930 and of the annual numbers in the youth age groups since 1945 revealed a high potential for fluctuation in the size of the youth labor force during the postwar period and in projections to 1995 (Chapters 2 and 8). Two main patterns emerged up to 1975–1980. One group of countries, those of Oceania (Australia and New Zealand) and North America, had prolonged periods of increase in the number of young people and thus in potential entrants to the labor market. In these countries, which are the newer nations and havens of settlement for migrants, the youth groups were considerably larger at the end of the period than at the beginning. Australia and New Zealand, in particular, showed steady growth. They also absorbed their rise in youth population with ease over the 1960s and, in fact, needed immigrants to supplement the labor force. In contrast, Canada and the United States found the bulging youth cohort a continuing problem from the 1960s onward, although Canada maintained heavy immigration in order to fill occupational and geographic needs in the labor force that its youth cohorts did not or could not meet.

The remaining eight countries had more irregular patterns, with shorter periods of growth, stability, and decline intermixed. In terms of the uncertainties and discontinuities produced by these changes, the second group of countries may have had an inherently more difficult accommodation, but all were affected by the changing numbers and shares of youth. In some countries, declines in the number or share of young people were as or more challenging than increases. In the context of actual economic developments, these countries, except for Italy, could have used additional young people in most of the years. Japan's declining share of youth in the population was seen as a serious labor market problem, given the vast expansion of employment, the desire of employers to recruit young people direct from school, and the aversion to imported labor.

Thus, the economic climate plays a basic role in national reactions to demographic changes. Concomitant recession and a rise in the youth population usually draw attention to demographic factors in youth unemployment. Secular or structural changes in the demand for youth in the labor market likewise cause demographic causes to be invoked. But identical demographic circumstances may be associated with diverse conditions in various countries, so that the demographic impact on employment and unemployment is not predictable without reference to changes in other parameters. Therefore, population projections to 1995 (Chapter 8), which show different trends and relationships among countries than in the earlier period, are only one ingredient in the future course of youth unemployment in this group of countries.

Educational enrollment rate (EER) trends are closely associated with medium-term trends in youth labor force participation rates (LFPR). Historically, the secular rise in enrollment rates appears to be the force that has curtailed LFPR (Chapter 3). In the postwar period, many countries had larger increases in enrollments in the quarter-century after the end of World War II than they had had in the previous century; this resulted from a combination of demographic and EER influences. An age of mass secondary education and rising enrollment rates in higher education, added to the average years of education completed, advanced the age of leaving full-time education and removed the younger age groups from the labor force, except to the extent that students combine school and work.

Educational institutions were modified in response to the strong, private demand for education and offered shorter, vocationally oriented courses, which attracted such groups as women, low-income youth, and minority youth more than traditional forms of higher education. Some reduction in the disparities in educational participation have occurred, especially for the two sexes and, in some countries, between geographic regions or other areas. In many countries the quantitative progress in educational attainment has been criticized as masking some deterioration of standards and devaluation of diplomas, degrees, and other credentials. Employers have adjusted the educational prerequisites of jobs accordingly, while students have retained their high aspirations and expectations of their labor market rewards, based on earlier experience.

While EER showed a wide range among the twelve countries, the general rise in EER narrowed the gap among nations toward the end of the period, especially since some of the leading countries had a pause or slowdown in the advance of EER. In explaining cross-national differences in EER and changes in EER from 1960 to 1975, regression analysis confirmed the hypothesis that the growth in EER was inversely related to growth in youth population, implying that countries which confronted large increases in the number of potential students were less able to raise EER than nations with smaller rises in numbers in the age group. Starting levels of EER were not a significant explanatory factor of cross-national differences, although the results showed the expected relation that countries with lower EER, which had more room to expand, actually did so. Introduction of per capita GNP as a variable showed, as expected, that differences in GNP levels among countries were related to differences in EER and explained 26 percent of the variation for teenagers and 19 percent for young adults, lower proportions than were explained by the population growth variable. A weaker but still positive relationship resulted when growth in EER was regressed on the rate of change in per capita GNP.

The common trend toward growth in EER in the postwar period was due in part to an extension of long-run factors that had operated before the war, and in part to a new sense of the importance of education for economic development, stimulating government expenditure on education and strong private demand, which tended to outrun public provision of educational places. The slowdown or reversal by the 1970s in some countries, especially among young adults and at the higher education level, had common elements. These revolved around the belief that the relative earnings, level of available jobs, job security, and immunity to unemployment, which earlier graduates enjoyed, were no longer available to potential new entrants because of temporary or longer-run oversupply in relation to the demand for such levels of education. Governments cut back on their financial support as the recession strained budgets. Although the continued rise in EER at the earlier pace did not continue through the 1970s in many countries, EER at the end of the 1970s was much higher than at the beginning of the postwar period.

Labor force participation rates for all age-sex groups of youth, except females aged 20–24, were predominantly on a declining trend, reflecting the growth of EER. Young adult females, as part of the female revolution, had a remarkable rise in LFPR among wives and mothers in most of the countries; simultaneously EER for the young adult females also increased. An upward trend in LFPR in Canada, the United States, and Sweden for teenagers from the mid-1960s reflected the growth in student LFPR and a pause in the ascent of EER. Rising student LFPR also was a factor in holding back the decline of young adult male LFPR in some countries.

The teenage share of the total labor force of the same sex had a fairly wide range at the start and continued to show diverse trends among the individual countries, with more change over time among females than males. Countries divided into those which had a growth in the size of their teenage labor force and those which had a decline. Young adult female shares of the total female labor force were in most cases more volatile than corresponding male shares, since adult females in the labor force also were increasing. Young adult males generally formed a rising share of the male labor force, as increasing fractions of older males retired at earlier ages.

Cross-national differences in trends in LFPR were closely associated with trends in EER, growth trends in population of the respective age groups, and starting LFPR rates, according to regression analysis. The decreasing proportion not in school or the labor force (NISLF) of young adult females was an important factor in expanding their LFPR. Earnings trends did not interact with LFPR in the way that is postulated for groups of secondary workers, a label which has frequently been applied to youth. Instead, the human capital explanation of young people's choice between pursuing education and entering the labor force appeared more consonant with the facts.

Conclusions about the youth labor force based on the number of individuals registered are an inexact way of reporting on the youth labor supply. Because the student proportion of the youth labor force varies among countries and over time within countries, and because students tend to work fewer hours per week and weeks per year than nonstudents, such factors should enter into the reckoning of full-time equivalents. Based on meager data, we concluded that the student share of the youth labor force was highest in the US reflecting both high EER and a high student LFPR. Since American students also tended to work more hours per year than students in other countries, the reduction of the total would not be as great as student LFPR first suggested. Existing data place Canada behind the US, followed by Australia and Sweden, with Japan exhibiting very little student labor force activity during the school term.

The same type of adjustment would reduce the female youth labor supply relative to the male. Again, insufficient data are available at present to modify the numbers in the labor force to represent full-time equivalents. Similar conclusions were reached in regard to comparisons of the youth and adult labor force, although it is not clear that nonstudent youth work fewer hours per year than adults. Evidence has also been presented that young people have disproportionate amounts of adverse working hours, such as shifts and Sundays, and noisy, dangerous, or repetitive work, which possibly explains the choice to work fewer hours in some countries.

The investigation of young people who were not in the labor force or in school (NISLF) revealed that only a small fraction of the male age group and declining proportions of female youth were in this category (Chapter 6). On the one hand, NISLF youth offered a small base for augmenting the youth labor force, especially for males. On the other hand, analysis of the NISLF group disclosed that a majority in Sweden, Japan, and the United States, three diverse types of countries, did not wish to work or were not able to work, making the potential of entry to the labor force irrelevant for them temporarily or for a quite long period. Our findings cause us to accept NISLF as a separate category, not to be added to the unemployed to form a new category called "nonemployed." We recognize, however, that there is a continuum between a segment of the youth unemployed who are not visibly searching for employment and a portion of NISLF youth who wish to work but are not searching because they are discouraged.

Cross-national differences in male NISLF are small, suggesting some irreducible minimum level. National affluence does not appear to be a valid source of national differences in NISLF rates for males. The common features found in the US, Canada, and Italy, countries with slightly higher male NISLF rates, are high youth unemployment rates and marked geographic, income and educational differences within the youth population. Females show clearly declining trends in NISLF. A reduction in the time devoted to household tasks and a smaller proportion kept at home by such duties has resulted in a rise in female LFPR and EER. Among teenage females, the EER has benefited most, while young adult females in some countries have favored one alternative more than the other. All signs point to a continued decrease in female NISLF rates.

If governmental social programs have had the unintended effect of weakening work incentives among youth and fostering abstention from labor force participation, as is often charged, two main kinds of evidence, which might have been expected to reveal this development, fail to do so. First, trends in the proportion of youth who are NISLF, neither in school nor the labor force, demonstrate that no upward trend was exhibited by males in any country and that females had a marked drop (Chapter 6). Second, the countries with the largest variety and most generous social programs did not have the highest NISLF rates. These findings do not imply that similar results would necessarily follow if the issue were the impact of government programs on the division of the youth labor force between employed and unemployed.

Striking similarities were discovered in a number of countries in the situation of some groups of minority youth, whether race, religion, or ethnic origin defines the group and whether the group has lived in the country for centuries or has recently arrived (Chapter 7). Examining educational and training opportunities, labor force participation, and the nature of employment, we found significant evidence of disadvantage whose full proportions still must be explored in most countries. All forecasts point to a rising share of youth from minority groups in the youth population and a persistence of existing problems, with some possible exacerbation. Each nation has had conflict and change of policy in determining whether the goal should be assimilation or biculturalism, with bilingualism in the schools.

Many countries hope that the achievement of the same educational levels as majority youth reach will all but eliminate differences between the groups. American experience which now shows about the same enrollment rates for black as white youth, nevertheless suggests that educational accomplishment and equality may be insufficient to overcome other inequality. This occurs in part because the quality of education still may not be equal for the various groups and in part because the labor market either discounts the education or discriminates against some minorities. Another problem identified by the more completely recorded American experience with black youth is that they tend to constitute a disproportionate share of NISLF youth. The overcoming of disparities, which is of policy interest in many countries, has called forth many national programs. Sharing of experience among countries appears to be potentially fruitful.

Data and Research Needs

Throughout this book we have called attention to the absence of certain types of data for some or most countries. Noncomparability of data because of minor or major differences in definitions and a paucity of historical series also have been cited repeatedly and need not be repeated here. Improvement of this situation lies primarily with the individual countries, but the international agencies OECD, ILO, EC, UN, UNESCO, which have already contributed toward achieving greater coverage and uniformity in national statistical reports, may be able to stimulate still greater efforts by member countries. While the international agencies have understandably concentrated on obtaining cross-sectional data, it may be timely and feasible for OECD and EC to organize conferences on another type of data base, longitudinal surveys. Such a conference would acquaint the persons planning and engaged in such activities in each country, or interested in starting them, with the efforts in other countries (Appendix 4:1). A valuable by-product might be some areas of agreement on procedures and content, which ultimately would facilitate comparative research.

On the basis of our diligent investigation of relevant national and international research studies available to 1979, we find several specific topics treated in our book that require further research in both national and comparative perspectives. Allowing for studies unknown to us, completed too late for our use, or still in progress, we suggest that research on the following subjects in a number of countries would add useful knowledge and enable comparative analysts to draw more reliable conclusions about medium-term trends in the youth labor force:

The impact of changes in cohort size on marriage and fertility rates, educational enrollment rates, labor force participation rates, employment patterns, relative earnings, and unemployment rates of youth.

The determinants of long and medium-term trends in educational enrollment rates by age groups and sex.

Out-of-pocket private costs of education as a proportion of total family income and resources at various educational and income levels and the relation to enrollment rates.

Educational attainment levels, educational standards, aspirations of youth, and labor market requirements.

Gross flows and cohort analyses to supplement youth labor force analysis based on cross-sectional data. In countries which conduct labor force surveys, a replication can be made of the Swedish study, which followed given samples for two-year periods, classifying them by their labor force pattern over that period (Chapter 1).

Factors influencing trends in the labor force participation rates of young adult females, including the effects of marriage and fertility rates, number and age of children, educational enrollment rates, educational attainment, urbanization, composition of employment, part-time job opportunities, relative earnings, and other relevant variables.

Competition in the labor market between youth and other age groups. Effects of changing youth shares of the total labor force on youth position. Youth hours and weeks of work compared to adults.

Participation in the labor force by students and comparison with nonstudents of the same age and sex through cross-sectional, longitudinal, and gross flows data. Hours and weeks of work by enrollment status, age, and sex. Type of employment held by students, relation to subjects of study, and to later full-time jobs. Earnings of students and nonstudents.

Effects of working during the term and number of hours worked on academic attendance, performance, completion of courses, progression to next educational level, choice of curriculum, extracurricular activities, etc.

Later labor market consequences of working or not working during the school years.

Direct and detailed studies of youth who are not in school or the labor force, from longitudinal and cross-sectional data, considering numbers and proportions in the category, characteristics, causes, desire to work, persistence of NISLF, later labor market position, effects of government programs on numbers.

Overlap between youth unemployed and youth not in the labor force. Differences between youth unemployed and discouraged workers. Gross flows between in-the-labor force and not-in-the-labor force for youth groups.

Comparisons of the educational and labor market position of distinct minority youth groups with (a) the majority or whole youth population, (b) other minority youth groups, and (c) adults of the same minority group. The precondition for conducting useful research studies on minority youth is the completion of basic research on the whole youth population.

We conclude this compilation, which is suggestive rather than exhaustive, by recommending that there should be replication of some of the studies described in earlier chapters and not specifically alluded to in this section. Countries in which the necessary data exist but where such studies have not yet been undertaken can find usable models.

The foregoing list contains subjects directly related to topics dealt with in our book. Building on this foundation, it appears desirable to broaden the scope of future comparative youth studies. A parallel analysis of medium-term trends that stresses demand-side variables would be valuable. A series of additional studies can be suggested that disaggregate the whole youth labor force into its components and analyze both the supply and demand aspects. Among the subnational divisions would be geographic areas, socioeconomic status, and minority groups. A division of the youth labor force into the employed and unemployed, with detailed comparative investigations into the two components separately, would be a desirable extension of our subject matter. While unemployment has had a fair degree of attention on a comparative basis, relatively little has been done on youth employment and earnings on a cross-national basis. The present authors will, in fact, undertake such studies of youth employment.

Implications

The trends and projections in the youth labor force outlined in this comparative analysis suggest potential problems for most of the countries we studied as well as for similar countries. These are problems that might be expected to arise, whether or not overall employment growth keeps pace with the size of the total labor force and its subdivisions by age and sex. However, an important general implication of this study is that greater attention should be given to the effects on youth employment of changing numbers in the youth supply, due to demographic and educational trends, rather than concentrating so heavily on changes on the demand side.

Policymakers in each nation might consider the relevance of these ten major issues, derived from our findings:

1. Fluctuating demand by young people for places in postcompulsory educational institutions, complicating educational planning in regard to financing, building construction, teacher training, assignment of students, provision of courses, improvement of educational standards, and utilization of excess or inadequate space.

2. Continued pressure to increase the educational participation rates of females, minorities, lower-income youth, disadvantaged geographical areas, and adults in the face of possible overall contraction or slow growth of numbers.

3. Lack of congruence between (1) the content and levels of education sought and achieved by young people and (2) the actual demand in the labor market for such large numbers with high attainment in liberal arts or certain specializations, at the same time as labor shortages are experienced at lower levels.

4. Rising labor force activity by students, induced by the prolongation of education and mounting private costs of education, which raise issues both for educational policy and the labor market, especially as regards the number and conditions of part-time jobs.

5. Deteriorating position in the labor market for youth with the lowest educational qualifications, which raises policy issues about improvement of basic education, knowledge of the world of work, preparation for work, occupational skills, and the transition from school to work, as well as measures to ameliorate the relevant job markets.

6. As educational enrollment rates rise, a growing proportion of the residual out-of-school young males remain out of the labor force for substantial periods of time or move in and out, frequently creating social as well as economic problems for youth and society, particularly as regards social benefits policy.

7. Pressures to give minority and female youth the same educational, training, and employment opportunities as enjoyed by the majority and male youth.

8. Growing disparity between the trends in labor force participation rates of

young males (declining or stationary) and young females (stable or rising), potentially elevating female unemployment rates relative to male.

9. Possibly intensified competition between adult women and youth in the labor market, affecting minimum wage provisions, child labor laws, health and safety laws, and other protective legislation, as well as youth unemployment rates.

10. Blocked access to promotions on career ladders for the smaller cohorts that follow the large cohorts now entering the prime-age work force.

In view of the wide range of problems disclosed, plus others that might be added, and in view of the substantial interrelations among these problems, it becomes all the more important for policymakers to formulate systematic, anticipatory plans. If they will undertake such planning in the knowledge that these issues are common to many countries, they will be more apt to seek joint consultation with other nations and thus be better prepared to cope with their own problems as they emerge. In that event, comparative research will have made a contribution beyond that of separate national studies.

Bibliography

Adams, V.A., and Mangum, G.L. 1978. *The Lingering Crisis of Youth Unemployment.* Kalamazoo, Michigan: W.E. Upjohn Institute.

American Educator. 1978. "London Schools: The View from Within." December.

Andersen, P. 1977. "Tax Evasion and Labor Supply." *Scandinavian Journal of Economics* 79, no. 2.

Anderson, B.E., and Sawhill, I.V., eds. 1980. *Youth Employment and Public Policy.* The American Assembly, Columbia University. Englewood Cliffs, New Jersey: Prentice-Hall.

Anderson, C.A.; Bowman, M.J.; and Tinto, V. 1972. *Where Colleges Are and Who Attends: Effects of Accessibility on College Attendance.* A report prepared for the Carnegie Commission on Higher Education. New York: McGraw-Hill.

Anderson, E. 1980. "Some Observations of Black Youth Employment" in Anderson, B.E., and Sawhill, I.V., eds. *Youth Employment and Public Policy.* Englewood Cliffs, New Jersey: Prentice-Hall.

Anderson, J.M. 1978. *Substitution Among Age Groups in the United States Labor Force.* Research Paper no. 18. Williams College. Williamstown, Massachusetts.

Antos, J.R., and Mellow, W.S. 1979. *The Youth Labor Market: A Dynamic Overview.* BLS Staff Paper 11. U.S. Department of Labor, Bureau of Labor Statistics. Washington: GPO.

Antos, J.R.; Mellow, W.S.; and Triplett, J.E. 1979. "What is a Current Equivalent to Unemployment Rates of the Past?" *Monthly Labor Review,* March.

Aoki, H., and Tomizawa, M. 1968. "An Analysis of the Decrease of Births in 1966." *Annual Reports of the Institute of Population Problems.* Tokyo: Ministry of Health and Welfare, Institute of Population Problems.

Ashenfelter, O. 1978. "What Do Teenage Employment Statistics Measure?" *Conference on Youth Unemployment: Its Measurement and Meaning. Supplementary Papers.* Washington: Department of Labor, Office of Assistant Secretary for Policy, Evaluation, and Research.

Ashenfelter, O., and Heckman, J.D. 1972. *Estimating Labor Supply Functions.* Working Paper no. 34, Industrial Relations Section. Princeton University. Princeton, New Jersey.

AUSTRALIA

1971-80. *The Labour Force.* Australian Bureau of Statistics (ABS). Canberra, annual.

1972-78. *Labour Force Experience.* Australian Bureau of Statistics (ABS). Canberra, biennial.

1974-80. *The Labour Force.* Australian Bureau of Statistics (ABS). Canberra, monthly.

1978. *Employment Status of Teenagers, August 1978.* Australian Bureau of Statistics (ABS). Canberra.

1979. *Persons Not in the Labour Force, March 1979.* Australian Bureau of Statistics (ABS). Canberra.

1979a. *Education, Training and Employment.* Report of the Committee of Inquiry into Education and Training. 3 vols. Canberra: Australian Government Publishing Service.

Bancroft, G. 1958. *The American Labor Force.* New York: W. Ley.

Barber, A. 1980. "Ethnic Origin and the Labour Force." Great Britain Department of Employment *Gazette,* August.

Baudot, J.; Desmotte, S.F.; and Vimont, C. 1968. *Conditions de vie et d'emploi des jeunes travailleurs* [Conditions of Life and Work of Young Workers]. INED (Institut d'études démographiques). Résultats de deux enquêtes. Travaux et documents. Cahier no. 50. Paris: Presses universitaires de France.

Bazelly, J.P. 1977. "Les sorties du système scolaire" [Exits from the Educational System]. *Economie et statistique,* September.

Beck, R.H. 1971. *Change and Harmonization in European Education.* Minneapolis, Minnesota: University of Minnesota Press.

Becker, G.S. 1965. "A Theory of the Allocation of Time." *Economic Journal,* September.

Beckerhoff, D. 1976. *Individual Demand for Education. Case Study: Germany.* SME/ET/76.24. Paris: OECD.

Bednarzik, R.W., and Klein, D.P. 1977. "Labor Force Trends: A Synthesis and Analysis." *Monthly Labor Review,* October.

Benjamin, B. 1978. *The Decline in the Birthrate: Towards a Better Quality of Life.* London: Birth Control Trust.

Bergendal, G. 1977. *Higher Education and Manpower Planning in Sweden.* Stockholm: The National Swedish Board of Universities and Colleges.

Bertrand, S. 1975. *Analysis of the Labour Force Participation Rate Among Young People in Canada.* Research Projects Groups, Strategic Planning and Research Division. Ottawa: Department of Manpower and Immigration.

Beruf und Bildung [Occupation and Education]. 1974-1980. Zeitschrift für Ausbildung und Fortbildung im Handwerk. Deutscher Handwerkskammertag. Bad Wörishofen, Germany: Hans Holzmann, monthly.

Best, F. 1980. *Exchanging Earnings for Leisure: Findings of an Exploratory National Survey on Work Time Preferences.* R&D Monograph 99, Employment and Training Administration. Washington: U.S. Department of Labor.

Bielby, W.T.; Hawley, C.B.; and Bills, D. 1977. *Research Uses of the National Longitudinal Surveys.* Special Report no. 18, Institute for Research on Poverty. Madison, Wisconsin: University of Wisconsin.

Birtig, G. 1976. "Employment Problems and the Educational System in Italy." *International Labour Review,* July-August.

Bishop, J. 1977. "The Effect of Public Policies on the Demand for Higher Education." *Journal of Human Resources,* Summer.

Blau, P.M. 1980. "Implications of Growth in Services for Heterogeneity, Inequality and Integration." *Social Science Quarterly,* June.

Blaug, M. 1966. "An Economic Interpretation of the Private Demand for Education." *Economica,* May.

_____. 1968-69. *Economics of Education.* Penguin Modern Economics Readings, 2 vols. Baltimore: Penguin Books.

Blinder, A.S., and Weiss, Y. 1976. "Human Capital and Labor Supply: A Synthesis." *Journal of Political Economy,* May.

Blomqvist, L. 1980. "Second Generation Issues Are the Most Important in Swedish Immigration Policy Today." *Social Change in Sweden* 15. New York: Swedish Information Service.

Bogue, D.J., and Tsui, A.O. 1979. "Zero World Population Growth?" *The Public Interest,* Spring.

Borjas, G.J., and Heckman, J.J. 1978. *Labor Supply Estimates for Public Policy Evaluation.* Working Paper no. 299. Cambridge, Massachusetts: National Bureau of Economic Research.

Borus, M.; Mott, F.; and Nestel, G. 1978. "Counting Youth: A Comparison of Youth Labor Force Statistics in the Current Population Survey and the National Longitudinal Surveys." *Conference Report on Youth Unemployment: Its Measurement and Meaning.* Office of Assistant Secretary for Policy, Evaluation, and Research and Employment Training Administration. Washington: Department of Labor.

Bowen, W.G.; and Finegan, T.A. 1969. *The Economics of Labor Force Participation.* Princeton, New Jersey: Princeton University Press.

Bowers, J.K. 1975. "British Activity Rates: A Survey of Research." *Scottish Journal of Political Economy,* February.

Bowers, N. 1979. "Young and Marginal: An Overview of Youth Employment." *Monthly Labor Review,* October.

_____. 1980. "Probing the Issues of Unemployment Duration." *Monthly Labor Review,* July.

Bullock, P. 1973. *Aspirations vs. Opportunity: "Careers" in the Inner City.* Ann Arbor, Michigan: Institute of Labor and Industrial Relations.

Burn, B.B. 1971. *Higher Education in Nine Countries—A Comparative Study of Colleges and Universities Abroad.* A General Report prepared for the Carnegie Commission on Higher Education. New York: McGraw-Hill.

Busch, G. 1975. "Inequality of Educational Opportunity by Social Origin in Higher Education." *Education, Inequality and Life Chances,* vol. 1. Paris: OECD.

Butz, W.P., and Ward, M.P. 1979. "The Emergence of Countercyclical U.S. Fertility."

American Economic Review, June.

Byrne, E.M. 1979. *Equality of Education and Training for Girls (10–18 years).* Education Series no. 9. Brussels: Commission of the European Communities.

Cain, G.G. 1966. *Married Women in the Labor Force.* Chicago: University of Chicago Press.

_____ . 1971. "Issues in the Economics of a Population Policy for the United States." *American Economic Review,* May.

_____ . 1977. *Determinants of the Level and Composition of Labour Supply.* Experts' Meeting on Structural Determinants of Employment and Unemployment. Paris: OECD.

_____ . 1978. *Labor Force Concepts and Definitions in View of Their Purposes.* Background Paper no. 13, U.S. National Commission on Employment and Unemployment Statistics. Washington: GPO.

_____ . 1979. "The Unemployment Rate as an Economic Indicator." *Monthly Labor Review,* March.

Cain, G.G., and Watts, H.W. 1973. *Income Maintenance and Labor Supply.* Chicago, Illinois: Rand-McNally.

Campbell, A.A. 1974. "Beyond the Demographic Transition." *Demography,* November.

Campbell, D.T., and Stanley, J.C. 1963. *Experimental and Quasi-Experimental Designs for Research.* Chicago: Rand-McNally.

Campbell, R., and Siegel, B.N. 1967. "The Demand for Higher Education in the United States, 1919–1964." *American Economic Review,* September.

CANADA

1971. *Requirements and Salaries, University Graduates 1971.* Ottawa: Department of Manpower and Immigration.

1973. *Immigration and Working Age Population.* Strategic Planning and Research Division. Research Projects Group. Ottawa: Department of Manpower and Immigration.

1974–80. *Historical Labour Force Statistics—Actual Data, Seasonal Factors, Seasonally Adjusted Data.* Ottawa: Statistics Canada, Labour Force Survey Division, annual.

1975–80. *Research Papers.* Labour Force Survey Division. Ottawa: Statistics Canada, occasional.

1976–80. *The Labour Force.* Ottawa: Statistics Canada, Labour Force Survey Division, monthly.

1976a. *People and Jobs.* Economic Council of Canada. Ottawa: Information Canada.

1976b. *Labor Market Flows in Canada.* Strategic Planning and Research Division. Research Projects Group. Ottawa: Department of Manpower and Immigration.

1976c. *Conceptual, Definitional, and Methodological Changes in the Labour Force Survey.* Labour Force Survey Division. Ottawa: Statistics Canada.

1976d. *Youth Employment in Canada: A Detailed Analysis.* Project R-128. Strategic Planning and Research Division. Ottawa: Department of Manpower and Immigration.

1977a. *Part-time Employment in 1975 and 1976.* Research Paper no. 12, Labour Force Survey Division. Ottawa: Statistics Canada.

1977b. *Labour Force Activities and Characteristics of Students.* Research Paper no. 14, Labour Force Survey Division. Ottawa: Statistics Canada.

1978a. *Out of School—Into the Labour Force.* Cat. 81-570E Occasional. Ottawa: Ministry of Industry, Trade and Commerce.

1978b. *Historical Compendium of Educational Statistics. From Confederation to 1975.* Ottawa: Statistics Canada.

1978c. *1971 Census of Canada. Profile Studies. Labour Force Participation in Canada.* Cat. no. 99-712. Vol. V, pt. 2. Ottawa: Statistics Canada.

1979a. *Persons Not in the Labour Force: Job Search Activities and the Desire for Employment.* Research Paper no. 21, Labour Force Survey Division. Ottawa: Statistics Canada.

1979b. *The Class of 2001. The School-Age Population—Trends and Implications—1961 to 2001.* (Clark, W.; Devereaux, M.S.; Zsigmond, Z.) Ottawa: Statistics Canada.

1979c. *Guide to Labour Force Survey Data.* Ottawa: Statistics Canada.

1979d. *Education in Canada. A Statistical Review for 1977-78.* Ottawa: Statistics Canada.

1980a. *Persons Not in the Labour Force: Job Search Activities and the Desire for Employment—1979.* Research Paper no. 23, Labour Force Survey Division. Ottawa: Statistics Canada.

1980b. *The Labour Force.* Ottawa: Statistics Canada.

Cardenas, G. 1979. *Hispanic Youth and Public Policy: Data Problems, Issues and Needs.* Paper prepared for the Vice-President's Task Force on Youth Employment. Washington.

Carnoy, M., and Marenbach, D. 1975. "The Return to Schooling in the United States 1939–69." *The Journal of Human Resources,* Summer.

Castro-Almeida, C. 1979. "Problems Facing Second Generation Migrants in Western Europe." *International Labour Review,* November–December.

Chazalette, A., with Michaud, P. 1977. "La deuxième génération d'immigrants dan la région Rhône-Alpes" [The Second Generation of Immigrants in the Rhone-Alps Region]. *Migration-Etudes,* no. 4.

Cherry, N. 1976. "Persistent Job Changing—Is It a Problem?" *Journal of Occupational Psychology,* December.

Christensen, S.; Melder, J.; and Weisbrod, B.A. 1975. "Factors Affecting College Attendance." *Journal of Human Resources,* Spring.

CHRR (Center for Human Resource Research). 1979. *The National Longitudinal Surveys Handbook,* revised. Columbus, Ohio: Ohio State University.

Cibois, P. 1976. *Individual Demand for Education: Case Study France.* SME/ET/76.16. Paris: OECD.

Clark, K.B., and Summers, L.H. 1978a. *Labor Force Transitions and Unemployment.* Working Paper no. 277. Cambridge, Massachusetts: National Bureau of Economic Research.

———. 1978b. *The Dynamics of Youth Unemployment.* Working Paper no. 274. Cambridge, Massachusetts: National Bureau of Economic Research.

———. 1978c. *Social Insurance, Unemployment and Labor Force Participation: The Reporting Effect.* Employment and Training Administration. Office of Assistant Secretary for Policy, Evaluation, and Research. Washington: Department of Labor.

———. 1979a. "Labor Market Dynamics and Unemployment: A Reconsideration." *Brookings Papers on Economic Activity,* no. 1. Washington: Brookings Institution.

———. 1979b. *The Dynamics of Youth Unemployment.* Paper prepared for the National Bureau of Economic Research Conference on Youth Unemployment, Airlie, Virginia, May.

———. 1979c. *Labor Force Participation—Timing vs. Persistence.* Technical Analysis Paper no. 60, Office of the Assistant Secretary for Policy, Evaluation, and Research. Washington: Department of Labor.

———. 1979d. *The Demographic Composition of Cyclical Variations in Employment.* Technical Analysis Paper no. 61, Office of the Assistant Secretary for Policy, Evaluation, and Research. Washington: Department of Labor.

Coale, A.J. 1960. "Introduction." *Demographic and Economic Change in Developed Countries.* National Bureau of Economic Research. New York: Columbia University Press.

Conlisk, J. 1969. "Determinants of School Enrollment and School Performance." *Journal of Human Resources,* Spring.

Corcoran, M. 1979. *The Employment, Wage and Fertility Consequences of Teenage Women's Nonemployment.* Paper prepared for National Bureau of Economic Research Conference on Youth Unemployment, Airlie, Virginia, May.

Council of Europe. *Newsletter.* 1977–1980. Documentation Centre for Education in Europe. Strasbourg, monthly.

———. 1979. *Education and Equality of Opportunity for Girls and Women.* Standing Conference of European Ministers of Education. CME/XI (79). Strasbourg.

Courbin, J. 1978. "Quel avenir pour les jeunes migrants?" [What Future for the Young Migrants?] *Revue française des affaires sociales.* Paris: Ministère de la Santé et de la Famille and Ministère du Travail et de la Participation, April–June.

Courtheoux, J.-P. 1977. "Pertes en population active et restitution d'activité" [Flows In and Out of Economic Activity]. *L'orientation scolaire et professionnelle,* no. 2.

Crean, J.F. 1973. "Forgone Earnings and the Demand for Education: Some Empirical Evidence." *Canadian Journal of Economics,* January–February.

Creech, F.R.; Freeberg, N.E.; Rock, D.A.; Wilson, K.M.; and Young, K. 1977. *Comparative Analysis of Postsecondary Occupational and Educational Outcomes for the High School Class of 1972.* Princeton, New Jersey: Educational Testing Service.

Cripps, F., and Tarling, R. 1973. "Is Labour Really Scarce?" *New Society,* November 22.

Danziger, S.; Haveman, R.; and Plotnick, R. 1980. *Retrenchment or Reorientation: Options for Income Support Policy.* Discussion Paper no. 597, Institute for Research on Poverty. Madison, Wisconsin: University of Wisconsin.

Davis, N.H.W. 1971. *Cycles and Trends in Labour Force Participation, 1953–1968.* Special Labour Force Studies, Series B, no. 5. Ottawa: Dominion Bureau of Statistics.

de Francesco, C. 1978. "Occupational Choice and Motivation of Youth in Italy." *Youth Unemployment and Vocational Training: Motivation of Young People: Their Vocational Training and Employment Prospects.* Surveys of Member States of the European Communities. Berlin: CEDEFOP (Centre européen pour le développement de la formation professionnelle).

Denison, E.F., with Poulliet, J.-P. 1967. *Why Growth Rates Differ: Postwar Experience in Nine Western Countries.* Washington: Brookings Institution.

Denton, F. 1973. "A Simulation Model of Month-to-Month Labor Force Movement in Canada." *International Economic Review,* June.

Denton, F.T.; Feaver, C.H.; and Robb, A.L. 1976. *The Short-run Dynamics of the Canadian Labour Market.* Ottawa: Economic Council of Canada.

Dessaur, C.I., and Van Vleuten, C.E. 1979. *Education and Equality of Opportunity for Girls and Women.* Standing Conference of European Ministers of Education, 11th Session. Document CEM/XI(79)4. Strasbourg: Council of Europe.

Devens, R.M. 1979. "Unemployment Among Recipients of Food Stamps and AFDC." *Monthly Labor Review,* March.

Deville, J.C. 1977. "Fécondité et activité féminine" [Fertility and Female Activity]. *Économie et statistique* 93, October.

Dohnanyi, K. von. 1978. *Education and Youth Employment in the Federal Republic of Germany.* Berkeley, California: Carnegie Council on Policy Studies in Higher Education.

Donaldson, A. 1979. *The British Unemployment Figures in Context.* IIM/dp 79-2. Berlin: International Institute of Management.

Dossou, F. 1980. "Un bilan des mécanismes et des modes d'insertion professionnelle des jeunes à 20–22 ans" [An Evaluation of Techniques and Modes of Occupational Entry of Youth Aged 20–22]. *Jeunes et premiers emplois.* Cahiers du centre d'études de l'emploi, no. 20. Paris: Presses universitaires de France.

Douglas, J.W.B., and Cherry, N. 1977. "Does Sex Make Any Difference?" *Times* (London) *Educational Supplement.* December 9.

Dresch, S.P. 1975. "Demography, Technology, and Higher Education: Toward a Formal Model of Educational Adaptation." *Journal of Political Economy,* June.

Driver, G. 1980. "West Indians and School." *New Society,* January 17.

Duncan, B. 1965. "Family Factors and School Dropouts: 1920–1960." Final Report, Cooperative Research Project no. 2258, U.S. Office of Education. Ann Arbor, Michigan: University of Michigan.

————. 1967. "Early Work Experience of Graduates and Dropouts." *Demography,* February.

Durand, J. 1948. *The Labor Force in the United States, 1890–1960.* New York: Social Science Research Council.

————. 1960. "Comment." In *Demographic and Economic Change in Developed Countries.* National Bureau of Economic Research. New York: Columbia University Press.

Dyer, C. 1977. *Population and Society in Twentieth Century France.* London: Hodder & Stoughton.

Easterlin, R.A. 1968. *Population, Labor Force, and Long Swings in Economic Growth.* General Series no. 86, National Bureau of Economic Research. New York: Columbia University Press.

————. 1973. "Relative Economic Status and the American Fertility Swing." In Sheldon, E.B., ed. *Family Economic Behavior.* Philadelphia, Pennsylvania: Lippincott.

————. 1978. "What Will 1984 Be Like? Socioeconomic Implications of Recent Twists in Age Structure." *Demography,* November.

————. 1980. *Birth and Fortune. The Impact of Numbers on Personal Welfare.* New York: Basic Books.

Easterlin, R.A., and Condran, G.A. 1976. "A Note on the Recent Fertility Swing in Australia, Canada, England and Wales and the United States." In Richards, H., ed. *Population, Factor Movement and Economic Development*. Cardiff: University of Wales.

Easterlin, R.A.; Wachter, M.L.; and Wachter, S.M. 1978. "Demographic Influences on Economic Stability: The United States Experience." *Population and Development Review* 4.

_____. 1979. "Here Comes Another Baby Boom." *Wharton Magazine,* Summer.

EC (EUROPEAN COMMUNITIES)

1975-78. *Labour Force Sample Survey*. Luxembourg: Eurostat, biennial.

    a. 1973.

    b. 1975.

    c. 1977.

    d. Methods and Definitions.

1976. *Youth Unemployment and Vocational Training. A Conference Report*. West Berlin: CEDEFOP.

1977a. *Censuses of Population in the Community 1968-1971*. Luxembourg: Eurostat.

1977b. *Demographic Statistics, 1960-1976*. Luxembourg: Eurostat.

1977c. *Working Conditions in the Community 1975*. Luxembourg: Eurostat.

1977d. *The Children of Migrant Workers*. Studies, Education Series no. 1. Brussels: Commission of the European Communities.

1978a. *Education Statistics 1970/71-1976/77*. Luxembourg: Eurostat.

1978b. *Youth Unemployment and Vocational Training. Occupational Choice and Motivation of Young People, Their Vocational Training and Employment Prospects—Surveys on Member States of the European Communities*. West Berlin: CEDEFOP.

1979a. *Hours of Work. Main Results of Surveys at Community Level*. Demographic and Social Statistics 3-1979. Luxembourg: Eurostat.

1980a. "What do Europeans Think About Their Children?" *Euroforum*. 23 May.

1980b. *Labour Force Sample Survey 1973, 1975, 1977*. Luxembourg: Eurostat.

1980c. *Education and Training 1970/71-1977/78*. Luxembourg: Eurostat.

Edwards, L.N. 1975. "The Economics of Schooling Decisions: Teenage Enrollment Rates." *Journal of Human Resources,* Spring.

_____. 1976. "School Retention of Teenagers Over the Business Cycle." *Journal of Human Resources,* Spring.

_____. 1977a. "An Empirical Analysis of Compulsory Schooling Legislation, 1940-1960." Unpublished.

_____. 1977b. "The Effect of Compulsory School Attendance Legislation on Teenage Unemployment." Unpublished.

Ehrenberg, R.G. 1979a. "The Demographic Structure of Unemployment Rates and Labor Market Transitions." Paper prepared for the National Commission for Employment Policy, July.

_____. 1979b. "The Demographic Structure of Unemployment Rates and Labor Market Transitions: Empirical Evidence." Paper prepared for the National Commission for Employment Policy, August.

El-Khawas, E.H., and Biscenti, A.S. 1974. *Five and Ten Years After College Entry*. ACE Research Reports vol. 9, no. 1. Washington: American Council on Education.

Ellwood, D. 1979. *Teenage Unemployment: Permanent Scars or Temporary Blemishes*. Working Paper no. 399. Cambridge, Massachusetts: National Bureau of Economic Research.

EUROPE

1979. "The Netherlands—Member State Report." Brussels: European Communities, bimonthly, November-December.

Evans, P. 1980. "A Place of Refuge." *Sweden Now,* no. 2.

Eversley, D. 1980. "Social Policy and the Birth Rate." *New Society,* April 3.

Faguer, J.-P. 1980. "L'entrée dans la vie active de la génération 1955. L'emploi après les études secondaires" [The Entrance into Working Life of the Generation of 1955. Employment after Secondary School]. In *Jeunes et premiers emplois*. Cahiers du centre d'études de l'emploi, no. 20. Paris: Presses universitaires de France.

Faguer, J.-P.; Dossou, F.; and Kandel, I. 1977.
    a. "L'entrée des jeunes dans la vie active: la génération 55" [The Entrance of Young People into Working Life: The Generation of 1955]. In *L'entrée dans la vie active*. Cahiers du centre d'études de l'emploi, no. 15. Paris: Presses universitaires de France.
    b. Unpublished data for 1976 survey.

Fair, R.C. 1971. "Labor Force Participation, Wage Rates, and Money Illusion." *Review of Economics and Statistics,* May.

Farm, A. 1979. "Future Nordic Labour Market Statistics—Draft Principles for the Development Work of the 1980s." *Statistik Tidskrift,* no. 4.

Featherman, D.L., and Carter, T.M. 1976. "Discontinuities in Schooling and Socio-economic Life Cycle" in Sewell, W.H.; Hauser, R.M.; and Featherman, D.L., eds. *Schooling and Achievement in American Society.* New York: Academic Press.

Feldstein, M., and Ellwood, D. 1979. *Teenage Unemployment: What is the Problem?* Working Paper no. 393. Cambridge, Massachusetts: National Bureau of Economic Research.

Ferguson, T., and Cunnison, J. 1951. *The Young Wage Earner.* Oxford, England: Oxford University Press.

Finegan, T.A. 1972. "Labor Force Growth and the Return to Full Employment." *Monthly Labor Review,* February.

———. 1978. *The Measurement, Behavior, and Classification of Discouraged Workers.* Background Paper no. 12. National Commission on Employment and Unemployment Statistics. Washington: GPO.

Fisher, M.R. 1971. *The Economic Analysis of Labour.* London: Weidenfeld & Nicolson.

Flaim, P.O. 1969. "Persons Not in the Labor Force: Who They Are and Why They Don't Work." *Monthly Labor Review,* July.

———. 1973. "Discouraged Workers and Changes in Unemployment." *Monthly Labor Review,* March.

———. 1979. "The Effect of Demographic Changes on the Nation's Unemployment Rate." *Monthly Labor Review,* March.

Flaim, P.O., and Fullerton, H.N. 1978. "Labor Force Projections to 1990: Three Possible Paths." *Monthly Labor Review,* December.

Flanagan, J.C.; Shaycoft, M.F.; Richards, J.M., Jr.; Claudy, J.G. 1971. *Project Talent Five Years After High School.* Pittsburgh, Pennsylvania: University of Pittsburgh and American Institutes for Research.

Fleisher, B.M. 1971. "The Economics of Labor Force Participation: A Review Article." *Journal of Human Resources,* Spring.

Fleisher, B.M.; Parsons, D.O.; and Porter, R.D. 1972. *Dynamic Analysis of the Labor Force Behavior of Men and Youth.* PB 218-939. Springfield, Virginia: NTIS (National Technical Information Service).

Fogelman, K., ed. 1976. *Britain's Sixteen-Year-Olds.* London: National Children's Bureau.

Folger, J.K., and Nam, C.B. 1967. *Education of the American Population.* U.S. Bureau of the Census. Washington: GPO.

FRANCE

1971. *Recensement général de la population de 1968, population active* [General Census of Population, 1968, Labor Force]. INSEE (Institut national de la statistique et des études économiques). Paris: Imprimerie nationale.

1976-79. *L'observatoire national des entrées dans la vie active* [National Survey of the Entrance to Working Life]. Paris: CEREQ. (Centre d'études et de recherches sur les qualifications).
    a. Note d'information, no. 32, 15 March 1976.
    b. Note d'information, no. 41, 20 May 1977.
    c. Note d'information, no. 49, 25 June 1978.

1977a. *Les universités et le marché du travail* [The Universities and the Labor Market]. Dossier no. 14. CEREQ (Centre d'études et de recherches sur les qualifications). Paris: La documentation française.

1977-79. *Tableaux de l'observatoire national des entrées dans la vie active* [Statistical Tables of the National Survey of the Entrance to Working Life]. CEREQ (Centre d'études et de recherches sur les qualifications). Paris: La documentation française.
    a. vol. 1, D.U.T., B.T.S., B.T.S.A., December 1977.

b. vol. 2, CAP-BEP, April 1978.

c. vol. 3, les universités scientifiques, December 1978.

1978a. *Enquête sur l'emploi de Mars 1977* [Labor Force Survey]. Résultats détaillés. Les collections de l'INSEE, no. 250, Series D 53. INSEE (Institut nationale de la statistique et des études économiques). Paris: Imprimerie nationale.

1978b. *Enquêtes sur l'emploi 1975–1976* [Labor Force Surveys 1975–1976]. Résultats détaillés. Les collections de l'INSEE, no. 265, Series D 57. INSEE (Institut national de la statistique et des études économiques). Paris: Imprimerie nationale.

1978c. *Projection de population active à horizon 1990–2000* [Projection of the Labor Force to 1990–2000]. 2nd version. Note no. 1370/431. INSEE (Institut national de la statistique et des études économiques). Paris.

1978–79. *Formation-qualification-emploi* [Training-Qualifications-Employment]. Cahiers de l'observatoire national des entrées dans la vie active. CEREQ (Centre d'études et de recherches sur les qualifications). Paris: La documentation française.

a. no. 1. les universités scientifiques, October 1978.

b. no. 2. les C.A.P., December 1978.

1979a. *Enquête sur l'emploi de Mars 1978* [Labor Force Survey March 1978]. Résultats détaillés. Les collections de l'INSEE, no. 287, Series D 61. INSEE (Institut national de la statistique et des études économiques). Paris: Imprimerie nationale.

1979b. *Projection de population totale pour la France 1975–2020* [Population Projection for France, 1975–2020]. Les collections de l'INSEE, no. 303, Series D 63. INSEE (Institut national de la statistique et des études économiques). Paris: Imprimerie nationale.

1979c. *Formation-qualification-emploi* [Training-Qualifications-Employment]. Notes d'information du CEREQ, no. 56. CEREQ (Centre d'études et de recherches sur les qualifications). Paris.

1979d. *Population active* [The Economically Active Population]. France 1975 Census. Les collections de l'INSEE, no. 328, Series D 67. INSEE (Institut national de la statistique et des études économiques). Paris: Imprimerie nationale.

1980a. *E.V.A.: Observatoire national des entrées dans la vie active* [National Survey of the Entrance to Working Life]. Bulletin formation-qualification-emploi no. 60. CEREQ (Centre d'études et de recherches sur les qualifications). Paris.

1980b. *Les activités du CEREQ en 1980* [The Activities of CEREQ in 1980]. Bulletin formation-qualification-emploi no. 62. CEREQ (Centre d'études et de recherches sur les qualifications). Paris.

Freeman, R.B. 1975. "Overinvestment in College Training?" *Journal of Human Resources,* Summer.

———— . 1976a. *The Overeducated American.* New York: Academic Press.

———— . 1976b. "Teenage Unemployment: Can Reallocating Educational Resources Help?" *The Teenage Unemployment Problem: What Are the Options?* Report of a Congressional Budget Office Conference, April 30. Washington: GPO.

———— . 1977. "The Decline in the Economic Rewards to College Education." *Review of Economics and Statistics,* February.

———— . 1979a. *Economic Determinants of Geographic and Individual Variation in the Labor Market Position of Young Persons.* Paper prepared for National Bureau of Economic Research Conference on Youth Unemployment, Airlie, Virginia, May.

———— . 1979b. *The Effect of Demographic Factors on Age-Earning Profiles.* Working Paper no. 316. Cambridge, Massachusetts: National Bureau of Economic Research.

———— . 1980a. "The Facts About the Declining Economic Value of College." *Journal of Human Resources,* Winter.

———— . 1980b. "Why is There a Youth Labor Market Problem?" in Anderson, B.E., and Sawhill, I.V., eds. *Youth Employment and Public Policy.* The American Assembly, Columbia University. Englewood Cliffs, New Jersey: Prentice-Hall.

———— . 1980c. *The Evolution of the American Labor Market 1948–1980.* Working Paper no. 446. Cambridge, Massachusetts: National Bureau of Economic Research.

Freeman, R.B., and Holloman, J.H. 1975. "The Declining Value of College Going." *Change,* September.

Freeman, R.B., and Medoff, J. 1978. *The Youth Labor Market Problem in the United States: An Overview.* Cambridge, Massachusetts: National Bureau of Economic Research.

_____ . 1979. *Why Does the Rate of Youth Labor Force Activity Differ Across Surveys?* Paper prepared for National Bureau of Economic Research Conference on Youth Unemployment, Airlie, Virginia, May.

Freeman, R.B., and Wise, D., eds. 1980. *The Youth Employment Problem: Its Nature, Causes and Consequences.* Chicago, Illinois: University of Chicago Press.

Frey, L. 1978. *"Black Labor" and Italian Employment Policy.* Paper prepared for Conference on Recent European Manpower Policies. Rome: Centro di Ricerche Economiche.

Friedlander, S.L. 1972. *Unemployment in the Urban Core: An Analysis of Thirty Cities with Policy Recommendations.* New York: Praeger.

Fuà, G. 1977. "Employment and Productive Capacity in Italy." *Banca Nazionale Lavoro Quarterly Review,* September.

Garfinkel, I. and Masters, S. 1974. *The Effect of Income and Wage Rates on the Labor Supply of Young Men and Women.* Institute for Research on Poverty. Madison, Wisconsin: University of Wisconsin.

Gathorne-Hardy, J. 1978. *The Old School Tie: The Phenomenon of the English Public School.* New York: Viking Press.

GB (GREAT BRITAIN)

1952–57. *Census 1951.* General Register Office. London: HMSO.
  a. One Percent Sample Tables, Part II.
  b. Classification of Occupations (1956).
  c. Classification of Industries (1952).
  d. Industry Tables (1957).
  e. Occupation Tables (1956).

1959. *15 to 18.* A Report of the Central Advisory Council for Education—England. Vol. 2. Ministry of Education. London: HMSO.

1966. *Census 1961.* General Register Office. Summary Tables. London: HMSO.

1968a. *Sample Census 1966.* General Register Office. Economic Activity Tables, Part I. London: HMSO.

1968b. *Young School Leavers.* Schools Council. Report of an enquiry carried out for the Schools Council by the Government Social Survey. London: HMSO.

1969–80. Department of Employment *Gazette.* London: HMSO, monthly.
  a. May 1975, pp. 395–99.
  b. May 1976, pp. 455–60.
  c. March 1969, pp. 213–17.
  d. April 1978, pp. 426–27.
  e. June 1978, pp. 662–71.
  f. June 1980, pp. 497–508.
  g. July 1979, pp. 671–77.

1973. *Social Trends, no. 4.* Office of Population Censuses and Surveys. London: HMSO.

1973–79. *The General Household Survey.* Office of Population Censuses and Surveys. London: HMSO.
  a. Introductory Report.
  b. 1972 Report.
  c. 1973.
  d. 1974.
  e. 1975.
  f. 1976.

1975. *Census 1971.* Office of Population Censuses and Surveys. Economic Activity, Part II. London: HMSO.

1976. *Thirteenth Annual Report, Statistical Supplement.* UCCA (Universities' Central Council on Admissions). Cheltenham, England.

1977. *Social Trends, no. 7.* Central Statistical Office. London: HMSO.

1978a. *Population Trends.* Office of Population Censuses and Surveys. London: HMSO.

1978b. *Social Trends, no. 8.* Central Statistical Office. London: HMSO.

1978c. *Population Projections.* Series PP2, no. 9. Government Actuary and Registrars General. London: HMSO.

1978d. *Higher Education Into the 1990s. A Discussion Document.* Department of Education and Science and the Scottish Education Department. London and Edinburgh.

1978e. *Young People and Work.* Manpower Studies no. 19781. London: Manpower Services Commission.

Gendreau, N. 1974. *Short-term Variations in Student and Non-student Labour Force Participation Rates, 1966–73.* Special Labour Force Studies, Series B, no. 6. Statistics Canada. Labour Division. Manpower Research and Development Section. Ottawa: Information Canada.

GERMANY

1963–78. *Stand und Entwicklung der Erwerbstatigkeit* [Status and Development of the Labor Force]. Mikrozensus (1 Percent Sample Survey). SB (Statistics Bundesamt). Wiesbaden.

1970–80. *Bildung und Wissenschaft* [Education and Science]. INPS (Inter Nationes Press Service). Bonn.
   a. no. 5/78, pp. 105-7.
   b. no. 1/79, pp. 3-4.
   c. no. 6/74, p. 91.
   d. no. 1–2/80, pp. 8-11.
   e. no. 8-9/79, pp. 123-24.
   f. no. 4/80, pp. 69-74.
   g. no. 1/74, p. 5.
   h. no. 2/79, pp. 25-27.

1973–80. *Bulletin,* no. 116, pp. 1081-83. PIB (Presse -und Informationsamt der Bundesregienung). Bonn, weekly.

1975–80. *Informationen-Bildung Wissenschaft* [News-Education/Science]. BMBW (Der Bundesminister für Bildung und Wissenschaft). Pressereferat. Bonn, monthly.
   a. Dec. 1978, p. 239.
   b. Jan. 1980.
   c. April 1980.

1976a. *Arbeiterkinder in Bildungssystem* [Working Class Children in the Educational System]. BMBW (Der Bundesminister für Bildung und Wissenschaft). Bonn: Druckhaus Bayreuth.

1977. *Materialen aus der Arbeitsmarkt-und Berufsforschung.* (Mat AB), no. 9. IAB (Institut für Arbeitsmarkt-und Berufsforschung der Bundesanstalt für Arbeit). Nürnberg.

1978a. *International Labour Market: Employment Patterns and Trends in the Federal Republic of Germany and Other Countries.* Quint. AB 9. IAB (Institut für Arbeitsmarkt-und Berufsforschung der Bundesanstalt für Arbeit). Nürnberg.

1978–80. *Arbeits-und Sozial-statistik* [Work and Social Statistics]. BAS (Der Bundesminister für Arbeit-und Sozialordnung). Bingen: Robert Schulz, annual.

1979. *Grund-und Struktur Daten 1979* [Basic and Structural Data 1979]. BMBW (Der Bundesminister für Bildung und Wissenschaft). Bonn, annual.

1979–80. *Sozialpolitische Informationen* [Social and Political Information]. BAS (Der Bundesminister für Arbeit-und Sozialordnung). Bonn, weekly.
   a. Feb. 27, 1979.
   b. April 9, 1979.
   c. May 3, 1979.
   d. March 27, 1980.
   e. April 24, 1980.
   f. Dec. 20, 1979.

1980a. *Bundestag Paper* 8/1703. Bonn.

Ghez, G., and Becker, G.S. 1975. *The Allocation of Time and Goods Over the Life Cycle.* New York: National Bureau of Economic Research.

Gibb, S.J. 1907. *The Problem of Boy Work.* London: W. Gardner, Darton.

Gibson, G. 1977. "The Elusive Rise in the American Birthrate." *Science,* April 29.

Gille, H. 1960. "An International Survey of Recent Fertility Trends" in National Bureau of Economic Research, *Demographic and Economic Change in Developed Countries.* New York: Columbia University Press.

Gordon, A., and Williams, G.L. 1976. *Individual Demand for Education. Case Study: United Kingdom.* SME/ET/76.21. Paris: OECD.

_____ . 1977. *Attitudes of Fifth and Sixth Formers to School, Work and Higher Education.* Report submitted to the Department of Education and Science. Institute for Research and Development in Post-compulsory Education. Lancaster, England: University of Lancaster.

Gordon, R.A., and Gordon, M.S., eds. 1966. *Prosperity and Unemployment.* New York: John Wiley.

Gramm, W.L. 1975. "Household Utility Maximization and the Working Wife." *American Economic Review,* March.

Grant, J.H., and Hamermesh, D.S. 1980. *Labor Market Competition Among Youths, White Women and Others.* Working Paper no. 519. Cambridge, Massachusetts: National Bureau of Economic Research.

Grasso, J.T. 1977. "On the Declining Labor Market Value of Schooling." *Proceedings* of the American Education Research Association.

Grasso, J.T., and Shea, J.R. 1979. *Vocational Education and Training: Impact on Youth.* A Technical Report. Berkeley, California: Carnegie Council on Policy Studies in Higher Education.

Grauman, J.V. 1960. "Comment" in National Bureau of Economic Research, *Demographic and Economic Change in Developed Countries.* New York: Columbia University Press.

Greenberger, E., and Steinberg, L.D. 1979. *Part-Time Employment of In-School Youth: A Preliminary Assessment of Costs and Benefits.* Washington: National Institute of Education.

Greenhalgh, C. 1977. "A Labour Supply Function for Married Women in Great Britain." *Economica,* August.

_____ . 1979. "Male Labour Force Participation in Great Britain." *Scottish Journal of Political Economy,* November.

Gregory, P.R.; Campbell, J.M.; and Cheng, B.S. 1972. "A Simultaneous Equation Model of Birth Rates in the United States." *Review of Economics and Statistics,* August.

Griliches, Z. 1977a. "Estimating Returns to Schooling: Some Econometric Problems." *Econometrica,* January.

_____ . 1977b. "Schooling Interruptions, Work While in School, and the Returns from Schooling." Unpublished.

Gronau, R. 1973. "The Effect of Children on the Housewife's Value of Time." *Journal of Political Economy,* Supplement, March–April.

Grubel, H., ed. 1978. *The Effects of Unemployment Insurance on Unemployment.* Vancouver: Frazer Institute.

Guardian Weekly (The). 1979–80. Manchester, England.
  a. April 1979.
  b. July 1, 1979, *12.*
  c. October 28, 1979. "Immigrants to France Feel New Twist of the Screw."

Gustman, A.L., and Steinmeier, T.L. 1979. "The Impact of the Market and Family on Youth Enrollment and Labor Supply." Hanover, New Hampshire: Dartmouth College.

Hall, R.E. 1970. "Why is the Unemployment Rate so High at Full Employment?" *Brookings Papers on Economic Activity,* no. 3. Washington: Brookings Institution.

_____ . 1971. "Prospects for Shifting the Phillips Curve Through Manpower Policy." *Brookings Papers on Economic Activity,* no. 3. Washington: Brookings Institution.

_____ . 1972. "Turnover in the Labor Force." *Brookings Papers on Economic Activity,* no. 3. Washington: Brookings Institution.

_____ . 1978. "The Nature and Measurement of Unemployment." Working Paper no. 252. Cambridge, Massachusetts: National Bureau of Economic Research.

Hallaire, J. 1968. *Part-time Employment: Its Extent and Its Problems.* Paris: OECD.

Hamel, H.R. 1979. "Two-fifths of Discouraged Sought Work During Prior 6-month Period." *Monthly Labor Review,* March.

Hamermesh, D.S. 1977. *Jobless Pay and the Economy.* Baltimore: Johns Hopkins University Press.

_____ . 1978. "Unemployment Insurance, Short-time Compensation and the Workweek" in *Work Time and Employment.* Special Report no. 28, National Commission for Manpower Policy. Washington: GPO.

Hansen, W.L., and Weisbrod, B.A. 1969. *Benefits, Costs and Finance of Public Higher*

Education. Chicago, Illinois: Markham.

Hanushek, E.A., and Jackson, J.E. 1977. *Statistical Methods for Social Scientists.* New York: Academic Press.

Härnqvist, K. 1976. *Individual Demand for Education: Background Analytical Report.* ED(76)15. Paris: OECD.

Harrisson, J.A.C. 1978. *The Future Supply of School-Leavers.* Client Note no. 134, Institute of Manpower Studies. Brighton, England.

Harrisson, J.A.C., and Hersleb, A. 1978. *The Future Supply of Graduates: A Review of Current Projections.* Client Note no. 123, Institute of Manpower Studies. Brighton, England.

Hause, J.C. 1971. "Ability and Schooling as Determinants of Lifetime Earnings or If You're So Smart, Why Aren't You Rich?" *American Economic Review,* May.

Heckman, J.J. 1978. "A Partial Survey of Recent Research on the Labor Supply of Women." *American Economic Review,* May.

Hecquet, I.; Verniers, C.; and Cerych, L. 1976. *Recent Student Flows in Higher Education.* New York: International Council for Educational Development.

Hedges, J.N. 1973. "Absence From Work—A Look at Some National Data." *Monthly Labor Review,* July.

———. 1977. "Absence From Work—Measuring the Hours Lost." *Monthly Labor Review,* October.

Hedges, J.N., and Sekscenski, E. 1979. *Workers on Late Shifts in a Changing Economy.* Special Labor Force Report 232, Bureau of Labor Statistics. Washington: Department of Labor.

Herriot, R.A. 1979. "The 1980 Census: Countdown for a Complete Count." *Monthly Labor Review,* September.

Hilaski, H. 1968. "The Status of Research on Gross Changes in the Labor Force." *Employment and Earnings,* October.

Hill, M.S. 1978. "Family Status and Labor Force Patterns." *Conference on Youth Unemployment: Its Measurement and Meaning. Supplementary Papers.* Office of Assistant Secretary for Policy, Evaluation, and Research. Washington: Department of Labor.

Hills, S., and Thompson, J. 1980. "Unemployment Compensation and the Transition from School to Work." A report for the U.S. National Commission on Unemployment Compensation.

Hirsch, W.Z. 1961. "Income Elasticity of Public Education." *International Economic Review,* September.

Hoagland, J. 1977. "Europe's Illegal Workers: Ducking Welfare Costs." *Washington Post,* September 11.

Hoeppner, M. 1978. *Early Adolescent Childbearing: Some Social Implications.* P. 5831/1. Santa Monica, California: Rand Corporation.

Holden, K., and Peel, D.A. 1979. "The Benefit/Income Ratio for Unemployed Workers in the United Kingdom." *International Labour Review,* September–October.

Holmberg, I. 1978. "Births Down, Aging Up: What's the Impact?" *Social Change in Sweden,* no. 4. New York: Swedish Information Service.

Holt, C.C., and David, M.H. 1966. "The Concept of Job Vacancies in a Dynamic Theory of the Labor Market." *The Measurement and Interpretation of Job Vacancies.* National Bureau of Economic Research. New York: Columbia University Press.

Hopkins, T. 1974. "Higher Education Enrollment Demand." *Economic Review,* March.

Huet, M. 1977. "Emploi et activité entre 1968 et 1975" [Employment and Activity 1968–1975]. *Economie et Statistique,* no. 94. Paris: INSEE.

Hunter, L.C. 1970. "Some Problems in the Theory of Labour Supply." *Scottish Journal of Political Economy* 17.

Husén, T. 1972. *Social Background and Educational Career.* Paris: OECD.

———. 1975. *Social Influences on Educational Attainment.* Centre for Educational Research and Innovation (CERI). Paris: OECD.

Hutton, M., and Polianski, A.N. (n.d.). *Gross Movements in the Labour Force.* Report no. 1, Manpower Supply Studies. Ottawa: Department of Manpower and Immigration.

Iden, G. 1980. "The Labor Force Experience of Black Youth: A Review." *Monthly Labor Review,* August.

ILO (International Labour Office). 1960-80. *Yearbook of Labor Statistics.* Geneva, annual.
_____ . 1975-80. *Social and Labour Bulletin.* Geneva, quarterly.
_____ . 1977. *Labour Force Estimates and Projections 1950-2000.* 6 vols. Geneva.
    a. Vol. I, Asia.
    b. Vol. IV, Europe, North America, Oceania, USSR.
    c. Vol. VI, Methodological Supplement.
ILR (International Labour Review.) 1957a. "Demographic Trends in Western Europe and Their Implications for the Employment Market." Geneva, February.
_____ . 1957b. "The Influx of Young People into the Employment Market in Western and Northern Europe." Geneva, April.
IMS Monitor. 1973. "The Effects of the Raising of the School-Leaving Age (ROSLA) on Labour Supply." *Journal of the Institute of Manpower Studies* 2, no. 2. London: Chapman & Hall.
ITALY
1961-80. *Annuario di Statistiche del Lavoro* [Yearbook of Labor Statistics]. Rome: ISTAT (Instituto Centrale di Statistica).
JAPAN
1956-80. *Annual Report on the Labour Force Survey.* Tokyo: Office of the Prime Minister. Bureau of Statistics.
1958-80. *Basic Survey of the Wage Structure.* Tokyo: Ministry of Labour.
1960-78. *Employment Status Survey.* Tokyo: Office of the Prime Minister. Bureau of Statistics.
1971a. *Educational Standards in Japan 1970.* MEJ 4238. Tokyo: Ministry of Education.
1971b. *Education in 1968-70.* Tokyo: Ministry of Education.
1971c. *Education in Japan 1971.* Ministry of Education. Tokyo: Government Printing Bureau.
1972. *Basic Guidelines for the Reform of Education.* Report of the Central Council for Education. Tokyo: Ministry of Education.
1976a. *Educational Standards in Japan, 1975.* MEJ 4257. Tokyo: Ministry of Education, Science and Culture.
1978. *Japan Statistical Yearbook 1978.* Tokyo.
1979a. *Statistical Abstract of Education, Science and Culture.* Tokyo: Ministry of Education, Science and Culture.
Japan Labor Bulletin. Tokyo: Japan Institute of Labour, monthly.
    a. December 1979.
    b. January 1980.
    c. May 1979.
    d. October 1980.
Jewkes, J. and S. 1938. *The Juvenile Labour Market.* London: Victor Gollancz.
Job, B.C. 1979. "How Likely Are Individuals to Enter the Labor Force?" *Monthly Labor Review,* September.
Johnson, N.E. 1979. "Minority-Group Status and the Fertility of Black Americans, 1970: A New Look." *American Journal of Sociology,* May.
Johnson, R.W. 1978. "Generation Game." *New Society,* July 20.
Johnson, T. 1978. "Time in School: The Case of the Prudent Patron." *American Economic Review,* December.
Johnston, D.F., and Wetzel, J.R. 1969. "Effect of the Census Undercount on Labor Force Estimates." *Monthly Labor Review,* March.
Jones, L.Y. 1980. *Great Expectations. America and the Baby Boom Generation.* New York: Coward, McCann & Geoghegan.
Jusenius, C., and von Rabenau, B. 1979. *Unemployment Statistics in the United States and the Federal Republic of Germany: Problems of International Comparisons.* Background Paper no. 29, National Commission on Employment and Unemployment Statistics. Washington: GPO.
Kalachek, E. 1969. *The Youth Labor Market.* Ann Arbor, Michigan: University of Michigan–Wayne State University, Institute of Labor and Industrial Relations.
_____ . 1978. *Longitudinal Surveys and Labor Market Analysis.* Background Paper no. 6, National Commission on Employment and Unemployment Statistics. Washington: GPO.

———. 1979. *Longitudinal Surveys and the Youth Labor Market.* Steering Group of the Manpower and Social Affairs Committee on Youth Unemployment. SME/YU(79)3. Paris: OECD.

Kaser, M.C. 1966. "Education and Economic Progress in Industrialized Market Economies." In Robinson, E.A.G., and Vaizey, J., *The Economics of Education.* London: Macmillan.

Kato, H. 1978. *Education and Youth Employment in Japan.* Berkeley, California: Carnegie Council on Policy Studies in Higher Education.

Keeley, M.C.; Robins, P.K.; Spiegelman, R.G.; and West, R.W. 1978. "The Estimation of Labor Supply Models Using Experimental Data." *American Economic Review,* December.

Keyfitz, N. 1978. "The Impending Crisis in American Graduate Schools." *The Public Interest,* Summer.

King, E.J.; Moor, C.N.; and Mundy, J.A. 1974. *Post-Compulsory Education: A New Analysis in Western Europe.* London: Sage Publications.

Kirk, D. 1946. *Europe's Population in the Inter-War Years.* Geneva: League of Nations.

———. 1960. "The Influence of Business Cycles on Marriage and Birth Rates." In National Bureau of Economic Research, *Demographic and Economic Change in Developed Countries.* New York: Columbia University Press.

Kitagawa, E.M. 1955. "Components of a Difference Between Two Rates." *Journal of the American Statistical Association,* December.

Klein, D. 1970. "Determining the Labor Force Status of Men Missed in the Census." *Monthly Labor Review,* March.

Korbel, J. 1966. "The Labor Force Entry and Attachment of Young People." *Journal of the American Statistical Association,* March.

Koshiro, K. 1978–79. "Labor Productivity and Recent Employment Adjustment Programs in Japan: Are We Workaholics?" I and II. *Japan Labor Bulletin,* December and January.

Kühlewind, G.; Mertens, D.; and Tessaring, M. 1976. *Zur drohenden Ausbildungskrise in nächsten Jahrzeit — eine Modellrechnung. Schülerberg und Ausbildung* [The Coming Crisis in Vocational Training]. Stuttgart.

Kuznets, S. 1960. "Population Change and Aggregate Output" in National Bureau of Economic Research, *Demographic and Economic Change in Developed Countries.* New York: Columbia University Press.

Lampman, R. 1979. *Labor Supply and Social Welfare Benefits in the United States.* National Commission on Employment and Unemployment Statistics. Final Report, *Counting the Labor Force.* Appendix vol. 1. Washington: GPO.

Landes, W.M., and Solmon, L.D. 1972. "Compulsory Schooling Legislation: An Economic Analysis of Law and Social Change in the Nineteenth Century." *Journal of Economic History,* March.

Layard, R. 1979. *Youth Unemployment in Britain and the U.S. Compared.* Paper prepared for National Bureau of Economic Research Conference on Youth Unemployment, Airlie, Virginia, May.

Layard, R.; King, J.; and Moser, C. 1969. *The Impact of Robbins.* Harmondsworth, England: Penguin Education Special.

Leicester, C. 1978. *Increased Labour Force Participation and the Growing Employment Opportunities for Women.* General Note no. 115, Institute of Manpower Studies. Brighton, England.

Lenhardt, G., ed. 1979. *Der Hilflose Sozialstaat, Jugendarbeitslosigkeit, und Politik* [The Bankrupt Welfare State, Youth Unemployment and Policy]. Frankfurt am Main: Edition Suhrkamp.

Leon, C. 1978. "Young Adults: A Transitional Group with Changing Labor Force Patterns." *Monthly Labor Review,* May.

Leroy, R. 1977. Comments on Cain paper at Experts' Meeting on Structural Determinants of Employment and Unemployment. Paris: OECD.

Leveson, I. 1979. *Generational Crowding: Economic, Social and Demographic Effects of Changes in Relative Cohort Size, an Examination of Some Recent Evidence.* Paper presented at the American Statistical Association, August.

Levin, H.M. 1976. *Equal Educational Opportunity in Western Europe: A Contradictory Relation.* Paper presented to American Political Science Association, September.

Lindert, P. 1977. *Fertility and Scarcity in America.* Princeton, New Jersey: Princeton University Press.

Link, C.R., and Ratledge, E.C. 1975. "Social Returns to Quantity and Quality of Education: A Further Statement." *Journal of Human Resources,* Winter.

Lloyd, C.B., and Niemi, B. 1978. "Sex Differences in Labor Supply Elasticity: The Implications of Sectoral Shifts in Demand." *American Economic Review,* May.

Long, C.D. 1958. *The Labor Force Under Changing Income and Employment.* Princeton, New Jersey: Princeton University Press.

Lucas, R. 1974. "The Distribution of Job Characteristics." *Review of Economics and Statistics,* November.

Mack, J. 1975. "The School Non-Leavers." *New Society,* October 2.

Madden, J.F. 1978. "Economic Rationale for Sex Differences in Education." *Southern Economic Journal,* April.

Maddison, A. 1975. "Education, Inequality and Life Chances: The Major Policy Issues." *Education, Inequality and Life Chances,* I. Paris: OECD.

Mallar, C.D. 1976. "Estimating a Simultaneous Probability Model: The School and Labor Force Participation Decisions of Youth." *Proceedings,* American Statistical Association, Business and Economic Section.

Mangum, G.L., and Seninger, S.F. 1978. *Coming of Age in the Ghetto. A Dilemma of Youth Unemployment.* Baltimore, Maryland: The Johns Hopkins University Press.

Mare, R.D. 1977a. *Social Background and School Continuation Decisions.* Discussion Paper no. 462-77, Institute for Research on Poverty. Madison, Wisconsin: University of Wisconsin.

_____. 1977b. *Social Background Composition and Educational Growth.* Discussion Paper no. 471-77, Institute for Research on Poverty. Madison, Wisconsin: University of Wisconsin.

_____. 1978a. *Market and Institutional Sources of Educational Growth.* Discussion Paper no. 494-78, Institute for Research on Poverty. Madison, Wisconsin: University of Wisconsin.

_____. 1978b. "Sources of Educational Growth in America." *Focus,* Winter.

Mare, R.D., and Winship, C. 1980. *Changes in the Relative Labor Force Status of Black and White Youths: A Review of the Literature.* Special Report Series 26, Institute for Research on Poverty. Madison, Wisconsin: University of Wisconsin.

Marsden, D. 1979. *A Study of Changes in the Wage Structure of Manual Workers in Industry in Six Community Countries Since 1966, and Proposals for the Development of Future Community Surveys.* Sussex European Research Centre. University of Sussex, England.

Marston, S. 1976. "Employment Instability and High Unemployment Rates." *Brookings Papers on Economic Activity,* no. 1. Washington: Brookings Institution.

Masnick, G., and Bane, M.J. 1980. *The Nation's Families: 1960-1990.* Cambridge, Massachusetts: Joint Center for Urban Studies of MIT and Harvard University.

Mattila, J.P. 1978. "G.I. Bill Benefits and Enrollments." *Social Science Quarterly,* December.

_____. 1979a. "Youth Labor Markets, Enrollments, and Minimum Wages" in *Proceedings,* Industrial Relations Research Association.

_____. 1979b. *Final Report on the Impact of Minimum Wages on School Enrollment and Labor Force Status of Youths.* Employment and Training Administration. Office of Research and Development. Washington: U.S. Department of Labor.

MDRC. 1979. *Schooling and Work Among Youths from Low-Income Households.* A Baseline Report from the Entitlement Demonstration. New York: Manpower Demonstration Research Corporation.

Mendelievich, E. 1979. "Child Labour." *International Labour Review,* September–October.

Meyer, J.W.; Tyack, D.; Nagel, J.; and Gordon, A. 1979. "Public Education as Nation-Building in America: Enrollments and Bureaucratization in the American States, 1870-1930." *American Journal of Sociology,* November.

Meyer, R.H., and Wise, D.A. 1979. *High School Preparation and Early Labor Force Experience.* Working Paper no. 342. Cambridge, Massachusetts: National Bureau of Economic Research.

Miller, L.S., and Radner, R. 1975. *Demand and Supply in United States Higher Education.* Berkeley, California: Carnegie Commission on Higher Education.

Mincer, J. 1962. "Labor Force Participation of Married Women." *Aspects of Labor Economics.* National Bureau of Economic Research. Princeton, New Jersey: Princeton University Press.

_____. 1966. "Labor Force Participation and Unemployment: A Review of Recent Evidence." In Gordon, R.A., and Gordon, M.S., eds. *Prosperity and Unemployment.* New York: John Wiley.

_____. 1976. "Unemployment Effects of Minimum Wages." *Journal of Political Economy,* August, Part 2.

Mincer, J., and Leighton, L. 1980. *Effect of Minimum Wages on Human Capital Formation.* Working Paper no. 441. Cambridge, Massachusetts: National Bureau of Economic Research.

Mincer, J., and Polachek, S. 1974. "Family Investments in Human Capital: Earnings of Women." *Journal of Political Economy,* March/April, Part 2.

Mitchell, A.M. 1977. *Career Development Needs of Seventeen Year Olds: How to Improve Career Development Programs.* Washington: National Advisory Council for Career Education.

Moore, C.G. 1977. *Baby Boom Equals Career Bust.* Monographs on Career Education. U.S. Office of Education, Office of Career Education. Washington: GPO.

Moore, K.A.; Hofferth, S.L.; Caldwell, S.B.; and Waite, L.J. 1979. *Teenage Motherhood: Social and Economic Consequences.* Washington: Urban Institute.

Morrison, P.A. 1978. *Overview of Demographic Trends Shaping the Nation's Future.* P-6128. Santa Monica, California: Rand Corporation.

Mott, F.L. 1978. *Racial Differences in Female Labor Force Participation: Trends and Implications for the Future.* Center for Human Resource Research. Columbus, Ohio: Ohio State University.

_____. 1979. *The Socioeconomic Status of Households Headed by Women.* R&D Monograph 72, Employment and Training Administration. Washington: Department of Labor.

Mott, F.L., and Shaw, L.B. 1978. "Work and Family in the School Leaving Years: A Comparison of Female High School Graduates and Dropouts." Revised paper, Conference on Young Women and Employment. U.S. Women's Bureau and Office of Youth Programs. Washington: Department of Labor.

Motuz, C. 1974. *Sociological Factors Influencing Labour Force Participation Rates—An Overview.* Research Projects Group, Strategic Planning and Research Division. Ottawa: Department of Manpower and Immigration.

MRC (Medical Research Council, London School of Economics). 1971. *Young School-Leavers at Work and College.* The National Survey of Health and Development. Final Report to the Social Science Research Council. London, unpublished.

Myers, S.C. 1977. "Labor Force Participation and the Probability of Completing College." *Proceedings,* American Statistical Association, Business and Economic Section.

McCabe, L.G. 1973. "Short-term Forecasting of Labour Force Participation by Major Demographic Groups." *Canada Manpower Review,* no. 2.

McCarthy, P.J. 1978. *Some Sources of Error in Labor Force Survey Estimates from the Current Population Survey.* Background Paper no. 15, National Commission on Employment and Unemployment Statistics. Washington: GPO.

McGill, I. 1979. *Enrollment Projections for Primary and Secondary Education: A Review of Past Projections, Current Methodology and Some Resource Implications.* Paper for the New Zealand Demographic Society Conference, June 29.

Maclure, S. 1979. *Education and Youth Employment in Great Britain.* Berkeley: Carnegie Council on Policy Studies in Higher Education.

McNabb, R. 1977. "The Labour Force Participation of Married Women." *Manchester School of Economic and Social Studies,* September.

Macredie, I., and Petrie, B. 1976a. "The Canadian Labour Force Survey." Paper presented at the 10th Annual Meeting of the Canadian Economics Association, Laval University, Quebec.

_____. 1976b. *The Canadian Labour Force Survey.* Ottawa: Statistics Canada, Labour Force Survey Division.

Nakamura, M.; Nakamura, A.; and Cullen, D. 1979. "Job Opportunities, the Offered Wage and the Labor Supply of Married Women." *American Economic Review,* December.

NBER (National Bureau of Economic Research). 1960. *Demographic and Economic Change in Developed Countries.* A Conference of the Universities – National Bureau Committee for Economic Research, Special Conference Series no. 11. New York: Columbia University Press.

NETHERLANDS

1967-79. *De Nederlandse Jeugd en Haar Onderwijs* [Netherlands Youth in Education]. The Hague: CBS (Centraal Bureau voor de Statistiek).

1976a. *De toekomstige demografische ontwikkeling in Nederland na 1980* [Future Demographic Trends in the Netherlands After 1980]. CBS (Centraal Bureau voor de Statistiek). The Hague: Staatsuitgeverij.

1977a. *De Nederlandse Jeugd. Een Inventarisatie van Statistische Gegevens* [Youth in the Netherlands. A Compilation of Statistical Data]. Deel 2: Onderwijs en arbeid [Vol. 2: Education and Employment]. The Hague: CBS (Centraal Bureau voor de Statistiek).

1979. *Ontwikkelingslÿnen Leerlingen, onderwÿzend Personeel en Schoolgebouwen tot 2050* [Projection Statistics for Education and Science]. SCP-Cahier no. 2. The Hague: CBS (Centraal Bureau voor de Statistiek).

Newman, M.J. 1978. "A Profile of Hispanics in the U.S. Work Force." *Monthly Labor Review,* December.

———. 1979. "The Labor Market Experience of Black Youth, 1954-78." *Monthly Labor Review,* October.

New Society. London, weekly.
    a. "Futures That Got Away." April 1, 1976.
    b. Untitled article. May 26, 1977.
    c. Report "Class in Schools," March 9, 1978.
    d. Untitled article. June 29, 1978.
    e. "Blue Stockings." February 15, 1979.
    f. Untitled article. November 1, 1973.
    g. "A Degree of Confusion." November 15, 1979.
    h. "The End of an Era for Higher Education?" January 24, 1980.
    i. "Sixth Form Wages." June 19, 1980.
    j. "West Indians and School." January 24, 1980; February 7, 1980; February 14, 1980.
    k. "Action or Rhetoric?" July 17, 1980.
    l. "Births by Mothers' Birthplace." February 21, 1980.
    m. "Beyond a Fad." June 26, 1980.
    n. "Why is the Press so Obsessed with Welfare Scroungers?" October 20, 1978.
    o. "Welfare Scroungers." November 30, 1978.

Newsweek. 1978. "Black Youth: A Lost Generation?" August 7.

New York Times.
    a. June 11, 1978.
    b. "Britain Considering Cut in Immigration." November 15, 1979; July 10, 1979.
    c. "Panel Proposes Broad Changes in Education and Job Preparation." November 28, 1979.
    d. December 27, 1978.
    e. "Colleges Pressed for Students Grow Less Selective." April 1, 1980.
    f. "New Scandal Arises in Japanese Schools." May 20, 1980.
    g. "The Educated Black: Caught in a Self-Fulfilling Prophecy." April 20, 1980.
    h. "Canada Says Gap Persists Between Indians and Whites." June 29, 1980.
    i. "Youth Unrest All Over." July 2, 1980.
    j. "Swedes Discover Their Dark Side: Racism." February 24, 1980.
    k. "U.S. Study Finds Higher Jobless Levels in Youth Ranks." February 29, 1980.
    l. "New Peak for Women in Doctorates in U.S." September 2, 1980.
    m. "The Winter Hunt for a Summer Job." November 20, 1980.
    n. "Teen Jobs Raise Concerns." April 30, 1978.

NEW ZEALAND

1976. *Primary and Secondary School Enrollment Projections 1977-1991. Technical Notes.* Wellington: Department of Education.

1978a. *New Zealand Official Yearbook 1978.* Wellington: Department of Statistics.

1978b. *New Zealand Population and Labour Force Projections, 1979-2011.* Technical Appendix. Wellington: Department of Statistics.

1979. Thompson, B., and Endres, T. "The Relationship Between Registered Unemployment and Census Unemployment." *Labour and Employment Gazette,* December.

Nolfi, G. et al. 1978. *Analysis of the National Longitudinal Study of the High School Class of 1972.* Cambridge, Massachusetts: University Consultants.

OECD (ORGANIZATION FOR ECONOMIC COOPERATION AND DEVELOPMENT)

1955. *Economic Effects of Population Trends.* Manpower Committee. MO(55)36. Paris.

1957. *Employment Problems of Young Workers.* Manpower Committee. MO(57)15. Paris.

1969. *Development of Secondary Education. Trends and Implications.* Paris.

1970a. *Conference on Policies for Educational Growth, Background Study No. 1. Educational Expansion in OECD Countries Since 1950.* Committee for Scientific and Technical Personnel. Paris.

1970b. Conférence sur les politiques d'expansion de l'enseignement, rapport de base no. 4. Disparités entre les groupes en matière de participation à l'enseignement [Group Disparities in Educational Participation]. Comité du personel scientifique et technique. Paris.

1970c. *Development of Higher Education 1950-1967, Analytical Report.* Education Committee. Paris.

1970d. *Development of Higher Education 1950-1967. Statistical Survey.* Education Committee. Paris.

1971a. *Japan.* Reviews of National Policies for Education. Paris.

1971b. *Intergovernmental Conference on the Utilization of Highly Qualified Personnel. Evolution of the Structure of the Labor Force in Japan.* Document no. 5, Education Committee. Paris.

1972a. *Economic Surveys: Australia.* Paris.

1972b. *An Exploration of the Relationship Between GNP Per Capita and School Enrollment in Age Groups 15-19 and 20-24.* Directorate for Scientific Affairs. Working Groups of the Education Committee on the Review of Methods of Educational Financing and on Educational Statistics and Indicators. DAS/EID 72.30. Paris.

1973a. *Short-Cycle Higher Education — A Search for Identity.* Paris.

1973b. *Educational Policy and Planning — Japan.* Directorate for Scientific Affairs. Paris.

1974a. *Towards Mass Higher Education — Issues and Dilemmas.* Conference on Future Structures of Post-Secondary Education. Paris.

1975a. *Education Statistics Yearbook.* Vol. II, Country Tables. Paris.

1975b. *Education, Inequality and Life Chances.* 2 vols. Paris.

1976a. *Individual Demand for Post-Compulsory Education. Summary and Implications.* Education Committee. ED(76)18. Paris.

1976b. *Public Expenditure on Education.* Studies in Resource Allocation. Paris.

1976c. *Methodological and Conceptual Problems of Measuring Unemployment in OECD Countries.* Directorate for Social Affairs, Manpower and Education. Paris.

1976d. *Students in Short-Cycle Higher Education — France, Great Britain and Yugoslavia.* Paris.

1976-77. *Country Replies to Questionnaire on Employment and Unemployment Statistics.* Working Party on Employment and Unemployment Statistics. MAS/WP7 (76) 6/01-23. Paris.

1977a. *Towards Full Employment and Price Stability.* Paris.

1977b. *Educational Statistics in OECD Member Countries.* Working Party of the Education Committee on Educational Statistics and Indicators. ED/WP1(77)2. Paris.

1978a. *Migration, Growth and Development.* Manpower and Social Affairs Committee. MAS(78)5. Paris.

1978b. *Full-Time School Enrollment 1960-80.* Working Party of the Education Committee on Educational Statistics and Indicators. ED/WP1(77)1 (1st Revision). Paris.

1978c. *Demographic Trends: Their Labour Market and Social Implications.* Manpower and Social Affairs Committee. MAS(77)1, 1st revision. Paris.

1978d. *Review of Student Support Schemes in Selected OECD Countries* (M. Woodhall). Paris.

1978e. *Educational Trends: Analytical Report.* Meeting of the Education Committee at Ministerial Level. Education Committee. Paris.

1978f. "The Rise in Public Expenditure—How Much Further Can It Go?" *OECD Observer,* May.

1978g. "Declaration on Future Educational Policies in the Changing Social and Economic Context." *OECD Observer,* November.

1978h. "Unemployment Compensation: A Comparison of Six Countries." *OECD Observer,* November.

1978i. *Youth Unemployment,* 2 vols. Paris.

1979a. *Demographic Trends: Their Labour Market and Social Implications.* Manpower and Social Affairs Committee. Paris.

1979b. *Full-Time School Enrollment 1960–80.* Working Party of the Education Committee on Educational Statistics and Indicators. ED/WP1(77)1 (2nd Revision). Paris.

1979c. *Trends in Labor Supply: Analytical Report.* Manpower and Social Affairs Committee. MAS(79)29. Paris.

1979d. *Demographic Trends 1950–1990.* Paris.

1980a. "Migrant Workers in the Current Economic Context." *OECD Observer,* May.

1980b. "Young Foreigners and the Working World." *OECD Observer,* July.

O'Keefe, D.J. 1975. "Some Economic Aspects of Raising the School Leaving Age in England and Wales in 1947." *Economic History Review,* August.

Olneck, M.R., and Wolpe, B.L. 1978. "A Note on Some Evidence on the Easterlin Hypothesis." *Journal of Political Economy,* October.

Olsen, L.S. 1975. An Analysis of the Decision to Take Formal, Post-Secondary Vocational School Training. Ph.D. dissertation, University of Rochester.

Ondeck, C.M. 1978. "Discouraged Workers' Link to Jobless Rate Reaffirmed." *Monthly Labor Review,* October.

Ornstein, M.D. 1976. *Entry into the American Labor Force.* New York: Academic Press.

Osterman, P. 1978. "Racial Differences in Male Youth Unemployment." Paper prepared for Conference on Employment Statistics and Youth, sponsored by the Department of Labor at the Institute of Industrial Relations, UCLA.

———— . 1979. *The Causes of the Worsening Employment Situation of Black Youth.* Office of Assistant Secretary for Policy, Evaluation, and Research. Washington: U.S. Department of Labor.

———— . 1980. *Getting Started: The Youth Labor Market.* Cambridge, Massachusetts: MIT Press.

Owen, J.D. 1978. "Hours of Work in the Long Run: Trends, Explanations, Scenarios, and Implications" in *Work Time and Employment: A Conference Report.* Special Report no. 28, National Commission for Manpower Policy. Washington: GPO.

———— . 1979. *Working Hours: An Economic Analysis.* Lexington, Massachusetts: D.C. Heath.

Parke, R. 1979. "Population Changes that Affect Federal Policy: Some Suggestions for Research." *Social Science Research Council Items,* March.

Parnes, H.S. 1970. "Labor Force and Labor Markets." *A Review of Industrial Relations Research,* vol. 1. Industrial Relations Research Association. Madison, Wisconsin: University of Wisconsin.

———— . 1972. "Longitudinal Surveys: Prospects and Problems." *Monthly Labor Review,* February.

———— . 1975. "The National Longitudinal Surveys: New Vistas for Labor Market Research." *American Economic Review,* May.

Parsons, D.O. 1974. "The Cost of School Time, Foregone Earnings, and Human Capital Formation." *Journal of Political Economy,* March.

———— . 1975. "Intergenerational Wealth Transfers and the Educational Decisions of Male Youth." *Quarterly Journal of Economics,* November.

Passin, H. 1965. *Society and Education in Japan.* New York: Columbia University, Teachers College.

Passow, A.H.; Noah, H.J.; Eckstein, M.A.; and Mallea, J.R. 1976. *The National Case Study: An Empirical Comparative Study of Twenty-One Educational Systems.* International Studies in Evaluation, VII. New York: John Wiley.

Pearl, R. 1963. "Gross Changes in the Labor Force: A Problem in Statistical Measurement." *Employment and Earnings,* April.

Peng, S.S.; Stafford, C.E.; and Talbert, R.J. 1977. *Review and Annotation of Study Reports.* NCES 78-238. National Center for Education Statistics. Washington: U.S. Department of Health, Education and Welfare.

Perrella, V.C. 1971. *Students and Summer Jobs, October 1969.* Special Labor Force Report 128, Bureau of Labor Statistics. Washington: Department of Labor.

Perry, G.L. 1970. "Changing Labor Markets and Inflation." *Brookings Papers on Economic Activity,* no. 3. Washington: Brookings Institution.

———. 1972. "Unemployment Flows in the U.S. Labor Market." *Brookings Papers on Economic Activity,* no. 2. Washington: Brookings Institution.

———. 1977. "Potential Output and Productivity." *Brookings Papers on Economic Activity,* no. 1. Washington: Brookings Institution.

Peterson, L. 1979. "Work and Socioeconomic Life Cycles: An Agenda for Longitudinal Research." *Monthly Labor Review,* February.

Petrie, B. 1978. *Synopsis of Country Replies to Questionnaire on Employment and Unemployment Statistics.* OECD Working Party on Employment and Unemployment Statistics. MAS/WP7(77)2 (1st Revision). Paris.

Pettenati, P. 1979. *Illegal and Unrecorded Employment in Italy.* OECD Working Party on Employment and Unemployment Statistics. MAS/WP7(79)6. Paris, February.

Pissarides, C.A. 1979. *Staying on at School in England and Wales—And Why 9% of the 1976 Age Group Did Not.* Discussion Paper no. 63, Centre for Labour Economics. London: London School of Economics.

———. 1980. *The Demand for Higher Education in Britain, 1955-77.* Discussion Paper no. 70, Centre for Labour Economics. London: London School of Economics.

Poignant, R. 1973. *Education in the Industrialised Countries.* Project 1: Educating Man for the 21st Century. The European Cultural Foundation. The Hague: Martinus Nijhoff.

Polachek, S.W. 1978. "Sex Differences in College Major." *Industrial and Labor Relations Review,* July.

Position. 1975-80. Magazin für Berufsausbildung [Magazine for Occupational Training]. Deutscher Industrie -und Handelstag (DIHT). Bonn, quarterly.

a. "Die zweite Ausländergeneration-Ausbildungsprobleme und-perspectiven" no. 4, 1978.

Praderie, M.; Salais, R.; and Passagez, M. (1967). "Une enquête sur la formation et la qualification des français (1964)—La mobilité sociale en France: liaison entre la formation reçue et l'activité professionnelle" [An Inquiry into the Training and Qualifications of the French in 1964]. *Etudes et Conjoncture,* Fevrier. Paris: INSEE.

Princeton University. 1968. *The Transition from School to Work.* A Report Based on the Princeton Manpower Symposium May 9-10, 1968. Research Report Series no. 111, Industrial Relations Section. Princeton, New Jersey: Princeton University.

Prost, A. 1968. *Histoire de l'enseignement en France, 1800-1967* [History of Education in France, 1800-1967]. Paris: Armand Colin.

Purdue Opinion Panel. 1972. *Vocational Plans and Preferences of Adolescents.* Report of Poll no. 94, Measurement and Research Center. Lafayette, Indiana: Purdue University.

———. 1973. *Sources of Information for Career Decisions.* Report of Poll no. 98, Measurement and Research Center. Lafayette, Indiana: Purdue University.

Radner, R., and Miller, L.S. 1975. *Demand and Supply in U.S. Higher Education.* A report prepared for the Carnegie Commission on Higher Education. New York: McGraw-Hill.

Ragan, J.F., Jr. 1977. "Minimum Wages and the Youth Labor Market." *Review of Economics and Statistics,* May.

Rãsević, M.; Mulina, T.; and Macura, M. 1978. *The Determinants of Labour Force Participation in Yugoslavia.* Geneva: International Labor Office.

Rea, S.A., Jr. 1977. "Investment in Human Capital Under a Negative Income Tax." *Canadian Journal of Economics,* November.

Rees, A., and Gray, W. 1979. *Family Effects in Youth Employment.* Working Paper no. 396. Cambridge, Massachusetts: National Bureau of Economic Research.

Reid, W.A. 1974. "Choice and Selection: The Social Process of Transfer to Higher Education." *Journal of Social Policy,* October.

Reubens, B.G. 1977a. *Bridges to Work: International Comparisons of Transition Services.* Montclair, New Jersey: Allanheld, Osmun.

_____ . 1977b. "College and Jobs. International Problems." In Vermilye, D.W., ed. *Relating Work and Education*. San Francisco, California: Jossey-Bass.

_____ . 1978. "The Measurement and Interpretation of Teenage Unemployment in the United States and Other Countries." *Conference on Youth Unemployment: Its Measurement and Meaning. Supplementary Papers*. Office of Assistant Secretary for Policy, Evaluation, and Research. Washington: Department of Labor.

Ribich, T., and Murphy, J.L. 1975. "The Economic Returns to Increased Educational Spending." *Journal of Human Resources*, Winter.

Ritzen, J.M.M. 1977. *Higher Education and Manpower Planning in the Netherlands*. World Employment Programme Working Paper. Geneva: International Labor Office.

Roberts, K. 1967. "The Incidence and Effects of Spare-time Employment Amongst School-Children." *The Vocational Aspect*, Summer.

Root, N., and Hoefer, M. 1979. "The First Work-Injury Data Available From New BLS Study." *Monthly Labor Review*, January.

Rosen, H.S. 1979. *What is Labor Supply and Do Taxes Affect It?* Working Paper no. 411. Cambridge, Massachusetts: National Bureau for Economic Research.

Rosen, S. 1977. "Human Capital: A Survey of Empirical Research." In Ehrenberg, R.G., ed. *Research in Labor Economics*, vol. 1. Greenwich, Connecticut: JAI Press.

Rousselet, J.; Faguer, J.-P.; Kandel, I.; and Dossou, F. 1975. "L'entrée des jeunes dans la vie active: la génération 1955" [The Entrance of Young People into Working Life: The Generation of 1955]. *Les Jeunes et l'Emploi*. Cahiers du centre d'études de l'emploi, no. 7. Paris: Presses universitaire de France.

Rumberger, R.W. 1980. "The Economic Decline of College Graduates: Fact or Fallacy." *Journal of Human Resources*, Winter.

Russell, L.B. 1980. *The Macroeconomic Effects of Changes in the Age Structure of the Population*. Technical Series T-020. Washington: Brookings Institution.

Ryder, N.B. 1974. "The Family in Developed Countries." *Scientific American*, September.

Ryscavage, P.M. 1979. "BLS Labor Force Projections: A Review of Methods and Results." *Monthly Labor Review*, April.

Sandell, S.H. 1978. "Young Women's Decisions to Attend College: Desires, Expectations and Realizations." In Mott, F.L., ed. *Women, Work and Family*. Lexington, Massachusetts: D.C. Heath.

Sanders, D.P., and Barth, P.S. 1968. "Education and Economic Development." *Review of Educational Research*, June.

Saterdag, H., and Kraft, H. 1979. "Ausbildungs-und Berufsperspektiven der Jugendlichen gegen Ende der 9. Klasse" [Educational and Occupational Outlook of Youth at the End of the Ninth School Year]. *Mitteilungen aus der IAB*, no. 2. Nürnberg.

Saterdag, H., and Stegmann, H. 1980. *Jugendliche beim Übergang vom Bildungs-in das Beschäftigungssystem. Bericht über die Ergebnisse der Basiserhebungen einer Längsschnitt-Untersuchung* [Youth in the Transition from School to the Employment System. A Report on the Basic Survey for a Longitudinal Study]. Beiträge zur Arbeitsmarkt-und Berufsforschung, no. 41. Nürnberg: IAB.

Schuessler, K. 1973. "Ratio Variables and Path Models." In Goldberger, A.S., and Duncan, O.D., eds. *Structural Equation Models in the Social Sciences*. New York: Seminar Press.

Schultz, T.P. 1975. *The Estimation of Labor Supply Functions for Secondary Workers*. R-1265-NIH/EDA. Santa Monica, California: The Rand Corporation.

Schwartz, E., and Thornton, R. 1980. "Overinvestment in College Training?" *Journal of Human Resources*, Winter.

Simon, J.L. 1977. *The Economics of Population Growth*. Princeton, New Jersey: Princeton University Press.

Simon, J.L., and Pilarski, A.M. 1979. "The Effect of Population Growth Upon the Quantity of Education Children Receive." *Review of Economics and Statistics*, November.

Skoulas, N. 1974. *Determinants of the Participation Rate of Married Women in the Canadian Labour Force: An Econometric Analysis*. Ottawa: Statistics Canada.

Smith, J.P., and Welch, F. 1978. *Race Differences in Earnings: A Survey and New Information*. Santa Monica, California: Rand Corporation.

Smith, R.E. 1974. *Dynamic Determinants of Labor Force Participation: Some Evidence from Gross Change Data*. Working Paper 350-49. Washington: Urban Institute.

————. 1977. "A Simulation Model of the Demographic Composition of Employment, Unemployment, and Labor Force Participation." In Ehrenberg, R.G., ed. *Research in Labor Economics,* vol. 1. Greenwich, Connecticut: JAI Press.

————. 1979a. *Women in the Labor Force in 1990.* Washington: The Urban Institute.

Smith, R.E., ed. 1979b. *The Subtle Revolution: Women at Work.* Washington: The Urban Institute.

Smith, R.E., and Holt, C.C. 1974. "Recession and the Employment of Demographic Groups." *Brookings Papers on Economic Activity,* no. 3. Washington: Brookings Institution.

Smith, R.E., and Vanski, J.E. 1978a. "The Volatility of the Teenage Labor Market: Labor Force Entry, Exit, and Unemployment Flows." *Conference Report on Youth Unemployment: Its Measurement and Meaning.* Office of Assistant Secretary for Policy, Evaluation, and Research and Employment Training Administration. Washington: Department of Labor.

————. 1978b. *Gross Change Data: The Neglected Data Base.* Background Paper no. 11, National Commission on Employment and Unemployment Statistics. Washington: GPO.

Smith, S.P. 1976. "The Changing Composition of the Labor Force." Federal Reserve Board of New York, *Quarterly Review,* Winter.

Solon, G. 1979. "Labor Supply Effects of Extended Unemployment Benefits." *Journal of Human Resources,* Spring.

Sørensen, A.B. 1978. *The Organizational Differentiation of Students in Schools.* Discussion Paper no. 480-78, Institute for Research on Poverty. Madison, Wisconsin: University of Wisconsin.

Sorrentino, C. 1981. *Youth Unemployment: An International Perspective.* Bureau of Labor Statistics. Department of Labor. Washington: GPO.

Spencer, B.G., and Featherstone, D.C. 1970. *Married Female Labour Force Participation: A Micro Study.* Special Labour Force Studies Series B, no. 4. Ottawa: Dominion Bureau of Statistics.

Spies, U. 1978. *Die Zweite Generation* [The Second Generation]. Discussion Paper no. 78-78. Berlin: International Institute for Management.

Spindler, Z., and Maki, D. 1975. "The Effect of Unemployment Compensation on the Rate of Unemployment in Great Britain." *Oxford Economic Papers,* December.

Sproat, K. 1979. "Using National Longitudinal Surveys to Track Young Workers." *Monthly Labor Review,* October.

Stamas, G.D. 1979. "Long Hours and Premium Pay, May 1978." *Monthly Labor Review,* May.

————. 1980. "Percent Working Long Hours Shows First Post-recession Decline." *Monthly Labor Review,* May.

Standing, G. 1976. "Education and Female Participation in the Labour Force." *International Labour Review,* November–December.

————. 1978. *Labour Force Participation and Development.* A World Employment Project study. Geneva: International Labor Office.

Stegmann, H. 1980. "Studenten in den Anfangssemestern. Einstellungen zum Studium und zum zukünftigen Beruf" [Students in the First Semester. Their Attitudes Toward Their Studies and Future Occupations]. *Mitteilungen aus der Arbeitsmarkt-und Berufsforschung,* no. 1. Nürnberg.

Stegmann, H., and Holzbauer, I. 1978. "Die Nachfrage nach Ausbildungsplätzen und ihre Realisierung bei Absolventen und Abgängern allgemeinbildender Schulen" [Demand for Training Places and Actual Training Possibilities for Graduates and Early School-leavers from the General Education System]. *Mitteilungen aus der Arbeitsmarkt-und Berufsforschung,* no. 2. Nürnberg.

Stein, R.L. 1967. "Reasons for Non-participation in the Labor Force." *Monthly Labor Review,* July.

Stein, R.L. 1980. "National Commission Recommends Changes in Labor Force Statistics." *Monthly Labor Review,* April.

Stephenson, S., Jr. 1977. *The Prediction of School Enrollment and Labor Force Participation Using a Multinomial Logit Model.* Department of Economics. University Park, Pennsylvania: The Pennsylvania State University.

_____. 1978a. *The Occupational and Education Effects of Early Work Experience.* Department of Economics. University Park, Pennsylvania: The Pennsylvania State University.

_____. 1978b. *The School-to-Work Transition of Young Men.* Office of Assistant Secretary for Policy, Evaluation, and Research. Washington: Department of Labor.

_____. 1978c. "The Transition from School to Work with Job Search Implications." *Conference Report on Youth Unemployment: its Measurement and Meaning.* Office of Assistant Secretary for Policy, Evaluation, and Research and Employment Training Administration. Washington: Department of Labor.

Stephenson, S., Jr., and McDonald, J. 1979. "Disaggregation of Income Maintenance Impacts on Family Earnings." *Review of Economics and Statistics,* August.

Stevenson, W. 1978. "The Relationship Between Youth Employment and Future Employability and Earnings." *Supplementary Papers from the Conference on Youth Employment: Its Measurement and Meaning.* Office of Assistant Secretary for Policy, Evaluation, and Research and Employment Training Administration. Washington: Department of Labor.

Stewart, C.T., Jr.; and Avery, K. 1978. "College Enrollment in Response to Fluctuations in Unemployment and Income." *College and University,* September.

Stigler, G.J. 1950. *Employment and Compensation in Education.* Occasional Paper no. 33. New York: National Bureau of Economic Research.

Sum, A.M. 1977. "Women in the Labor Force: Why Projections Have Been Too Low." *Monthly Labor Review,* July.

Swan, N. 1974. "The Response of Labour Supply in Canadian Regions." *Canadian Journal of Economics,* August.

_____. 1975. "Unemployment Insurance and Labor Force Participation with Applications to Canada and Its Maritime Provinces." *Proceedings,* Industrial Relations Research Association, Spring.

SWEDEN

1963-79. *Arbetskraftsundersökningen.* Råtabeller. [Labor Force Surveys. Raw Tables]. Stockholm: SCB (Statistiska Centralbyrån).
   a. annual averages.
   b. November.

1965-80. *Meddelanden från Utredningsbyrån* [Reports from the Research Bureau]. Stockholm: Arbetsmarknadsstyrelsen (AMS) (Later called Meddelanden från Utredningsenheten and issued from Solna).

1969-79. *Arbetskraftens Utbildningsstruktur* [Educational Characteristics of the Labor Force]. Stockholm: SCB (Statistiska Centralbyrån).

1971a. *Labor Resources 1965-1990.* Information i prognosfrågor 1971:5. Stockholm: SCB (Statistiska Centralbyrån).

1972-79. *Grundskolan. Elevuppföljning. Studier, Förvärvsarbete etc.* [Follow Up Studies of Comprehensive School Pupils]. Series U: 1972 no. 3; 1974 nos. 6,8; 1976 no. 35; 1978 nos. 21, 29; 1979 no. 24. Stockholm: SCB (Statistiska Centralbyrån).

1973. *Arbetskraftsresursernas utveckling 1965-1972* [Labor Market Resources 1965-1972]. Promemorior 1973:3. Stockholm: SCB (Statistiska Centralbyrån).

1973-75. *Folk-och bostadsräkningen 1970* [Population and Housing Census 1970]. Stockholm: SCB (Statistiska Centralbyrån).
   a. Vol. 10. Näringsgren, yrke och utbildning. Definitioner, jämförbarhet och utveckling m m.
   b. Vol. 13. Sysselsättning och utbildning. Definitioner, jämförbarhet och utveckling m m.

1974a. *Trender och prognoser 1974* [Trends and Forecasts—Population, Education and Labour Market in Sweden]. Information i prognosfrågor 1974:8. Stockholm: SCB (Statistiska Centralbyrån).

1974b. *Utbildningsstatistik 1960-1973* [Educational Statistics 1960-1973]. Promemorior 1974:3. Stockholm: SCB (Statistiska Centralbyrån).

1974c. *Swedish Educational Statistics 1960-1973.* Promemorior 1974:3. Appendix. Stockholm: SCB (Statistiska Centralbyrån).

1974-79. *Gymnasieskolan. Elevuppföljning. Studier, förvärvsarbete etc.* [Follow-up Studies of Integrated Upper Secondary School Pupils]. Series U: 1974 nos. 4, 5; 1976 no. 1; 1979 no. 11. Stockholm: SCB (Statistiska Centralbyrån).

1975-79. *Högskolan. Elevuppföljningar, Studier, Förvärvsarbete etc. after examen* [Follow-up Studies of Higher Education Graduates]. Series U: 1975 nos. 11, 16, 28, 33, 37, 46, 51; 1976 nos. 18, 24, 25, 29, 47; 1977 nos. 14, 26; 1978 nos. 1, 10; 1979 nos. 7, 17, 29. Stockholm: SCB (Statistiska Centralbyrån).

1976a. *Arbetskraftsresurserna 1965-2000* [Labor Market Resources 1965-2000]. Main Report. Information i prognosfrågor 1976:1. Stockholm: SCB (Statistiska Centralbyrån).

1976b. *Arbetskraftsresursernas utveckling 1965-2000* [Labor Market Resources 1965-2000]. Tabellbilaga till Information i prognosfrågor 1976:1 [Statistical Appendix to IPF report 1976:1]. Promemorior 1976:1. Stockholm: SCB (Statistiska Centralbyrån).

1976c. *Högskolestatistik II — Social Bakgrund för Studerande vid universitet och högskolor 1962/63-1972/73* [Swedish University Education II — Statistics on Social Background for Students at Universities and Specialized Colleges 1962/63-1972/73]. Promemorior 1976:5. Stockholm: SCB (Statistiska Centralbyrån).

1976d. *Studerandes ålder höstterminen 1975* [Age Distribution of Students in the 1975 Autumn Semester]. Statistiska Meddelanden U 1976:39. Stockholm: SCB (Statistiska Centralbyrån).

1977a. *Trender och prognoser 1977* [Trends and Prognoses 1977]. Information i prognosfrågor 1977:1. Stockholm: SCB (Statistiska Centralbyrån).

1977b. *Förvärsarbetande Befolkning Hösten 1975 Enligt Arbetskraftsundersökningarna. Resultat anpassade till: Folk-och-bostadsräkningen 1975 anvanda begrepp* [1975 Labor Force Survey Results Adapted to Definitions Used in the Census 1975]. Statistiska Meddelanden, Am 1977:1.1. Stockholm: SCB (Statistiska Centralbyrån).

1977c. *Förvärsarbetande Befolkning Hösten 1976 Enligt Arbetskraftsundersökningarna. Resultat anpassade till i Folk-och-bostadsräkningen 1975 anvanda begrepp* [1976 Labor Force Survey Results Adapted to Definitions Used in the Census 1975]. Statistiska Meddelanden, Am 1977:1.2. Stockholm: SCB (Statistiska Centralbyrån).

1977d. *Utbildning Statistik 1970-1975* [Education Statistics 1970-1975]. Promemorior 1977:5. Stockholm: SCB (Statistiska Centralbyrån).

1977e. *Elevströmmarna genom utbildningsväsendet och utflödet till arbetsmarknaden. Framskrivning till 1990* [Student Flows Through the Educational System and Number of Students Entering the Labor Market. Projection up to 1990]. Information i prognosfrågor 1977:4. Stockholm: SCB (Statistiska Centralbyrån).

1977f. *Statistical Abstract of Sweden 1977*, vol. 64. Stockholm: SCB (Statistiska Centralbyrån).

1977g. *Elever: Icke-Obligatoriska Skolor 1864-1970* [Pupils in Secondary Schools in Sweden 1864-1970]. Promemorior 1977:11. Stockholm: SCB (Statistiska Centralbyrån).

1978a. *Deltidsarbete* [Part-time Work]. Meddelanden från Utredningsenheten no. 1978:20. Solna: AMS (Arbetsmarknadsstyrelsen).

1978b. *Folkmängd (Population)*, 31 Dec. 1977. Stockholm: SCB (Statistiska Centralbyrån).

1978c. *Arbetskraftsundersökningarna 1963-1975* [The Labor Force Surveys 1963-1975]. Statistiska Meddelanden Am 1978:32. Stockholm: SCB (Statistiska Centralbyrån).

1978d. *Utflödet av utbildade och arbetsmarknadens rekryteringsbehov — prognos till 1990* [Number of Students Leaving the Educational System and the Labor Market Recruitment Need of Manpower — Forecast to 1990]. Information i prognosfrågor 1978:3. Stockholm: SCB (Statistiska Centralbyrån).

1978e. *Arbetsmarknads politik i förändring*. Betänkande av expertgruppen för utredningsverksamhet i arbetsmarknadsfrågor (EFA). [Labor Market Policy In Transition. A Report from the Expert Group for Labor Market Research at the Swedish Ministry of Labor]. Stockholm: SOU.

1978f. *Utbildnings statistik årsbok 1978* [Education Statistics Yearbook 1978]. Stockholm: SCB (Statistika Centralbyrån).

1978g. *Arbetskraftsresurserna 1977-2025* [Labor Force Resources 1977-2025]. Working draft of *promemorior*, unpublished. Stockholm: SCB (Statistiska Centralbyrån).

1978h. *Grundskolan och gymnasieskolan 1977-78. Invandrarelever och invandrarundervisning i grundskola och gymnasieskola varen 1978* [Comprehensive School and Integrated Upper Secondary School 1977-78. Immigrant Pupils in the Comprehensive School and the Integrated Upper Secondary School, Spring 1978]. Statistiska Meddelanden U 1978:26. Stockholm: SCB (Statistiska Centralbyrån).

1978i. *Labour Market Policy in Transition*. Summary of a report from the Expert Group for Labour Market Research. Ministry of Labour. Stockholm: LiberForläg.

1979a. *Strömmarna till och från arbetskraften 1970-1977* [The Flows To and From the Labor Force 1970-1977]. Information i prognosfrågor (IPF) 1979:3. Stockholm: SCB (Statistiska Centralbyrån).

1979b. *Förvärvsarbete Parallellt med Studier på Grundskolans Högstadium* [Working and Studying at the Same Time in the Last Year of Basic School]. Report P 1979:1. Stockholm: SÖ (Skolöverstyrelsen).

1979c. *Förvärvsarbete vid sidan av studierna Elever på gymnasieskolans 3-och 4-åriga finjer* [Work While Studying. Students in the 3 and 4 Year Lines at the Gymnasium School]. Rapport P1 1979:6. Stockholm: SÖ (Skolöverstyrelsen).

1979d. *Social bakgrund och yrkesval för 1957, 1962 och 1967 års studenter* [Graduates from Upper Secondary School 1957, 1962 and 1967—Social Background and Occupation]. Information i prognosfrågor 1979:1. Stockholm: SCB (Statistiska Centralbyrån).

1979e. *Studerandes ålder höstterminen 1978* [Age Distribution of Students in the 1978 Autumn Term]. Statistiska Meddelanden U 1979:28. Stockholm: SCB (Statistiska Centralbyrån).

1979f. *Ung 79* [Youth 79]. Promemorior från SCB 1979:6. Stockholm: SCB (Statistiska Centralbyrån).

1979g. *Årssysselsättningen 1978 och Utbildningsnivån Februari 1979* [Work Experience in 1978 and Educational Level February 1979]. Solna: AMS (Arbetsmarknadsstyrelsen).

1979h. *Pressmeddelande* [Press Release] no. 1979:360. Stockholm: SCB (Statistiska Centralbyrån).

1979i. *Löner 1978* [Wages 1978], vol. 2. Stockholm: SCB (Statistiska Centralbyrån).

1979j. *The Swedish Budget 1979/80. A Summary.* Ministry of Economic Affairs and the Ministry of the Budget. Stockholm: LiberFörlag.

1980a. *Högskolan 1977. Social och utbildningsmässig bakgrund bland för första gangen registerade i högskolan (högskolenybörjare) per 15 September 1977* [Higher Education 1977. Socioeconomic and Educational Background Among Those Who for the First Time Entered Higher Education and Were Registered on 15 September 1977]. U 1980:2. Stockholm: SCB (Statistiska Centralbyrån).

Swinton, D.H. 1979. *Toward Defining the Universe of Need for Youth Employment Policy.* Paper prepared for the Vice-President's Task Force on Youth Employment. Washington.

SWITZERLAND

1977. *Intégration sociale des étrangers par l'intermédiaire de la scolarisation de leurs enfants* [Social Integration of Foreigners through the Intermediary of Educating their Children]. Federal Consultative Commission for Foreigners Questions. Berne.

Taeuber, K.E. 1976. "Demographic Trends Affecting the Future Labor Force." In National Commission for Manpower Policy, *Demographic Trends and Full Employment.* Special Report no. 12. Washington: National Commission for Manpower Policy.

Taylor, D.E. 1979. *Absence from Work—Measuring the Hours Lost, May 1978.* Special Labor Force Report 229, Bureau of Labor Statistics. Washington: Department of Labor.

Tessaring, M., and Werner, H. 1977. *Die Entwicklung der Beschäftigungsmöglichkeiten für akademisch ausgebildete Arbeitskräfte im Vergleich zu anderen Arbeitskräftegruppen in Ländern mit starkes Bildungsexpansion* [The Development of Employment Opportunities for Academically Trained Labor Force Compared to Other Labor Force Groups in Countries with Strong Educational Expansion]. Studie in Auftrage der Kommission für Wirtschaftlichen und Sozialen Wandel. Göttingen: O. Schwartz.

Thomas, M.W. 1945. *Young People in Industry 1750-1945.* London: Thomas Nelson & Sons.

Thomas, R., and Wetherell, D. 1974. *Looking Forward to Work.* Office of Population Censuses and Surveys. London: HMSO.

⸻. *Starting Work and After.* Office of Population Censuses and Surveys. London: HMSO, (forthcoming).

Tippelt, R. 1978. "Children of Migrant Workers in the Federal Republic of Germany." Surveys of Member States of the European Communities in *Youth Unemployment and Vocational Training. Occupational Choice and Motivation of Young People: Their Vocational Training and Employment Prospects.* Berlin: CEDEFOP (European Centre for the Development of Vocational Training).

Toikka, R.S.; Scanlon, W.J.; and Holt, C.C. 1977. "Extensions of a Structural Model of the Demographic Labor Model." In Ehrenberg, R.G., ed. *Research in Labor Economics,* vol. I. Greenwich, Connecticut: JAI Press.

Tolley, G.S., and Olson, E. 1971. "The Interdependence between Income and Education." *Journal of Political Economy,* May–June.

Tsui, A.O., and Bogue, D.J. 1978. "Declining World Fertility: Trends, Causes, and Implications." *Population Bulletin,* October. Washington: Population Reference Bureau.

Tufte, E.R. 1974. *Data Analysis for Politics and Policy.* Englewood Cliffs, New Jersey: Prentice-Hall.

Twentieth Century Fund. 1971. *The Job Crisis for Black Youth.* Task Force on Employment Problems of Black Youth. Background Paper by S. Levitan and R. Taggart III. New York: Praeger.

Umetani, S. 1977. "The Labor Market for College Graduates in Postwar Japan." *Japan Labor Bulletin,* March.

UN (UNITED NATIONS)

1956. *Economic Survey of Europe in 1955.* Geneva: Economic Commission for Europe.

1958–80. *Demographic Yearbook.* New York, annual.

1970–80. *Monthly Bulletin of Statistics.* New York.

1973. *The Determinants and Consequences of Population Trends.* Population Studies no. 50, 2 Vols. Department of Economic and Social Affairs. New York.

1975. *Economic Survey of Europe in 1974.* Part II. Post-war Demographic Trends in Europe and the Outlook Until the Year 2000. New York.

US (UNITED STATES)

1946–79. *School Enrollment — Social and Economic Characteristics of Students.* Department of Commerce. Bureau of the Census. Current Population Reports. Series P-20. Washington: GPO, annual.

1950–79. *Statistical Abstract of the United States.* Department of Commerce. Bureau of the Census. Washington: GPO, annual.

1960–77. *Employment of School-age Youth.* Department of Labor. Bureau of Labor Statistics. Special Labor Force Reports. Washington: GPO, annual.

1960–79a. *Students, Graduates and Dropouts in the Labor Market.* Department of Labor. Bureau of Labor Statistics. Special Labor Force Reports. Washington: GPO, annual.

1960–79b. *Educational Attainment of Workers.* Department of Labor. Bureau of Labor Statistics. Special Labor Force Reports. Washington: GPO, annual.

1963. *Census of Population 1960.* United States Summary, Detailed Characteristics. Department of Commerce. Bureau of the Census. Washington: GPO.

1964–79. *Work Experience of the Population.* Department of Labor. Bureau of Labor Statistics. Special Labor Force Reports. Washington: GPO, annual.

1965–78. *Estimates of the Population of the United States.* Department of Commerce. Bureau of Census. Series P-25 nos. 311, 519, 704, 706, 721. Washington: GPO.

1970. *Youth Unemployment and Minimum Wages.* Department of Labor. Bulletin 1657, Bureau of Labor Statistics. Washington: GPO.

1970–79. *Career Thresholds: A Longitudinal Study of the Educational and Labor Market Experience of Male Youth.* Department of Labor. Employment and Training Administration (formerly Manpower Administration). 7 vols. Vols. 1–4: Manpower Research Monograph no. 16, 1970, 1971, 1974. Vols. 5–7: R&D Monograph no. 16, 1976, 1977, 1979. Washington: GPO.

1971–80. *Employment and Earnings.* Department of Labor. Bureau of Labor Statistics. Washington, monthly.
  a. July 1971.
  b. July 1974.
  c. January 1977.
  d. January 1978.
  e. January 1979.
  f. January 1980.

1971–81. *Years for Decision: A longitudinal study of the educational and labor market experience of young women.* Department of Labor. Employment and Training Administration (formerly Manpower Administration). 5 vols. Vols. 1–2: Manpower Research Monograph no. 24, 1971, 1974. Vols. 3–5: R&D Monograph 24, 1976, 1978, 1980. Washington: GPO.

1972. *Projections of School and College Enrollment: 1971 to 2000.* Department of Commerce. Bureau of the Census. Current Population Reports. Population Estimates and Projections. Series P-25 no. 473. Washington: GPO.

1973a. *1970 Census of Population.* United States Summary, Detailed Characteristics. Department of Commerce. Bureau of the Census. Washington: GPO.

1973b. *1970 Census of Population. Employment Status and Work Experience.* Department of Commerce. Bureau of the Census. Washington: GPO.

1973c. *Vital Statistics of the United States 1972,* vol. 1. Washington: Department of Health, Education and Welfare.

1974. *Estimates of Coverage of Population by Sex, Race and Age: Demographic Analysis.* Department of Commerce. Bureau of the Census. PHC(E)-4. Washington: GPO.

1975a. *Accuracy of Data for Selected Population Characteristics as Measured by the 1970 CPS-Census Match.* Department of Commerce. Bureau of the Census. PHC(E)-11. Washington: GPO.

1975b. *Digest of Educational Statistics, 1974 Edition.* Department of Health, Education and Welfare. National Center for Education Statistics. Washington: GPO, annual.

1975–80. *The Condition of Education.* Department of Health, Education and Welfare. National Center of Education Statistics. Wasington: GPO.
   a. 1975 ed.
   b. 1976 ed.
   c. 1977 ed.
   d. 1978 ed.
   e. 1979 ed.
   f. 1980 ed.

1976a. *The Teenage Unemployment Problem: What are the Options?* Congressional Budget Office. Report of a Conference April 30, 1976. Washington: GPO.

1976b. *Concepts and Methods Used in Labor Force Statistics Derived from the Current Population Survey.* Department of Commerce. Bureau of the Census and Department of Labor. Bureau of Labor Statistics. BLS Report no. 463 and Bureau of the Census Series P-23, no. 62. Washington: GPO.

1976c. *Policy Options for the Teenage Unemployment Problem.* Background Paper no. 13, Congressional Budget Office. Washington: GPO.

1976–79. *National Longitudinal Study of the High School Class of 1972.* Department of Health, Education and Welfare. National Center for Education Statistics. Washington: GPO.
   a. Tabular summary of first follow up questionnaire data. 1976.
   b. Tabular summary of second follow up questionnaire data, 2½ years after high school. 1977.
   c. Tabular summary of third follow up questionnaire data. 1978.
   d. Base year, first and second follow up data file users manual, preliminary. 1976.
   e. National longitudinal study data collection activities for the third follow up (July 1976 through June 1977). 1979.

1977a. *Employment in Perspective: A Critical Analysis of Gross Flows in the Labor Force.* Department of Labor. Report 508, Bureau of Labor Statistics. Washington: GPO.

1977b. *Health 1976–1977.* Department of Health, Education and Welfare. Washington: National Center for Health Statistics.

1977c. *Withdrawal from Institutions of Higher Education.* Department of Health, Education and Welfare. National Center for Education Statistics. Washington: GPO.

1977d. *Fulfillment of Short-term Educational Plans and Continuance in Education.* Department of Health, Education and Welfare. Washington: National Center for Education Statistics.

1978a. *International Comparisons of Unemployment.* Department of Labor. Bulletin 1979, Bureau of Labor Statistics. Washington: GPO.

1978b. *Characteristics of American Children and Youth: 1976.* Department of Commerce. Bureau of the Census. Current Population Reports. Series P-23 no. 66. Washington: GPO.

1978c. *Conference Report on Youth Unemployment: Its Measurement and Meaning.* Office of the Assistant Secretary for Policy, Evaluation, and Research and Employment Training Administration. Washington: Department of Labor.

1978d. *Indicators of Youth Unemployment and Education in Industrialized Nations.* Working Paper, National Center for Education Statistics. Washington: GPO.

1978e. *Domestic Consequences of United States Population Change.* House of Representatives, Select Committee on Population. 95th Congress, 2nd Session. 35-6650. Washington: GPO.

1978f. *The Educational Disadvantage of Language—Minority Persons in the United States, Spring 1976.* NCES Bulletin no. 78, National Center for Education Statistics. Washington: GPO.

1978g. *Projections of Education Statistics to 1986–87.* National Center for Education Statistics. Washington: GPO.

1979a. *Draft-Fact Book.* Department of Labor. Washington: GPO.

1979b. *Employment and Training Report of the President* 1979. Department of Labor. Washington: GPO.

1979c. I. *Counting the Labor Force: Preliminary Draft Report.* II. *Final Report.* National Commission on Employment and Unemployment Statistics. Washington: GPO.

1980a. *Population Profile of the United States: 1979.* Department of Commerce. Bureau of the Census. Current Population Reports. Series P-20, no. 350. Washington: GPO.

1980b. *Employment and Training Report of the President* 1980. Department of Labor. Washington: GPO.

Vaizey, J.; with Norris, K., and Sheehan, J. 1972. *The Political Economy of Education.* London: Duckworth.

Venieris, Y.P.; Sebold, F.D.; and Harper, R.D. 1973. "The Impact of Economic, Technological and Demographic Factors on Aggregate Births." *Review of Economics and Statistics,* November.

Wachter, M.L. 1972. "A Labor Supply Model for Secondary Workers." *Review of Economics and Statistics,* May.

———. 1974. "A New Approach to the Equilibrium Labour Force." *Economica,* February.

———. 1976. "The Demographic Impact on Unemployment: Past Experience and the Outlook for the Future." In National Commission for Manpower Policy, *Demographic Trends and Full Employment.* Special Report no. 12. Washington: National Commission for Manpower Policy.

———. 1977. "Intermediate Swings in Labor-Force Participation." *Brookings Papers on Economic Activity,* no. 2. Washington: Brookings Institution.

———. 1980. "The Dimensions and Complexities of the Youth Unemployment Problem." In Anderson, B.E., and Sawhill, I.V., eds. *Youth Employment and Public Policy.* The American Assembly, Columbia University. Englewood Cliffs, New Jersey: Prentice-Hall.

Wachter, M.L., and Kim, C. 1979. *Time Series Changes in Youth Joblessness.* Working Paper no. 384. Cambridge, Massachusetts: National Bureau of Economic Research.

Wadensjö, E. 1978. *Ungdomsarbetslösheten* [Youth Unemployment]. Department of Economics, University of Lund, Sweden.

Waite, L.J., and Moore, K.A. 1978. "The Impact of an Early First Birth on Young Women's Educational Attainment." *Social Forces,* March.

Ward, M.P., and Butz, W.P. 1978. *Completed Fertility and its Timing: An Economic Analysis of U.S. Experience Since World War II.* R-2285-NICHD. Santa Monica, California: Rand Corporation.

Watts, H.W., and Skidmore, F. 1978. *The Implications of Changing Family Patterns and Behavior for Labor Force and Hardship Measurement.* Special Report 21, Institute for Research on Poverty. Madison, Wisconsin: University of Wisconsin.

Weightman, G. 1978. "The Tricky Game of Population Trends." *New Society,* February 16.

Weinschrott, D.J. 1977. *Demand for Higher Education in the United States: A Critical Review of the Empirical Literature.* R-2195-LE. Santa Monica, California: Rand Corporation.

Welch, F. 1975. "Human Capital Theory: Education, Discrimination, and Life Cycles." *American Economic Review,* May.

———. 1979. "Effects of Cohort Size on Earnings: The Baby Boom Babies' Financial

Bust." *Journal of Political Economy*, pt. 2., October.

Werner, H. 1980. *Employment Problems of University Graduates in an International Comparison*. CC-PU(80)11. Strasbourg: Council of Europe, Division for Higher Education and Research.

West, E.G. 1967. "The Political Economy of American Public School Legislation." *Journal of Law and Economics*, October.

Westcott, D.N. 1976. "Youth in the Labor Force: An Area Study." *Monthly Labor Review*, July.

_____ . 1977. "The Nation's Youth: An Employment Perspective." *Worklife*, June.

Wickens, M.R. 1974. "Towards a Theory of the Labour Market." *Economica*, August.

Willauer, E.T., Jr. 1974. *The Demand for Youth Labor: A Cross-Sectional Approach*. CAC Document no. 132, Center for Advanced Computation. Urbana-Champaign: University of Illinois.

Williams, G. 1974. "Higher Education Deflated." *New Society*, November 21.

Willis, R.J. 1973. "A New Approach to the Economic Theory of Fertility Behavior." *Journal of Political Economy*, Supplement, March/April.

Wilson, S.R., and Wise, L.L. 1975. *The American Citizen: 11 Years After High School*. Palo Alto, California: American Institutes for Research.

Winston, G. 1966. "An International Comparison of Income and Hours of Work." *Review of Economics and Statistics*, February.

Witmer, D.R. 1980. "Has the Golden Age of American Higher Education Come to an Abrupt End?" *Journal of Human Resources*, Winter.

Wool, H. 1978. *Discouraged Workers, Potential Workers, and National Employment Policy*. Special Report no. 24. Washington: National Commission for Manpower Policy.

Yamaguchi, K. 1967. "Recent Fertility Trends, Particularly the Fertility Decline in the Year of 'Hinoeuma.' " In *Annual Reports of the Institute of Population Problems, 1967*. Tokyo: Ministry of Health and Welfare.

Young, A. McD. 1978. "Students, Graduates and Dropouts in the Labor Market, October 1977." *Monthly Labor Review*, June.

_____ . 1979. "The Difference a Year Makes in the Nation's Youth Work Force." *Monthly Labor Review*, October.

Zsigmond, Z.E., and Rechnitzer, E. (n.d.). "Projected Potential Labour Force Entrants from the Canadian Educational Systems 1971 to 1985." Ottawa: Statistics Canada.

Index

The Authors

BEATRICE G. REUBENS is a Senior Research Associate at Conservation of Human Resources, Columbia University, and has published extensively on comparative labor market issues.

JOHN A. C. HARRISSON is a Research Associate at Conservation of Human Resources, Columbia University. A graduate of Oxford University, he holds an M.A. in labor economics from the University of Sussex and was a Research Fellow, specializing in youth, at the Institute of Manpower Studies in England.

KALMAN RUPP received his PhD. in economics from Budapest University in 1971, earned an M. Phil. in sociology from Columbia University in 1978, and has been an NIMS post-doctoral fellow. He has published papers on social mobility and employment.